Informatik – Fachberichte

Band 189: B. Wolfinger (Hrsg.), Vernetzte und komplexe Informatik-Systeme. Industrieprogramm zur 18. Jahrestagung der GI, Hamburg, Oktober 1988. Proceedings. X, 229 Seiten. 1988.

Band 190: D. Maurer, Relevanzanalyse. VIII, 239 Seiten. 1988.

Band 191: P. Levi, Planen für autonome Montageroboter. XIII, 259 Seiten. 1988.

Band 192: K. Kansy, P. Wißkirchen (Hrsg.), Graphik im Bürobereich. Proceedings, 1988. VIII, 187 Seiten. 1988.

Band 193: W. Gotthard, Datenbanksysteme für Software-Produktionsumgebungen. X, 193 Seiten. 1988.

Band 194: C. Lewerentz, Interaktives Entwerfen großer Programmsysteme. VII, 179 Seiten. 1988.

Band 195: I. S. Bátori, U. Hahn, M. Pinkal, W. Wahlster (Hrsg.), Computerlinguistik und ihre theoretischen Grundlagen. Proceedings. IX, 218 Seiten. 1988.

Band 197: M. Leszak, H. Eggert, Petri-Netz-Methoden und -Werkzeuge. XII, 254 Seiten. 1989.

Band 198: U. Reimer, FRM: Ein Frame-Repräsentationsmodell und seine formale Semantik. VIII, 161 Seiten. 1988.

Band 199: C. Beckstein, Zur Logik der Logik-Programmierung. IX, 246 Seiten. 1988.

Band 200: A. Reinefeld, Spielbaum-Suchverfahren. IX, 191 Seiten. 1989.

Band 201: A. M. Kotz, Triggermechanismen in Datenbanksystemen. VIII, 187 Seiten. 1989.

Band 202: Th. Christaller (Hrsg.), Künstliche Intelligenz. 5. Frühjahrsschule, KIFS-87, Günne, März/April 1987. Proceedings. VII, 403 Seiten, 1989.

Band 203: K. v. Luck (Hrsg.), Künstliche Intelligenz. 7. Frühjahrsschule, KIFS-89, Günne, März 1989. Proceedings. VII, 302 Seiten. 1989.

Band 204: T. Härder (Hrsg.), Datenbanksysteme in Büro, Technik und Wissenschaft. GI/SI-Fachtagung, Zürich, März 1989. Proceedings. XII, 427 Seiten. 1989.

Band 205: P. J. Kühn (Hrsg.), Kommunikation in verteilten Systemen. ITG/GI-Fachtagung, Stuttgart, Februar 1989. Proceedings. XII, 907 Seiten. 1989.

Band 206: P. Horster, H. Isselhorst, Approximative Public-Key-Kryptosysteme. VII, 174 Seiten. 1989.

Band 207: J. Knop (Hrsg.), Organisation der Datenverarbeitung an der Schwelle der 90er Jahre. 8. GI-Fachgespräch, Düsseldorf, März 1989. Proceedings. IX, 276 Seiten. 1989.

Band 208: J. Retti, K. Leidlmair (Hrsg.), 5. Österreichische Artificial-Intelligence-Tagung, Igls/Tirol, März 1989. Proceedings. XI, 452 Seiten. 1989.

Band 209: U. W. Lipeck, Dynamische Integrität von Datenbanken. VIII, 140 Seiten. 1989.

Band 210: K. Drosten, Termersetzungssysteme. IX, 152 Seiten. 1989.

Band 211: H. W. Meuer (Hrsg.), SUPERCOMPUTER '89. Mannheim, Juni 1989. Proceedings, 1989. VIII, 171 Seiten. 1989.

Band 212: W.-M. Lippe (Hrsg.), Software-Entwicklung. Fachtagung, Marburg, Juni 1989. Proceedings. IX, 290 Seiten. 1989.

Band 213: I. Walter, Datenbankgestützte Repräsentation und Extraktion von Episodenbeschreibungen aus Bildfolgen. VIII, 243 Seiten. 1989.

Band 214: W. Görke, H. Sörensen (Hrsg.), Fehlertolerierende Rechensysteme / Fault-Tolerant Computing Systems. 4. Internationale GI/ITG/GMA-Fachtagung, Baden-Baden, September 1989. Proceedings. XI, 390 Seiten. 1989.

Band 215: M. Bidjan-Irani, Qualität und Testbarkeit hochintegrierter Schaltungen. IX, 169 Seiten. 1989.

Band 216: D. Metzing (Hrsg.), GWAI-89. 13th German Workshop on Artificial Intelligence. Eringerfeld, September 1989. Proceedings. XII, 485 Seiten. 1989.

Band 217: M. Zieher, Kopplung von Rechnernetzen. XII, 218 Seiten. 1989.

Band 218: G. Stiege, J. S. Lie (Hrsg.), Messung, Modellierung und Bewertung von Rechensystemen und Netzen. 5. GI/ITG-Fachtagung, Braunschweig, September 1989. Proceedings. IX, 342 Seiten. 1989.

Band 219: H. Burkhardt, K. H. Höhne, B. Neumann (Hrsg.), Mustererkennung 1989. 11. DAGM-Symposium, Hamburg, Oktober 1989. Proceedings. XIX, 575 Seiten. 1989

Band 220: F. Stetter, W. Brauer (Hrsg.), Informatik und Schule 1989: Zukunftsperspektiven der Informatik für Schule und Ausbildung. GI-Fachtagung, München, November 1989. Proceedings. XI, 359 Seiten. 1989.

Band 221: H. Schelhowe (Hrsg.), Frauenwelt – Computerräume. GI-Fachtagung, Bremen, September 1989. Proceedings. XV, 284 Seiten. 1989.

Band 222: M. Paul (Hrsg.), GI – 19. Jahrestagung I. München, Oktober 1989. Proceedings. XVI, 717 Seiten. 1989.

Band 223: M. Paul (Hrsg.), GI – 19. Jahrestagung II. München, Oktober 1989. Proceedings. XVI, 719 Seiten. 1989.

Band 224: U. Voges, Software-Diversität und ihre Modellierung. VIII, 211 Seiten. 1989

Band 225: W. Stoll, Test von OSI-Protokollen. IX, 205 Seiten. 1989.

Band 226: F. Mattern, Verteilte Basisalgorithmen. IX, 285 Seiten. 1989.

Band 227: W. Brauer, C. Freksa (Hrsg.), Wissensbasierte Systeme. 3. Internationaler GI-Kongreß, München, Oktober 1989. Proceedings. X, 544 Seiten. 1989.

Band 228: A. Jaeschke, W. Geiger, B. Page (Hrsg.), Informatik im Umweltschutz. 4. Symposium, Karlsruhe, November 1989. Proceedings. XII, 452 Seiten. 1989.

Band 229: W. Coy, L. Bonsiepen, Erfahrung und Berechnung. Kritik der Expertensystemtechnik. VII, 209 Seiten. 1989.

Band 230: A. Bode, R. Dierstein, M. Göbel, A. Jaeschke (Hrsg.), Visualisierung von Umweltdaten in Supercomputersystemen. Karlsruhe, November 1989. Proceedings. XII, 116 Seiten. 1990.

Band 231: R. Henn, K. Stieger (Hrsg.), PEARL 89 – Workshop über Realzeitsysteme. 10. Fachtagung, Boppard, Dezember 1989. Proceedings. X, 243 Seiten. 1989.

Band 232: R. Loogen, Parallele Implementierung funktionaler Programmiersprachen. IX, 385 Seiten. 1990.

Band 233: S. Jablonski, Datenverwaltung in verteilten Systemen. XIII, 336 Seiten. 1990.

Band 234: A. Pfitzmann, Diensteintegrierende Kommunikationsnetze mit teilnehmerüberprüfbarem Datenschutz. XII, 343 Seiten. 1990.

Band 235: C. Feder, Ausnahmebehandlung in objektorientierten Programmiersprachen. IX, 250 Seiten. 1990.

Band 236: J. Stoll, Fehlertoleranz in verteilten Realzeitsystemen. IX, 200 Seiten. 1990.

Band 237: R. Grebe (Hrsg.), Parallele Datenverarbeitung mit dem Transputer. Aachen, September 1989. Proceedings. VIII, 241 Seiten. 1990.

Band 238: B. Endres-Niggemeyer, T. Hermann, A. Kobsa, D. Rösner (Hrsg.), Interaktion und Kommunikation mit dem Computer. Ulm, März 1989. Proceedings. VIII, 175 Seiten. 1990.

Band 239: K. Kansy, P. Wißkirchen (Hrsg.), Graphik und KI. Königswinter, April 1990. Proceedings. VII, 125 Seiten. 1990.

Informatik-Fachberichte 285

Herausgeber: W. Brauer
im Auftrag der Gesellschaft für Informatik (GI)

Subreihe Künstliche Intelligenz
Mitherausgeber: C. Freksa
in Zusammenarbeit mit dem Fachbereich 1
„Künstliche Intelligenz" der GI

Th. Christaller (Hrsg.)

GWAI-91
15. Fachtagung für Künstliche Intelligenz

Bonn, 16. - 20. September 1991

Proceedings

Springer-Verlag Berlin Heidelberg GmbH

Herausgeber

Thomas Christaller
Gesellschaft für Mathematik und Datenverarbeitung (GMD)
Institut für Angewandte Informationstechnik, Forschungsbereich KI
Schloß Birlinghoven, W-5205 Sankt Augustin 1

GWAI-91
15. Jahrestagung „Künstliche Intelligenz"

Veranstaltet vom Fachbereich 1 „Künstliche Intelligenz" der GI

Programmkomitee

L. Bonsiepen (Bremen)
L. Dreschler-Fischer (Hamburg)
U. Furbach (Koblenz)
J. Grabowski (Berlin)
C. Kemke (Saarbrücken)

D. Koch (Berlin)
C. Lischka (Sankt Augustin)
H. Marburger (Darmstadt)
C. Reddig (Saarbrücken)
S. Wrobel (Sankt Augustin)

Programmkomiteevorsitz und Tagungsleitung

Th. Christaller

CR Subject Classification (1991): I.2.0-4, I.2.6-8

ISBN 978-3-540-54558-3   ISBN 978-3-662-02711-0 (eBook)
DOI 10.1007/978-3-662-02711-0

Vorwort

Die diesjährige GWAI ist die 15. Fachtagung für Künstliche Intelligenz. Sie ist ein weiterer Schritt, um die GWAI einerseits attraktiv für alle wissenschaftlich Interessierten in der Künstlichen-Intelligenz-Forschung zu halten und andererseits der Tatsache Rechnung zu tragen, daß inzwischen für viele Teilgebiete eigene Veranstaltungen existieren und die Anzahl der KI-Tagungen insgesamt gestiegen ist. Aufgrund der Diskussionen über ein neues Konferenzkonzept für den Fachbereich Künstliche Intelligenz habe ich mit Hilfe der Erfahrungen der letzten beiden GWAIs einige Veränderungen verstärkt.

Eine nur auf den ersten Blick vordergründige Veränderung ist der Tagungsort. Bis 1983 fand die GWAI in Bad Honnef statt. Es mußte dann aber aufgrund der höheren Teilnehmerzahl eine neue Tagungsstätte gefunden werden. Nach einigen Experimenten – Dassel, Wingst, Dassel, Ottenheim – etablierte sich die GWAI in Eringerfeld bei Geseke. Der diesjährige Tagungsort Bonn ist auf jeden Fall leichter erreichbar als alle bisherigen. Die Tagungsstätte selbst wurde unter dem Gesichtspunkt, daß möglichst alle Teilnehmer in demselben Gebäude untergebracht werden können, in dem auch genügend geeignete Tagungsräume sein sollten, ausgewählt.

Das Tagungsprogramm gliedert sich in vier große Blöcke: vier Einführungsveranstaltungen, vier Hauptvorträge, neunundzwanzig Fachvorträge und sieben Workshops. Daneben gibt es eine Reihe von Sitzungen der Teilgliederungen des Fachbereichs Künstliche Intelligenz und der Fachbereichsleitung. Die Hauptvorträge wurden von mir unter dem Eindruck ausgewählt, daß außerhalb der KI und deren "traditionellen" Nachbardisziplinen wie Philosophie, Psychologie und Linguistik, neue Zugänge der Beschreibung und Erklärung kognitiver Phänomene ermöglicht werden. Diese sind durch Neurophysiologie, Evolutionsbiologie und andere wissenschaftliche Disziplinen geprägt. Mir erschien es wichtig, den punktuell vorhandenen Dialog durch die GWAI auf eine breitere Basis zu stellen.

Der vorliegende Tagungsband enthält die Texte der 29 Fachvorträge. Die angesprochenen Themenbereiche dabei sind: Deduktion (5), Maschinelles Lernen (2), Planen (1), Sprachverarbeitung (6), Wissensrepräsentation (6), Expertensysteme (5), Automatisches Programmieren (1) und Konnektionismus (3). Damit setzt sich der Trend fort, den Heinz Marburger schon in seinem Vorwort zur GWAI-90 beschrieben hat. Die Schwerpunkte der eingereichten und auch angenommenen Beiträge liegen auf Deduktion, Sprachverarbeitung, Wissensrepräsentation und Expertensysteme. Andere Teilgebiete wie beispielsweise Bildverarbeitung, gesprochene Sprache oder Robotik sind im Vortragsprogramm nicht vertreten. Allerdings finden dieses Jahr wieder Einführungen und Workshops statt, die sich speziellen Fragestellungen auch in diesen Teilgebieten widmen.

Die GWAI ist seit vielen Jahren auf einem konstant hohen wissenschaftlichen Niveau. Auch die diesjährige GWAI konnte dies Dank des großen Engagements derjenigen erreichen, die die insgesamt 69 Arbeiten einreichten, die als Mitglieder des Programmkomitees und Nebengutachter gewirkt haben. Außerdem danke ich den vier Referenten der eingeladenen Hauptvorträge, den Organisatoren der Workshops und den Referenten der Einführungsveranstaltungen.

Jede Veranstaltung erfordert Unterstützung bei der Vorbereitung und Durchführung, und aufgrund eines persönlichen Mißgeschicks war dies für die GWAI-91 besonders notwendig. So ist es mir eine angenehme Pflicht, mich dafür zu bedanken: bei der GMD, die mir die Übernahme der Tagungsleitung ermöglicht hat; bei den Firmen, durch deren Spenden Studenten unterstützt werden konnten; bei den Mitgliedern des Programmkomitees, die über das übliche Maß sich engagiert haben; bei meinen Mitarbeiterinnen und Mitarbeiter Ulli Teuber, Monika Wendel und Brigitte Hönig für ihre tatkräftige Hilfe; bei Christine Harms und Lucia Sassen-Hesseler für die professionelle und angenehme Tagungsorganisation.

St. Augustin, im Juli 1991   Thomas Christaller

Albrecht, Andreas
Allgayer, Jürgen
André, Elisabeth

Becker, Barbara
Beick, Hans-Rainer
Berger, Frank
Böcker, H.-D.
Bonsiepen, Lena
Bosenink, Thorsten
Bothe, Klaus
Brewka, Gerd
Bruns, F. W.
Bry, Francois
Brzoska, Christoph
Busse, Joachim

Christaller, Thomas
Claussen, Ute
Coy, Wolfgang
Cunis, Roman

Dahr, Michael
Decker, Hendrik
Diederich, Joachim
Dreschler-Fischer, Leonie
Dressler, Oskar

Emde, Werner
Endres-Niggemeyer, Brigitte

Florath, Peter
Freitag, Hartmut
Freksa, Christian
Friedrich, Horst
Furbach, Ulrich

Gehne, Jürgen
Geske, Ulrich
Goltz, Hans-Joachim
Gordon, Thomas F.
Grabowski, Jan
Graf, Winfried
Günter, Andreas
Güsgen, Hans-Werner

Haarslev, Volker
Habel, Annegret
Hallendoorn, Hans
Hecht, Angelika
Hein, Manfred
Heinz, Wolfgang
Heitsch, Wolfram
Herre, Heinrich
Hertzberg, Joachim

Hille, Gunter
Hoeppner, Wolfgang
Hölldobler, Steffen
Hönisch, Ulf
Horz, Alexander
Hub, Albrecht
Huwig, Clemens

Janeztko, Dietmar
Jansen-Wenkeln, Roman

Kemke, Christel
Kietz, Jörg-Uwe
Kindermann, Jörg
Kobsa, Alfred
Koch, Dietrich
Kockskämper, Sabine
Kreyß, Jutta

Lange, Harald
Lau Stefanie
Lefebvre, Alexandre
Letz, Reinhold
Linster, Marc
Lischka, Christoph
Ludwig, Oliver

Marburger, Heinz
Martial, Frank v.
Matiasek, Johannes
Menzel, Wolfgang
Möller, Jens-Uwe
Möller, Ralf
Müller, Wolfgang

Nebel, Bernhard
Neitzke, Michael
Nerbonne, John
Neumann, Bernd
Neumann, Günter
Noack, J.

Owsnicki-Klewe, Bernd

Reddig, Carola
Rehbold, Robert
Reimer, Ulrich
Reithinger, Norbert
Rist, T.

Schieck, Matthias
Schild, Klaus
Schmidt, Karl-Heinrich
Schnepf, Uwe
Selbig, Joachim

Sprengel, Rainer
Stein, Thorsten v.
Stiehl, H. Siegfried

Trost, Harald

Ultsch, A.

Werner, Eric
Wirth, Rüdiger
Wrobel, Stefan

Zercher, Kai

INHALTSVERZEICHNIS

5. Wissensrepräsentation

6. Expertensysteme

7. Automatisches Programmieren

8. Konnektionismus

1. DEDUKTION

Generalized Earley Deduction and its Correctness

Clemens Beckstein
CS Department #8 (IMMD VIII)
University of Erlangen-Nuremberg
8520 Erlangen, W. Germany

Michelle Kim
IBM Research Division
T.J. Watson Research Center
Yorktown Heights, NY 10598

Abstract

This paper describes a deduction method that works both top-down and bottom-up. The method can be viewed as an extension of a well-known approach—Earley deduction—to handle negation-as-failure. We show that with respect to the stratified model theory of [1] the method is sound, that it is strongly complete (terminating) for function-free programs with negation, and complete for programs without negation if function symbols are allowed.

The method uses the call graph of a program to represent static dependencies, and a Truth Maintenance System to store dynamic dependencies between partial lemmas generated by the deduction method. We argue by means of examples that these dependencies allow the method to avoid some redundant deductions, and that they are useful in forward reasoning in the presence of negation-as-failure.

1 Introduction

Whether a logic program should be processed bottom-up or top-down has been much discussed in the literature. The two approaches have been compared and contrasted mainly on strong (i.e. terminating) completeness over programs without function symbols, weak (non-terminating) completeness, coverage and efficiency.

The top-down approach is goal directed, often a good feature for efficiency. However, it has been shown that strict top-down approaches cannot be strongly complete over programs without function symbols [4]. Vieille has described top-down approaches in which lemmas are used to obtain termination over programs without function symbols, and there is a completeness proof for one of his methods (see [13]). The bottom-up approach is complete and terminating over programs without function symbols, but used naively computes the entire deductive closure of a program in order to answer any question, so it is not usually efficient. Various methods based on 'magic sets' (cf. [12]) have been proposed to guide bottom-up deduction, but appear to sometimes need very large numbers of auxiliary 'magic rules' (see [2]).

Pereira and Warren proposed a mixed bottom-up and top-down deduction method (in [11]), which is based on an algorithm by Earley which parses context-free grammars [7] and techniques developed in the context of chart-parsing [9]. Earley deduction, while combining the bottom-up and top-down approaches, has not (to our knowledge) been extended to cover negation-as-failure.

In this paper we take the basic Earley deduction framework, extend it to handle negation-as-failure, and provide (strong) completeness and soundness proofs for the method. The method uses the call graph of a DATALOG program to constrain deduction in the presence of negation, and the ATMS [6] to maintain important data about the ongoing deduction process. It has been implemented as a meta-interpreter in PROLOG.

2 The Nature of Earley Deduction

Earley deduction works by utilizing two kinds of deduction steps: Instantiation and Reduction. We can think of instantiations as backward chaining steps (top-down) and reductions as forward chaining (bottom-up) steps. Backward chaining steps identify rules relevant to a given query and forward chaining steps compute the consequences of those rules. In Earley deduction backward and forward chaining are interleaved and partly grounded rules, as well as fragments of partly grounded rules (the lemmas), are maintained.

An Earley prover operates on two sets of definite clauses: the given program (input clauses) and a so-called state. The state is a collection of derived clauses (conditional lemmas). It is initialized with a query and describes the progress made by the prover in its attempt to derive answers to this query. At any moment a selection function distinguishes a certain literal of every non-unit clause in the state upon which either an instantiation or a reduction is performed.

In order to perform an *instantiation*, a clause in the current state is chosen whose selected body literal L unifies with the head of a non-unit clause $H \leftarrow B$ in the program. In this situation a new clause C' with $C' = (H \leftarrow B)\sigma$ is added to the state where $\sigma = \mathrm{mgu}(L, H)$ (the most general unifier of L and H). A *reduction step* involves a non-unit clause C of the state and a unit clause F from either the program or the state. If C' is the clause C with its selected body literal L removed, then the new clause added to the state is $C'\sigma$ where $\sigma = \mathrm{mgu}(L, F)$. In both cases a check whether the new clause is subsumed by an older clause in the state is made before the clause is added.

As can be seen from these definitions, Earley deduction computes only part of the fixpoint of a logic program. It combines the goal-directedness of backward operating proof procedures like SLD resolution with the robustness of forward operating procedures. Earley deduction can be realized in many different ways: the method itself does not define a strategy that determines when to perform an instantiation and when to do a reduction if there is a choice. In order to simplify proofs about Earley deduction we reformulate Earley deduction as a meta-program E for a meta-interpreter that operates bottom-up[1]:

$$fact(Q) \leftarrow lemma(Q \leftarrow B) \wedge fact(B) \qquad (E1)$$
$$query(B) \leftarrow lemma(Q \leftarrow B) \wedge B \neq (C_1 \wedge C_2) \qquad (E2)$$
$$query(B_1) \leftarrow lemma(Q \leftarrow B_1 \wedge B_2) \qquad (E3)$$
$$lemma(Q \leftarrow B) \leftarrow query(Q) \wedge rule(Q \leftarrow B) \qquad (E4)$$
$$lemma(Q \leftarrow B_2) \leftarrow lemma(Q \leftarrow B_1 \wedge B_2) \wedge fact(B_1) \qquad (E5)$$

The variables in this meta-program range over atoms or conjunctions of atoms in the language of the object-program. $fact(Q)$ is considered true if either Q is a fact of the program or $fact(Q)$ was deduced earlier by rule (E1). $rule(Q \leftarrow B)$ is true if $(Q \leftarrow B)$ is a rule of the object-program. Rules (E1) and (E5) realize reduction steps whereas rule (E4) is responsible for instantiations. Rules (E3) and (E5) make up a left-to-right selection strategy.

The following is a suitable bottom-up operating meta-interpreter (called demo and written in VM-PROLOG). We will need it later for termination considerations:

```
demo(Q,P,Ans) <-                                        (F1)
    vunion([query(Q)],P,S1) &
    iterate(S1,S2) &
    set_of(A, member(fact(A),S2) &
            is_instance_of(A,Q),Ans).
iterate(S1,S2) <-                                       (F2)
    step(S1,S3) &
    S1 =/ S3 &
    iterate(S3,S2).
iterate(S,S).                                           (F3)
step(S1,S2) <-                                          (F4)
    set_of(H, meta_rule(H <- B) & known(B,S1) &
            not(contained_in(H,S1)),N) &
    vunion(S1,N,S2).
known(B1 & B2,S) <- / &                                 (F5)
    known(B1,S) & known(B2,S).
```

---

[1] We assume that $\wedge$ associates to the right.

```
known(B1 =/ B2,S) <- / &                                          (F6)
     B1 =/ B2.
known(B,S) <- member(B,S).                                        (F7)
```

The first argument of the demo predicate is the (atomic) query given to the object-program. The second argument P denotes the object-program which the Earley prover E operates on. We assume it to be already in a processable form, i.e. all facts F in P are replaced by fact(F) and all rules R by rule(R). Since P is represented as a PROLOG-list we also assume that no two distinct clauses in P use the same variable. The third argument eventually is the list of answers for q computed by demo wrt. P. A literal is_instance_of(A,Q) shall be true if and only if A is a substitution instance of Q; and meta_rule(C) looks up a clause C in the program being interpreted—in this case the meta-program E. contained_in(H,S1) is true if a variant of the term H occurs in the list S1. vunion is like the PROLOG standard predicate union but uses contained_in instead of member to do its membership tests. set_of(T,G,L) computes the list L of all templates T such that generator G succeeds. It always succeeds (possibly producing an empty list of solutions).

Here is an example for an Earley deduction. Let P be the program

```
p(X) <- q(X) & r(X).
q(X) <- s(X).
r(a).
s(a).  s(b).
```

The query p(b) will then result in the following iteration steps:

```
            query(p(b)).                              (user)
Step 1:     lemma(p(b) <- q(b) & r(b)).     (E4)      (instantiation)
Step 2:     query(q(b)).                    (E3)
Step 3:     lemma(q(b) <- s(b)).            (E4)      (instantiation)
Step 4:     fact(q(b)).                     (E1)      (reduction)
            query(s(b)).                    (E2)
Step 5:     lemma(p(b) <- r(b)).            (E5)      (reduction)
Step 6:     query(r(b)).                    (E2)
```

Step 7 does not produce any new queries, facts or lemmas. Thus p(b) is not deducible. In the course of the deduction only one new fact was derived (q(b))—the rest of P's fixpoint (q(a), p(a)) was irrelevant to the evaluation of the query and therefore not taken into account by the prover.

Plain Earley deduction can only handle object-programs consisting of definite clauses. This restriction cannot be relaxed easily as long as the state is represented just as a set of lemmas without information about interdependencies between those lemmas. The interdependencies really become important as soon as programs with negation are to be processed and—as we show in [10]—when explanations for failed queries are to be generated.

3   Constraining the Amount of Deduction

In this section we will show that Earley deduction automatically uses only those rules of a positive logic program for inferences, that—according to the call graph—are relevant to a given query. In the following discussion about negation we describe how Earley deduction for programs with negation can be made to work more efficiently by using information in the call graph.

Informally the call graph for a given logic program P is the directed graph representing the *refers to* relation between the relation symbols of P (for a formal definition cf. [1]): The edges leaving a node r of the call graph depict which other relations make up the *definition* of r (i.e. the set of the clauses in P that have the relation symbol r in their head). We write $q \leq p$ iff p refers to q or if there are $p_1, \ldots, p_n$ such that $p_1 \leq \ldots \leq p_n$ (i.e. $\leq$ is transitively closed).

Applied to Horn clause programs, Earley deduction instantiates only those clauses to the state that are—according to the call graph—relevant to the query:

Lemma 1 *Given a Horn clause program P and a query q with relation symbol r_q, then for any clause C in the current state, with r_C the relation symbol in the head of C, we have: $r_C \leq r_q$.*

PROOF By induction: Reductions only introduce lemmas for relations that are already represented in the state and therefore—wrt. the call graph—must be below any query present in the state. Instantiations by their very definition can only yield lemmas for relations referred to by the lemmas in the state that triggered the respective instantiation. $\square$

Hence, if we abbreviate the set $\{q\sigma \mid q\sigma$ is ground and derivable from P using (E1)-(E5)$\}$ with $Ans_P(q)$, the following consequence is immediate:

Corollary 1 *Let P be a Horn clause program and q be a query in the language of P with relation symbol r_q and let $P' := P - \{C \mid r_C \not\leq r_q$, where r_C is the relation symbol of C and $C \in P\}$. Then $Ans_P(q) = Ans_{P'}(q)$.*

In other words, given a Horn clause program P and a query q with relation symbol r_q, an Earley prover can and does safely ignore any definition for relations where the relation symbol is r and $r \not\leq r_q$.

Earley deduction performs better than one would get by just using the information in the call graph, since it also propagates partial instantiations from the goal to the clauses that could help to prove it.

4 The Treatment of Negation

One of the major drawbacks of plain Earley deduction is its limitation to definite clauses. Especially the lack of negation seems to be problematic. In this section we will describe how Earley deduction can be generalized to handle logic programs with negative literals in clause bodies.

For this purpose, we augment the meta-program E by two additional rules to get the program E_{neg} for Earley deduction with negation:

$$fact(Q) \leftarrow lemma(Q \leftarrow \neg B) \wedge assumable(\neg B) \tag{E6}$$
$$lemma(Q \leftarrow B_2) \leftarrow lemma(Q \leftarrow \neg B_1 \wedge B_2) \wedge assumable(\neg B_1) \tag{E7}$$

The predicate *assumable* provides the self referential link to the meta-interpreter necessary to do proofs via negation-as-failure. An evaluation of the new meta-predicate *assumable* does no variable bindings; it results in an invocation of a new instance of the meta-interpreter on the query B whenever the question $assumable(\neg B)$ has to be answered. If the new instance is unable to prove an instance of the query B given to it then, and only then, does the parent instance interpret $assumable(\neg B)$ as being true[2]. Since Earley deduction is lemma-generating, only the first of two $\neg B$ tests for the same B is expensive: upon evaluating $\neg B$ the second time, either $assumable(\neg B)$ was deduced previously and is now available in the state, or a counter example to $\neg B$ (namely a ground instance of B) is known.

As can be seen from these definitions, the evaluation of the negative literal to be reduced has to be done in its entirety before a decision whether to reduce the clause or not can be made. That is the only way we can do it if we do not fix the search strategy in advance[3]. Our way of treating negation-as-failure is therefore designed for use with programs that are stratified (cf. [1]), because otherwise the prover could get lost in an infinite chain of goals from p to $\neg p$ and back to p.

---

[2]We will investigate this treatment of the *assumable* predicate in some more detail later in this paper.
[3]E.g. by means of local selection functions.

We assume that the reader knows what it means that a DATALOG program P has a stratification $P = P_1 \dot{\cup} \ldots \dot{\cup} P_n$ (cf. [1]). In this case we use $P[i]$ as an abbreviation for $P_1 \dot{\cup} \ldots \dot{\cup} P_i$ with ($i \leq n$). We also define a function *stratum* on the set of relation symbols with $stratum(r) := \min_i \{r \text{ is defined in } P[i]\}$. Relation symbols for which there is no definition in P by default have the lowest stratum number assigned to them.

The following lemma can easily be shown by using the fact that the call graph of a stratified program can not have cycles containing a negative edge:

Lemma 2 *If P is a stratified program mentioning relation symbols p and q, then $q \leq p$ entails* $stratum(q) \leq stratum(p)$.

We therefore add the following clause to the known predicate of the PROLOG program demo which realizes our bottom-up meta-interpreter:

```
known(assumable(not(B)),P) <- prune(P,B,pruned_P) & demo(B,pruned_P,[]).      (F8)
```

Here not(B) is just the PROLOG notation for $\neg B$ and [] the empty set, and given a stratified program P and a literal B the PROLOG predicate prune computes $pruned\_P := P[stratum(B)]$. Corollary (1) and lemma (2) ensure that demo can now process the meta-program E_{neg} consisting of (E1)–(E5) and (E6)–(E7) which implements Earley deduction for programs with negation.

Our decision to realize negation via recursive instances of the prover now confronts us with a subtle design problem: should every instance of the prover maintain its own state? Or should all instances share one global state? It is of course desirable that the instances know about lemmas that were deduced by their parent instances. The following little program fragment tries to justify this claim:

$$a \leftarrow c \land \neg b \qquad\qquad\qquad (D1)$$
$$b \leftarrow c \qquad\qquad\qquad (D2)$$

Let the query be a and let us assume that c can be proven by some lengthy deduction performed while evaluating rule (D1). Then the instance evaluating $\neg b$ (using rule (D2)) can come up much faster with a (negative) answer if it knows that its parent instance already positively answered c. Thus starting a new instance with an empty state would be an inefficient solution.

It is also desirable that information deduced by child instances is made available to their parents, as the following program fragment illustrates:

$$a \leftarrow \neg b \qquad\qquad\qquad (U1)$$
$$a \leftarrow c \qquad\qquad\qquad (U2)$$
$$b \leftarrow c \qquad\qquad\qquad (U3)$$

Again, the query shall be a and we assume that c can be proven by some lengthy deduction. We also assume that rule (U1) is tried first. The instance evaluating $\neg b$ fails, but in rule (U3) it also deduces the lemma c which could be used by its parent instance to instantly complete a proof for a.

Having a global state would also be bad: if a child instance I_d of an instance I_p could access all the lemmas of its parent I_p, then amongst those lemmas also is the lemma which triggered the invocation of I_d (or a collection of lemmas that allows the deduction of a lemma that can trigger an invocation of I_d). An attempt by I_d to reduce this lemma would result in the invocation of a child instance of I_d equivalent to I_d itself, which could try the same thing. This can not happen if an instance does not have access to program clauses (and lemmas eventually depending on program clauses) which belong to strata above the stratum it is operating on.

We therefore have to address two problems:

1. how to represent the state so that different instances of the meta-interpreter can share lemmas relevant to all of them and

2. how to constrain the amount of information that flows between those instances.

Both problems can be solved by utilizing a subset of the truth-maintenance techniques provided by an ATMS [6] together with the call graph and stratification information.

5 Earley Deduction and Truth-Maintenance

Our Earley prover is assisted by a so called Assumption-Based Truth Maintenance System (ATMS, cf. [6]). Its role is—drastically simplified—to behave like an "intelligent" notebook: it efficiently stores reasoning steps made by the prover and maintains dependencies between these steps. For this purpose noteworthy data of the prover is mapped onto *nodes* in the ATMS. These nodes contain information as to whether their data are currently believed in and as to how they are involved in the reasoning of the problem solver—in other words, how they are *justified* by other nodes of the ATMS. There are distinguished nodes—so-called *assumptions*—which are not justified by other nodes. In the ATMS, justifications have the form of propositional Horn clauses: If $x_1, \ldots, x_n$ and y_n are nodes then for $(n > 0)$ the formula $x_1, \ldots, x_n \Rightarrow y$ means that the prover believes in the data represented by the *consequent node* y (the justified node), whenever there is evidence for the data represented by the *antecedent nodes* $x_1, \ldots, x_n$.

Our prover reports justifications to the ATMS and expects it to efficiently answer the question whether a given node holds wrt. to a given *context*, represented by a set of assumptions (also called an *environment*). For this purpose the ATMS computes $\vdash$, the derivability relation induced by the $\Rightarrow$ relation:

Definition 1 *A node n is derivable from a set of assumptions A (a context) and a set of justifications J, written $(A, J) \vdash n$, if there is a sequence of sets $S_1, \ldots, S_m$ such that*

$$A = S_1, \ S_{i+1} = S_i \cup \{y \mid \exists\, (x_1, \ldots, x_k \Rightarrow y) \in J \text{ with } x_j \in S_i \text{ for } (1 \leq j \leq k)\}, \text{ and } n \in S_m.$$

A node holds wrt. to a given context, if it is derivable from this context and the currently known justifications.

The data describing the current state of the proof consist of the object-program and a growing collection of lemmas. Each clause C in the state is represented by exactly one node n_C in the ATMS. Clauses which are just variants of each other are mapped onto the same ATMS node (they are *normalized*). Program clauses are represented by assumptions; the set A_P of all the assumptions for clauses in the program P is called the *program context* of P.

Whenever the prover performs an instantiation or reduction step, it also informs the ATMS about a corresponding justification. For Horn clause programs these justifications are obtained as follows. Let C be the selected state clause and L be the literal in the body of C the prover chooses for the next deduction step: If $H \leftarrow B$ is a non-unit program clause used for an instantiation with $\sigma = \mathrm{mgu}(L, H)$, then the justification $n_{(H \leftarrow B)} \Rightarrow n_{(H \leftarrow B)\sigma}$ is reported to the ATMS. If C' is the clause C with its selected literal L removed and F a unit clause used for a reduction with $\sigma = \mathrm{mgu}(L, F)$, then the justification $n_F, n_C \Rightarrow n_{C'\sigma}$ is transmitted to the ATMS.

Each instance of the prover maintains a private context. This context, its *positive context*, is always a subset of A_P and specifies the part of the program that the instance can use for deduction steps. The positive context $Pos(q, P)$ of an instance is completely determined by the query q that invoked this instance[4]:

Definition 2 *Let P be a logic program and L be a literal in the language of P with relation symbol r_L. If r_C is the relation symbol of the program clause C associated with the assumption $a_C \in A_P$, then: $a_C \in Pos(L, P)$ iff $r_C \leq r_L$.*

To process programs containing negation, the system also maintains a global context $Neg(P)$, the so-called *negative context*. This context is common to all instances of the prover. It represents the set of all propositions $\neg B$ where an attempt to prove B was unsuccessful. Thus, whenever the prover deduces a negative lemma $assumable(\neg B)$ for an atom B a *new* assumption $a_{\neg B}$ is created and associated with the node $n_{\neg B}$ and the negative context is augmented by $a_{\neg B}$. The negative context is initialized with the empty set.

---

[4] Recall that an instance of the prover, working on the query q—according to corollary 1—only needs to look at clauses with assumptions in $Pos(q, L)$.

Adding an assumption to the negative context amounts to assuming it by default (there was no way to produce evidence against it). For stratified programs there can be no default conflicts. That is why we could make the negative context global (common to all instances of the prover). The described treatment of negation therefore can not easily be extended to non-stratified programs.

We call $Ctxt(q, P) := Pos(q, P) \cup Neg(P)$ *the context* of an instance of the prover. It specifies which part of the program is visible to it. Hence, if the dependency net contains the justifications in set J, then an instance for query q can see a clause C only if it is accessible via its context, i.e. if C *holds* in $Ctxt(q, P)$: $(Ctxt(q, P), J) \vdash n_C$. Since any clause in the state is eventually justified by a set of program clauses (better, their corresponding assumptions), or is assumed by default (i.e. by an assumption in the negative context), the context hides exactly that part of the state which was not derived by the program fragment specified via the context and which therefore is not relevant to the query posed to the instance.

It is now clear how our coupling of an Earley prover with an ATMS solves the two problems stated in the previous section:

1. The dependency net of the ATMS is a global data structure storing information about the program, the state for each prover instance and the dependencies between clauses.

2. Each instance has its own limited view of this shared data structure. It sees exactly that part relevant to it.

3. All the lemmas deduced by an instance become automatically known to all other instances for which they could become relevant.

Our approach works independently of the particular search strategy. It leaves ample space for fine-tuning the Earley prover by a good choice of deduction strategies.

6 Soundness and Completeness Considerations

We will now show that Earley deduction has at least the power of a PROLOG-style prover, i.e. we will give a formal proof of the soundness and completeness of Earley deduction. We will also show *strong* completeness for DATALOG programs (i.e. we will prove that the interpreter halts once it has computed all correct answers to a query).

Let us first handle the case for definite clause programs. Another look at the meta-program for plain Earley deduction (rules (E1)–(E5)) reveals that this program can also be interpreted as a specification of a fixpoint operator T_e for Earley deduction[5]: an application of T_e is defined by exactly one iteration of the step predicate in the demo meta-interpreter for the meta-program E.

We assume that the reader is familiar with the well-known immediate consequence operator T for Horn databases. As usual, if T is an operator on a set S with $P \subseteq S$, we write $T{\uparrow}^\omega(P) := \bigcup_{n \in \omega} T{\uparrow}^n(P)$ where $T{\uparrow}^0(P) := P$ and $T{\uparrow}^{n+1}(P) := T(T{\uparrow}^n(P)) \cup T{\uparrow}^n(P)$ for $n \in \omega$. We also use the abbreviation

$$\bar{P} := \{fact(F) \mid F \in P\} \cup \{rule(H \leftarrow B) \mid (H \leftarrow B) \in P\}.$$

With this notation the following lemma about Earley deduction holds (for a proof see [3]):

Lemma 3 *Let P be a Horn clause program and A be an atom in the language of P that is made ground by a substitution τ. Then for all $P' \supseteq \bar{P}$ and all $n \in \omega$:*

$$A\tau \in T{\uparrow}^n(P) \text{ and } query(A) \in T_e{\uparrow}^\omega(P') \implies fact(A\tau) \in T_e{\uparrow}^\omega(P').$$

Using this lemma we now can establish the soundness and completeness of Earley deduction:

---

[5] For a general discussion of specifying operators as bottom-up meta-interpreters see [5].

9

Theorem 1 *Let P be a Horn clause program and A be an atom in the language of P that is made ground by a substitution τ:*

$$A\tau \in T{\uparrow}^{\omega}(P) \quad \text{iff} \quad \mathit{fact}(A\tau) \in T_e{\uparrow}^{\omega}(\bar{P} \cup \{query(A)\}).$$

PROOF The sufficient condition (Soundness) is evident (a reduction is a resolution step, and an instantiation is of course also truth preserving!).

In order to show necessity (Completeness) we use lemma (3). Let $A\tau \in T{\uparrow}^{\omega}(P)$. Then $\mathit{fact}(A\tau) \in T_e{\uparrow}^{\omega}(P')$ follows immediately if we choose $P' := \bar{P} \cup \{query(A)\}$ and apply this lemma. $\qquad\Box$

For recursive but function-free programs (also called DATALOG programs) we also know that answers to a query can be found in a finite number of steps—the proof procedure always terminates:

Corollary 2 *Let P be a function-free logic program. Then for all queries* q, *programs* P *and computed answer sets* A, demo(q,P,A) *applied to E stops in a finite number of steps.*

PROOF Obvious, therefore only informal: The program P given to the meta-interpreter is finite. Hence the predicates step and known of the interpreter are recursive[6]. The predicate step is monotone in its first argument; thus the step iteration in the iterate predicate defines a strictly monotone sequence of sets S_i. This sequence of sets must be finite, since all the S_i are subsets of the fixpoint of $\bar{P}$, which is finite itself, since P is a function-free program. Thus iterate and therefore demo is recursive as well. $\qquad\Box$

How generalized Earley deduction handles negation ensures that the analogous result for SLDNF-Resolution can be established, at least if we restrict our attention to stratified DATALOG (recursive, function-free programs with NAF)—cf. [1]. For this purpose we interpret the meta-program consisting of rules (E1)–(E5) and (E6)–(E7) as the specification of a fixpoint operator—this time the operator T_{neg}. Again one application of T_{neg} corresponds to one iteration of the step predicate—this time in the enhanced demo meta-interpreter ((F1)–(F7), (F8)) for the meta-program E_{neg}. But it is not immediate that the program indeed defines a unique operator, since the *assumable* predicate is defined by reference to the meta-interpreter itself.

If B is an atom in the language of program P, then the desired logical property of the *assumable* predicate can be stated as follows:

$$\begin{array}{c} assumable(\neg B) \in T_{neg}{\uparrow}^{\omega}(\bar{P} \cup \{query(\neg B)\}) \\ \text{iff} \\ \text{there is a ground substitution } \tau \text{ such that: } \mathit{fact}(B\tau) \notin T_{neg}{\uparrow}^{\omega}(\bar{P} \cup \{query(B)\}) \end{array} \qquad (1)$$

Although it is easy to see that this property is effectively decidable for DATALOG programs (the Herbrand universe of a DATALOG program is always finite), it is not exactly the property we ought to discuss. A look back at our informal description of how the meta-predicate *assumable* is handled by the prover reveals that its actual semantics—the one usually found in standard PROLOG processors—is different:

$$\begin{array}{c} assumable(\neg B) \in T_{neg}{\uparrow}^{\omega}(\bar{P} \cup \{query(\neg B)\}) \\ \text{iff} \\ \text{there is no ground substitution } \tau \text{ such that: } \mathit{fact}(B\tau) \in T_{neg}{\uparrow}^{\omega}(\bar{P} \cup \{query(B)\}) \end{array} \qquad (2)$$

Fortunately it recently has been shown (in [8]) that any DATALOG program P can be effectively transformed into a logically equivalent DATALOG program P' where the execution of P' by a standard PROLOG processor preserves the logical meaning of the negations in P and negative literals are only evaluated when they were previously made ground. Thus we can have the logical meaning, if we prefer it to the operational meaning as exhibited by standard PROLOG systems, by making sure that the programs to be processed by our system first undergo this transformation. For the transformed programs, the *assumable* predicate

---

[6]I.e. computable and finitely decidable.

is applied only to ground literals B, i.e. conditions (1) and (2) coincide. In the remainder of this paper we will adhere to the logical meaning.

Now let us assume that the program P, which contains negation, is a stratifiable DATALOG program: $P = P_1 \,\dot\cup\, \ldots \,\dot\cup\, P_n$. Based on corollary (1) and lemma (2), we then get the following lemma, which immediately follows from the definitions of the predicate demo ((F1)–(F7) and (F8)) and the meta-interpreter E_{neg}:

Lemma 4 *Let P be a stratifiable DATALOG program and B be a ground literal in the language of P. Then:*

$$assumable(\neg B) \in T_{neg}\!\uparrow^\omega(\bar{P} \cup \{query(\neg B)\})$$
$$iff$$
$$fact(B) \notin T_{neg}\!\uparrow^\omega(\overline{P[stratum(B)]} \cup \{query(B)\}).$$

Looking closer at the enhanced interpreter, we can make two more observations:

1. The definition of B is in a lower stratum than the rule that contained the $\neg B$ literal which triggered the test of assumability. Therefore $\overline{P[stratum(B)]}$ in the RHS of (F8) is a proper subset of $\bar{P}$. Hence (F8) evaluates the *assumable* predicate by a course-of-values recursion that eventually (after a maximum of n recursions) reduces the right-hand side to a test over the lowest stratum of $\bar{P}$, where clauses do not contain negative literals and derivability is well defined (as in the E meta-program).

2. Also for DATALOG programs the set $T_{neg}\!\uparrow^\omega(\bar{P} \cup \{query(B)\})$ is finite, because for them $T\!\uparrow^\omega(P)$ and $T_e\!\uparrow^\omega(\bar{P} \cup \{query(B)\})$ are finite.

Thus $assumable(\neg B)$ is a well-defined and effectively decidable concept if we apply it to stratified DATALOG programs.

A simple generalization of the argument in corollary (2) together with lemma (4) shows that the meta-interpreter for Earley deduction always terminates after a finite number of steps:

Lemma 5 *Let P be a DATALOG program with negation. Then the predicate* demo(q,P,A) *computed by the meta-interpreter for E_{neg} is recursive.*

We assume that the reader is familiar with the definition of the standard model M_P of a stratifiable DATALOG program P. Then the following theorem ensures the (strong) correctness (soundness and completeness) of Earley deduction for DATALOG programs with negation-as-failure (a detailed proof is contained in [3]):

Theorem 2 *Let P be a DATALOG program with stratification $P_1 \,\dot\cup\, \ldots \,\dot\cup\, P_n$ and A be a ground atom in the language of P:*

1. $A \in M_P$ iff $fact(A) \in T_{neg}\!\uparrow^\omega(\bar{P} \cup \{query(A)\})$.

2. $A \notin M_P$ iff $assumable(\neg A) \in T_{neg}\!\uparrow^\omega(\bar{P} \cup \{query(\neg A)\})$.

7 Conclusions

We have described a deduction method that works both top-down and bottom-up. It can be seen as an extension of Earley deduction to handle negation-as-failure. Wrt. to the stratified model theory of [1] the method is sound, strongly complete (terminating) for function-free programs with negation, and complete for programs without negation if function symbols are allowed.

The deduction method uses the call graph of an object-program to represent static dependencies, and a Truth Maintenance System to store dynamic dependencies between partial lemmas generated by the deduction method. We have argued that these dependencies allow the method to avoid some redundant deductions, and that they are useful in forward reasoning in the presence of negation-as-failure.

A more substantial advantage of maintaining dependencies may be realized when they are used to generate explanations of both successful and failing deductions. As we show in [10], the ATMS allows us to overcome many of the difficulties with classical tree-based approaches to explanation and to generate useful explanations, by maintaining suitable intermediate results.

8 Acknowledgements

The authors are indebted to Adrian Walker and Franciso Corella for their many valuable suggestions. We also thank B. Grosof, L. Morgenstern, and P. Sheridan for their helpful comments on the draft.

References

[1] Apt, K.R., Blair, H.A., Walker, A., *Towards a Theory of Declarative Knowledge*, In: Minker, J. (Ed.), *Foundations of Deductive Databases and Logic Programming*, Morgan Kaufman Publ., Los Altos, California, 1988

[2] Balbin, I., Meenakshi, K., *A Query Independent Method for Magic Set Computation on Stratified Databases*, Proc. Int. Conf. on Fifth Generation Computer Systems, Tokyo, Japan, 1988, pp. 711–718

[3] Beckstein, C., Kim, M. *A Mixed Top-Down and Bottom-Up Deduction Method and its Correctness*, IBM Research Report RC 14965, Yorktown Heights, New York, 1989

[4] Brough, D., Walker, A., *Some practical properties of logic programming interpreters*, Proc. Int. Conf. on Fifth Generation Computer Systems, Institute for New Generation Computer Technology, Tokyo, Japan, 1984, pp. 149–156

[5] Bry, F., *Query Evaluation in Recursive Databases: Bottom-up and Top-down Reconciled*, Research Report IR-KB-64, ECRC, Munich, 1989

[6] deKleer, L., *An Assumption-Based Truth Maintenance System*, AI-Journal 28, 1986, pp. 127–162

[7] Earley, J., *An Efficient Context-Free Parsing Algorithm*, CACM, Vol. 13, 1970, pp. 94–102

[8] Foo, N., Rao, A., Taylor, A., Walker, A., *Deduced Relevant Types and Constructive Negation in Logic Programming*, IBM Research Report RC 13407, Yorktown Heights, New York, 1988

[9] Kay, M., *Algorithm Schemata and Data Structures in Syntactic Processing*, Tech. Rep., XEROX PARC, Palo Alto, California, 1980

[10] Kim, M., Beckstein, C., *Logical Explanations of Deductions*, IBM Research Report RC 15348, Yorktown Heights, New York,1990

[11] Pereira, F.C.N., Warren, D.H.D., *Parsing as Deduction*, Proc. 21st Annual Meeting of the ACL, MIT, Cambridge, 1983

[12] Ullman, J.D., *Bottom-Up Beats Top-Down for DATALOG*, Proc. 8th ACM SIGACT-SIGMOD-SIGART Symp. on Principles of Database Systems, Philadelphia, Pennsylvania, 1989, pp. 140–149

[13] Vieille, L., *A database-complete proof procedure based on SLD-resolution*, Proc. 4th Int. Conf. on Logic Programming, Melbourne, Australia, May 1987, pp. 74–103

A Completeness Proof Technique for
Resolution with Equality

Peter Baumgartner
Institut für Informatik
Universität Koblenz
Rheinau 3-4
5400 Koblenz

Net: peter@infko.uucp

Abstract. *We present a new proof technique for proving completeness of resolution calculi with equality. It is a direct proof technique in the tradition of the well-known semantic trees. We will show how to enumerate E-interpretations with a device called semantic E-tree and show how such a tree can be used as a basis for a refutation of a given unsatisfiable clause set. As a side effect of our proof technique we obtain new high-level inference rules for treating equality; these rules combine multiple equations during one single inference step. It is a design goal of our technique to be compatible with modern trends in automated reasoning, such as ordering restrictions and general theory reasoning. This work is intended as a basic step forwards in that direction.*

Keywords: Resolution, Equality, Semantic Tree

1 Introduction

The resolution principle is an important and well investigated proof calculus in automated reasoning. It is known to be correct and refutationally complete for clause sets ([Rob65]); while correctness is immmediately clear from the rules of the calculus, completeness is harder to prove. A classical completeness proof is based on *semantic trees*, an elegant device which has become very familiar by now ([CL73]).

Equational reasoning can be found in nearly every branch of mathematics and deduction systems; being of that fundamental importance, it deserves special treatment in automated reasoning. For that purpose, the *paramodulation* inference rule was developed already in the early days ([RW69]) as an additional inference rule for the resolution calculus. Now an important question is: is this new calculus still complete, relative to the intended equality models? Fortunately the answer to this question is "yes"; however, the traditional proof (see e.g. [CL73]) is complicated and not very elegant: it relies on the fact that the equational axioms can be expressed in clauses, and that every PI-refutation of a clause set which is enhanced with the equational axioms has an isomorphic refutation using resolution and paramodulation (a PI-refutation is a refutation using PI-resolution, a highly specialized variant of ordinary resolution ([CL73])). Thus, completeness of PI-resolution has to be shown as a prerequisite.

In this paper we will present a new proof technique for establishing completeness results for resolution with equality. In contrast to the technique based on PI-resolution, our proof technique is a *direct* one in the tradition of the abovementioned semantic trees. Similar trees for completeness proofs were proposed by [HR87, Pet83] (see also the discussion in the last section). Another work emphasizing a direct proof technique is ([FHS89b]); there, a completeness result for Horn equational logic via least fixpoints is established.

In our calculus equality will be treated by inference rules à la SLDE-Resolution ([Höl89]) where syntactically different but semantical equal terms are resolved in one single inference step.

be unsatisfiable; hence we can apply our E-reflection inference rule which joins all the clauses involved but cuts out the unsatisfiable literal set. In the example the resulting clause is $\neg P(f(a))$. Note that this clause is falsified by an *ancestor node* $P(f(a))$ of $P(f(b))$; hence there exists a shorter semantic tree falsifiying the clause set. Repeating this procedure will eventually yield an empty tree which falsifies the empty clause. Thus there exists a refutation for the initial clause set.

In this text we will present only the ground versions of our inference rules. Although lifting to the non-ground case is possible, we will not do so, because the main emphasis lies on the proof technique and it does not change when lifted.
Every refutation with our calculus can be modelled by a resolution and paramodulation refutation. Thus, as a side effect, we will proof completeness of the the original resolution and paramodulation calculus.

The advantages of our proof technique are: for the first, it is elegant and gives a better intuition for equational proofs (at least for us); for the second, it constitutes the bases for certain restriction strategies (e.g. enumerating the interpretations in some fixed ordering, i.e. *ordered resolution* which assign weights to predicate symbols; its completeness can be shown by appropriate tree reconstruction); for the third, it is extendable to other theories than equality, e.g. partial orders.

The rest of this article is structured as follows: in section 2 the calculus is defined; in section 3 we will introduce semantic E-trees and establish the neccessary facts for the subsequent completeness proof. Finally, we will discuss related work and suggest some improvements.

2 An Equational Calculus

DEFINITIONS

It is well known (see e.g. [CL73]) that it is sufficient to consider Herbrand-interpretations only, which assign a fixed meaning to all language elements short of atoms; thus we define a *(Herbrand-) interpretation* I to be any total function from the set of atoms to $\{true, false\}$ and denote I by the set of literals $H_I :=$ $\{A|I(A) = true\} \cup \{\neg A|I(A) = false\}$. Note that no H_I can contain both, A and $\neg A$. By abuse of notation we will identify I with H_I in the sequel. The motivation for the explicit representation of positive *and* negative literals lies in the ability to conveniently define partial interpretations; a *partial interpretation* is simply a subset of an interpretation. (Partial) interpretations are extended to homomorphisms on literals, clauses and clause sets by interpreting the logical connectives as usual. A clause set M is *satisfiable* iff there exists an interpretation which assigns *true* to all its clauses. Since the truth value of M depends from the interpretation of its literals only, it is sufficient to restrict the domain of interpretations to the literals of M. Therefore we define the *atom set of M*, $\mathcal{A}(M)$ ([CL73]) as the set consisting of all atoms A where A or $\neg A$ occurs in M. An *interpretation for M* is a partial interpretation which is total on the set $\{A, \neg A|A \in \mathcal{A}(M)\}$. Henceforth all interpretations are understood in this narrow sense and where M should be clear from the context. A literal set S is *consistent* iff it can be extended to an interpretation I (iff $I(S) = true$). Let X be a ground literal or a ground term. Then $X[s]$ means that X contains the term s and $X[s/t]$ means replacement of any occurence of s in X by t. Often we will write $X[t]$ instead if confusion is less likely. An *E-interpretation* is an interpretation satisfying the axioms of reflexivity, transitivity, symmetry and substitution of equal subterms. It is well known, that even for E-interpretations it is sufficient to restrict to Herbrand-E-Interpretations (see e.g. [CL73]). Since we deal with E-interpretations only we will omit the prefix E- in the sequel.

Equations are written infix using the symbol "$\approx$". Below we will relate our calculus to paramodulation. Let us therefore briefly recall the paramodulation rule. Let $C_1 \equiv s \approx t \vee R_1$ and $C_2 \equiv L[s] \vee R_2$ be two clauses. Then the *paramodulant of C_1 into C_2* is the clause $L[s/t] \vee R_1 \vee R_2$. A *symmetric variant* of a clause $s \approx t \vee R$ is the clause $t \approx s \vee R$. We write $s \Rightarrow_C t$ to denote the fact that s is paramodulated into t using a clause C or the symmetric variant of C.

As usual, * denotes the reflexive and transitive closure of a relation.

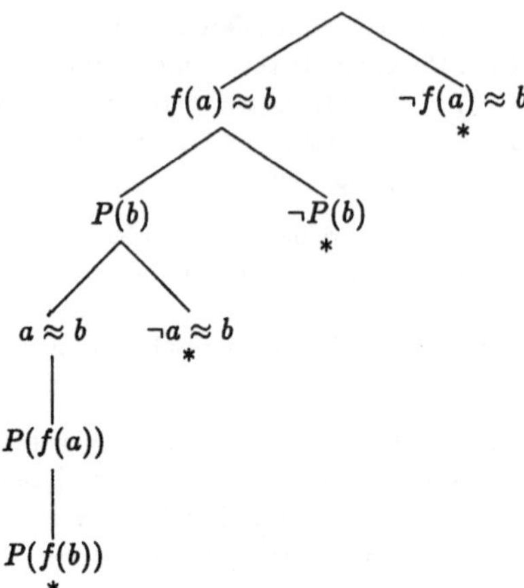

Figure 1: A semantic E-tree for M

In ([FHS89a]) a calculus similar to ours for Horn-logic is presented. The authors propose paramodulation and reflection inference rules modulo some equational theory. Our inference rules can be viewed as an extension of their rules towards non-Horn clauses.

The idea of our proof techique is best be described in comparison to ordinary semantic trees: an ordinary semantic tree enumerates (general) interpretations for ground instances of a given clause set, and by the Skolem-Herbrand-Gödel theorem it follows that this process comes to an end for unsatisfiable clause sets. The resulting semantic tree can be used to design a resolution refutation for the clause set. In our technique, we will keep this strategy, but we will not enumerate general interpretations, but only such interpretations which constrain the equality symbol to the intended interpretation of an equality relation (i.e. a transitive, reflexive and symmetry relation, closed under subterm replacement).

It reminds the question which inference rules to be employed in the refutation. In principle our semantic trees can be used to prove the completeness of the original resolution and paramodulation calculus. This plan, however, requires slightly more complicated semantic trees than those we would like to present. Hence we have decided to design inference rules which keep the trees simple. These inference rules (called E-reflection and E-lemma) are more "high-level" than paramodulation in the sense that they combine multiple equations during one single inference step.

In order to get an intention for our trees, let us give a simple example. Suppose the following equality unsatisfiable clause set M as given:

$$M = \{f(a) \approx b,\ a \approx b,\ P(b),\ \neg P(f(a)) \vee \neg P(f(b))\}$$

Now consider the tree in figure (1). Its nodes are labelled with literals, and the collection of all labels along a path forms a partial equality interpretation. Since M is unsatisfiable, every interpretation must falsify at least one clause in M; indeed, this is the case for the tree shown: it is easy to see that every leaf falsifies (i.e. is complementary to) a clause in M. Hence this tree is a sufficient basis for a refutation of M. How did we come to this tree ? It is constructed by starting with the empty tree and repeatedly appending on a leaf l in one of two ways: in the first way, l will be appended with a binary branch (which means a case analyses wrt. a given literal; cf. $P(b), \neg P(b)$ in figure (1)); in the second way an equational consequence of the interpretation given so far is appended as a single new son of l (cf. $P(f(a))$ in figure (1)). Now suppose the construction to be completed with the tree shown. Next we will outline how to design a refutation of the clause set based on the tree. Consider the node $P(f(b))$ which is an equational consequence of some other nodes along the branch (i.e. of $P(b), f(a) \approx b$ and $a \approx b$). Now, these nodes have complementary brothers $\neg P(b), \neg f(a) \approx b$ and $\neg a \approx b$. Using an appropriate induction argument it can be assured that these nodes are leaves; then there must exist clauses containing complementary literals $P(b), f(a) \approx b$ and $a \approx b$ again. Similarly, there must exist a clause containing the literal $\neg P(f(b))$ complementary to the node $P(f(b))$ (it is the clause $\neg P(f(b)) \vee \neg P(f(a))$). Now, the literal set $\{f(a) \approx b,\ P(b),\ a \approx b,\ \neg P(f(b))\}$ must

THE INFERENCE RULES

Definition 2.1 *(E-consequence)* Let I_p be a partial interpretation and L be a literal. Then L *is a logical E-consequence of* I_p iff $I_p \models L$ iff every E-interpretation extending I_p is a model of L.
We will write $S \models \Box$ for the fact that the literal set S is not consistent (inconsistent).

Definition 2.2 *(Ground Equational Resolution)* The inference rules of the *ground equational resolution calculus* are defined as follows:

E-reflection:

$$s_1 \approx t_1 \vee R_1$$
$$\vdots$$
$$s_n \approx t_n \vee R_n$$

if $\{s_1 \approx t_1 \ldots s_n \approx t_n \neg s \approx t\} \models \Box$:
$$\frac{\neg s \approx t \vee R}{R_1 \vee \ldots \vee R_n \vee R}$$

E-lemma:

$$s_1 \approx t_1 \vee R_1$$
$$\vdots$$

if $\{s_1 \approx t_1 \ldots s_n \approx t_n\} \models s \approx t$:
$$\frac{s_n \approx t_n \vee R_n}{s \approx t \vee R_1 \vee \ldots \vee R_n}$$

A *refutation* of a clause set M is defined to be a derivation of the empty clause $\Box$ from M.

Note that the inference rules are based on the purely model-theoretical notions of E-consequence, resp. E-inconsistency. The next lemma provides an equivalent operational semantics; it tells us that ground paramodulation is a sound and complete calculus for ground equational reasoning.

Lemma 2.1 *Let F be a set of positive equations, s and t be two ground terms. Then $\models s \approx t$ iff $s \Rightarrow_F^* t$*

But also note that the inference rules are not neccessarily bound to paramodulation. Indeed every equational calculus which is correct and complete for the conditions in the inference rules is admissible.

NON-EQUATIONS

When treating logic with equality the set of literals is usually divided into equations and non-equations. We will give up this distinction and deal with equations only. The advantage of this approach is that the semantic tree data structure and the proofs will be considerably simpler due to less case analyses.

Note that this approach causes no harm because every non-equation $P(s_1, \ldots, s_n)$ can be read as a "macro" expanding to $P(s_1, \ldots, s_n) \approx \top$, where $\top$ is a new constant symbol (with the meaning of "true"). Then a binary resolution step with the two parent clauses $P(s_1, \ldots, s_n) \vee R_1$ and $\neg P(s_1, \ldots, s_n) \vee R_2$ yielding $R_1 \vee R_2$ can be modelled by the following derivation wrt. ground equational resolution:

$$\frac{P(s_1, \ldots, s_n) \approx \top \vee R_1 \qquad \neg P(s_1, \ldots, s_n) \approx \top \vee R_2}{R_1 \vee R_2}$$

(by E-reflection, since $\{P(s_1, \ldots, s_n), \neg P(s_1, \ldots, s_n)\} \models \Box$ in every equational theory)

Furthermore, the substitution into non-equations is obviously subsumed by the substitution into equations. Suppose $P(s_1, \ldots, s_n) \approx \top$ and $Q(t_1, \ldots, t_m) \approx \top$ as given. Then the $E - lemma$ inference rule allows to derive the literal $P(s_1, \ldots, s_n) \approx Q(t_1, \ldots, t_m)$. However no binary resolution step resolving the corresponding non-equational literals exists. Consequently this E-lemma step is unneccessary and can be omitted. Thus, from an operational viewpoint, treating non-equations as equations does not cause any extra search space.

The rest of this text always assumes this transformation; hence we will deal with equations only, and the term *atom* is a synonym for *equation* and a *literal* is a (possibly negated) equation.

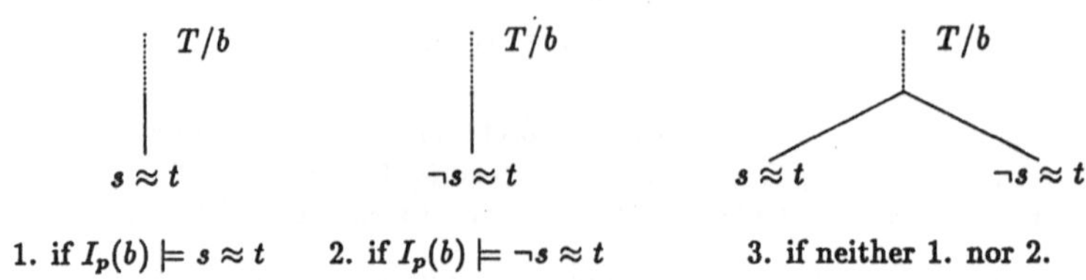

Figure 2: Definitional rules for semantic E-trees

3 Completeness

This section covers the main ideas, which are *semantic E-trees* and their application to completeness proofs. We will proceed as follows: In the first subsection semantic E-trees are formally defined. Then we will supply construction rules for semantic trees and record the neccessary facts. Next we will show that the trees constructed this way enumerate E-interpretations. Such trees will be used in the second subsection for the completeness proof.

SEMANTIC E-TREES AND THEIR PROPERTIES

As indicated in the introduction we are concerned with trees. More specifically, our trees have a branching factor ≤ 2 and the nodes are labelled with literals. More formally, let T be a tree and n be a node of T. Then the labelling function is denoted by $l_T(n)$ (or $l(n)$ for short). A *path* in T is a sequence $n_0 \circ n_1 \ldots$, where n_0 is the root and n_{i+1} is a son of n_i. A branch in T is a *finite* prefix of a path in T and is notated by T/n_k where n_k is the last node in the sequence. The *literal set* of a branch $b = n_0 \circ \ldots \circ n_k$, $L_T(b)$ is defined as $L_T(b) := \{l_T(n_i) | 0 \leq i \leq k\}$.

Definition 3.1 *(Semantic E-tree)* A *semantic E-tree* (or *semantic tree* for short) for a clause set M is a tree where every literal set is an interpretation for M and the root is labelled by the special atom $\top$ meaning *"true "*. For a given branch b we define the corresponding partial interpretation $I_p(b) = L(b)$, and we say b *satisfies* (*falsifies*) a clause C iff C is *true* (*false*) under $I_p(b)$.

Definition 3.2 *(Tree extension)* Let T be a semantic tree, b be a branch in T and E be an atom. Then T' is an *extension of b in T with E* if the following is obeyed (cf. figure (2)):

1. If $I_p(b) \models E$ then b is appended with one son labelled with E.

2. If $I_p(b) \models \neg E$ then b is appended with one son labelled with $\neg E$.

3. If neither 1. nor 2. does apply then b is appended with two sons labelled by E and $\neg E$.

The new nodes are called *derived nodes* in cases 1. and 2. and *original nodes* in case 3.

It is our intention to enumerate E-interpretations using trees. The next proposition states that the tree extension rules do not contradict this plan.

Proposition 1 *Let T' be obtained from T by tree extension. Then T' is a semantic tree.*

Proof.   Let b in T be extended with E. We have to show that the new branch b' in T' is a partial interpretation. We do a case analyses wrt. the definition rules of semantic trees:

1. Here $I_p(b') = I_p(b) \cup \{E\}$. Since $I_p(b) \models E$ any interpretation I satisfying $I_p(b)$ also satisfies E and thus satisfies $I_p(b')$. Hence $I_p(b')$ is a partial interpretation.

2. Here $I_p(b') = I_p(b) \cup \{\neg E\}$. Same argument as in case 1.

3. Suppose, to the contary, that $I_p(b') = I_p(b) \cup \{E\}$ were no partial interpretation, that is, there exists no interpretation which contains E. Then every interpretation extending $I_p(b)$ contains $\neg E$ and hence $I_p(b) \models \neg E$. So case 2. would have applied and not case 3. Contradiction. For symmetry reasons the same argumentation can be used for the other branch.

In our sematic trees the logical consequences of the partial interpretation constructed so far in a branch are *not* forced to be added to the tree (in [HR87] such an approach is taken). However, every branch can be extended to an interpretation. This is the main fact about semantic trees and shall be shown next.

Proposition 2 *Let M be a finite clause set. Then there exists a finite semantic tree such that*

1. *every branch is an interpretation for M, and*

2. *every interpretation for M is contained in some branch in T.*

Proof. The proof is by induction on the size n of the atom set $S = \mathcal{A}(M)$ of M. If $n = 0$ then the empty tree satisfies both conditions. Otherwise let $S = S' \cup \{E\}$ and suppose by the induction hypotheses that there exists a semantic tree T' with the desired properties for S'. Since T' is a semantic tree we can extend every branch in T' with E (definition (3.2)). Call the resulting tree T and let b be any branch in T. Note first that by proposition (1) b is a a partial interpretation. Since the case analyses in definition (3.2) is exhaustive b will contain either E or $\neg E$ and thus assign a truth value to E and $\neg E$. Hence $I_p(b)$ is an interpretation for S and 1. is proved. In order to prove 2. suppose to the contrary that there exists an interpretation $I = I' \cup \{E\}$ which is not contained in some branch b (The case $I = I' \cup \{\neg E\}$ is totally symmetric). By the induction hypotheses I' is contained in some branch b' in T' and by 1. b' must have been appended with a derived node $\neg E$. Then by definition (3.2) we have $I_p(b) \models \neg E$ and consequently $\neg E \in I$. This however contradicts to the assumption that $E \in I$ since no interpretation can contain both, E and $\neg E$. $\qquad\Box$

Lemma 3.1 *Let I_p be a partial interpretation and E_1 and E_2 be equations. Then*

$$I_p \cup \{E_1\} \models E_2 \text{ iff } I_p \cup \{\neg E_2\} \models \neg E_1$$

The following lemma will be important below in the construction of our semantic trees. It is a simple consequence of the fact that equality can be axiomatized as a set of definite clauses.

Lemma 3.2 *(Definiteness of logical consequences) Let I_p be a partial interpretation, L be a literal and suppose $I_p \models L$. Then one of the following cases applies:*

1. *Either L is positive and there exists an $I'_p \subseteq I_p$ such that $I'_p \models L$ and I'_p does not contain a negative literal, or else*

2. *L is negative and there exists an $I'_p \subseteq I_p$ such that $I'_p \models L$ and I'_p contains exactly one negative literal.*

The next lemma states that adding an equational consequence as a new axiom does not alter the theory. An application of the lemma follows immediately.

Lemma 3.3 *Let I_p be any partial interpretation, L_1 be a literal and suppose that $I_p \models L_1$. Then for all literals L_2:*

$$I_p \cup \{L_1\} \models L_2 \text{ iff } I_p \models L_2$$

The next lemma tells us that only original nodes have to be considered in the extension of derived nodes.

Lemma 3.4 *Let $b' = b \circ n$ be a branch ending in a derived node $l(n) = L$. Then there exist original nodes $L_1 \ldots L_n$ with $L_i \in I_p(b)$ such that*

$$\{L_1 \ldots L_n\} \models L$$

Proof. L is a derived node and by definition (3.2) $I_p(b) \models L$. Similarly, for every derived node $L' \in I_p(b)$ it holds that $I_p(b) \models L'$. Now apply lemma (3.3) and obtain $I_p(b) - \{L'\} \models L$. Then repeatedly apply this procedure until all derived nodes are removed. $\qquad\Box$

This lemma completes the neccessary facts about the declarative contents of E-trees. Now we will turn our attention towards the application of E-trees.

Semantic E-trees in Completeness Proofs

The completeness argument for our calculus consists of two parts: in the first part it is shown that for every unsatisfiable clause set there exists a finite semantic tree which can be used in the second part as a basis for a refutation. The neccessary facts for the first part are almost all developed in the preceeding subsection, so that we can turn now to the second part.

Definition 3.3 *(Closed semantic tree)* Let M be a finite ground clause set, and let T be a semantic tree for M. A branch b in T is *closing* iff there exists a clause in M which is falsified by b and no proper prefix of b falsifies a clause in M. T is *closed* iff each of its branches is closing.

In their traditional form semantic trees may be pruned starting with *any* pair of brother nodes which are both closing. In our case however we have to begin with the "shortest rightmost" branch which ends in a derived node. More precisely, we select a branch which ends in a derived node n such that the brother nodes of all positive ancestors of n are leaves (if existent). This branch is computed by the function f in the next definition.

Definition 3.4 Let n be a node tree T.   Suppose n has two sons. Then $left(n)$ denotes the positive son of n, $right(n)$ denotes the negative son of n. If n has one son it is denoted by $next(n)$. Now we define $f(n)$ as:

$$f(n) = \begin{cases} n & \text{if } n \text{ is a leaf.} \\ n \circ f(next(n)) & \text{if } next(n) \text{ exists.} \\ n \circ f(left(n)) & \text{if } right(n) \text{ exists and is a leaf.} \\ \\ n \circ f(right(n)) & \text{else.} \end{cases}$$

We note that f is a computable function and total on the nodes of T.

Proposition 3 *Let T be a finite closed semantic tree for a clause set M. Then there exists a derivation of M' from M wrt. the ground equational calculus such that M' is closed by a tree T' which contains strictly less nodes than T.*

Proof.   Let r be the root node of T and $b = f(r)$, C be a clause falsified by $I_p(b)$ and n be the leaf of b. We show how to derive a clause C' which is closed by a true prefix b' of b. Then the tree T' which is identical to T but b is replaced by b' is still closing and contains strictly less nodes than T.
Three cases have to be distinguished:

1. n labels a derived positive literal E (cf. figure (3)). By lemma (3.4) there exist original nodes $E_1 \ldots E_n$ such that $\{E_1, \ldots, E_n\} \models E$. By lemma (3.2) all $E_1, \ldots, E_n$ are positive. Hence all their brothers $\neg E_1, \ldots, \neg E_n$ are negative. It follows from the definition of f that all $\neg E_1, \ldots, \neg E_n$ are leaves (because otherwise, $f(r)$ yields a branch including one of these nodes). Let b_i denote the branch ending in $\neg E_i$ ($i = 1, \ldots, n$). Every b_i is closing a clause C_i and hence there is no shorter path which falsifies a clause. Hence C_i must contain the literal E_i, i.e. $C_i = E_i \vee R_i$. Similarly, b must falsify a clause $C = \neg E \vee R$. Since $E_1, \ldots, E_n \models E$ iff $\{E_1, \ldots, E_n \neg E\} \models \square$ we can apply an E-reflection step (definition 2.2):

$$\begin{array}{c} E_1 \vee R_1 \\ \vdots \\ E_n \vee R_n \\ \neg E \vee R \\ \hline R_1 \vee \ldots \vee R_n \vee R \end{array}$$

Since the resulting clause $C' = R_1 \vee \ldots \vee R_n \vee R$ does not contain one of $\{E_1, \ldots, E_n\}$, it contains only literals which are falsified by b. Furthermore, since b does not contain $\neg E$, C' is even falsified by some proper prefix b' of b.

2. In this case n labels a derived negative literal $\neg E$ (cf. figure (4)). This case is similar to 1. but the clause C falsified by b is of the form $C = E \vee R$. By lemma (3.2) there exist nodes $\{E_1, \ldots, E_n, \neg E'\}$ such that $\{E_1, \ldots, E_n, \neg E'\} \models \neg E$, and by lemma (3.1) it holds that $\{E_1, \ldots, E_n, E\} \models E'$. Thus we can apply the following $E - lemma$ step:

$$E_1 \vee R_1$$
$$\vdots$$
$$E_n \vee R_n$$
$$E \vee R$$
$$\overline{E' \vee R_1 \vee \ldots \vee R_n \vee R}$$

As in case 1. the resulting clause $C' = E' \vee R_1 \vee \ldots \vee R_n \vee R$ is falsified by a proper prefix b' of b.

3. In this case n labels an original literal E (cf. figure (5)). As a consequence of the definition of f, the brother of n is a leaf, too. The two clauses falsified by these two branches are of the form $C_1 = E \vee R_1$ and $C_2 = \neg E \vee R_2$. Since $\{E, \neg E\} \models \square$ we can apply the following $E - reflection$ step:

$$E \vee R_1$$
$$\neg E \vee R_2$$
$$\overline{R_1 \vee R_2}$$

Since $C' = R_1 \vee R_2$ does contain neither E nor $\neg E$, it is falsified by a proper prefix of b'.

$\square$

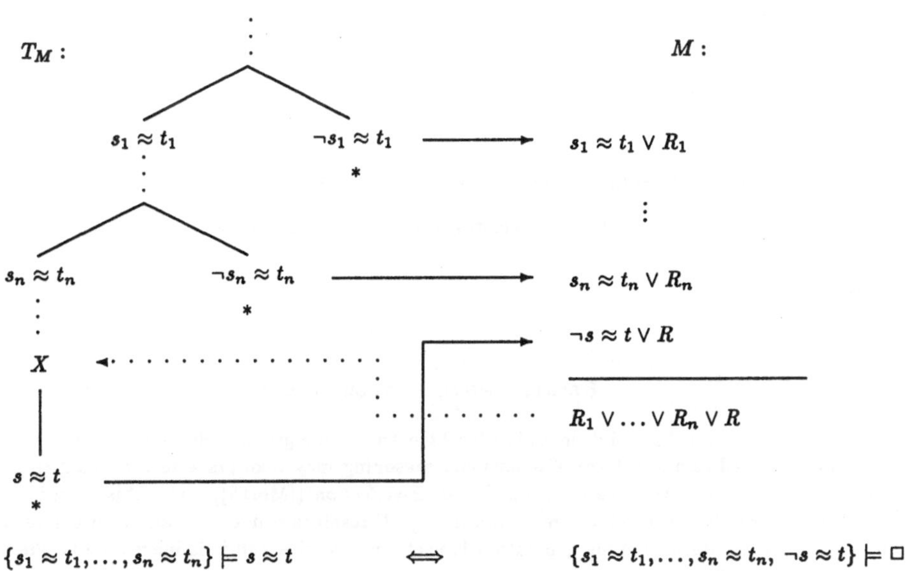

Figure 3: Refuting a derived positive node

Now we can turn to our main theorem.

Theorem 3.1 (Completeness) *Let M be an E-unsatisfiable set of ground clauses. Then there exists a refutation of M wrt. the ground equational resolution calculus.*

Proof.   Note first that by the definition of unsatisfiability, M is unsatisfiable iff every interpretation I for M falsifies M iff I falsifies at least one clause in M.

By the Skolem-Herbrand-Gödel theorem we may assume M to be finite. By proposition (2) there exists a semantic tree T with every branch being an interpretation for M, and every I being contained in some branch of T. Since every I falsifies a clause in M, every branch can be pruned to a closing branch. Thus there exists a finite closed semantic tree for M. By repeated application of proposition 3 this tree can be pruned by application of our inference rules until the empty tree is reached. Since the only clause which is falsified by the empty tree is the empty clause, we have constructed a refutation for M. $\square$

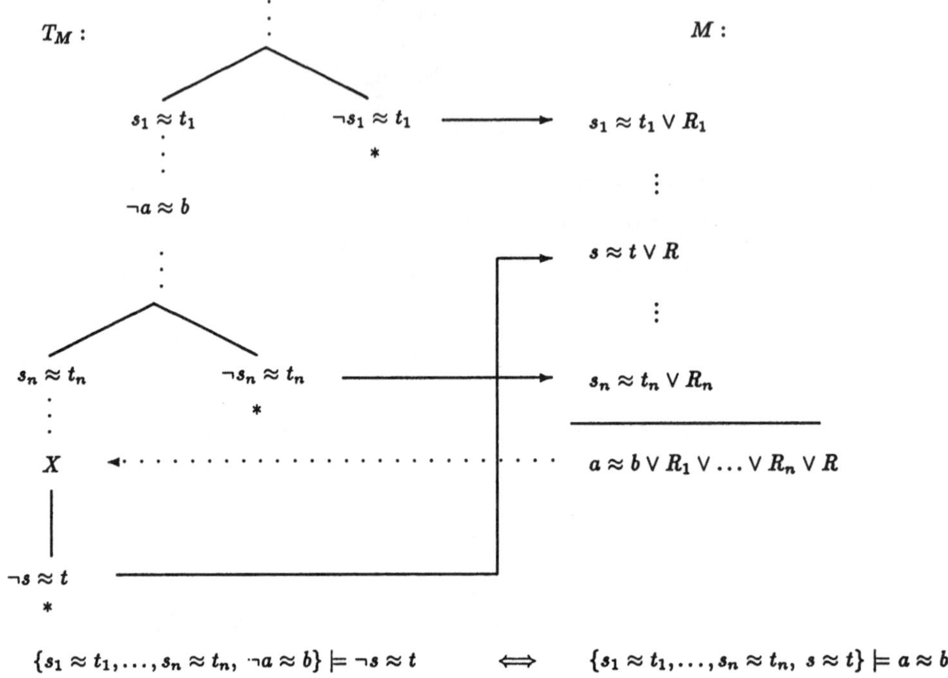

$$\{s_1 \approx t_1,\ldots,s_n \approx t_n,\ \neg a \approx b\} \models \neg s \approx t \qquad \Longleftrightarrow \qquad \{s_1 \approx t_1,\ldots,s_n \approx t_n,\ s \approx t\} \models a \approx b$$

Figure 4: Refuting a derived negative node

4 Discussion

Related work – other calculi

The ground resolution calculus builds in a high-level treatment of equations: by our inference rules, multiple equations may be used and any form of equational reasoning may take place in the "background" during one inference step; thus, our calculus is much like *E-reflection* ([Mor69]) wrt. this high-level property. As a difference, E-resolution produces no lemmas, e.g. E-resolution does not allow to derive $a \approx c$ from $\{a \approx b,\ b \approx c \ldots\}$. However, lemma generation is useful in practice and it is inevitable in the presence of strong ordering restrictions.

The *paramodulation* inference rule was already recalled in the introduction. As the main difference to our inference rules, a paramodulation inference step performs one single equality replacement using one single equation. Using the well-known Birkhoff completeness result (as formulated in lemma 2.1) it can be shown that one single step with our inference rules can be simulated by a sequence of paramodulation steps.

Related work – generalized semantic trees

The idea of enumerating E-interpretations in semantic trees can also be found in [Pet83]. As a major difference, this author is not free in the order of enumerating the members of the interpretations, whereas we are totally free. To be more precise, he relies on an extra concept of a well founded ordering on terms which is order isomorphic to the natural numbers. Now, he forbids to enumerate an equation which can be used to simplify a term enumarated before. This can already be demonstrated in the tree in the introduction (figure (1)). There, $f(a) \approx b$ is enumerated before $a \approx b$, but $a \approx b$ can be used to simplify $f(a) \approx b$ (independent from $a > b$ or $b > a$ in the ordering). However we recognize that this work shows that the functional reflexive axioms are unneccessary – a problem which we have to deal with when lifting the calculus to full first order logic.

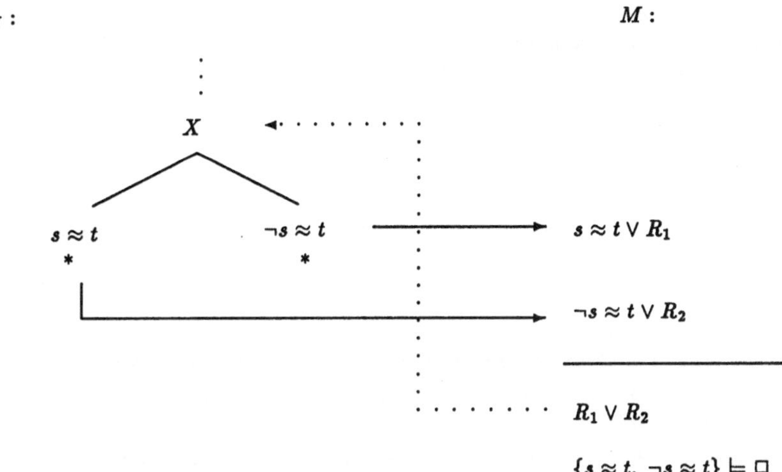

Figure 5: Refuting original nodes

Transfinite trees ([HR87]) obey a similar restriction on the enumeration ordering, however the ordering need not be order isomorphic to the natural numbers. In these trees, every consequence of a set of equations in a branch is forced to be added immediately to that branch. For example if

$$M = \{f(a) \approx a,\ P(a),\ P(b),\ \neg P(b)\}$$

and if a branch starts with $P(a)$, $f(a) \approx a$, then this branch will be extended infinitely with $P(f(a))$, $P(f(f(a)))$, ... and "after" this infinite process (hence the name "transfinite"), two branches $P(b)$ and $\neg P(b)$ can be added to close the branch. In our approach, we apply the Skolem-Herbrand-Gödel theorem and always obtain finite trees. Therefore we can apply simple induction techniques. As a further difference, the inference rules used there are single-step replacements a la paramodulation. However, this author proves a more restricted calculus (ordering restrictions) to be complete than our calculus.

IMPROVEMENTS AND FURHER WORK

In the definitions section we have noted that it suffices to restrict to partial interpretations for the atom set of the input clauses. Hence it is not neccessary to derive (via E-lemma steps) literals which do not appear in any of the input clauses. For example, if the clause set is

$$M = \{a \approx b,\ b \approx c,\ \neg a \approx b\}$$

then it is not neccessary to derive $a \approx c$ from M because $a \approx c$ is not in the atom set of M (whereas paramodulation allows to derive $a \approx c$).

A second, and much more powerful source for improvement comes from the enumeration of the atoms: given an enumeration $A_0 \ldots A_k$ of an atom set resulting in a closed semantic tree. In the proof of proposition (3) no assumption was made which A_i is to be selected for the next tree extension step. Hence A_i can be selected arbitrarily. Why is this observation useful? The enumeration can be carried out in increasing order wrt. a given literal ordering $<_L$. The corresponding tree to such an enumeration will carry ever greater literals wrt. $<_L$ towards the leaves. Now recall that in inferences only the literals corresponding to leaf positions are considered. Thus, it suffices to consider only the greatest literal in a clause. This idea has already been developed in ([KH69]) in the context of non-equational resolution and also by [HR87].

In ([Sti83, Sti85]) a very general extension of the resolution principle is defined. There, reasoning for arbitrary theories and not just equational theories takes place during one resolution step. We are aiming at such arbitrary theories, too. In fact it is a major criteria in our proof technique to be extendable in that sense. Consequently our proof does not need any special properties of the equality relation, as e.g.

substitution. The only neccessary property is that the theory must be defined by a set of *definite* clauses. We feel that generalized theory reasoning in combination with the abovementioned ordering restrictions will yield substantial improvements wrt. expressiveness and search space. A detailed treatment of this matter in combination with ordering restrictions is currently in preparation.

ACKNOWLEDGEMENTS

Many thanks to U. Furbach for critical comments and to W. Hower for general remarks.

References

[CL73]   C. Chang and R. Lee. *Symbolic Logic and Mechanical Theorem Proving*. Academic Press, 1973.

[FHS89a]   U. Furbach, S. Hölldobler, and J. Schreiber. Paramodulation modulo equality. In *Proc. GWAI'89*, pages 107–116. Springer, IFB 216, 1989.

[FHS89b]   Ulrich Furbach, Steffen Hölldobler, and Joachim Schreiber. Horn equational theories and paramodulation. *Journal of Automated Reasoning*, 3:309–337, 1989.

[Höl89]   Steffen Hölldbler. *Foundations of Equational Logic Programming*, volume 353 of *Lecture Notes in Artificial Intelligence. Subseries of Lecture Notes in Computer Science*. Springer, 1989.

[HR87]   J. Hsiang and M. Rusinowitch. On word problems in equational theories. In *Proc. ICALP'87*, pages 54–71. Springer, LNCS 267, 1987.

[KH69]   R.A. Kowalski and P. Hayes. Semantic Trees in Automatic Theorem Proving. In Meltzer and Mitchie, editors, *Machine Intelligence 5*. Edinburg University Press, 1969.

[Mor69]   J. B. Morris. E-Resolution: An Extension of Resolution to include the Equality Relation. In *Proc. IJCAI*, pages 287–294, 1969.

[Pet83]   G. Peterson. A Technique for Establishing Completeness Results in Theorem Proving with Equality. *SIAM Journal on Computing*, 12(1):82–100, February 1983.

[Rob65]   J.A. Robinson. A machine-oriented logic based on the resolution principle. *JACM*, 12(1):23–41, January 1965.

[RW69]   G. A. Robinson and L. Wos. Paramodulation and Theorem Proving in First Order Theories with Equality. In Meltzer and Mitchie, editors, *Machine Intelligence 4*. Edinburg University Press, 1969.

[Sti83]   M.E. Stickel. Theory Resolution: Building in Nonequational Theories. SRI International Research Report Technical Note 286, Artificial Intelligence Center, 1983.

[Sti85]   M. E. Stickel. Automated deduction by theory resolution. *Journal of Automated Reasoning*, pages 333–356, 1985.

Answers for disjunctive logic programs

Ulrich Furbach

University of Koblenz
Rheinau 3 – 4
D 5400 Koblenz
E-mail: uli@infko.uucp

Abstract

In this paper indefinite answers for disjunctive logic programs are investigated. A fixpoint semantics which is known from the literature is discussed and a result concerning its correspondence to a minimal model semantics is improved. As an operational semantics V-resolution is proposed and its answer correctness and completeness is proved. Finally the use of the splitting rule for computing answers for disjunctive logic programs is depicted.

Keywords: Automated reasoning, logic programming

Introduction

Logic programming research and development has been based to a large extend on Hornclause logic, a subset of predicate logic. This has the advantage that the logic programs can be interpreted, and even compiled, efficiently. On the other hand, in automated theorem proving research there have been developed powerful full first order theorem provers which can be used as logic programming system, extending the Hornclause-based approach significantly. Such a system is SETHEO, a first order prover based on model elimination [LSBB89]; it contains data structures and numerous built-in functions and, moreover, it is implemented by employing efficient WAM-techniques. These features show that the system is not only a theorem prover, it can be used as a logic programming system as well. Although it has a well defined operational semantics, i.e. the underlying proof procedure, there is a lack of understanding the declarative semantics of formulas in clause form as a programming language.

During the last years, however, there is work aiming in that direction: e.g. Minker and Rajasekar gave a fixpoint semantics of disjunctive logic programs as well as a question answering procedure ([MR90, MR88]) and Loveland came with the idea of near-Horn programs ([Lov87]) and of using the splitting rule as a base for an efficient implementation([Lov78]). Others like Herre ([Her88]) and Casanova et.al. ([CGS89]) investigate proof procedures for disjunctive logic programs which compute (indefinite) answer substitutions instead of answering only *yes* or *no* to a query. In this context there arises a fundamental question: should one allow programs that can only be answered in an indefinite way, such as "It is the case that $p(a) \vee p(b)$ holds, but I do not no whether it is $p(a)$ or $p(b)$" or should these indefiniteness be forbidden. The latter approach is taken in [WP88] or [LBSF89], where only programs with definite answers are considered to be useful.

We believe that the real advantage of full first order clauses as a programming language is just that fact that indefinite answers can be handled.[1]

---

[1]This is why indefinite clauses are used in the deductive database area.

The aim of this paper is twofold: Firstly, we want to discuss and improve the fixpoint theory for disjunctive logic programs as it is given in [MR90]. There, Minker and Rajasekar gave a transformation operator T^I which acts on states, i.e. positive clauses that may be formed by using atoms from the Herbrand base. They argue that their fixpoint semantics corresponds to the minimal model semantics given in [Min82]. We will show that the formulation of this correspondence can be improved by employing a result on deduction completeness for resolution.

Secondly, this paper addresses the question of an appropriate calculus for computing indefinite answers. For this we use the well-known (?) V-resolution calculus from [CL73], which, although being designed for other purposes, already has incorporated the necessary machinery for memorizing substitutions during deductions. We will give correctness and completeness results with respect to answers.

In the following section we introduce the concept of disjunctive logic programs together with an example which will be used throughout this paper. In section two we discuss the fixpoint semantics and in section three we attend to proof procedures.

1 Disjunctive logic programs

In this paper we are dealing with *disjunctive logic programs*, i.e. consistent sets of clauses derived from a first order predicate formula which is transformed in conjunctive normal form. Clauses are written as

$$A_1, \ldots, A_n \leftarrow B_1, \ldots, B_m$$

where the A_i's and B_i's are atoms. Hence a clause can be written alternatively as $A_1 \vee \ldots \vee A_n \vee \neg B_1 \vee \ldots \vee \neg B_m$. We will feel free to switch between these two notations throughout this paper; the arrow notation is used whenever the programming aspect is relevant, while in proofs it seems to be more convenient to use the latter notation.

A *query* is a clause of the form

$$\leftarrow B_1, \ldots, B_m$$

The set of variables, occurring in a query $\leftarrow Q$ are called the *query variables*. The query variables are assumed to be existentially quantified. As usually an *answer substitution* for a query $\leftarrow Q$ is a substitution for the query variables of $\leftarrow Q$. An *answer* for a query $\leftarrow Q$ is a formula of the form

$$Q\sigma_1, \ldots, Q\sigma_n \leftarrow$$

where each σ_i is an answer substitution. Hence, answers are disjunctions of the query-clause Q, which is a conjunction. And finally we have a *correct answer* C for a program P and a query Q, if C is an answer for $\leftarrow Q$ and C is a logical consequence of P.

As an example take the program P (taken from [WP88]):

$$
\begin{array}{rcll}
symptom(S) & \leftarrow & & (1) \\
cause(C_1), cause(C_2) & \leftarrow & symptom(S) & (2) \\
treatment(T_0) & \leftarrow & cause(C_1) & (3) \\
treatment(T_1) & \leftarrow & cause(C_1) & (4) \\
treatment(T_0) & \leftarrow & cause(C_2) & (5) \\
treatment(T_2) & \leftarrow & cause(C_2) & (6)
\end{array}
$$

Together with the query $\leftarrow treatment(x)$ the following clauses are answers

$$treatment(T_0) \leftarrow$$
$$treatment(T_1), treatment(T_2) \leftarrow$$
$$treatment(T_1) \leftarrow$$

of which only the first two are correct answers.

From this example one can see that there are programs which allow both, definite and indefinite answers to a given query. In [WP88] emphasis is put to the question how to find out whether a program computes a definite answer. There, it is shown, that linear ordered resolution refutations, where the entry clause is used only once, yield definite answers.

We believe that it is an advantage of disjunctive logic programs to allow indefinite answers and we propose to further investigate the semantics of those programs.

In the following two sections we deal with the task of characterizing correct answers by a fixpoint operator respectively by V-resolution.

2 Fixpoint semantics

The fixpoint semantics for disjunctive logic programs given in this section follows [MR90].

As in the case of Horn programs a closure operator T operating on a set S is defined, however, instead of choosing S to be the set of (Herbrand-)interpretations the closure operator takes sets of disjunctions of ground atoms. The underlying concept is that of an *extended Herbrand base*:

$\text{EHB}^k(P)$ is the set of all positive clauses formed by taking disjunction of k distinct ground atoms from the Herbrand base of the program P. Then

$$\text{EHB}_k(P) = \bigcup_{i=1}^{k} \text{EHB}^i(P)$$

and the extended Herbrand base of a program P, $\text{EHB}(P)$, is given by

$$\text{EHB}(P) = \text{EHB}_\infty(P) = \bigcup_{i=1}^{\infty} \text{EHB}^i(P).$$

A *state of a program* P is a subset of the extended Herbrand base of P. The set of all states of a program P is the power set of the extended Herbrand base, namely $\mathcal{P}(\text{EHB}(P))$; it is a complete lattice under the partial order of set inclusion with bottom element $\emptyset$ and top element $\text{EHB}(P)$.

The closure operator $T_P^I(S) : \mathcal{P}(\text{EHB}(P)) \to \mathcal{P}(\text{EHB}(P))$ is given by

$$T_P^I(S) = \{C \in \text{EHB}(P) \mid C' \leftarrow B_1, \ldots, B_n \text{ is a ground instance}$$
$$\text{of a program clause in } P \text{ and}$$
$$B_1 \vee C_1, \ldots, B_n \vee C_n \text{ are in } S \text{ and}$$
$$C'' = C' \vee C_1 \vee \ldots \vee C_n, \text{ where}$$
$$\forall 1 \leq i \leq n : C_i \text{ can be null and}$$
$$C \text{ is the smallest factor of } C'' \}$$

In [MR90] Minker and Rajasekar have proven that T_P^I is continuous and that its least fixpoint is the set of clauses derivable from C:

$$lfp(T_P^I) = \{C \mid C \text{ is derivable from } P\}$$

The authors use LUST-resolution as an operational semantics of programs, but in the context of fixpoints they base the notion of derivability on unrestricted resolution, so that the above set can be written as well as $\{C \mid P \vdash C\}$.

Let us shortly sketch the least fixpoint with our running example program. For this and in the following we abbreviate predicate names by their first letter, whereas the indices I and P from T_P^I are omitted:

$$T^0 = \emptyset$$
$$T^1 = \{s(S) \leftarrow\}$$
$$T^2 = T^1 \cup \{c(C_1), c(C_2) \leftarrow\}$$
$$T^3 = T^2 \cup \{t(T_0), c(C_2) \leftarrow,$$
$$t(T_1), c(C_2) \leftarrow,$$
$$c(C_1), t(T_0) \leftarrow,$$
$$c(C_1), t(T_2) \leftarrow\}$$
$$T^4 = T^3 \cup \{t(T_0) \leftarrow,$$
$$t(T_0), t(T_2) \leftarrow,$$
$$t(T_1), t(T_0) \leftarrow,$$
$$t(T_1), t(T_2) \leftarrow\}$$
$$T^5 = T^4 = T^\omega = lfp(T)$$

In order to relate this semantics to model theory it is necessary to discuss minimal Herbrand models.[2] It is easy to see that in contrast to Hornclauses there is no unique model which can be used to characterize disjunctive logic programs. A *minimal model M* of a program P is a model such that no proper subset of M is also a model of P. In the following $MM(P)$ denotes the set of minimal models of P.

The following theorem is from [MR90]:

Theorem 1 *Given a program P and a positive clause C. Then*

$$P \models C \text{ iff } \forall M \in MM(P) : M \models C$$

This theorem is stated incorrectly in [MR90], where it is given as $P \vdash C$ iff $\forall M \in MM(P) : M \models C$, which would imply deduction completeness of resolution. Take as an example the clause $s(S) \vee t(T_0)$, which is a logical consequence of our sample program, however it cannot be derived from it. From this and the discussion in the paper of Minker and Rajasekar we conclude that our version of the theorem is the intended one. It is important to note that the condition that C is positive is necessary for this theorem: non-positive clauses can be true in a minimal and false in a model which is an extension of that minimal one. Take as an example the minimal model $\{p(a)\}$ of the clause set $\{p(a) \vee p(b)\}$, then $\neg p(b)$ is obviously *true* in this minimal model — extending this to the non-minimal model $\{p(a), p(b)\}$ shows the non-monotonic effect, namely that $\neg p(b)$ is now *false*.

An immediate consequence of the above theorem and a fixpoint property of derivable states is

Lemma 2 *Given a program P and a positive clause C. Then*

$$\forall M \in MM(P) : M \models C \text{ iff } lfp(T) \models C$$

Again, this lemma is a corrected version of the one from Minker and Rajesakar; they wrote $\forall M \in MM(P) : M \models C$ iff $lfp(T) \vdash C$, as a consequence of the incorrect version of the above theorem.

In our small example it is clear that $s(S) \vee t(T_0)$ is a logical consequence from $lfp(T)$, however, it can not be derived from it.

---

[2]Since we are considering only Herbrand models we henceforth speak only of models.

As a consequence of this discussion we see that the above lemma does not offer an equivalence of fixpoint and model theoretic semantics; moreover it contains the rather trivial statement that the least fixpoint of a program contains the same "logical information" as the program itself.

In the remainder of this section we will show that it is possible to get a better result if we use a folklore-like theorem about resolution, namely that resolution is deduction complete modulo subsumption and tautology reduction. Although there is a proof from scratch in Lee's thesis [Lee67], we will give a simple proof for our special case which uses refutation completeness of resolution. Together with that completeness result we are able to give a closer correspondence of least fixpoints and minimal models.

For this we need a switching lemma for unit resolution steps.

Lemma 3 (Switching) *Let C be a positive clause such that their exists a refutation of $P \cup \{C\}$. If the following are two successive resolution steps*

$$(C_1 \vee B)\sigma \text{ is a resolvent of } C_1 \vee B \vee A \text{ and } \neg A'$$
$$(C_1\sigma \vee C_2)\theta \text{ is a resolvent of } (C_1 \vee B)\sigma \text{ and } C_2 \vee \neg B'$$

then there exist resolution steps, such that

$$(C_1 \vee C_2 \vee A)\theta' \text{ is a resolvent of } C_1 \vee A \vee B \text{ and } C_2 \vee \neg B'$$
$$(C_1 \vee C_2)\theta'\sigma' \text{ is a resolvent of } (C_1 \vee C_2 \vee A)\theta' \text{ and } \neg A'$$

Furthermore $C_1\sigma \vee C_2\theta$ and $(C_1 \vee C_2)\theta'\sigma'$ are variants.

Proof: From $B\sigma\theta = B'\theta$ and the fact that B' and $C_1 \vee A \vee B$ do not have variables in common we conclude $B\sigma\theta = B'\sigma\theta$.

Hence, $\sigma\theta$ is a unifier of B and B'. With θ' being mgu of B and B' we know that there exists a τ with $\theta'\tau = \sigma\theta$. From

$$A'\theta'\tau = A'\sigma\theta = A\sigma\theta = A\theta'\tau$$

it follows that A' and $A\theta'$ can be unified. With σ' being the mgu we conclude

$$\sigma\theta = \theta'\sigma'\tau' \tag{*}$$

From $A\theta'\sigma' = A'\theta'\sigma'$ and the fact that σ is an mgu of A and A' we know that there exists a substitution τ' such that $\sigma\tau' = \theta'\sigma'$. From

$$B\sigma\tau' = B\theta'\sigma' = B'\theta'\sigma' = B'\sigma\tau' = B'\tau'$$

we see that τ' is a unifier of $B\sigma$ and B' and hence there exists σ'' such that $\sigma\theta\sigma'' = \theta'\sigma'$. Together with equation (*) we conclude that $\theta'\sigma'$ and $\sigma\theta$ are variants.

q.e.d.

Theorem 4 (Deduction completeness) *Let P be a consistent program and $C \equiv A_1 \vee \ldots \vee A_n$ a positive clause, then the following holds:*

$$P \models C \text{ implies that there exists } C' : P \vdash C' \text{ and } C' \models C$$

Proof: From $P \models C$ and the refutation completeness of resolution we conclude

$$P \cup \{\neg A'_1\} \cup \ldots \cup \{\neg A'_n\} \vdash \square$$

where A_i' differs from A_i insofar as variables are substituted by Skolem constants. This is necessary because every variable in C is implicitly all-quantified and, hence, by negating C variables become existentially quantified.

Now assume a refutation of $P \cup \{\neg A_1'\} \cup \ldots \cup \{\neg A_n'\}$. Since P is consistent some resolution steps involving facts from $\{\neg A_1'\} \cup \ldots \cup \{\neg A_n'\}$ have to occur during this refutation. From the above switching lemma we conclude that this refutation can be transformed such that all resolution steps with these facts are delayed as long as possible, i.e. there exists a clause C' with

$$P \vdash C' \text{ and}$$
$$\{\neg A_1'\} \cup \ldots \cup \{\neg A_n'\} \cup \{C'\} \vdash \Box$$

From $C' \cup \{\neg A_1'\} \cup \ldots \cup \{\neg A_n'\} \vdash \Box$ we conclude that $C' \equiv B_1 \vee \ldots \vee B_m$ such that

$$\forall i \exists j : B_i \sigma_i = A_j' \sigma_i$$

where the σ_i's are the mgu's from this last resolution steps.

This means $C' \models A_1' \vee \ldots \vee A_n'$; remember that the A_i's contain Skolem constants instead of variables. From the theorem of constants [Sch67] we can conclude that $C' \models A_1 \vee \ldots \vee A_n$ holds, which completes our proof.

q.e.d.

It is interesting to note that the condition $C' \models C$ in the above lemma can be changed to "C' subsumes C if C does not contain a subclause which is a tautology".

Now we can give a sharpened version of lemma 2:

Theorem 5 *Given a program P and a positive clause C. Then*

$$\forall M \in MM(P) : M \models C \text{ iff there exists } C' \in lfp(T) : C' \models C$$

Proof: From theorem 1 and lemma 2 we conclude

$$P \models C \text{ iff } lfp(T) \models C$$

and together with our deduction theorem we have equivalently

$$\exists C' : P \vdash C' \text{ and } C' \models C$$

Since $lfp(T)$ consists exactly of the clauses derivable from the program P, we conclude that $\exists C' \in lfp(T) : C' \models C$.

The opposite direction follows directly from the correctness of resolution.

q.e.d.

3 Proof theory

In order to work towards an operational semantics for disjunctive logic programs we choose the calculus of *V-resolution* as it is introduced in [CL73]. V-resolution is a kind of Herbrand proof procedure, where the variables occurring in a clause are *not* treated to be universally quantified. Instead one has to work with a sufficient number of copies for each clause.

For this we have to start with an *alleged unsatisfiable* set of clauses S, which is obtained from an unsatisfiable set of clauses S' by adding variants of clauses to S, such that there exists a ground substitution θ with $S\theta$ is unsatisfiable.

A central notion for the definition of V-resolution is that of *consistent substitutions*: Let $\theta = \{x_1/s_1, \ldots, x_n/s_n\}$ and $\sigma = \{y_1/t_1, \ldots, y_m/t_m\}$ be two substitutions, then we define the two expressions

$$E_1 = (x_1, \ldots, x_n, y_1, \ldots y_m) \text{ and } E_2 = (s_1, \ldots, s_n, t_1, \ldots, t_m).$$

θ and σ are called consistent, iff E_1 and E_2 are unifiable. Their mgu is called a *combination*. This definition is generalized in an obvious way to more than two substitutions.

In V-Resolution each clause is augmented by a substitution; the clauses from S are augmented by the empty substitution $\emptyset$. Hence clauses are written as

$$C \mid \theta.$$

A V-resolvent is defined as follows. Let $C_1 \mid \theta_1$ and $C_2 \mid \theta_2$ be clauses, such that θ_1 and θ_2 are consistent with combination α; if L_1 and L_2 literals in C_1 and C_2, respectively, such that L_1 and $\neg L_2{}^3$ are unifiable with mgu σ and if α and σ are consistent with combination θ the clause

$$\{(C_1\sigma - L_1\sigma) \cup (C_2\sigma - L_2\sigma)\} \mid \theta$$

is called a *binary V-resolvent* of the parent clauses $C_1 \mid \theta_1$ and $C_2 \mid \theta_2$. In the same obvious manner the factoring rule is defined, which finally gives us the usual notion of V-refutations. From [CL73] we get a completeness-result for V-resolution.

In our running example we construct the following refutation of the goal $\leftarrow t(x)$:

$$\leftarrow t(x') \mid \emptyset$$
$$\downarrow \quad (4)$$
$$\leftarrow c(C_1) \mid \{x'/T_1\}$$
$$\downarrow \quad (2)$$
$$c(C_2) \leftarrow s(S) \mid \{x'/T_1\}$$
$$\downarrow \quad (1)$$
$$c(C_2) \leftarrow \mid \{x'/T_1\}$$
$$\downarrow \quad (6)$$
$$t(T_2) \leftarrow \mid \{x'/T_1\}$$
$$\downarrow \quad \text{goal with new query variable } x''$$
$$\square \mid \{x'/T_1, x''/T_2\}$$

The reader verifies easily, that alternative choices of input clauses during the deduction would result in the refutation:

$$\leftarrow t(x') \mid \emptyset \quad \xrightarrow{\,\ast\,} \quad \square \mid \{x'/T_0\}$$

---

[3] The operator $\neg$ will be used as negation and as complement-operator

The two answers computed in the above refutations are $t(T_1), t(T_2) \leftarrow$ and $t(T_0) \leftarrow$, respectively. In the following we describe how answers can be constructed from refutations.

Given a query $\leftarrow Q$ with query variables $\overline{x} = (x_1, \ldots, x_n)$ and a refutation $\leftarrow Q \mid \emptyset \xrightarrow{\;*\;} \square \mid \theta$. Let the domain of θ be such that x_i^j is the j-th new variant of x_i; we furthermore assume, that if there exists a j-th variant of a variable x_i, this is the case for all query variables (if not, we extend θ by the appropriate identity substitutions). With $\overline{x}^j$ denoting the tuple of the j-th variant of $\overline{x}$ and θ_j denoting the restriction of θ to the variables from $\overline{x}^j$, we have as a *computed answer* :

$$Q\theta_1, \ldots, Q\theta_n \leftarrow$$

From this example it should be clear that V-resolution offers a means of keeping track of the substitutions which are performed during a deduction; it is a fully worked out calculus, which is well-known in the literature. Though it was originally invented to narrow the search space for resolution procedures, it is very well suited for our purposes, namely an analysis of answer substitutions.

Theorem 6 (Correctness) *Given a program* P*, a query* $Q \leftarrow$ *and a computed answer* $C \equiv Q\theta_1, \ldots Q\theta_n \leftarrow$*, then* C *is a correct answer, i.e.* $P \models C$*.*

Proof: There exists a refutation

$$P \cup \neg Q(\overline{x}^1) \cup \ldots \cup \neg Q(\overline{x}^n) \vdash \square \mid \theta$$

By the definition of V-resolution the query variables are treated as constants; we therefore can apply the substitution θ throughout the whole deduction, obtaining

$$P \cup \neg Q(\overline{s}^1) \cup \ldots \cup Q(\overline{s}^n) \vdash \square \mid \theta$$

From the correctness of V-resolution we can conclude

$$P \models Q(\overline{s}^1) \vee \ldots \vee Q(\overline{s}^n)$$

Together with the theorem of constants ([Sch67]) we conclude the claim of the theorem.   q.e.d.

Theorem 7 (Completeness) *Given a program* P*, a query* $Q \leftarrow$ *and a correct answer* $Q(\overline{x}^1)\theta_1, \ldots, Q(\overline{x}$
Then there exists a refutation

$$P \cup \neg Q(\overline{x}^1) \cup \ldots \cup \neg Q(\overline{x}^n) \vdash \square \mid \theta'$$

such that θ' *restricted to those variables, which are variants of the query variables is* $\theta_1' \ldots \theta_n'$ *with* $\forall 1 \leq i \leq n : \theta_i' \geq \theta_i$*.*

Proof: From the completeness of V-resolution we have

$$P \cup \neg Q(\overline{x}^1)\sigma_1 \cup \ldots \neg Q(\overline{x}^n)\sigma_n \vdash \square \mid \emptyset$$

with $Q(\overline{x}^i)\sigma_i$ being a ground instance of $Q(\overline{x}^i)\theta_i$. Applying the usual lifting lemma for resolution (its formal proof for this context is omitted here), we learn that there exists a refutation

$$P \cup \neg Q(\overline{x}^1) \cup \ldots \cup \neg Q(\overline{x}^n) \vdash \square \mid \theta'$$

where in θ' each substitution for variants of a query variable is more general then the corresponding substitution in θ_i.

q.e.d.

Discussion

We have presented a discussion of the declarative and operational semantics of disjunctive logic programs. We have shown that the least fixpoint semantics is closely related to the minimal model semantics. As an operational semantics we have proposed V-resolution in order to develop the notion of computed answer substitutions. We are aware that this calculus is not the best candidate to be the kernel of a logic programming system. Rather it was chosen for this study because it allows to construct answers from refutations without modifications of the calculus. In [CGS89], e.g. a weak model elimination calculus is used to compute answers. For this the authors had to modify the notion of chains and they had to introduce an extra machinery to register substitutions. Certainly one has to proceed in such a way when implementing a system, for an understanding of disjunctive logic programming, however, we prefer our resolution approach.

Another promising approach for defining the semantics is based on the splitting rule ([Lov78, Lov87]). The idea is simply, that $P \cup \{A, B \leftarrow C\} \models L$ if $P \cup \{A \leftarrow C\} \models L$ and $P \cup \{B \leftarrow C\} \models L$. Thus, it is possible to transform a non-Horn program into a set of Horn programs, where a query as to be proven with each of those programs. In our example we get two Horn programs, which differ only in the clause $cause(C_1) \leftarrow symptom(S)$ and $cause(C_2) \leftarrow symptom(S)$, respectively. Using SLD-resolution and the query $\leftarrow treatment(x)$ one can get the two answer substitutions $\theta_1 = \{x/T_1\}$ and $\theta_2 = \{x/T_2\}$, which finally can be combined to yield the answer $treatment(T_1), treatment(T_2) \leftarrow$. In general, however, the Horn programs cannot be interpreted independently – if the positive literals from a splitted clause share variables, the substitutions into these variables must be compatible in each SLD-proof.
Besides proof theory based on the splitting rule, there are even first attempts to define a fixpoint theory, which is based on case-analysis, i.e. splitting ([RS90]).

Let us finally remark that most papers on disjunctive logic programming introduce a second kind of negation, which is based on a closed world assumption. We have done it without that, because we think that logic programming with first order clauses has to be investigated more detailed, before it is complicated by negation as failure or default theories. Questions like "What is an appropriate calculus for implementations?" or "How to write logic programs, i.e. what is the intuitive meaning of a program?" are topics of further research.

Acknowledgements

This work was very much inspired by discussions with Reinhold Letz and Bertram Fronhöfer about the question whether indefinite answers should be allowed. Robert Demolomb I want to thank for drawing my attention to Lee's thesis and Peter Baumgartner and Walter Hower for many fruitful discussions.

References

[CGS89] M.A. Casanova, R. Guerreiro, and A. Silva. Logic programming with general clauses and defaults based on model elimination. In *Proc. of the 11th IJCAI*, pages 395–400. Morgan Kaufmann, 1989.

[CL73] C. L. Chang and R. C. T. Lee. *Symbolic Logic and Mechanical Theorem Proving*. Academic Press, 1973.

[Her88] H. Herre. Negation and constructivity in logic programming. *J. New Gener. Comput. Syst.*, 1(4):295–305, 1988.

[LBSF89] R. Letz, S. Bayerl, J. Schumann, and B. Fronhöfer. The Logic Programming Language LOP. Technical report, ATP–Report, Technische Universität München, 1989.

[Lee67] C. Lee. *A completeness theorem and a computer program for finding theorems derivable from given axioms.* PhD thesis, UCB, 1967.

[Lov78] D.W. Loveland. *Automated Theorem Proving: A logical basis.* North-Holland, 1978.

[Lov87] D.W. Loveland. Near-Horn Prolog. In J.-L. Lassez, editor, *Proc. of the 4th Int. Conf. on Logic Programming*, pages 456–469. The MIT Press, 1987.

[LSBB89] R. Letz, J. Schumann, S. Bayerl, and W. Bibel. SETHEO: A High-Performance Theorem Prover. Technical report, ATP–Report, Technische Universität München, 1989. To appear in Journal of Automated Reasoning.

[Min82] J. Minker. On definite databases and the closed world assumption. In *LNCS 138*, pages 292–308. Springer, 1982.

[MR88] J. Minker and A. Rajasekar. Procedural interpretation of non-horn logic programs. In Lusk and Overbeek, editors, *Proc. of the 9th CADE*, pages 279–293. Springer LNCS 310, 1988.

[MR90] J. Minker and A. Rajasekar. A fixpoint semantics for disjunctive logic programs. *J. Logic Programming*, 9:45–74, 1990.

[RS90] D.W. Reed and B.T. Smith. A case-analysis based fixpoint semantics for disjunctive propgrams. Extended abstract for the Workshop on 'Non-Hornclause programming' during NACLP'90, 1990.

[Sch67] J. Schoenfield. *Mathematical Logic.* Addison-Wesley, 1967.

[WP88] T. Wakayama and T.H. Payne. Case inference in resolution-based languages. In Lusk and Overbeek, editors, *Proc. of the 9th CADE*, pages 313–322. Springer LNCS 310, 1988.

Zur Steuerung und Optimierung der SIP-Auswahl in der Magic Set Transformation

Günther Specht, Oliver Krone

Technische Universität München
Institut für Informatik
Orleansstrasse 34
D-8000 München 2

e-mail: {specht,krone}@informatik.tu-muenchen.de

Abstract

Eine der wichtigsten Optimierungen bottom-up auswertender Logikprogrammiersysteme ist die Magic Set Transformation. Die Güte dieser Transformation wird durch die SIP-Auswahl (sideways information passing) entscheidend beeinflußt. In bisherigen Systemen wird vor allem ein regellokaler reiner links-rechts SIP verwendet. In diesem Papier wird eine Datenstruktur, der AND/OR-SIP Graph, und ein kombinierter Such- und Generierungsalgorithmus darauf, der HSB-SIP Algorithmus, vorgestellt, der über eine Kostenfunktion eine optimale SIP-Auswahl trifft. Dadurch werden beliebige, auch regelglobale SIP-Strategien unterstützt.

1. Einleitung

Deduktive Datenbanken und Logikprogrammiersysteme, die bottom-up auswerten, erlangen immer größere Bedeutung. Im Gegensatz zu top-down auswertenden Systemen mit backtracking Mechanismen, wie z.B. Prolog, errechnen sie immer alle Lösungen zu einer Query und sind dabei unabhängig von der Aufschreibungsreihenfolge sowohl der Regeln, als auch der Subgoals innerhalb der Regeln.

Eine der wichtigsten Optimierungen bottom-up auswertender Logikprogrammiersysteme ist die Magic Set Transformation. Sie propagiert Bindungen so, daß frühzeitig eine Eingrenzung der nach oben aufsteigenden Tupel erreicht wird. Durch die Magic Set Transformation können sogar Programme mit unendlichen Fixpunkt, wie z.B. member oder append bottom-up berechenbar werden, denn sie simuliert eine top-down Auswertung des ursprünglichen Programms.

Die Steuerung und damit die Güte der Magic Set Transformation wird durch die Auswahl, wie und welche Bindungen propagiert werden, bestimmt. Das Propagieren der Bindungen wird *Sideways Information Passing* (SIP) genannt, die Auswahl unter mehreren möglichen SIPs wird durch die *SIP-Strategie* getroffen. Ausgehend vom Bindungsmuster (=Adornment) des Kopfes einer Regel werden Bindungen seitwärts auf Rumpfliterale übertragen, welche dann wiederum Kandidaten für das Weiterpropagieren von neuen Bindungen sind.

Die Wahl einer geeigneten SIP-Strategie zu einem Logikprogramm mit seiner Query ist immer noch ein offenes Problem: Alle uns bekannten bottom-up Logikprogrammiersysteme wie ADITI (Uni Melbourne), LDL (MCC, Texas), LOLA (TU München), NAIL! (Stanford University) und RDL (Inria, France) benutzen daher einen regellokalen links-rechts SIP, entsprechend der Regelaufschreibung.

In diesem Papier wird die SIP-Auswahl genauer untersucht. Dazu wird zuerst eine geeignete Datenstruktur, der AND/OR-SIP Graph, zur Darstellung und Bewertung der verschiedenen SIPs definiert. Das Generieren aller möglichen SIPs, d.h. das vollständige Aufbauen des AND/OR-SIP Graph ist i.A. viel zu teuer und ineffizient. Der hier vorgestellte Algorithmus expandiert den Graphen nur soweit, wie dies zur Wahl eines "optimalen" SIP's nötig ist. Der Heuristic Search Best (HSB) SIP Algorithmus ist also ein verschränkter Generierungs- und Suchalgorithmus auf dem AND/OR-SIP Graphen. Die Auswahl, welcher Teil-SIP weiterverfolgt, d.h. welcher Knoten weiterexpandiert und welcher SIP letztendlich für die Magic Set Transformation ausgewählt werden soll, bestimmt eine Kostenfunktion. Sie ist der Hauptparameter des HSB-SIP Algorithmus, über sie können sowohl regellokale als auch regelglobale SIP-Strategien priorisiert werden. Über die Kostenfunktion kann auch erreicht werden, daß SIPs, die Programme erzeugen, die nicht auswertbar sind, weil sie z.B. die Stratifikation oder die Safety verletzen, wieder verworfen werden. Damit gehen die Möglichkeiten des hier vorgestellten Verfahrens weit über reine links-rechts SIPs hinaus.

Der Rest des Papieres ist wie folgt gegliedert: Kap.2 führt den AND/OR-SIP Graphen als Datenstruktur ein. Kap.3 beschreibt den HSB-SIP Algorithmus als kombinierten Such- und Generierungsalgorithmus für den AND/OR-SIP Graphen und Kap.4 stellt verschiedene Kostenfunktionen für die SIP-Strategien vor. Mit ihnen kann der HSB-SIP Algorithmus gesteuert werden.

Diese Arbeit entstand im Rahmen des DFG-Projekts "Effiziente Deduktion", in dem die Logiksprache LOLA ([Freitag et al. 91], [Specht 89]) entwickelt wird. Soweit nötig, werden die bottom-up Auswertung von Logikprogrammen (siehe etwa [Bancilhon/ Ramamohanarao 86], [Ullman 89]) und die Magic Set Transformation (siehe etwa [Beeri/ Ramakrishnan 87], [Balbin et al. 87] etc.) als bekannt vorausgesetzt.

2. Datenstruktur: Der AND/OR-SIP Graph

Bei globalen SIP-Strategien reichen die herkömmlichen Datenstrukturen, die nur isoliert Regelrümpfe betrachten, nicht mehr aus. Darum wird zunächst als neue Datenstruktur ein gerichteter azyklischer AND/OR-SIP Graph definiert, auf dem der heuristische Suchalgorithmus arbeitet. Der Graph besteht aus verschiedenen Knotentypen, denen, um eine Auswahl treffen zu können, Kosten zugewiesen werden. Diese Kosten sind das Eintscheidungskriterium, welche SIPs für ein gegebenes Logikprogramm verwendet werden.

Definition: AND/OR-SIP Graph

Der AND/OR-SIP Graph G zu einem Logikprogramm P mit Query q sei definiert:

(1) Der Startknoten entsteht aus der augmentierten Query q^a und wird als Initnode $I(q,a)$ bezeichnet. Keiner dieser Initnodes ist ein Goalnode (Definition siehe (5)).

(2) Ein Initnode $I(p,a)$ hat n AND-Nachfolger. Diese werden auch als n-successor eines Knoten bezeichnet, wobei n gleich der Anzahl der Regeln aus P ist, deren Kopfprädikat p ist. Diese Knoten werden Rulenodes genannt R $[p,a']$.

(3) Ein Rulenode R $[p,a]$ hat k OR-Nachfolger, mit k gleich der Anzahl der aus einer regellokalen SIP-Generierung hervorgegangenen SIPs. Ein Rulenode hat dementsprechend k 1-successor. Diese Knoten werden Sipnodes genannt.

(4) Ein Sipnode hat entsprechend der Anzahl der Rumpfliterale in einer Regel r und der durch den SIP erreichten Literale m AND-Nachfolger. Sie stellen gleichzeitig wieder neue Initnodes dar.

(5) Ein Initnode $I(s,a)$ heißt Goalnode genau dann, wenn:
- s ein Basisprädikat ist oder wenn
- I bereits in G enthalten ist.
Andernfalls wird der Initnode entsprechend den Schritten 1-4 expandiert. Mit der zweiten Bedingung wird Zyklenfreiheit im Graphen garantiert.

(6) Jedem Knoten aus G wird mit Hilfe einer Kostenfunktion C eine positive reelle Zahl oder ∞ zugeordnet. Es gilt: je größer die zugeordnete Zahl ist, desto "schlechter" ist der Knoten bewertet. Ist der Wert ∞, so läßt sich die zugrunde gelegte SIP-Strategie bottom-up nicht auswerten (z.B. wegen offener Basisfakten, Stratifikationsverletzung, etc.)

Den prinzipiellen Aufbau eines AND/OR-SIP Graphen[1] zu einem Logikprogramm zeigt die Abb. 1. Eine Instantiierung dieses Graphen mit dem same-generation Beispiel zeigt die Abb. 2.

Aufgabe eines heuristischen Suchalgorithmus ist es, in diesem Graphen, ausgehend vom Startknoten, einen optimalen Pfad bis zu den Goalnodes zu generieren.

Definition: Lösungspfad im AND/OR-SIP Graphen

Ein Pfad L im AND/OR-SIP Graphen ist ein Lösungspfad genau dann wenn:

(1) Sei $n \in L$. Ist n ein AND-Knoten, so muß gelten: $\forall\, k \in$ successor(n): Der Pfad ausgehend von k führt zu einem Goalnode.

(2) Sei $n \in L$. Ist n ein OR-Knoten so muß gelten: $\exists\, k \in$ successor(n): Der Pfad ausgehend von k führt zu einem Goalnode.

(3) Sei $n \in L$. $C(n) < \infty$.

---

[1] Beachte: bei diesem AND/OR Graphen wechseln sich AND und OR Knoten nicht streng ab, wie sonst oft standardmäßig verlangt.

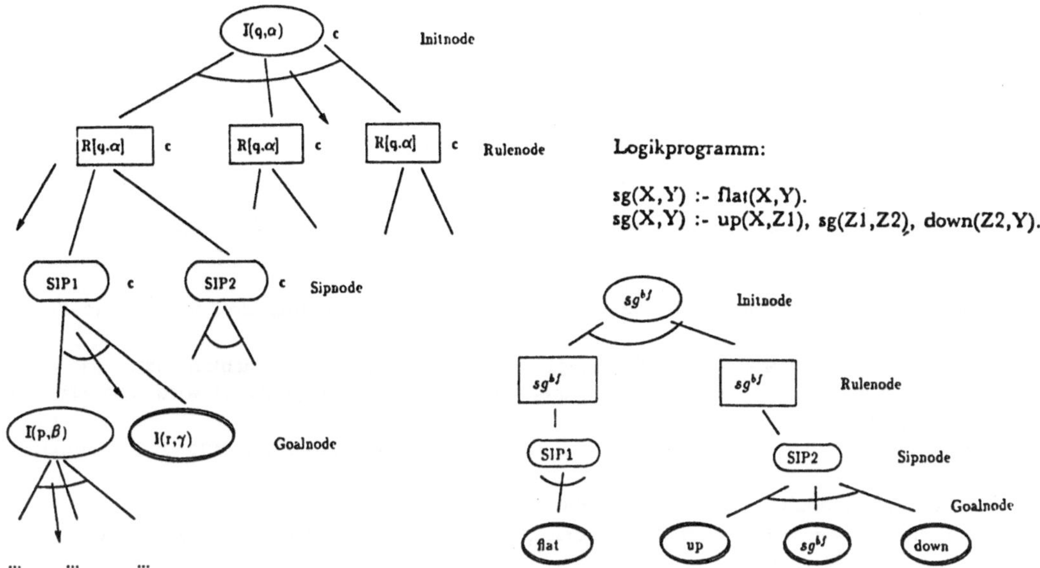

Abb. 1: Allgemeiner Aufbau eines AND/OR-SIP Graphen

Abb. 2: AND/OR-SIP Graph für das same-generation Beispiel

Legende: Initnodes sind durch Ellipsen dargestellt, Rulenodes durch Rechtecke sowei Sipnodes durch Ovale. Die Kosten der jeweiligen Knoten sind rechts am Knoten markiert. Ein Goalnode ist durch seine doppelte Umrandung gekennzeichnet. AND Verbindungen sind durch eine kreisförmige Verbindung untereinander markiert, OR Verbindungen stellen alle anderen übrigen Verbindungslinien dar. Ein gerade betrachteter Pfad ist im AND/OR-SIP Graphen durch Pfeile markiert.

Zu Sipnodes führen immer Oder-Verzweigungen. Der Sipnode mit den kleinsten Kosten $C(n)$ ist der optimale.

Definition: Ein Pfad L im AND/OR-SIP Graphen ist der optimale Lösungspfad, wenn er an allen OR Verzweigungen den Knoten mit den kleinsten Kosten $C(n)$ enthält und somit die Gesamtkosten für L minimal sind.

Beispiel 1: Beispiel zur Kostenfunktion
Eine erste einfache Bewertungsfunktion besteht in der Bevorzugung von SIPs mit möglichst vielen gebundenen Argumentpositionen:
Sei $C(s)$ definiert als das Verhältnis von freien Argumentpositionen zur Stelligkeit eines Prädikates und dies summiert über alle Rumpfliterale einer Regel r. Für diese spezielle Kostenfunktion gilt also, je kleiner $C(s)$, desto "besser" ist der SIP bewertet. C definiert eine regellokale SIP-Strategie.

Zu folgender Regel gibt es u.a. diese zwei SIP Möglichkeiten:
```
    p_bb(X,Y) :- s(X,T,U,V), t(X,Y,T,Z,K).
```

```
SIP1:  {p_bb(X,Y)} --------------------{X}------> s_bfff(X,T,U,V).
       {p_bb(X,Y),s_bfff(X,T,U,V)}----{X,Y,T}--> t_bbbff(X,Y,T,Z,K).
```

```
SIP2:  {p_bb(X,Y)} --------------------{X,Y}--> t_bbfff(X,Y,T,Z,K).
       {p_bb(X,Y),t_bbfff(X,Y,T,Z,K)}---{X,T}--> s_bbff(X,T,U,V).
```

Die Bewertung von SIP1 mit obiger Kostenfunktion ergibt:

$$C(\text{SIP 1}) = \sum_{i=1}^{2} \frac{freeArgs(p_i)}{Arity(p_i)} = 3/4 + 2/5 = 23/20$$

für SIP2 ergibt sich:

$$C(\text{SIP 2}) = \sum_{i=1}^{2} \frac{freeArgs(p_i)}{Arity(p_i)} = 3/5 + 2/4 = 22/20$$

Es gilt $C(\text{SIP2}) < C(\text{SIP1})$. Hier wird also SIP2 bevorzugt!

3. Ein kombinierter Such- und Generierungsalgorithmus für AND/OR-SIP Graphen

3.1. Die Arbeitsweise des HSB-SIP Algorithmus

(HSB = Heuristic Search Best) Der jetzt vorgestellte Algorithmus muß drei wesentliche Funktionen erfüllen:

(1) Generierung des AND/OR-SIP Graphen, wobei darauf zu achten ist, daß aus Effizienzgründen nicht der gesamte theoretisch mögliche Graph generiert wird, sondern nur ein Teilgraph davon.

(2) Bewertung der einzelnen Knoten, insbesonders der Sipnodes mit Hilfe einer Kostenfunktion C.

(3) Suche nach optimalen Pfaden im Graphen.

Die Suche im Graphen nach optimalen Pfaden gliedert sich wiederum in zwei Operationen:

(1) Ein top-down Vorgang:
Ausgangsbasis sind die Initnodes. Eine Expansion dieser Knoten führt zu neuen Sipnodes, welche aus einer regellokalen SIP-Generierung für die durch die Rulenodes angesprochenen Regeln entstehen. Diese Sipnodes werden mit Hilfe einer Kostenfunktion C bewertet. Der regellokal beste Sipnode wird weiterexpandiert.

(2) Ein bottom-up Vorgang:
Ausgehend von den entstandenen Rulenodes werden dessen Kosten berechnet und bottom-up im Graphen nach oben propagiert. Gleiches gilt für die GOAL-Eigenschaft eines Knoten, sodaß bei Terminierung des Algorithmus der Startknoten die GOAL-Eigenschaft besitzt. Das bottom-up Abändern der Knotenkosten ist kombiniert mit einer Auswahl des aktuellen Pfades im AND/OR-SIP Graphen. Unter Umständen kann dies dazu führen, daß Backtracking erforderlich wird.

3.2. Der HSB-SIP Algorithmus

Gegeben sei ein Logikprogramm P mit Query q. Ein Knoten im AND/OR-SIP Graphen G wird in Komponentendarstellung beschrieben: In <...> geklammerte Ausdrücke stellen in der jeweiligen Implementierungssprache noch weiter zu verfeinernde Anweisungen dar, ihre Semantik ist aber durch die intuitive Beschreibung klar.

```
G.label = GOAL oder NIL      /* Ist dies ein Goalnode? */
G.succ  = <Nachfolgermenge>
G.cost  = C(G)               /* Kosten                 */
G.type  = AND oder OR        /* AND bzw. OR Knoten     */
G.name  = Initnode, Rulenode, Sipnode
```

Außerdem seien folgende Funktionen gegeben:

parent(N): Gibt den Vorgängerknoten eines Knoten N ∈ G.

successor(N): Liefert die Nachfolgerknoten eines Knoten N ∈ G.

ruleOf(S): Liefert Regel r ∈ P für einen Sipnode S.

adornedLiteral(r): Liefert augmentiertes Rumpfliteral zu einer Regel r.

adornment(l): Gibt Augment eines Literals l.

head(r): Liefert Kopf einer Regel r.

Algorithmus:
Input: Logikprogramm P mit augmentierter, atomarer Query q und Adornment a
Output: Optimaler Pfad im AND/OR-SIP Graphen

begin
```
    G := <leerer SipNode>
```

```
InitNodes := {(i,a) | i ∈ adornedLiteral(q), a = adornment(i)}
RuleNodes := {[r,a] | r = head(rule), r = i,(i,a) ∈ InitNodes, rule ∈ P}
k := |InitNodes|

<installiere InitNodes als k-successors von G>
n := |RuleNodes|
<installiere RuleNodes als n-successors der InitNodes>
while (G.label ≠ GOAL)
do
    while (InitNodes ≠ ∅)
    do
        I ∈ InitNodes /* Wähle einen InitNode */
        InitNodes := InitNodes \ {I}
        M := successor(I)
        while (M ≠ ∅)
        do
            R ∈ M /* Wähle einen RuleNode */
            M := M \ {R}
            R.cost = C(R)
            if R = Basisprädikat ∨ (R ∈ G ∧ R.cost ≠ ∞ )
            then
                R.label := GOAL
            else
                <generiere lokal SIPs für R: ergibt x neue SipNodes>
                <installiere SipNodes als x 1-successor von R>
                <für jeden SipNode berechne seine Kosten>
            fi
        od
    od

    /* bottom-up Kosten abändern und GOAL-Eigenschaft nach oben reichen */
    S := RuleNodes
    while (S ≠ ∅)
    do
        m ∈ S
        S := S \ m
        for every k-successor t of m
        do
            <berechne neue Kosten von t: C(t) >
        od
        <markiere besten successor>
        m.cost = C(<bester successor>)
        <lösche vorhergehenden markierten Pfad falls unterschiedlich>
        if for every k-successor t of m holds: t.label = GOAL
        then
            m.label := GOAL
        fi
        S := {p | p = parent(m) ∧ (<Kosten von m haben sich verändert> ∨ m.label = GOAL)}
    od
    <verfolge gerade markierten Pfad; Ergebnis: SipNodes SIP>
    for every s ∈ SIP
    do                          /* SipNodes expandieren */
        InitNodes := {(i,a) | i = adornedLiteral(ruleOf(s)), a = adornment(i)}
        k := |InitNodes|
        <installiere InitNodes als k-successors von s>
        RuleNodes := {[r,a] | r = i,(i,a) ∈ InitNodes, r = head(ruleOf(s))}
        for every I(i,a) ∈ InitNodes do
            for every R[r,a] ∈ RuleNodes do
                <initialisiere R als successor von I mit r=i>
```

```
      od   od
   od
od
   return(G)
end
```

3.3. Beispiel zum HSB-SIP Algorithmus

Die Arbeitsweise des Algorithmus soll mit Hilfe eines ausführlichen Beispiels erläutert werden. Gegeben sei ein Ausschnitt aus einem Logikprogramm P mit Query p(a,X):

Logikprogramm:
```
r1:  p(X,Y)    :- q(X,V,Z), g(Z,U,V).
r2:  g(Z,U,V)  :- oq(Z,U,V),k(U).
r3:  oq(Z,U,V).
     k(U)      :- ...
     q(X,V,Z)  :- ...
```

Zur Bewertung der SIP-Auswahl im Algorithmus muß nun eine Kostenfunktion definiert werden:

Kostenfunktion:

Sei $C(N)$, $N \in G$, G ein AND/OR-SIP Graph induktiv über die zu betrachtenden Knotentypen definiert als:

(1) $C(N) = k$, k sei die Anzahl der freien Argumentpositionen eines Prädikates p, N sei ein Initnode oder ein Rulenode aber kein Goalnode.

(2) $C(N) = \sum_{i=1}^{l} C(m_i)$, N sei ein Sipnode, mit l-successor m

(3) $C(N) = \infty$, $N=(p,a)$, p Basisprädikat (d.h. N Goalnode) sowie p ist offenes Fakt und mindestens eine Argumentposition ist nicht gebunden.

Ablauf: Zu Beginn der äußeren while-Schleife ergibt sich die Situation: InitNodes = {(p,bf)}, RuleNodes = {[p,bf]}. Als Anfangskosten für die Initnodes bzw. Rulenodes ergibt sich jeweils der Wert 1. Die regellokale SIP-Generierung ermittle für Regel r1 z.B. folgende drei unterschiedliche Sipnodes als successor Knoten für den Rulenode [p,bf]:
```
SIP1:   {p_bf(X,Y)} ------{X} -------↓
        {g_fff(Z,U,V)} ---{V,Z} ---> q_bbb(X,V,Z)

SIP2:   {p_bf(X,Y)} ----------------{X} ----> q_bff(X,V,Z)
        {p_bf(X,Y),q_bff(X,V,Z)} --{V} ----> g_ffb(Z,U,V)

SIP3:   {p_bf(X,Y)} ----------------{X} ----> q_bff(X,V,Z)
        {p_bf(X,Y),q_bff(X,V,Z)} --{V,Z} --> g_bfb(Z,U,V)
```

Die Kosten für die einzelnen Sipnodes berechnen sich aus der Summe der freien Argumentpositionen für die Rumpfliterale der betrachteten Regel. Da alle drei Sipnodes identische Kosten haben, wird ein beliebiger, z.B. der erste Sipnode SIP1 weiterexpandiert. Die Situation ist in Abbildung 3 dargestellt.

Als neue Initnode- bzw. Rulenode-Menge ergeben sich: InitNodes = {(q,bbb),(g,fff)} , RuleNodes = {[q,bbb],[g,fff]}. Im Gegensatz zu diesem Beispiel gilt nicht immer: InitNodes = RuleNodes. Wird ein Rumpfliteral in einem Logikprogramm (= Initnode) durch mehrere Regeln definiert, so entstehen entsprechend mehr Rulenodes.

Für das Beispiel genügt es, wenn nur der Rulenode [g,fff] weiter betrachtet wird. Es muß nun ein SIP für die Regel r2 gefunden werden, denn g ist Kopf von r2. Die SIP-Generierung liefere z.B.:
```
SIP4:   {k_f(U)} ---{U} ---> oq_fbf(Z,U,V).
```

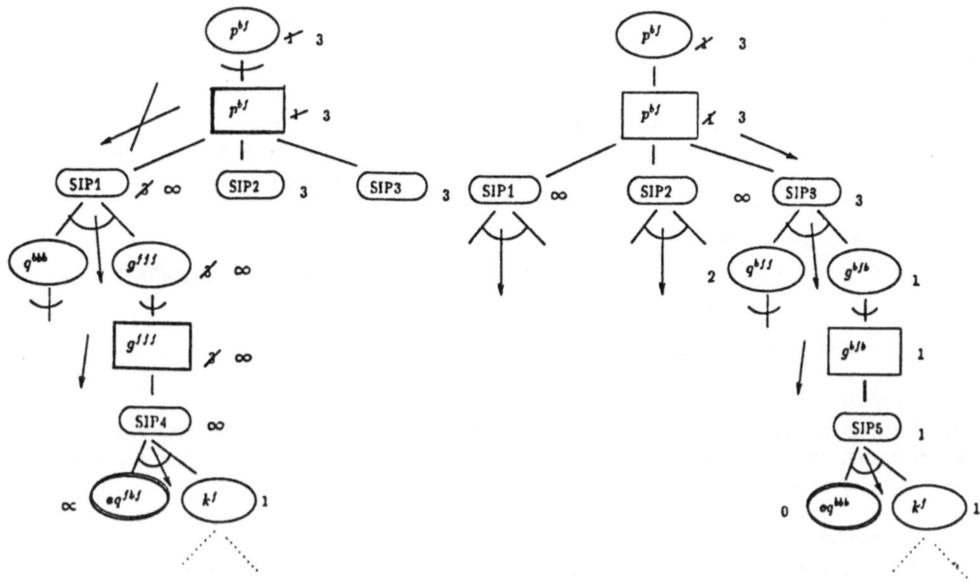

Abb. 3: AND/OR-SIP Graph nach Expansion des ersten Sipnodes

Abb. 4: AND/OR-SIP Graph nach Expansion des dritten Sipnodes

Wird jetzt der neue Initnode (oq,fbf) expandiert, so wird dieser Knoten als Goalnode markiert, da oq ein Basisprädikat in P ist. Dessen Kosten ergeben sich zu ∞, denn oq ist ein offenes Fakt und nicht alle seine Argumentpositionen sind durch den SIP gebunden worden. Ein Adornment fbf ist für dieses Prädikat bei bottom-up Evaluierung nicht möglich. Die Situation ist in Abbildung 3 dargestellt.

Jetzt setzt Backtracking ein: Die Kosten werden nun bottom-up im Graphen nach oben propagiert, was dazu führt, daß der ausgewählte SIP1 für Regel r1 verworfen wird, da seine Kosten jetzt zu ∞ steigen. Der bereits markierte Weg im Graphen wird verändert und als neuer Knoten der Sipnode SIP2 für r1 expandiert. Anloges Vorgehen für diesen Sipnode liefert wiederum keine Lösung. Diesmal entsteht der Goalnode (oq,fbb), dessen Kosten ebenfalls ∞ betragen. Die dritte Alternative führt zum Ziel. Es entsteht der Goalnode (oq,bbb), dessen Kosten 0 betragen (Abbildung 4). Der HSB-SIP Algorithmus liefert für Regel r1 den SIP3 als Ergebnis.

In diesem Beispiel wurde, um den HSB-SIP Algorithmus im vollen Detail zu zeigen, absichtlich jeweils der nächst schlechtere Fall gewählt. Durch den Nichtdeterminismus in der Auswahl bei gleichen Kosten kann auch gleich günstiger verzweigt werden.

3.4. Eigenschaften des HSB-SIP Algorithmus

Es lassen sich interessante Aussagen über einen Lösungspfades im AND/OR-SIP Graphen machen:

Satz 1:
Sei L ein Lösungspfad im AND/OR-SIP Graphen und aus Algorithmus HSB-SIP entstanden, dann gilt für L:
∀ N in L: N.label = GOAL

Satz 2: Zur Größe des transformierten Programmes
Sei L ein Lösungspfad im AND/OR-SIP Graphen und aus Algorithmus HSB-SIP entstanden, dann gilt für L:

- Die Größe des augmentierten Regelsystems S^{aug} ergibt sich zu
  $|S^{aug}| \geq |\{N \mid N$ ist ein Rulenode, $N \in L \}|$
- Die Größe des daraus entstehenden MST-transformierten Programmes S^{mst} ergibt sich zu
  $|S^{mst}| \geq |S^{aug}| + |\{N \mid N = $ Sipnode, N in L $\}| + 1$

Beweis: zu beiden Sätzen folgt direkt aus der Definition für AND/OR-SIP Graphen, bzw. durch Induktion über den Aufbau eines Lösungspfades im AND/OR-SIP Graphen.

4. Sideways Information Passing Strategien und ihre Kostenfunktionen

In diesem Kapitel sollen nun einige konkrete SIP-Strategien für den HSB-SIP Algorithmus aufgezeigt werden. SIP-Strategien lassen sich prinzipiell in zwei Kategorien einteilen:

(1) Strategien über die Struktur der Regeln

(2) Strategien über die Mächtigkeit der Relationen

wobei die erste Kategorie eine weitere Unterteilung in regellokale und regelglobale Strategien zuläßt.

4.1. Strategien über Regelstrukturen

4.1.1. Regellokale Strategien

Diese SIP-Strategien betrachten ausschließlich den Aufbau einer Regel eines Logikprogrammes. Jeglicher Kontext, in dem die Regel eingebetet ist, bleibt unberücksichtigt (im Gegensatz zu regelglobalen Strategien).

4.1.1.1. Basisprädikate vor definierende Prädikate

Heuristik: Bei der Auswahl eines geeigneten Kandidaten für das Weiterreichen von Bindungen werden Basisprädikate vor definierenden Prädikaten berücksichtigt. Dadurch sollen möglichst viele Argumentpositionen von definierenden Prädikaten frühzeitig gebunden werden.
C könnte folgendermaßen definiert werden:

$$C(\text{Sipnode}) = \sum_{\forall \text{Tail} \in \text{Sipnode}} \sum_{\forall p \in \text{Tail}} \text{if } p = \text{Basisprädikat then } 0 \text{ else } 1$$

4.1.1.2. Verhältnis der bound/free Augmente eines Prädikates

Heuristik: Bei der Kandidatenauswahl für die Weitergabe von Bindungen soll dasjenige Prädikat bevorzugt werden, dessen Verhältnis von gebundenen zu freien Argumentpositionen am größten ist. So ist garantiert, daß auch weniger gebundene Prädikate Bindungen erhalten und bereits errechnete Information möglichst früh weitergegeben wird.
C wird definiert zu:

$$C(\text{Sipnode}) = \sum_{\forall \text{Tail} \in \text{Sipnode}} \sum_{\forall p \in \text{Tail}} \frac{freeArgs(p)}{allArgs(p)}$$

4.1.1.3. Beachtung der Aufschreibungsreihenfolge der Rumpfliterale

Heuristik: Diese Heuristik propagiert Bindungen gemäß der Aufschreibungsreihenfolge der Rumpfliterale in einer Regel, also von links nach rechts.

$$C(\text{Sipnode}) = \text{if links} - \text{rechts SIP} \quad \text{then } 0 \quad \text{else} \sum \text{Anzahl Abweichungen}$$

4.1.2. Regelglobale Strategien

4.1.2.1. Minimierung der Größe des augmentierten Regelsystems

Heuristik: Diese Strategie versucht das entstehende augmentierte Regelsystem möglichst klein zu halten. Bei dieser Heuristik kommt die Stärke des HSB-SIP Algorithmus erstmals voll zum Tragen. Läßt man bei der Berechnung der Kostenfunktion C die Anzahl der Rulenodes eines gerade betrachteten Lösungsweges mit einfließen, so läßt sich damit eine, was die Größe des entstehenden augmentierten Regelsystems angeht, optimale Lösung im AND/OR-SIP Graphen finden. Die Rulenodes sind gerade die Köpfe der neu entstehenden augmentierten Regelmenge. Ein gravierender Nachteil ist jedoch zu beachten: wird die Anzahl der Rulenodes mit in C verwendet, wird unter Umständen der gesamte AND/OR-SIP Graph aufgebaut, da Kosten in diesem Graphen nach oben propagiert werden, und an den jeweiligen Rulenodes der gerade expandierten Sipnodes ein möglichst kostengünstiger Pfad gesucht wird. Durch das Einbeziehen der Rulenodes in C wächst C garantiert mit jeder weiteren Expansion von im Graphen weiter unten liegenden Knoten. Deswegen kann es an OR-Knoten, durch den kostenabändernden bottom-up Prozeß, zu ständig wechselnden Lösungspfaden kommen. Der Algorithmus "schwingt".

4.1.2.2. Beachtung von mode Deklarationen

Heuristik: Mode Deklarationen stellen eine Möglichkeit dar, wie der Programmierer direkt in die SIP-Generierung eingreifen kann, Durch eine Deklaration wie z.b. `$mode(member,[f,b])`. wird dem System mitgeteilt, daß für das member-Prädikat nur die Augmente f,b erlaubt sind.

$$C(\text{Sipnode}) = \text{if } \exists \text{ Arg} \in \text{Argumentposition} : \text{Adornment}(\text{Arg})=f \text{ and } \text{mode}(\text{Arg})=b, \text{then } \infty \text{ else } 0$$

4.1.2.3. Vermeidung von offenen Fakten

Heuristik: Durch offene Fakten können Variablenlöcher entstehen. Wird für die SIP-Generierung der vorgeschlagene Algorithmus verwendet, so lassen sich diese Nachteile vermeiden; die Kostenfunktion C ermittelt, falls sie auf offene Fakten als Goalnodes trifft, die nicht vollständig gebunden sind, den Wert ∞ und somit wird die SIP Struktur, die zu dieser Bindung geführt hat, verworfen.

4.1.2.4. Erhaltung der Stratifikation

Heuristik: Es lassen sich Kriterien angeben, die bereits für Logikprogramm und gewählten SIP entscheiden, ob nach der Magic Set Transformation das erzeugte Programm noch stratifizierbar ist. (Für Details siehe [Argenton 90], [Krone 91]). SIPs die zu einem nichtstratifizierbaren Programm führen werden mit $C = \infty$ belegt.

4.2. Strategien über Relationengrößen

Diese Strategien haben prinzipiell regelglobalen Charakter.

4.2.1. Extension der Prädikate

Heuristik: Diese Heuristik berücksichtigt die Extension der für einen SIP relevanten Prädikate. Ziel ist es Bindungen von kleineren Relationen auf größere Relationen zu übertragen. Für Basisrelationen ist die Berechnung relativ einfach. Die Größe eines derivierten Prädikats läßt sich aber a priori nur mit sehr großem Aufwand abschätzen. Ein Ansatz, wie die Relationengröße von derivierten Prädikaten abgeschätzt werden kann, findet sich in [Lenz 90]. Sinnvoller ist die Einführung und Verwendung von benutzergegebener Metainformation über das zu verarbeitende Logikprogramm.

4.2.2. Selektivität der Argumente

Heuristik: Diese Heuristik bevorzugt Kandidaten für die Weitergabe von Bindungen, deren gebundene Argumentpositionen eine möglichst hohe Selektivität aufweisen. Durch einen hohen Selektivitätswert werden entstehende magic-Relationen klein gehalten. Auch hier gelten die in der vorhergehenden Heuristik angesprochenen Einschränkungen. Die Selektivität einer Argumentposition ist als der reziproke Wert der Mächtigkeit der Extension der Argumentposition definiert. Auch hier können geeignete benutzergegebene Metainformationen die Bestimmung der Selektivität einer Argumentposition erleichtern.

Die Kostenfunktion $C(\text{Sipnode})$ definiert sich zu:

$$C(\text{Sipnode}) = \sum_{\forall \text{Tail} \in \text{Sipnode}} \sum_{\forall p \in \text{Tail}} \frac{\text{freeArgs}(p)}{\text{allArgs}(p)} \langle \text{Selektivität der boundArgs(p)} \rangle$$

4.3. Kombination der Heuristiken

Eine Kostenfunktion für einen Sipnode S, die alle aufgeführten Heuristiken berücksichtigt, wird als die gewichtete Summe aller zu den jeweiligen Heuristiken gehörende Teilkostenfunktion definiert:

$$C(S) = \sum_{i=1}^{|\text{Heuristiken}|} g_i \, C_i(S)$$

Durch unterschiedliche g_i kann der Anwender bestimmte Heuristiken bevorzugen, indem er ihnen einen kleineren Wert zuordnet. Die Verteilung der g_i Werte sollte experimentell ermittelt werden.

5. Zusammenfassung und Bewertung der Heuristiken

Die aufgezeigten Heuristiken stellen ein wirkungsvolles Instrumentarium dar, um die SIP-Generierung entscheidend zu beeinflussen. Eine ausgewogene SIP-Generierung besteht aus der Implementation folgender Heuristiken:
- Beachtung von Mode-Deklarationen für Built-In Prädikate
- Erhaltung der Stratifikation
- Basisprädikate vor definierte Prädikate
- Verhältnis der bound/free Augmente eines Prädikates
- Beachtung der Aufschreibungsreihenfolge der Rumpfliterale
- Der Bindungsfluß muß nicht notwendigerweise vom Kopf der Regel bzw. von der Query aus starten, sondern kann auch von ausgezeichneten Rumpfliteralen ausgehen.

6. Danksagung

Wir möchten Herrn Prof. R. Bayer sowie Herrn H. Schütz und Herrn B. Freitag für ihre Diskussionsbereitschaft danken.

Literatur:

[Argenton 90]   Argenton H.: *Stratifikationsbehandlung innerhalb der Magic-Set Transformation*, Diplomarbeit, Institut für Informatik, TU-München 1990

[Balbin et al. 87]Balbin I., Port G.S., Ramamohanarao K.: *Magic Set Computation for Stratified Databases*, Technical Report 87/3, Department of Computer Science, University of Melbourne

[Balbin et al. 88]Balbin I., Meenakshi K., Ramamohanarao K.: *An Effizient Labelling Algorithm for Magic Set Computation on Stratified Databases*, Technical Report 88/1, Department of Computer Science, University of Melbourne

[Bancilhon/Ramakrishnan 86] Bancilhon F., Ramakrishnan R.: *An Amateurs Introduction to Recursive Query Processing Strategies*, Proceedings ACM SIGMOD, 1986

[Beeri/Ramamohanarao 87] Beeri C., Ramamohanarao K.: *On the Power of Magic*, ACM SIGMOD-SIGART, Symp. on Principles of Database Systems, 1987

[Freitag et al. 90]Freitag B., Schütz H., Specht G.: *LOLA A Logic Language for Deductive Databases and its Implementation*, Proc. of 2nd Int. Symposium on Database Systems for Advanced Applications (DASFAA), Tokyo 1991

[Holzner 89]   Holzner J.: *Optimierung rekursiver Logik-Programme durch die Magic-Set Methode*, Diplomarbeit, Institut für Informatik, TU-München 1989

[Kemp et al. 89]Kemp D.B., Meenakshi K., Ramamohanarao K., Balbin I.: *Propagating Constraints in Recursive Deductive Databases*, Technical Report 89/6, Department of Computer Science, University of Melbourne

[Krone 91]   Krone O.: *Optimierende SIP-Auswahl innerhalb der Magic-Set Transformation für die Logiksprache LOLA*, Diplomarbeit, Institut für Informatik, TU-München 1991

[Lenz 90]   Lenz T.: *Index Optimierung für einen Übersetzer für die Logisprache LOLA*, Diplomarbeit, Institut für Informatik, TU-München 1990

[Lloyd 87]   Lloyd J.W.: *Foundations of Logic Programming* Springer Verlag 1987

[Specht 89]   Specht G.: *Die Logiksprache LOLA und ihre interne Darstellung durch Relationen*, Technischer Report TUM-I8910, TU-München 1989

[Ullman 89]   Ullman J.D.: *Principles of Database and Knowledge-Base Systems, Volume II.* Computer Science Press, Rockville, 1989

NON-MONOTONIC REASONING FOR CLAUSE LOGIC PROGRAMMING IN A GENERAL SETTING

HEINRICH HERRE

Universität Leipzig

Sektion Informatik

Augustusplatz 10-11, 7010 Leipzig

A b s t r a c t

This survey paper is concerned with a unifying approach to non-monotonic
reasoning in clause logic programming. An outline of a general theory of
non-monotonic reasoning is given that synthesizes several semantical and
syntactical approaches that are aimed at a foundation of this area. Some
typical results are presented within this framework and problems related to
logic programming are discussed.

1. INTRODUCTION

A semantics can be defined by an operator Φ associating to every first order
theory T a class of models $\Phi(T) \subseteq \text{Mod}(T)$. For every such operator Φ a family
of inference operations C: $\text{Pow}(L)$ -> $\text{Pow}(L)$ can be generated by taking
suitable subsets of $\text{Th}(\Phi(T))$, $T \subseteq L$. Inference operations which are derived
from such model operators Φ are said to be model-based. Classical examples
of model-based inference operations which are distinct from the classical
consequence operation are those related to ω-logic [Sh 67] and to standard
models of second order theories. All these inference operations are
monotonic.

A new class of inference operations arose in the area of
artificial intelligence and logic programming. Typical examples are
presented by the semantics of a definite program P defined by the least
Herbrand model of P, by the closed world assumption and by the sceptical
closure of a default theory. From all these examples the notion of a model
operator can be abstracted whose derived inference operations are in general
not monotonic. Such general inference operation were studied on an abstract
level in [Ma 89], [Th 89], [Ja 88]. The idea to develop a general theory of
inference operations goes back to Tarski [Ta 56]. The contribution of the
present theory consists in synthesizing all these approaches and to develop
a framework for the study of the semantical and syntactical aspects of
non-monotonic reasoning. We assume familarity with the first-order

predicate calculus and the standard notions of set theory. A *general program clause* has the form $L \leftarrow L_1,\ldots,L_n$, where $L,L_1,\ldots,L_n$ are literals. A *clause* C is a formula having the form $C := A_1 \vee \ldots \vee A_m \vee \neg B_1 \vee \ldots \vee \neg B_n$, where A_i, B_j are atomic formulas. A *query* G is a program clause of the form $\leftarrow L_1,\ldots,L_n$ and let $\wedge G$ be the formula $L_1 \wedge \ldots \wedge L_n$. A *universal theory* is a set of clauses. For a universal theory S let $cl(S)$ be the set of all general program clauses generated from S. This set is defined as follows. Let $C := L_1 \vee \ldots \vee L_n$ be a clause; then $cl(C) =$
$\{\, L_i \leftarrow \neg L_1,\ldots, \neg L_{i-1}, \neg L_{i+1},\ldots,\neg L_n\colon i \in \{1,\ldots,n\}\}$ and $cl(S) = \bigcup_{C \in S} cl(C)$.

The *signature* of a universal theory P , denoted by $\Sigma(P)$, is the set containing the relational, functional and constant symbols appearing in P. $L(\Sigma)$ is the first order language based on Σ. If Σ is not specified we write L. For a set $S \subseteq L$ let $S^C = \{\neg A\colon A \in S\}$. B(P) denotes the *Herbrand base* of P, i.e. the set of all ground atoms of the signature of P. U(P) is the set of all variable-free terms of $\Sigma(P)$. A substitution λ is an operation which replaces occurrences of variables by a term throughout an expression E. The result is denoted by $E\lambda$ and is called an instance of E. We use the notion of an interpretation for P as a relational structure A, which associates a declarative meaning to the symbols of $\Sigma(P)$. A structure A is a model for P if every formula A in P is true in A, denoted by $A \models A$. Let Mod(P) be the class of all models of P. A *Herbrand model* for P is one for which the universe equals U(P). Herbrand models can be represented by subsets $I \subseteq B(P)$. For a class of K of structures let $Th(K) = \{F\colon F \in L(K)$ and $K \models F\}$. The classical consequence relation is denoted by $\models$. A Herbrand model I is said to be *minimal* for S if I is a model of S and no proper subsets of I represents a model of S. Min(S) is the set of all minimal Herbrand models of S. A universal theory (or general program) is said to be consistent if it has a model; then it has always a Herbrand model.

2. MODEL-BASED INFERENCE OPERATIONS

An *inference operation* C is a function from Pow(L) in Pow(L) satisfying the condition $T \subseteq C(T)$ for every theory T. A *model operator* Φ is a function from Pow(L) in Pow(Mod(L)) satisfying following conditions for $S \in$ Pow(L):
(1) $\Phi(S) \subseteq$ Mod(S); (2) if $S \subseteq T \subseteq Th(\Phi(S))$ then $\Phi(S) = \Phi(T)$.
If only the condition (1) is assumed then Φ is said to be a *weak model operator*. A model operator Φ is said to be a *Herbrand operator* if every model from $\Phi(S)$ is a Herbrand model. Φ is said to be *minimal* if every model

in $\Phi(S)$ is minimal. For every model operator Φ we introduce the inference operation C_Φ defined by $C_\Phi(S) = Th(\Phi(S))$. Let be $S \models_\Phi F$ iff $F \in C_\Phi(S)$, and $C_0(S) = \{F : S \models F\}$. For every sublanguage $S \subseteq L$ and model operator Φ there is the following inference operation $C_{\Phi,S}(T) = T \cup (C_\Phi(T) \cap S)$. $C_{\Phi,S}$ is called the restriction of C_Φ to S. In particular, following sublanguages are considered: NL(T) is the set of all negative ground literals of $L(T)$, GL(T) is the set of all ground literals of $L(T)$ and GC(T) the set of all ground clauses in $L(T)$. C *generates literal extensions* if for every T: $C(T) = T \cup V$, $V \subseteq GL(T)$. The notion "C generates clause extensions" is defined analogously. C_1 is bounded by C_2 if for all T: $C_1(T) \subseteq C_2(T)$.

PROPOSITION 1 [He 91]

If Φ is a model operator then C_Φ satisfies the following conditions:
(1) $S \subseteq C_\Phi(S)$ and $C_0(C_\Phi(S)) = C_\Phi(S)$ for every S;
(2) if $S \subseteq T \subseteq C_\Phi(S)$ then $C_\Phi(S) = C_\Phi(T)$;
(3) $C_\Phi(C_\Phi(S)) = C_\Phi(S)$.

If Φ is a model operator then C_Φ is a cumulative inference operation satisfying the stronger condition (1) which is called in [Ma 90] *right absorption*. Every inference operation C: $Pow(L) \rightarrow Pow(L)$ satisfying the condition (1) of proposition 1 can be represented by an operation C_Φ for a certain operator Φ, [He 91]. A model operator Φ is said to be *strongly compact* if for every set S of sentences and every sentence A the following is satisfied: assume that for every finite subset $S_0 \subseteq S$ holds $\Phi(S_0) \cap Mod(A) =/ \emptyset$. Then $\Phi(S) \cap Mod(A) =/ \emptyset$. Φ satisfies the *finiteness theorem* if for for every set S of sentences and sentence A the following holds: if $S \models_\Phi A$ then there is a finite subset $S_0 \subseteq S$ such that $S_0 \models_\Phi A$. The following proposition is a typical result that can be formulated within the general theory.

PROPOSITION 2 [He 91]

Let Φ be a model operator. Then C_Φ satisfies the finiteness theorem if and only if Φ is strongly compact.

Let Φ be a minimal operator and S an universal theory. We introduce the following sets: $NL(\Phi,S) := Th(\Phi(S)) \cap NL(S)$, $GL(\Phi,S) := Th(\Phi(S)) \cap GL(S)$, $GC(\Phi,S) := Th(\Phi(S)) \cap GC(S)$. We summarize some approaches in non-monotonic reasoning that can be analysed within the general theory.

Default Logic. Given any set D of closed default rules in the sense of Reiter [Re 80], we may define an inference operation C: Pow(L) -> Pow(L) by $C(T) = \bigcap E(T)$, T an universal theory, where $E(T)$ is the set of all extensions introduced in [Re 80]. C(T) satisfies left absorption and if we define $\Phi(T) = \text{Mod}(C(T))$, then $C_\Phi(T) = C(T)$. Φ is a weak model operator because C is not cumulative. There are many model operators Φ defining the same inference operation C; finding out the "intensionally correct" one is an open problem.

Finite Failure Extensions. Let S be a set of definite clauses and FF(S) the finite failure set for S. Let $C(S) = S \cup FF(S)^C$, and comp(S) the predicate completion of S in the sense of Clark [Ll 87]. Define $\Phi(S) = \text{Mod}(\text{comp}(S))$; then $C(S) = (C_\Phi(S) \cap GL(S)) \cup S$. C(S) is bounded by $C_\Phi(S)$. C is also bounded by the ˙generalized closed world assumption and by circumscription operations.

Circumscription. Let $\Phi(S) := \text{Min}(S)$ and $C(S)=\text{Th}(\Phi(S))$, C(S) describes the first order theory of the minimal models of S; C(S) contains the circumscription schema Circ(S) for S, [MC 80]. If $\Phi^*(S) := \text{GMin}(S)$ (=the class of all general minimal models of S), then $C_\Phi*(S) \subseteq C_\Phi(S)$. A model operator Φ can be defined satisfying for every finite universal theory S the condition $C_\Phi(S) = C_0(\text{Circ}(S))$. The inference operations derived from the concept of circumscription are cumulative.

Generalized closed world assumption [Mi 82]. Let T be an universal theory. Then GCWA(T) is defined as the set $NL(\Phi,T)$, where $\Phi(S) := \text{Min}(T)$. The GCWA-operation is defined by $C_{gwa}(T) = T \cup NL(\Phi,T)$. It is bounded by the inference operation $C_m(T) = \text{Th}(\text{Min}(T)$; C_{gwa} does not satisfy left absorption but is cumulative.

Similarly, other approaches can be classified within the general theory. The wellfounded semantics [Prz 88], e.g., can be described as an inference operation that generates literal extensions for normal programs and satisfies a property of local cumulativity.

3. CONDITIONS OF CONSTRUCTIVITY

Let Φ be a model operator, $F := \exists x G(x)$, F an existential sentence, S an universal theory. We introduce the following constructive versions of $\models_\Phi$:

(1) $S \models_{\Phi}^{C} F$ iff there is a ground substitution σ such that $S \models_{\Phi} G\sigma$.
σ is said to be a definite Φ-solution for G in S.
(2) $S \models_{\Phi}^{WC} F$ iff there are substitutions $\sigma_1,\ldots,\sigma_n$ such that $S \models_{\Phi} V_{i \leq n} G\sigma_i$.
The set $\{\sigma_1,\ldots,\sigma_n\}$ is said to be an indefinite Φ-solution of G in S.

A model operator Φ is said to be *downward closed* if for every universal theory S the following holds: if $A \in \Phi(S)$ and $B \subseteq A$ then $B \in \Phi(S)$. Φ is said to be Δ_0-compact if for every set X of quantifier free sentences and every theory S holds: If for every finite subset $Y \subseteq X$ the condition $\Phi(S) \cap \text{Mod}(Y)$ =/ $\emptyset$ is satisfied then it follows $\Phi(S) \cap \text{Mod}(X)$ =/ $\emptyset$. Φ is called *weakly constructive* if for all universal S and existential sentences F we have:
$S \models_{\Phi}^{WC} F$ iff $S \models_{\Phi} F$. Again, we have the following typical result.

PROPOSITION 3 [He 91]
Let Φ be a model operator which is downward closed and Δ_0 - compact. Then C_{Φ} is weakly constructive (satisfies Herbrand' s theorem).

The constructive versions of the relation $\models_{\Phi}$ can be relatively axiomatized (with respect to existential sentences) by adding certain sets of variable free sentences to the theory S. This observation is crucial, because it shows that for logic programming those inference operations are the most important that generate literal and clause extensions for universal theories.

PROPOSITION 4
Let S be a universal theory, Φ a minimal operator, F an existential sentence. Then the following conditions are satisfied:
    (1) $S \models_{\Phi}^{C} F$ if and only if $S \cup GL(\Phi,S) \models^{C} F$.
    (2) $S \models_{\Phi}^{WC} F$ if and only if $S \cup GC(\Phi,S) \models F$.

To generate indefinite solutions for existential sentences it is sufficient to apply a complete proof calculus to the set $S \cup GC(\Phi,S)$. For definite solutions one has to formalize the relation $"\models^{C}"$. This case can be handled by the following propositions. Here the SLD-resolution is formally generalized to program clauses from cl(T) as in [He 88].

PROPOSITION 5 (Correctness) [He 91]

Let Φ be a minimal operator , S an universal theory, $S_1 = S \cup GL(\Phi,S)$, G a query. Assume there is a SLD-refutation of $(cl(S_1),G)$ generating a substitutiton σ. Then S $\models_\Phi \wedge G\sigma$.

PROPOSITION 6 (Completeness) [He 91]

Let Φ be a minimal operator, G a query, S an universal theory, $S_1 = {}'S \cup GL(\Phi,S)$. Let σ be a ground substitution satisfying $var(G) \subseteq dom(\sigma)$ and S $\models_\Phi \wedge G\sigma$. Then there is a SLD-refutation of $(cl(S_1),G)$ generating a substitution δ such that $\delta = \sigma$ on $var(G)$.

References

[He 88] Herre,H.: Negation and Constructivity in Logic Programming. J. New Gener. Comput. Syst. 1 (1988), 295 - 305

[He 91] Herre,H.: Nonmonotonic Reasoning and Logic Programs (Workshop on Nonmonotonic and Inductive Logic, 4.-7.12.1990, Karlsruhe) (Ed. P.Schmitt)

[Ja 88] Jäger,G.: Non-monotonic reasoning by axiomatic extensions,in: J.E. Fenstad,I.T. Frolow,R. Hilpinen, Proc. 8th International Congress in Logic, Methodology and Philosophy of Sciences, North-Holland, Amsterdam, 1989

[Ll 87] Lloyd,J.W.: Foundations of Logic Programming, Springer 1987

[Ma 89] Makinson,D. General Theory of Cumulative Inference, in: Reinfrank,M. (Ed.) Non-monotonic Reasoning Berlin Springer Verlag, 1989, 1-18

[Ma 90] Makinson,D.: General Patterns in Nonmonotonic Reasoning; in: Handbook of Logic in Artificial Intelligence and Logic Programming

[MC 80] McCarthy,J.: Circumscription, A.I., vol. 13 (1980), 27-39

[Mi 82] Minker,J.: On indefinite databases and the closed world assumption. In: 6th Conference obn Automated Deduction; Proceedings 1982, LNCS 138

[Pr 88] Przymusinski,T.: Every Logic Program has a natural Stratification and an iterated fixed point model. TR (1988), Departm. of Math. Univ. of Texas at El Paso, TX 79968

[Re 80] Reiter,R.: A Logic for Default Reasoning; AI 13 (1980), 81-132

[Sh 67] Shoenfield,J.R.: Mathematical Logic, Addison-Wesley, 1967

[Ta 56] Tarski,A.: Logic, Semantics, Metamathematics. Papers from 1923 - 1938. Clarendon Press, Oxford, 1956

[Th 89] Thiele,H. : Monotones und nichtmonotones Schließen; in: Grabowski,J., Jantke,H.-J., H. Thiele: Grundlagen der Künstlichen Intelligenz, 80 - 160, Akademie-Verlag, Berlin 1989

2. MASCHINELLES LERNEN

Feature Construction during Tree Learning

Gerhard Mehlsam[*], Hermann Kaindl[*¶] and Wilhelm Barth[¶]

[*] Siemens AG Österreich   [¶] Technische Universität Wien
Programm- und Systementwicklung   Inst. für Computergraphik
Gudrunstraße 11   Karlsplatz 13/186
A—1100 Vienna / Austria   A—1040 Vienna / Austria

Abstract

This paper addresses the "problem of new terms" in the context of learning decision trees using the approach based on ID3. We discuss an algorithm for efficiently constructing new features from given primitive features and relate it to *constructive induction*. In our approach, feature construction is integrated with selecting a (new) feature for building the decision tree in *one* process. Hence, appropriate features are constructed *during* tree generation. The representation of constructed features is based on sets. While the search space of possible features is *exponential*, we use a geometric interpretation to show that this algorithm provides *linear* time and space complexity. Moreover, we show that it finds features with *optimal* value for the tree construction procedure of ID3. Results of experiments are reported, and besides of considerations related to the size of the generated trees we also discuss the important issue of how comprehensible these trees are. In particular, we are interested in the intelligibility of the discovered features.

1 Introduction

In the sub-field *machine learning* of *artificial intelligence*, so-called learning by example plays a prominent role. For long, *empirical* learning of a "rule" which generalizes a given set of examples has dominated this area. One of the first approaches was called CLS by Hunt *et al.* [6], which was designed to learn decision trees for tasks of classifying examples into "concepts". This approach has strongly influenced later work, in particular the well-known ID3 of Quinlan (see e.g. [18] and [17]).

The basis is a universe of *objects* which are described in terms of *attributes* (often synonymously called *features*) taking certain *values*. Each object belongs to one of a set of mutually exclusive *classes*. The task is to develop a *decision tree* that can determine the class of any object from its feature values.

Of course, compared to the more recently developed methods for *analytic* learning (mainly *explanation-based generalization* or *learning* (EBG or EBL), see e.g. [13]), *empirical* learning like that in ID3 utilizes very little domain knowledge. However, it should be clear that the complex features which are normally used for tests in the decision trees represent very important knowledge for making the trees tractable.

While humans with sufficient knowledge about the domain in question can provide appropriate features after serious work, machines themselves usually cannot. This was recognized as the "problem of new terms". Michalski [11] called the approach for constructing new features automatically *constructive induction.* Recently, also the names *constructive deduction* [12], *constructive compilation,* and *feature construction* [8] have been used for variations of the general theme, especially in order to denote whether induction is actually involved or not.

There may be different goals for constructing new features. Since the primitive features used for describing the instances would lead to very large trees for classification tasks of realistic size, there is actually a need for more appropriate features in order to achieve smaller trees. Also the process of tree generation is much easier then. Another point is the issue of intelligibility of the generated trees for humans. While too large trees will typically be difficult to understand, unfortunately also small ones are not necessarily intelligible.

While it is clear that for real practicability also for the process of constructing useful features a large amount of domain knowledge is necessary, we investigate here an approach of "discovering" them. (Combination with methods like those described by Matheus [7] is possible, however.) This approach has been implemented in a system called FEACON, which was used for experiments. While the methods described are fairly general, for these experiments the domain of the chess ending KPK (king and pawn against king) has been chosen. We also use it as a running example for explaining our approach.

First, we describe the basic representation used, which resembles approaches used in the systems CART [3] and ASSISTANT (see [2] and [4]). While to our best knowledge this approach has not yet been related to feature construction, we show how it fits into the general framework of Matheus and Rendell [8]. As a matter of fact, this approach to feature construction has to cope with an exponential search space. Then we discuss an algorithm of CART [3] with *linear* time and space complexity which can be applied to a wide variety of such problems. We use a geometric interpretation to show that it finds *optimal* features in the sense defined below. Thereafter, we present some experimental results of using this algorithm. Finally, we discuss our approach and relate it to the literature.

Major part of this paper is based on part of the first author's doctoral dissertation [9], where more details can be found.

2   Basic Representation

While CLS of Hunt *et al.* is restricted to binary tests of the form "attribute A has value A_i,", Quinlan's ID3 also involves tests of multi-valued attributes. However, the usual evaluation function for selecting the attribute-based test (using information theory and introduced by ID3) tends to favor attributes with many values. This has been observed by Kononenko *et al.* experimenting with ASSISTANT, and Quinlan [16] analyses this problem in more abstract terms. Since a bias is introduced this way, ASSISTANT uses a "subset criterion". A multi-valued attribute is "binarised" by partitioning its value set S into two subsets S_L and S_R so that each subset is treated as one value of the resulting binary attribute. In subsequent tests these subsets can be partitioned further. Unfortunately, a set with n values has 2^n subsets, and even when removing trivial and symmetric subsets, there are still $2^{n-1} - 1$ different ways of partitioning [17]. The splits of "categorial" variables in CART are performed in the same way.

Now let us fit this approach into the framework for feature construction of Matheus and Rendell [8]. Let $\mathcal{F}$ be the set of (primitive) *features* given. Ideally, these would be the ones used to describe the instances. Another view of a "primitive" feature is related to its complexity and its ease of being evaluated (cf. the *operationality criterion* of EBG). *Constructive operators* are applied to $\mathcal{F}$, resulting in a set of new features. Since the representation of a constructed feature in ASSISTANT and in FEACON is a *set*, the constructive operator used is the "inclusive or": $or(binary, binary)$. It is usually applied several times in sequence during one step of feature construction.

However, the nominal features with multiple values (more than two) first have to be converted into Boolean expressions. As an example of a primitive feature in KPK, let F be the position of the white king within the range of 64 squares. The conversion results in 64 Boolean expressions of the form $equal(F, F_i)$. It is interesting to note, that this is reminiscent to the binary tests of CLS.

In the approach we adopt, however, these expressions are not directly used for the tests in the tree. They only serve as the basis for constructed features, which are more conveniently viewed as sets of feature values. For instance, $\{F_i, F_j, F_k\}$ can be constructed by $or(or(equal(F, F_i), equal(F, F_j)),$ $equal(F, F_k))$. In KPK such a set can represent some "critical squares", each of which is equivalent for a given piece.

Since the resulting tests are still binary, actually there are two complementary subsets constructed. This view of construction is dual to the one of "partitioning" or "splitting" described in [2]. We prefer still another view for the description of our algorithm. Beginning with the given set $S = S_R$ and its empty complement S_L, one element is removed from S_R and put into S_L, in effect "moving" it from S_R to S_L. This way the question which binary features to combine using the or-operator—or equivalently which partition to chose—can be reformulated to the question of which element to move. Besides of the more convenient way of looking at the problem in terms of a geometric interpretation (presented below), it has the technical advantage of allowing for incremental (and therefore cheaper) computations.

Consequently, binarisation can be viewed as a special case of feature construction. Of course, the latter is in general more ambitious, and besides of using several constructive operators other aspects can be involved as well. However, the special case of binarisation still deserves special attention. In fact, it can very efficiently provide useful results, while the general case is usually intractable.

3 Feature Generation

Matheus and Rendell [8] and Pagallo [15] propose iterations of tree learning and feature construction. Our approach integrates more tightly in constructing features *during* tree generation. In our system FEACON, we integrated selecting a feature for generating the decision tree and creating this feature into *one* process. First, features are constructed using the method described below. Immediately thereafter these features are used for the normal procedure of test selection in ID3. Currently, features are always generated from the primitive features given. This approach could be extended to also build upon generated ones.

Using the values of a given nominal feature as a basis, a space of features to be constructed is defined as described above. This space is traversed by systematically moving elements from one set to the other. The evaluation is done using the information-based function of ID3 itself. Due to certain properties of this function it is possible to find an feature in this space with minimal value of this function without backtracking. The key idea is to order the elements appropriately before "moving". While Breiman *et al.* [3] present similar results, we emphasize the algorithmic aspect and a geometric interpretation.

First, we describe an algorithm for feature construction in the context of *single-concept learning*, i.e. there is only a distinction between positive and negative instances, or between two classes.

Due to the exponential search space of features and sets with a typical cardinality of 64 (the number of chess squares) or larger, (up to 225 in our experiments), no blind algorithm can do a complete search within reasonable time. A heuristic best-first search for a feature with an optimal value requires too much storage (and still too much time). In such a situation, some sort of hill-climbing often serves as a last resort. A straight-forward approach is to determine at each step the element which results in the best evaluation when moved, and to proceed by moving an element from one set to the other as long as there is improvement. While such a procedure can efficiently find solutions (features), there is no guarantee that they are optimal (in any sense), due to the well-known disadvantages of hill-climbing (in particular getting stuck on local minima). Moreover, even if the procedure does not stop when there is no immediate improvement, sub-optimal solutions may be found.

We tried to have a closer look on the properties of the information-based function. The formula for the *expected information requirement* $E_F(a,b)$ after testing a feature F in the decision tree can be written as follows, for the case of 2 classes A and B (*single-concept learning*) and 2-valued features. This function is to be minimized, and a and b are the numbers of objects which show up the feature F.

$$
\begin{aligned}
E_F(a,b) \;=\; & \frac{1}{n_A+n_B} \cdot \big((a+b)\cdot \mathrm{ld}(a+b) - a\cdot \mathrm{ld}(a) - b\cdot \mathrm{ld}(b) + \\
& + (n_A - a + n_B - b)\cdot \mathrm{ld}(n_A - a + n_B - b) - \\
& - (n_A - a)\cdot \mathrm{ld}(n_A - a) - (n_B - b)\cdot \mathrm{ld}(n_B - b) \big)
\end{aligned}
$$

$$
\begin{aligned}
a \;\;&\ldots\;\; \text{number of objects of class } A \text{ in the left branch} \\
b \;\;&\ldots\;\; \text{number of objects of class } B \text{ in the left branch} \\
n_A \;\;&\ldots\;\; \text{total number of objects of class } A \text{ in the left and} \\
& \quad\quad \text{in the right branch together (constant)} \\
n_B \;\;&\ldots\;\; \text{total number of objects of class } B \text{ in the left and} \\
& \quad\quad \text{in the right branch together (constant)}
\end{aligned}
$$

There actually exists a property of E_F which allows for a very efficient method of finding features with optimal value. It can probably best be understood using a geometric interpretation of the function and the procedure of moving elements. Therefore, see Fig. 1 for a plot of an example. It indicates that values become smaller the closer they are to the boundary. This is indeed an important property, since it implies that there are no minima at an inner point of a closed area.

Now let us relate this to a geometric interpretation of our approach of moving elements from one set to the other. Each element of such a set (i.e., a binary feature) has associated with it a certain number of objects of class A and a certain number of objects of class B (which show up this feature). Hence, it corresponds to a point in the a,b-plane (see also Fig. 2). If several such elements are in a

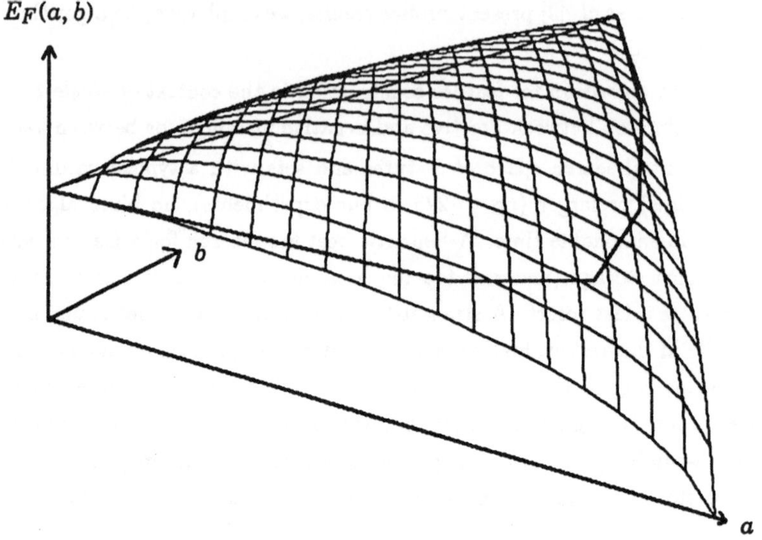

Figure 1: A plot of the function $E_F(a, b)$

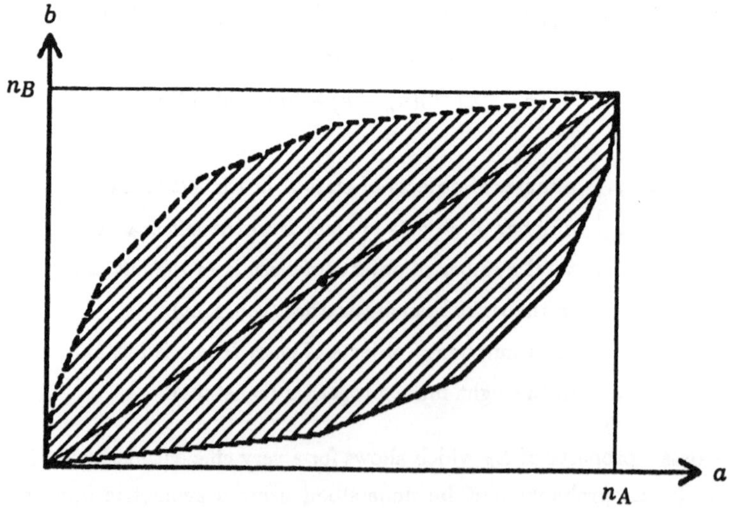

Figure 2: Area of the points corresponding to subsets

set, the numbers of their associated objects are summed up, and the whole set again corresponds to a point. Consequently, we can visualize the procedure of adding (removing) an element from (to) a set as moving from one point in the a,b-plane to another. We connect two such points by a straight line. The whole procedure of adding the elements of one set (S_R) to the other (S_L, which is initially empty) can be visualized as a polygonal line.

Note, that the dual procedure of moving the elements from set S_L to the initially empty set S_R is represented by another polygonal line which is symmetric to the opposite one (see Fig. 2). Related to this is the obvious property $E_F(a,b) = E_F(n_A - a, n_B - b)$, implying that symmetric points have the same value of E_F.

The key idea is now to identify a closed polygon which contains all points in the a,b-plane corresponding to subsets. In fact, it is easy to see that this can be achieved in the following way. If at each step the element with the straight line of steepest ascent is chosen, no point above this line can correspond to a subset. Symmetrically, the opposite part of the polygon is found by going back along the steepest descent.

This polygon determines a closed area of those points which actually correspond to subsets and hence can be achieved by moving elements. If the conjecture stated above is true (it is, as the proof sketch below shows) the minimum value of E_F in this area is on the boundary. Due to the symmetry it occurs (at least) twice, and more precisely at those points of the polygon where the direction changes. The following algorithm X uses these properties for efficiently finding features with optimal value.

Definition. A constructed feature F is E_F-*optimal* if its associated value E_F is minimal compared to the competing features. ∎

Although this optimality of a feature does not necessarily imply that its use results in a decision tree of minimal size, this definition is reasonable in the sense that ID3 selects features for tests according to the same criterion.

Algorithm X. Before actually moving elements, they are ordered according to their corresponding quotient $b/(a + b)$. Then they are actually moved in this order, and each time an element has been moved, E_F is computed for the resulting partition. This procedure does not stop on its route until all the elements have been moved. A partition with the minimal value of E_F found corresponds to an E_F-optimal feature. ∎

Proposition 1. Algorithm X has *linear* time and space complexity. ∎

This proposition is obviously true, and it is also worth noting that the actual computations performed are even less than those for hill-climbing. However, it is less obvious that this algorithm also finds E_F-*optimal* features, minimizing E_F as its evaluation function. Especially, this depends on the properties of E_F. Therefore, we state some propositions below and sketch their proofs (more elaborate proofs can be found in [9]).

Lemma. The function $E_F(a, b)$ is concave in the whole domain $0 < a < n_A$, $0 < b < n_B$. This is equivalent to

$$2 \cdot E_F(a,b) \geq E_F(a + x, b + y) + E_F(a - x, b - y)$$

for every a, b, x, y, as long as all arguments are in the domain.

Proof sketch: x and y determine s and α by $x = s \cdot \cos \alpha$ and $y = s \cdot \sin \alpha$. We can prove that $\frac{d^2 E_F}{ds^2} \leq 0$ holds for all angles α. From this the stated inequality follows directly. ∎

Proposition 2. For any part of the a,b-domain surrounded by a polygon the function $E_F(a,b)$ takes its minimum only on the polygon itself, more precisely on the vertices.

Proof sketch: The lemma shows that along any straight line through (a,b) the function $E_F(a,b)$ decreases in the one or in the other direction (or remains constant). Consequently, there is no local minimum at an inner point of the domain. This also holds for the edges of the polygon with the exception of the vertices. Therefore, all the local minima are on the vertices, hence also the global minimum. ∎

Proposition 3. Algorithm X finds an E_F-optimal feature, i.e. a subset corresponding to a partition with minimal value of E_F.

Proof sketch: Algorithm X builds the subset representing the constructed feature by adding one element after each other. At each step, it takes the element associated with the steepest ascent. The sequence of straight lines constructed this way lies above all points corresponding to subsets. The polygonal line as constructed by algorithm X is above the center of symmetry of E_F. Together with its symmetric "dual" it constructs a complete polygon. The points of all other partitions lie strictly within this boundary. According to Proposition 2, the minimum is at a vertex of this polygon, and it is consequently found by algorithm X. ∎

Since a key point in this argumentation is that E_F is a concave function, the question may arise, why the hill-climbing approach mentioned above (without the specific ordering mechanism) does *not* work for guaranteeing E_F-optimality. In order to answer this, it is necessary to note that the arguments a and b denote numbers of objects in class A and B, respectively. The hill-climbing approach tries to minimize the information content related to a one-ply look-ahead of moving one element. Movement of an element, however, may add an arbitrary number of associated objects of both classes, in effect allowing for large "jumps" in the space of a and b. Additionally, the direction of such a jump may be different from the direction chosen by algorithm X. Moreover, the hill-climbing procedure may proceed along some sequence of straight lines not visiting all vertices visited by algorithm X. Therefore, without the possibility of backtracking (taking back some element) it may miss the optimum. Moreover, sub-optimal features may also be constructed due to stopping at a local minimum on the boundary.

Having found an efficient procedure for the case of two classes, the question arises whether algorithm X can be generalized for *multi-concept learning*, i.e. making the distinction between more than two classes. Analogously to the considerations in the 2-dimensional space, the principal arguments should also be valid in an n-dimensional space defined by n classes. Therefore, such a generalisation should be possible in principle. However, the exact method is not clear yet, and such a procedure would again be rather costly. After all, a search in a space with $n-1$ dimensions would be necessary.

Hence, the straight-forward way of transforming the multi-concept learning problem into a sequence of single-concept learning problems is a pragmatic way to do it. Unfortunately, this approach does not guarantee optimal solutions, even though all the single-concept problems are solved by algorithm X.

4 Experimental Results

Due to lack of space, we can only give a qualitative summary here. Quantitative data and an elaborate discussion can be found in [9]. For the experiments a data base containing complete and reliable information on the chess ending KPK (king and pawn against king) has been generated and used. For instance, the work by Beal and Clarke [1] can be seen as an indication that the task of generating decision rules for classification of such endgame positions has been a challenge for humans. Moreover, they used much chess knowledge in their approach of designing such rules "by hand". In addition to the problem of whether a position is a win or a draw (*single-concept learning*), we also made experiments with our approach for the more difficult problem of determining the number of moves to a (possible) win, given "optimal" play of both sides (*multi-concept learning*). It might be interesting to compare human results on the latter task, for which they probably have much less knowledge available since in chess practice it is usually not important to win in a minimal number of moves.

We provided the program with simple features (of chess positions), and restricted these to *static* features (i.e., using none which would require search in the problem space). The most simple ones are the *absolute* positions of the pieces on the board (given as the codes of the squares they are located). Possible features to be created from these are sets of squares, e.g. lines, rows, or arbitrary regions, and even unions of different regions. Additionally, the *relative* positions of the pieces have been used (i.e., coding the distances, which amounts to providing additional knowledge). For further experiments also distances to specific (key) squares were taken into account, and finally schemata of the form "piece A is closer to square x than piece B", with A and B fixed, while x was a variable parameter to be determined automatically by the machine. When only providing such simple features to the original ID3, the given problem is intractable within practical time and space limits. The same is true for applying the subset criterion with an exponential search.

For the reported experiments we always had the system learn complete information, hence there was *no induction* involved. Moreover, for reasons of simplicity we did not employ the iterations with "windows" of ID3. The primary measure for comparison is the number of nodes in the generated decision trees. 14 example problems of varying difficulty based on KPK were defined, fixing the position of the pawn on specific squares. From these, 7 are single- and 7 multi-concept learning problems, depending on whether the number of moves to a (possible) win is taken into account. To give an idea of the relative difficulty (for the machine), the factors in tree size between corresponding pairs of problems varied between 1.6 up to about 4 (using only the absolute positions of the pieces as given features).

Generally, with more complicated features given initially, better features could be constructed, and the trees became smaller, but not as much as could have been expected. The given procedure can already create reasonable trees with only the absolute positions of the pieces as a given primitive feature, which is readily available from the instance descriptions. Using all the features described above, the decision tree generated for the complete KPK domain had a total number of 733 nodes, or 366 internal nodes with associated decisions using constructed features. This is only larger by a factor of 7.6 than the best known decision procedure created manually (see [1]), which uses 48 much more complicated criteria, and these represent a lot of domain knowledge especially provided by the human creators.

In addition to the size of the generated trees, an important point is also how intelligible they are to humans. There are many factors involved, such as the branching of the trees, of course also their size, the intelligibility of the features used for the tests, and their distribution within the trees. While Shepherd [20] conjectures that multi-branching trees may have an advantage in this regard over binary trees, Cestnik *et al.* [4], report that due to binarisation the trees became smaller and for this reason also more intelligible to human experts. A potential problem with this approach is that the parts of the original multi-valued feature may appear "scattered" to humans, when they occur in various subsets distributed over the whole tree. Of course, the general issue of comprehensible trees deserves further attention. We were particularly interested in the aspect, how intelligible the discovered *features* are.

Careful inspection of some of the generated trees revealed both features corresponding to known chess concepts as well as features which could not be interpreted by us. From this experience, we realized more and more that this interpretation of discovered features is strongly related to "matching" them with already existing domain knowledge. While we do not claim that every feature constructed here is really important, appearently there are many of them worth a closer look. In general, if a discovered feature is not known by the human user, it may be useful for him to learn the underlying concept. For this purpose the system should be able to present examples via an appropriate user interface. Such procedures have some potential of "creativity". For instance given the primitive features described above, FEACON (re-)discovered the "rule of the square". (Since no generalization is done yet, it is discovered and represented for each position of a pawn anew.)

5 Discussion and Related Work

While Michalski [11] investigated constructive induction in the framework of AQ11, Quinlan [18] made first attempts with ID3 discovering patterns from statistics of a complete set of instances and generalising these patterns. Bratko and Kononenko [2] employed binarisation using set partitioning, but they did not present an efficient method for doing it with larger sets. Interestingly, the relationship of this approach to feature construction has not been mentioned before. Quinlan [16] made extensive experiments with it, but lacking an efficient method only small sets could be handled. For this reason, in ASSISTANT a hill-climbing approach is used for features with more than four values, and exhaustive search is performed for fewer values [4].

Similar work has been performed independently by Breiman *et al.* [3] in the context of *classification* and *regression trees* (CART). As a matter of fact, in this book no reference is made to [6] and [18]. Conversely, the ASSISTANT group and Quinlan were obviously unaware of important results in [3]. In fact, also our work reported here was performed without knowledge of the CART system. Nevertheless, binarization is reminiscent of the method of dealing with "categorial" variables in this system. Moreover, a major result in [3] essentially proves our proposition 3. While their proof is more general, our geometric interpretation appears to be much more understandable. In addition, our lemma shows that the information theoretic function so often used in tree learning systems in the field of AI in fact has the required property.

Matheus and Rendell [8] provide a general framework for feature construction, and we have shown how the subset approach fits into it. Now let us briefly discuss, how our system relates to the four aspects they have identified. First, FEACON has no explicit step for *detection* of when construction is required. Due to the linear complexity of the employed algorithm X the method of construction is very efficient, and it may be more costly to try detecting the need than just doing it. Since FEACON uses only one constructive operator, the question of constructor *selection* boils down to the question of which operands to chose. Again, this is very efficiently done by this algorithm without the need for domain knowledge (though it could be included). Currently, there is no *generalization* of selected constructors in FEACON.

Finally, for *evaluation* of the new features, FEACON uses the same criterion as it does for deciding which feature to select as a test during tree formation. Hence, this evaluation is fully compatible to the process it is designed to support. Moreover, it is specific for the part handled at each node, since it is performed *during* tree generation. This way it can avoid potential disadvantages of evaluating features according to their utility on the entire training set. This latter issue is discussed for the system CITRE by Matheus and Rendell [8], since this system performs iterations of tree learning and feature construction.

In both CITRE and the system FRINGE by Pagallo [15], iterations of tree learning and feature construction are used to achieve trees that are *less tall*. In FEACON, feature construction is done *during* tree learning in order to achieve *less bushy* trees. Hence, combinations of these approaches appear to be both easy from an algorithmic view as well as useful in adding the effects. In particular, Pagallo reports on using FRINGE in Boolean domains, which are constructed from multiple values by FEACON. Moreover, an integration of the approach of Matheus [7] into FEACON would be useful as a means to include domain knowledge.

In fact, there exist many more systems doing some form of feature construction, for instance Muggleton's DUCE [14], Rendell's PLS0 [19], MIRO by Drastal *et al.* [5], and a system by Watanabe and Elio [21]. While these appear to be not so directly related to our approach, still considerations on combining the ideas will be useful. Finally, the geometric interpretation using "inverted spaces" by Mehra *et al.* [10] may help in this respect.

6 Conclusion

We put the "subset criterion" (as used in CART and ASSISTANT and now in FEACON) into the framework for feature construction of [8]. Due to the combinatorial explosion inherent in this approach, an efficient method is necessary to make it practicable for sets of realistic size. Algorithm X constructs E_F-*optimal* features efficiently with *linear* time and space complexity. While we have experimented with it in the KPK subdomain of chess, its general applicability is only determined by the following conditions. The nominal features must have a finite number of values greater than two, and a concave evaluation function (like the common information-based one) must be used. (For instance, ASSISTANT has been applied for medical and technical diagnostic tasks.) When more than two classes are to be distinguished, optimal solutions are not guaranteed, but the method can still serve as a very efficient means of handling the single-concept problems involved in solving the multi-concept learning problem.

We have not studied the effects of *induction* in this context (i.e., the performance on "unseen cases"), since this had already been done by Quinlan [16]. The results from theses experiments as well as the experience reported from the use of ASSISTANT suggest that the accuracy is improved by binarisation, which is related to the reductions of the size of the generated decision trees. Algorithm X allows to do it efficiently. Still it may be useful to study the effect of using E_F-optimal vs. non-optimal features on the accuracy. Also the influence of noisy data would be of interest.

Moreover, *generalization* of discovered features is an interesting issue here. The already achieved results as well as these extensions, are to be seen as steps towards fully automatic generation of decision trees, which should be based only on (primitive) features as given for the description of the instances. There should be no need for hand-crafted features, though the inclusion of domain knowledge in some form will be necessary for larger problems.

Acknowledgment

We would like to thank Holger G. Ziegeler for his aid in mastering TₑX for the production of this paper.

References

[1] D. F. Beal and M. R. B. Clarke. The construction of economical and correct algorithms for king and pawn against king. In M. R. B. Clarke, editor, *Advances in Computer Chess 2*, pages 1–30, Edinburgh University Press, Edinburgh, U.K., 1980.

[2] I. Bratko and I. Kononenko. Learning diagnostic rules from incomplete and noisy data. In B. Phelps, editor, *Interactions in Artificial Intelligence and Statistical Method*, pages 142–153, London, England, 1986.

[3] L. Breiman, J.H. Friedman, R.A. Olshen, and C.J. Stone. *Classification and Regression Trees*. Wadsworth, Belmont, 1984.

[4] B. Cestnik, I. Kononenko, and I. Bratko. ASSISTANT 86: A knowledge-elicitation tool for sophisticated users. In I. Bratko and N. Lavrac, editors, *Progress in Machine Learning*, pages 31–45, Sigma Press, Wilmslow, England, 1987.

[5] G. Drastal, G. Czako, and S. Raatz. Induction in an abstraction space: A form of constructive induction. In *Proceedings of the Eleventh International Joint Conference on Artificial Intelligence*, pages 708–712, Morgan Kaufmann, Detroit, MI, August 1989.

[6] E. B. Hunt, J. Marin, and P. T. Stone. *Experiments in Induction*. Academic Press, New York, NY, 1966.

[7] C. J. Matheus. Adding domain knowledge to SBL through feature construction. In *Proceedings of the Eighth National Conference on Artificial Intelligence*, pages 803–808, AAAI, AAAI Press and MIT Press, Boston, MA, July/August 1990.

[8] C. J. Matheus and L. A. Rendell. Constructive induction on decision trees. In *Proceedings of the Eleventh International Joint Conference on Artificial Intelligence*, pages 645–650, Morgan Kaufmann, Detroit, MI, August 1989.

[9] G. Mehlsam. *Automatisches Erzeugen von Klassifikationskriterien*. Doctoral Dissertation, Technische Universität Wien, Vienna, Austria, August 1989.

[10] P. Mehra, L. A. Rendell, and B. W. Wah. Principled constructive induction. In *Proceedings of the Eleventh International Joint Conference on Artificial Intelligence*, pages 651–656, Morgan Kaufmann, Detroit, MI, August 1989.

[11] R. S. Michalski. Pattern recognition as rule-guided inductive inference. *IEEE Transactions on Pattern Analysis and Machine Intelligence*, PAMI-2(4):349–361, July 1980.

[12] R. S. Michalski and Y. Kodratoff. Research in machine learning: Recent progress, classification of methods, and future directions. In Y. Kodratoff and R. S. Michalski, editors, *Machine Learning: An Artificial Intelligence Approach, Volume III*, chapter 1, pages 3–30, Morgan Kaufmann, San Mateo, CA, 1990.

[13] T. M. Mitchell, R. M. Keller, and S. T. Kedar-Cabelli. Explanation-based generalization: A unifying view. *Machine Learning*, 1:47–80, 1986.

[14] S. Muggleton. Duce, an oracle based approach to constructive induction. In *Proceedings of the Tenth International Joint Conference on Artificial Intelligence*, pages 287–292, Morgan Kaufmann, Milan, Italy, August 1987.

[15] G. Pagallo. Learning DNF by decision trees. In *Proceedings of the Eleventh International Joint Conference on Artificial Intelligence*, pages 639–644, Morgan Kaufmann, Detroit, MI, August 1989.

[16] J. R. Quinlan. Decision trees and multi-valued attributes. In J. E. Hayes, D. Michie, and J. Richards, editors, *Machine Intelligence 11*, chapter 13, pages 305–318, Clarendon Press, Oxford, England, 1988.

[17] J. R. Quinlan. Induction of decision trees. *Machine Learning*, 1:81–106, 1986.

[18] J. R. Quinlan. Learning efficient classification procedures and their application to chess end games. In R. S. Michalski, J. G. Carbonell, and T. M. Mitchell, editors, *Machine Learning: An Artificial Intelligence Approach*, chapter 15, pages 463–482, Tioga, Palo Alto, CA, 1983.

[19] L. A. Rendell. Substantial constructive induction using layered information compression: Tractable feature formation in search. In *Proceedings of the Ninth International Joint Conference on Artificial Intelligence*, pages 650–658, Morgan Kaufmann, Los Angeles, CA, August 1985.

[20] B. A. Shepherd. An appraisal of a decision tree approach to image classification. In *Proceedings of the Eighth International Joint Conference on Artificial Intelligence*, pages 473–475, Morgan Kaufmann, Karlsruhe, FRG, August 1983.

[21] L. Watanabe and R. Elio. Guiding constructive induction for incremental learning from examples. In *Proceedings of the Tenth International Joint Conference on Artificial Intelligence*, pages 293–296, Morgan Kaufmann, Milan, Italy, August 1987.

Using Integrated Knowledge Acquisition to Prepare Sophisticated Expert Plans for Their Re-Use in Novel Situations[*]

Franz Schmalhofer, Ralph Bergmann, Otto Kühn, Gabriele Schmidt

German Research Center for Artificial Intelligence
University Bldg 57
Erwin-Schrödinger Str.
D-6750 Kaiserslautern
Germany
e-mail: schmalho@informatik.uni-kl.de

Abstract: Plans which were constructed by human experts and have been repeatedly executed to the complete satisfaction of some customer in a complex real world domain contain very valuable planning knowledge. In order to make this compiled knowledge re-usable for novel situations, a specific integrated knowledge acquisition method has been developed: First, a domain theory is established from documentation materials or texts, which is then used as the foundation for explaining how the plan achieves the planning goal. Secondly, hierarchically structured problem class definitions are obtained from the practitioners' highlevel problem conceptualizations. The descriptions of these problem classes also provide operationality criteria for the various levels in the hierarchy. A skeletal plan is then construced for each problem class with an explanation-based learning procedure. These skeletal plans consist of a sequence of general plan elements, so that each plan element can be independently refined. The skeletal plan thus accounts for the interactions between the various concrete operations of the plan at a general level. The complexity of the planning problem is thereby factored in a domain-specific way and the compiled knowledge of sophisticated expert plans can be re-used in novel situations.

1. MOTIVATION

Like other synthetic tasks, planning problems are inherently intractable [Georgeff87]. In a complex real world domain such as production planning in mechanical engineering, expert systems can consequently not be based on planning from first principles [Koehler91]. It is also not surprising that in at least 80 percent of all mechanical engineering planning tasks, even human planners re-use old plans by adapting them to the new planning problem [Spur79; ThobenSchmalhofer90].

Expert plans have not only been developed with much effort, but were also carefully tested and have proven their sophistication during numerous successful executions in the real world. Preparing such human planning solutions for their re-use in novel situations can provide an important basis for the development of a successful planning system.

This paper describes a general procedure by which concrete human expert plans can be generalized into skeletal plans [FriedlandIwasaki85]. A skeletal plan provides a partitioning of the enormous search space of the complete planning problem into a number of subproblems with small search spaces. The skeletal plans constructed by this procedure are indexed by the various application conditions so that they can be re-used in novel situations.

---

[*] This research was funded by "Bundesministerium für Bildung und Wissenschaft" under grant ITW 8902 C4 and in part by grant Schm 648/1 from "Deutsche Forschungsgemeinschaft".

Explanation-based learning [MitchellKeller86] is applied to find an appropriate generalisation of a concrete case consisting of the description of a manufacturing problem and its solution. It is embedded into an integrated knowledge acquisition method [SchmalhoferKuehn+91] which provides the domain theory and allows the specification of domain-adequate operationality criteria for the construction of skeletal plans.

We will first outline the integrated knowledge acquisition framework, which is based on a quite general model of expertise. The general model describes the overall structure of the future expert system. We will then describe the skeletal plan construction procedure and its implementation in some detail. The application of the procedure to the production planning of a rotational part will be described and the results will be discussed.

2. INTEGRATED KNOWLEDGE ACQUISITION FOR PLAN RE-USE

The problem of production planning in mechanical engineering consists of finding an adequate production plan for a given workpiece which is to be manufactured in some factory. For the manufacturing of a rotational part, the production plan consists of a sequence of chucking and cutting operations by which the workpiece can be manufactured.

The general structure of the expert system which is being developed can be described by the model of expertise [BreukerWielinga89] shown in Figure 1. From the concrete description of the workpiece and the available manufacturing environment more abstract feature descriptions are first constructed. These abstractions are then associated with an appropriate skeletal plan that has been stored stored in the knowledge base. The skeletal plan is finally refined with the help of the workpiece and the factory description into the concrete production plan.

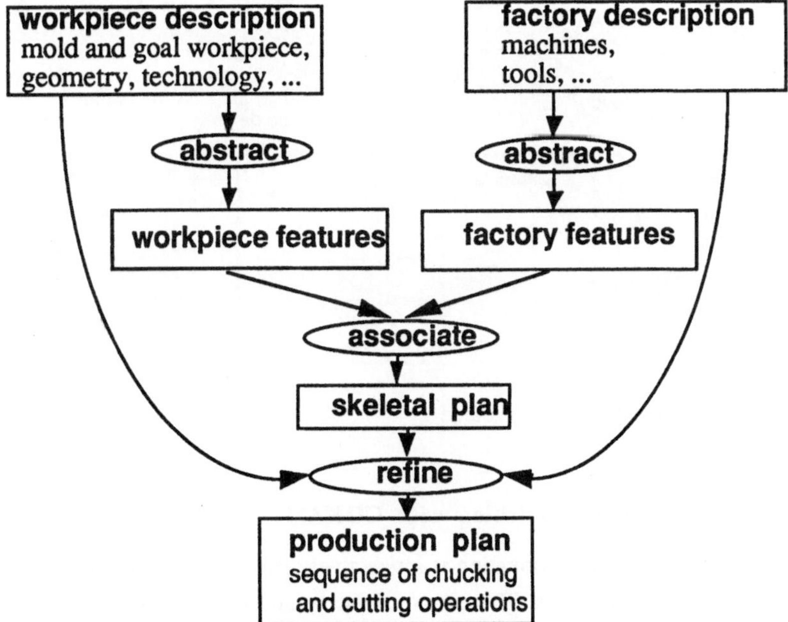

Figure 1: Model of expertise for production planning

The model of expertise specifies what kind of knowledge has to be acquired for the expert system, namely abstraction rules, refinement rules and skeletal plans which are associated with features of the problem description. In addition, a model of mechanical engineering actions is presumed as a general domain model. This model requires chucking and cutting operations to be described by some typology and their preconditions and effects.

An integrated knowledge acquisition method is used to coordinate knowledge from texts, previously solved planning problems (cases) and the expert's respective memories. The knowledge acquisition tools COKAM (Case-Oriented Knowledge-Acquisition Method from Text) [SchmidtSchmalhofer90; KuehnLinster+91] and CECoS (Case-Experience Combination System) [BergmannSchmalhofer91] are applied to the same set of cases so that the knowledge acquired with the two tools will complement one another. The domain and common sense knowledge supplied by COKAM and the definition of production classes obtained through CECoS, can then be utilized to automatically construct skeletal plans and associated application conditions through the explanation-based learning procedure SPGEN (Skeletal Plan Generation Procedure).

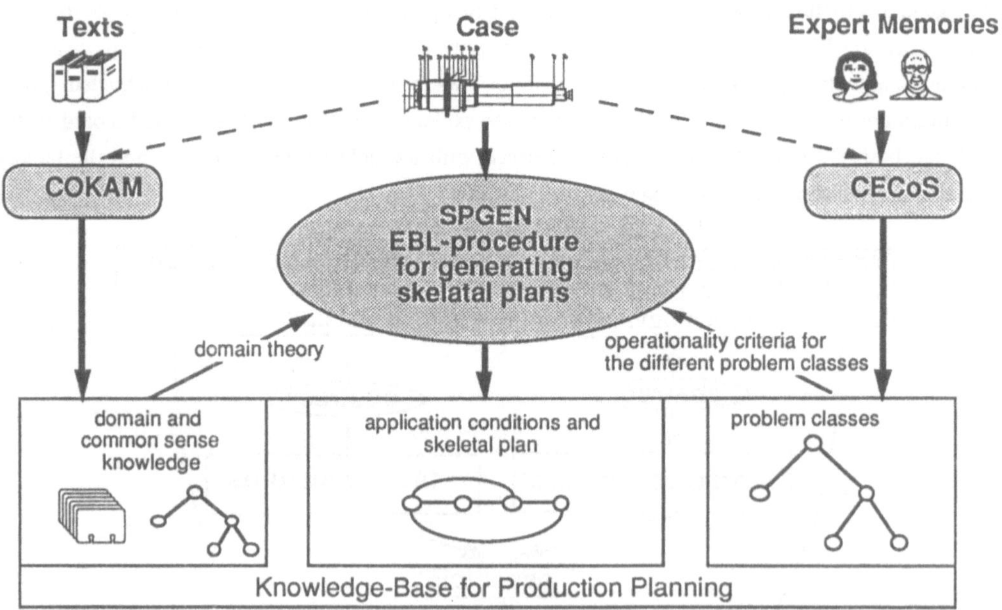

Figure 2: Integrated knowledge acquisition method

2.1. Case oriented knowledge acquisition with COKAM

With the interactive tool COKAM information is interactively extracted from a text and subsequently enhanced by the expert's elaborations. The extracted information is then mapped to the model of mechanical engineering actions (domain model). The so collected knowledge thus provides an explanation of each step in the production plan and specifies the conditions which are required for its application and the resulting consequences. Table 1 shows a sample of text information and expert elaborations, which are relevant for determining the preconditions and consequences of a specific cutting operation. The mapping of the 3rd knowledge unit of Table 1 into the model of mechanical engineering actions, which will be described in section 3.1 shows that the extracted information needs to be properly interpreted.

1. For rough cutting the cutting speed should be 400 to 600 m/minute.
2. When the mold has been forged, bezeling is required, if ceramic cutting tools are to be used.
3. The surface roughness Rt depends on the cutting feed f and the corner radius r_e of the cutting tool and can be computed by the formula $R_t = f^2/8r_e$.
4. When thin workpieces are manufactured with a high cutting force, vibrations may occur.
5. When high tolerances are required, a very hard cutting material must be used for fine turning.

Table 1: A sample of text information extracted with COCAM

2.2. Acquisition of problem classes with CECoS

With the interactive tool CECoS a hierarchically structured set of problem classes is obtained from a set of prototypical cases and human expert judgements. The problem classes are defined so that a useful skeletal plan will exist for each problem class. From explicit and implicit memories, the expert first establishes an extensional definition of the various problem classes with respect to selected prototypical cases. The so established production classes are then intensionally and thereby generally defined.

Because the class definitions are based on expert judgements, the classes should be defined at the right level of generality: They should be general enough so that a large number of specific problems fall into the different classes and they should be specific enough to provide operational knowledge for production planning.

Figure 3 shows a section of the hierarchy of production classes which was obtained for some prototypical shafts. Class A is defined by the features which all three cases have in common. The more specific class B inherits all the features from class A and has some additional features which apply to the cases M5 and M4 but not to M3.

The features of each class may refer to the geometry (long workpiece) and technology (hardened steel) of the workpiece, to the factory (one tool revolver), or to the production plan (2 chucking fixations). As will be shown later, the features referring to the problem description (i.e. the workpiece or the factory) are utilized for the specification of the application conditions, whereas the features referring to the production plan are used for the definition of the operator classes in the skeletal plans.

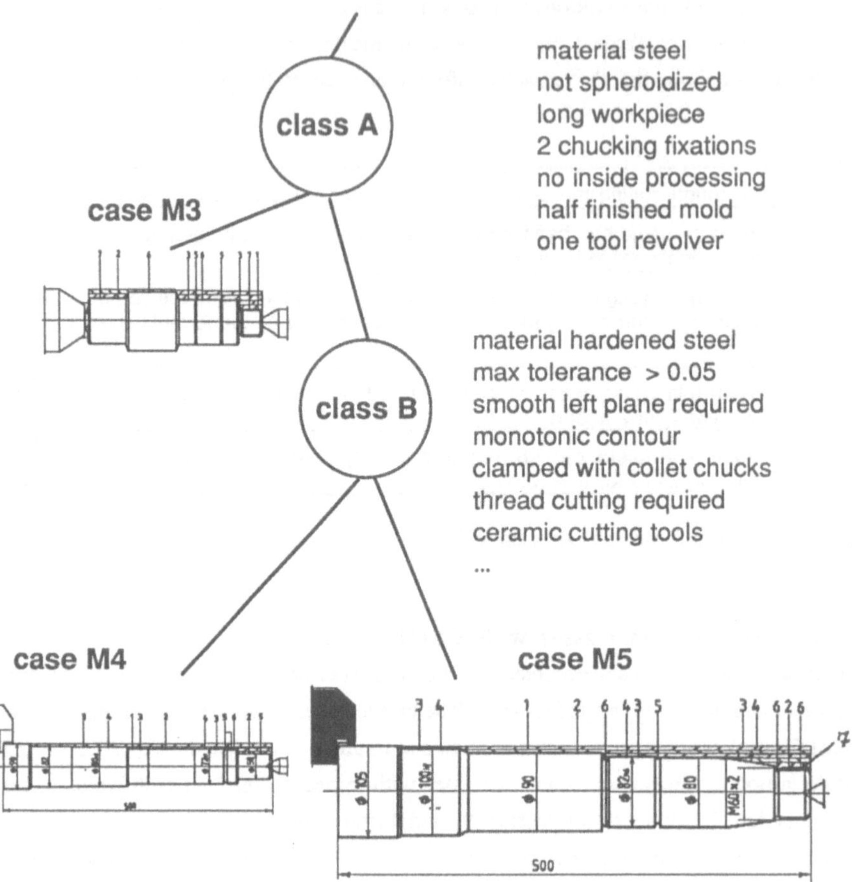

Figure 3: A section of a hierarchy of problem classes acquired with CECoS

3. PROCEDURE FOR GENERATING SKELETAL PLANS

SPGEN is based on explanation-based generalization as described by [MitchellKeller86]. The domain and common sense knowledge acquired with COKAM is thereby used as domain theory and the hierarchy of problem classes is employed to specify operationality criteria. Depending upon the selected problem class and the respective operationality criteria, a more or less general skeletal plan will be obtained from a given case.

A skeletal plan is constructed by SPGEN in four phases:

1. In the first phase the execution of the source plan is simulated and explanations for the effects of the individual operations are constructed.

2. In the second phase the generalization of these explanations is performed with respect to a criterion of operationality, that specifies the vocabulary for defining abstract operators for the skeletal plan.

3. In the third phase, a dependency analysis of the resulting operator effects unveils the substantial interactions of the concrete plan at the more general level of the skeletal plan.

4. In the forth phase the concept descriptions for the abstract operators of the skeletal plan are formed by collecting and normalizing the important constraints for each operation that were indicated by the dependencies.

For describing the SPGEN procedure we will use a simplification of the case M5 from Figure 3. The input and the (intermediate) results of the procedure will be presented in a PROLOG-like notation in which unquoted strings beginning with an upper-case character denote variables.

The formal representation of the case M5 which is used as input to SPGEN is shown in Table 2. The left side of the table shows the representation of the problem description which consists of the representation of the to be manufactured workpiece, the mold and the factory. The geometry of the workpiece and the geometry of the mold is represented by elementary surfaces. The technology is represented by a specification of the tolerances, the material, the heat-treatment, etc. These specifications may apply to individual or to all surfaces. The production plan is represented as a sequence of chucking and cutting operations with various parameters.

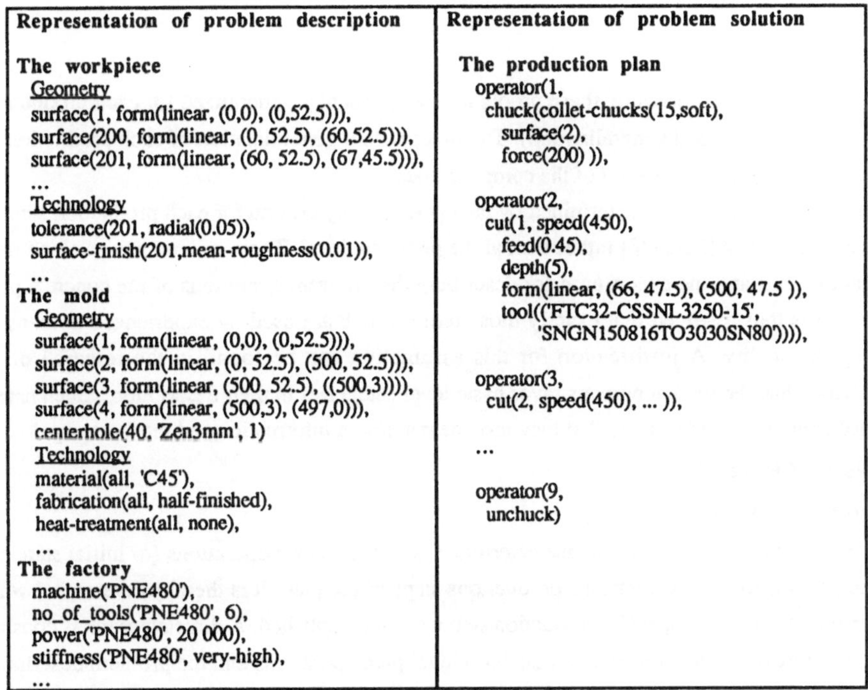

Representation of problem description	Representation of problem solution

The workpiece
  <u>Geometry</u>
  surface(1, form(linear, (0,0), (0,52.5))),
  surface(200, form(linear, (0, 52.5), (60,52.5))),
  surface(201, form(linear, (60, 52.5), (67,45.5))),
  ...
  <u>Technology</u>
  tolerance(201, radial(0.05)),
  surface-finish(201,mean-roughness(0.01)),
  ...
The mold
  <u>Geometry</u>
  surface(1, form(linear, (0,0), (0,52.5))),
  surface(2, form(linear, (0, 52.5), (500, 52.5))),
  surface(3, form(linear, (500, 52.5), ((500,3)))),
  surface(4, form(linear, (500,3), (497,0))),
  centerhole(40, 'Zen3mm', 1)
  <u>Technology</u>
  material(all, 'C45'),
  fabrication(all, half-finished),
  heat-treatment(all, none),
  ...
The factory
  machine('PNE480'),
  no_of_tools('PNE480', 6),
  power('PNE480', 20 000),
  stiffness('PNE480', very-high),
  ...
	The production plan
	  operator(1,
	    chuck(collet-chucks(15,soft),
	      surface(2),
	      force(200))),
	
	  operator(2,
	   cut(1, speed(450),
	     feed(0.45),
	     depth(5),
	     form(linear, (66, 47.5), (500, 47.5)),
	     tool(('FTC32-CSSNL3250-15',
	       'SNGN150816TO3030SN80')))),
	
	  operator(3,
	   cut(2, speed(450), ...)),
	
	  ...
	
	  operator(9,
	   unchuck)

Table 2: Partial representation of a case used as input for SPGEN

3.1. Simulation and Explanation

In the first phase of SPGEN, the plan execution is simulated on the basis of the available domain theory. The simulation of the plan is performed by sequentially determining the effects of each operator $Op_1,...,Op_n$ of the plan. In order to determine the effects of the sequence of operators, the intermediate processing states from the initial state S_0 (the mold) to the final state S_n (which will contain the target workpiece if the domain theory is sufficient) are computed as follows:

$$S_0 \xrightarrow{\ Op_1\ } S_1 \xrightarrow{\ Op_2\ } S_2 \; .... \; S_{n-1} \xrightarrow{\ Op_n\ } S_n$$

The effects of the operator are represented by a set of rules with STRIPS like add- and delete actions. The execution of these rules thus create the successor world state. For example, knowledge unit 3 from table 1 is represented by the following rule:

IF operator(I,cut(speed(S),feed(F),depth(D),form(Form), tool(T)),
    corner_radius(T,R),
    produces_roughness(F,R,Roughness),
    is_surface(Form,Surface),
  THEN ADD(roughness(Surface,Roughness))

By applying all the rules for each operator, the various consequences of the individual operations of the plan are calculated. If the domain theory is sufficient, a complete explanation of the plan will be obtained. The proofs that exist for the applicability of each operator rule can now be seen as an explanation of each effect that depends on operator attributes as well as world state attributes, from the initial or intermediate states.

3.2. Generalization

In the second phase of the procedure, these proofs are independently generalized for each production step of the plan (explanation based generalization). The independent generalization of each production step is necessitated because of the complexity of the complete plans.

The degree of generalization is determined by the operationality criteria for each production step, which are defined at the concept [Hirsh88] rather than at the predicate level. These criteria are obtained from the terms, which the texts and the expert used for describing the different operations of the concrete plan at a general level. It is thus assumed that exactly those terms which are used by experienced humans would determine operationality. A justification for this assumption can be found in the research of Rosch [Rosch78]: Rosch has shown that humans favor basic level categories in their descriptions. Such categories can be termed operational in the sense that they provide maximum information and the least cognitive effort for achieving some task goal.

3.3. Dependency Analysis

The dependency analysis of the third phase determines which previous operations (or initial state affairs) achieved the prerequisites for the various productions steps of the plan. It is thereby determined when the prerequisites for performing a specific production step were accomplished. A directed graph is constructed, in which all existing dependencies between the individual plan operations and the problem description are denoted by arcs. These problem descriptions, which were obtained through CECoS determine the generality of the skeletal plan to be constructed. The operationality criteria are provided by the features of the problem classes which were acquired from the human expert with the knowledge acquisition tool CECoS.

With the hierarchy of problem classes shown in figure 3, either the features of class B (and its subclasses) or the features of class A (and its subclasses) can be specified as being operational. In the first case a rather specific skeletal plan which applies to the problems of class B will be constructed, whereas in the latter case a more general skeletal plan for class A will be obtained.

Figure 4 shows a graphical representation of a part of the dependency graph that results from the analysis of the case M5. For example, cut 1 depends on the workpiece being chucked (for subsequent cuts this obvious dependency is no longer shown in the graph), on the geometry and the technology of the mold, and on the availability of ceramic cutting tools in the factory. It can also be seen from figure 4 that the first three cuts produce intermediate surfaces which are needed for the subsequent cut respectively but are no longer present in the final workpiece. The required geometry and technol6gy of the goal workpiece is produced exclusively by the cuts 4 to 7, each of which produces some particular feature. The lack of a dependency between the cuts 5 to 7, furthermore indicates that they could be executed in any sequence.

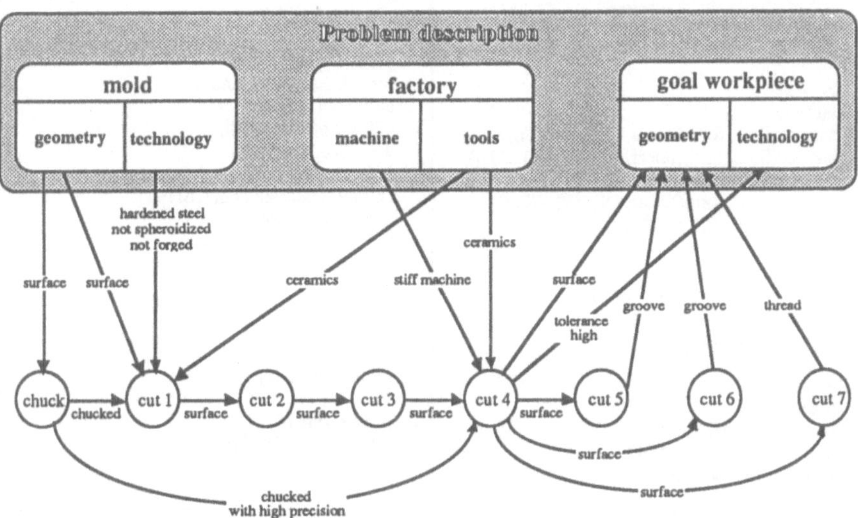

Figure 4: Partial dependency graph for the case M5

3.4. Normalization

This last phase builds the skeletal plan in its final representation by identifying independently solvable sub-formulas from the dependency graph which expresses only local constraints on one operator. By analyzing the occurrence of variables in the graph the dependencies are separated into:

- one set $\mathcal{R}_{Enable}$ that collects all dependencies that only relate to features of the problem description,

- one set $\mathcal{R}_{Opi}$ for each operator Op_i where the dependencies refer to parameters of the operator Op_i

- one set $\mathcal{R}_{Dependent}$ where the dependencies refer to the possible orderings of the operator classes.

The set of constraints $\mathcal{R}_{Enable}$ formally describes the class of problems for which the skeletal plan can be used: it specifies the application conditions for the skeletal plan. The application conditions may refer to the mold, the goal workpiece or the manufacturing environment, as indicated in Figure 4. The skeletal plan itself consists of the set of operator classes $Op_1,...,Op_n$ with the constraints $\mathcal{R}_{Opi}$ and $\mathcal{R}_{Dependent}$ which specify the possible sequences in which they may be applied.

For the case M5 the skeletal plan with application conditions shown in Table 3 is generated for the problem class B. The skeletal plan for the problem class A would be somewhat more general. For instance, it would allow any chucking tool with two fixations instead of collet chucks and would not require the material to be hardened steel.

<table>
<tr><td>Application conditions concerning</td><td>The skeletal plan</td></tr>
<tr><td>

the workpiece
<u>Geometry</u>
   surface(S1, form(linear, (0,0), (0,Z1))),
   10 =< Z1 < 120,
   surface(S2, form(linear, (0, Z1), (X1,Z1))),
   ...
<u>Technology</u>
   tolerance(S2, radial(Rt1)), Rt1 >= 0.025,
   surface-finish(201,mean-roughness(MR)),
   MR >= 0.01,
   ...
the mold
<u>Geometry</u>
   surface(Sm1, form(linear, (0,0), (0,Z1))),
   surface(Sm2, form(linear, (0, Z1), (X1, Z1))),
   surface(Sm3, form(linear, (X1,Z1), ((X1,Z2)))),
   surface(Sm4, form(linear, (X1,Z2), (X2,0))),
   centerhole(Sm5,Type,Depth), ...
<u>Technology</u>
   material(all, Mat),
   mat_type(Mat,hardened_steel),
   fabrication(all, half-finished),
   heat-treatment(all, none),
   ...
the factory
   machine(M),
   no_of_tools(M,N), N >= 6,
   power(M,P), P >= 15000,
   stiffness(M, very-high),
   ...

</td><td>

operator(1,
  chuck(collet-chucks(Width,soft),
   surface(S2),
   force(Force1))),
   10 =< Width < 20,
   200 =< Force1 < 300,
   ...
operator(2,
  cut(speed(Speed1),
   feed(Feed1),
   depth(Depth1),
   form(linear, Star1,End1),
   tool(Tool1))),
   400 < Speed1 < 600,
   3 =< Feed1 < 5,
   1 =< Depth1 < 6,
   cutting_material(Tool1,'SN80'),
   rake_angle(Tool1,45),
   tool_phase(Tool1,Phase1),
   2 =< Phase1 < 3,
   ...
operator(3, ...),
   ...

operator(9,unchuck)

Dependencies
  see bottom half of Figure 4

</td></tr>
</table>

Table 3: Partial skeletal plan generated from case M5 for problem class A

A first version of SPGEN has been implemented in LPA-PROLOG on a MAC II computer [Bergmann90]. It can construct skeletal plans from simplified cases such as those shown in Figure 3. The current implementation deals mostly with the geometrical aspects and does not yet adequately take into account the technological and economical aspects of production planning.

4. DISCUSSION

The re-use of previously established solutions to hard problems has been suggested in the area of Artificial Intellegence [RiesbeckSchank89] as well as for software development in general [Fischer87; Standish84]. In the area of Artificial Intelligence most approaches to the re-use of established solutions are discussed within the framework of case-based reasoning [Koehler91]. In case-based reasoning, the modification of an old case to a new problem is typically performed at the time when the new problem arises. By suggesting to systematically prepare sophisticated expert plans already during the knowledge acquisition process for an expert system these approaches are extended in the current paper.

Unlike case-based planning, the preparation of a case for its re-use is thus performed in ignorance of a specific new problem. It basically consists in analyzing and explaining a prototypical case in terms of a model of expertise and supplementary domain knowledge. Additionally, the features of problem classes which supposedly constitute the base level categories of human experts [Rosch78] are used to determine operationality criteria for concepts in an explanation-based generalization procedure.

e skeletal plans and application conditions constructed with SPGEN, provide a combination of owledge-based and heuristic abstractions of a concrete plan. For novel problems, which satisfy the lication conditions, the skeletal plan will provide a knowledge-based partitioning of the novel problems o appropriate subproblems, which can then be solved more easily.

REFERENCES

[Bergmann90] Bergmann, R. (1990). Generierung von Skelettplänen als Problem der Wissensakquisition. Universität Kaiserslautern, Germany.

[BergmannSchmalhofer91] Bergmann, R., & Schmalhofer, F. (1991). CECoS: A case experience combination system for knowledge acquisition for expert systems. Behavior Research Methods, Instruments, & Computers. in press.

[BreukerWielinga89] Breuker, J., & Wielinga, B. (1989). Models of expertise in knowledge acquisition. In Guida, G., & Tasso, C. (Eds.), Topics in expert system design, methodologies and tools (pp. 265 - 295). Amsterdam: North Holland.

[Fischer87] Fischer, G. (1987, July). Cognitive view of reuse and redesign. IEEE Software, 60-72.

[FriedlandIwasaki85] Friedland, P.E., & Iwasaki, Y. (1985). The concept and implementation of skeletal plans. Journal of Automated Reasoning, 161-208.

[Georgeff87] Georgeff, M.P. (1987). Planning. Annual Reviews in Computing Science, (2), 359-400.

[Hirsh88] Hirsh, H. (1988). Reasoning about operationality for explanation-based learning. Proceedings of the 5th International Conference on Machine Learning, 214 - 220.

[Koehler91] Köhler, J. (1991). Approaches to the reuse of plan schemata in planning formalisms (Technical Memo No. TN-91-01). Kaiserslautern, Germany: German Research Center for Artificial Intelligence.

[KuehnLinster+91] Kühn, O., Linster, M., & Schmidt, G. (1991, May). Clamping, COKAM, KADS, and OMOS: The construction and operationalization of a KADS conceptual model. Proceedings of EKAW 91 (Crieff).

[MitchellKeller86] Mitchell, T.M., Keller, R.M., & Kedar-Cabelli, S.T. (1986). Explanation-based generalization: A unifying view. Machine Learning, (1), 47 - 80.

[RiesbeckSchank89] Riesbeck, C.K., & Schank, R.C. (1989). Inside case-based reasoning. Hillsdale Lawrence Earlbaum.

[Rosch78] Rosch, E. (1978). Principles of categorisation. In Rosch, E., & Lloyd, B. (Eds.), Cognition and categorisation. Hillsdale, New Jersey: Lawrence Erlbaum.

[SchmalhoferKuehn+91] Schmalhofer, F., Kühn, O., & Schmidt, G. (in press). Integrated knowledge acquisition from text, previously solved cases, and expert memories . Applied Artificial Intelligence.

[SchmidtSchmalhofer90] Schmidt, G., & Schmalhofer, F. (1990). Case-oriented knowledge acquisition from texts. In Wielinga, B., Boose, J., Gaines, B., Schreiber, G., & van Someren, M. (Eds.), Current trends in knowledge acquisition (pp. 302-312). Amsterdam: IOS Press.

[Spur79] Spur, G. (1979). Produktionstechnik im Wandel. München: Carl Hanser Verlag.

[Standish84] Standish, T.S. (1984). An essay on software reuse. IEEE Transactions on Software Engineering, 10 (5), 494 - 497.

[ThobenSchmalhofer90] Thoben, J., & Schmalhofer, F. (1990). Wiederholungs- Varianten- und Neuplanung bei der Fertigung rotationssymmetrischer Teile (Interner Bericht des ARC-TEC-Projektes). Kaiserslautern, Germany: German Research Center for Artificial Intelligence.

3. PLANEN

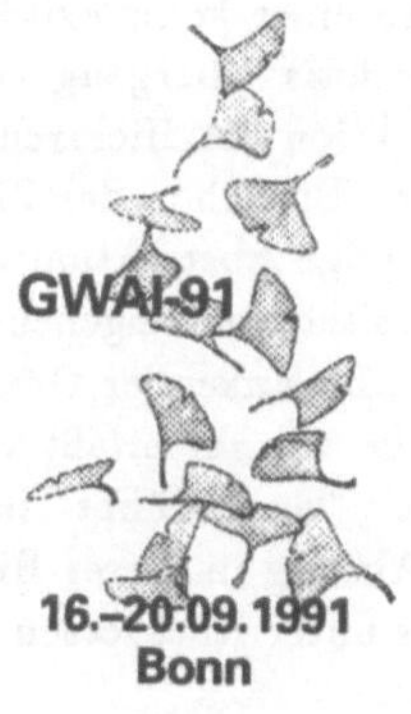

Problemzerlegung als optimalitätserhaltende Operatorabstraktion

FRITZ MÄDLER

HAHN-MEITNER-INSTITUT BERLIN GMBH
PROJEKT SOLEIL
BEREICH D/ABTEILUNG D1
GLIENICKER STR. 100
W 1000 BERLIN 39
MAEDLER@VAX.HMI.DBP.DE

Zusammenfassung

Abstraktionstechniken im Sinne von Sacerdoti [Sac74], [Sac77] und Wilkins [Wil84], [Wil86] haben eine strukturelle Entsprechung im Zustandsraum. Wir deuten in dieser Arbeit ein in der Praxis erprobtes, anwendungsunabhängiges Zerlegungsprinzip [MäG90] als optimalitätserhaltende Abstraktion der atomaren Operationen. Die Definitions- und Bildbereiche der Operatorabstraktionen werden als Extension von Zuständen gewonnen, deren Klassifikation eine intensionale Beschreibung der Planungsoperatoren für die Abstraktionsstufe erzeugt. Wir sehen die hier vorgestellte Methode als einen Schritt in Richtung eines allgemein tragenden Prinzips zur Akquisition von "Problemzerlegungswissen" an, das sich über Induktion mit Lerntechniken verbinden läßt.

1 Hintergrund

Suchraumbeschränkung und Steuerung der Suchprozesse stellen für jeden Planungsansatz eine kritische Hürde dar. Freie Suche über allen kombinatorischen Möglichkeiten bedeutet exponentielles Wachstum beim Suchaufwand und bei den Antwortzeiten, die schnell jenseits tolerabler Grenzen liegen. Durch Maßnahmen und Strategien zur Reduktion des Aufwands, zusammengefaßt im Begriff Heuristik, läßt sich die Effizienz der Programme beim Problemlösen steigern.

Abstraktionstechniken liefern Ansätze zu einer komplexitätssenkenden Gliederung der Suchprozesse. Das klassische Beispiel ist Sacerdotis Übergang vom Planungssystem STRIPS zu ABSTRIPS [Sac74]. Dort bedeutet Abstraktion die Hierarchisierung der situationsbeschreibenden Merkmale nach ihrer Wichtigkeit für das Erreichen der Ziele. Allgemeiner definiert Wilkins in [Wil86] hierarchische Planung als mehrstufige Abstraktion von Details in der Repräsentation (vgl. auch [Her89]). Jede Abstraktionsstufe besitzt einen eigenen Satz von Prädikaten mit einem für sie typischen Grad an Detail-Genauigkeit. Mit sinkender Granularität der Beschreibung vergrößert sich die Zahl der möglichen Zustände, die von ihr erfaßt werden. Man geht davon aus, daß der Suchraum auf der obersten Stufe so weit "ausgedünnt" ist, daß sich das abstrahierte Problem behandeln läßt. Planung ist dann der Abstieg in dieser Hierarchie; auf jeder Abstraktionsebene werden fehlende Details ergänzt, notfalls unter Rücksetzen auf höheren Stufen, bis auf der untersten Ebene ein vollständiger Plan gelingt.

Durch eine Abstraktionshierarchie läßt sich eine implizite Bindung zwischen Start- und Zielzuständen herstellen, die den Suchaufwand entscheidend reduzieren kann. Korf hat diese Senkung der Komplexität untersucht [Kor88]: Im Mittel entspricht der Gesamtaufwand bei Abstraktion der *Summe* der Aufwände auf den einzelnen Abstraktionsstufen, während man es sonst mit deren *Produkt* zu tun hätte. Dieses Ergebnis wird durch die (wenigen) empirischen Daten aus dem Vergleich von STRIPS und ABSTRIPS im großen und ganzen bestätigt.

Abstraktion ist auch bei den Operationen durchführbar [Sac77]. Dazu werden in den Operatorbedingungen Prädikate vernachlässigt (oder zuerst verfeinert und dann teilweise gestrichen). Zusätzlich lassen sich Operatorabstraktionen mit sogenannten "plots" ausstatten [Wil84], mit Zwischenzielen für Teilpläne, in die der Operator im Laufe der Planung zu expandieren ist. Auch dies erweitert Definitions- und Bildbereich eines Operators im Sinne von Abstraktion. Man schafft auf diese Weise Makro-Operatoren, die auf Teilgraphen des Zustandsraumes anwendbar sind. Die detaillierte Expansion hängt dann vom Startzustand beim Aufruf des Operators ab.

Obwohl die Komplexitätsreduktion unumstritten ist, steht die automatische Erzeugung geeigneter Operatorabstraktionen erst am Anfang. Unter der einschränkenden Voraussetzung der Serialisierbarkeit [Kor88] haben Cheng und Irani einen Algorithmus zur Vorordnung von Teilzielen angegeben [ChI89]. Horz beweist die Äquivalenz dieses operationenorientierten Ansatzes zu einem graphenorientierten Ansatz von Joslin und Roach [JoR89] durch Angabe einer geeigneten Abstraktion vom Ausgangsproblem [Hor90]. Als weiterer Schritt in Richtung eines allgemein tragenden Prinzips zur Problemzerlegung deuten wir in dieser Arbeit ein in einer Anwendung erprobtes Meta-Prinzip [MäG90] als Operatorabstraktion. Dieses Zerlegungsprinzip ist optimalitätserhaltend auf den Teilen des Zustandsraumes, die zur Gewinnung der Abstraktionen herangezogen werden. Die interessierenden Teilgraphen werden mit Hilfe der elementaren Operationen erzeugt und liefern im Falle einer sogenannten Nadelöhr-Konstellation die Vor- und Nachbedingungen sowie die Zwischenziele der abstrakten Operatoren. Die Bedingungen sind zunächst extensional in Form von Zustandsmengen gegeben, ihre intensionale Beschreibung wird aber durch Klassifikation auf die trennenden Merkmale reduziert und auf diese Weise vereinfacht. Aus Gründen, die im nächsten Abschnitt deutlich werden, kann man diese Vorgehensweise als *strukturelle Abstraktion* ansehen.

2 Die zentrale Idee

Die grundlegende Idee läßt sich anhand einer Blockwelt mit drei Blöcken veranschaulichen.

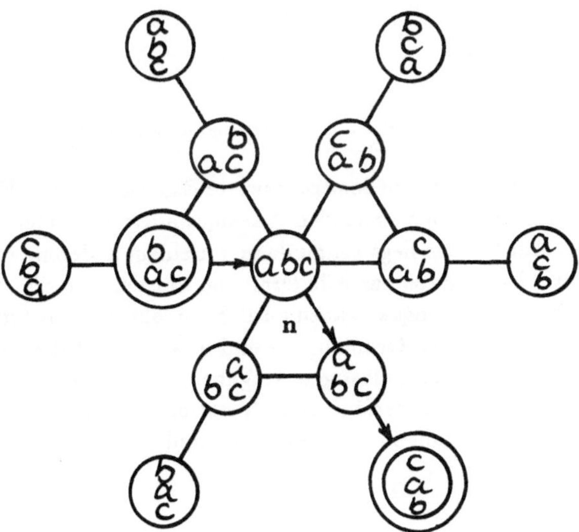

Abbildung 1 : Zustandsgraph und optimale Lösungen einer Planungsaufgabe

Die Knoten im Zustandsgraphen der Abbildung 1 repräsentieren die Stellung der Blöcke zueinander und zur Unterlage. Die Kanten stehen für die Handlung, mit der ein Zustand aus einem benachbarten hervorgeht.

Viele der Planungsaufgaben dieses Bereichs besitzen die Eigenschaft, in allen ihren optimalen Lösungen den mittleren Knoten n als Zustand zu enthalten. Sie sind hier von besonderem Interesse, weil sie sich in n zerlegen lassen. Eine dieser Aufgaben ist samt ihren optimalen Lösungen als gerichteter Teilgraph eingezeichnet. Weil der Zerlegungsknoten im optimalen Plan enthalten ist, liefert die Verkettung optimaler Teillösungen ein optimales Gesamtergebnis.

Offensichtlich besitzt der Knoten n diese günstige Zerlegungseigenschaft für eine Vielzahl von Aufgaben, insbesondere auch für die längeren; in Abbildung 2 wurde eine Auswahl getroffen. Jede Kombination eines Knotens aus der Startmenge S mit einem Ziel aus der Menge G führt zu einem in n zerlegbaren Planungsproblem. Die gerichteten Teilgraphen geben alle optimalen Lösungen aller beteiligten Aufgaben wieder.

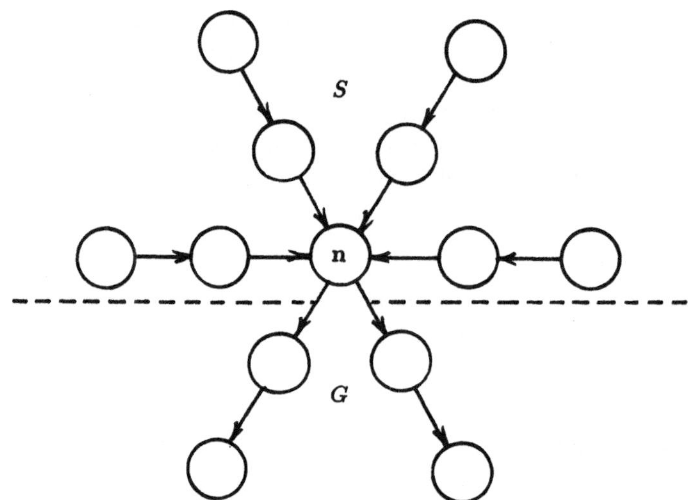

Abbildung 2 : Zerlegung einer Aufgabenmenge durch den Knoten n

Die gewählte Aufgabenmenge besitzt eine bemerkenswerte Eigenschaft: Die Kanten repräsentieren nicht nur die Zustandsübergänge in den optimalen Plänen, sondern auch eine *partielle Ordnung* auf der Menge der Zustände. Ein Knoten liegt genau dann vor einem anderen, wenn er in einem optimalen Plan früher auftritt. Es ist diese partielle Ordnung, mit der sich die Zerlegungseigenschaft von n auf eine ganze Schar von Planungsaufgaben ausdehnen läßt: Sie gilt für jede Aufgabe, deren Startknoten im Sinne dieser partiellen Ordnung *vor* und deren Ziel *hinter* dem Zerlegungsknoten n liegt. Bei der Zusammenstellung der zulässigen Aufgabenmenge spielt das Bereichswissen keine Rolle. Es steckt zwar implizit in den verfügbaren Operationen, mit denen sich die Teilgraphen erzeugen lassen. Ob aber eine Aufgabe in n zerlegbar ist und hinzugenommen werden kann oder nicht, wird allein bestimmt

- durch den Teilgraphen aller ihrer optimalen Lösungen

- und durch die Forderung nach einer partiellen Ordnung, in der der Zerlegungsknoten im Inneren aller Lösungen aller Aufgaben liegt.

Weil die Zerlegungseigenschaft in diesem Sinne nicht aus dem Bereichswissen sondern aus der *Struktur* des Zustandsgraphen abgeleitet wird, haben wir die Vorgehensweise *strukturelle Abstraktion* genannt. Ihr Ergebnis sind abstrakte Operatoren, auf dieser Stufe und in unserem Beispiel etwa von folgender Bauart (als Prolog-Klausel notiert[1]):

```
abs_operator( decompose( N ),[ Start | Plan_in ],[ Goal | Plan_out ])
    :-
        decomposition( N, S, G),        % input: States
        member( Start, S ),
        member( Goal,  G ),
        plan( [ Start | Plan_in ], [ N | Plan_tmp ] ),
        plan( [ N | Plan_tmp ], [ Goal | Plan_out ] ).
```

Die Aufgabe wird unter Problemzerlegung im Zustand N gelöst, wenn die *Vorbedingungen* erfüllt sind, wenn nämlich Start und Goal zu einer zulässigen Aufgabe gehören. Das Prädikat plan steht für die "plots" [Wil84], [Her89] des Operators und erweitert den Eingangsplan um die beiden Teilpläne (Start,N) und (N,Goal). Der zurückgegebene Gesamtplan ist optimal, sobald die Teilpläne es sind. Als *Nachbedingung* gilt der Zustand Goal.

Glücklicherweise muß man sich mit dieser extensionalen, un-detaillierten und den Speicher beanspruchenden Form der Abstraktion nicht zufrieden geben. Das weitere Ziel dieser Arbeit ist die Darstellung einer Methode, durch Induktion zu möglichst einfachen, intensionalen Beschreibungen solcher Operatoren zu gelangen (Abschnitt 4). Dazu sind zunächst die Formalien des zugrunde liegenden Zerlegungsprinzips zu behandeln. Insbesondere bedeutet dies die Befreiung von den idealisierenden Annahmen über den zentralen Knoten n im obigen Beispiel. Jeder der formalen Schritte des folgenden Abschnitts besitzt aber eine einfache Entsprechung in der Vorgehensweise bei diesem Beispiel.

3   Nadelöhrmengen

Eine notwendige Bedingung für die Optimalität eines Planes ist die Optimalität aller seiner Teilpläne. Diese als Bellman-Prinzip bekannte diskrete Fassung eines allgemeinen Optimalitätsprinzips [Bel57] hat einschneidende Konsequenzen für die Gewinnung von Operatorabstraktionen: Um die Optimalität eines Planes überhaupt erreichen zu können, müssen die durch Abstraktion gewonnenen Teilpläne bereits optimal sein.

Betreibt man die Abstraktion wie im obigen Beispiel durch Problemzerlegung, so läßt sich diese Optimalitätserhaltung nur auf einem eng eingegrenzten Typ von Zwischenzielen erreichen: Die Verkettung von optimalen Lösungen zweier Planungsaufgaben (s,n) und (n,g) ist genau dann optimal, wenn es eine optimale Lösung zur Aufgabe (s,g) durch den Zwischenzustand n gibt. Dies motiviert die Begriffsbildungen dieses Abschnitts.

Zunächst wird das in [MäG90] vorgeschlagene Zerlegungsprinzip durch eine abgeschwächte Definition der "Nadelöhrmengen" erweitert und damit sein Geltungsbereich vergrößert. Außerdem konnte eine hinreichende Bedingung an Aufgabenmengen gefunden werden, aus der sich eine Ordnungsrelation zur Verkettung solcher Zerlegungsmengen herleiten läßt. Das Hauptergebnis dieses Abschnitts ist Satz 2, nach dem sich die optimalen Pläne einer Menge von Planungsaufgaben aus Teilplanungen über zerlegten Problemen gewinnen lassen.

Mit $\Pi_{opt}(s,g)$ bezeichnen wir die Menge aller optimalen Lösungen zur Planungsaufgabe (s,g), mit $Z_{opt}(s,g)$ die Menge der beteiligten Zustände. Für letztere kann stets eine partielle Ordnung

---

[1] Der SOLEIL-Planer ist in Prolog geschrieben [MäG90].

angegeben werden: Zwei Zustände stehen in einer Relation $z \prec z'$, wenn z in einem optimalen Plan $p \in \Pi_{opt}(s,g)$ vor z' auftritt. Diese asymmetrische und transitive Relation ist eine partielle Ordnung für die Zustände $Z_{opt}(s,g)$. Wir schreiben $z \preceq z'$, falls $z \prec z'$ oder $z = z'$ gilt.

Zu zwei in dieser Weise geordneten Zuständen z, z' gibt es einen wohldefinierten, gerichteten Abstand $l(z,z')$ in Form der Länge der optimalen Pläne in $\Pi_{opt}(z,z')$.

Definition 1: Eine Teilmenge $N \subset Z_{opt}(s,g)$ von Zuständen $n \in N$, $s \prec n \prec g$, heißt *Nadelöhr zur Planungsaufgabe* (s,g), wenn gilt:

1. Jeder Plan $p \in \Pi_{opt}(s,g)$ verläuft durch genau einen Zustand n des Nadelöhrs N.

2. Die Zustände n des Nadelöhrs N haben alle den gleichen Abstand vom Startzustand s.

Die erste Bedingung wird benötigt, um im folgenden Satz 1 die Umkehrbarkeit des Bellman-Prinzips beweisen zu können. Die zweite Bedingung ist erforderlich, um ein analoges Resultat für Aufgaben*mengen* und Mehrfach-Zerlegung zu gewinnen (siehe Satz 2).

Satz 1: Sei N ein Nadelöhr zur Planungsaufgabe (s,g). Dann besitzt die Menge der optimalen Pläne eine Darstellung als Cartesisches Produkt

$$\Pi_{opt}(s,g) \overset{f_N}{\approx} \bigcup_{n \in N} \Pi_{opt}(s,n) \times \Pi_{opt}(n,g)$$

unter der Bijektion $f_N((s,...,n,....,g)) = ((s,...,n),(n,....,g))$.

3.1 Ordnung der Zustände bei c-abgeschlossenen Aufgabenmengen

Die Zerlegungseigenschaften von Nadelöhren lassen sich durch Übergang zu Nadelöhr*mengen* auf Mengen von Aufgaben ausdehnen. Um die dafür benötigte Ordnungsrelation zu gewinnen, kann man sich an einer weiteren bemerkenswerten Eigenschaft der Zustandsmenge $Z_{opt}(s,g)$ orientieren; sie ist im folgenden Sinne abgeschlossen gegenüber Verkettung: Falls zwei Pläne $p = (s,z_1,z_2,..,z_j,z_{j+1},..,z_{l-1},g)$ und $p' = (s,z_1',z_2',..,z_j',z_{j+1}',..,z_{l-1}',g)$ einen gemeinsamen inneren Zustand $z_j = z_j'$ haben, liefert auch ihre "Überkreuzung" in z_j optimale Pläne von s nach g, nämlich $q = (s,z_1,z_2,..,z_j,z_{j+1}',..,z_{l-1}',g)$ und $q' = (s,z_1',z_2',..,z_j,z_{j+1},..,z_{l-1},g)$.

Für eine Menge S von Startzuständen und eine Menge G von Zielen sei $P(S,G) \subset S \times G$ eine Aufgabenmenge. Ihre nähere Festlegung geschieht so, daß die Menge $Z_{opt}(S,G)$ der in optimalen Plänen $\Pi_{opt}(S,G)$ auftretenden Zustände partiell geordnet werden kann. Eine Aufgabenmenge heißt *c-abgeschlossen*, wenn folgende Eigenschaften gelten: Es gilt für je zwei Pläne $p \in \Pi_{opt}(s,g)$ und $p' \in \Pi_{opt}(s',g')$ mit $(s,g),(s',g') \in P(S,G)$ und einem gemeinsamen Zustand z

1. die gekreuzten Aufgaben gehören ebenfalls zur Aufgabenmenge

$$(s,g'),(s',g) \in P(S,G)$$

2. die gekreuzten Pläne sind optimal

$$q := (s,..,z,.....,g') \in \Pi_{opt}(s,g'), \quad q' := (s',....,z,...,g) \in \Pi_{opt}(s',g)$$

Bei c-abgeschlossenen Aufgabenmengen $P(S,G)$ lassen sich die Zustände ihrer optimalen Lösungen in ihrer Gesamtheit partiell ordnen: Die Definitionen

$$z \prec z' :\Longleftrightarrow j_z < j_{z'} \quad \text{bzw.} \quad z \preceq z' :\Longleftrightarrow j_z \le j_{z'}$$

liefern partielle Ordnungen auf $Z_{opt}(S,G)$, wenn j_z und $j_{z'}$ die Positionen von z bzw. z' in einem gemeinsamen optimalen Plan $p = (s, .., z, ..., z', .., g) \in \Pi_{opt}(S,G)$ sind.

Für jede Aufgabe $(s,g) \in P(S,G)$ stimmen die Einschränkungen dieser partiellen Ordnungen mit den weiter oben auf $Z_{opt}(s,g)$ benutzten Ordnungen überein. Damit steht für c-abgeschlossene Aufgabenmengen das Nadelöhr-Konzept zur Verfügung, und in einem weiteren Schritt lassen sich nun Nadelöhr*mengen* definieren und ordnen. Dazu bestehe für ein Mengensystem $\mathcal{N}$ aus der Potenzmenge $\mathcal{P}(Z_{opt}(S,G))$ und Zustandsmengen $N \in \mathcal{N}$ die Klasse $P_N \subset P(S,G)$ aus all denjenigen Planungsaufgaben (s,g), die eine Teilmenge $N' \subset N$ als Nadelöhr im Sinne der Definition 1 besitzen. $N \in \mathcal{N}$ heißt *Nadelöhr zu P_N*.

Definition 2: $\mathcal{N}$ heißt *Nadelöhrmenge zur Aufgabenmenge $P(S,G)$*, wenn die Nadelöhre $N \in \mathcal{N}$ paarweise disjunkt sind und die Klassen $\{P_N \mid N \in \mathcal{N}\}$ eine nicht-triviale, vollständige und disjunkte Überdeckung der Aufgabenmenge darstellen, wenn also gilt:

(a) $P_N \ne \emptyset \quad$ für $N \in \mathcal{N}$

(b) $P(S,G) = \bigcup_{N \in \mathcal{N}} P_N$

(c) $P_{N_1} \cap P_{N_2} = \emptyset \quad$ für $N_1, N_2 \in \mathcal{N}$ mit $N_1 \ne N_2$

Die folgenden Beispiele veranschaulichen die Definition:

Beispiel 1: Im Blockweltbeispiel aus Abschnitt 2 ist $\mathcal{N} = \{\{n\}\}$ eine Nadelöhrmenge zur Aufgabenmenge $P(S,G) = S \times G$ mit dem einzigen, einelementigen Nadelöhr $N = \{n\}$ (Abb. 2).

Beispiel 2: Abbildung 3 auf der nächsten Seite zeigt eine Hälfte einer der Nadelöhrmengen, die in der SOLEIL-Anwendung zur Problemzerlegung benutzt werden. Jede Nummer steht für einen von insgesamt 88 Zuständen. Es gibt vier Partitionsmengen oder "Spalten", von denen aus Platzgründen nur zwei dargestellt sind. Die beiden fehlenden Teile mit den zweiten 44 Zuständen erhält man durch Spiegelung entlang der rechten Achse. Die Aufgabenmenge wurde vollständig exploriert, sie ist c-abgeschlossen. Alle Kanten sind abwärts gerichtet und repräsentieren die oben eingeführte Ordnung der Zustände. Die Abbildung gibt, ebenso wie die Abbildung 2, das "Hasse-Diagramm" [Bir61] für die partiell geordnete Menge $(Z_{opt}(S,G), \prec)$ wieder.

Die zusätzlich eingezeichnete Nadelöhrmenge $\mathcal{N}$ besteht aus vier einelementigen Nadelöhren. Sie zerlegt jede der 360 Planungsaufgaben, deren Start als Zustand oberhalb $\mathcal{N}$ und deren Ziel unterhalb $\mathcal{N}$ aus der gleichen Spalte gewählt werden kann. Insgesamt lassen sich 1152 optimale Pläne in zerlegter Form erzeugen. 40 der Aufgaben sind in dem Sinne extremal, daß sie als Start bzw. Ziel bezüglich der betrachteten Ordnung minimale bzw. maximale Elemente verwenden, etwa (1,8).

Beispiel 3: Nadelöhre im Sinne der obigen Definition müssen nicht einelementig sein. Man erhält eine Nadelöhrmenge, wenn man in $\mathcal{N}$ das Nadelöhr $\{4\}$ durch das Nadelöhr $\{9, 11, 3\}$ ersetzt (oder durch eine andere Zwischenschicht seiner Spalte).

Nadelöhre werden so gewählt, daß sie die Komplexität in ausreichendem Maße reduzieren und zu möglichst einfachen intensionalen Beschreibungen im Sinne des Abschnitts 4 führen. Häufig haben Verengungen im Zustandsraum für den Bereichsexperten eine plausible Bedeutung. Problemzerlegung an derartigen Engstellen überträgt diese Bedeutung auf die Nadelöhre (so auch im Beispiel der Abbildung 3, siehe unten). Zerlegung kann aber auch an weniger plausiblen Stellen stattfinden, etwa wenn weitere Komplexitätssenkung geboten ist.

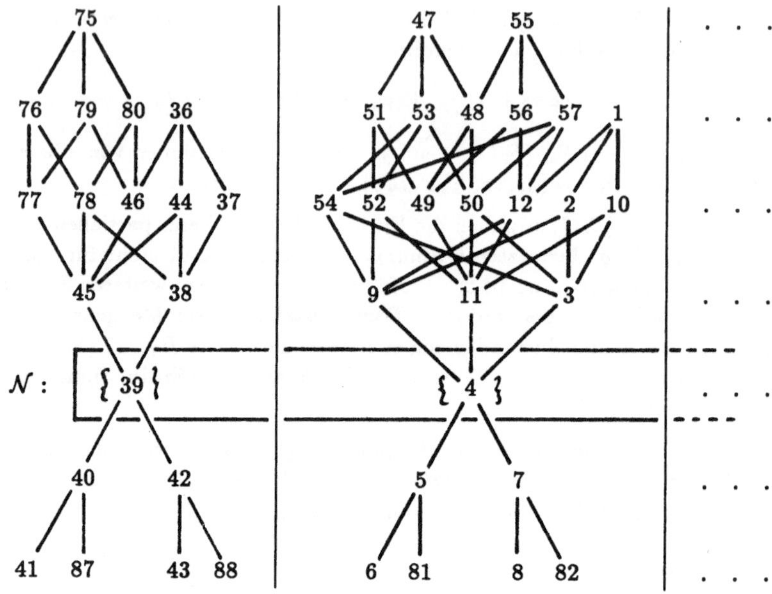

Abbildung 3: Teil einer SOLEIL-Nadelöhrmenge

3.2 Zerlegung durch Ketten aus Nadelöhrmengen

Um mit Nadelöhrmengen Mehrfach-Zerlegung betreiben zu können, müssen sie zuvor partiell geordnet werden: Zwei Nadelöhrmengen $\mathcal{N}, \mathcal{N}' \subset \mathcal{P}(Z_{opt}(S, G))$ stehen in einer Relation $\mathcal{N} \prec^* \mathcal{N}'$, wenn für je zwei ihrer Nadelöhre $N \in \mathcal{N}$ bzw. $N' \in \mathcal{N}'$ und je zwei unter $\prec$ vergleichbare Zustände $n \in N$ bzw. $n' \in N'$ die Relation $n \prec n'$ gilt.

Bezüglich $\prec^*$ können Ketten $\mathcal{K} := \{\mathcal{N}_1, \mathcal{N}_2, ..., \mathcal{N}_m\}$ vorhanden sein, also vollständig geordnete Systeme von Nadelöhrmengen zu $P(S, G)$. Wie zuvor kann die Aufgabenmenge (mit Hilfe von Multi-Indizes $(N_1, N_2, ..., N_m) \in \mathcal{N}_1 \times \mathcal{N}_2 \times ... \times \mathcal{N}_m$) in Klassen eingeteilt werden

$$P_{N_1, N_2, ..., N_m} := \{(s, g) \mid \forall i : N_i \text{ enthält Nadelöhr zu } (s, g)\}$$

wobei für gewisse Indizes leere Klassen auftreten, wenn es zu ihnen keine Aufgaben gibt. Dann erhält man in Verallgemeinerung des Satzes 1 durch vollständige Induktion [Mäd91]:

Satz 2: Sei $P(S, G)$ eine c-abgeschlossene Aufgabenmenge und $\mathcal{K} = \{\mathcal{N}_1, \mathcal{N}_2, ..., \mathcal{N}_m\}$ bzgl. $\prec^*$ eine Kette aus Nadelöhrmengen zu $P(S, G)$. Dann gibt es eine Darstellung für die optimalen Pläne

$$\Pi(S, G) \stackrel{f_{\mathcal{K}}}{\approx} \bigcup_{(N_1, .., N_m) \in \mathcal{N}_1 \times .. \times \mathcal{N}_m} \bigcup_{(s, g) \in P_{N_1, ..., N_m}} \bigcup_{(n_1, .., n_m) \in N_1 \times .. \times N_m} \Pi(s, n_1) \times \Pi_{l_{N_1, N_2}}(n_1, n_2) \times .. \times \Pi(n_m, g)$$

unter der Bijektion

$$f_{\mathcal{K}}((s, .., n_1, .., n_m, .., g)) = ((s, .., n_1), (n_1, .., n_2), ..., (n_m, .., g)) \ .$$

Dabei sondert auf der rechten Seite der Index $l_{N_j,N_{j+1}}$ für $j = 1, .., m - 1$ Teilpläne aus, die zu lang sind und keine Entsprechung in der Menge links haben: Für Zustandsmengen N_1, N_2 mit vergleichbaren Elementen $n_1 \in N_1$ bzw. $n_2 \in N_2$ sei $l(N_1, N_2) := min\{l(n_1, n_2) \mid n_1 \in N_1, n_2 \in N_2\}$ der gerichtete Abstand von N_1 nach N_2. Wir setzen $\Pi_{l_{N_1,N_2}}(n_1, n_2) := \emptyset$, falls $l(n_1, n_2) \neq l(N_1, N_2)$ und sonst $\Pi_{l_{N_1,N_2}}(n_1, n_2) := \Pi(n_1, n_2)$ (der Index opt wurde unterdrückt).

Eine Kette $\mathcal{K}$ aus Nadelöhrmengen im Sinne dieses Satzes beschreibt (wie im Blockweltbeispiel aus Abschnitt 2) einen abstrakten Operator in seiner extensionalen Form. Die Operatorbedingungen stecken in den explizit aufgezählten Zustandsmengen vor, zwischen und hinter den Nadelöhrmengen. Zumindest auf diesen Teilen des Zustandsraumes verhält sich die Abstraktion als wohldefinierte Abbildung mit präzisiertem Definitions- und Bildbereich. Die Expansionen oder "plots" sind dabei in Form einer Schleife über die Nadelöhrmengen-Kette gegeben.

Durch den Übergang zu einer intensionalen Fassung erhält das in Nadelöhrmengen akquirierte "Problemzerlegungswissen" seine handhabbare Form.

4 Induktion einer intensionalen Beschreibung

Bis zu dieser Stelle wurden nur rein *strukturelle* Argumente benutzt, indem die in der Definition einer Nadelöhrmenge festgelegte strukturelle Konstellation im Zustandsgraphen oder abstrakte Prinzipien wie Optimalität, Ordnung, Abstand und c-Abgeschlossenheit herangezogen wurden. Hinter den aufgezählten Zuständen verbergen sich jedoch im konkreten Fall Merkmale mit Werten, aus denen durch Induktion [Qui86] eine intensionale Beschreibung der Operatorabstraktionen erzeugt werden kann.

Dies sei am Beispiel der Nadelöhrmenge aus der Abbildung 3 illustriert. Sie stammt vom SOLEIL-Prototyp, bei dem ein Ausschnitt einer Plasma-Depositionsanlage zur Erzeugung von photovoltaischen Schichten modelliert wurde [MäG90]. Zur Steuerung dieses Anlagenteils wurden 13 Merkmale benötigt, die Anzahl ihrer Werte lag zwischen 2 (Ventile, Pumpen, Positionierungen etc.) und 9 (abgeleitete Parameter wie Prozeßkammerzustände, Gas-/Druckzustände in Leitungen, die qualitativ modelliert wurden).

Eine Planungsaufgabe wird in der Nadelöhrmenge $\mathcal{N}$ zerlegt, wenn Start und Ziel der gleichen Spalte angehören ("horizontale Koordinate") und zwischen ihnen ein Nadelöhr liegt ("vertikale Koordinaten" von Start bzw. Ziel). Klassen für die horizontale Induktion sind in diesem Fall die vier Spalten (vgl. Def. 2). Man gewinnt vier Regeln, von denen beispielsweise eine lautet:

```
rule( truth_horizontal , rule_number( 2 ) , class( 2 ) , State )
    :-   status( State , turbopumpe( aus ) ),
         status( State , ventil_15( zu ) ).
```

Die Regel ordnet den Zustand State der Spalte 2 zu (also dem Nadelöhr $N_2 = \{4\}$), wenn seine Merkmale turbopumpe und ventil_15 die Werte aus bzw. zu haben. Die vier möglichen Wertkombinationen aus/auf, aus/zu, an/auf, an/zu bestimmen die horizontale Klasse eines jeden der 88 beteiligten Zustände und ändern sich entlang dieser Klasse nicht.

Bei der vertikalen Induktion wird die Klasse start von den Schichten 0 bis 3, das Zwischenziel inter von der Nadelöhrmenge $\mathcal{N}$ auf der Schicht 4 und die Klasse goal von den Schichten 5 und 6 gebildet. ID3 induziert weitere fünf Regeln, eine davon für die Nadelöhrmenge:

```
rule( truth_vertical , rule_number( 6 ) , class( inter ) , State )
    :-   status( State , prozesskammer( luft_1 ) ),
         status( State , balgzugschieber( auf ) ),
         status( State , ventil_8( auf ) ).
```

Die vier Nadelöhre werden in diesem Fall durch eine gemeinsame Regel beschrieben. Das in ihr ausgedrückte Wissen erscheint dem Experten natürlich; ohne einen gewissen Niederdruckwert (luft_1) in der Prozeßkammer sind die bei dieser Nadelöhrmenge möglichen Ziele nicht zu erreichen. Daß - unabhängig von den beteiligten Startzuständen und Zielen - für die Optimalität der Pläne rechtzeitiges Öffnen von Balgzugschieber und Ventil 8 nötig sind, mag schon nicht mehr so klar gewesen sein. Jedenfalls wurde per Induktion eine anwendungsunabhängige Wissensform, nämlich die strukturelle Konstellation "Nadelöhrmenge", mit einer konkreten Bedeutung aus der Anwendung versehen und als komplexitätssenkendes Planungszwischenziel plausibel gemacht.

Eine auf einer vollständig explorierten Nadelöhrmenge induzierte intensionale Beschreibung erlaubt die korrekte Identifikation aller zugehörigen Planungsaufgaben und ihre Zerlegung. Umgekehrt liefert die Induktion auf einer nur teilweise vorliegenden Nadelöhrmenge wertvolle Hypothesen über Start-Ziel-Paarungen, die als Erweiterung hinzugenommen werden dürfen, sofern sie die c-Abgeschlossenheit und damit die Ordnung der optimalen Zustandsmenge Z_{opt} bewahren.

In diesem Zusammenhang ist auf ein Phänomen aufmerksam zu machen, das bei Nadelöhrmengen mehr oder minder ausgeprägt auftritt und sich zu ihrer Gewinnung nutzen läßt. Abbildung 4 zeigt nochmals die Nadelöhrmenge aus Abbildung 3, unter Hervorhebung gewisser Zustände.

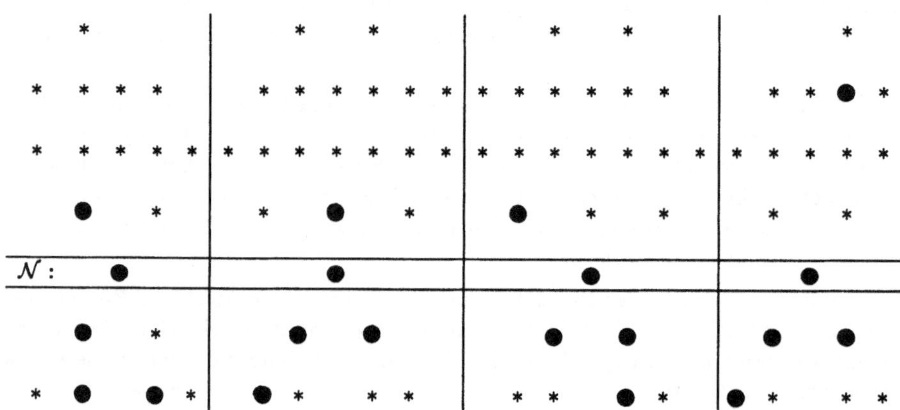

Abbildung 4: "Hologramm-Effekt" bei Nadelöhrmengen

Induziert man auf den schwarz ausgezeichneten Zuständen *einer beliebig gewählten Spalte,* so erhält man bereits einen korrekten Satz von Regeln zur vollständigen Beschreibung *der gesamten Nadelöhrmenge* entlang der Vertikalen. Das Gleiche gilt für die Klassifikation entlang der Horizontalen (nicht eingezeichnet): Man erhält zum Beispiel einen korrekten, vollständigen Regelsatz bereits durch Induktion über den Zuständen einer einzelnen waagerechten Schicht. Weil so gesehen das Ganze (nämlich die korrekte und vollständige Information zur Beschreibung aller Aufgaben und ihrer Zerlegungen) bereits in seinen kleineren Einheiten enthalten ist und sich im Gitter der senkrechten und waagerechten Induktion sichtbar machen läßt, liegt eine Art "Hologramm-Effekt" vor, der nicht etwa nur ein Spezifikum der SOLEIL-Anwendung ist. So erfolgt die Entkopplung der Spalten einer Nadelöhrmenge beispielsweise schon dann, wenn es Merkmale mit konstanten Werten entlang der Senkrechten gibt, wobei diese Werte die zugehörige Spalte bestimmen und sonst keine Rolle in den Abhängigkeiten spielen. Solche Merkmale liegen gewissermaßen orthogonal zu anderen, die in die Abhängigkeiten eingehen und die Übergänge in den Plänen der einzelnen Spalten beschreiben. Diese Form der Orthogonalität in den Attributen und die Redundanz in der Extension der an einer Nadelöhrmenge beteiligten optimalen Zustände sind dafür verantwortlich, ob und in welchem Ausmaß das Phänomen auftritt; beides sind "Meta-Aspekte", die für *jede* Anwendung untersucht werden können, beispielsweise durch Explorationen im Zustandsraum.

Die in [MäG90] angegebene Grundvariante zur Explikation von Nadelöhrmengen wird zur Zeit um eine induktive Komponente erweitert, mit der Hypothesen für die Hinzunahme weiterer Planungsaufgaben gebildet werden können und die intensionale Beschreibung aus der extensionalen Form induziert wird. Der "Hologramm-Effekt" wird genutzt, um die relevanten Teile einer Aufgabenmenge möglichst früh zu erkennen und die Herleitung redundanter Teile einzusparen.

Literatur:

[Bel57]   Bellman, R. E.: Dynamic Programming, Princeton, NJ, 1957

[Bir61]   Birkhoff, G.: Lattice Theory, Amer. Math. Soc., 1961

[ChI89]   Cheng, I. / Irani, K.: Ordering Problem Subgoals, Proceedings of the 11th International Joint Conference on Artificial Intelligence (IJCAI-89), pp 931 - 36, 1989

[Her89]   Hertzberg, J.: Planen, BI-Wiss.-Verl., Mannheim 1989

[Hor90]   Horz, A.: Über die Serialisierung von Teilzielen beim Planen, in Kratz, N. / Günter, A. / Hertzberg, J. (eds): Beiträge zum 4. Workshop Planen und Konfigurieren, FAW-B-90008, Universität Ulm, Mai 1990

[JoR89]   Joslin, D. / Roach, J.: A Theoretical Analysis of Conjunctive-Goal Problems, Artificial Intelligence 41, 1989

[Kor88]   Korf, R. E.: Optimal Path Findings Algorithms, in Kanal,L. / Kumar, V. (eds): Search in Artificial Intelligence, Springer 1988

[MäG90]   Mädler, F. / Gust, H.: Über ein Meta-Prinzip zur Explikation von Kontrollwissen, in Marburger, H. (ed): 14th German Workshop on Artificial Intelligence (GWAI-90), Eringerfeld, September 1990

[Qui86]   Quinlan, J. R.: Induction of decision trees, Machine Learning, Vol. 1, Nr. 1, 1986

[Sac74]   Sacerdoti, E. D.: Planning in a hierarchy of abstraction spaces, Artificial Intelligence 5(2), 1974

[Sac77]   Sacerdoti, E. D.: A Structure for Plans and Behavior, Elsevier Computer Science Library, Elsevier North-Holland 1977

[Wil84]   Wilkins, D.: Domain-Independent Planning: Representation and Plan Generation, Artificial Intelligence 22, 1984

[Wil86]   Wilkins, D.: Hierarchical Planning: Definition and Implementation, in Proceedings of the 7th European Conference on Artificial Intelligence (ECAI-86), Brighton July 1986

Ein internes Arbeitspapier enthält Ergänzungen und Beweise:

[Mäd91]   Mädler, F.: Nadelöhrmengen, ein Konzept zur Induktion von Problemzerlegungen, Dokument SOLEIL-06-PLN-02-AA, HMI Berlin 1991

4. SPRACHVERARBEITUNG

A Frame-Based Computational Model of Generic Generalisations

Gerhard Heyer

TA Triumph-Adler AG
Forschung
Fürtherstr. 212
D-8500 NÜRNBERG
heyer@triumph-adler.de

Summary

The paper describes a system for updating and querying an extended PROLOG knowledge base with generic generalisations. It describes a referential semantics of generic generalisations, and explains the principles of its implementation. It argues against an analysis of generic generalisations by means of a default logic and shows how semantics and knowledge structures can meaningfully be seperated.

Keywords: Natural Language Processing, Knowledge Representation, Generic Generalisations, Semantics

1. Introduction

During the past ten years, a number of formalisms have emerged that are based on logic, but that by using methods and results of AI and Cognitive Science have sufficiently been enriched to also serve as knowledge encodings (/Moore 1981/). Most of these formalisms are explicitly based on the assumption that a theory of knowledge and a theory of meaning can, for the purposes of AI, be considered identical (/Habel 1986/), and aim at a combination of a definition of truth with a systematic account of language understanding (/Kamp 1981/).

Putting such theories to practice, generic reference has been a particularly prominent example in the semantics of natural language where it has been claimed that a knowledge encoding of generic generalisations by way of a default logic is more adequate than a plain truth-conditional semantics (/Krifka 1988/, /Asher & Morreau 1990 and 1991/). In what follows, I want to show, however, that any such approach does not contribute to a solution of the semantic problems of generic reference, and that it, rather, rests on a confusion of semantics and epistemology. Alternatively, a computational model of generic reference is presented where semantics and knowledge structures are seperated, while the close relation that generic generalisations bear to default reasoning is still adequately explained.

2. Generic Generalisations

Generic generalisations are statements such as the following:

> *I. Singular definite NPs,*
> 1. The horse occasionally mates with the donkey.

> *II. Plural definite NPs,*
> 2. The horses have a flowing mane and tail.

> *III. Singular indefinite NPs,*
> 3. A horse occasionally mates with a donkey.

> *IV. Plural indefinite NPs (bare plurals),*
> 4. Horses occasionally mate with donkeys.

> *V. Mass terms,*
> 5. Gold is a precious metal,

> *VI. Quantified NPs,*
> 6. Some cats, namely the lion and the tiger, are beasts of prey,
> 7. Noah saved all animals in his Arch.

> *VII. Habituals,*
> 8. John smokes.

Generic generalisations are well known to pose at least two problems. First, generic generalisations do not constitute a referentially homogeneous group. There appear to be two basic aspects of generic reference, one related to reference to kinds and the other to reference to default representatives, or typical representatives, of a kind. In general, generic expressions involving a reference to the default representatives of a kind - called default generics for short - allow for the substitution of the determiner of the singular or plural generic expression by the singular indefinite article (given that the sentential predicate does not require a collective reading, and assuming a corresponding change with respect to number of the respective noun when necessary). Conversely, generic expressions involving reference to kinds - henceforth called kind generics for short - in general do not allow for this substitution. The first question, then, is whether or not both kinds of generic generalisations can be dealt with by the same semantics. In particular, this question is related to the problem of how to assign determiners like the definite or indefinite article a homogenuous semantics that explains their meaning under generic as well as non-generic readings.

The second problem concerns the question of how to deal with the fact that generic generalisations typically allow for exceptions, as is evident from statements like (9) and (10),

> 9. Dogs bark,
> 10. The Scotsman drinks Whisky.

In contrast to statements involving universal quantification, the rule of universal instantiation clearly is not applicable here: If Fido is a dog, and if dogs bark, it does not strictly follow that Fido barks, unless it is assumed (by way of a conversational maxime, for example), or explicitly stated, that Fido is a typical dog. Nevertheless, on the basis of the generic generalisation that dogs bark one can reasonably expect that Fido barks. Both considerations are closely related, for when a generic generalisation is understood as a default rule, and not as a universal statement, it naturally must allow for exceptions. Notice, however, that only generic statements referring to default representatives can be understood as default rules, as is clear from statements like (11) and (12),

> 11. Man set foot on the moon in 1969,
> 12. The musk-rat was imported into Europe in 1905.

3. Informal Semantics of Generic Generalisations

Leaving aside mass terms and kind generic readings of quantifiers and numerals (such as in (6) and (7) above), the intuitively available readings of the bare plural, the definite, and indefinite article can be summarized as follows:

Determiner	*Reading*			
	generic			existential
bare plural	kind	or	default	collective or distributive
definite article	kind	or	default	unique_referent
indefinite article	--		default	distributive

Thus, we stipulate a basic distinction between generic and non-generic readings of the determiners in question. The non-generic readings are called existential, because they generally involve an existential presupposition. Within the category of existential readings the usual distinctions between collective or distributive can be applied. Notice, however, that the distinction between kind generics and default generics is a distinction only within the category of generic readings.

Considering e.g. an expression like "the dog", any semantics of generic generalisations must now be capable of explaining of how its three readings, viz. unique_referent (e.g. "the dog has bit the postman"), kind generic (e.g. "the dog is widespread in Europe"), and default generic (e.g. "the dog barks"), can be interrelated. Carlson (1978) has attempted a unifying approach to generic and existential readings of the bare plural construction (in English) by taking expressions under a generic reading to refer to kinds, and under an existential reading to refer to instances of kinds. The choice of the preferred reading is supposed to be determined by the verb. Corresponding to the distinction between kinds and instances of kinds, episodic and habitual predicates are distinguished such that episodic predicates are always thought to induce a non-generic, existential reading, while habitual predicates are always thought to induce a generic reading. Thus, generic generalisations are treated essentially the same as habitual sentences. This analysis meets with difficulties, however, when confronted with generic statements that contain episodic predicates like (11) and (12). It also cannot be upheld for the general case of kind generics not involving any quantification over cases. In consequence, Krifka (1987) submits to deal with kind generics and default generics by two different and completely unrelated analysis, one involving simple reference to kinds, the other involving default quantification. Given, however, that there are substantial arguments in favour of a unified analysis of the determiners (/Hawkins 1978/, /Loebner 1985/), an approach that preserves our semantic intuition of the unity of the articles should be preferred.

On our approach, the generic interpretation of a determiner expression is (with the exception of kind-predicates) independent from the interpretation of the sentential predicate. Based on findings that generic generalisations behave syntactically like proper names (/Carlson 1978/ and /Heyer 1990/),it is assumed that determiner expressions can be assigned by the semantics either a generic or an existential reading. If a generic expression is assigned a generic reading, its reference is taken to be a generic individual, or kind. Once a determiner expression is interpreted generically, however, it does depend on the sentential predicate whether the determiner expression has a kind generic or default generic reading, and, similarly, whether a plural expression has a collective or distributive non-generic reading. Generic individuals are thought to have two kinds of properties: those that apply to the kind itself (kind-level and event predicates), and those that determine certain properties of the representatives - as representatives - of that kind (dispositions). Kind reference of generic expressions is then explained as reference to a generic individual in the context of a predicate that only allows (in that context) the predication of the property to the generic individual itself. Default reference of generic expressions is explained on the basis of kind reference in the context of a disposition. The idea is that representatives of a kind have certain dispositional properties because they are representatives of that kind. (Vice versa, being a representative of a kind determines which dispositional properties the individual representative of a kind can have). Those representatives of a kind that have the characteristic properties of a kind are called the typical representatives of that kind. Thus, default reference of generic expressions is explained as a reference to the typical representatives of a kind.

For the referential semantics of generic expressions it is important to realize that the exact extension of the set of typical representatives of a kind need not be known to a speaker: by way of a general division of linguistic labour, the extension of a generic term will in general be fixed by the experts on the particular domain (/Putnam 1975/). To decide the question whether or not a particular individual is contained in the set of typical representatives of a kind may therefore require further knowledge and reasoning.

A formal semantics of generic descriptions on the basis of the informal semantics sketched above has been described in /Heyer 1985/. For the purposes of implementing this semantics, we shall assume a frame-structured model with a hierarchy of objects and classes, and inheritance of properties within this hierarchy. The system allows for the representation of hierarchies of frames with strict subclass relations as well as slots (with slot values) that frames typically possess. Defeasible and undefeasible links can be represented, but chains of defeasible inferences are not allowed.

As Brewka (1987) has shown, the logic of such inheritance systems can be described by a first order logic formalisation with the addition of the three-place predicate *exceptional* whose extension is minimized by variable circumscription. However, using this default logic as the basis for a semantics of generic generalisations would blurr the distinction between semantics and epistemology, contrary to our intuition that the exact extension of concepts need not be known by every speaker. Semantics would be impossible if we ask that the semantics have built into it always a complete world model. The guiding idea of our implementation, therefore, is to translate the semantic representation of generic expressions into frames in the knowledge base as a partial model for the referential semantics. Even though the model behaves as described by the default logic, the default reasoning based on the knowledge structures, by our approach, is not part of the semantics of generic generalisations.

4. Implementation

The ideas sketched above have been implemented as an extension of a system described in /Covington 1988/, i.e. a programme (in PROLOG) for updating and querying a PROLOG knowledge base. The system comprises a simple DCG parser that generates semantic representations, a translation of these semantic representations into a frame extended PROLOG knowledge base, and a frame representation and management system based on work done within ESPRIT I project ACORD (/Heyer et.al. 1990/).

The semantic representation consists of terms

> *assertion(EntityList, Predicate),*
> *question(EntityList, Predicate),*

where *EntityList* is a list of entity terms

> *entity(Name,Determiner,Reading,Reference,Condition).*

The variable *Name* either is a variable, in which case *Condition* is a structure with that variable as argument, or it is an atom, i.e. the proper name of an individual or a kind, in which case *Condition* simply is the atom true. *Determiner* can be any of the three atoms *plural, the,* or *a*; the variable *Reading* can be instantiated to the atoms *generic* or *existential*, and *Reference* can be any of the atoms *kind, default, unique, collective,* or *distributive.*

Using PROLOG unification in order to check semantic congruence with respect to the arguments *Determiner, Reading,* and *Reference,* the programme generates e.g. the following semantic representations for determiner expressions and proper names:

proper name
    John   *entity(john,_,existential,unique_referent,true)*

generic generalisations
    the dog   *entity(dog,the,generic, kind | default,true)*
    bare plural   *entity(dog,plural,generic, kind | default,true)*
    a dog   *entity(dog,a,generic,default,true)*

definite description
    the dog   *entity(dog,the,existential,unique_referent,true)*

bare plural
    dogs   *entity(X,plural,existential,collective|distributive,dog(X))*

indefinite description
    a dog   *entity(X,a,existential,distributive,dog(X))*

As has been outlined in the above semantics of generic generalisations, these semantic structures are generated by taking the generic reading of a determiner expression as default, and then determining the kind of reference, i.e. kind reference or default reference in the case of a generic reading, or unique, collective or distributive reference in the case of an existential reading. The information required for checking semantic congruence is provided by the lexicon. Thus, for each verb and noun we also list the semantic information which kind of reference the entry will require:

common_noun(lion,default,_,[lion|X],X).
comon_noun(species,kind,_,[species|X],X).
generic_name(lion,_,_,[lion|X],X).
individual_name(leo,_,_,[leo|X],X).

transitive_verb(come,event,distributive,[comes|X],X).
transitive_verb(come,event,collective,[comes|X],X).
transitive_verb(suckle,event,distributive,[suckles|X],X).
transitive_verb(suckle,disposition,distributive,[suckles|X],X).

As has been pointed out above, if a determiner expression has been assigned a generic reading, then an event reference of the verb phrase will induce a kind reference, and a disposition reference of the verb phrase will induce a default reference of the generic noun phrase.

The complete parser output for simple cases like (8) and (9) results in the structures (8') and (9'),

8. John smokes,
9. Dogs bark,

8' assertion(entity(john,_,existential,unique_reference,true),
smokes(entity(john,_,existential,unique_reference,true))).

9' assertion(entity(dog,plural,generic,default,true),
bark(entity(dog,plural,generic,default,true))).

The translation of semantic representations into PROLOG proceeds as follows. Statements about entities referred to by the atom unique_reference, i.e. statements containing proper names and definite descriptions, are asserted as PROLOG facts. Given the general format of the semantic representation, viz. *assertion(EntityList,Predicate)*, the algorithm simply asserts the value of the variable *Predicate*, which in the above example is the structure *smokes(entity(john,_,existential, unique_reference,true))*.

Statements involving reference to a generic object, i.e. semantic representations where the variable Reading has the value generic, lead to the creation of new frames, or the extension of already created frames, in the knowledge base. The structure of a frame is defined by five arguments:

frame(FRAME, SLOTTYPE, SLOTNAME, ASPECT, FACET, VALUE)

where FRAME takes as value the name of the frame, SLOTTYPE and SLOTNAME define the slots of the frame, ASPECT indicates the kind of value, FACET describes the behaviour of the value with respect to inheritance, i.e. whether or not a value can be bequeathed, or whether or not it has been inherited, and VALUE is the value itself. SLOTTYPE and SLOTNAME can only take values in a number of predefined (obligatory or facultative) slots, including a slot called *generalisation* for recording all father frames of a frame, and a slot called *property* for marking the slots that specify the properties of the frame. Thus, the semantic representation of (9) leads to a change in the knowledge base such that the structure *frame(dog,property,bark,value,[new,bequeath],[bark])*

either is created, or added to the frame with the name dog. As the semantic representation of (9) indicates a default generic reading, the facet of the property slot with slotname bark is set to *bequeath*. Therefore, the value *bark* will be inherited by all typical instances of the frame dog in the knowledge base. However, if for an individual instance (and, in the present implementation, only for individual instances) the negation of a default property has explicitly been specified, it will override the default property. Kind generic readings are treated analogously. Thus, if the semantic representation of a statement indicates a kind generic reading, as is the case with statement (13),

13. The lion is a species,

13' assertion(entity(lion,the,generic,kind,true),
species(entity(lion,the,generic,kind,true)))

then the facet of the property slot in the respective frame is set to *[new, not_bequeath]*, i.e. the predicated property only is a property of the frame, and cannot be inherited by any of its instances.

Statements about individual instances of frames, like statement (14),

14. Fido is a dog,

14'assertion(entity(fido,_,existential,unique_referent,true),
dog(entity(fido,_,existential,unique_referent,true)))

lead to the addition of the related PROLOG fact (e.g. *dog(entity(fido,_,existential,unique_referent,true)))* to the knowledge base, as is the case with all statements involving a proper name or definite description as explained above.

In addition, a PROLOG fact is created that asserts Fido as an instance of the frame dog, viz. *instance(entity(fido,_,existential,unique_referent,true),frame(dog,_,_,_,_,_))*. This relation induces the consequence that every instance of a frame also is an instance of the generalisations of that frame; it also gives rise to the expectation that the default properties of a frame also hold for its instances. However, in order to keep a clear distinction between semantics and knowledge base, the conclusion that, e.g., Fido barks, is no logical consequence in the model, as the knowledge base contains too little information about Fido. In the present implementation this conclusion is licensed only if it has explicitly been asserted that e.g. Fido is a typical dog, leading to the assertion of *typical_instance(entity(fido,_,existential,unique_referent,true), frame(dog,_,_,_,_,_))* to the knowledge base. For all entities that are typical instances of a frame it is then guaranteed that all default properties, or characteristics, are inherited.

Finally, existential readings of the indefinite article and the bare plural, i.e. semantic representations of the kind

entity(X,a | plural,existential,_,Condition),

are translated into the knowledge base in the same fashion, except that Skolem constants, or dummy variables, of the form *entity(dummyN,_,existential,_,true)* are added to the knowledge base in place of a proper name or a definite description. Thus, the existential reading of (14), resulting in the semantic representation (15'),

15. A dog barks,

15' assertion(entity(X,a,existential,distributive,dog(X)),
bark(entity(X,a,existential,distributive,dog(X)))),

yields the knowledge base update

bark(entity(dummy1,a,existential,distributive,dog(dummy1))).

In addition, in order to link that fact with the frame dog, and thus with all the knowledge that is available about dogs in the knowledge base, the fact *instance(entity(dummy1,a,existential, distributive, dog(dummy1)),frame(dog_,_,_,_,_))* is created. Again, this linkage gives rise to reasonable expectations, but does not, without additional knowledge, license further logical consequences.

4. Conclusion

The implementation is based on a strict seperation of semantic representation and knowledge base, where, in fact, the knowledge base can be considered a partial model for the semantic representations. It can be considered, therefore, as providing us with a referential semantics for generic generalisations that validates a unified approach to kind generic and default generic readings of generic generalisations, and also explains how generic generalisations can allow for exceptions without proposing a default logic for the semantics. The basic notions that are needed for a semantics of generic generalisations are the notion of a generic object, and the notion of kind and default properties of such generic objects. In our implementation, these notions have been realized by frames, and inheritance of slot values, and this formal structure appears to be sufficient for a truth conditional semantics of generic generalisations. However, the implementation also shows that the completion of this structure by common sense and domain knowledge, and the processing of this knowledge, clearly can be regarded as not itself belonging to the semantics.

Literature

/Asher & Morreau 1990/, A Dynamic Modal Semantics for Default Reasoning and Generics, in: Brewka and Freitag (eds.), Proceedings of the Workshop on Nonmonotonic Reasoning 1989, Arbeitspapiere der GMD 443, St.Augustin 1990

/Asher & Morreau 1991/, What some Generic Sentences Mean, DYANA Deliverable R2.5.B, Edinburgh

/Brewka 1987/, The Logic of Inheritance in Frame Systems, IJCAI

/Carlson 1978/, Reference to kinds in English, Bloomington; repr. 1982, N.Y.

/Covington 1988/, Prolog Programming in depth, Scott, Foresman & Co, Glenview

/Habel 1986/, Prinzipien der Referentialität, Springer

/Hawkins 1978/, Definiteness and Indefiniteness, London

/Heyer 1985/, Generic Descriptions, Default Reasoning, and Typicality, Theoretical Linguistics 12

/Heyer 1990/, Semantics and Knowledge Representation in the Analysis of Generic Descriptions, Journal of Semantics 7/1

/Heyer et.al. 1990/, The knowledge base component in the final ACORD system: Its contribution to NL-processing, in: G.Bez (ed.), ACORD - Construction and interrogation of knowledge bases using natural language text and graphics, Berlin/Heidelberg/New York, to appear

/Kamp 1981/, A Theory of Truth and Semantic Representation, in: Groenendijk and Stokhoff, Truth, Interpretation, and Information, Dordrecht 1984

/Krifka 1988/ Genericity in Natural Language, Proceedings of the 1988 Tübingen Conference, SNS-Bericht 88-42, Tübingen

/Loebner 1985/, Definites, Journal of Semantics 4

/Moore 1981/, Problems in Logical Form, ACL Proceedings 19th Annual Meeting, Urbana-Champaign

/Putnam 1975/, The meaning of meaning, in: Mind, Language, and Reality, Philosophical Papers Vol.2, Cambridge

TOWARDS FINDING THE REASONS BEHIND - GENERATING THE CONTENT OF EXPLANATION

HELMUT HORACEK

Universität Bielefeld
Fakultät für Linguistik und Literaturwissenschaft
Postfach 8640, D-4800 Bielefeld 1
Tel.: (0521) 106-3678

ABSTRACT

This paper presents a constructive method for generating the propositional content of natural language explanations which aim at providing insights into the reasons behind the solution of a constraint-satisfaction problem. The generation process attempts to achieve certain goals comprising the relevance of the arguments included, the appropriateness of the associated degree of detail, and the adequacy of the presentation structure, which we believe to be important criteria for high quality explanations. The method is based on a retrospective analysis of the problem solving trace produced by an expert system, and it aims at focussing on the reasons underlying those aspects of the system´s decision which are addressed by a particular explanation seeking request. In addition, the relations between the propositional specifications selected and natural language texts adequate to convey the content expressed by the propositions are discussed.

1. INTRODUCTION

The task of providing informative natural language explanations for illustrating the results produced by various kinds of decision support systems, in particular by expert systems, is assessed as being a problem of significant and strongly increasing importance. One of the reasons for this judgement is that knowledge about a system´s problem solving behavior and understanding the decisive criteria underlying its solution leads towards a better understanding of the system´s competence and limitations and is an important prerequisite for assessing the relevance of the results produced.

Furthermore, common agreement about the importance of high quality explanations correlates with the assessment of the difficulty of the associated generation process. In fact, explaining the solution of a problem apparently requires more competence than merely solving the associated problem itself. Quite frequently, it is possible to solve a certain problem by applying some elementary operations and by following some simple search technique, without a deeper understanding of the reasons underlying this procedure (this is why computers work). However, *understanding* a problem requires insights in the influence that given facts and domain regularities exhibit on the solution of the associated problem. Once these relations have been analysed to a sufficient degree, the dependencies recognized can be exploited for reasoning about processes concerned with answering a particular explanatory request.

Pursuing the aim of improving current explanation techniques we have designed and implemented a constructive explanation mechanism that combines aspects of relevance and well-structuredness for selecting and organizing the propositional content of explanations. The resulting propositional specifications are an important prerequisite for the production of natural language utterances which appropriately convey the meaning expressed by these specifications. The mechanism developed is based on a retrospective analysis of partial results recorded in the trace of an expert system, and it is capable of producing propositional specifications of varying degrees of complexity.

The applicability of our method is restricted to constraint-satisfaction problems. Hence, the primary goal is to find out which of the constraints defining a problem are really relevant for (certain aspects of) the solution and how they should be presented in an informative way. Despite constraint-satisfaction methods have already been applied to real world problems (e. g., [19]), this is a new research goal, since giving explanations has never been about the topics of interest in that research area. Expanding the power of current explanation techniques, which are moderately well suited for treating explanatory requests on the level of *'How did you find that ... ?'*, our contribution lies in approaching the potential of answering the fundamentally deeper question *'What are the reasons for ... ?'*

After an overview of related research we introduce the expert system OFFICE-PLAN [11]. Next, we describe in detail the constructive mechanism that generates specifications for explaining certain aspects of the expert system´s decision. In addition, relations between these propositional specifications and natural language texts, and a more global view of the intuition behind the mechanism are discussed.

2. RELATED RESEARCH

As for the scientific goal of generating informative explanations automatically, research in the area of natural language processing contributes to this aim in mainly two respects:

- Some approaches focus on determining the content and the structure of explanations in and of themselves. This includes, among others, tasks concerned with structuring an explanation´s content [18], applying content and discourse planning devices [5], and selecting an appropriate type of explanation on the basis of the actual context [13]. All these approaches take the information seeking person´s knowledge into account; the latter two also strongly advocate for a reactive explanation strategy.

- Other approaches are concerned with tailoring the presentation of explanations to the conversational setting and to the particular needs of their addressees. This comprises the selection among alternative object descriptions [16], the presentation of taxonomic knowledge [15], and the choice of a presentation mode suiting the intended purpose of the explanation (reasoning or debugging) [1].

However, despite the considerable effort invested in providing informative explanations and presenting them to the addressee´s best convenience, comparably little success has yet been achieved in adequately explaining why an expert system comes up with a certain solution. Usually, the meaning of an inference rule is expressed by associating it with a text template or by straightforwardly transforming it into a piece of natural language text [4]. These conventional techniques prove to be essentially insufficient to support adequate explanations with the exception of illustrating very local associative relations - without providing evidence for deeper reasons. Motivated by these shortcomings Swartout has argued that explanation supporting mechanisms must be foreseen explicitly, i.e, ´explanation cannot be an afterthought, it must be designed-in´. Hence, in the design of the expert systems XPLAIN [17] and EES [14], different kinds of knowledge (terminological, factual, and control knowledge) are explicitly separated to be better exploitable for generating a system reaction constructively.

However, in all systems discussed so far, the information that is relevant for generating explanations is or can be pre-structured somehow. The knowledge needed is represented statically (used for describing the parts and the functionality of objects [5]), it can easily be transformed into a hierarchy of facts and justifications [18], or the context to be considered is comparably local so that relatively little additional analysis is needed to select an adequate content of the explanation [14, 17].

Our goal, however, lies in treating explanation seeking requests which address significantly larger contexts. Hence, it seems to be intuitively plausible that more sophisticated techniques than the present ones must be applied to enable high quality explanations in such cases. In particular, we feel that a retrospective analysis of the intermediate results produced in the course of the problem solving process is among the techniques required. To the best of our knowledge, only the system BKG [2], which is an explanatory device attached to a backgammon playing program, re-analyses all parameters involved in its decision for illustrating the underlying reasons. It explicitly compares judgements associated with two competing problem states in order to filter out the decisive factor(s) constituting the preference of one of them over the other. The basis of comparison, however, is in terms of quantitative rather than of qualitative measures, so that the methods applied in that system can hardly be expected to be beneficial for our purposes.

3. THE PROBLEM SOLVING COMPONENT

OFFICE-PLAN is an application of the expert system work bench BABYLON [6] which has a built-in constraint-satisfaction mechanism called CONSAT [8] that is particularly useful to tackle assignment problems. The system is applied to solve room assignment problems in offices (as described in [11]), which are represented as constraint-satisfaction problems where employees correspond to components and rooms correspond to slots. OFFICE-PLAN applies a least commitment strategy using a global constraint-satisfaction algorithm ([7], [8], [12]). Given a partial assignment of rooms to a certain set of employees, the system attempts to find adequate rooms for another set of employees while satisfying requirements concerned with supporting communication, providing the necessary resources, avoiding social conflicts, etc. Basically, the employees to be assigned to rooms are ordered according to a given preference list. One after the other, they are assigned to the set of rooms in a way that is consistent with the constraints evaluated so far in addition to those constraints associated with the employee currently integrated. At the end, this procedure results in sets of assignments which constitute all solutions of the associated problem.

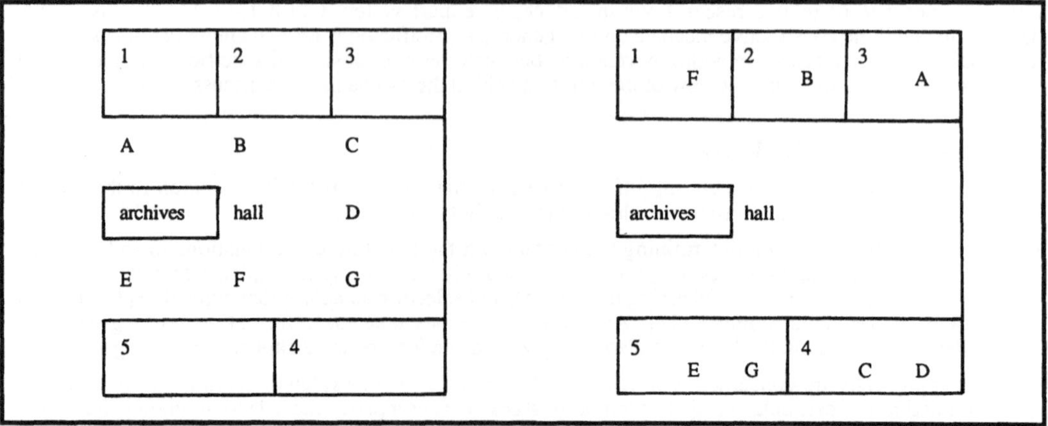

Figure 1: An office-planning problem   Figure 2: The solution of the office-planning problem

1 A in single room	7 E in room different from D´s room	13 F in room different from C´s room
2 B in next door room to A´s room	8 E in room different from C´s room	14 F in room different from B´s room
3 C in room near to A´s room	9 E in room different from B´s room	15 F in room different from A´s room
4 C in room different from B´s room	10 E in room different from A´s room	16 G in room different from F´s room
5 D in room near to A´s room	11 F in room different from E´s room	17 G in room different from D´s room
6 D in room different from B´s room	12 F in room different from D´s room	18 G in room different from A´s room

Figure 3: The associated set of constraints for the office-planning problem

<u>components integrated and requirements associated</u>	<u>sets of feasible assignments</u>
A A in single room, because A is a groupleader	{(A/1), (A/2), (A/3)}
B B in next door room to A´s room, because B is A´s secretary	{(A/1,B/2), (A/2,B/1), (A/2,B/3), (A/3,B/2)}
C C in room near to A´s room, because C is a project leader of A´s group C in room different from B´s room, in order to respect different frequencies	{(A/1,B/2,C/3), (A/2,B/1,C/3), (A/2,B/3,C/1), (A/3,B/2,C/1), (A/3,B/2,C/4)}
D D in room near to A´s room, because D is a project leader D in room different from B´s room, in order to respect different frequencies	{(A/3,B/2,C/1,D/4), (A/3,B/2,C/4,D/1), (A/3,B/2,C/4,D/4)}
E E in room different from D´s room, in order to respect different frequencies E in room different from C´s room, because they work on the same project E in room different from B´s room, in order to respect different frequencies E in room different from A´s room, because they work on the same project	{(A/3,B/2,C/1,D/4,E/5), (A/3,B/2,C/4,D/1,E/5), (A/3,B/2,C/4,D/4,E/5), (A/3,B/2,C/4,D/4,E/1)}
F F in room different from E´s room, because of smoker non-smoker aversion F in room different from D´s room, because they work on the same project F in room different from C´s room, because of smoker non-smoker aversion F in room different from B´s room, in order to respect different frequencies F in room different from A´s room, because they work on the same project	{(A/3,B/2,C/4,D/4,E/5,F/1), (A/3,B/2,C/4,D/4,E/1,F/5)}
G G in room different from F´s room, because of smoker non-smoker aversion G in room different from D´s room, because they work on the same project G in room different from A´s room, because they work on the same project	{(A/3,B/2,C/4,D/4,E/5,F/1,G/5)}

Figure 4: The trace of the process solving the office-planning problem

A constraint is derived from a requirement by reducing it to the restriction imposed and leaving out the associated justification. For instance, the requirement ´if an employee (with instance A) is a group leader, he/she must be in a single room´ breaks down into a constraint part ´the employee (A) must be in a single room´ and into a justification part ´(because) he/she is a group leader´. Despite most of the explanation generation processes refer to the constraints only, the link to the associated justifications is never removed. They are taken into account again in context with the presentation of constraints as parts of explanations.

We demonstrate the functionality of the system by the following small example. The employees A to G are to be assigned to the rooms 1 to 5 (1, 2 , and 3 are single rooms, 4 and 5 are double rooms). Two rooms are considered to be *near-to* each other if the hall or at most one other room is physically located in between them. Figure 1 shows the topological relations of this office-planning problem. Figure 2 represents the only possible solution in view of the set of constraints listed in Figure 3. The order in which the employees are assigned to rooms is determined by a preference list built by role abstraction. It proposes to integrate first the head of group (A), followed by the secretary (B), the project leaders (C and D), and the ordinary employees (E, F, and G). The problem solving process is illustrated in Figure 4 by an abbreviated trace. It contains the employees and the requirements associated in the order these employees are assigned to rooms. In addition, the sets of feasible room assignments resulting after integration of the employee assigned most recently are included. When presenting our explanation mechanism we frequently refer to this example.

4. GENERATING EXPLANATIONS

4.1 Support provided by the expert system

In this section we present a constructive mechanism for selecting an explanation´s propositional content, which is partially supported by the structuring facilities of the KADS methodology [3] applied in developing the system OFFICE-PLAN. Similar to Swartout´s approach, KADS distinguishes between several types of knowledge (i.e., domain, inference, task, and strategic knowledge). Figure 5 shows the system´s control structure (the *inference layer* in KADS) in terms of the knowledge sources contributing to the assignment *task* and the meta classes referred to (and partially updated) by each of the knowledge sources involved. The associated representation facilities can be used to determine the relevance of meta classes for answering some types of explanation seeking requests, for instance questions about changes of meta classes. In this paper, we concentrate our efforts on elaborating methods to answer questions of the type

´Why is <set1 of person/room assignments> feasible (and not <set2 of person/room assignments>)?´

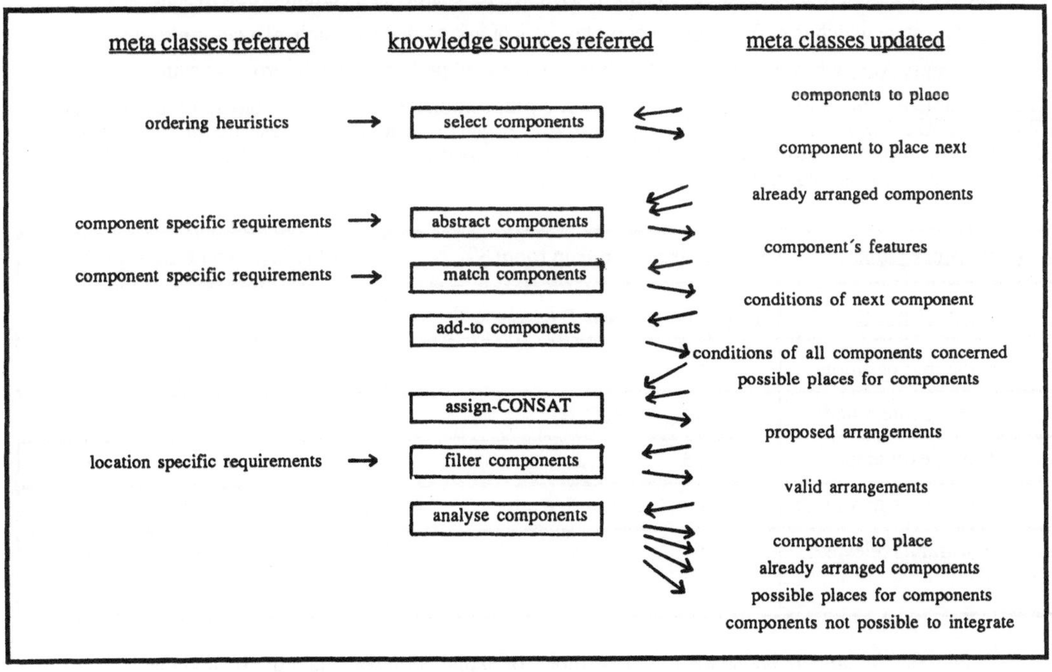

Figure 5: The control structure of OFFICE-PLAN

which refer to the meta class *already arranged components*. When determining the knowledge sources involved, we have to consider the sequence of knowledge sources enclosed between *abstract components* (where *already arranged components* is an <u>input parameter</u>) and *analyse components* (where *already arranged components* is an <u>output parameter</u>). Hence, the set of meta classes referred to in the course of this sequence enclosed consists of <u>*component specific requirements*</u> and <u>*location specific requirements*</u>. Because, in the scope of this paper, we disregard requirements concerning resources (for reasons of simplicity), the location specific requirements are reduced to the parameters expressing the size of a room (i.e., single or double room). For the time being we neglect the room sizes in the associated explanations because we assume that this information can usually be inferred from assertions about room categories and occupancies mentioned in an explanation.

4.2 The overall explanation strategy

The purpose of our explanation mechanism is to establish a set of *really relevant* requirements (with respect to the properties addressed by a concrete request) to identify the reasons for the system´s decision, which is done by a retrospective analysis of the associated problem solving trace. This analysis consists of several procedures each of which serves the purpose of attacking certain subproblems associated with the goal of achieving high quality explanations:

- First of all, the set of <u>potentially relevant</u> requirements is determined taken out of the complete set of requirements involved in the whole problem solving process (pursuing goals of *relevance*).

- Next, this set is <u>pre-structured</u> into potentially <u>several partitions</u> according to the influence of its elements on the solution aspect addressed to by an explanation seeking request (pursuing goals of *structuring*).

- Within each partition, an attempt is made to <u>reduce</u> the set of requirements included such that all remaining elements have a genuine contribution to the solution (pursuing goals of *relevance*).

- At the end, a decision is made according to the expected <u>degree of complexity</u> of the associated explanation as to which partitions are to be described by the set of requirements included, and which ones are only summarized (pursuing goals of adapting to different *degrees of complexity*).

The resulting propositional specification of an explanation may consist of several types of structures:

- <u>a set of requirements</u> which contribute to the identification of the reasons for the system´s decision,

- <u>a set of assignments</u> (<u>a set of rooms</u> is sufficient for a single employee) which identify the places <u>the employees referred to by a request</u> can still be assigned to feasibly at a certain problem state,

- <u>a problem state</u> which is defined by the <u>complete</u> sets of assignments feasible at a certain stage,

- <u>a set of employees</u> which comprise all employees integrated prior to a certain problem state.

The mechanism applied to generate an explanation´s propositional content is demonstrated by the requests *Why is person A in room 3?´* and *Why is person F in room 1?´*, which also illustrate the differences that may occur in replys to similar looking requests. The intermediate results obtained after each subprocess completed are summarized in Figure 6.

<u>explanatory request</u>	1: Why is person A in room 3?		2: Why is person F in room 1?			
<u>relevant trace part</u>	up to the integration of D (constraint 6)		complete trace - all constraints			
<u>division into partitions</u>	1	2	1	2	3	4
persons integrated:	A	B, C, D	A, B	C	D, E, F	G
rooms excluded:	4, 5	1, 2	2	3	4	5
constraints involved:	1	2, 3, 4, 5, 6	1, 2	3, 4	5 - 15	16
constraints relevant:	1	2, 3, 5	1, 2	3	5, 7, 8 11, 12, 13	16

Figure 6:   A comparison between two examples of explanation seeking requests and the intermediate results obtained in creating propositional specifications of the replys

4.3 Preselection of relevant information

So, let us consider the procedures applied in more detail. Determination of the set of <u>potentially relevant requirements</u> is done by identifying the <u>first</u> problem state S (in the trace) where the conditions imposed by the request (referred to by A_f and A_n, as sets of assignments required to be feasible or not, respectively) are completely satisfied. Hence, $\forall a_f \varepsilon A_f, \forall a_n \varepsilon A_n$: *contains* (S, a_f) & $\neg$ *contains* (S, a_n) must hold, where *contains* (S, a) expresses that an assignment a is consistent with at least one of the assignments that belong to S. If the request is consistent with the solution (i.e., the request does not contain presupposition failures - $\forall S$ in the trace, $\forall a_f \varepsilon A_f$: *contains* (S, a_f) holds - which we assume throughout the paper), the subsequent part of the problem solving process has no further influence on the solution aspect to be explained. Thus, the relevant part of the trace which entails the constraints in question is enclosed by the very beginning of the trace and by the problem state just identified.

Although this measurement may not have large reduction effects for some complicated instances of requests, the amount of information to be considered further may be substantially reducible in some occasions. Most trivially, when confronted with the request *'Why is A in a single room?'* applied to the problem defined by Figures 1 and 3, only constraint 1 is relevant because the problem state resulting after integration of this constraint (i.e., by integrating person A to obtain the set of rooms A can consistently be assigned to) consists of exactly the single rooms 1, 2, and 3. Notice that the test is performed on the basis of the set of feasible room assignments and not by comparing the constraint integrated and the conditions imposed by the request itself, which are identical in that particular case.

If, however, the decision´s properties referred to by request 1 in Figure 6 *'Why is A in room 3?'* (and, which is also asked implicitly, not in any of the other rooms) is to be explained, the relevant part of the trace includes all constraints up to those derived from the requirements associated with person D. After integrating that person, A´s feasible assignments are limited to room 3 only, whereas the other single rooms have still been feasible assignments before integrating D. Referring to the other request in Figure 6 *'Why is F in room 1?'*, no reduction of the part of the trace to be considered is possible because F´s feasible assignments are not yet restricted to room 1 before integrating the last person, G, into the constraint-satisfaction process (which inhibits F´s otherwise feasible assignment to room 5).

4.4 Structuring the preselected information

We continue with the procedure responsible for achieving <u>structuring measurements</u>, which can be considered as an extention of the method presented above. These measurements are accomplished by identifying *transition states* within the relevant trace part. We define a problem state T to be a transition states if, caused by the requirements associated with the person integrated most recently, a reduction of the set of feasible assignments of the persons P referred to by the request occurs in comparison to the assignments valid at the preceeding problem state S. Hence, $\exists p \varepsilon P$: *rooms* $(S, p) \supset$ *rooms* (T, p) must hold, where *rooms* (S, p) yields the set of rooms employee p can be assigned to according to any of the assignments that belong to S.

Then, all constraints enclosed between two transition states, between the head of the trace and the first transition state, or between the last transition state and the end of the relevant trace part become substructures of the relevant trace part, which we call *partitions*. In addition, a partition is defined completely by the assignments valid at the partition´s starting boundary (i.e., by the preceeding problem state). For description purposes, the assignments concerning the persons referred to by a certain request are sufficient.

For instance, referring again to the request *'Why is A in room 3?'* the state resulting after assigning person A is identified as a transition state because that person is restricted to be assigned to one of the single rooms 1, 2, and 3 (apparently, the feasible assignments have been unrestricted before assigning A at all, thus also including rooms 4 and 5). The resulting set of feasible assignments with respect to A remains unchanged until person D is integrated (eliminating rooms 1 and 2 from the set of assignments feasible before), which also constitutes the end of the relevant trace part. Hence, constraint 1 makes up the first partition of the relevant trace part, whereas constraints 2 to 6 constitute the second one.

As for the other request under discussion *'Why is F in room 1?'* the structuring process results in a more pronounced division into partitions, each of which is responsible for excluding one room from the set of assignments feasible for F. After the integration of the requirements associated with persons A and B, which make up the first partition, room 2 is assigned to either of these persons. When integrating person C, which constitutes the next partition, person A is definitely assigned to room 3. The integration of persons D, E, and F leads to the assignment of the two places in room 4 to the group leaders C and D (therefore, the associated constraints constitute the third partition). And, finally, integration of person G, which constitutes the last partition, restricts person F from being in room 5.

4.5   Determining the relevance of information

The next procedure of the explanation mechanism consists in reducing the set of constraints contained in each of the partitions as far as their inclusion in the propositional specifications is concerned. The procedure aims at <u>eliminating</u> those <u>constraints</u> which prove to be <u>irrelevant</u> for the resulting assignments within the partition they belong to. A constraint c is considered to be <u>irrelevant</u> within a certain partition, if its integration into the constraint-satisfaction process does not contribute to a further reduction of the set of feasible assignments (of the persons P focussed on by the request) which has been established at the problem state S that constitutes the starting boundary of the respective partition. Hence, $\forall p \; \varepsilon \; P$: $rooms$ (S, p) = $rooms$ (S_c, p) must hold, where S_c is obtained by evaluating c in S.

This condition applies, for instance, to constraints 4 and 6 when treating request 1 in Figure 6. As, in consequence of person A´s assignment, the assignments of person B are restricted to the single rooms 1 to 3, no other person (including, in particular, C and D) can conceivably share his/her room with B, which are exactly the conditions imposed by constraints 4 and 6, respectively. Therefore, the set of relevant constraints belonging to trace partition 2 consists of constraints 2, 3, and 5. When eliminating irrelevant constraints for treating request 2 in Figure 6 we are confronted with rather similar cases. Constraints 4, 6, 9, 10, 14, 15, and 18 are eliminated because they disallow persons integrated later to share a room with either of the persons A and B, which are assigned to single rooms at an early stage of the problem solving process. The elimination of constraint 17 is justified because, in addition to the other group leader, C, person D is definitely assigned to room 4 before constraint 17 is evaluated.

4.6   Adapting to different degrees of complexity

So far, a set of relevant constraints is obtained and structured by applying selection, partitioning, and reduction processes. As the size of this set may vary significantly in dependency of the problem´s properties and of the explanatory request, the amount of information specified may occasionally be too complex to be conveyed in all details in a single utterance. Therefore, we provide options to select an appropriate degree of detail of the information to be included in the explanation, which is done by focussing on the most important constraints and by only summarizing the effect of the others. In concrete, a certain problem state is chosen as a cut-off point, which means that all constraints that belong to preceeding partitions are excluded from the explanation´s specification.

In addition to the relevant requirements integrated after the cut-off point a summary of the results obtained at that stage is included in the message. This summary contains a description of the problem state (i.e, the cut-off point) in terms of the set of employees integrated previously and the sets of assignments feasible. This technique is similar to BLAH´s [18] option which consists in pruning the hierarchy of arguments at a higher level to shorten the associated explanation at the price of reducing the degree of detail. In concrete, we consider about 5 constraints (or 2 partitions) to be a reasonable choice for the maximal amount of information to be conveyed in full details. In addition, there is always an option of including just constraints instead of entire requirements in the explanation, which is preferably done if a set of constraints with similarities among the constraints is to be conveyed.

Consider, for instance, the request *'Why is person A in room 3?´*, where constraint 1 constitutes the first partition and constraints 2, 3, and 5 the second one. As the number of constraints is small enough, both partitions are preferably uttered explicitly. They are connected by the property of the joining problem state containing the feasible assignments of A, which is the person referred to by the request. If, however, the request is *'Why is person F in room 1?´* the underlying reasons are more complex due to many indirect influences on the feasible assignment of F caused by the assignments of other employees. In this case, we consider the explicit presentation of two partitions and a summary of the preceeding partitions to be a reasonable choice. These results are presented in Figure 7.

4.7   From propositional specifications to natural language texts

´Simple´ text versions are included in Figure 7 in order to demonstrate that, in principle, the generated specifications can be converted into pieces of natural language text without considerable effort (e.g., a more or less straightforward application of text templates appears to be sufficient). However, the quality of the text is apparently to be improved, which certainly requires the natural language specific generation processes to exhibit some extraordinary capabilities. The ´fluent´ text versions may give the reader a flavor of how the quality may be improved and what the most difficult problem areas are:

- finding appropriate groupings of constraints (respectively, requirements) with partially overlapping content; this helps keeping the resulting text portions concise by supporting the creation of gapping, pronominalization, and conjugated expressions; for instance *neither - nor*, and *or* in the text above,

<table>
<tr><td colspan="2" align="center"><u>final specifications for the explanatory requests</u></td></tr>
<tr><td>1: Why is person A in room 3?</td><td>2: Why is person F in room 1?</td></tr>
</table>

<table>
<tr><td colspan="2" align="center"><u>problem state the explanation applies to</u></td></tr>
<tr><td>no assignments made yet</td><td>{(A/1,B/2,C/3), (A/2,B/1,C/3), (A/2,B/3,C/1), (A/3,B/2,C/1), (A/3,B/2,C/4)}</td></tr>
<tr><td colspan="2" align="center"><u>employees already integrated</u></td></tr>
<tr><td>no employees integrated so far</td><td>A, B, C integrated</td></tr>
</table>

<table>
<tr><td colspan="2" align="center"><u>feasible assignments of the employees focussed on by the request</u></td></tr>
<tr><td>A may be assigned to any room</td><td>F may be assigned to room 1, 4, or 5</td></tr>
</table>

<table>
<tr><td colspan="2" align="center"><u>set of constraints in partition 1</u></td></tr>
<tr><td>A in single room</td><td>D in room near to A´s room   E in room different from D´s room
E in room different from C´s room   F in room different from E´s room
F in room different from D´s room   F in room different from C´s room</td></tr>
</table>

<table>
<tr><td colspan="2" align="center"><u>feasible assignments of the employees focussed on by the request</u></td></tr>
<tr><td>A may be assigned to 1, 2, and 3</td><td>F may be assigned to 1 and 5</td></tr>
</table>

<table>
<tr><td colspan="2" align="center"><u>set of constraints in partition 2</u></td></tr>
<tr><td>B in next door room to A´s room
C in room near to A´s room
D in room near to A´s room</td><td>G in room different from F´s room</td></tr>
</table>

<table>
<tr><td colspan="2" align="center"><u>´simple´ natural language text</u></td></tr>
<tr><td>A must be in a single room. Among the rooms 1, 2, and 3 only 3 is feasible, since B must be next door to A, C must be near to A, and D must be near to A.</td><td>After integrating the employees A, B, and C the following set of assignments is feasible: A in 1, B in 2, C in 3; or A in 2, B in 1, C in 3; or A in 2, B in 3, C in 1; or A in 3, B in 2, C in 1; or A in 3, B in 2, C in 4. Among the rooms 1, 4, and 5, 4 is excluded because D must be near to A, E in a room different from D´s room E in a room different from C´s room, F in a room different from E´s room, F in a room different from D´s room, and F in a room different from C´s room. Among the rooms 1 and 5, only 1 is feasible since G must be in a room different from F´s room.</td></tr>
</table>

<table>
<tr><td colspan="2" align="center"><u>´fluent´ natural language text</u></td></tr>
<tr><td>A as a group leader must be in one of the single rooms 1, 2, and 3. Among them only 3 provides a place in a next door room for the secretary B and two places in near rooms for the group leaders, C and D.</td><td>After integrating the employees A, B, and C, the single rooms are occupied by these employees with the exception of the set of assignments where C is in room 4 instead of room 1, leaving only the rooms 1, 4, and 5 as feasible ones for assigning F. Because A must be near to D, neither E nor F may share a room with C or D, and E´s room must be different from F´s room, F is restricted to rooms 1 and 5. Only 1 remains since F must not share G´s room.</td></tr>
</table>

Figure 7: Two examples of propositional specifications of replys to explanation seeking requests

- generating appropriate quantifying expressions referring to objects of the same category (if the same property is asserted to some of them); for instance, *(one of) the single rooms, with the exception of,*

- applying measurements to achieve coherence by ordering expressions referring to the same object near each other to support the generation of pronouns; for instance, *the single rooms - among them,*

- selecting that justification which correlates best with others, if several of them are associated with a certain constraint (i.e., identical constraints are derived from several requirements).

5. DISCUSSION OF THE INTUITION BEHIND

When designing our explanation mechanism we have attempted to attack rather general goals in generating an explanation´s content. The methods actually applied are intended to be formal reconstructions of aspects of the intuitively characterized explanation giving skills outlined below.

- <u>Aspects of **relevance**</u>: Apart from rather trivial instances, problems are usually characterized by a considerably sized set of parameters (here, constraints). As we have seen in the examples, the significance they bear for the solution may strongly differ for each of them, and several kind of dependencies may hold between them. Currently, we are already able to treat the simple cases where constraints are irrelevant at all for the request to be answered (see section 4.1) or within the context of a certain partition (when a constraint does not contribute to restrict feasible assignments, see section 4.3). The more complicated cases, when some set of constraints is less influencial on the feasibility of the solution than some other set (in the sense that the less influential constraints do not change the sets of feasible assignments once the other constraints are integrated), constitute a further source for reducing the set of constraints to be included in the explanation´s specification. Occasionally, the effects of two sets of constraints equalize each other, which imposes the additional choice of which of the sets is to preferred as an argument to be used in the explanation (the decisions can be based on similarities with other constraints or on similarities of the associated justifications).

- <u>Aspects of **structure**</u>: Structuring an explanation´s content is motivated by the goal of discharging the addressee´s attention capability. Applying this measurement is usually necessary in a typical real world problem, because the reasons underlying its solution may occasionally be rather complex. In our approach, we have presented a method for partitioning the justifications that contribute to the reasons asked for by a particular request (see section 4.2). However, the criterion selected for building these partitions is not the only reasonable choice. In particular, building less partitions than indicated by this criterion may occasionally be profitable, because the subprocess responsible for testing the relevance of constraints may yield better reductions in a larger context (see the example below). Moreover, partitioning according to, for instance, the roles of employees appears to be intuitively plausible because it is based on considerations of the problem as a whole.

- <u>Aspects of **complexity**</u>: Occasionally, the specifications of an explanation´s content may still be considered too complex (even in a well-structured form), so that the explanation has to be given in less degree of detail. Preferably, only the most decisive factors are to be presented in a very accurate manner, while the others are only summarized - e.g, according to partition boundaries (see section 4.6). If the explanation seeking person is interested in knowing more details, he/she can initiate follow-up questions to get acquainted with the underlying reasons more precisely, thus following the reactive strategy favored in ([5], [13]). Furthermore, taking the addressee´s knowledge into account may be a reason for dropping parts of the specifications generated. In addition, the effects of the natural language specific processes - which can be imagined to produce texts of strongly varying complexity in dependency of the assumptions made about the particular user - have an influence on the decision concerned with only summarizing parts of the specifications or presenting them in detail. Again, it is worth analysing dependencies across the boundaries of the subprocesses involved.

Consider, as an example for possible generalizations, a review of one of the requests discussed in the preceeding sections - ´Why is person F in room 1?´ If a different kind of partitioning is chosen by integrating partitions 3 and 4 into a single one, the constraints relevant for restricting F´s assignment to room 1 (from the set consisting of the rooms 1, 4, and 5) can be reduced to 4 instead of 7 by the aid of an improved procedure for testing the relevance of sets of constraints (only constraints 11, 12, 13, and 16 remain). The resulting explanation

"Rooms 2 and 3 are occupied after integration of the employees A, B, and C. Because F cannot share a room with any other employee, he/she must be assigned to 1, which is the only remaining single room"

is apparently better than those based on the specifications given in Figure 7: it is simpler, and the underlying reasons are identified more clearly.

6. CONCLUSION AND FUTURE RESEARCH

The explanation mechanism described has been implemented in Common Lisp on a SUN4 as a stand-alone version because OFFICE-PLAN is currently available on Macintoshs only. In the future, we will integrate these two subsystems with the natural language generator we are currently developing. Parts of this generator are derived from the WISBER system [9], some explanation-specific devices [10] are incorporated, and it will be enhanced by capabilities described in section 4.7. Further effort will also be invested in obtaining better propositional specifications. Potential areas for improvements in this direction comprise the exploitation of relations between the influence of sets of constraints on the feasibilty of assignments and dependencies among subprocesses. In addition, facilities that take the listeners expectations and knowledge into account can be included in some of the subprocesses described. Finally, if the problem defintion leads to a set of solutions instead of a single one, it is worth examining the effects on explanations.

Despite the considerable progress already achieved and still expandable, we think that good human experts can even do better in producing informative explanations. They are very skillful in exploiting general concepts for descriptions used in explanations (i.e., by building *abstractions*, introducing, for instance, ´flexibility´ as an argument for a particular assignment) and in adapting their techniques to different kinds of problems and to various species of users, which we feel to be among the most severe problems to be attacked in building explanation generating facilities.

REFERENCES

[1] J. Bateman, C. Paris: *Phrasing a Text in Terms the User can Understand*. In IJCAI-89, Detroit, pp. 1511-1517, 1989.

[2] H. Berliner, D. Ackley: *The QBKG System: Generating Explanations from a Non-Discrete Knowledge Representation*. In AAAI-82, 1982.

[3] J. Breuker, et al.: *Model-Driven Knowledge Acquisition: Interpretation Models*. Memo 87, Esprit project 1098, VF Project Knowledge Acquisition in Formal Domains, 1986.

[4] B. Buchanan, E. Shortliffe: Rule-Based Expert Systems *The MYCIN Experiments of the Stanford Heuristic Programming Project*. Addison-Wesley Publ. Comp., Massachussets, 1984.

[5] A. Cawsey: *Generating Explanatory Discourse*. In Current Issues in Natural Language Generation, R. Dale, C. Mellish, M. Zock (eds.), pp. 75-102, Academic Press, 1990.

[6] T. Christaller, F. di Primio, A. Voss: *Die KI-Werkbank BABYLON*. Addison Wesley, Bonn, 1989.

[7] R. Dechter, J. Pearl: *Network-Based Heuristics for Constraint-Satisfaction Problems*. In Artificial Intelligence, 34(1), pp. 1-38, 1988.

[8] H.-W. Güsgen: *CONSAT: A System for Constraint Satisfaction*. Research Notes in Artificial Intelligence, Pitman Publishing, London, 1989.

[9] H. Horacek: *The Architecture of a Generation Component in a Natural Language Dialog System*. In Current Issues in Natural Language Generation, R. Dale, C. Mellish, M. Zock (eds.), pp. 193-227, Academic Press, 1990.

[10] H. Horacek: *Exploiting Conversational Implicature For Generating Concise Explanations*. In EACL-91, J. Kunze (ed.), pp. 191-193, 1991.

[11] W. Karbach, M. Linster, A. Voß: *OFFICE-PLAN: Tackling the Synthesis Frontier*. In GWAI-89, Metzing D. (ed.), Springer, Berlin, pp. 379-387, 1989.

[12] A. Macworth: *Consistency in Networks of Relations*. In Artificial Intelligence, 8, pp. 99-118, 1977.

[13] J. Moore, W. Swartout: *A Reactive Approach to Explanation*. In IJCAI-89, Detroit, pp. 1504-1510, 1989.

[14] R. Neches, W. Swartout, J. Moore: *Enhanced Maintenance and Explanation of Expert Systems Through Explicit Models of Their Development*. In IEEE Transactions on Software Engineering SE-11(11), pp. 1337-1351, 1985.

[15] C. Paris: *Tailoring Object Descriptions to a User´s Level of Expertise*. In Computational Linguistics 14, pp. 64-78, 1988.

[16] E. Reiter: *Generating Descriptions that Exploit a User´s Domain Knowledge*. In Current Issues in Natural Language Generation, R. Dale, C. Mellish, M. Zock (eds.), pp. 257-285, Academic Press, 1990.

[17] W. Swartout: *XPLAIN: A System for Creating and Explaining Expert Consulting Systems*. In Artificial Intelligence, 21(3), pp. 285-325, 1983.

[18] J. Weiner: *BLAH: A System which Explains its Reasoning*. In Artificial Intelligence, 15(1), pp. 19-48, 1980.

[19] H. Ziegeler, H. Kaindl: *A Cyclic Pattern Resulting From a Constraint-Satisfaction Search*. To appear in CAIA-91, 7th IEEE Conference on AI Applications, February 1991, Miami Beach, Florida.

Fokusmodellierung durch Sichtabhängigkeitsgraphen bei der Interpretation natürlichsprachlicher Datenbank-Updates

Jörg Noack, Johannes Wings
Lehrstuhl für Angewandte Mathematik insbesondere Informatik,
Ahornstr. 55, D-5100 Aachen

Abstract

Die besonderen Schwierigkeiten bei der Interpretation von Updates in einer natürlichsprachlichen Datenbank-Schnittstelle resultieren daraus, daß dem Benutzer in der Regel nur ein Ausschnitt der in der Datenbank modellierten Diskurswelt bekannt ist. Updates, die für den Benutzer sinnvoll und eindeutig formuliert sind, können häufig nicht direkt in eine Änderung der Datenbank übersetzt werden. Wir schlagen ein Benutzermodell vor, in dem der Fokus eines Datenbank-Dialogs in einem Sichtabhängigkeitsgraphen festgehalten wird. Eine Update-Äußerung kann dann als Update der im Graphen dargestellten Sicht aufgefaßt werden, wodurch sich das natürlichsprachliche Update-Problem auf das View-Update-Problem in relationalen Datenbanken zurückführen läßt.

1 Einleitung

Obwohl es bereits umfassende Arbeiten über natürlichsprachliche Anfragesysteme zu Datenbanken gibt, beschäftigen sich bis heute nur wenige mit der Fragestellung des natürlichsprachlichen Updates (Salveter 84, Davidson 87). Wir skizzieren, wie die transportable Datenbank-Schnittstelle NATHAN so erweitert werden kann, daß in Dialogen mit dem System auch Äußerungen zugelassen sind, die durch Update-Operationen der formalen Anfragesprache SQL interpretiert werden. Grundkenntnisse über relationale Datenbanken (Vossen 91) werden vorausgesetzt.

Die Arbeit ist wie folgt aufgebaut. In Abschnitt 2 wird eine kurze Bestandsaufnahme von NATHAN vor der Erweiterung um eine Update-Komponente gegeben. Abschnitt 3 erläutert die Notwendigkeit eines Fokusmodells. In Abschnitt 4 zeigen wir, wie die aktuelle Benutzersicht in diesem Modell durch sogenannte Sichtabhängigkeitsgraphen festgehalten werden kann. Abschnitt 5 beschreibt die Übersetzung von natürlichsprachlichen Updates mit Hilfe dieser Graphen. Schließlich gehen wir in Abschnitt 6 auf die notwendigen Erweiterungen von NATHAN ein und skizzieren zum Schluß in Abschnitt 7 die universellen Einsatzmöglichkeiten des vorgestellten Ansatzes. Sämtliche Beispiele im Text beziehen sich auf einen Ausschnitt der Wohnungsmarkt-Datenbank, der im Anhang A dargestellt ist.

2 Architektur von NATHAN

NATHAN wird über eine menuegesteuerte Akquisitionskomponente (Noack 89b) von einem Datenbankexperten an einen neuen Diskursbereich angepaßt. Dabei liegt ein konzeptuelles Modell zugrunde, das auf einem erweiterten Entity-Relationship-Modell aufbaut. In der Akquisitionsphase werden die Informationen für den anwendungsspezifischen Teil des Lexikons festgelegt. Zu den einzelnen Lexemen werden verschiedene morphologische, syntaktische und semantische Merkmale wie Kasus, Numerus, Genus, Wortklasse etc. erhoben, wobei vom Datenbankexperten nur linguistisches Grundwissen und keine Kenntnisse über Grammatikformalismus oder interne Repräsentationen verlangt werden. Außerdem sind die anwendungsspezifischen Wörter mit sogenannten *Datenbanktoken* zu verknüpfen, welche die Konzepte des Datenmodells repräsentieren. Datenbanktoken werden intern durch die Bezeichner für Relationen, Attribute und Domains dargestellt.

Die Dialogkomponente beginnt mit einer morphologisch-lexikalischen Analyse. Die nachfolgende Syntaxanalyse bedient sich einer DCG-Grammatik, die breite Teile der deutschen Sprache überdeckt. Das Ergebnis dieser Analyse wird als Strukturbaum dargestellt. Lexikalische Mehrdeutigkeiten werden anschließend mit Hilfe eines heuristischen Verfahrens aufzulösen versucht. Dieses Verfahren verwendet als Input den im Strukturbaum festgehaltenen Satzkontext und das als Graph kodierte Datenbankschema (Noack 89a). Parallel dazu wird nach einer eindeutigen Zuordnung zwischen Datenbankwerten und den Domains des Datenmodells gesucht. Dies ist nötig, da Datenbankwerte bei NATHAN nicht im Lexikon eingetragen werden müssen und deshalb nach der lexikalischen Analyse zunächst noch unbekannt sein können. Die Aufgabe der semantischen Analyse besteht darin, die durch Datenbanktoken repräsentierten Konzepte des Datenmodells, eventuelle Ausgabeattribute, Vergleiche und quantifizierende Informationen im Strukturbaum zu erkennen und in eine interne Repräsentation zu überführen. NATHAN verzichtet auf eine logische Repräsentation, die noch unabhängig vom verwendeten Datenmodell ist. Stattdessen wird für die in einer Anfrage enthaltenen Datenbanktoken zunächst eine Zusammenhangskomponente berechnet, die als Eingabe für den Algorithmus zur Bestimmung des Quantorenskopus dient. Dieser generiert schließlich eine vom Datenbankschema abhängige, prädikatenlogische Darstellung, die unmittelbar in die formale Anfragesprache SQL übertragen werden kann (Noack 90).

3 Ein einfaches Benutzermodell

Die Benutzer eines natürlichsprachlichen Systems erwarten einen Gesprächspartner, mit dem sie in gewohnter Weise einen Dialog führen können. Eine erfolgreiche Kommunikation kann aber nur dann stattfinden, wenn beide Gesprächspartner gegenseitig begreifen, was der andere meint. Ein interaktives System muß daher versuchen, die Intentionen seines Benutzers bzw. Gesprächspartners zu erkennen. Zugleich sind Antworten zu generieren, aus denen der Benutzer schließen kann, daß das System seine Intention verstanden hat. Dabei sind Annahmen über fehlendes oder aber bereits vorhandenes Vorwissen des Benutzers zu berücksichtigen, so daß Unverständlichkeit und Redundanz vermieden werden können.

KI-Systeme (Wahlster und Kobsa 89, Rich 89) verwenden daher ein *Benutzermodell*, in dem sämtliche Aspekte, die über einen Benutzer a priori oder durch sein Dialogverhalten bekannt sind, festgehalten werden. Bei der Behandlung von Updates in einem natürlichsprachlichen Datenbank-Interface sind wir (gemäß Rich 89) an einem impliziten, individuellen und kurzfristigen Benutzermodell interessiert, d.h. an einem solchen, welches aus dem Dialogverhalten des individuellen Benutzers inferiert werden kann und sich dynamisch an das aktuelle Gesprächsthema anpaßt.

Da wir es bei NATHAN mit einem transportablen System zu tun haben, das vor allem Computerlaien einen Zugang zu Datenbanken ermöglichen soll, können wir nicht davon ausgehen, daß der Benutzer- wie bei der Verwendung von formalen Anfragesprachen üblich - das zugrunde liegende Datenbankschema kennt. Default-Annahmen (Wahlster und Kobsa 89), wie sie etwa bei einem Hotelreservierungssystem sinnvoll sind, spielen hier keine Rolle, da typische Datenbank-Interaktionen keinem allgemeinen Muster folgen. Als primäre Wissensquelle für das benötigte Benutzermodell dient das augenblickliche Gesprächsthema, der *Fokus*. Die Konstruktion unseres Modells, das i.w. aus einem Dialoggedächtnis besteht, umfaßt drei Aspekte:

- die Repräsentation des Fokus,

- eine Methode zur Ableitung und Wartung des Fokus während des Benutzer-System-Dialogs und

- einen Mechanismus zur Verwendung der Fokusrepräsentation bei der Interpretation oder Antwortgenerierung.

In unserem Modell fassen wir die letzte Anfrageäußerung als die aktuelle Benutzersicht auf. Wenn der zu ändernde Wert einer nachfolgenden Update-Äußerung in der Benutzersicht vorkommt, so wird die Update-Äußerung als Update dieser Benutzersicht interpretiert, andernfalls wird aus der Update-Äußerung eine neue Sicht generiert.

4 Die Benutzersicht

Der Zusammenhang zwischen Benutzersicht und Datenbankschema kann wie in Abbildung 1 dargestellt werden. $V(D)$ repräsentiert den aktuellen Ausschnitt der Datenbankextension D, die dem Benutzer bekannt ist. Wenn der Benutzer einen Update u ausführen möchte, erwartet er gemäß seiner Sicht $u(V(D))$ als Resultat dieses Updates. Die Aufgabe der Update-Komponente der natürlichsprachlichen Schnittstelle besteht nun darin, für die Datenbankextension D eine Übersetzung $T(u)$ zu finden, so daß $V(T(u)(D)) = u(V(D))$ ist.

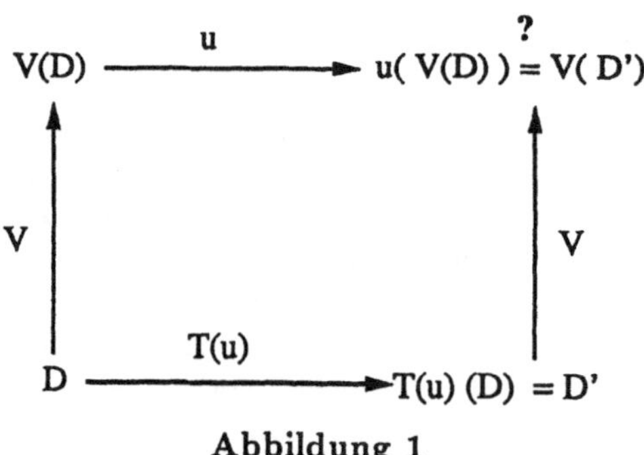

Abbildung 1

Die Abbildung $V : D \to V(D)$ induziert einen Homomorphismus. Es sei $v \in V(D)$ ein Tupel aus der Benutzersicht und u die Update-Operation, die auf v ausgeführt werden soll. Da u nicht direkt auf v ausgeführt werden kann, muß ein Datenbanktupel $t \in D$ bestimmt werden, so daß gilt: $V(T(u)(t)) = u(v)$. Wäre V ein Isomorphismus, dann könnte mit $V^{-1}(v)$ immer ein eindeutiges $t \in D$ bestimmt werden. Daß es sich bei V i.a. nicht um einen Isomorphismus handelt, zeigt Beispiel 1.

Beispiel 1
(a) Ben: "Wer vermietet was?"

(b) Sys:

VNR	WNR
V2	W1
V2	W2
V3	W3
V4	W4
V5	W6

(c) Ben: "Ersetze den Vermieter der Wohnung W2 durch V1!"

Das Tupel $v = (V2, W2) \in V(D)$ soll geändert werden. Da $V^{-1}(v) = \{t_1, t_2\}$ mit $t_1 = (V2, Oezer, Schurzelterstr., 549, 5300, Bonn)$ und $t_2 = (W2, T1, V2, G2, Kastanienweg, 4, 5300, Bonn, 105, 300.00, 100.00)$ gibt es keine eindeutige Übersetzung $T(u)$. Die Änderung könnte also auf t_1 oder t_2 ausgeführt werden. Wenn im Tupel t_2 das Attribut VNR in $V1$ geändert wird, so ergibt sich eine korrekte Übersetzung der natürlichsprachlichen Update-Äußerung, d.h. es gilt $V(T(u)(D)) = u(V(D))$. Wird hingegen in t_1 das Attribut VNR in $V1$ geändert, so ändert sich auch der Vermieter der Wohnung $W1$ in $V1$. Wir haben es dann mit einem *Seiteneffekt* zu tun, den der Benutzer nicht explizit angegeben hat. Da damit gilt $V(T(u)(D)) \neq u(V(D))$, liegt keine korrekte Übersetzung vor.

Zur Darstellung der Benutzersicht verwenden wir - wie in (Davidson 87) - sogenante Sichtabhängigkeitsgraphen. Diese basieren auf den *View Dependency Graphs*, die in (Dayal und Bernstein 82) bei der Behandlung des View-Update-Problems in relationalen Datenbanken eingeführt wurden. In einem Sichtabhängigkeitsgraphen werden sämtliche Attribute, die von NATHAN während der semantischen Interpretation für eine Anfrage berechnet wurden, sowie die zwischen ihnen geltenden funktionalen Abhängigkeiten festgehalten. NATHAN ermittelt verschiedene Listen, in denen die Ausgabeattribute, selektierende Bedingungen und Quantifikationen für einen Eingabesatz zusammengefaßt werden. Zusätzlich bestimmt der Tokeninterpreter (Noack 90) die Verbindungen für die Datenbankentoken, die im Eingabesatz aufgetreten sind.

Sei F eine natürlichsprachliche Anfrage eines Benutzers und PL, SL und JL die dazu bestimmten Listen der Projektionsattribute, Selektions- und Jointerme. Der *Sichtabhängigkeitsgraph* $G = (V, E)$ mit der Knotenmenge V und der Kantenmenge E ergibt sich wie folgt:

- Für jedes Attribut $Xi.A \in PL$ gibt es Knoten $Xi.A$ und $Xi.A_v$ und Kanten $(Xi.A, Xi.A_v)$ von $Xi.A$ nach $Xi.A_v$ und $(Xi.A_v, Xi.A)$ von $Xi.A_v$ nach $Xi.A$.

- Für jeden Jointerm $(Xi.A = Xj.B) \in JL$ gibt es Knoten $Xi.A$ und $Xj.B$ und Kanten $(Xi.A, Xj.B)$ von $Xi.A$ nach $Xj.B$ und $(Xj.B, Xi.A)$ von $Xj.B$ nach $Xi.A$.

- Für jeden Selektionsterm $(Xi.AopC) \in SL$ mit $op \in \{=, <, >, \leq, \geq, \neq\}$ gibt es Knoten $Xi.A$ und C und Kanten $(Xi.A, C)$ von $Xi.A$ nach C und $(C, Xi.A)$ von C nach $Xi.A$.

- Gilt zwischen der Attributmenge $A = \{Xi.A_1, ..., Xi.A_m\}$ und dem Attribut $Xi.B$ die funktionale Abhängigkeit $A \rightarrow_{Xi} B$, so gibt es für jedes $Xi.Aj$ $(1 \leq j \leq m)$ eine Kante $(Xi.A_j, Xi.B)$ von $xi.Aj$ nach $xi.B$.

Die Attribute aus PL und aus den Selektionstermen in SL heißen *sichtbar*. Die Attribute der Jointerme aus JL, die die Verbindungen zwischen den beteiligten Relationen herstellen und die nicht sichtbar sind, heißen *innere* Attribute. Sichtbare Attribute werden durch o dargestellt, innere Attribute durch •, und die Attribute und qualifizierenden Konstanten der Benutzersicht durch □.

5 Update-Übersetzung anhand der aktuellen Benutzersicht

Beispiel 2
(a) Ben: "Zeige mir den Wohnungstyp und das Stadtviertel von jeder Aachener Wohnung!"

Semantische Analyse:
$PL = [X0.WNR, X1.BEZEICHNUNG, X2.NAME]$
$SL = [X0.ORT = "Aachen"]$
$JL = [X0.TYPNR = X1.TYPNR, X0.GNR = X2.GNR]$
$RL = [(WOHNUNG, X0), (WOHNUNGSTYP, X1), (WOHNGEBIET, X2)]$

PL, SL, JL sind die gefundenen Listen der Ausgabeattribute, Selektions- und Jointerme. Die Liste RL enthält die betroffenen Relationen des Datenbankschemas zusammen mit den intern benutzten Referenzvariablen.

Sichtabhängigkeitsgraph:

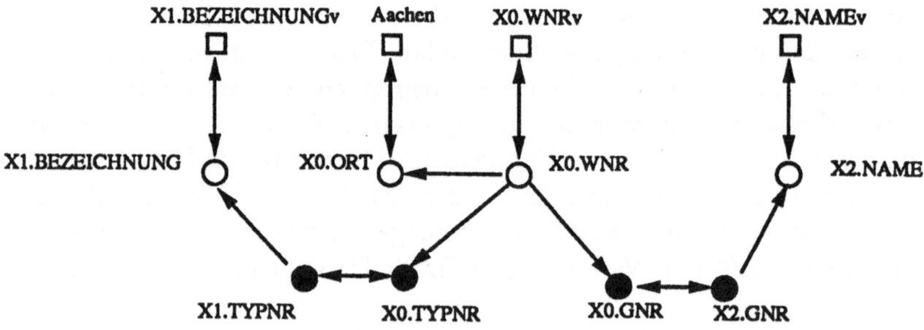

(b) Aktuelle Benutzersicht:

Sys:

WNR	BEZEICHNUNG	NAME	ORT
W1	Appartement	Burtscheid	Aachen
W5	Wohngemeinschaft	Horn	Aachen
W6	Appartement	Zentrum	Aachen

(c) "Entferne den Wohnungstyp Appartement im Stadtviertel Burtscheid!"

$PL = [X1.TYPNR]$
$SL = [X1.BEZEICHNUNG = "Appartement", X2.NAME = "Burtscheid"]$
$JL = [X0.TYPNR = X1.TYPNR, X0.GNR = X2.GNR]$
$RL = [(WOHNUNG, X0), (WOHNUNGSTYP, X1), (WOHNGEBIET, X2)]$

Das Ziel der Update-Äußerung ist das Löschen des Tupels ($W1$, *Appartement*, *Burtscheid*, *Aachen*) aus der Benutzersicht. Gesucht ist dabei eine Übersetzung, die den vom Benutzer gewünschten Update so exakt wie möglich ausführt. NATHAN bestimmt zunächst diejenigen der an der Benutzersicht beteiligten Relationen, deren Änderung zu einer Realisierung der Update-Äußerung führt. Im obigen Beispiel sind das die Relationen WOHNUNG und WOH-

NUNGSTYP. Anhand des Sichtabhängigkeitsgraphen läßt sich feststellen, ob eine Änderung in einer dieser Relationen zu einem Seiteneffekt führt. Der von uns verwendete Algorithmus, der in (Wings 90) vollständig beschrieben ist, benutzt dazu die vorhandenen funktionalen Abhängigkeiten, die im Sichtabhängigkeitsgraphen festgehalten werden. Im Gegensatz zu (Davidson 87) werden dabei auch Existenzabhängigkeiten berücksichtigt. Falls eine Realisierung ohne Seiteneffekt möglich ist, dann wird diese als die korrekte Übersetzung interpretiert. Andernfalls wird über eine Heuristik nach der Änderung mit dem "geringsten" Seiteneffekt gesucht. Die von NATHAN generierte, korrekte Übersetzung der natürlichsprachlichen Update-Äußerung in Beispiel 2(c) lautet wie folgt:

```
DELETE
FROM WOHNUNG X0
WHERE X0.ORT="Aachen" AND X0.WNR IN
(SELECT X0.WNR
FROM WOHNUNG X0, WOHNUNGSTYP X1, WOHNGEBIET X2
WHERE X1.BEZECHNUNG="Appartement" AND X2.NAME="Burtscheid" AND
X0.TYPNR=X1.TYPNR AND X0.GNR=X2.GNR);
```

Obwohl in der Update-Äußerung in Beispiel 2(c) der Wohnungstyp als Zielattribut erwähnt wurde, wird die Löschung realisiert, indem die Wohnung des entsprechenden Typs aus der Datenbank entfernt wird. Eine Elimination des Wohnungstyps Appartement hätte nämlich zur Folge gehabt, daß auch die Wohnung $W6$ in der aktuellen Benutzersicht verschwindet und ebenfalls alle anderen Wohnungen vom Typ Appartement, die für den Benutzer nicht sichtbar sind. Diese Seiteneffekte entsprechen aber nicht der explizit geäußerten Absicht des Benutzers.

Beispiel 3
(a) Ben: "Zeige alle Wohnungen des Vermieters V5!"

Semantische Analyse:
$PL = [X1.WNR]$
$SL = [X0.VNR = "V5"]$
$JL = [X0.VNR = X1.VNR]$
$RL = [(VERMIETER, X0), (WOHNUNG, X1)]$

Sichtabhängigkeitsgraph:

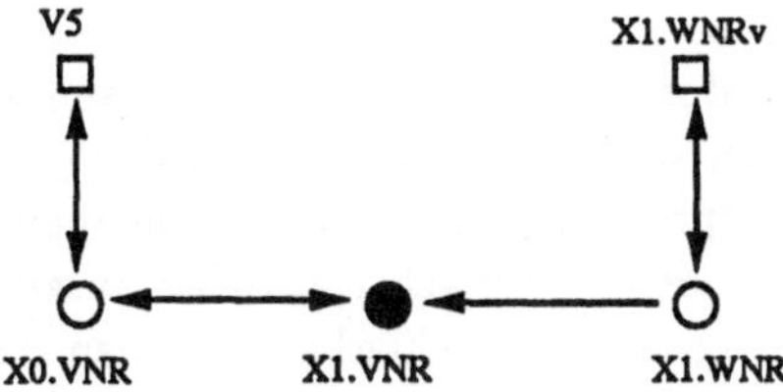

(b) Benutzersicht:

Sys:

WNR	VNR
W5	V5
W6	V5

(c) Ben: "Ersetze den Vermieter durch V6!"

$PL = [X0.VNR]$
$SL = []$
$JL = []$
$RL = [(VERMIETER, X0)]$

Das Ziel des Benutzeräußerung ist eine Änderung des Vermieterattributs in den Tupeln
$(W5, V5)$ und $(W6, V5)$. Diese Änderung kann aber erst dann ausgeführt werden, wenn der
Benutzer den neuen Vermieter $V6$ in die Relation VERMIETER eingetragen hat. Die weiteren Attributwerte des neuen Vermieters werden deshalb von NATHAN automatisch erfragt.
Die von NATHAN generierte, korrekte Update-Übersetzung lautet wie folgt:

```
UPDATE WOHNUNG
SET VNR="V6"
WHERE X1.VNR IN
(SELECT X1.VNR
FROM VERMIETER X0, WOHNUNG X1
WHERE X0.VNR="V5" AND X0.VNR=X1.VNR);
```

Man beachte, daß Wohnungen in der Benutzeräußerung gar nicht explizit erwähnt wurden. Trotzdem wird der Update realisiert, indem die Tupel in der Relation WOHNUNG
geändert werden. Auch hier wird die aktuelle Sicht dazu benutzt, um den vom Benutzer
gewünschten Update so exakt wie möglich zu realisieren. Eine Änderung des Attributs VNR
in der Relation VERMIETER würde nämlich zu einem unerwünschten Seiteneffekt führen,
der sogar außerhalb der Benutzersicht liegt.

6   Erweiterung von NATHAN

Die freie Formulierbarkeit von Updates wird vorerst eingeschränkt, da Äußerungen wie Beispiel 4 zu bisher unbekannten Problemen für die Analysekomponente von NATHAN führen.

Beispiel 4
Ben: "Die Wohnung W1 bekommt einen neuen Vermieter zugeordnet."

Zwar ist NATHAN sehr wohl in der Lage, Diskontinuitäten wie in dem obigen Verbkomplex "zugeordnet bekommen" zu verarbeiten, hier tritt jedoch eine *pragmatische Ambiguität*
auf, die bei der bisherigen Interpretation von Benutzereingaben durch SQL-Anfragen keine
Rolle spielte. Der Verbkomplex deutet zunächst auf eine auszuführende Update-Operation
hin. Es ist jedoch nicht eindeutig, ob es sich hierbei um einen Änderungs- oder Einfügungs-
wunsch des Benutzers handelt. Eine Interpretation als Änderung würde eine Rückfrage
nach dem Namen bzw. nach der Vermieternummer erfordern. Bei einer Einfügung muß
gewährleistet sein, daß der neue Vermieter auch in der Relation VERMIETER vorhanden
ist. Das System hat dafür Sorge zu tragen, daß die Integrität der Datenbank gewährleistet
bleibt.

Die bereits implementierten Syntax- und Semantikanalysekomponenten von NATHAN reichen jedoch völlig aus, wenn man die Formulierungsmöglichkeiten für natürlichsprachliche Updates gezielt einschränkt. Aufgrund von Lexikoninformationen kann zunächst entschieden werden, ob eine Anfrage- oder Update-Äußerung vorliegt. Im anwendungsunabhängigen Teil des Lexikons wird eine vom Umfang her restringierte, jedoch aus pragmatischer Sicht eindeutige Sub-Klasse von Verben eingeführt, die eine Interpretation als Update indizieren. Wir verwenden momentan "löschen", "streichen", "entfernen", "eintragen", "einfügen", "ersetzen" und "ändern". Die dazu benötigten Erweiterungen von NATHAN lassen sich leicht implementieren, so daß die schnelle Transportierbarkeit unseres Systems erhalten bleibt (Wings 90).

7 Schlußbemerkungen

Mit diesem Ansatz wurde die natürlichsprachliche Datenbank-Schnittstelle NATHAN um eine Update-Komponente erweitert. Dadurch wird ein Benutzer, der zwar Entscheidungskompetenz besitzt und dem bisher die Kenntnisse formaler Methoden fehlten, in die Lage versetzt, im beschränkten Rahmen Manipulationen an der Datenbank vorzunehmen. Die hier skizzierte Komponente unterstützt neben dem Löschen und Ändern von Einträgen auch das Einfügen von einzelnen Entitäten (Wings 90).

Die Benutzersicht, die momentan vom System manipuliert werden kann, läßt sich mit Hilfe von Selektions- und Jointermen beschreiben. Dabei wird die linguistische Überdeckung der Anfragekomponente von NATHAN (Noack 89b) noch nicht vollständig ausgenutzt. Die Anfragekomponente allein interpretiert auch quantifizierende Informationen, wie sie als Denotate von Determinatoren und Negationspartikeln, die sich nicht durch *konjunktive Anfragen* darstellen lassen, gegeben sind. Diese Aspekte sind in der von uns verwendeten Theorie der View-Updates noch nicht ausreichend theoretisch verankert. Deshalb beschränkten wir uns zunächst auf einfache Benutzersichten und deren Updates.

Zur Verbesserung der Dialogfähigkeiten von NATHAN soll in Zukunft eine freiere Formulierbarkeit von natürlichsprachlichen Updates ermöglicht werden, indem update-indizierende Verben über eine lernende Akquisitionskomponente erfaßt werden. NATHAN ist dann so zu erweitern, daß auch die bisher ausgeschlossenen pragmatischen Ambiguitäten behandelt werden können.

Die Realisierung eines Vorerwähntheitsgedächtnisses mit Hilfe von *Sichtabhängigkeitsgraphen* kann auch bei der Auflösung von Ellipsen und anaphorischen Referenzen eingesetzt werden, wie das abschließende Beispiel 5 erläutert.

Beispiel 5
(a) Ben: "Liste alle Wohnungen in Aachen auf."

$$PL = [X0.WNR]$$
$$SL = [X0.ORT = "Aachen"]$$
$$JL = []$$
$$RL = [(WOHNUNG, X0)]$$

(b) Benutzersicht:
Sys:

WNR	ORT
W1	Aachen
W5	Aachen
W6	Aachen

(c) Ben: "Welche haben eine Kaltmiete, die höher als 300 DM ist?"

Da das Attribut X0.WNR in der aktuellen Benutzersicht als Fokus festgehalten ist und eine syntaktische Kongruenz von "Wohnungen" zu "welche" vorliegt, kann angenommen werden, daß der Benutzer immer noch die Antworttupel in (b) fokussiert. Die entsprechende SQL-Interpretation lautet daher:

```
SELECT X0.WNR
FROM WOHNUNG X0
WHERE X0.ORT="Aachen" AND X0.KALTMIETE > 300.0;
```

(d) Ben: "Lösche sie."

Da sich der Fokus immer noch nicht geändert hat, ergibt sich für die Update-Äußerung nach Auflösung der anaphorischen Referenz, die sich hier auf ein Attribut der aktuellen Benutzersicht bezieht, folgende Interpretation:

```
DELETE
FROM WOHNUNG
WHERE ORT="Aachen" AND KALTMIETE > 300.0;
```

Erst wenn eine Anfrage gestellt worden ist, die neue oder neu qualifizierte Zielattribute einführt, muß eine neue Benutzersicht generiert werden.

8 Literatur

Davidson, J.E. (1987): Interpreting Natural Language Database Updates, Report CS-87-1152, Department of Computer Science, Stanford University

Dayal, U., P.A. Bernstein (1982): On the Correct Translation of Update Operations on Relational Views, ACM Transactions on Database Systems 8 (3), 381–416

Noack, J. (1989a): Kontextdisambiguierung in natürlichsprachlichen Anfragen an relationale Datenbanken, in H. Burkhardt, K.H. Höhne, B. Neumann (Hrsg.): Mustererkennung 1989, IFB 219, Springer Verlag, 512–517

Noack, J. (1989b): NATHAN: Ein transportables Front-End zur Interpretation deutschsprachiger Anfragen an ein relationales Datenbanksystem, Dissertation, RWTH Aachen

Noack, J. (1990): Die Behandlung von semantisch unvollständigen Anfragen in einer transportablen natürlichsprachlichen Datenbank-Schnittstelle, in H. Marburger (Hrsg.): GWAI 1990, IFB 251, Springer Verlag, 221 - 230

Rich, E. (1989): Stereotypes and User Modelling, in W. Wahlster, A. Kobsa (eds.): User Models in Dialog Systems, Springer Verlag, Berlin, 35–51

Salveter, S. (1984): A Transportable Natural Language Database Update System, ACM SIGACT-SIGMOD Symposium on Principles of Database Systems, 239–247

Vossen, G. (1991): Data Models, Database Languages and Database Management Systems, Addison Wesley, Wokingham, England

Wahlster, W., A. Kobsa (1989): User Models in Dialog Systems, in W. Wahlster, A. Kobsa (eds.): User Models in Dialog Systems, Springer Verlag, Berlin, 4–34

Wings, J. (1990): Übersetzung natürlichsprachlicher Datenbank-Updates durch Sichtabhängigkeitsgraphen, Diplomarbeit, RWTH Aachen

A   Wohnungsmarkt-Datenbank

WOHNGEBIET:

GNR	NAME	BEWERTUNG
G1	Burtscheid	1a
G2	Kullen	1b
G3	Zentrum	1c
G4	Frankenbergerviertel	1d
G5	Hörn	1e

WOHNUNG:

WNR	TNR	VNR	GNR	STRASSE	HAUSNR	PLZ	ORT	FLAECHE	KALTMIETE	NEBENKOSTEN
W1	T1	V2	G1	Vaalserstr.	150a	5100	Aachen	42	280.00	70.00
W2	T1	V2	G2	Kastanienweg	4	5300	Bonn	105	300.00	100.00
W3	T3	V3	G1	Hauptstr.	1	5000	Köln	33	500.00	150.00
W4	T4	V4	G4	Robbenstr.	3	5300	Bonn	24	400.00	90.00
W5	T4	V5	G5	Ahornstr.	55	5100	Aachen	200	950.00	500.00
W6	T1	V5	G3	Mauerstr.	24	5100	Aachen	100	450.00	200.00

VERMIETER:

VNR	VNAME	STRASSE	HAUSNR	PLZ	ORT
V1	Itani	Schurzelterstr.	549	5100	Aachen
V2	Oezer	Schurzelterstr.	549	5300	Bonn
V3	Hemmelrath	Schurzelterstr.	553	5000	Köln
V4	Noack	Oppenhoffallee	75	5100	Aachen
V5	Wings	Heuvel	77	6291	Vaals

WOHNUNGSTYP:

TYPNR	BEZEICHNUNG
T1	Appartement
T2	Studio
T3	Einzelzimmer
T4	Wohngemeinschaft

The Morphological Principle

A Proposal for Treating Russian Morphology
within an HPSG Framework

Renate Henschel
Zentralinstitut für Sprachwissenschaft
Prenzlauer Promenade 149, O-1071 Berlin

Abstract

In this paper a new declarative approach for treating morphology is proposed. Inflectional morphology is integrated in the uniform HPSG grammar representation formalism using principles, rules and a lexicon. Lexical rules are not necessary furthermore, because they are replaced by a new principle and new types of lexicon entries. This enables us to give up an extra implementation for lexical rules. The main exemplification is taken from Russian verb and noun inflection, where a remarkable removal of redundancy is achieved.

1. Introduction

Universal principles, grammar rules, lexical rules and lexical entries can be considered as the four substantial components of the HPSG framework. A grammar can be represented by unification/disjunction of universal principles, grammar rules and lexical entries. This approach has gained attractivity in that only one unified formalism is able to solve parsing and generation tasks, and to handle syntax and semantics with the same formal account. The lexical rules have a distinguished character. They serve to provide the full-form lexicon from ground forms. This requires the implementation of an extra module.

In this paper a first step is made to integrate the work done by lexical rules into the uniform grammar formalism, so that no separate module will be necessary furthermore. To achieve this, lexical rules are eliminated and substituted by a new principle and new types of lexical entries. This is carried out for inflectional lexical rules. The main exemplification is taken from Russian. Besides saving the lexicon expansion module, a remarkable removal of redundancy what is to be found in the traditional inflection paradigms of Russian can be achieved.

2. HPSG - an overview

In this paper I refer to HPSG as published in [POLLARD 1987] with some revisions from later drafts. HPSG uses as its representation of linguistic objects typed feature structures, which are partially ordered in a subsumption lattice with unification as the lattice meet and disjunction as the lattice join. The types themselves are ordered in a subsumption lattice - the inheritance hierarchy.

HPSG distinguishes two major types, the lexical-sign denoting word forms with their linguistic properties as they are written in a full-form lexicon, and the phrasal-sign coding the tree structure of phrases:

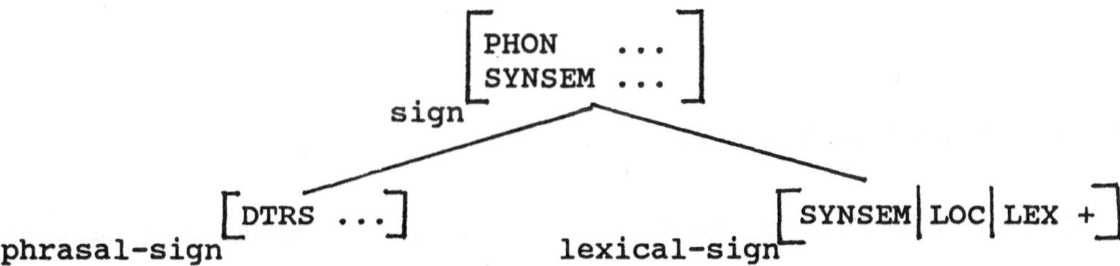

Here PHON bears as value an inflected word form in the case of a lexical-sign and a list of word forms in the case of a phrasal-sign. Phrasal signs represent phrase structure trees, the terminal nodes of which are lexical signs. Phrasal signs are constructed out of lexical signs according to the SUBCATegorization Principle:

$$(1) \quad \begin{bmatrix} \text{SYNSEM} \mid \text{LOC} \mid \text{SUBCAT} \; \boxed{1} \\ \text{DTRS} \; \begin{bmatrix} \text{HEAD-DTR} \mid \text{SYNSEM} \mid \text{LOC} \mid \text{SUBCAT} \; (\text{append} \; \boxed{1} \; \boxed{2}) \\ \text{COMP-DTRS} \; \boxed{2} \end{bmatrix} \end{bmatrix}_{\text{headed-structure}}$$

$\boxed{1}$ and $\boxed{2}$ are lists of signs (lexical or phrasal). Besides the SUBCAT-Principle P_1, HPSG posits other language-universal principles $P_2 \ldots P_m$ (e.g. the Head-Feature Principle and the Semantics Principle). A grammar then can be described with the help of only one datatype, the feature structure, and two operations, unification and disjunction, operating on feature structures:

$$(2) \quad G = P_1 \cap \ldots P_m \cap (P_{m+1} \cap \ldots P_n) \cap (R_1 \cup \ldots R_\ell \cup L_1 \cup \ldots L_q).$$

Here $R_1 \ldots R_\ell$ are language dependent grammar rules, $P_{m+1} \ldots P_n$ language specific principles and $L_1 \ldots L_q$ lexical entries of a full-form lexicon of this language.

3. Treatment of Morphology within HPSG

To reduce the number of necessary lexical entries, the lexicon in HPSG is also organized in a type lattice: Much of the redundancy of lexical information can be eliminated by factoring out shared properties and defining a type for it. Some properties of a lexical sign can thus be inherited by the subsumption relation from defined more general types. POLLARD and SAG call this elimination of "vertical" redundancy. But the lexicon still contains massive horizontal redundancy: inflectional paradigms, derivational relationships, polyvalency patterns. This kind of redundancy is handled with the help of lexical rules. The lexicon type hierarchy consisting of base forms is viewed as input domain for rules which output the whole range of a full-form lexicon. Hence lexical rules have a distinguished status and need another treatment than the type controlled unification formalism.

4. The Morphological Principle

To handle inflectional morphology within the grammar framework in the same way as syntactic and semantic composition as in formula (2), I propose in this paper a new treatment of inflection without using lexical rules, but by vertical type inheritance. This is not only of interest from a formalistic point of view, but also provides an elegant redundancy-free representation of morphology as a type lattice for languages with rich inflection.

We introduce new types of signs, the inflected sign and the stem and the suffix sign:

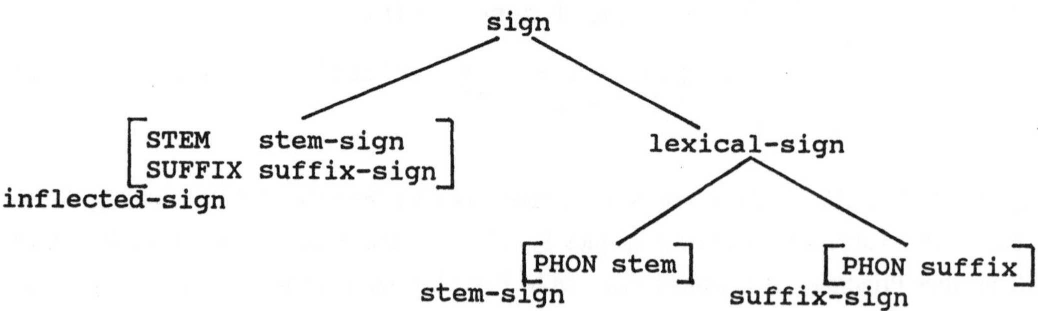

Phrases consist of inflected signs. Lexical signs now denote the entries of a stem lexicon, not a full-form lexicon as previously. The relation between them and inflected signs is organized by a new posited principle:

(3)   M O R P H O L O G I C A L PRINCIPLE

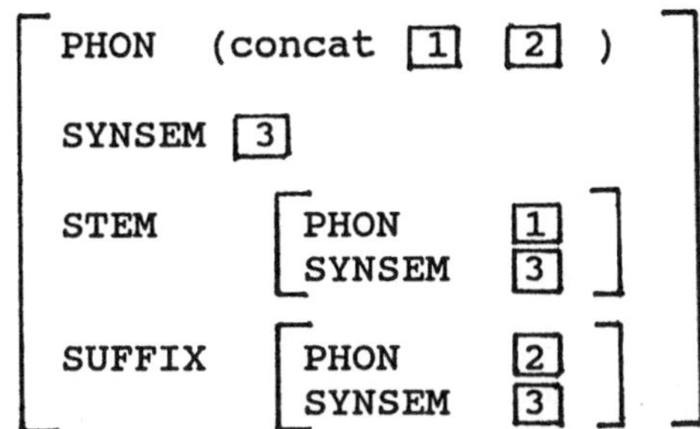

`inflected-sign`

The information of a lexical sign of the POLLARD & SAG type is split up into stem relevant information and inflectional information. The stem contains the features category, gender, subcategorization, etc. The suffix consists of all grammatical properties that are expressed by inflectional endings, in Russian case and number for nouns, number, person and tense for verbs. Some features play the role of a glue between stems and suffixes. That ensures the right unification. The function "concat" is a language dependent one (It does not fit for arabian-semitic languages or languages with vowel harmony).

As we will see in the next section, we avoid the special "horizontal" treatment of lexical entries by lexical rules. The grammar description (2) is changed to

$$(4) \quad G = P_1 \cap \ldots P_m \cap (MP \cap P_{m+1} \ldots P_n) \cap (R_1 \cup \ldots R_\ell \cup L_1 \ldots L_q \cup S_1 \ldots S_k)$$

```
     MP - Morphological Principle
     S₁...Sₖ   - Suffixes
```

Lexical rules concerning inflectional derivation are not necessary furthermore. Lexical rules of other kind are not included in this consideration until now.

5. Type Hierarchy for Russian Morphology

5.1. Nouns

Nominal inflection in Russian is highly systematic. The relevant features to distinguish are gender, number, case, animateness, which are all features embedded in the SYNSEM structure. The suffix type can be divided into different kinds of subtypes with regard to gender, number, case, animateness and phonology. Gender, number, case and animateness are freely combinable. But the combination with the PHON feature introduces serious

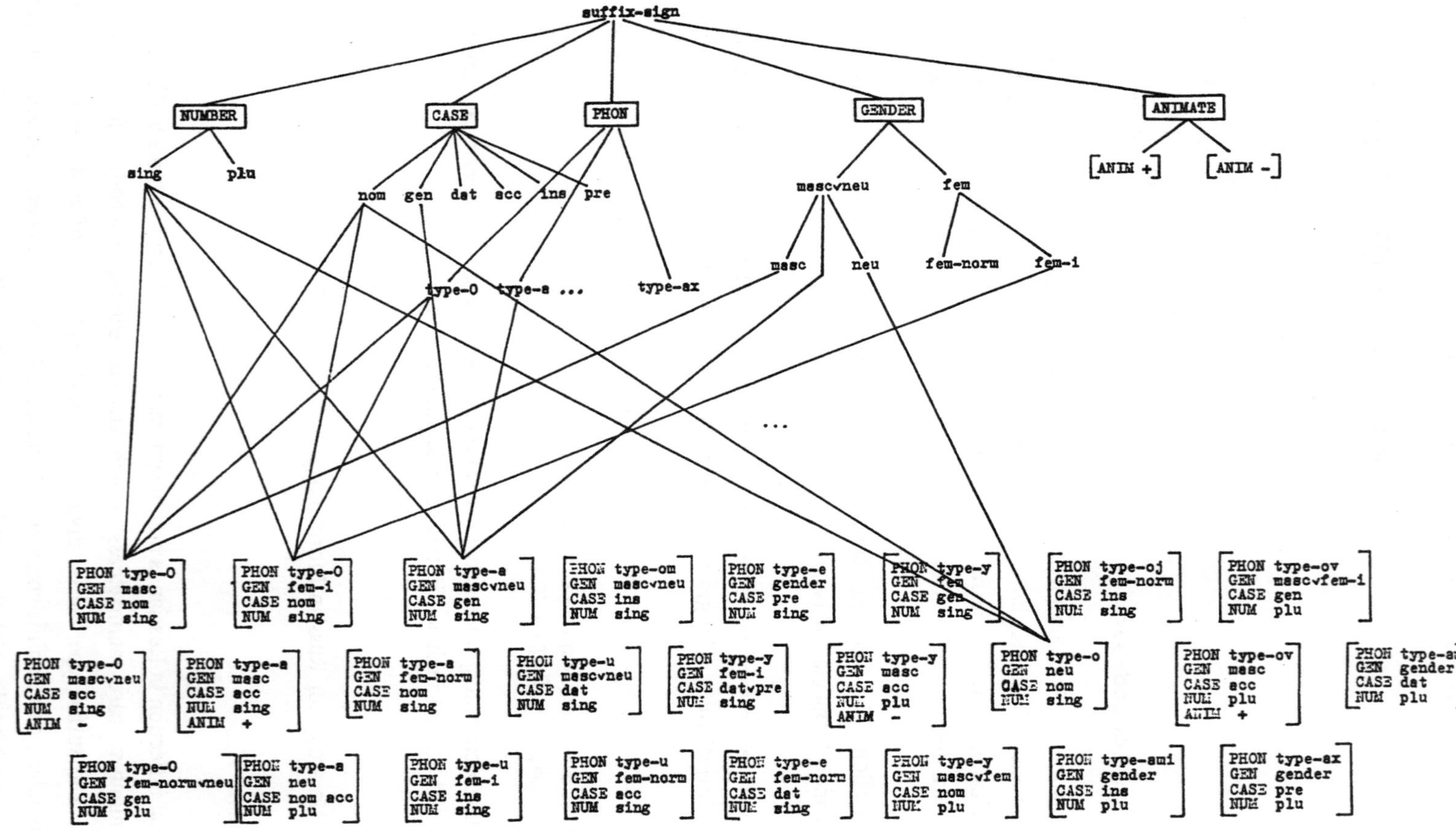

Figure 1:   Lexical hierarchy of nominal suffix signs

constraints. There are then 25 minimal elements in the suffix type lexical hierarchy, which provide the appropriate constraints for Russian noun inflection (see figure 1). For simplicity all relevant features are written here at top level, even if they are deeper embedded in the actual implementation. They represent 17 declension paradigms at 6x2 inflectional endings each taken from our earlier treatment of Russian sentence generation within the VIRTEX MT system [BUSCHBECK et al. 1990].

With regard to the PHON feature, the suffix type has 12 subtypes. The actual phonological realization of them depends further on phonological properties. Here the last character (LC) of the stem and information about the paradigm type (PARA) - in Russian we distinguish the "hard" and the "soft" declension paradigm - are taken into account. For that reason, the PHON feature is split into

```
                    ┌                              ┐
                    │       ┌ SUFFIX     suffix   ┐ │
                    │ PHON  │ PARA       binary   │ │
                    │       │ LAST-CHAR  character │ │
                    │       └                     ┘ │
     suffix-sign    └                              ┘
```

An interesting part of the suffix-PHON-type hierarchy is shown in figure 2.

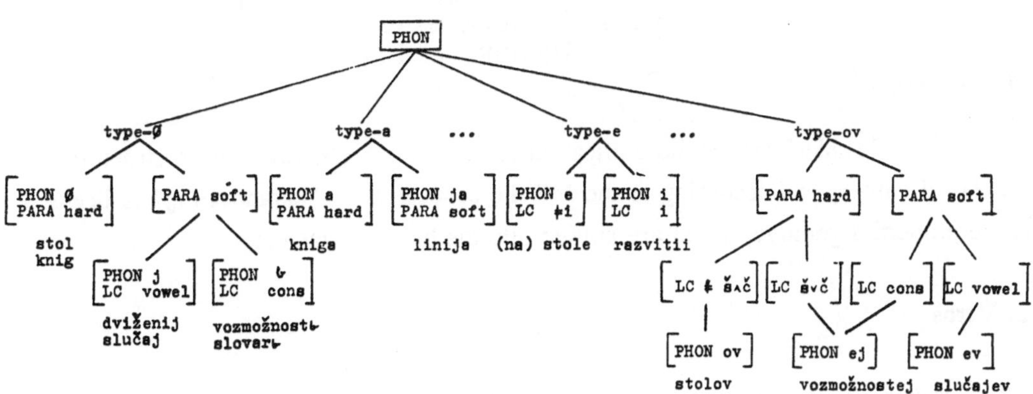

Figure 2:   Suffix types for Russian nouns

This has to be incorporated in the Morphological Principle as follows:

(5)

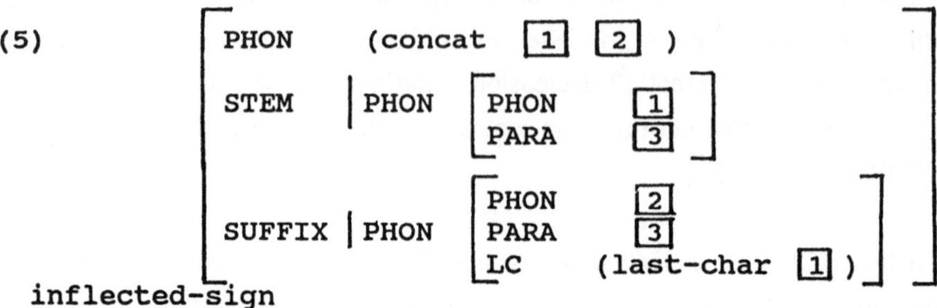

As an example let us consider the lexical entries for the noun "karandaš" and the suffix-type "ov":

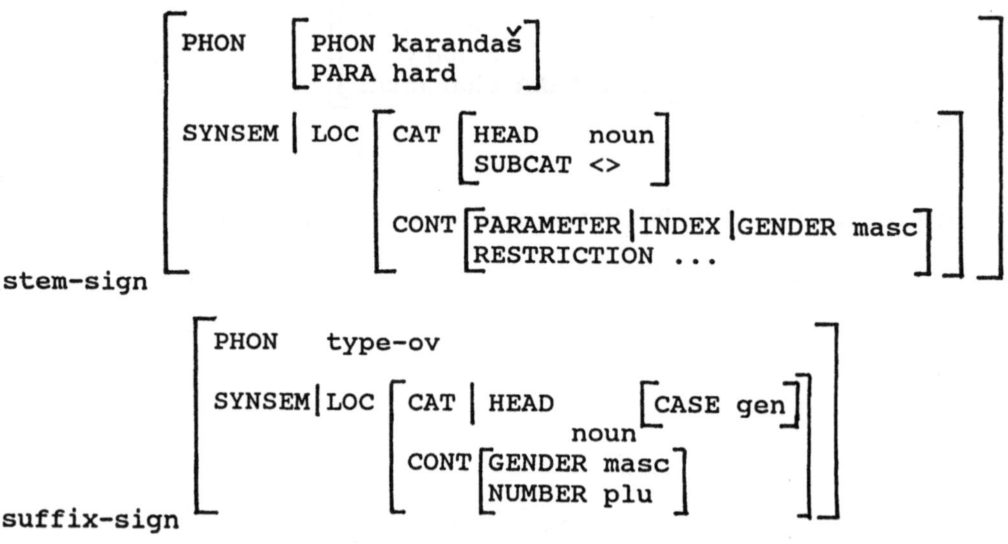

The glue item "gender" causes the unification between the SYNSEM feature structures of both lexical entries, and according to the MP the concatenation "karandaš+ej" is licensed and the properties genitive, plural are unified into the built inflected-sign.

5.2. Verbs

The paradigms of Russian verb inflection are not as systematic as of noun declension. E.g. we have to take into account special information about a phonem substitution at the end of the stem. This is done here by a suffix-controlled insertion of a string (the so-called quasi-suffixes Q-S-1 or Q-S-2), which has to be given in the stem sign. How this can be organized, is shown in a more complex version of the Morphological Principle below:

(6)

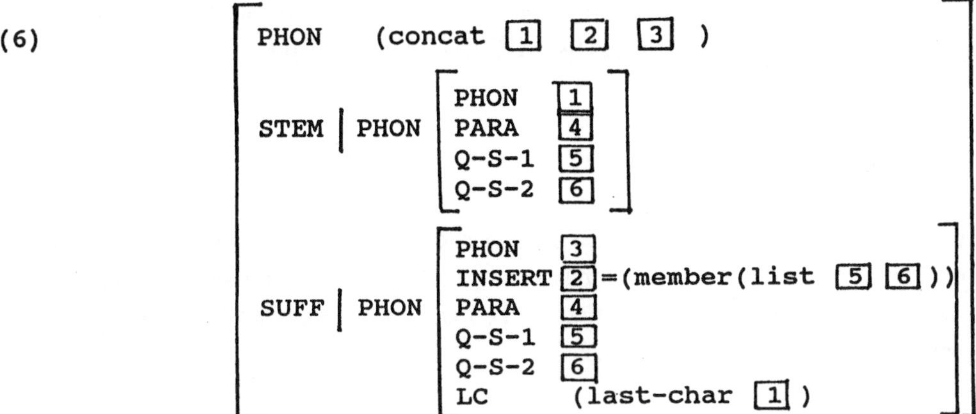

inflected-sign

In addition to that, the traditional conjugation type is a relevant stem feature (represented with attribute PARA, values i or e). The inflected verb features, which are expressed by suffixation, are gender, number in the case of past tense, and person and number in the case of present tense. Figure 3 shows the mutual constraints of them.

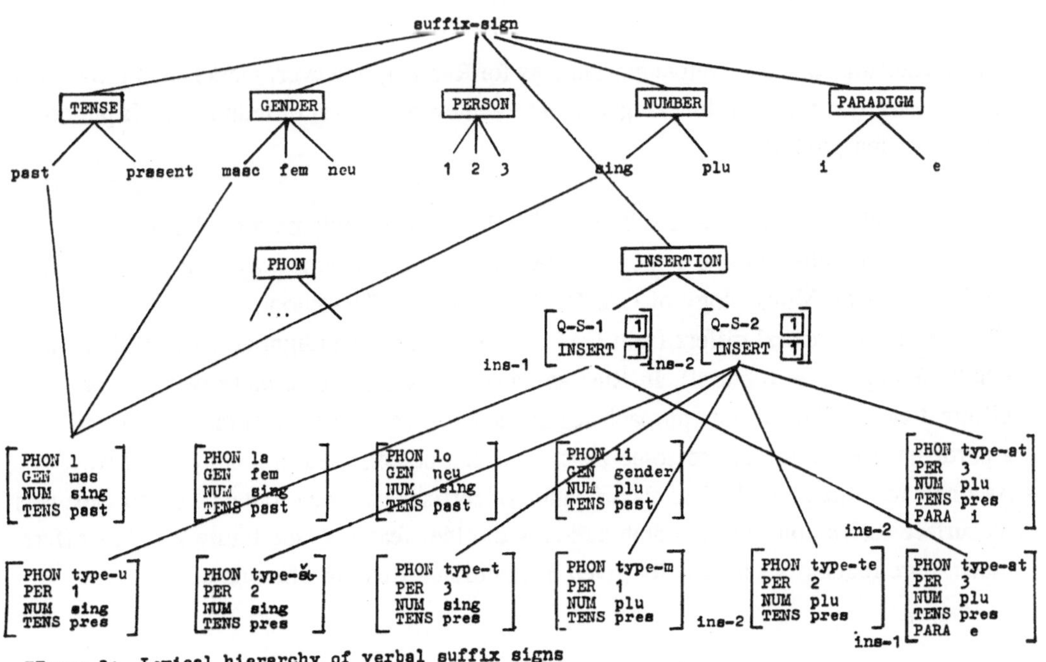

Figure 3: Lexical hierarchy of verbal suffix signs

The presented inflection type lattices are implemented using the TFS software developed by EMELE and ZAJAC (cf. [EMELE/ZAJAC 1990], [ZAJAC 1991]).

6. Conclusion

In the proposed treatment of inflection some phenomena are left for further investigation. The problem of o-insertion and -deletion in noun paradigms may be possibly managed in the same way as the insertion of quasi-suffixes. The handling of irregularities is not integrated until now.

The proposal of a declarative approach to morphology is not, in itself, new. It is closely related to Paradigmatic Morphology [CALDER 1989], the DATR-formalism developed by [EVANS/GAZDAR 1990] and the Prosodic Inheritance model of [REINHARD/GIBBON 1991].These are pure lexicon handling models and lack an integration into grammatical parsing/generation formalisms. Certain attempts have been made to combine DATR and PATR [KILBURY 1991], but this requires a conversion procedure from one framework to the other and vice versa. The combination of two different formalisms is not as elegant as the integration of the lexical component into the grammatical component, by only using the means of the latter. The current proposal has the above mentioned advantage that neither a full-form lexicon nor an extra module for lexicon expansion (the lexical rules) are necessary furthermore. The treatment of morphology is done by identical formal means as the treatment of syntax and semantics in the grammar. A similar approach for Japanese is to be found in [WHITELOCK 1987].

The formulation of a declarative morphology for Russian, however, marks an improvement over previous treatments for that language. The achieved removal of redundancy is put down to the following properties:

- The introduction of super- and subtypes of inflectional paradigms provides the for inheritance formalisms usual removal of redundancy in the same way as it is proposed in the Paradigmatic Morphology of CALDER or in the DATR-school.
- The presented proposal differs from CALDER's in that a paradigm is not considered as a whole (6 singular + 6 plural). In Russian some suffixes serve to mark two or more different cases. The current approach regards suffixes independent from their affiliation to a particular paradigm, and so some constraints can be collected in a convenient way.
- As a new result, a phonological classification of suffixes has been found. A suffix type gets its surface realization only in combination with other features (see figure 2). This offers much more regularities as usually given in traditional Russian grammars.

Acknowledgement

I would like to thank the VIRTEX group, especially Gerda Klimonow, for the contribution of the Russian data and clarifying discussions.

References

[BUSCHBECK et al. 1990] B.Buschbeck, R.Henschel, I.Höser, G.Klimonow, A.Küstner, I.Starke: VIRTEX - a German-Russian Translation Experiment. In: Proceedings of COLING 1990, Helsinki.

[CALDER 1989] Jonathan Calder: Paradigmatic Morphology. In: Proceedings of EACL 1989, Manchester.

[EMELE/ZAJAC 1990] Typed Unification Grammars. In: Proceedings of COLING 1990, Helsinki.

[EVANS/GAZDAR 1990] Roger Evans & Gerald Gazdar. The DATR Papers: February 1990. Cognitive Science Research Paper No. 139. University of Sussex.

[KILBURY 1991] James Kilbury, Petra Närger, Ingrid Renz: DATR as a lexical component for PATR. In: Proceedings of EACL, Berlin.

[POLLARD 1987] Carl Pollard & Ivan S. Sag: Information-based Syntax and Semantics. Volume 1: Fundamentals. CSLI Lecture Notes, Number 13, Stanford 1978.

[REINHARD/GIBBON 1991] Sabine Reinhard, Dafydd Gibbon: Prosodic Inheritance and Morphological Generalisations. In: Proceedings of EACL 1991, Berlin.

[WHITELOCK 1987] A Feature-Based Categorial Morpho-Syntax for Japanese. In: Uwe Reyle and Christian Rohrer (1987) Natural Language Parsing and Linguistic Theories. Reidel, Dordrecht.

[ZAJAC 1991] Remi Zajac. Notes on the Typed Feature System. Version 4 - January 1991. IMS Stuttgart.

Evaluation von Grammatiken für die Analyse natürlicher Sprache durch Generierung einer repräsentativen Satzmenge[1]

Karl Gregor Erbach
Roman Georg Arens
Universität des Saarlandes, FR 8.7 Computerlinguistik
Im Stadtwald, W-6600 Saarbrücken
e-mail: erbach / arens@coli.uni-sb.de

Abstract

Ein Mechanismus, um beliebige unifikationsbasierte Grammatiken dadurch zu evaluieren, daß Sätze, die von der in Frage stehenden Grammatik beschrieben werden, generiert werden und so zu einer Überprüfung zur Verfügung stehen.

1 Motivation

Wird in einem NL-Projekt eine Grammatik geschrieben, so dient im Allgemeinen eine Menge von Testsätzen dazu, diese zu evaluieren. Sicherzustellen ist so die Vollständigkeit, nicht aber die Korrektheit: Ein Übergenerieren kann im allgemeinen nicht ausgeschlossen werden. Zu diesem Zweck wird dem Grammatikentwickler ein Generator als Werkzeug zur Verfügung gestellt. Dessen Ausgaben werden hier als Sätze bezeichnet, können aber auch beliebige andere Strukturen (z.B. NP's) sein. Die Unterscheidung zwischen akzeptablen und unerwünschten Sätzen muß allerdings manuell erfolgen.

2 Überlegungen zur Theorieunabhängigkeit

Welcher Theorie die zu prüfende Grammatik[2] folgt, ob es eine Kategorialgrammatik ist oder eine in der Art der HPSG konzipierte Grammatik, darf für den Generator keine Rolle spielen — ebensowenig (für manche Algorithmen unangenehme) Eigenschaften wie Links- oder Rechtsrekursion. ID/LP-Regeln werden gegenwärtig nicht unterstützt. Ansonsten muß der Generator jede Unifikationsgrammatik verarbeiten und soll dabei nicht bei einer *hinterlistigen Nominalphrase,* einer *hinterlistigen, hinterlistigen Nominalphrase* oder gar einer *hinterlistigen, hinterlistigen, hinterlistigen Nominalphrase* hängenbleiben. Es scheint nahezuliegen, solche Konstruktionen auszuschließen und es stellt sich die Frage, wie dies zu bewerkstelligen ist. Denn die mehrfache Anwendung der gleichen Regel darf keineswegs ausgeschlossen werden, da sonst beispielsweise Kategorialgrammatiken, bei denen (idealerweise) die funktionale Applikation die einzige Regel ist, nicht angewendet werden können.

---

[1] Die Arbeit ist im Rahmen des LILOG-Projektes der IBM Deutschland GmbH entstanden.

[2] Es wird eine Unifikationsgrammatik verlangt, die in STUF (Bouma et al. 1988) notiert ist. Der Generator ist in Prolog geschrieben und verwendet den Abstrakten Datentyp von STUF (STUFADT). Andere Teile der LILOG-Entwicklungsumgebung (LEU2) werden nicht verwendet.

Entgegen dem ersten Eindruck dürfen die obigen Beispiele jedoch tatsächlich nicht ausgeschlossen werden, da sonst die Aufgabe des Generators nicht gewährleistet wäre. Es ist die Aufgabe der Grammatik und nicht des Generators, unsinnige Phrasen auszuschließen. Auch ist es nicht Aufgabe des Generators, festzustellen, ob und wie eine Grammatik sich effizient parsen läßt, vielmehr soll der Generator jede gegebene Grammatik möglichst effizient verarbeiten.

Die oben genannten Beispiele müssen also generiert werden, aber eben nicht nur diese, sondern auch die Repräsentanten für Sätze, die nicht dem Muster Adjektiv* + Nomen entsprechen. Die Reihenfolge der Generierung wird daher so geregelt, daß zunächst alle satzwertigen oder nicht satzwertigen Strukuren generiert werden, die aus einem Wort bestehen, danach diejenigen aus zwei Wörtern und so fort. Lexikon und Regelmenge sind endlich.

Dieses Vorgehen bedingt, daß lange Sätze erst spät generiert werden, auch wenn sie wegen linguistischer Interessantheit möglichst früh gewünscht werden. Einerseits jedoch bestehen lange Sätze aus kürzeren Strukturen, die zuvor erzeugt werden müssen, andererseits gibt es auch keinen Algorithmus, der bestimmt, ob eine Wortkette ein interessantes Phänomen darstellt; insbesondere, wenn nicht einmal die Art der verwendeten Grammatik bekannt ist.

Ein Problem dieses Verfahrens sind Regeln, die auf der rechten Seite nur ein Element verlangen. Diese vergrößern die Anzahl der überspannten Wörter nicht, so daß es zu einer endlosen Rekursion kommen kann. Diese Regeln werden deswegen separiert und ihre Anwendung mit einem Test auf zyklische Strukturen verbunden. Ist der Test erfolgreich, so wird der betroffene Generierungspfad nicht weiter verfolgt und eine Warnung ausgegeben, da in diesem Falle möglicherweise nicht alle analysierbaren Strukturen erzeugt werden.

3 Abwägungen zu Rechenzeit und Speicherbedarf

Nicht nur Rechenzeit und Speicherplatz wachsen exponential,[3] sondern auch die Größe des Ergebnisses. Um die Anzahl der ausgegebenen Sätze in einer handhabbaren Größenordnung zu halten, müssen die Wortmenge, die Regelmenge und die Satzlänge stark eingeschränkt werden. Sinnvoll erscheint es, jeder vermuteten Klasse von lexikalischen Einträgen nur einen Vertreter im Lexikon zuzugestehen. Allerdings hängt es stark sowohl von der (natürlichen) Sprache als auch von der (Feinheit der) Grammatik ab, ob zum Beispiel bestimmte Artikel Dativ Femininum Singular und bestimmte Artikel Genitiv Femininum Singular derselben Klasse obiger Art angehören oder nicht.

Unabhängig von den obigen Überlegungen, die sich auf die Anwendung des Generators beziehen, ist die Designentscheidung zu treffen, ob der Generator bezüglich Rechenzeit oder Speicherbedarf optimiert sein soll. Einmal errechnete Strukturen werden nicht verworfen, sondern im Speicher gehalten und bei Bedarf in größeren Strukturen wiederverwendet. Grundsätzlich gibt es die Möglichkeit, die Merkmalstruktur selbst zu speichern (kürzere Rechenzeit) oder nur eine Beschreibung, wie die Merkmalstruktur erzeugt wird. Per Default werden nur rekursive Beschreibungen der Merkmalstrukturen abgespeichert. Wenn genug Speicherplatz vorhanden ist, können häufig benutzte Merkmalstrukturen aber auch in expandierter Form gespeichert werden.

4 Funktion des Programms

Eine Möglichkeit der Realisierung ist ein Parser, der mit einer unterdeterminierten Eingabe versorgt wird. Einen solchen Chart-Parser, der analysiert und generiert, beschreibt Erbach 1991. Hier wurde jedoch ein reiner Generator realisiert, der nicht parsen kann. Der Generator ähnelt in einigen Punkten

---

[3]Exponential zur Länge der ausgegebenen Sätze! Lexikon und Grammatik sind konstant, eine Eingabe (bei einem Generator klassischerweise eine semantische Beschreibung) gibt es nicht. Oder um es mit einem Witz zu sagen: Der Generator erzeugt in unendlicher Zeit mit unendlichem Speicher unendlich viele Sätze. Ergo ist er effizient.

einem Earley-Parser, kennt jedoch nur passive Items. Der für Analyse nötige Overhead (Position einer abgeleiteten Teilstruktur in der Eingabe) wird eingespart.

Nach Laden des Generators arbeitet dieser zunächst auf der ganzen Grammatik und dem ganzen Lexikon. Der Generator stellt Funktionen zur Verfügung, um bestimmte Wörter und Regeln aus vorhandenem Lexikon und Grammatik zu erlauben oder auszuschließen.

```
allow_word( +Wort_als_PrologAtom ).        forget_word( +Wort_als_PrologAtom ).
allow_rule( +Regelname_als_PrologAtom ).   forget_rule( +Regelname_als_PrologAtom ).
```

Zunächst ist das ganze Lexikon und Grammatik für den Generator verfügbar. Nach erstmaliger Verwendung einer der Funktionen wird nur noch die Teilmenge der explizit erlaubten Wörter und Regeln berücksichtigt. Einige Beispiele für Aufrufe und die jeweils resultierende Datenstruktur:

```
allow_word( die ).                         a_word( die ).
allow_rule( 'SLASH_INTRODUCTION' ).        rule_1( 'SLASH_INTRODUCTION' ).
allow_rule( 'LEFT_COMPLEMENTATION1' ).     a_rule( 'LEFT_COMPLEMENTATION1' ).
```

Die Regeln liegen nicht in einer Normalform vor. SLASH_INTRODUCTION ist unär, die andere Beispielregel ist nicht unär. Wird die Generierung angestoßen, so prüft der Generator, bis zu welcher Länge bereits Strukturen generiert wurden und erzeugt dann die um ein Wort längeren. Im Anschluß werden die jeweils nächstlängeren Strukturen aufgebaut, bis gegebenenfalls eine zuvor vorgegebene Abbruchlänge erreicht wird. Die Ergebnisse werden in Beschreibungsstrukturen abgespeichert, die die Länge einer (auch unvollständigen) Phrase in Wörtern, eine eindeutige Identifikation und eine Ableitungsbeschreibung enthalten. Beispiele sind:

```
beschreibungs_struktur( 1 , i1 , [ 'SLASH_INTRODUCTION' , ist ] ).
beschreibungs_struktur( 2 , i47 , [ 'LEFT_COMPLEMENTATION1' , geschehen , ist ] ).
beschreibungs_struktur( 2 , i48 , [ 'SLASH_INTRODUCTION' , i47 ] ).
beschreibungs_struktur( 2 , i49 , [ 'LEFT_COMPLEMENTATION1' , geschehen , i1 ] ).
beschreibungs_struktur( 4 , i213 , [ 'LEFT_COMPLEMENTATION1' , i53 , i47 ] ).
```

Das vierte Beispiel unterscheidet sich vom zweiten durch einen rekursiven Verweis auf die Struktur beschreibungs_struktur(_ , i1 , _) (das erste Beispiel). Soll die Rechenzeit verringert werden und steht genügend Speicherplatz zur Verfügung, so können häufig gebrauchte Beschreibungsstrukturen ermittelt und expandiert werden. Expandierte Beschreibungsstrukturen enthalten anstelle der Beschreibung die Merkmalstruktur.

Um die Strukturen der Länge n zu erzeugen, wird für jede der zugelassenen mehrstelligen Regeln versucht, diese auf alle Kombinationen aus zugelassenen lexikalischen Einträgen und (expandierten) Beschreibungsstrukturen anzuwenden, für die gilt, daß die Summe der Wörter, die sie enthalten, n ist. Ist ein Versuch erfolgreich, wird das Ergebnis als Beschreibungs-Struktur gespeichert. Dann wird geprüft, ob die Struktur die Satzbedingung erfüllt (d.h. ob das Startsymbol der Grammatik erreicht ist). Ist das der Fall, so wird die Wortfolge und eine Ableitungsbeschreibung ausgegeben. Außerdem wird versucht, jede unäre Regel auf die Struktur anzuwenden. Ist das möglich, wird die resultierende Struktur ebenfalls abgespeichert, auf die Satzbedingung getestet, gegebenenfalls ausgegeben und das gleiche Verfahren auch auf die resultierende Struktur angewendet. Allerdings wird ab diesem Punkt ein zusätzlicher Test vor dem Abspeichern einer weiteren Beschreibungs-Struktur ausgeführt: Wenn in einer ununterbrochenen Reihe von unären Regelanwendungen der gleiche Regelname zweimal benutzt wird, wird die Struktur zurückgewiesen und eine Warnung an den Benutzer ausgegeben, da nun nicht mehr garantiert werden kann, daß wirklich alle analysierbaren Sätze auch generiert werden.

Ein Sonderfall sind die Sätze und Strukturen (aus lexikalischen Regeln) der Länge eins, die überhaupt nur durch Anwendung einer unären Regel entstehen können. Um dies zu ermöglichen, wird bei der Generierung dieser Sätze der oben beschriebene Prozeß der Anwendung unärer Regeln auf alle erlaubten Lexikon-Einträge angewendet. Befinden sich im Lexikon Einträge, die bereits satzwertig sind, so erscheinen diese nicht in der Ausgabe.

5 Zusammenfassung und Ausblick

Um den Umfang der Ausgabe handhabbar zu halten, ist es unverzichtbar, die zu prüfende Grammatik auf ihre (unter einer bestimmten Problemstellung) interessanten Teile einzuschränken. Diese Einschränkung durchzuführen, ohne dabei auch die (unerwünschten) Effekte der Grammatik, die ja gerade erst durch den Generator gefunden werden sollen, auszuschließen, gerät leicht zu einem Glücksspiel. Daher kann das Programm vermutlich nur für einen erfahrenen Linguisten ein Hilfsmittel sein.

Der Generator erlaubt es jeweils nach der Vollendung der Sätze einer Länge, Veränderungen an den Einstellungen vorzunehmen. So können Beschreibungsstrukturen, die bis zu diesem Punkt besonders häufig verwendet wurden, expandiert werden, um die Rechenzeit zu verringern. Eine Erweiterung des Programms soll es auch erlauben, Strukturen, die sehr viel kürzer als die gegenwärtige Satzlänge sind und die nie verwendet wurden, zu löschen. Es ist jedoch auch möglich, an dieser Stelle Wörter oder Regeln zu erlauben oder zu verbieten. Der Zweck eines solchen manuellen Eingriffs in „die laufende Maschine" könnte sein, uninteressante Ergebnisse zu vermeiden. Die Gefahr, Inkonsistenzen zu verursachen und dadurch das Generierungsergebnis zu entwerten, ist jedoch enorm (das gilt auch für die Löschung von Strukturen).

6 Literatur

Gosse Bouma, Esther König, Hans Uszkoreit 1988, A flexible graph-unification formalism and its Application to Natural-Language Processing, IBM Journal of Research and Development 32.(2) 170-184

Jochen Dörre, Roland Seiffert 1991, A Formalism for Natural Language — STUF, In: Integrating Computational Linguistics and Artificial Intelligence: Text Understanding in LILOG, Otthein Herzog, Claus Rollinger (eds.), Springer

Karl Gregor Erbach 1991, A Bottom-Up Algorithm for Parsing and Generation, unveröffentlicht

Jochen Dörre, Ingo Raasch 1991, The Stuttgart Type Unification Formalism — User Manual, IWBS Report 168

On the Representation of Speech Acts in Situation Semantics[*]

Elizabeth Garner
Wolfgang Heinz

Austrian Research Institute for Artificial Intelligence
Schottengasse 3, A-1010 Vienna

Email: {elizabeth, wolfgang}@ai-vie.uucp

Abstract

In this paper a method of representing speech acts is outlined which is suitable for implementation in a natural language consulting system. Speech acts are classified according to the discourse situation in which they arise and the change in the discourse situation they incur. The approach is formulated in a Situation Semantics framework.

1 Introduction

A natural language consulting system such as the one we are building in the VIE-$\mathcal{DU}$ project, designed to provide information about available subsidies for housing improvements (Buchberger & al. (1991)), needs to be able to correctly determine the intentions and beliefs of a user from her utterances and to react to them in an appropriate manner. Speech act theory offers a natural means of achieving these goals.

In order to ground speech acts in a theory of rational action, Cohen & Levesque (1990b) have developed a formalism in which the properties of speech acts are analysed in terms of the primitives *goal* and *belief*. In an analogous approach, we show how to account for the illocutionary differences between the major sentence-types which occur in German, as well as the five types of performative verbs suggested by Searle & Vanderveken (1985).

Our approach has much in common with that of Werner (1988), as well as that adopted in the WISBER project (Sprenger & Gerlach (1988)). In the project VIE-$\mathcal{DU}$ however, we have chosen to adopt Situation Semantics as our semantic theory. In this paper, we show how our analysis of sentence-types, performative verbs, and the relations between them, can be elegantly captured within a Situation Semantics framework.

2 The Basic Framework

Our approach to speech acts seeks to reformulate them in the traditional plan framework of preconditions, actions and effects. A speech act is an action (the utterance) which occurs in a particular discourse environment (which includes the preconditions) and which extends the discourse situation (by the effects). While speech acts are linguistic activities, there is nothing inherent in the theory which precludes the utterance being replaced by a non-linguistic action. The theory therefore accords with the requirement of Cohen & Levesque (1990b) that speech act theory be grounded in a more general theory of non-communicative action.

To implement such a framework we have chosen to adopt a semantic theory that allows for the integration of context—Situation Semantics (cf. Barwise & Perry (1983), Barwise (1989), Cooper, Mukai & Perry (1990)). Meaning in Situation Semantics is considered relational, i.e. the meaning of a (declarative) expression ϕ is 'a relation $u[\phi]e$ between situations u where ϕ is uttered and situations e described by such utterances. This relation constrains both u and e.' (Barwise & Perry (1983), p. 120).

We may now define our basic form of speech acts using the conditional constraints introduced in Barwise (1989), Chapter 5.

$$(1) \qquad A \Rightarrow E \mid B$$

$$(2) \qquad A = [\dot{s} \mid \dot{s} \models \langle\!\langle \dot{t}_\phi; \mathrm{Utter}, \dot{s}p, \phi \rangle\!\rangle]$$

The conditional constraint (1) is a constraint relativised to some background condition B. If we have a background situation of this type, the constraint holds. For our purposes we identify A with the *action*, i.e. the situation of the utterance (2). In this situation, (represented by $\dot{s}$), the speaker, ($\dot{s}p$), utters ϕ at the utterance time $\dot{t}_\phi$.[1] If the *preconditions* given by B are met, we have the *effect* given by E.

---

[*] This research has been sponsored by the Austrian *Fonds zur Förderung der wissenschaftlichen Forschung*, Grant No. P7986-PHY. Many thanks to the anonymous referees for helpful comments and to J. Matiasek for fruitful discussions. Thanks also to Prof. R. Trappl for continuing support.

[1] $\dot{s}$ is used in Situation Semantics to represent an indeterminate of type *situation*, $\dot{s}p$ an indeterminate with the role *speaker*, etc.

A general effect of speech acts is:

$$(3) \qquad E = [\dot{s} \mid \dot{s} \models \langle\!\langle t_\phi + \delta; \mathrm{MutBel}, \dot{sp}, a\dot{d}d, B\rangle\!\rangle]$$

i.e. that immediately after the felicitous utterance $(t_\phi + \delta)$ the speaker and the addressee $(a\dot{d}d)$ mutually believe that the background conditions hold.

2.1 Sentential Mood

In this section we will look at the preconditions and effects associated with the three major clause types in German, declarative, interrogative and imperative. For all three, we will assume that general sincerity conditions hold.

A precondition of declarative sentences is that the speaker believe the truth of the proposition expressed in the utterance. We may state this as follows:

$$(4) \qquad ds \models SC \text{ with } SC = \langle\!\langle t_\phi; \mathrm{Bel}, \dot{sp}, e\rangle\!\rangle$$

(4) says that in the discourse situation ds the following has to hold: at the utterance time the speaker has to believe the propositional content e of his declarative utterance ϕ. This represents a kind of sincerity condition which we call SC and which forms part of B in (1).

The effect of the declarative utterance is that the speaker $\dot{sp}$ and addressee $a\dot{d}d$ mutually believe the speaker's belief SC:

$$(5) \qquad ds \models \langle\!\langle t_\phi + \delta; \mathrm{MutBel}, \dot{sp}, a\dot{d}d, SC\rangle\!\rangle$$

This represents a special case of (3).

Interrogative and imperative sentences (hereafter *directives*) share the precondition that the speaker before the utterance has as a goal that the hearer perform some action. In the case of interrogatives this action is usually linguistic, in the case of imperatives it is usually non-linguistic. An order to open the door in the imperative mood imposes the constraint:[2]

$$(6) \qquad ds \models \langle\!\langle t_\phi; \mathrm{Goal}, \dot{sp}, (s \models \langle\!\langle t_\phi + \delta; \mathrm{Open}, a\dot{d}d, door\rangle\!\rangle)\rangle\!\rangle$$

i.e. it is the goal of the speaker that the addressee open the door at a time after the utterance.

The effect of a successful directive is that the addressee is aware of this goal of the speaker, i.e. that the speaker and addressee mutually believe that the goal of the speaker is that the addressee open the door. In addition, following Cohen & Levesque (1990a) directives constitute attempts by the speaker to cause the addressee to fulfil this goal. The success of such an attempt depends on a number of conditions, including, for example, whether the addressee is competent to perform the action and whether her attitude towards the speaker is cooperative.

To model the effect of a directive under *cooperativity* we have:[3]

$$(7) \qquad \begin{aligned} ds &\models \langle\!\langle \mathrm{Bel}, a\dot{d}d, (s_1 \models \langle\!\langle \mathrm{Goal}, \dot{sp}, (s \models \langle\!\langle \mathrm{Open}, a\dot{d}d, door\rangle\!\rangle)\rangle\!\rangle)\rangle\!\rangle \Rightarrow \\ ds &\models \langle\!\langle \mathrm{Goal}, a\dot{d}d, (s \models \langle\!\langle \mathrm{Open}, a\dot{d}d, door\rangle\!\rangle)\rangle\!\rangle \end{aligned}$$

where $\Rightarrow$ represents the relation *involves*, a type of constraint.[4]

3 Performatives

Searle & Vanderveken (1985) distinguish between five types of performative verbs: assertive, directive, commissive, expressive and declarative. In this section we will look at how the performative and non-performative uses of these verbs can be represented within our framework.

3.1 Assertives

An example of an assertive verb in German is *behaupten* as in (8a) (the performative use) and (8b) (the non-performative use).

(8) a) *Ich behaupte, daß ich kommen werde.*
'I assert that I will come.'

b) *Hans hat behauptet, daß er kommen wird.*
'Hans asserted that he would come.'

Behaupten is associated with a precondition that the agent of the verb believe the truth of the following proposition and an effect that the agent and the audience, which need not be explicitly specified, mutually believe that the agent believes the proposition.

---

[2] While the example sentences have been chosen on the basis of simplicity of exposition all the sentence-types mentioned do regularly occur in our domain, cf. the assertive *Mein Nachbar behauptet, daß der Einbau von Zentralheizung gefördert wird.* 'My neighbour asserts that central heating installation is subsidised.'

[3] We omit time locations for the sake of brevity

[4] While limitations of space prevent us from offering a detailed account of indirect speech acts, *constraints* provide us also with a mechanism for treating them. For example, an utterance of 'Can you open the door?' can be constrained by an *involves* relation to be interpreted as an imperative, in addition to its receiving its literal interrogative interpretation.

In our lexical entry for *behaupten* we require that the verb be associated with an asserting-situation via the relation type *Assert*.

(9) $$[ag, theme \mid \langle\!\langle i; \text{Assert}, ag, theme \rangle\!\rangle]$$

The semantic argument positions *ag* and *theme* are linked to the syntactic argument positions (the subcategorization frame) of *behaupten* indirectly by their thematic roles and syntactic case indices as given in Heinz & Matiasek (1991). This analysis also uses thematic situation types (as proposed by Larson (1988)) to link the Assert relation to a more general believe relation that now forms part of the background modelling the precondition.

(10) $$\langle\!\langle \Rightarrow, e \models \langle\!\langle i; \text{Assert}, \dot{a}g, \dot{theme} \rangle\!\rangle, B \models \langle\!\langle i; \text{Bel}, \dot{a}g, \dot{theme} \rangle\!\rangle \rangle\!\rangle$$

Our treatment of indirectly linking syntactic and semantic arguments via their thematic roles overcomes a problem mentioned in Cohen & Levesque (1990b), p. 85. If the agent is associated directly with the syntactic subject (as in their analysis) passivisation destroys the linking. In our analysis only the syntactic Case index is altered, but the link to the thematic role of Agent remains intact.

Another problem mentioned in Cohen & Levesque (1990b) is the possibility of uttering performatives in the first person plural. This problem is solved by using the framework developed in Heinz & Matiasek (1990) for the treatment of non-singular terms. The condition on the applicability of the preconditions is loosened from requiring the identity of agent and speaker to an individual part relation between them (a more general notion subsuming identity).

The effect of the assertion mentioned above is defined in (11):

(11) $$E \models \langle\!\langle t \dot{+} \delta; \text{MutBel}, \dot{a}g, \dot{a}ud, (s \models \langle\!\langle i; \text{Bel}, \dot{a}g, \dot{theme} \rangle\!\rangle) \rangle\!\rangle$$

Moreover, a further precondition on (8a) and (8b) is that the *speaker* believe that the agent asserted the proposition, with the corresponding effect that the speaker and the addressee mutually believe that the speaker believes this. In fact this corresponds exactly to the preconditions and effects of declarative sentences, given in (4), and hence does not require an explicit reformulation. (8a) and (8b) differ because the agent of *behaupten* in (8a) is also the speaker, whereas in (8b) they refer to different individuals. Furthermore in (8a) the asserting event and the uttering event coincide. This illustrates the difference between the performative and non-performative usage of the illocutionary verbs.

3.2 Directives

An example of a directive verb in German is *befehlen*. As with the assertives, directive verbs are not always used performatively.

(12)   a) *Ich befehle dir, die Tür zu öffnen.*
        'I order you to open the door.'

      b) *Maria hat Peter befohlen, die Tür zu öffnen.*
        'Maria ordered Peter to open the door.'

The precondition associated with *befehlen*, namely that the goal of the speaker is that the addressee perform the action identified by the complement clause, is given in (13).

(13) $$\langle\!\langle \Rightarrow, e \models \langle\!\langle i; \text{Order}, \dot{a}g, \dot{p}at, \dot{theme} \rangle\!\rangle, B \models \langle\!\langle i; \text{Goal}, \dot{a}g, \dot{theme}(\dot{p}at) \rangle\!\rangle \rangle\!\rangle^5$$

Notice that when used performatively, *befehlen* corresponds to an imperative, and when used non-performatively it does not. This can be easily accounted for. When the time parameter is anchored to the utterance time and the argument roles are anchored to the speaker and the addressee this situation corresponds to our precondition for directives with the effect that the addressee adopt a goal to fulfil the directive. Otherwise, as with assertives, it corresponds to our general case for declarative sentences, and has as effect simply a new belief state of the speaker and addressee.

3.3 Commissives, Expressives and Declaratives

Commissives, expressives and declaratives[6] may for the most part be treated in an analogous manner to assertives and directives. To deal with expressives, however, we need to add an extra parameter to our descriptions of the preconditions of verbs, which we will call Val(uation). Our entry for the expressive *bedauern*, 'regret' contains

(14) $$\langle\!\langle \Rightarrow, e \models \langle\!\langle i; \text{Regret}, \dot{a}g, \dot{theme} \rangle\!\rangle,$$
$$B \models \langle\!\langle i; \text{Assert}, \dot{a}g, \dot{theme} \rangle\!\rangle \wedge \langle\!\langle i; \text{Val}, \dot{a}g, \dot{theme}, \dot{v} \rangle\!\rangle \wedge \langle\!\langle <, \dot{v}, NeutralValue \rangle\!\rangle \rangle\!\rangle$$

(15) $$E \models \langle\!\langle t \dot{+} \delta; \text{MutBel}, \dot{a}g, \dot{a}ud, B \rangle\!\rangle \rangle\!\rangle$$

Declaratives serve to bring about a change in the state of the world (Searle & Vanderveken (1985)). The effect of a declarative is thus twofold; firstly that the agent and his audience mutually believe the goal of the agent was to

---

[5] *theme*(*pat*) is short for a parametric situation type *theme* where *pat* fills the role.
[6] not to be confused with declarative mood

perform the action, and secondly that the speaker and his audience mutually believe the action now holds. (16) and (17) show the representation of *ernennen* 'declare', as in 'I declare you Chairman'.[7]

$$(16) \qquad \langle\!\langle \Rightarrow, e \models \langle\!\langle i; \text{Declare}, \dot{a}g, \dot{t}h\dot{e}me \rangle\!\rangle, B \models \langle\!\langle i; \text{Goal}, \dot{a}g, e \rangle\!\rangle \rangle\!\rangle$$

$$(17) \qquad E \models \langle\!\langle t \dot{+} \delta; \text{MutBel}, \dot{a}g, \dot{a}ud, B \rangle\!\rangle \wedge \langle\!\langle t \dot{+} \delta; \text{MutBel}, \dot{a}g, \dot{a}ud, \dot{t}h\dot{e}me \rangle\!\rangle \rangle\!\rangle$$

Commissives, expressives and declaratives, just as assertives and directives, all correspond to the general description of preconditions and effects given for declarative sentences. That is to say, at the utterance situation, they each represent beliefs of the speaker that the preconditions of the performative do/did hold at the time of the action. The effect, then, of all three types of performatives is to raise this belief of the speaker to a mutual belief of speaker and addressee.

4   Implementation

The above framework is currently being implemented in the VIE-*DU* project employing a unification-based formalism (cf. Johnson (1988), Shieber (1986)). A major advantage of such an approach is its neutrality with regard to analysis and generation; we intend to make use of the above descriptions for both. The syntactic component of the grammar has been constructed within the framework of HPSG (Heinz & Matiasek (1991)).[8] For the incorporation of semantic and pragmatic features we take the situation schemata of Fenstad et al. (1987) as a starting point. As an example (18) can be used to represent a partial (simplified) description of the utterance situation of (8a). The description consists of sets of constraints, relating to e, B and E described above. Such an attribute-value structure allows us to provide a uniform representation of contextual and linguistic information simplifying the integration of constraints at all levels.[9]

(18)

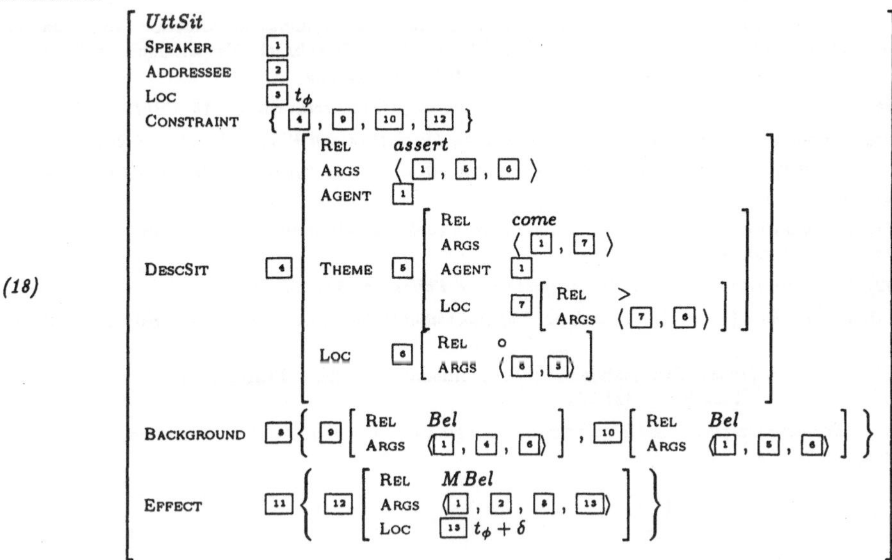

5   Summary

We have presented a formalism for speech acts within the framework of Situation Semantics for implementation in a natural language consulting system. Speech acts are recast by means of primitives such as *belief* and *goal* in the traditional plan framework of preconditions, actions and effects. This enables us to describe speech acts in terms of their communicative properties and their impact on the discourse situation. The formalism is able to provide an analysis for the three major sentence types of German, as well as the five types of performative verbs suggested by Searle & Vanderveken (1985).

This approach has a number of advantages. Defining speech acts simply in terms of preconditions and effects allows for the possibility pointed out by Evans (1981) that a speech act may span over several sentences. The approach offers an explanation to the problem posed by Searle (1989): why is it that illocutionary verbs are in some cases indicators of illocutionary force and in others part of the propositional content. Finally, the approach provides some justification for the analysis of performatives as declarative utterances on the basis of their effects on the discourse situation.

---

[7] Assuming further preconditions on the social position of the agent hold
[8] For an overview of HPSG see Pollard & Sag (1987).
[9] $>$ represents the relation *temporally follows* and o *temporally overlaps*.

References

Barwise, J. (1989) *The Situation in Logic*, CSLI Lecture Notes 17, CSLI, Stanford

Barwise, J. and J. Perry (1983) *Situations and Attitudes*, MIT Press, Cambridge, Mass.

Buchberger, E., Garner, E., Heinz, W., Matiasek, J., and Pfahringer, B. (1991) 'VIE-*DU* — Dialogue by Unification', in *Proceedings of the 7. Österreichische Artificial Intelligence Tagung*, Springer, Berlin

Cohen, P.R. and H.J. Levesque (1990a) 'Rational Interaction as the Basis for Communication', in P.R. Cohen, J. Morgan and M.E. Pollack (eds.) *Intentions in Communication*, MIT Press, Cambridge, Mass.

Cohen, P.R. and H.J. Levesque (1990b) 'Performatives in a Rationally Based Speech Act Theory', in *Proceedings of the 28th Annual Meeting of the Association for Computational Linguistics*, Pittsburgh, Pennsylvania, 79-88

Cooper, R., K. Mukai and J. Perry, eds. (1990) *Situation Theory and its Applications*, Vol. 1, CSLI Lecture Notes 22, CSLI, Stanford

Evans, David A. (1981) 'A Situation Semantic Approach to the Analysis of Speech Acts', in *Proceedings of the 19th Annual Meeting of the Association for Computational Linguistics*, Stanford University, Stanford, CA, 113-116

Fenstad, J.E., P.-K. Halvorsen, T. Langholm and J. van Benthem (1987) *Situations, Language and Logic*, Reidel, Dordrecht

Heinz, W. and J. Matiasek (1990) 'A Framework for Treating Non-Singular Terms in a Natural Language Consulting System', to appear in *Proceedings of the Workshop "Semantisch-Pragmatische Verarbeitung von Pluralen und Quantoren in NLP", Eringerfeld (Sept. 1990)*, also available as Technical Report TR-90-15, Austrian Research Institute for Artificial Intelligence, Vienna

Heinz, W. and J. Matiasek (1991) 'Case-Assignment in a Computational Grammar for German', to appear in *Proceedings der 3.Fachtagung der Sektion Computerlinguistik der DGfS*, Osnabrück, also available as Technical Report TR-91-5, Austrian Research Institute for Artificial Intelligence, Vienna

Johnson M. (1988) *Attribute–Value Logic and the Theory of Grammar*, CSLI Lecture Notes 16, CSLI, Stanford

Larson, R.K. (1988) 'Implicit Arguments in Situation Semantics', *Linguistics and Philosophy* 11, 169-201

Pollard, C. and I. Sag (1987) *Information-Based Syntax and Semantics, Vol. 1: Fundamentals*, CSLI Lecture Notes 13, CSLI, Stanford

Shieber, S. M. (1986) *An Introduction to Unification-based Approaches to Grammar*, CSLI Lecture Notes Series, Chicago University Press, Chicago

Searle, J.R. (1989) 'How Performatives Work', in *Linguistics and Philosophy* 12, 535-558

Searle, J.R. and D. Vanderveken (1985) *The Foundations of Illocutionary Logic*, Cambridge University Press, Cambridge

Sprenger, M. and M. Gerlach (1988) 'Expectations and Propositional Attitudes - Pragmatic Issues in WISBER', *Proceedings of the ICSC-88*, Hong Kong, 327-334

Werner E. (1988) 'A Formal Computational Semantics and Pragmatics of Speech Acts', in *Proceedings of the 12th COLING*, Budapest, 744-749

5. WISSENSREPRÄSENTATION

Entwicklung von Wissensbankbetriebssystemen

Wolfgang Oertel
Institut für Datenbanken und Künstliche Intelligenz
Fakultät für Informatik
Technische Universität Dresden
Mommsenstr.13
O-8027 Dresden

Zusammenfassung

Mit der Arbeit ist die Zielstellung verbunden, über die Entwicklung von Konzepten bzw. Systemen zur Modellierung und Verwaltung von Wissensbeständen Grundlagen zu schaffen für die Herausbildung einer Wissensbanktechnologie. Dabei steht nicht die Frage der Abbildung eines Diskursbereiches im Mittelpunkt, sondern die systemtechnische Behandlung des Wissens. Den Ausgangspunkt bilden Untersuchungen zum prinzipiellen Aufbau eines Wissensmodells und die Einordnung existierender Wissensmodelle in das daraus resultierende Schema. Aus diesen Arbeiten lassen sich Anforderungen an Wissensbankbetriebssysteme ableiten. Diese Systeme müssen sowohl die rein syntaktische Handhabung von Wissensbeständen als auch ihre semantische Interpretation ermöglichen. Sie besitzen intern eine heterogene Struktur, stellen jedoch nach außen hin, der Forderung nach Wissensunabhängigkeit Rechnung tragend, ein einheitliches System dar. Die vorgestellte Arbeit ist konzeptioneller Natur. Sie wird begleitet durch die Entwicklung eigener Basissoftware zur Wissensverarbeitung und deren ständige Erprobung in praxisrelevanten Anwendungssystemen.

1 Einleitung

Mit der Datenbanktechnologie hat sich in den letzten Jahren eine Wissenschaftsdisziplin herausgebildet, die über hocheffiziente Mittel und Methoden zur Verwaltung von Massendatenbeständen verfügt. Dagegen ist die Ausdruckskraft der bereitgestellten Datenmodelle zur Beschreibung eines Diskursbereiches relativ gering. Seit einiger Zeit existieren Anstrengungen, die Potenzen der Datenbanktechnologie bei der Verwaltung großer Datenbestände mit der Ausdruckskraft der in der Künstlichen Intelligenz vorliegenden Wissensmodelle zu verbinden ([1],[3]).

Der vorliegende Artikel stellt Arbeitsergebnisse aus dem Grenzgebiet zwischen beiden Disziplinen vor. Es wird eine Wissensbanktechnologie angestrebt, die ausgeht von einer Basisprogrammiersprache der Künstlichen Intelligenz und über die Entwicklung von Werkzeugen und Werkbanken zur Wissensverarbeitung hin zu Wissensbankbetriebssystemen führt. Dabei gilt es spätestens in der letzten Phase, Datenbanktechniken einzubeziehen (Abb. 1). Die Vorgehensweise stellt Wissensbestände als zentrale Ressource in den Mittelpunkt und schafft Möglichkeiten, diese Bestände langfristig zu entwickeln, zu warten und einer breiten Nutzung zugänglich zu machen.
Gegenwärtig liegen zahlreiche Systeme zur Wissensverarbeitung mit Werkbankcharakter vor

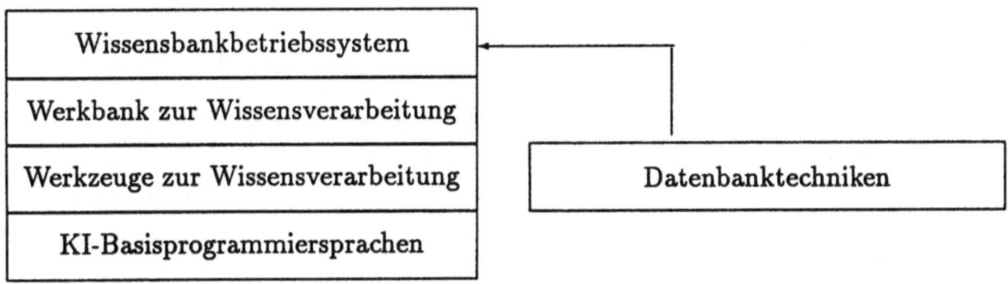

Abbildung 1: Entwicklung von Basissoftware zur Wissensverarbeitung

(z. B. [4]). Sie bieten komfortable Methoden zur Wissensmodellierung an, schenken jedoch dem Verwaltungsaspekt weniger Beachtung.
Es zeigt sich, daß die separate Behandlung von Wissensbeständen, insbesondere, wenn der Umfang der Wissensbasen ein bestimmtes Maß übersteigt, eigenen Gesetzen unterliegt und schwer mit herkömmlichen Programmiertechniken zu bewältigen ist. So stehen Fragen der Strukturierung der Wissensbestände, ihrer Integrität, Sicherung und Änderbarkeit sowie geeigneter Speicherungsformen und Zugriffsverfahren - kurz, der Modellierung und Verwaltung des Wissens.

Im Abschn. 2 der vorliegenden Arbeit werden Grundzüge der Wissensverarbeitung dargestellt und im Abschn. 3 daraus Anforderungen an ein zu entwickelndes Wissensbankbetriebssystem abgeleitet. Abschn. 4 stellt Konzepte vor, die als Grundlage für derartige Systeme dienen können. Schließlich zeigt der letzte Abschnitt bereits erzielte praktische Ergebnisse.

2 Problematik der Wissensverarbeitung

Das Ziel der Wissensverarbeitung besteht darin, einen Diskursbereich in einem wissensbasierten System abzubilden, um Nutzern Informationen über den Diskursbereich bereitzustellen. Dabei sind Zustände, Prozesse und Gesetzmäßigkeiten darzustellen. Der Diskursbereich ist in der Regel unendlich. So erfolgt die Abbildung stets auf bestimmten Abstraktionsniveaus gemäß unterschiedlicher Aspekte in Nutzeranforderungen.
Die Art und Weise der Abbildung wird durch das dem System zugrunde liegende Wissensmodell bestimmt. Es legt mögliche explizite und implizite Wissenselemente, Operationen und Inferenzverfahren als Beschreibungsmittel fest (Abb. 2).

Explizite Wissenselemente stellen Zustände des Diskursbereiches - Entitäten und Beziehungen zwischen ihnen - dar. Je nachdem, ob diese selbst oder Vorschriften zu deren Generierung existieren, unterscheidet man deklarative und prozedurale Form der Elemente. Implizite Wissenselemente sind Abbilder von Gesetzmäßigkeiten des Diskursbereiches. Während man bei Integritätsbedingungen die auftretende Redundanz nutzt, um die Konsistenz der Abbildung zu überprüfen (Analyse), verwendet man deduktive Regeln konstruktiv, um implizite Abbilder aus expliziten Abbildern abzuleiten (Synthese).
Anfrageoperationen stellen mit Hilfe des Wissens Informationen über den Diskursbereich bereit, und Änderungsoperationen gestatten es, Prozesse, die im Diskursbereich ablaufen, in seinem Abbild nachzuvollziehen oder vorwegzunehmen.
Inferenzverfahren letztlich geben an, wie insbesondere implizite Wissenselemente in das Ausführen von Operationen einbezogen werden. Dabei beschreiben Schlußregeln Klassen syntaktischer Transformationen von Wissenselementen unter Beibehaltung deren Semantik. Such-

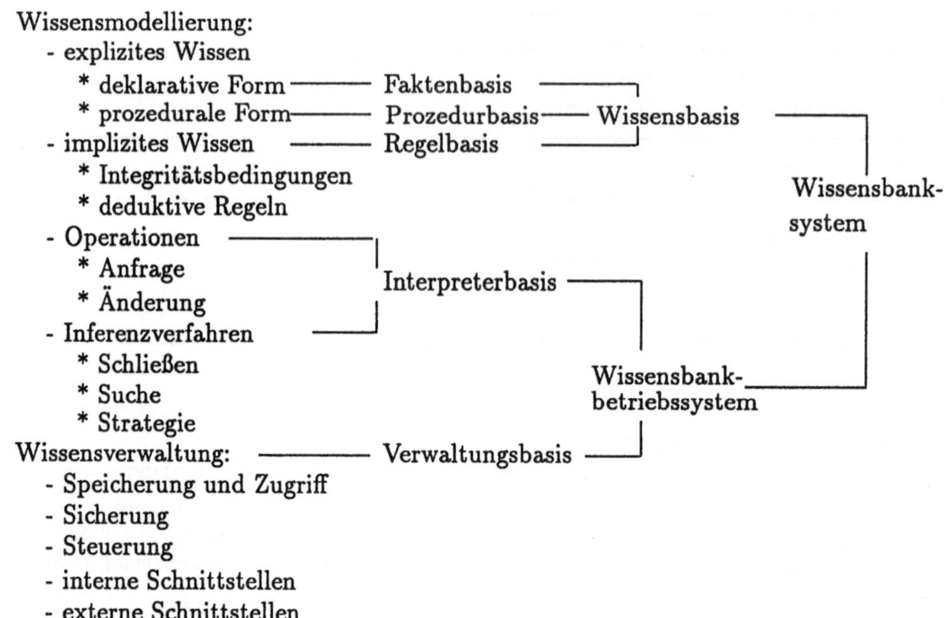

Abbildung 2: Wissensmodellierung und Wissensverwaltung

verfahren geben an, wie bei Vorliegen alternativer Schlußmöglichkeiten zu verfahren ist, und die Strategie legt die generelle Vorgehensweise im Inferenzprozeß fest. Das Inferenzverfahren erlaubt es damit, implizit gespeichertes Wissen explizit verfügbar zu machen, was einem Problemlösungsprozeß gleichkommt. Die Zulassung impliziten Wissens bedeutet eine Vervielfachung der im System speicherbaren Informationen zu Lasten des Verarbeitungsaufwandes.

Neben der Modellierung von Wissensbeständen spielt bei der Entwicklung praxisrelevanter Systeme die systemtechnische Handhabung des Wissens eine entscheidende Rolle. Zu dieser Wissensverwaltung gehören Speicherungsformen, Zugriffsverfahren, die Sicherung der Bestände sowie die Steuerung der gesamten Verarbeitung. Unabdingbar ist weiterhin die Beschreibung interner und externer Schnittstellen, die verschiedene Verfahren zur Modellierung und Verwaltung des Wissens aufeinander abbilden bzw. die Interaktion interner Verfahren mit der Umgebung des Systems spezifizieren.

Den einzelnen Teilgebieten der Wissensverarbeitung lassen sich jeweils Systemkomponenten zuordnen (vgl. Abb. 2). Die Abbildung auf unterschiedlichen Abstraktionsniveaus erfordert in letzter Konsequenz die Zulassung unterschiedlicher Wissensmodelle. Damit werden entscheidend die Adäquatheit, die Effizienz und die Akzeptanz von Abbildern bestimmt. Neben klassischen Wissensmodellen, wie logik-, produktionsregel-, netzwerk- und frameorientierten Modellen, die sich leicht in die angegebene Systematik einordnen lassen, existieren Modelle, die über nur sehr eingeschränkte oder keine inferentiellen Möglichkeiten verfügen, wie z. B. prozedurale, relationale, netzwerk- oder objektorientierte Modelle.

3 Merkmale von Wissensbankbetriebssystemen

Aus der in Abb. 2 dargestellten Systematik zur Wissensverarbeitung und der Analyse konkreter Wissensmodelle lassen sich Kriterien ableiten, die für die Entwicklung von Wissensbankbetriebssystemen relevant sind.

(1) Syntaktische Manipulation von Wissen
Auf rein syntaktischer Ebene stellen sämtliche Wissenselemente komplexe, konnektive Strukturen dar, d. h. Strukturen, die aus einer beliebigen Anzahl beliebig tief verschachtelter Unterstrukturen bestehen, die ihrerseits wieder mit anderen Strukturen in Beziehung stehen. Es sind Komponenten erforderlich, die eine Darstellung und Manipulation von Mengen komplexer, konnektiver Strukturen gestatten.

(2) Semantische Interpretation von Wissen
Semantisch wird zwischen expliziten und impliziten Wissenselementen unterschieden. Das Explizieren von impliziten Wissen bedeutet das Realisieren von syntaktischen Transformationen als Schlußregeln, von Verfahren zur Navigation im Suchraum und von Steuerungsstrategien. Es sind Komponenten erforderlich, die syntaktische Wissensstrukturen unterschiedlich interpretieren, d. h., ihnen verschiedene Bedeutungen zuweisen.

(3) Hybride Systemstruktur
Aus der Vielzahl bereits existierender und darüber hinaus potentiell möglicher Wissensmodelle, die von einem System zu unterstützen sind, ergibt sich zwangsläufig die Notwendigkeit einer heterogenen Modellierung, die nur durch eine hybride interne Systemstruktur zu realisieren ist. Diese ist durch folgende Merkmale gekennzeichnet:

- Bereitstellung einer Menge selbständiger Komponenten,

- Schnittstellen zwischen den Komponenten,

- Nutzung zentraler Komponenten,

- Generierbarkeit neuer Komponenten.

(4) Zentrale Verwaltung großer Wissensbestände
Im Mittelpunkt des Systems stehen nicht Anwendungen, sondern Wissensbasen, die als zentral nutzbare Ressourcen über einheitliche Verwaltungskomponenten gespeichert, gesichert, einer Manipulation oder Interpretation zugänglich gemacht und unterschiedlichen Nutzern bereitgestellt werden.

(5) Wissensbasierte Selbstorganisation
Es wird gefordert, daß die wissensbasierte Organisation nicht nur für die Beschreibung des eigentlichen Diskursbereiches, sondern gleichermaßen für die systeminterne Arbeit verwendet wird. Die Notwendigkeit ergibt sich daraus, daß es keine eiheitlichen Definitionen für Wissensmodelle und schon gar nicht für Schnittstellen zwischen ihnen gibt. Die eigenständige Repräsentation von Wissen in Wissensbasis, Interpreterbasis und Verwaltungsbasis sichert eine hohe Flexibilität des Gesamtsystems und schafft gleichzeitig die Voraussetzung für eine weitestgehende Selbstorganisation.

(6) Wissensunabhängigkeit
Um das System für Nutzer bzw. Anwendungsprogramme trotz der internen heterogenen Modellierung handhabbar zu machen, muß eine Struktur vorliegen, die es ermöglicht, Problemlösungsprozesse zu spezifizieren unabhängig davon, wie das zur Lösung erforderliche Wissen konkret in der Wissensbasis abgelegt ist. Diese Unabhängigkeit bezieht sich auf alle Wissenselemente und betrifft sowohl die Speicherung und den Zugriff als auch das verwendete Wissensmodell (physische bzw. logische Wissensunabhängigkeit).

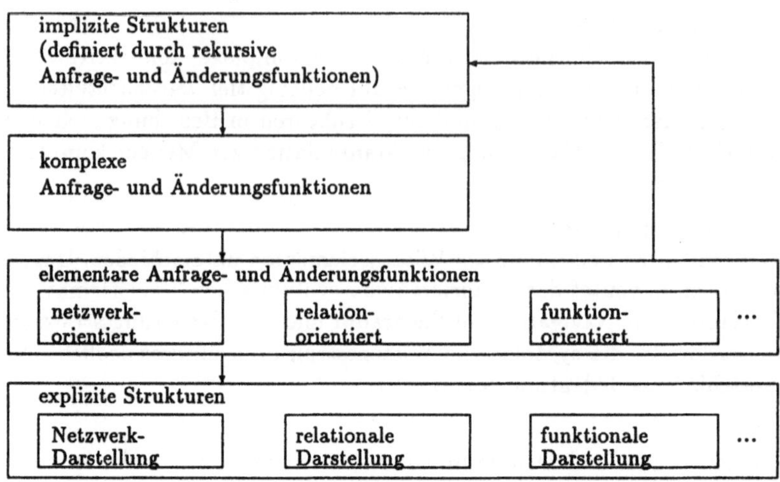

Abbildung 3: Funktionales Wissensmodell

4 Basiswerkzeuge zur Wissensverarbeitung

In diesem Abschnitt werden Basiswerkzeuge zur Wissensverarbeitung und mit ihnen verbundene Konzepte vorgestellt, die dem Aufbau von Systemen gemäß der im Abschn. 3 angegebenen Forderungen dienen. Aus Effizienzgründen wird versucht, soweit wie möglich Konzepte der Basisprogrammiersprache selbst in die Werkzeuge einzubinden. Verwendet man LISP als Basisprogrammiersprache, so stehen bereits elementare Funktionen sowohl für die Manipulation komplexer, vernetzter Strukturen als auch für die Zuordnung einer Semantik zu diesen Strukturen zur Verfügung, auf die mit vertretbarem Aufwand entsprechende komplexere Funktionen aufgesetzt werden können.

4.1 Funktionales Wissensmodell

Das funktionale Wissensmodell ([5]) ist eine Verallgemeinerung des traditionellen relationalen Datenmodells in Richtung Funktionalität, Rekursivität und Heterogenität. Es erlaubt, Strukturen unterschiedlich darzustellen (z. B. als Relation, Netzwerk, Funktion). Das Modell ist offen für weitere Darstellungen. Über strukturspezifische elementare Anfrage- und Änderungsoperationen können Elemente der Strukturen abgefragt bzw. geändert werden. Mengenorientierte komplexe Operationen greifen auf ganze Unterstrukturen zu oder ändern diese im Komplex. Dabei sind die Mengenoperationen so definiert, daß keine einschränkenden Forderungen bezüglich der Struktur der Elemente der Mengen nötig sind. Elemente von Mengen können z. B. sein unstrukturiert, Tupel, Relationen, Prozeduren, Regeln. Schließlich gestatten es rekursive Funktionen, rekursive (implizite) Strukturen in Abhängigkeit expliziter Strukturen zu definieren. Diese rekursiven Strukturen werden im Falle der Änderung physisch erzeugt oder vermitteln im Falle der Anfrage lediglich eine andere Sicht auf bereits existierende Strukturen (Abb. 3).

Das Funktionale Wissensmodell bildet die Grundlage für die syntaktische Manipulation von Wissensbeständen. Die Operationen können manuell oder zur Definition von Schlußregeln in Inferenzverfahren verwendet werden. Weiterhin bietet es sich an für die Definition von Schnittstellen zwischen verschiedenen Modellen sowie zur externen Verwaltung von Wissensbeständen.

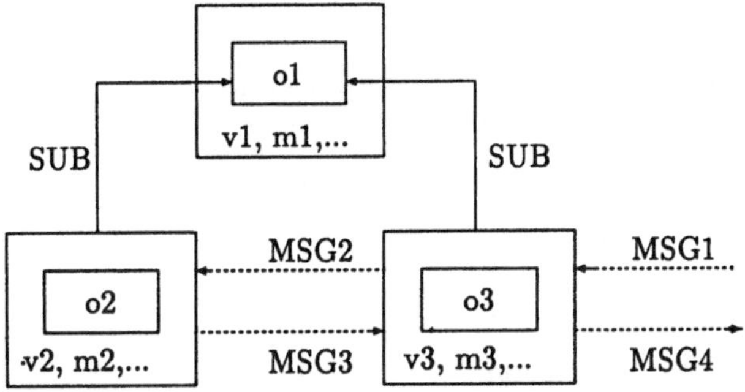

Abbildung 4: Objektorientiertes Wissensmodell

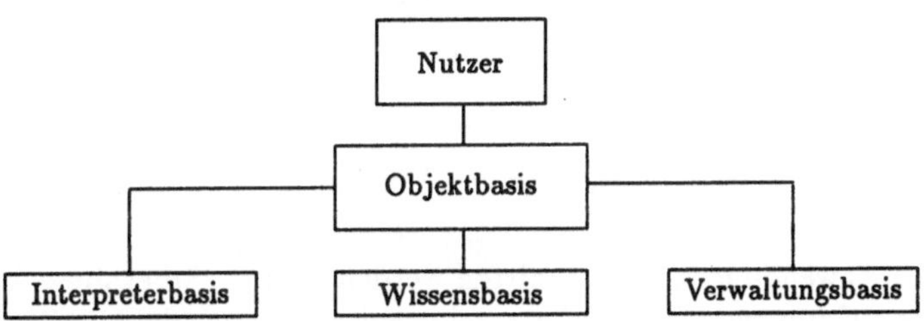

Abbildung 5: Systemstruktur eines hybriden wissensbasierten Systems

4.2 Objektorientiertes Wissensmodell

Das Wesen des objektorientierten Modells besteht darin, daß zunächst eine Menge von Objekten existiert, die jeweils einen Namen o und eine lokale Umgebung mit Variablen v (statische Elemente) und Methoden m (dynamische Elemente) besitzen. Objekte können von außen nur über das Senden von Nachrichten MSG aktiviert werden. Ein aktives Objekt kann seine lokale Umgebung ändern oder ebenfalls Nachrichten versenden. Das Einordnen von Objekten in eine Subordinationshierarchie SUB gestattet die Vererbung von lokalen Umgebungen (Abb. 4).

Das objektorientierte Wissensmodell erlaubt die Beschreibung aller im System anfallenden Steuerungsaufgaben. Es lassen sich objektorientiert organisieren die Wissensbasis, der Inferenzprozeß oder das hybride System mit seinen Komponenten als Ganzes.
Für die objektorientierte Organisation eines hybriden Systems eignet sich die in Abb. 5 angegebene Systemstruktur. Die Objektbasis enthält ausschließlich Informationen über Kooperationsmöglichkeiten zwischen Nutzeranforderungen, Wissensbeständen, Interpretern und Verwaltungskomponenten. Eine derartige Struktur sichert eine hohe Flexibilität des Systems und bereits ein gewisses Maß an Wissensunabhängigkeit.

4.3 Externe Verwaltung

Für die externe Verwaltung von Wissen wird ein Verfahren vorgestellt, das auf einer rein syntaktischen Speicherung von Wissensbeständen in sequentiellen Dateien in der jeweiligen vom Modell festgelegten Form aufbaut, unabhängig von jeglicher Interpretation. Um dennoch die schnelle Verfügbarkeit des Wissens, insbesondere im Inferenzprozeß (dynamischer Zugriff), zu sichern, sind komfortable Zugriffshilfen bereitzustellen, die natürlich generierbar sind und

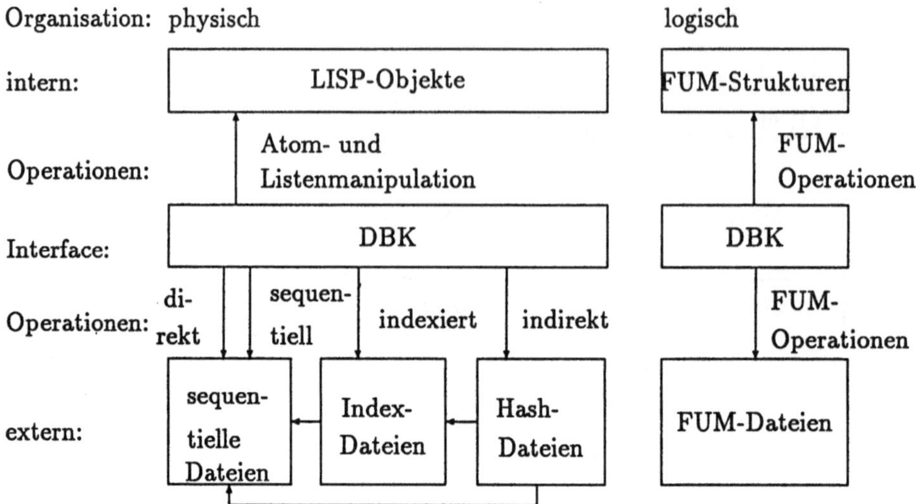

Abbildung 6: Externe Verwaltung von Wissen

so auf konkrete Interpreter oder Anwendungen zugeschnitten werden können. Über diese Methode ist eine Speicherhierarchie aufzubauen, die die Wissenselemente z. B. nach der Häufigkeit ihrer Verwendung oder Änderung ordnet und daran verschiedene Speicherungs- und Zugriffsverfahren bindet. Im einfachsten Fall ist eine Kombinationen zwischen interner und externer Verwaltung zu erreichen (Abb. 6).

Auf logischem Niveau sind Strukturen und Operationen des funktionalen Wissensmodells (FUM) ausreichend auch für die externe Verwaltung. Eine Datenbankkomponente (DBK) steuert das Zusammenwirken der internen und externen Operationen.

4.4   Sicherungsverfahren

Die Sicherung von Wissensbeständen untergliedert sich in drei Klassen. Deren Ziel besteht jeweils darin, die Adäquatheit der Abbildung des Diskursbereiches in der Wissensbasis zu jedem Zeitpunkt zu gewährleisten.

(1) Semantische Integrität beinhaltet die Sicherung der Bestände gegenüber Nutzereinwirkungen. Als Verfahren existieren

- statische Sicherung (Konsistenzüberprüfung) und

- dynamische Sicherung (Zulassen nur konsistenter Änderungen).

(2) Physische Integrität beinhaltet die Sicherung der Bestände bei Ausfällen des Basissystems. Als Verfahren existieren

- Sicherungsabzüge (punktuelle Sicherung),

- Protokollführung (Vorwärts-Sicherung),

- Backtrack-Verfahren (Rückwärts-Sicherung),

- Generationskonzept.

Jedem Verfahren ist ein Wiederanlaufkonzept zugeordnet. Es ermöglicht die Wiederherstellung eines bestimmten Zustandes ausgehend von Sicherungspunkten durch Vorwärts- oder Rückwärts-Änderung.

(3) Operationale Integrität beinhaltet die Sicherung der Bestände im Mehrnutzerbetrieb. Hierzu zählt das Transaktionskonzept.

Alle angegebenen Verfahren können sowohl manuell als auch zur Organisation von Inferenzprozessen eingesetzt werden. Sie sind getrennt für interne und externe Bestände zu realisieren. Eine ausreichende Sicherung erhält man nur durch die geeignete Kombination mehrerer Verfahren. Es sei darauf hingewiesen, daß sich Wissensverarbeitung und Sicherungskonzepte wechselseitig beeinflussen. So bietet der wissensbasierte Ansatz sehr gute Möglichkeiten für die Realisierung von Sicherungsverfahren selbst.

4.5 Unterstützung von Wissensmodellen

Um die eigentliche Abbildung von Diskursbereichen in der Wissensbasis zu ermöglichen, enthält ein System zunächst eine repräsentative Menge von Wissensmodellen. Dabei ist darauf zu achten, daß qualitativ verschiedene Modelle angeboten werden, die jeweils bestimmte Aspekte der Abbildung betonen.
Neben typischen Wissensmodellen (Regeln, Logik, Netzwerke, Frames) kann auf konventionelle Verarbeitungsmodelle nicht vollkommen verzichtet werden. Sämtliche Verwaltungskomponenten müssen unterstützend für jedes Modell bereitstehen.

Damit verschiedene Modelle zur Lösung einer Aufgabe eingesetzt werden können, bedarf es Schnittstellen zwischen den Modellen. Man unterscheidet die Schnittstellen nach

- dem Niveau: physisch - logisch,

- der Verantwortlichkeit: explizit - implizit,

- der Komplexität: elementar - komplex - rekursiv und

- dem Transformationsobjekt: Operationen - Wissenselemente.

Da es kaum eine eindeutige Zuordnung zwischen den Bestandteilen zweier Wissensmodelle gibt, können Schnittstellen nur über Transformationsregeln, also selbst wissensbasiert, definiert werden. Der Schnittstellenproblematik kommt besondere Bedeutung bei der Gewährleistung der Wissensunabhängigkeit zu. Probleme treten bei der Abbildung verschiedener Inferenzverfahren aufeinander auf.

Um die Flexibilität des Systems hinsichtlich der Modellierung zu sichern, muß die Möglichkeit bestehen, neue Wissensmodelle hinzuzufügen. Das bedeutet, daß im System Wissensmodelle unter Nutzung von Basiswerkzeugen generierbar sind. Es wird die Auffassung vertreten, daß mit Hilfe des funktionalen und des objektorientierten Wissensmodells sowie der angegebenen Sicherungsverfahren Wissensmodelle mit vertretbarem Aufwand nachgebildet werden können. Dabei lassen sich Wissenselemente und Operationen über entsprechend definierte FUM-Strukturen bzw. FUM- Operationen realisieren. Inferenzverfahren enthalten FUM-Operationen als Schlußregeln, Sicherungsverfahren zur Organisation der Suche und letztlich eine objektorientierte Steuerung. Abb. 7 zeigt dazu einen typischen Inferenzprozeß unter dem Aspekt der Anwendung von Sicherungsverfahren. Nahezu alle angegebenen Operationen greifen auf Sicherungsverfahren zurück.

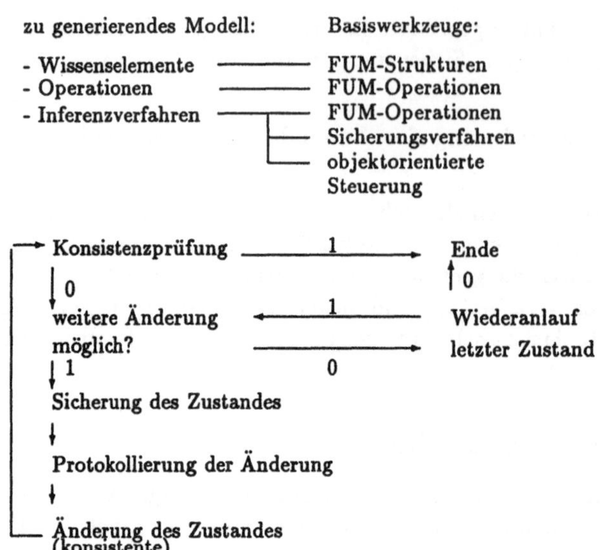

Abbildung 7: Generierung von Wissensmodellen

5 Erzielte praktische Ergebnisse

Die im Abschn. 4 vorgestellten Konzepte sind Bestandteil eines auf Basis der Sprache Common Lisp erstellten Werkzeugsystems zur Wissensverarbeitung ETA-L ([6]), das an der TU Dresden entwickelt wurde. Das System ist gegenwärtig sowohl auf UNIX-Workstations als auch auf PC unter MS-DOS lauffähig. Dabei zwangen insbesondere die Restriktionen der PC-Umgebung zu starker Systematisierung (Verwendung generischer Funktionen, Modularisierung, externe Verwaltung). Es kann im Rahmen dieser Arbeit nur auf einige Aspekte und Erfahrungen bei der Implementation und Nutzung des Systems eingegangen werden.

Das System enthält zunächst in Form separat nutzbarer Werkzeuge Implementationen traditioneller Wissensmodelle, die im Abschn. 4 angegebenen Basiswerkzeuge sowie Hilfskomponenten zur Graphik- und Dialogarbeit.
Als verbindendes Element zwischen den Komponenten wurde eine Objektbasis geschaffen, die gemäß Abb. 5 eine konkrete Systemstruktur definiert. Auf diese Weise wurden mehrere wissensbasierte Anwendungssysteme geschaffen, darunter ein System zur Konstruktion mehrstufiger Zahnradgetriebe, ein Auskunfts-, Simulations- und Planungssystem für den Straßenbahnfahrplan der Stadt Dresden sowie ein System zur Diagnose und Therapie von Waldkrankheiten.
Es hat sich sehr bald gezeigt, daß Teile der Objektbasis eines Anwendungssystems ohne größeren Aufwand auf andere Anwendungen übertragbar sind. So kristallisierte sich nach und nach eine Objektstruktur heraus, die ab einer gewissen Ebene aufwärts in der Objekthierarchie nur noch allgemeingültige Modellierungs- und Verwaltungskomponenten enthält, die als Ausgangsform eines Wissensbankbetriebssystems gedeutet werden können. Daneben existieren Teilstrukturen, die für bestimmte Anwendungsklassen stehen, z. B. Auskunft, Klassifikation, Konstruktion, Planung, Simulation.

Physische Schnittstellen zwischen einzelnen Komponenten bereiten bei der einheitlich verwendeten Basissprache und der offenen Systemstruktur kaum Schwierigkeiten. Interessant sind logische Schnittstellen, die ganze Wissensmodelle aufeinander abbilden. So wurde ein Schnittstellenkomplex Logik geschaffen, der prädikatenlogische Formeln 1. Ordnung transformiert in

Prolog- Klauseln, Operationen des funktionalen Wissensmodells, Integritätsbedingungen oder Datenbankoperationen. Logische Formeln können sich auf beliebige FUM-Strukturen beziehen. Ein ähnlicher Komplex existiert für Produktionsregeln.

Nach der Methode in Abb. 7 wurden im System zusätzlich ein Produktionsregel- und ein Netzwerk-Interpreter unter Verwendung der Basiswerkzeuge generiert. Als vorteilhaft erweist sich dabei, daß man FUM-Strukturen und Sicherungsverfahren dem zu lösenden Problem anpassen und damit wesentlich die Effizienz des Inferenzverfahrens steuern kann.

Ein großer Teil der Arbeiten befaßte sich mit der Problematik der externen Verwaltung und Sicherung von Wissensbeständen. Die in Abb. 6 angegebene Struktur wurde im wesentlichen realisiert und verwendet, um sowohl statisch als auch dynamisch zu externen Beständen zuzugreifen. Zu verschiedenen Datenbankbetriebssystemen wurden Schnittstellen hergestellt. Während der ausschließlich dynamische Zugriff zu Datenbankbetriebssystemen sich nicht bewährt hat, hat sich gezeigt, daß eine externe Verwaltung des Wissens bei Verwendung zielgerichteter Zugriffsverfahren nicht notwendigerweise eine Verschlechterung der Effizienz des Gesamtsystems auch bei dynamischem Zugriff zur Folge hat. Bewährt hat sich ferner die strikte Trennung zwischen rein syntaktischer (z. B. Editieren) und semantischer Behandlung der Bestände. Erforderlichenfalls wurden Transformationskomponenten zwischengeschaltet, um eine Anpassung an existierende Interpreter zu erreichen.

Die implementierten Verfahren zur Sicherung der semantischen und physischen Integrität stellen eine wertvolle Hilfe bei der praktischen Arbeit mit Wissensbasen dar. Sie sind allerdings gezielt einzusetzen, um die Effizienz des Systems nicht zu gefährden.

Insgesamt kann eingeschätzt werden, daß mit der vorliegenden Implementation ein System geschaffen wurde, das bereits Aspekte der im Abschn. 3 aufgestellten Forderungen 1 bis 4 erfüllt. Dagegen stehen die Forderungen 5 und 6 weiterhin auf der Tagesordnung.

6 Schlußbemerkungen

Mit der vorliegenden Arbeit wurde das Anliegen verfolgt, grundlegende Aspekte der Schaffung von Wissensbankbetriebssystemen zu diskutieren. Es wurden wesentliche Merkmale derartiger Systeme herausgearbeitet. Die im Abschn. 4 vorgestellten Konzepte stellen lediglich einen ersten Schritt in die angegebene Richtung dar. Für die Entwicklung einer umfassenden Wissensbanktechnologie ist neben der Schaffung von Basissoftware zur (systemtechnischen) Wissensverarbeitung ein zweiter Schwerpunkt zu setzen - die wissensbasierte Modellierung von Diskursbereichen, d. h. die Unterstützung des Prozesses der wissensbasierten Aufbereitung von Anwendungsgebieten (Wissenserwerb). Hier liegt mit der KADS- Technologie ([2]) eine leistungsfähige Methodologie vor. Erst die Verbindung von Basissoftware zur Wissensverarbeitung (Wissensbankbetriebssystem) mit einem für die Wissensverarbeitung aufbereiteten Diskursbereich (Wissensbasis) bildet ein Wissensbanksystem, das Nutzern ausreichend und effizient Informationen über einen Teil der Realität bereitstellt.

Literatur

[1] Altenkrüger, D.E.: KBMS: Aspects, Theory and Implementation. in: Information Systems 15(1990)1

[2] Breuker, J; Wielinga, B.; u.a.: Model-Driven Knowledge Acquisition: Interpretation Models. University of Amsterdam, 1987

[3] Brodie, M.L.; Mylopoulos, J.: On Knowledge Base Management Systems. Springer-Verlag, New York, 1986

[4] Christaller, T; Primio, F.; Voß, A.: Die KI-Werkbank BABYLON. Bonn: Addison-Wesley, 1989

[5] Oertel, W.: Eine funktionale Methode der Wissensrepräsentation. Dresden, Techn. Univ., 1988, Diss. A

[6] Oertel, W.: Ein System von Werkzeugen zur Wissensverarbeitung. in: Wissenschaftliche Tagungen der TU Karl-Marx-Stadt 6/1990

Konstruktion und Evaluation von Wissensbasen in textverstehenden Systemen

Thomas Pirlein

IBM Deutschland
Wissenschaftliches Zentrum
Institut für wissensbasierte Systeme
Postfach 80 08 80
7000 Stuttgart 80
Email: PIRLEIN@DS0LILOG.BITNET

Zusammenfassung

Diese Arbeit beschäftigt sich mit Aspekten der Aufbereitung von Hintergrundwissen für ein textverstehendes System. Es wird die These aufgestellt, daß man nur durch die Spezifikation eines *Szenarios* eine Wissensbasis für ein solches System entwickeln und evaluieren kann.

Ein *Szenario* eines wissensbasierten Systems wird definiert als eine konzeptuelle Rahmenbeschreibung, in der eine funktionale und kontextuelle Abgrenzung hinsichtlich des Aufgabenbereichs, Gegenstandsbereichs und der Modellierungsgranularität geschieht.

Ein solches Szenario dient also dazu, die Aufgabe, den Gegenstandsbereich und die Modellierungstiefe der Wissensmodellierung festzuhalten und dadurch einen Aufbau und eine Bewertung der Modellierung überhaupt zu ermöglichen. In diesem Papier wird gezeigt, wie ein Szenario definiert und in der Praxis angewendet werden kann.

Zuerst wird in Kapitel 2 die Wissensmodellierung für textverstehende Systeme von Modellierungen für andere Systeme abgegrenzt. Das Resultat dieser Analyse bildet ein Schema, mit dessen Hilfe man Wissensmodellierungen *charakterisieren* und *differenzieren* kann. Wie dieses Schema den *Aufbau* von Wissensbasen beeinflußt, ist Gegenstand des vierten Kapitels. Für das System LEU/2 im LILOG-Projekt wird ein prototypisches Szenario angegeben, anhand dessen eine exemplarische Modellierung erfolgt. Die anschließende Evaluation dieser Modellierung bildet den Abschluß der Arbeit (Kapitel 5).

1 Einleitung

Geht man von der in der Künstlichen Intelligenz angenommenen Hypothese aus, daß das Verstehen von natürlichsprachlichen Äußerungen ohne Wissen über die Regularitäten in der Welt nicht möglich ist, können textverstehende Systeme zu der Klasse der wissensbasierten Systemen gezählt werden. Trotz dieser grundlegenden Hypothese liegt bisher keine Methodik zur Aufbereitung eines zum Textverstehen notwendigen Weltausschnitts vor (siehe z.B. [Bra90]). Orientiert man sich an Vorschlägen aus dem Bereich der Expertensysteme, bemerkt man bald, daß die dort angewandten Vorgehensweisen nicht einfach übertragbar sind. Gründe für diese Inkompatibilität werden u.a. in dieser Arbeit diskutiert.

Grundlegend für die hier dargelegte Vorgehensweise ist die Spezifikation eines Szenarios. Dabei ergeben sich Parallelen zum Software Engineering: in der Spezifikationsphase wird bei der Entwicklung von (traditioneller) Software ein Übergang von einer unpräzisen Anforderungsumschreibung zu einer formalen Spezifikation beschrieben. Da eine formale Spezifikation im Bereich der Rekonstruktion von Wissen nicht möglich ist [Par89], soll ein Szenario ein Äquivalent zu dieser formalen Spezifikation bilden.

Meist wird bei der Konstruktion einer Wissensbasis für textverstehende Systeme (und auch anderer wissensbasierter Systeme) ein Szenario zwar *implizit* mitgeführt - um möglichst allgemeingültig und flexibel zu bleiben, wird aber auf eine Explizierung oft verzichtet. In diesem Papier wird dagegen der Standpunkt vertreten, daß nur durch eine explizite Diskussion eine Wissensmodellierung für eine Wissensbasis möglich ist.

Im folgenden wird deshalb versucht, vom Wissensbasisaufbau für textverstehende Systeme zu abstrahieren und allgemeine charakterisierende Eigenschaften von Wissensbasen auszudifferenzieren. Durch diese

Differenzierung soll ein Schritt in Richtung einer methodischen Vorgehensweise zur Klassifikation (Kapitel 2, 3), Konstruktion (Kapitel 4) und Evaluierung (Kapitel 5) von allgemeinen Wissensbasen und speziell Wissensbasen für textverstehende Systeme, gemacht werden.

2 Charakteristika wissensbasierter Systeme

Postuliert man, daß Wissen überhaupt repräsentierbar ist und daß es Strukturen geben muß, in denen Wissen explizit repräsentiert wird, kann man den Prozeß der Wissensrepräsentation als einen Modellbildungsprozeß interpretieren. Um Methoden für die systematische Rekonstruktion von Wissen für wissensbasierte Systeme zu finden, sollen deshalb Prinzipien der Modelltheorie betrachtet und in die Wissensrepräsentation transferiert werden.

Die Bildung eines Modellsystems läßt sich modelltheoretisch durch vier Merkmale charakterisieren (siehe beispielsweise [Sta73]):

1. **Abbildungsmerkmal:** Modelle sind stets Modelle von etwas und somit Abbildungen bestimmter natürlicher oder künstlicher Systeme.

2. **Subjektivierungsmerkmal:** Modelle erfüllen ihre Repräsentations- und Ersetzungsfunktion nur für *bestimmte Subjekte.*

3. **Verkürzungsmerkmal:** Modelle erfassen *nicht alle Eigenschaften von Entitäten* der durch sie repräsentierten Originalsysteme.

4. **pragmatisches Merkmal:** Modelle werden nach Zweckmäßigkeitsgesichtspunkten gewählt und sind abhängig von Sacherwägungen.

Überträgt man die letzten drei Punkte auf die Repräsentation von Wissen sind drei Fragestellungen interessant:

zu 2. **Gegenstandsbereich:** Wird bei der Modellierung nur ein bestimmter Ausschnitt der Welt betrachtet?

zu 3. **Granularität:** Wo wird die Grenze zwischen molarer und molekularer Ebene[1] gezogen bzw. welche Primitive werden in diesem Modell angenommen?[2]

zu 4. **Aufgabe:** Wird bei der Modellierung des Wissens über die Welt schon eine konkrete Problemstellung berücksichtigt?

Daraus ergeben sich folgende Aspekte der Wissensmodellierung, die man in drei Achsen aufspannen kann: (siehe Abb. 1):

1. **Gegenstandsbereichskomplexität:** den Umfang des Weltausschnitts bzw. Gegenstandsbereichs, der modelliert wird.

2. **Modellierungstiefe:** die Tiefe der Wissensmodellierung, in der modelliert wird.

3. **Aufgabenkomplexität:** die Komplexität der Aufgabe, für die modelliert wird.

2.1 Klassifikation von Wissensmodellierungen

Diese dreidimensionale, stetige Darstellung soll in zweierlei Hinsicht modifiziert werden. Zum einen soll die Einteilung diskret nach Gegensatzpaaren erfolgen. Zum anderen soll über die Beurteilung der Tiefe einer Modellbildung der menschliche Wissensbestand als Vergleichsmaßstab herangezogen werden. Das letzte Merkmal „Modellierungstiefe" teilt sich somit wiederum auf in Wissensbestände, die die Mehrzahl[3] der

---

[1] Wie 'feinkörnig' das Wissen über eine Entität ist bzw. auf welcher Abstraktionsebene die Primitiva gewählt werden, wird oft mit dem Begriff 'Granularität' bezeichnet. [MGP60] unterscheidet in diesem Zusammenhang zwischen der molaren und der molekularen Ebene: die molare Ebene setzt sich aus molekularen Bausteinen zusammen.

[2] Da ein absolutes Modell nicht angebbar ist, wird meist für einen Gegenstandsbereich Primitiva zu definieren, die bei Wechsel in einen anderen Gegenstandsbereich neu definiert oder ergänzt werden dürfen.

[3] D.h. Wissen, das von einer Subkultur bzw. einer Sprachgemeinschaft geteilt wird.

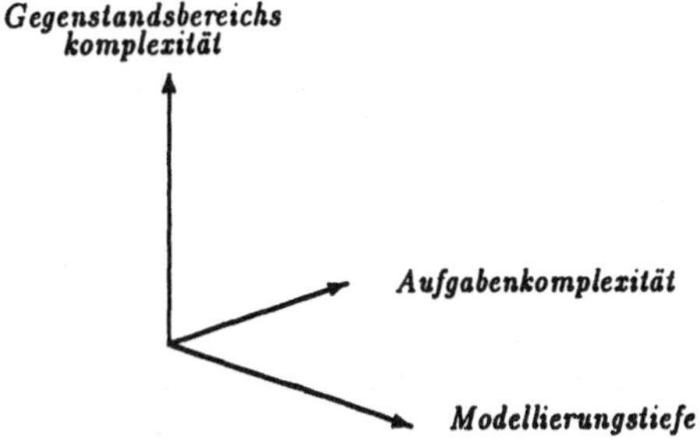

Abbildung 1: Aspekte der Wissensmodellierung (I)

Menschen besitzt[4] und in spezielles Wissen, welches meist in Wissenschaftsbereichen benötigt wird und somit hauptsächlich bei Fachexperten gefunden wird.

Spannt man nun dieses Schema mit den eingeführten Gegensatzpaaren auf, ergibt sich das Schaubild in Abbildung 2.

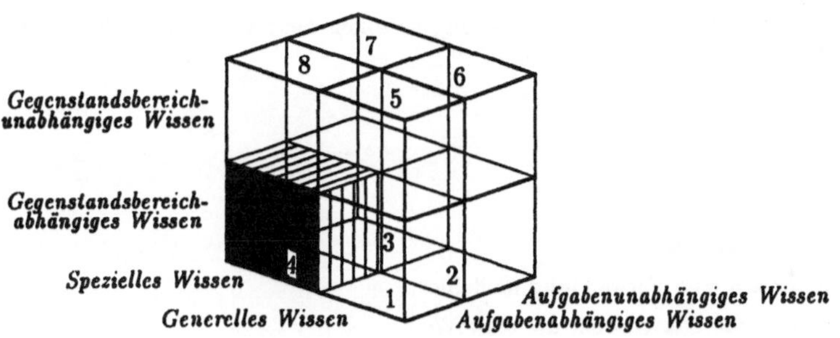

Abbildung 2: Aspekte der Wissensmodellierung (II)

Durch die Einführung dieser drei Merkmale werden in dem Würfel acht Teilquader definiert. Zur Veranschaulichung des Schemas ist Teilquader 4 schraffiert worden.

2.2 Beispielsysteme

Im folgenden sollen zu den Teilquadern Beispielsysteme angegeben und Problembereiche dieser Einteilung diskutiert werden. Die Durchnumerierung der folgenden Beispielsysteme stimmt mit der Numerierung der Teilquader in Abbildung 2 überein.

Beispielssysteme zu jedem Teilquader können wie folgt angegeben werden:

1. Blocks World [Win72]

- *Gegenstandsbereich*: Ansammlung von Blöcken in einem Raum
- *Aufgabe*: Planen von Bewegungssequenz für einen einarmigen Roboter
- *Modellierungstiefe*: generelles physikalisches, objekt- und raumorientiertes Problemlösewissen

---

[4][HM85] beispielsweise nennen dies „Kernwissen", d.h. Wissen, welches jeder intelligente Agent besitzt.

2. Liquids [Hay85]

- *Gegenstandsbereich*: relativ autonomer Teilbereich ('cluster') aus dem Alltagswissen: 'Flüssigke ten'
- *Aufgabe*: ohne Hinblick auf eine Verwendung modelliert
- *Modellierungstiefe*: generelles Wissen

3. Bitter Pills [SvLNP86]

- *Gegenstandsbereich*: Gebrauch, Anwendungsmöglichkeiten, Nebenwirkungen, Dosierungen etc von Arzneien
- *Aufgabe*: In einer bewußt unwissenschaftlichen Sprache soll Laien das fachspezifische Wissen au einer wissenschaftlichen Disziplin (Medizin, Pharmazie) nahegebracht werden.
- *Modellierungstiefe*: spezielles Wissen aus medizinischer Fachliteratur

4. klassische Expertensysteme

- *Gegenstandsbereich*: eng umrissenes Spezialgebiet
- *Aufgabe*: hohes Leistungspotential an *Problemlösefähigkeit*
- *Modellierungstiefe*: spezielles Fachwissen

5. Naive Semantics [Dah88]

- *Gegenstandsbereich*: gegenstandsbereichsunabhängig, es sollen neue Gegenstandsbereiche („businness, finance, ..") angebunden werden können
- *Aufgabe*: Textverstehen
- *Modellierungstiefe*: generelles, prototypisches Wissen

6. CYC [LG8b]

- *Gegenstandsbereich*: Alltagswissen
- *Aufgabe*: ohne Hinblick auf eine Verwendung modelliert
- *Modellierungstiefe*: generelle Fakten über die reale Welt

7. und 8. In diesem Quadermodell gibt es Bereiche, denen man keine existierende Wissensmodellierung zuordnen kann. Die Gründe dafür sind in der Charakteristikakombination 'gegenstandsbereichunabhängiges Wissen' und 'spezielles Wissen' zu suchen: In dieser Zusammenstellung wird für *jeden* Gegenstandsbereich Spezialwissen verlangt. Ansätze für eine Wissensmodellierung in diese Richtung bilden vielleicht flexible Ontologien, in denen besonderer Wert auf einfache Erweiterbarkeit der Wissensbasis durch neue Gegenstandsbereiche gelegt wird.

Ein weiterer zu beachtender Aspekt dieses Quadermodells ergibt sich aus der gewählten diskreten Einteilungsform: Beispielsweise haben die Aufgabenstellungen 'allgemeines Sprachverstehen in allen Gegenstandsbereichen' und 'Diagnose von Virusinfektionen' unterschiedliche Komplexität, werden aber in dieser Komplexität im Schema nicht voneinander unterschieden.

2.3 Eingrenzungsmöglichkeiten der Wissenmodellierung

Im letzten Kapitel wurde versucht, inhaltliche Aspekte der Wissensmodellierung aufzuzeigen und Kriterien zu geben, die bei der *Klassifikation* von Wissen in WBS behilflich sein können.

Will man nun bei der *Entwicklung* einer Wissenbasis ein ad-hoc-Vorgehen des Modellierers weitgehend vermeiden, müssen wiederum Kriterien gegeben sein, aus denen sich Modellierungsanforderungen ableiten lassen. Bis jetzt gibt es aber noch keinen allgemeinen Prinzipienkatalog, durch den man das Wissen in einer Domäne erschließen und strukturieren kann (siehe beispielsweise [SvLNP86, S.11]).

Als eine mögliche Vorgehensweise soll die Entwicklung einer Wissensbasis aus den Charakteristika 'Aufgabenabhängigkeit, Wahl des Gegenstandsbereichs und Tiefe der Modellierung' versucht werden. Wie ein solches Vorgehen in einem konkreten Beispiel aussehen kann, soll im folgenden behandelt werden. Die Systemkonzeption eines wissensbasierten Systems muß in Worte gefaßt werden. Dazu soll der Begriff *'Szenario'* einführt werden:

> Ein *Szenario* eines wissensbasierten Systems ist eine konzeptuelle Rahmenbeschreibung, in der eine funktionale und kontextuelle Abgrenzung hinsichtlich der Leistungsfähigkeit dieses Systems in Bezug auf Aufgabenbereich, Gegenstandsbereich und Modellierungsgranularität geschieht.

In einem Szenario können also implizit oder explizit Aussagen über Gegebenheiten in einem Gegenstandsbereich, die Spezifität dieser Gegebenheiten und Aufgaben- und Problemgebiete enthalten sein. Insofern bietet ein Szenario die Möglichkeit, die vorher angegebenen Kriterien direkt oder indirekt einzugrenzen.

Im weiteren soll nun der Einfluß eines Beispielszenarios auf den konkreten Prozeß der Wissensmodellierung untersucht werden.

3 Aspekte der Wissensmodellierung in LEU/2

Das Beispielszenario wurde im Rahmen des LILOG-Projekts (LInguistische und LOGische Methoden zur maschinellen Verarbeitung des Deutschen [HRS86]) der IBM Deutschland GmbH entwickelt. Innerhalb dieses Projekts wurde ein prototypisches natürlichsprachliches System LEU/2 (LILOG-Experimentier-Umgebung/2) entwickelt. Das Beispielszenario für LEU/2 sieht wie folgt aus ([vLMP89]):

> *Eine Gruppe von Geschäftsleuten hält sich zu einer einwöchigen Veranstaltung in Düsseldorf auf. Während dieser Veranstaltung ist ein freier Nachmittag vorgesehen, der durch Besichtigungen von Sehenswürdigkeiten in der Altstadt von Düsseldorf genutzt werden soll. Zur Information über diese Sehenswürdigkeiten sind textuelle Beschreibungen der jeweiligen Objekte in ein System eingegeben worden, die Nachfragen über die Texte im Sinne eines Auskunftssystems erlauben.*

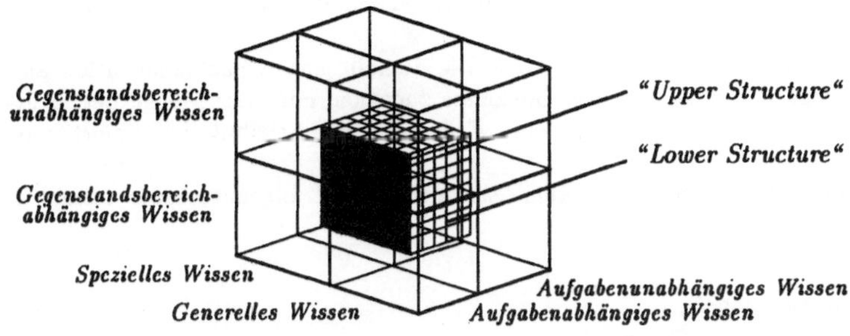

Abbildung 3: LEU/2

Die Einordnung aufgrund der Charakteristika von LEU/2 in den Quader kann man in Abbildung 3 sehen. Auf die Begriffe 'Upper Structure' und 'Lower Structure' soll später eingegangen werden.

Im folgenden wird begründet, wie die Definition eines Szenarios für die LEU/2-Wissensbasisentwicklung genutzt wurde. Dabei werden zwei Wege eingeschlagen. Zunächst wird das Szenario mit Modellierungsentscheidungen in der Hintergrundwissensbasis in Beziehung gesetzt. Im nächsten Schritt wird anhand des Szenarios eine Evaluierung des implementierten Prototypen und speziell der Wissensbasis skizziert.

4 Konstruktion anhand des Szenarios

Anhand der drei Dimensionen Aufgabenstellung, Gegenstandsbereich und Modellierungstiefe wird jetzt die Konstruktion der Wissensbasis diskutiert.

4.1 Modellierung anhand der Aufgabenstellung

In obigem Szenario sind Informationen über die Aufgabenstellung *explizit* enthalten: LEU/2 ist ein Auskunftssystem, welches Texte verstehen und natürlichsprachliche Anfragen beantworten soll.

Um Sprache verstehen zu können, kommt man automatisch mit den verschiedensten Domänen in Kontakt (siehe z.B. [Win72]) - eine Modellierung des benötigten Wissens sollte also möglichst bereichsunabhängig geschehen. Deshalb wurde in der Modellierung des Hintergrundwissens eine Zweiteilung in 'Upper Structure' und 'Lower Structure' vorgenommen.

In der 'Upper Structure' wird bereichsunabhängiges Wissen für Textverstehen modelliert, in der 'Lower Structure' wird stärker auf das Wissen über den spezifischen Gegenstandsbereich eingegangen.

Eine Modellierungsentscheidung war deshalb, die 'Upper Structure' in bereichsunabhängige Cluster einzuteilen, wie sie beispielsweise schon durch [Hay79] motiviert wurde. Das folgende Beispiel soll zeigen, wie die Wissensmodellierung für ein Cluster - das der Ereignisse - von der Aufgabendimension des Szenarios beeinflußt wurde.

Ereignisse unterscheiden sich von anderen Entitäten dadurch, daß sie nur in ihrem Verlauf in Raum und vor allem Zeit existieren und charakterisiert werden können. Ereignisse werden in natürlichsprachlichen Wissensquellen meist durch Verben eingeführt. Es war deshalb naheliegend, schon existierende Verbklassifikationen der Linguistik als Orientierungshilfe heranzuziehen. Eine der bekanntesten Verbklassifikationen wurde von Vendler angegeben [Ven67]. Vendler unterscheidet zwischen telischen und atelischen Prozessen/Zuständen bzw. Verben und nimmt folgende Verbklassen an:

- Zustände (states - Heinz kann Deutsch) und Handlungen

- Handlungen sind entweder Prozesse (activities - Heinz schreibt) oder Ereignisse.

- Ereignisse sind entweder ausgedehnt (accomplishments - Heinz schreibt einen Brief) oder punktuell (achievements - Heinz findet die Lösung).

Accomplishments (acc) und Achievements (ach) sind Ereignisse im engeren Sinne: beide haben ein inhärentes Ende und streben auf ein Ziel zu. Activities lassen sich auf minimale Intervalle, States sogar auf Punkte abbilden und besitzen also im Gegensatz zu zielgerichteten Ereignissen, die sogenannte 'Subintervall-Eigenschaft'.

Ereignisse sind also entweder zielgerichtet oder nicht. Es wurde deshalb eine Kreuzklassifikation aufgebaut und jedes Ereignis der Menge der zielgerichteten Ereignisse zuordnen oder der Menge der nicht-zielgerichteten Ereignisse. Ob ein Ereignis sein Ziel erreicht, wird durch ein Attribut 'kulminiert' ausgedrückt.

Somit kann man Ereignisse unter dem Charakteristikum 'Zielgerichtetheit' folgendermaßen formal in L_{LILOG} [5] strukturieren:

```
sort a-telisch-E      <  ereignis.
sort zielgerichtet-E  <  and(a-telisch-E,
                              ziel :: ereignis,
                              kulminiert : {j n}).
sort nicht-ziel-E     <  a_telisch-E;
                              disjoint zielgerichtet-E.
sort activity-E       <  nicht-zielgerichtet-E.
sort state-E          <  nicht-zielgerichtet-E;
                              disjoint  dynamisch-E.
```

Durch die Orientierung an der Aufgabenstellung ergab sich in der Wissensmodellierung die Möglichkeit, die linguistische Einteilung in telische und nichttelische Verben zu übernehmen. Diese Unterscheidung wurde codiert und in den Modulkorpus[6] zur Klassifikation von Ereignissen aufgenommen.

---

[5] L_{LILOG} ist der in LILOG benutzte Repräsentationsformalismus (siehe [PvL89])

[6] Der Modulkorpus zur Definition von Ereignissen besteht aus mehreren Modulen in der 'Upper Structure' die alle dazu dienen, die spezifischen Charakteristika von Ereignissen repräsentieren zu können: Zielgerichtetheit, Kulmination, Kausalität, Intention, zeitliches Verhalten, Wahrnehmbarkeit, Ortsmodifikationen, kulturelle Gebundenheit, etc.

4.2 Modellierung anhand der Gegenstandsbereich

Der Gegenstandsbereich ist zumindest räumlich reduziert auf die Düsseldorfer Altstadt - die notwendige Breite und Tiefe der Modellierung steckt aber *implizit* in der Szenariobeschreibung.

Das Wissen über den Gegenstandsbereich liegt in Form von Texten über die Düsseldorfer Altstadt vor. Das Szenario besteht also in erster Linie aus der Rahmengeschichte, manifestiert sich aber auch in den Texten.[7]

In dem Gegenstandsbereich bzw. den Texten tauchen oft geschichtliche Daten über Objekte auf: wichtig sind hier Vorgänge wie Planung, Entstehung, Restaurierung, Umbau etc. und ihre kausalen und temporalen Beziehungen untereinander. Modifikationen sind verändernde Prozesse an Entitäten, die destruktiv, konstruktiv oder variativ sein können und Einfluß auf das Erscheinungsbild dieser Entität haben. Dabei spielen Orts- und Zeitwechsel, die für Ereignisse sonst charakteristisch sind, keine Rolle.

Ortsmodifikationen erfassen die Veränderungen, die zwar das Wesen eines Objektes nicht beeinflußen, aber seine lokale Dimension. In LEU/2 wird oft von aktiven ('bummeln') und passiven ('fahren') Ortsveränderungen geredet.

Durch diese Analyse des Gegenstandsbereichs konnten Anforderungen an eine Ereignisklassifikation identifiziert werden. Orts- und Wesensmodifikationen wurden deshalb auch in den Modulkorpus der 'Upper Structure' aufgenommen (siehe Abbildung 4).

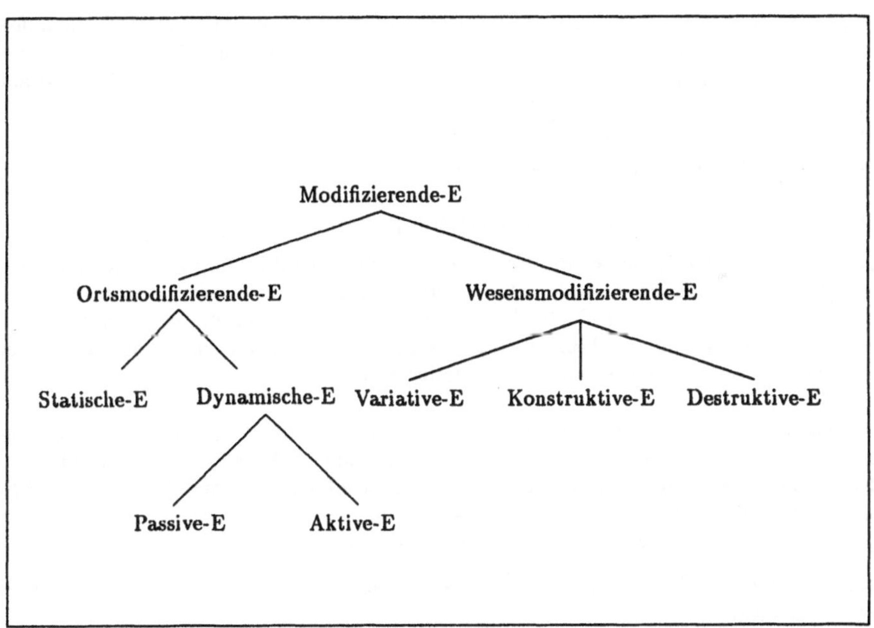

Abbildung 4: Modifikation von Ereignissen als Sortenstruktur

4.3 Modellierung anhand der Modellierungstiefe

Die Entscheidung über die Modellierungstiefe in der Wissensbasis läßt sich ebenfalls anhand des eben angegebenen Beispiels diskutieren.

Die Modellierungstiefe in dem Ereignischarakteristikum 'Modifikation' ergibt sich aus der Analyse der zu erwartenden Fragen von fiktiven Szenario-Geschäftsleuten und durch die Analyse des Textkorpus.

---

[7] Eine Analyse der Auswirkungen des Szenarios auf die gesamte Wissensrekonstruktion einer Ontologie soll wegen der Komplexität [Pir90] vorbehalten sein.

Wesensmodifizierende Ereignisse treten in den Texten hauptsächlich in Verbindung mit Sehenswürdigkeiten und räumlich modifizierbaren Objekten auf. Interessant hierbei ist, ob etwas geschaffen, zerstört oder variiert wurde. Wichtig ist deswegen in unserem Kontext, neben den obligatorischen Raum und Zeitangaben, welche Entitäten modifiziert wurden und wie bzw. durch wen sie modifiziert wurden. Wenn es sich um eine Variation handelt, ist noch wichtig, was variiert wurde, und ob es sich beispielsweise um eine Restauration, Renovierung, Umbau, Ersetzung des Objektes handelt. Auf konkrete Feinheiten eines Restaurationsvorgangs kann verzichtet werden.

Hier sind wieder Szenarien - beispielsweise der Baubranche oder des Antiquitätenhandels - denkbar, bei denen in diesen Bereichen tiefer modelliert werden müßte. Auch werden bei einer Ersetzung relevante Informationen über das ersetzte Teil nicht bei dem Ersetzungsereignis angegeben, sondern bei dem Objekt, welches in einem anderen Teil der Ontologie modelliert wird.

5 Evaluation anhand des Szenarios

Momentan wird versucht, die durch das Szenario festgelegten Anforderungen auf verschiedene Weise mit der erreichten Implementation zu vergleichen.

Durch die Aufgabe 'Textverstehen', die in der Rahmengeschichte festgelegt wurde, ist die Wissensbasis in ein System eingebunden, in dem Anforderungen aus den verschiedenen Schnittstellenbeziehungen an die Wissensbasis herangetragen werden und nach denen sich auch die Modellierung richten konnte. Hier gilt es zu bewerten, inwieweit die Anforderungen erfüllt und systematisch eingebracht werden konnten (siehe Kapitel 5.1).

Durch die Definition des Gegenstandsbereichs, der sich hauptsächlich in den Texten manifestiert, kann eine Evaluation geschehen, indem man beispielsweise die Veränderung des Textkorpus in dem zeitlichen Verlauf des Projektes betrachtet und durch vorgenommene Glättungen im Text Hinweise auf Modellierungsschwächen bekommt (siehe Kapitel 5.2).

Evaluiert man die Wahl der Granularität, interessieren u.a. wie flexibel die Modellierung ist, wenn man die Modellierungstiefe variiert (siehe Kapitel 5.3).

5.1 Evaluation anhand der Aufgabenstellung

Am naheliegensten ist die Evaluation der Modellierung indem man den Grad des Textverstehens durch rein empirische Methoden mißt. Dies wurde auf zweierlei Weise getan: zum einen kann man die Wissensbasis *statisch* evaluieren, indem man nur die Struktur der Wissensbasis betrachtet. Zum anderen kann man eine *dynamische* Evaluierung durchführen, indem man die Wissensbasis im laufenden System, d.h. im Zusammenspiel mit den anderen Komponenten, betrachtet.

Dynamische Evaluierung: Dazu wurde eine Sammlung von Frage/Antwort - Paaren mit dem Ziel zusammengestellt, die Antwortkapazität des Systems herauszufinden. Man versuchte, eine Menge von Fragen zu finden, die in diesem Szenario zu erwarten sind: z.B. 'Wie komme ich zum Hetjensmuseum?' oder 'Hat das Hetjensmusem dienstags geöffnet?'. Diese Fragen wurden durch systematische Analyse der verstandenen Texte gewonnen. Die Wissensbasis wurde beispielsweise dahingehend untersucht, ob

- 'tote Bereiche' d.h. Wissensbasisbereiche, die nie oder sehr selten angesprochen werden, identifiziert werden können.

- Fragen nicht beantwortet werden können, weil Definitionen fehlen oder unvollständig sind.

- die Modellierung uneffizient ist, d.h. durch umständliche Modellierung die Gesamtperformanz herabgesetzt wird.

- die Modellierung zu gegenstandsbereichsabhängig modelliert wurde. Dies würde dann der Fall sein, wenn die WB-Zugriffe häuptsächlich auf der 'Lower-Structure'-Ebene geschehen würde.

- die Zugriffsfunktionen der anderen Komponenten (Semantik, Generierung, ..) quantitativ und qualitativ unterstützt werden können. Die Wissensbasis wird somit als 'Servicekomponente' betrachtet.

Erst durch die Definition eines Szenarios mit einem definierten Textkorpus wurde die Möglichkeit gegeben, die oben genannten Punkte zu untersuchen und adäquate Fragen stellen zu können.

Statische Evaluierung: Die Wissensbasis wird nicht im laufenden System betrachtet, sondern aus statischer Perspektive. Als Kriterien waren statistische Auswertungen nach der Anzahl der Konzepte, Attribute und Axiome und deren Verhältnis untereinander von Interesse.

Von vorrangigem qualitativen Interesse im Blick auf die Aufgabendimension 'Sprachverstehen' stand das Problem der Entsprechung zwischen 'linguistischem Wissen' und 'Weltwissen'. Eine Analyse erbrachte eine eigentlich unbeabsichtigt Gliederung der 'Upper Structure' in Konzepte ähnlich der syntaktischen Wortklassenunterscheidung in 'Adjektive, Verben und Substantive'. Die momentane Arbeit konzentriert sich deshalb darauf, solche unscharfen bzw. unbewußt vollzogenen Unterscheidungen zu identifizieren und dokumentieren.

5.2 Evaluation anhand des Gegenstandsbereiches

Der Textkorpus wurde im Laufe der Projektdauer verändert und angepaßt um ad-hoc-Lösungen zu vermeiden. Konnten bestimmte Phänomene im Hinblick auf zu schwierige oder zu textspezielle Konstruktionen nicht behandelt werden, wurden die Texte geglättet. Eine Sammlung und Auswertung dieser Stellen gibt Aufschluß über die Leistungsfähigkeit des Prototypen im allgemeinen und über die Modellierungsproblematik im speziellen.

Beispiele:

- Schwierige syntaktische Konstruktionen wie Kopula-Konstruktionen und Patizipialkonstruktionen wurden geglättet (Projektfokus).

- Schwierigen adjektivische Beziehungen wurden geglättet (Modellierungsfokus).

- Vagheitsphänomene wurden weitgehend aus den Texten genommen, da aus verschiedenen Gründen keine adäquate Modellierung möglich war (Modellierungsfokus).

In engem Zusammenhang zur 'Upper Structure' steht natürlich die Ebene der 'Lower Structure' in dem der gegenstandsbereichsabhängige Teil der Modellierung ansetzte. Die folgenden Beispiele sollen ein Gefühl für die Zusammenhänge geben:

- Sind alle Entitäten die in diesem Gegenstandsbereich auftauchen können, im Modell enthalten (Vollständigkeit)? Dies kann beispielsweise durch alternative Texte aus der Domäne überprüft werden.

- Können alle Objekte aus der Domäne mit Konstrukten der 'Upper Structure' ausgedrückt werden? Wo mußten die Texte deswegen verändert werden?

5.3 Evaluation anhand der Modellierungstiefe

Ziel der Einführung der Modellierungtiefe war es, die Modellierung in Bezug auf das als 'normal' in unserem Szenario geltende Wissen beschränken zu können. Die Modellierung sollte aber dynamisch vertieft werden können, d.h. bei einem Übergang in eine andere Domäne oder beim Übergang in eine größere Granularität sollte sich die bisherige Modellierung nicht stark verändern.

Bei der Evaluation der Modellierung der Zielgerichtetheit von Ereignissen ergab sich der folgende Konflikt. Entitäten sind nur dann Zustände, wenn man sich für ihre innere Struktur nicht weiter interessiert, d.h. wenn die 'Subintervall-Eigenschaft' auf sie zutrifft. In unserem Szenario beispielsweise wird das Ereignis 'Projektsitzung' in seiner Struktur nicht weiter zerlegt. Es werden zwar Aussagen gemacht, die das Ereignis betreffen - es sind aber keine Aussagen über die interne Struktur (Begrüßung, Reden, Pausen, Verabschiedung,...) notwendig - woraus folgt, daß 'Projektsitzung' ein Zustand ist. Bei einer detaillierteren Modellierung dieses Konzepts müßte die Umkategorisierung auf sehr abstraktem Level in der 'Upper Structure' erfolgen - ein Effekt der nicht wünschenswert ist.

Eine mögliche Konsequenz ist, die linguistische Unterscheidung zwischen 'Zustand' und 'Nichtzustand' in LEU/2 nicht zu benutzen.

6   Schlußbemerkung

Es wurde gezeigt, wie sich der Vorgang der Wissensrekonstruktion auf einen Modellbildungsprozeß zurückführen läßt und wie man dadurch Charakteristika zur *Klassifikation* von Wissensbasen gewinnen kann. Diese Charakteristika wurden dazu benutzt, ein Szenario für ein konkretes natürlichsprachliches System anzugeben. Erst durch dieses Szenario war es möglich, die Anforderungen an die zu konstruierende Wissensbasis zu spezifizieren und Leitlinien für eine *Konstruktion* und *Evaluation* dieser Wissensbasis zu geben.

Bei der Entwicklung von LEU/2 zeigte sich, daß das Szenario eine wichtige Orientierungshilfe für die Wissensmodellierung war, ohne daß dadurch die allgemeine Verwendbarkeit der Wissensbasis eingeschränkt wurde.[8] Darüber hinaus bietet die Analyse der Veränderungen des Szenarios im Laufe der Entwicklung der Wissensbasis eine gute Grundlage, um das System zu bewerten und zu verbessern.

Literatur

[Bra90] R. J. Brachman. The future of knowlege representation. *ACM Transactions on Programming Languages and Systems*, pages 1082–1092, 1990.

[Dah88] Kathleen Dahlgren. *Naive Semantics for Natural Language Understanding*. Kluwer international series in engineering and computer science. Natural language processing and machine translation. Kluwer Academic Publishers, Boston, etc., 1988.

[Hay79] Patrick J. Hayes. The naive physics manifesto. In D. Michie, editor, *Expert Systems in the Microelectronic Age*. Edinburgh Univ. Press, 1979.

[Hay85] Patrick J. Hayes. Naive physics I: Ontology for liquids. In J. R. Hobbs and R. C. Moore, editors, *Formal Theories of the Commonsense World*, pages 71–108. Ablex Publishing Corporation, Norwood, NJ, 1985.

[HM85] J.R. Hobbs and R.C. Moore. Formal theories of the commonsense world. *Ablex Publishing Corporation*, 1985.

[HRS86] O. Herzog, C.-R. Rollinger, and P. (et.al.) Schmitt. *LILOG - Linguistische und logische Methoden für das maschinelle Verstehen des Deutschen*. LILOG-REPORT 1. IBM Deutschland GmbH, August 1986.

[LG8b] Doug Lenat and R.V. Guha. The world according to cyc, September 1988b. MCC Technical Report No. ACA-AI-300-88.

[LP91] Kai von Luck and Thomas Pirlein. Constructing a Context for LEU/2. In O. Herzog and C. Rollinger, editors, *Text Understanding in LILOG*. Springer-Verlag, Berlin, Heidelberg, 1991. to appear.

[vLMP89] Kai von Luck, Ralf Meyer, and Thomas Pirlein. Die logische Rekonstruktion eines Gegenstandsbereiches. In Retti and Leidlmair, editors, *Proceedings of ÖGAI-89*, pages 278–287. Springer Verlag, Berlin, Heidelberg, 1989.

[MGP60] G.A. Miller, E. Galanter, and K.H. Pribram. *Plans and the Structure of Behaviour*. The Free Press, Holt, 1960.

[Par89] Derek Partrige. *KI und das Software Engineering der Zukunft*. McCraw-Hill, Hamburg, etc., 1989.

[Pir90] Thomas Pirlein. *Rekonstruktion von Hintergrundwissen für ein wissensbasiertes textverstehendes System*, volume 129 of *IWBS-REPORT*. IBM Deutschland GmbH, Stuttgart, 1990.

[PvL89] Udo Pletat and Kai von Luck. Knowledge Representation in LILOG. In Karl-Hans Bläsius, Uli Hedtstück, and Claus Rollinger, editors, *Sorts and Types in Artificial Intelligence*. Springer Verlag, Berlin, Heidelberg, 1989.

[Sta73] H. Stachowiak. *Allgemeine Modelltheorie*. Springer Verlag, Wiesbaden, 1973.

[SvLNP86] Albrecht Schmiedel, Kai von Luck, Bernhard Nebel, and Christof Peltason. 'bitter pills'—a case study in knowledge representation. KIT Report 39, Technische Universität Berlin, Berlin, August 1986.

[Ven67] Zeno Vendler. *Linguistics in Philosophy*. Cornell University Press, Ithaca, N. Y., 1967.

[Win72] Terry Winograd. *Understanding natural language*. BI, Massachusetts, 1972.

---

[8]siehe [LP91]

Vivid Logic and Directly Skeptical Inheritance

Gerd Wagner

Gruppe Logik, Wissenstheorie und Information

Institut für Philosphie, Freie Universität Berlin

Habelschwerdter Allee 30, 1000 Berlin 33

Abstract

Vivid logic as a nonmonotonic system of partial logic can be used to represent and reason with inheritance nets. We show how both ambiguity-blocking and ambiguity-propagating skeptical inheritance can be modelled in this framework. Furthermore, we discuss possible generalizations of inheritance nets which are straightforward on the basis of vivid logic.

1 Introduction

In [Wagner 1990a,b] we reported on a nonmonotonic system of partial logic with two kinds of negation, called *weak* and *strong*, respectively. Referring to Levesque's idea of *vivid knowledge*[1] we called this system *vivid logic* (VL), since it is specifically designed to model information processing in a vivid knowledge base. Unlike classical logic, VL offers several options how to deal with inconsistency. We shall discuss three of them in this paper in connection with inheritance theory. Each of them leads to a particular version of VL which we call *liberal*, *conservative* and *skeptical*, respectively.

Conservative and skeptical vivid logic can be viewed as generalizations of ambiguity-blocking and ambiguity-propagating inheritance. Since there is a direct translation from a net into a corresponding vivid knowledge base, inheritance nets[2] can be considered as simple vivid knowledge bases. Notice that this view fits well with the conclusion of Thomason and Horty [1988] that a nonmonotonic logic for inheritance must be based on some kind of four-valued logic. The partial semantics we propose is basically four-valued.

In order to keep this paper self-contained we repeat all relevant definitions of VL appropriateley restricted to inheritance reasoning. We also present here some new model-theoretic definitions, namely those of a conservative, resp. skeptical, model of a vivid knowledge base.

For methodological reasons we shall pursue a two-step logical reconstruction of inheritance reasoning based on VL. The first step is to define a formalism which captures the logic of defeasible inheritance arguments without preemption. Then, in a second step, this formalism has to be extended by adding an appropriate preemption mechanism.

Many problems discussed in the literature, like "floating conclusions" and "zombie paths" (see [Makinson & Schlechta 1991]), are not related to preemption but only to plain defeat. These problems, therefore, should be solved in step one of the above reconstruction independently from the resp. preemption mechanism. Also, a satisfying formal account of 'common sense preemption' seems to be an especially difficult task. The problems arising here should be decoupled from other more basic ones.

---

[1] cf. [Levesque 1986]

[2] We are only concerned here with bipolar, homogeneous multiple inheritance systems where all links are defeasible and the net structure is acyclic.

2   Vivid Logic

The language of vivid logic consists of the logical operator symbols $\wedge, \vee, \sim, -$ and 1 standing for conjunction, disjunction, strong negation, weak negation and the verum, respectively; the predicate symbols $p, q, r, \ldots$; the constant symbols $c, d, \ldots$ and variables $x, y, \ldots$. Notice that in VL we do not have functional terms but only variables and constants.[3] Also, there are no explicit quantifiers in VL.

An *atom* is an atomic formula, it is called *proper*, if it is not 1. *Literals* are either atoms or strongly negated atoms. We use $a, b, \ldots, l, k, \ldots$ and $F, G, H, \ldots$ as metavariables for atoms, literals and formulas, respectively. A variable-free expression is called *ground*. The contrary of a literal l, denoted by $\tilde{l}$, is defined as $\tilde{a} = \sim a$ and $\widetilde{\sim a} = a$.

A vivid knowledge base (VKB) consists of inference rules (also called *clauses*) of the form $l \leftarrow F$ (read "l if F") where l is a proper literal and F an arbitrary formula. We consider such rules as *conditional facts*. A rule with premise 1 is also called a *fact*, and we also abbreviate $l \leftarrow 1$ by l.

Example 1   *The net*

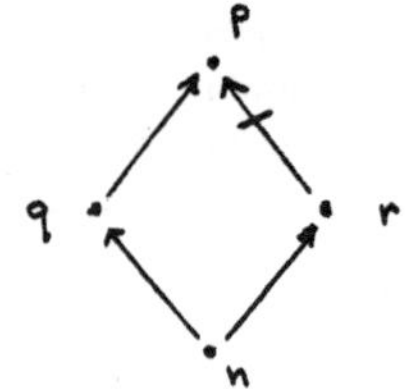

is translated into the following VKB,

$$V = \{q(n), r(n), p(x) \leftarrow q(x), \sim p(x) \leftarrow r(x)\}$$

In general, links between an individual c and a class p, $c \to p$, $c \not\to p$, are expressed as facts, $p(c)$ and $\sim p(c)$, respectively. Links between classes, $p \to q$, $p \not\to q$, are expressed as conditional facts, $q(x) \leftarrow p(x)$ and $\sim q(x) \leftarrow p(x)$, respectively. This translation procedure of a net leads to a VKB without weak negation where all clauses have the form $l \leftarrow a$, i.e. conclusions are literals and premises are atoms. Therefore, in the sequel, although we keep the general notation of a rule, $l \leftarrow F$, we restrict formulas F to atoms, $F = a$, in the context of ordinary inheritance, and to possibly weakly negated literals, $F = l | - l$, in the context of generalizations of inheritance.

A vivid knowledge base V containing non-ground conditional facts is a dynamic representation of the corresponding set of ground conditional facts formed by means of the current domain of individuals U and denoted by $[V]_U$. Formally,

$$[V]_U = \{l\sigma \leftarrow F\sigma \mid l \leftarrow F \in V \text{ and } \sigma : \mathrm{Var}(l, F) \to U\}$$

where σ ranges over all mappings from the set of variables of l and F into the set of all constant symbols U. We call σ a *ground substitution* for $l \leftarrow F$ and $[V]_U$ the *Herbrand expansion* of V with respect to a certain (finite) Herbrand universe U. We shall write $[V]$ for the Herbrand expansion of V with respect to the Herbrand universe U_V induced by V, i.e. the set of all constant symbols occuring in V. Instead of $[V]_{U(\mathcal{M})}$, where $U(\mathcal{M})$ is the Herbrand universe of some model $\mathcal{M}$, we shall simply write $[V]_{\mathcal{M}}$.

---

[3]This restriction guarantees that we deal with a finite Herbrand universe, and hence, essentially stay on the conceptual level of propositional logic.

3   Model Theory

Let $\mathcal{M} = \langle M^+, M^- \rangle$ be a partial Herbrand interpretation, that is, M^+ contains the positive facts which are believed to be true, whereas M^- contains the negative facts which are believed to be false (formally, both M^+ and M^- are sets of proper ground atoms). Following Langholm [1988], we shall speak of *proper* models when M^+ and M^- are required to be disjoint, as opposed to *general* models for which they may overlap (in the sequel, we shall frequently just say 'model' instead of 'general model').

A partial Herbrand interpretation gives rise to a model relation, defined as follows:

$$\mathcal{M} \models a \qquad \text{iff} \quad a \in M^+$$
$$\mathcal{M} \models \sim a \qquad \text{iff} \quad a \in M^-$$
$$\mathcal{M} \models -F \qquad \text{iff} \quad \mathcal{M} \not\models F$$

where a and F are ground. We also stipulate that for all interpretations $\mathcal{M}$, $\mathcal{M} \models 1$. There are two notions of falsity involved in this semantics each one underlying the respective negation: $\sim F$ stands for the explicit falsity of F, whereas $-F$ stands for the weak falsity of F given implicitly. In classical logic, where models are total (i.e. two-valued), $\sim F$ and $-F$ coincide.

The intuitive reading of $\sim p$ is 'p is falsifiable' or 'p is known to be false' whereas $-p$ would mean 'p is not verifiable' or 'p is not known to be true'. Likewise, $-\sim p$ can be read as 'p is not falsifiable' or 'p is not known to be false' which obviously does not reduce to p (not disliking something, for instance, does not amount to liking it !).

In order to simplify notation we shall also represent a model $\mathcal{M}$ as the set M of all ground literals supported by it, $M = \{l : l$ is a proper ground literal and $\mathcal{M} \models l\}$. M is also called the *diagram* of $\mathcal{M}$. Obviously, $M^+ = \{a : a \in M\}$, and $M^- = \{a : \sim a \in M\}$.

We call $\mathcal{M}'$ an *extension* of $\mathcal{M}$, symbolically $\mathcal{M}' \geq \mathcal{M}$, if $M \subseteq M'$. An extension of a model represents a growth of information since it assigns truth or falsity to formerly undetermined sentences. We could also consider total extensions of a model determining the truth or falsity of all sentences like classical two-valued models.

In [Thomason & Horty 1988] a four-valued logic for inheritance reasoning, N4, was presented. Instead of weak negation the language of N4 contains two pseudo-modal operators, both of which are easily definable in VL, namely 'necessarily', $\Delta := \sim -$, and 'possibly', $\nabla := -\sim$. N4 corresponds to liberal VL. It was shown to be adequate with respect to credulous inheritance without preemption. However, it cannot handle directly skeptical inheritance, which is the domain of application of conservative and skeptical VL.

We say that $\mathcal{M}$ is a *liberal model* of V, symbolically $\mathcal{M} \models_l V$ or $\mathcal{M} \in \mathrm{LMod}(V)$, if for all $l \leftarrow F \in [V]_{\mathcal{M}}$, $\mathcal{M} \models l$ whenever $\mathcal{M} \models F$.

A liberal model is a general model, that is, it may contain overdetermined information, or, in other words, assign both *true* and *false* simultaneously to an atom. It corresponds to the 4-valued assignments of some paraconsistent logics (see e.g. [Belnap 1977]). On the other hand, bot conservative and skeptical models are proper, i.e. they maintain a consistent state of affairs.

We say that $\mathcal{M}$ is a *conservative model* of V, symbolically $\mathcal{M} \models_c V$ or $\mathcal{M} \in \mathrm{CMod}(V)$, if for all $l \leftarrow F \in [V]_{\mathcal{M}}$, $\mathcal{M} \models l$ whenever $\mathcal{M} \models F$, and

(c) $\forall(\tilde{l} \leftarrow G) \in [V]_{\mathcal{M}} : \mathcal{M} \not\models G.$

We say that $\mathcal{M}$ is a *skeptical model* of V, symbolically $\mathcal{M} \models_c V$ or $\mathcal{M} \in \mathrm{SMod}(V)$, if for all $l \leftarrow F \in [V]_{\mathcal{M}}$, $\mathcal{M} \models l$ whenever $\mathcal{M} \models F$, and

(s) $\forall(\tilde{l} \leftarrow G) \in [V]_{\mathcal{M}} \exists \mathcal{N} \in \mathrm{LMod}(V) : \mathcal{N} \geq \mathcal{M} \ \& \ \mathcal{N} \not\models G.$

Notice that we have only one satisfaction relation between a model $\mathcal{M}$ and a formula F, $\mathcal{M} \models F$, but we have three kinds of model relation between a model and a VKB, $\models_l$, $\models_c$ and $\models_s$, all of them interpreting the conditional $\leftarrow$ as non-contrapositive (i.e. a model of $\{\sim p, p \leftarrow q\}$ does not necessarily satisfy $\sim q$). While $\models_l$ provides a 'context-free' interpretation of $\leftarrow$, the conservative and the skeptical model relations yield an interpretation of $\leftarrow$ within the context of the given VKB. The conservative (resp. skeptical) model condition commits a model to satisfy at least all literals which are supported by a rule (with a resp. satisfied premise) and are not doubted by a contrary rule (with a resp. satisfied premise).

Observation 1 *For a VKB V without weak negation we have: $LMod(V) \subseteq CMod(V) \subseteq SMod(V)$, i.e. a liberal model is also a conservative model, and a conservative model is also a skeptical model.*

Both inclusions follow by the strengthening of the condition for acceptance commitment. While this is obvious for the first inclusion, it is a straightforward consequence of the *permanence principle*[4] in the case of the second inclusion.

The following example illustrates the difference between ambiguity-blocking and ambiguity-propagating inheritance which was first reported in [THT 1987].

Example 2 *The net* 

corresponds to $V = \{p(c), \sim p(c), q(c), \sim q(x) \leftarrow p(x)\}$. *The least liberal model of V is* $\mathcal{M}_V^l = \{p(c), \sim p(c), q(c), \sim q(c)\}$. *Examples of conservative but not liberal models are* $\mathcal{M}_1^c = \{\sim p(c), q(c)\}$ *and* $\mathcal{M}_2^c = \{p(c)\}$. *Examples of skeptical but not conservative models are* $\mathcal{M}_1^s = \{\sim p(c)\}$ *and* $\mathcal{M}_V^s = \emptyset$.

According to ambiguity-blocking inheritance $q(c)$ does hold, whereas it does not hold according to ambiguity-propagating inheritance, where the propagation of the 'ambiguity' of $p(c)$ blocks the inference to $q(c)$. This situation is captured by the intended conservative model, $\mathcal{M}_V^c = \{q(c)\}$, and the intended skeptical model, $\mathcal{M}_V^s = \emptyset$, respectively.

In the absence of indefinite information a KB has a single intended model which serves as an *adequate model* in the sense that exactly those formulas are satisfied which are logical consequences. The KB can then be viewed as a specification of this model.

Claim 1 *Every vivid knowledge base V without weak negation has a least liberal model (denoted by $\mathcal{M}_V^l$), viz the meet of all its liberal models.*

The meet of two conservative (resp. skeptical) models need not be a conservative (resp. skeptical) model again. Consider, for instance $\mathcal{M}_1^c \cap \mathcal{M}_2^c = \emptyset$ from example 2. While the least liberal model is the intended one, the intended conservative and skeptical models have to be characterized differently because there are, in general, no least ones.

We call $\mathcal{M}$ a *conservatively*, resp. *skeptically*, *supported model* of V if for all $l \in M$ there exists $l \leftarrow F \in [V]_{\mathcal{M}}$, such that $\mathcal{M} \models F$ and (c), resp. (s), holds.

---

[4]see [Wagner 1990a]

Example 3   *The net*

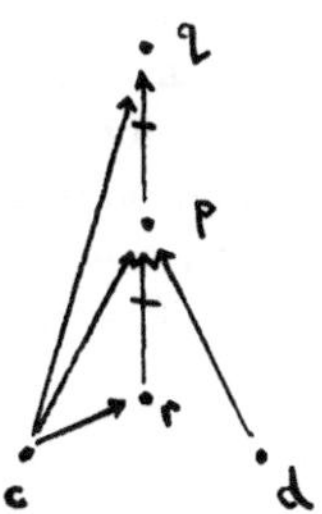

corresponds to

$$V \;=\; \left\{ \begin{array}{l} p(c),\; p(d),\; q(c),\; r(c) \\ \sim q(x) \leftarrow p(x) \\ \sim p(x) \leftarrow r(x) \end{array} \right.$$

Here $\mathcal{M}_1^c = \{q(c), r(d)\}$ is a conservative model which is not supported. V has a unique supported model, viz $\mathcal{M}_V^c = \{p(d), q(c), \sim q(d), r(c)\}$ which is also the intended one.

In general, a VKB may have more than one supported model.

Conjecture 1   *A VKB V without weak negation has a least conservatively and a least skeptically supported model (denoted by $\mathcal{M}_V^c$, resp. $\mathcal{M}_V^s$).*

4   Proof Theory

In [Wagner 1991] the key ideas of vivid reasoning with contradictory information are presented in an intuitive and informal way. Here we only repeat the formal definitions needed and discuss their application to inheritance reasoning.

We first stipulate that for any V, $V \vdash_* 1$ for $* = l, c, s$.

Concerning the recursive structure of a VKB, the most straightforward way to define *liberal derivability* for ground literals is the following

$$
\begin{array}{lll}
(l) & V \vdash_l l & \text{iff} \quad \exists (l \leftarrow F) \in [V] : V \vdash_l F \\
(-l) & V \vdash_l -l & \text{iff} \quad \forall (l \leftarrow F) \in [V] : V \vdash_l -F
\end{array}
$$

However, this definition only works for 'well-behaved' VKBs which we call *well-founded* according to the definition in [Wagner 1990a]. Acyclic inheritance nets correspond to *strongly well-founded* VKBs which are defined in [Wagner 1991]. Such VKBs permit the following simple definitions of conservative and skeptical derivability:

conservative derivability

$$
\begin{array}{lll}
(l) & V \vdash_c l & \text{iff} \quad \exists (l \leftarrow F) \in [V] : V \vdash_c F, \text{ and } \forall (\tilde{l} \leftarrow G) \in [V] : V \vdash_c -G \\
(-l) & V \vdash_c -l & \text{iff} \quad \forall (l \leftarrow F) \in [V] : V \vdash_c -F, \text{ or } \exists (\tilde{l} \leftarrow G) \in [V] : V \vdash_c G
\end{array}
$$

skeptical derivability

$$
\begin{array}{lll}
(l) & V \vdash_s l & \text{iff} \quad \exists (l \leftarrow F) \in [V] : V \vdash_s F, \text{ and } \forall (\tilde{l} \leftarrow G) \in [V] : V \vdash_l -G \\
(-l) & V \vdash_s -l & \text{iff} \quad \forall (l \leftarrow F) \in [V] : V \vdash_s -F, \text{ or } \exists (\tilde{l} \leftarrow G) \in [V] : V \vdash_l G
\end{array}
$$

Notice the difference between $\vdash_c$ and $\vdash_s$. In a conservative derivation all contrary rules are required to be conservatively non-applicable, whereas in skeptical derivations they are required to be liberally non-applicable. Therefore, in Ex. 2 above, the skeptical inference to $q(c)$ is blocked by the liberal derivability of a contrary premise, viz $p(c)$. Since $p(c)$ is not conservatively derivable, the conservative inference to $q(c)$ is not blocked. In skeptical VL 'ambiguities' (corresponding to the fourth truth-value *overdetermined* in liberal VL) are 'propagated', i.e. liberally overdetermined information is considered to have a contradicting force. In conservative VL 'ambiguities' are 'blocked', i.e. conservatively overdetermined information is discarded, which in turn may lead to 'promiscuous'[5] conclusions not doubted conservatively but liberally, and hence skeptically.

Denoting the resp. consequence operations by LC, CC and SC, i.e. $LC(V) = \{F : V \vdash_l F\}$, and correspondingly for CC and SC, we can make

Observation 2 $SC(V) \subseteq CC(V) \subseteq LC(V)$

Of course, we would like to establish the adequacy of our model and proof theory. This was done for liberal VL in [Wagner 1990a]. For conservative and skeptical VL this is still ongoing work, so we can only formulate it as

Conjecture 2   *(c)* $V \vdash_c F$ iff $\mathcal{M}_V^c \models F$

  (s) $V \vdash_s F$ iff $\mathcal{M}_V^s \models F$

5   Discussion: Is Ideal Skepticism Really Ideal ?

In one approach to skeptical inheritance, called *ideally skeptical* in [Stein 1989], a conclusion is considered as valid if it holds in all credulous extensions. Many authors take the legitimacy of this approach for granted, even though "it is not only conceptually indirect but also computationally costly", as Makinson and Schlechta [1991] admit. Ideal skepticism violates the two basic principles of vivid reasoning: cognitive adequacy (implying conceptual directness) and computational affordability. We, therefore, advocate a direct approach to skeptical inheritance, no matter whether it is able to capture the intersection of all credulous extensions or not.

Ambiguity-blocking inheritance (generalized by CC) allows for conclusions which are unsound according to the philosophy of ideal skepticism. This concerns, for instance, the conservatively valid conclusion $q(c)$ from Ex. 2 which is not in all credulous extensions. Makinson and Schlechta [1991] argue that direct approaches are intrinsically not able to account for this phenomena (which they call 'zombie paths'), and that this constitutes a severe problem for directly skeptical inheritance. Since in their considerations preemption is involved we cannot see whether their criticism also applies to ambiguity-propagating inheritance as generalized by SC.[6] Independently from that, conservative reasoning can be justified: if the point of mutual neutralization is taken seriously, overdetermined information has the same deductive force, whether positively or negatively, as undetermined (i.e. no) information.

It was argued in [Stein 1989] that ambiguity-blocking inheritance creates a certain 'parity' pattern constituting a severe anomaly. Although she does not explain it, Stein maintains that this would be counterintuitive. We do not see, however, why. Such patterns arising from rather artificial examples are acceptable if implied by the semantics. Their acceptance is less a question of intuition.

Whereas ambiguity-blocking inheritance is unsound, ambiguity-propagating inheritance is incomplete, according to the criticism of Stein [1989] and Makinson and Schlechta [1991]. This is revealed by the phenomena of 'floating conclusions' holding in all credulous extensions but not supported by one and the same path in all of them.

---

[5]cf. [Stein 1989]

[6]In skeptical VL 'zombie paths' have the force of a defeating counterargument.

Example 4   *Consider*

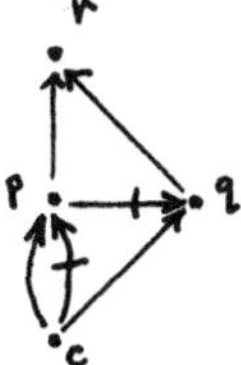

Although $r(c)$ is an ideally skeptical consequence (since it is supported by the path cpr in one extension, and by cqr in the other one), it is not derivable in skeptical VL.

However, why should it be intuitively clear that a floating conclusion has to be accepted ? A floating conclusion is not firmly grounded in non-contradictory information but only based on mutually incompatible credulous paths. So this question becomes an issue of whether to adopt a Platonic position (corresponding to ideal skepticism) or rather a constructivistic position (corresponding to the philosophy of vividness, i.e. to a direct and computational approach). The legitimacy of ideal skepticism is based on the Platonic principle *tertium non datur* constituting classical logic. The family of all credulous extensions represents all such Platonically valid alternatives $p(x)$ or $\sim p(x)$. Even if we don't know which one holds, one of them is assumed to hold.[7]

It follows from the above remarks that we don't see any non-debatable reason why ideal skepticism should be the ultimate measure for skeptical reasoning procedures. It rather represents a certain dogma which can be questioned (especially in the context of inheritance) and which was questioned many times in philosophy and logic.

6   Preemption

In order to take into account that more specific information should defeat less specific one, which is usually called 'preemption' in inheritance terminology, we extend our definitions of conservative and skeptical derivability, now requiring all contrary rules to be either non-applicable or preempted. Formally, in the case of conservative derivability,

$$
\begin{aligned}
(l) \quad & V \vdash_c l(c) \quad \text{iff} \quad \exists(l(x) \leftarrow a(x)) \in V : V \vdash_c a(c), \text{ and} \\
& \qquad\qquad\qquad \forall(\tilde{l}(x) \leftarrow b(x)) \in V : V \vdash_c -b(c) \text{ or } V, a(d) \vdash_c b(d) \\
(-l) \quad & V \vdash_c -l(c) \quad \text{iff} \quad \forall(l(x) \leftarrow a(x)) \in V : V \vdash_c -a(x), \text{ or} \\
& \qquad\qquad\qquad \exists(\tilde{l}(x) \leftarrow b(x)) \in V : V \vdash_c b(c) \text{ and } V, a(d) \vdash_c -b(d)
\end{aligned}
$$

where d is a newly introduced individual name not occuring in V. For skeptical derivability the extended definition is analogously.

Example 5   *The net*

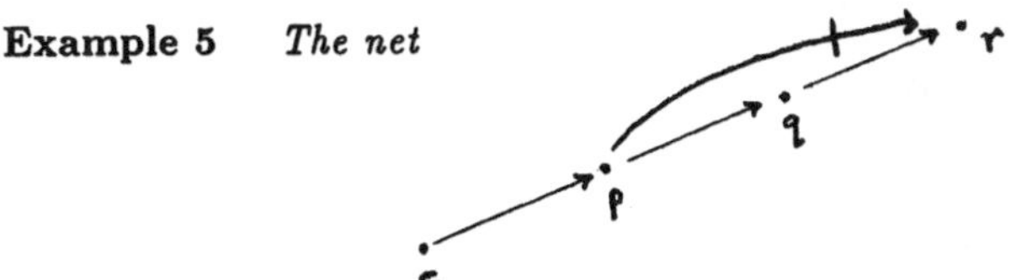

is translated to $V = \{p(c), q(x) \leftarrow p(x), r(x) \leftarrow q(x), \sim r(x) \leftarrow p(x)\}$. The conclusion $\sim r(c)$ is both conservatively and skeptically valid, since in both cases the inference from $q(c)$ and $r(x) \leftarrow q(x)$ to $r(c)$ is preempted by $V \cup \{p(d)\} \vdash q(d)$.

---

[7]Notice the resemblance between ideal skepticism and the supervaluation semantics in partial logic.

It was brought to the author's attention by one of the referees that this concept of specificity between two properties a and b is not adequate if the specific individual c is abnormal with respect to an intermediate property in the subsumtion chain from a to b. Such an abnormality would not be taken into consideration by the above two-place check,

$$a \text{ is more specific than } b \quad \text{iff} \quad V, a(d) \vdash_* b(d)$$

where d is not an argument but only an auxiliary symbol. We briefly mention one possible solution to this problem. What we need is to check whether $a(c)$ in some sense relevantly implies $b(c)$ on the basis of V. In order to make this precise we would have to modify the concept of conservative (resp. skeptical) derivation in the same way as the concept of an intuitionistic derivation has to be modified to yield the concept of a relevant derivation. In this way we would get a 3-place notion of specificity ordering relation between two properties with respect to a certain individual,

$$a \text{ is more specific than } b \text{ wrt } c \quad \text{iff} \quad V \vdash_* a(c) \rightarrow b(c)$$

7 Possible Generalizations of Inheritance

The expressiveness of VL suggests a number of possible generalizations of ordinary inheritance. First, negative premises, like in $p \leftarrow \sim q$, could be allowed. For this purpose we have to modify our notation of links. We get four different inheritance links:

rule	link
$p \leftarrow q$	$q \longrightarrow p$
$\sim p \leftarrow q$	$q \longrightarrow\!\!\!\!\cdot\, p$
$p \leftarrow \sim q$	$q \longmapsto p$
$\sim p \leftarrow \sim q$	$q \longmapsto\!\!\!\!\cdot\, p$

It is important to keep in mind the intuitive meaning of strong negation here: $\sim p$ does mean more than simply "something is not p", it rather means "something is definitely not p" or even "something is anti-p".

Example 6 *Communists are not ok. An anti-communist is ok. An anti-communist is an anti-leninist. A leninist is not a democrat. Democrats are ok. Leninists are not ok. Peter is a leninist and an anti-communist. Tom is a democrat.*

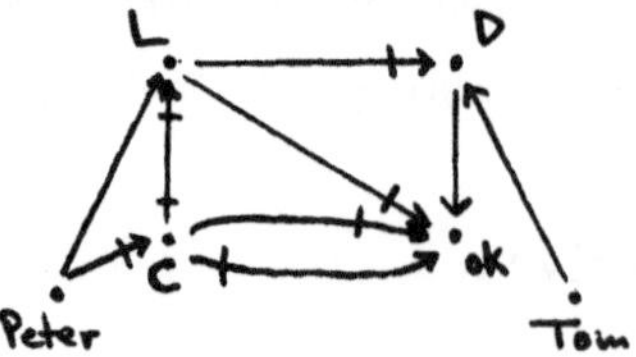

Both Peter and Tom are ok.

A further generalization would be to allow weakly negated premises, like in $p \leftarrow -\sim q$ (read "something is p if it is not non-q"). We get two new links:

rule	link
$p \leftarrow -q$	$q \longmapsto p$
$p \leftarrow -\sim q$	$q \longmapsto p$

Example 7   *We modify the above example by replacing "Communists are not ok" by "Not-anti-communists are not ok."*

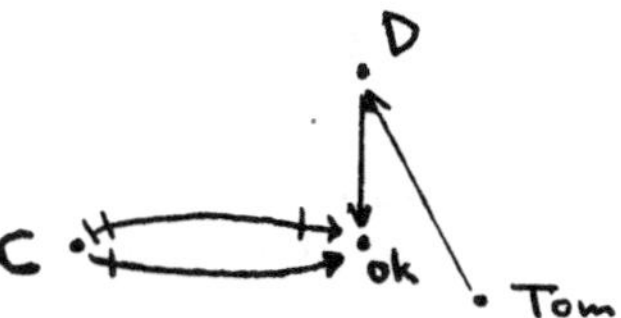

Now Tom is no longer ok, since he is not an anti-communist (although he is neither a communist). By mutual neutralization he is neither ok nor non-ok.

8   Concluding Remarks

Vivid logic can serve as a semantics of defeasible inheritance systems. We have shown that both ambiguity-blocking and ambiguity-propagating inheritance have a well-defined logical interpretation with a model and a proof-theory. Although these procedures of directly skeptical inheritance have been criticised for not being able to capture the intersection of all credulous extensions we believe that they express highly interesting principles of vivid reasoning with contradictory information. In fact, we claim that directly skeptical inheritance is cognitively more relevant than the intersection approach which is hardly imaginable as being pursued by an intelligent agent.

Thomason's and Horty's [1988] criticism of the default logic translation of nets suggested by [Etherington & Reiter 1983] does not apply to our proposed translation of nets into VL which is clearly modular and defined in a general way. The interpretation of nets as vivid knowledge bases has several benefits. It allows for generalizations such as sketched in the previous section. It relates the very basic level of inheritance to the higher level of general knowledge representation. And, as VL is closely related to logic programming, it might bring the ideas and results of inheritance research to the still evolving field of logic programming.

References

[Belnap 1977] N.D. Belnap: A Useful Four-valued logic, in G. Epstein and J.M. Dunn (Eds.), *Modern Uses of Many-valued Logic*, Reidel, 1977, 8–37

[Etherington & Reiter 1983] D. Etherington and R. Reiter: On inheritance hierarchies with exceptions, *Proc. of AAAI-83*, 104–108

[Langholm 1988] T. Langholm: *Partiality, Truth and Persistence*, CSLI Lecture Notes No. 15, University of Chicago Press, 1988

[Levesque 1986] H.J. Levesque: Making Believers out of Computers, *AI 30* (1986), 81-107

[Makinson & Schlechta 1991] D. Makinson and K. Schlechta, Floating Conclusions and Zombie Paths: Two Deep Difficulties in the "Directly Skeptical" Approach to Defeasible Inheritance Nets, *AI* 48 (1991), 199–209

[Nelson 1949] D. Nelson: Constructible falsity, *JSL 14* (1949), 16–26

[Stein 1989] L.A. Stein, Skeptical Inheritance: Computing the Intersection of Credulous Extensions, *Proc. of IJCAI-89*, 1153–1158

[Thomason & Horty 1988] R.H. Thomason and J.F. Horty: Logics for Inheritance Theory, *Proc. of 2nd Int. Workshop on Nonmonotonic Reasoning 1988*, Springer LNAI 346, 220–237

[THT 1987] D.S. Touretzky, J.F. Horty and R.H. Thomason. A Clash of Intuitions: The Current State of Nonmonotonic Multiple Inheritance Systems, *Proc. of IJCAI-87*, 476–482

[Wagner 1990a] G. Wagner: Vivid Reasoning with Negative Information, LWI Technical Report 8/1990, Freie Universität Berlin, also in W. van der Hoek and Y.H. Tan (Eds.), Proc. of Int. Workshop on Non-Monotonic Reasoning & Partial Semantics 1991, Free University Amsterdam

[Wagner 1990b] G. Wagner: The Two Sources of Nonmonotonicity in Vivid Logic – Inconsistency Handling and Weak Falsity, in G. Brewka and H. Freitag (eds.), *Proc. of the GMD Workshop on Nonmonotonic Reasoning 1989*, Gesellschaft für Mathematik und Datenverarbeitung, Bonn - St. Augustin, 1990

[Wagner 1991] G. Wagner: Ex contradictione nihil sequitur, forthcoming in *Proc. of IJCAI-91*, Morgan Kaufmann

TEMPO -
ein integrierter Ansatz zur Modellierung
qualitativer und quantitativer zeitlicher Informationen

Rainer Bleisinger

Deutsches Forschungszentrum für Künstliche Intelligenz GmbH
Postfach 2080, 6750 Kaiserslautern
Tel.: (0631) 205 - 3216, e-mail: bleising@dfki.uni-kl.de

Zusammenfassung

In diesem Papier wird eine Modellarchitektur vorgestellt, in der quantitative und qualitative Aspekte der Zeit integriert sind. An zeitlichen Informationen werden zum einen konkrete Daten als quantitative und relative Beziehungen bezüglich der Reihenfolge als qualitative Reihenfolgeangaben betrachtet. Zum anderen werden konkrete Zeitdauern als quantitative und relative Beziehungen bezüglich der Dauer als qualitative Zeitdauerangaben betrachtet. Das Modell ist in ein Repräsentationsmodell und ein Verarbeitungsmodell unterteilt. Dadurch wird es möglich, im Repräsentationsmodell deklarativ zu beschreiben, welche Werte verwendet werden, wie die Konsistenzbedingungen aussehen und welche Propagierungsbeschränkungen zu beachten sind. Die im Repräsentationsmodell beschriebenen Restriktionen ermöglichen eine modellbasierte Verarbeitung von zeitlichen Informationen und steuern die einzelnen, auf bestimmte zeitliche Angaben spezialisierten Zeitexperten. Das umfassende Modell wird im Überblick beschrieben und teils an einzelnen ausgewählten Beispielen vertieft diskutiert.

1. Motivation

Die Zeit stellt in unserer hektischen und schnellebigen Welt einen wichtigen Faktor dar. Ohne sie ist kein modernes gesellschaftliches System funktionsfähig. Bereits seit Jahrhunderten wird in verschieden wissenschaftlichen Disziplinen der Forschungsgegenstand "Zeit" untersucht. Auch in der Informatik wird und kann die Zeit nicht ignoriert werden. Hier steht die Frage im Vordergrund, wie Zeit adäquat zu repräsentieren und zu verarbeiten ist. Auf dem Gebiet der Datenbankentwicklungen sind z.B. Bestrebungen im Gange, sich über die Zeit verändernde Daten zu verwalten.

Starke Beachtung findet die Repräsentation und Verarbeitung von Zeit in besonderem Maße in der Künstlichen Intelligenz. Dies soll an den folgenden exemplarischen Arbeitsgebieten verdeutlicht werden.

Im Bereich der natürlichsprachlichen Analyse sind die vielfältigen Möglichkeiten zu berücksichtigen, zeitliche Informationen auszudrücken. So werden zeitliche Informationen z.B. durch die Verwendung unterschiedlicher Tempi, durch die Spezifikation zeitlicher Beziehungen mittels spezieller Worte oder durch die Angabe von konkreten Kalenderdaten bzw. Uhrzeiten formuliert.

Auf dem Gebiet der Planung sind zeitliche Aspekte ebenfalls wichtig. In einem Plan z.B. werden den spezifizierten Aktionen Zeitdauern zugeordnet, sind Aktivitäten in bestimmten zeitlichen Abfolgen durchzuführen oder Vorgänge zu bestimmten Terminen zu initiieren.

Eine sehr entscheidende Rolle spielt die Zeit im gesamten Umfeld der Büroautomatisierung. Die zwei Teilbereiche der rechnergestützten Dokumentanalyse und der Vorgangsplanung belegen dies. Um eine umfassende Dokumentanalyse durchzuführen muß der textuelle Inhalt, vor allem die zeitlichen Bezüge in den natürlichsprachlichen Formulierungen, untersucht werden. Nur so sind Verweise auf andere Dokumente zu ermitteln. Soll der Ablauf von Bürovorgängen modelliert werden, so sind diese auch hinsichtlich der zeitlichen Randbedingungen zu spezifizieren. In der Ausführung der Vorgänge ist ihr Zusammenspiel zu planen, der Plan durchzuführen und zu überwachen.

In all diesen Domänen ist zu beobachten, daß der Mensch in seine Schlußfolgerungen die Komponente Zeit sowohl implizit als auch explizit miteinbeziehen muß. Deshalb sind Modellierungen notwendig, in denen der Zeit eine besondere Stellung zugeordnet und zeitbehaftetes Schlußfolgern möglich wird.

2. Einleitung

Ziel dieser Arbeit ist der Entwurf eines Zeitrepräsentations- und -verarbeitungsmodells, in dem modellbasiertes zeitliches Schließen ermöglicht wird. Insbesondere werden dabei sowohl quantitative als auch qualitative zeitliche Repräsentationen und Schlußfolgerungen kombiniert. Die umfassende Modellarchitektur steht hierbei im Mittelpunkt der Betrachtungen, nur an einzelnen Beispielen wird zur Verdeutlichung der konkrete Bezug hergestellt.

Mit einem Modell wird ein Abbild der realen Welt geschaffen, das jedoch nur näherungsweise dem Original entspricht und immer unvollständig bleibt. Ein umfassendes Modell für zeitbehaftetes Wissen betrachtet besonders die Beziehungen der realen Welt zur Zeit. Viele allgemeine Modelle mit Zeitbezug [McDermott 82, Allen 84, Shoham 89, Galton 90] können, abstrakt betrachtet, in drei Ebenen unterteilt werden. Die drei Ebenen werden in Abbildung 1 verdeutlicht.

In der obersten Ebene wird die Darstellung des realen Weltausschnittes zeitunabhängig behandelt. Dazu werden die vorkommenden Objekte und Zustände genauer klassifiziert und jeweils klassenspezifisch in die zeitunabhängige Verarbeitung einbezogen.

In der untersten Ebene werden ausschließlich die Zeit betreffende Entitäten betrachtet. Es werden Objekte der Zeit bestimmt, deren Beziehungen zueinander festgelegt und spezielle Verarbeitungen vorgenommen.

Mit Hilfe der mittleren Ebene werden die Verbindungen von Zeit- und Weltobjekten hergestellt. Dazu werden in logik-basierten Modellen spezielle Prädikate definiert, die die Klassifizierung der Weltobjekte mit berücksichtigen (vergleiche Ansatz von Allen und dessen Erweiterung von Galton). Damit wird dem unterschiedlichen zeitlichen Verhalten bezüglich einer weitergehenden Verarbeitung Rechnung getragen.

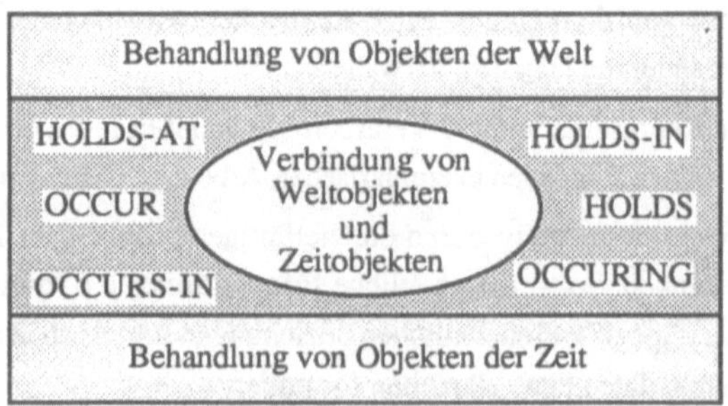

Abb.1: Ebenen eines allgemeinen Modells mit expliziter Zeit.

Dieses Papier konzentriert sich ausschließlich auf die unterste Ebene eines umfassenden Modells, also auf das Repräsentations- und Verarbeitungsmodell für die Zeit. In idealisierter Weise wird nur das betrachtet, was in der realen Welt mit zeitlichen Informationen behaftet ist. Darüberhinaus wird davon nur die Zeit

Betreffendes im Modell angesprochen und abstrakt als Zeitobjekt mit beschreibenden zeitlichen Angaben aufgefaßt. Da die mittlere und oberste Schicht eines allgemeinen Modells für die unberücksichtigt gebliebenen Teile verantwortlich sind geht durch diese Betrachtungsweise in keiner Hinsicht etwas verloren, sondern sie erleichtert eine konzentrierte und fokusierte Untersuchung der relevanten Details bezüglich der Zeit.

Im nächsten Kapitel werden die Anforderungen erarbeitet, denen ein solches Modell genügen sollte. Der Gesamtüberblick über den integrierten Ansatz wird in Kapitel 4 gegeben, unterteilt in das Repräsentationsmodell und das Verarbeitungsmodell.

3. Anforderungen an ein adäquates Modell

Die Entwicklung eines adäquaten Repräsentations- und Verarbeitungsmodells für Zeit muß möglichst anwendungsunabhängig sein. Dennoch sollte man sich beispielhaft an den Anforderungen verschiedener Anwendungen orientieren, um den Bezug zur "Realität" nicht zu verlieren. In diesem Papier wird als Anwendung auf die Büroautomatisierung zurückgegriffen, insbesondere die Dokumentanalyse[1] und die Planung von Softwareprojekten[2] (siehe [Bleisinger et al 91]).

Zur Beantwortung der Frage, welche zeitlichen Angaben in dem Anwendungsfeld der Büroautomatisierung zu beobachten sind, sollen die nachfolgenden Beispiele untersucht werden.

Beispiele für zeitliche Aspekte in der Büroautomatisierung:

"Die Besprechung wird entweder vor oder nach der Mittagspause abgehalten"

"Die Dienstreise findet vom 15.10.91 bis zum 20.10.91 statt"

"Die Konferenz dauert höchstens 5 Tage"

"Die Implementierungsphase in einem Softwareprojekt dauert länger als die Designphase"

"Die Testphase im Projekt X beginnt frühestens im Dezember 1991"

"Die Benutzerdokumentation wird spätestens 3 Tage nach Testende vorhanden sein"

Insgesamt wird deutlich, daß zeitliche Informationen in vielfältiger Form verwendet werden. Zum einen werden vage und unscharfe zeitliche Angaben benutzt, zum anderen werden sehr konkrete und detaillierte Angaben gegeben, z.B. mit Hilfe von Zahlen und Maßen oder genauen Reihenfolgebeziehungen.

Als Konsequenz läßt sich folgende Forderung aufstellen: Modelle für zeitliche Informationen müssen zum einen qualitative und quantitative Angaben integrieren und zum anderen sowohl sehr präzise als auch ungenaue Spezifikationen dieser erlauben.

Grundsetzlich lassen sich vier Typen von zeitlichen Angaben identifizieren:

qualitative Zeitreihenfolge

quantitative Zeitreihenfolge

qualitative Zeitdauer

quantitative Zeitdauer.

---

[1]In diesem Zusammenhang ist das vom BMFT geförderte Projekt ALV (Automatisches Lesen und Verstehen) zu nennen, das am DFKI durchgeführt wird und in dem als Forschungsaufgabe die Analyse von Geschäftsbriefen bearbeitet wird.

[2]Ein entsprechendes Projekt läuft an der Universität Kaiserslautern, in dem ein Tool zur Unterstützung von Softwareentwicklungsprozessen entworfen wird.

Bezogen auf ein kalendarisch-chronometrisches System (z. B. das gregorianische Kalendersystem erweitert durch das momentan verwendete Uhrzeitsystem) bilden diese Zeitangabentypen die Basis aller zeitlichen Informationen. Mit den Angaben zur Zeitreihenfolge wird entweder auf einem abstrakten Niveau eine relativ (qualitativ) oder auf einem konkreten Niveau eine numerisch (quantitativ) bestimmte zeitliche Ordnung auf den Objekten festgelegt. Mit den Angaben zur Zeitdauer wird analog eine relative bzw. numerische zeitliche Ausdehnung der Objekte definiert.

Beim Studium von Arbeiten in vergleichbaren Domänen ist festzustellen, daß oftmals nur einzelne dieser zeitlichen Angaben berücksichtigt werden [Allen 84, van Beek 90]. Umfassendere Ansätze beziehen zwei [Ladkin 86, Koomen 88] oder sogar drei [Vere 83, Rit 86, Faidt et al 89, Huber 90] der vorgenannten zeitlichen Angaben mit ein. Diese integrierenden Ansätze vernachlässigen oftmals das Problem der wechselseitigen Beziehungen der unterschiedlichen zeitlichen Angaben. Außerdem werden in vielen Arbeiten die Aspekte der Repräsentation und der Verarbeitung von zeitlichen Angaben nicht genügend getrennt.

Als Beispiel für eine separate Betrachtung ist die Arbeit von Allen [Allen 83] anzusehen, der einerseits in der "Transitivitätstabelle" deklarativ beschreibt, welche qualitativen Zeitreihenfolgen zugelassen sind und wie diese prinzipiell zusammenhängen. Andererseits gibt er einen Inferenzalgorithmus (Constraint Propagation) an, der mit Hilfe dieser Tabelle aktuelle zeitliche Informationen verarbeitet. Durch einen anwendungsbedingten Austausch der Tabelle kann mit dem gleichen Algorithmus ein anderes Propagierungsverhalten erzielt werden. Alternative Algorithmen, die sich auf die Repräsentation der Tabelle stützen, sind leicht dazuzunehmen.

Sowohl die Forderung nach einem Zeitmodell mit mindestens vier Typen für Zeitangaben als auch die oben aufgezeigten Defizite in bisherigen Arbeiten führten zur Entwicklung eines eigenen Modells. Einige grundlegende Ideen knüpfen an die in [Flohr et al 88] vorgestellten Ansätze an.

4. Das Zeitmodell TEMPO

Aus der bisherigen Diskussion läßt sich zwar unmittelbar bestimmen, was repräsentiert werden muß, jedoch noch nicht wie dies geschieht. Da zeitliche Angaben z. B. Aussagen über Zeitdauer und über das Überlappen von Objekten der realen Welt (Ereignissen) beinhalten, liegt der Schritt zu einer intervallbasierten Repräsentation nahe. Zudem kann als erster Ausgangspunkt auf die oben angesprochene Arbeit von Allen zurückgegriffen werden (in dieser Arbeit von Allen und in [Bleisinger et al 88] findet sich auch eine Diskussion bezüglich Zeitintervall und Zeitpunkt).

Im Mittelpunkt aller zeitlichen Betrachtungen steht damit das Intervall, dessen zeitlicher Charakter durch die vier Typen von Zeitangaben, d.h. Zeitreihenfolgeangaben und Zeitdauerangaben jeweils in qualitativer und quantitativer Form, beschrieben wird. An folgendem Beispiel wird die Verwendung von Intervallen und den Intervallen zugeordneten zeitlichen Zusatzinformationen in Form von Zeitangabentypen exemplarisch verdeutlicht.

Als Beispiel sei zu repräsentieren:

"Die einstündige Sitzung findet am 15.03.1991 nach einer verkürzten Mittagspause statt".

Für zwei Objekte der realen Welt sind Intervalle zu erzeugen, die die zugeordneten zeitlichen Informationen repräsentieren. Und nur diese Intervalle werden weiter betrachtet.

Sitzung = Intervall1,
Mittagspause = Intervall2.

Intervall1 wird weiter zugeordnet:

    quantitative Zeitreihenfolgeangabe: 15.03.1991,

    quantitative Zeitdauerangabe: 1 Stunde,

    qualitative Zeitreihenfolgeangabe: Intervall1 nach Intervall2,

    qualitative Zeitdauer: Intervall1 länger Intervall2.

Das Beispiel und die zentrale Stellung von Intervallen werden in Abbildung 2 verdeutlicht.

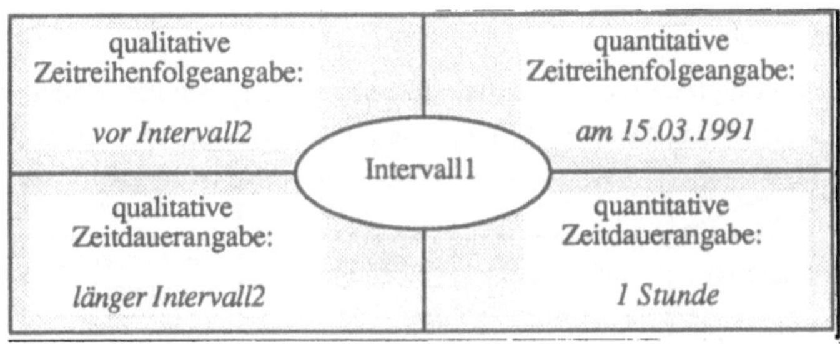

Abb. 2: Intervall und beschreibende Zeitangaben.

An diesem Beispiel wird auch die getrennte Verwendung von Intervallen als Zeitobjekte und von realen Objekten der Welt deutlich. Die Intervalle, mit den verschiedenen Zeitangabentypen, können durch die hier nicht betrachteten Schichten als zeitliche Informationen den realen Objekten der Welt zugeordnet werden.

Das Zeitmodell TEMPO setzt sich aus zwei Teilen zusammen, dem Repräsentationsmodell TERESA und dem Verarbeitungsmodell TEVERA. Durch die strikte Zweiteilung wird erreicht, daß die Repräsentation der Kriterien für Konsistenz und Propagierung deklarativ erfolgen kann und die algorithmische Ebene quasi als Interpreter dieser fungiert.

4.1 Das Repräsentationsmodell TERESA

TERESA ist ein 3-Schichten-Zeitrepräsentationsmodell, das eine qualitative, eine quantitative und eine integrierende Schicht beinhaltet. In TERESA wird für jeden Zeitangabentyp deklarativ beschrieben, welche Werte verwendet werden und wie diese zusammenspielen, d.h. welche wechselseitigen Restriktionen zwischen diesen bestehen. Damit werden die Grundlagen geschaffen für die Prüfung auf korrekte Eingaben, auf deren Konsistenz und für die Herleitung von zeitlichen Angaben.

Damit sind entsprechende Definitionen für die, in Abbildung 3 dargestellten, vier Typen von Zeitangaben als Minimalanforderung, samt den wechselseitigen Beziehungen, in TERESA zu repräsentieren.

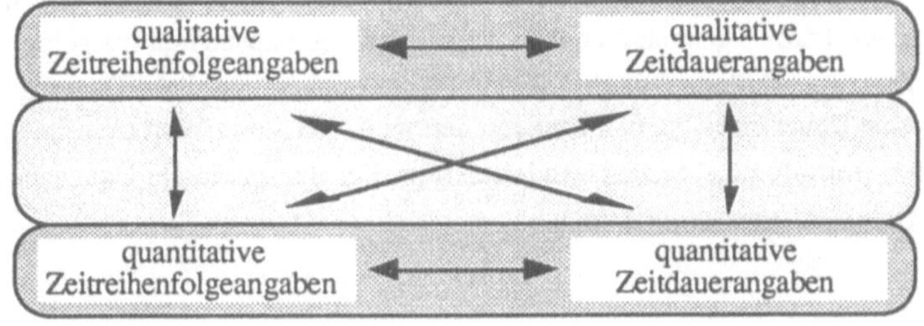

Abb. 3: In TERESA repräsentierte Zeitangabentypen und deren Beziehungen.

Nachfolgend wird sich auf den Teil der Zeitdauerangaben beschränkt. Es werden ausgewählte Beispiele für die qualitative und quantitative Zeitdauer sowie deren Beziehungen besprochen.

Qualitative Zeitdauer

Der Ansatz von Allen, der ganz speziell auf den Teil der qualitativen Zeitreihenfolge zugeschnitten ist, wird auf die qualitative Zeitdauer übertragen. Für die qualitativ genaue Zeitdauerbeziehung zweier Intervalle sind als Werte (Dauerrelationen, DR) zugelassen:

>   longer, shorter, equal.

Deren exklusiv-oder Verknüpfung wird als unscharfe Beschreibung benutzt. Mittels der modifizierten Transitivitätstabelle[3] in Abbildung 4 werden die Propagierungsbedingungen spezifiziert.

DR1 \ DR2	shorter	equal	longer
shorter	shorter	shorter	{shorter, equal, longer}
equal	shorter	equal	longer
longer	{shorter, equal, longer}	longer	longer

Abb.4: Transitivitätstabelle für Dauerrelationen.

Quantitative Zeitdauer

Für den Teil der quantitativen Zeitdauer wird beispielsweise festgelegt, daß zwei numerische Werte betrachtet werden, eine minimal und eine maximal mögliche Dauer:

>   min-dur, max-dur.

Die numerischen Werte, die für jede dieser quantitativen Angaben erlaubt sind, werden durch ein kalendarisch-chronometrischen Systems (KCS) vorgegeben [Lemke 91]. Zu bemerken ist, daß auch dieses KCS als Modell verstanden wird, daß prinzipiell beliebig austauschbar ist.

Als Konsistenzbedingungen können Restriktionen aufgestellt werden, die die zulässigen Beziehungen dieser numerischen Werte mittels Dauerrelationen beschreiben. So ist denkbar, daß die minimale mögliche Dauer immer kürzer oder gleichlang zu der maximal möglichen Dauer ist, um eine konsistente Wertebelegung zu erreichen:

>   min-dur {shorter, equal} max-dur.

Wird eine Verletzung dieser Restriktion entdeckt, kann durch eine entsprechende Propagierung versucht werden, die bestehende Inkonsistenz aufzuheben. Dazu muß noch zusätzlich festgelegt werden, wie die Werte *min-dur* und *max-dur* verändert werden dürfen. Da die minimal mögliche Dauer als größte bekannte untere Schranke für die Dauer eines Intervalls interpretiert wird, soll dieser Wert ($min-dur_{alt}$) nur durch eine neue, längere Dauer ($min-dur_{neu}$) ersetzt werden dürfen. Für die maximale Dauer wird analog vorgegangen. Als Restriktionen werden somit definiert:

---

[3]Die Tabelle ist folgendermaßen zu lesen: Seien I1, I2 und I3 Zeitintervalle. Zwischen I1 und I2 gilt die Dauerrelation DR1, zwischen I2 und I3 gilt DR2. Dann läßt sich zwischen I1 und I3 die Dauerrelation im Schnittfeld von DR1 und DR2 herleiten.

min-dur_{alt} {shorter} min-dur_{neu},

max-dur_{alt} {longer} max-dur_{neu}.

Beziehungen von qualitativer und quantitativer Zeitdauer

Für die integrierende Schicht muß festgelegt werden, welche Beziehungen zwischen der qualitativen und quantitativen Zeitdauer bestehen. Prinzipiell sind zwei Richtungen zu betrachten: zum einen wird als Ausgangspunkt eine zwischen zwei Intervallen festgelegte Zeitdauerrelation herangezogen, zum anderen bilden *min-dur* und *max-dur* die Bezugspunkte. Diese Beziehungen[4] werden sowohl zur Konsistenzüberprüfung herangezogen als auch zu Propagierungen.

Nachfolgend stehen I_1 und I_2 für Zeitintervalle, min-dur_{I_i} und max-dur_{I_i} für die quantitativen Zeitdauerangaben des Intervalls I_i.

Zuerst wird betrachtet, was von Zeitdauerrelationen ausgehend bezüglich der quantitativen Zeitdauerangaben *min-dur* und *max-dur* abgeleitet werden kann.

I_1 {shorter} I_2 $\rightarrow$ min-dur_{I_1} {shorter} max-dur_{I_2}

I_1 {equal} I_2 $\rightarrow$ min-dur_{I_1} {shorter, equal} max-dur_{I_2} und

max-dur_{I_1} {longer, equal} min-dur_{I_2}

I_1 {longer} I_2 $\rightarrow$ max-dur_{I_1} {longer} min-dur_{I_2}

Als nächstes wird untersucht, welche Auswirkungen die Behandlung von unscharfen Angaben, also Relationenmengen, haben.

I_1 {shorter, equal} I_2 $\rightarrow$ min-dur_{I_1} {shorter, equal} max-dur_{I_2}

I_1 {longer, equal} I_2 $\rightarrow$ max-dur_{I_1} {longer, equal} min-dur_{I_2}

I_1 {longer, shorter} I_2 $\rightarrow$ min-dur_{I_1} {shorter} max-dur_{I_2} oder

max-dur_{I_1} {longer} min-dur_{I_2}

I_1 {longer, equal, shorter} I_2 $\rightarrow$ ohne Einschränkung!

Abschließend muß noch der inverse Fall analysiert werden: ausgehend von quantitativen Zeitdauerangaben sollen Inferenzen bezüglich der qualitativen Zeitdauer gezogen werden. Dabei erfolgt eine Aufteilung in zwei Gruppen, jeweils die kreuzweisen Beziehungen von *min-dur* und *max-dur* der betrachteten zwei Intervalle:

min-dur_{I_1} {shorter} max-dur_{I_2} $\rightarrow$ I_1 {longer, equal, shorter} I_2

min-dur_{I_1} {equal} max-dur_{I_2} $\rightarrow$ I_1 {longer, equal} I_2

min-dur_{I_1} {longer} max-dur_{I_2} $\rightarrow$ I_1 {longer} I_2

max-dur_{I_1} {shorter} min-dur_{I_2} $\rightarrow$ I_1 {shorter} I_2

max-dur_{I_1} {equal} min-dur_{I_2} $\rightarrow$ I_1 {shorter, equal} I_2

max-dur_{I_1} {longer} min-dur_{I_2} $\rightarrow$ I_1 {longer, equal, shorter} I_2

Für alle anderen möglichen Kombinationen läßt sich die Menge aller Dauerrelationen herleiten:

I_1 {longer, equal, shorter} I_2.

---

[4]Die hier verwendete Auslegung dieser Beziehungen stellt nur eine mögliche Variante dar.

4.2 Das Verarbeitungsmodell TEVERA

In dem Repräsentationsmodell TERESA sind vier grundlegende Typen zeitlicher Angaben aufgenommen: qualitative und quantitative Zeitreihenfolgeangaben sowie qualitative und quantitative Zeitdauerangaben. Auf dieses Repräsentationsmodell abgestimmt wurden zeitliche Schlußfolgerungsverfahren entwickelt, die gleichzeitig eine Konsistenzanalyse durchführen. Hierbei sind die drei Bereiche qualitatives Schließen, quantitatives Schließen und insbesondere die Verbindung von beiden zu berücksichtigen. In der allgemeinen Übersicht in Abbildung 3 sind alle Beziehungen aufgeführt, die prinzipiell von dem Verarbeitungsmodell TEVERA abzudecken sind.

Das Verarbeitungsmodell TEVERA benutzt das entwickelte Zeitrepräsentationsmodell TERESA, um auf aktuell vorliegenden zeitlichen Angaben Konsistenztests durchzuführen und neue Zeitangaben herzuleiten (siehe Abbildung 5). Ausgehend von der Repräsentation der bestehenden zeitlichen Restriktionen bezüglich Konsistenz und Inferenz wurden erforderliche Verfahren entwickelt.

Um bezüglich zusätzlicher Zeitangaben (im Repräsentationsmodell TERESA), und den damit verbundenen neuen Verarbeitungsverfahren, ein offenes und leicht erweiterbares System zu erhalten, erfolgt eine modulare Vorgehensweise. Daher werden für jeden angeführten Zeitangabentyp spezifische Experten, d.h. auch mehrere pro Zeitangabentyp, für die Inferenz bzw. Konsistenz vorgesehen.

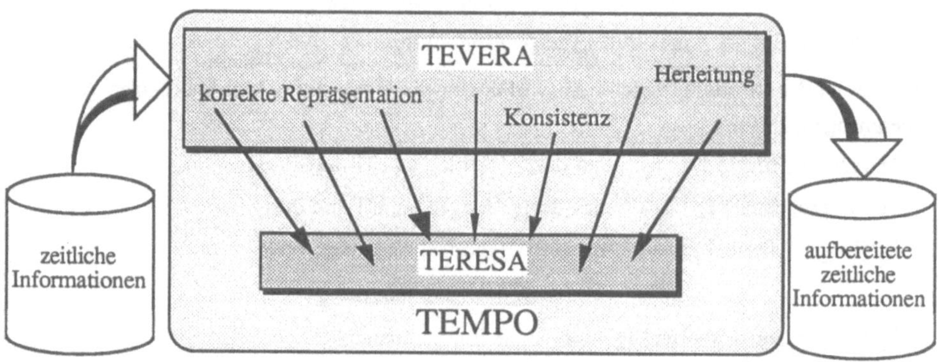

Abb. 5: Verarbeitung von zeitlichen Informationen in TEMPO.

Zusätzlich sind weiterhin die wechselseitigen Beziehungen zwischen einzelnen Zeitangaben zu berücksichtigen. Dazu werden diese in drei Gruppen unterteilt:

Beziehungen zwischen den quantitativen Zeitangaben

Beziehungen zwischen den qualitativen Zeitangaben

Beziehungen zwischen den qualitativen und quantitativen Zeitangaben.

Äußerst wichtig ist in diesem Zusammenhang die Entwicklung einer Gesamtstrategie, die festlegt, wie die einzelnen Zeitexperten sinnvoll und effizient entweder nacheinander oder verzahnt angewendet werden (statische Methode). Darüberhinaus eröffnet diese Vorgehensweise die Möglichkeit, die einzelnen Zeitexperten effizient bezüglich der vorliegenden zeitlichen Informationen einzusetzen, was zu situationsspezifischen Gesamtstrategien führt (dynamische Methode).

Nachfolgend werden grob die Prinzipien der Zeitexperten für qualitative und quantitative Zeitdauer sowie für die Beziehungen zwischen quantitativ und qualitativ in beiden Richtungen verbal beschrieben. Zum Abschluß wird eine statische Gesamtstrategie, bezogen auf diese vier Zeitexperten, aufgezeigt.

Der Experte für die qualitative Zeitdauer stützt sich auf die in TERESA modellierte Transitivitätstabelle. Da diese in Analogie zur Transitivitätstabelle von Allen erstellt wurde bietet sich die Übernahme des von Allen entwickelten Algorithmus an.

Der Experte für die quantitative Zeitdauer muß berücksichtigen, welche Werte für Zeitdauer laut TERESA verwendet werden. Unter Verwendung dieser Werte und der Beachtung der in TERESA spezifizierten Restriktionen bezüglich diesen muß auf die Konsistenz der eingetragen Daten geprüft werden. Im Falle einer entdeckten Inkonsistenz muß eine korrigierende Propagierung versucht werden. Gelingt diese nicht, so muß eine entsprechende Meldung gegeben werden.

Vorgehen: (Zeitexperte für quantitative Zeitdauerangaben)

    für alle Intervalle

        füge alle aktuellen Restriktionen eines Intervalls in Menge ein;

        solange eine Restriktion in Menge

            nimm eine Restriktion aus Menge

            führe Konsistenztest durch:

                Dauerrelation in Restriktionen $\in$ vorgegebene Dauerrelation(en) der entsprechenden Restriktionen in TERESA;

            falls nicht OK:

                versuche Inkonsistenz durch Propagierung zu beheben:

                    "constraint propagation algorithmus";

                falls geglückt:

                    füge alle aktuellen Restriktionen, an denen der veränderte Wert beteiligt ist, in Menge ein;

                falls nicht geglückt:

                    melde Inkonsistenz und Abbruch!;

Die Zeitexperten für die Integration von qualitativen und quantitativen Zeitdauern müssen in erster Linie die speziellen Restriktionen bezüglich der wechselseitigen Beziehungen berücksichtigen, die in TERESA formuliert sind. Zusätzlich müssen sie auch einige Restriktionen mit einbeziehen, die sich nur auf die quantitativen bzw. qualitativen Angaben beziehen. So z.B. die Propagierungsbedingungen für die quantitativen Angaben.

Als Gesamtstrategie ist momentan eine statisch festgelegte Vorgehensweise implementiert. Zuerst wird lokal für jedes Intervall der Experte für die quantitative Zeitdauer angewendet. Danach wird der Experte für die qualitative Zeitdauer gestartet, der immer drei Intervalle zusammen betrachtet. Ausgehend von der relationalen Dauerbeziehungen werden anschließend Werte für die quantitativen Angaben hergeleitet. Nach jeder Veränderung der Dauerrelationen wird der qualitative Zeitdauerexperte erneut angewendet. Abschließend wird der inverse Fall betrachtet, bei dem nach jeder quantitativen Werteänderung der entsprechende Experte aufgerufen wird.

Zum isolierten Testen der einzelnen Zeitexperten und um verschiedene Gesamtstrategien manuell durchzuspielen wird zur Zeit eine interaktive Entwicklerumgebung aufgebaut. Mit Hilfe der maus- und menuegesteuerten Window-Oberfläche werden statistische Daten ermittelt. Zum einen wird evaluiert wie sich die speziellen Experten auf den unterschiedlichsten zeitlichen Eingabeinformationen verhalten und zum anderen wie das Zusammenspiel der Zeitexperten zu bewerten ist.

5. Schlußbemerkungen

In TEMPO wird durch die integrierte Betrachtung von quantitativen und qualitativen Zeitreihenfolge- und Zeitdauerangaben eine Basis geschaffen, um zeitliche Informationen umfassend zu repräsentieren und zu verarbeiten. Die konsequente Zweiteilung in das Repräsentationsmodell TERESA und das Verarbeitungsmodell TEVERA ermöglicht eine deklarative Beschreibung der erlaubten Werte, deren Konsistenzbedingungen und deren Propagierungsrestriktionen. Durch die Idee der Zeitexperten, die sich auf die Beschreibungen in TERESA stützen, wird darüberhinaus eine Erweiterung des Modells erleichtert.

Bislang wurden Zeitexperten sowohl für die qualitative Ebene ([Braun 91]) als auch für die quantitative Ebene ([Lemke 91]) jeweils für Zeitreihenfolge- und Zeitdauerangaben sowie deren Beziehungen implementiert. An der integrierenden Schicht wird gearbeitet.

Schwerpunkt zukünftiger Aktivitäten bildet zum einen der Ausbau der integrierenden Schicht. Zum anderen wird die Entwicklung von dynamischen Gesamtstrategien für die Verarbeitung vorangetrieben, die gezielt in Abhängigkeit der Eingabeinformationen vorgehen.

Literatur

[Allen 83] Allen, J.F.: *Maintaining Knowledge about Temporal Intervals*, Communications of the ACM, 26, Nr. 11, Nov. 1983, S. 832-843.

[Allen 84] Allen, J.F.: *Towards a General Theory of Action and Time*, Artificial Intelligence, 23, Nr. 2, Juli 1984, S. 123-154.

[Bleisinger et al 88] Bleisinger, Rainer; Faidt, Klaus; Flohr, Stephan: *Zeitintervalle und Zeitpunkte*, WISDOM-Forschungsbericht FB-AGB-88-21, Juli 1988.

[Bleisinger et al 91] Bleisinger, Rainer; Knauber, Peter; Schramm, Wolfgang; Verlage, Martin: *Software Process Description and Enactment Considering Temporal Constraints*, eingereicht zum 4th Int. Symp. on AI, Cancun, Mexiko, 1991.

[Braun 91] Braun, Norbert: Qualitatives zeitliches Schließen, Projektarbeit, Uni Kaiserslautern, 1991.

[Flohr et al 88] Flohr, Stephan; Bleisinger, Rainer; Faidt, Klaus: *Verarbeitung von zeitlichem Wissen*, WISDOM-Forschungsbericht FB-AGB-88-26, Dezember 1988.

[Faidt et al 89] Faidt, Klaus; Flohr, Stephan; Bleisinger, Rainer: *Repräsentation und Verarbeitung von zeitlichem Wissen*, Proc. of 5th OEGAI, 1989, S. 303-312.

[Galton 90] Galton, Antony: *A Critical Examination of Allens Theory of Action and Time*, Artificial Intelligence, 1990, S. 159-188.

[Huber 90] Huber, Alfred: *Wissensbasierte Überwachung und Planung in der Fertigung*, Erich Schmidt Verlag, Berlin, 1990.

[Koomen 88] Koomen, Johannes A.G.M.: *The TIMELOGIC Temporal Reasoning System*, Technical Report 231, University of Rochester, 1988.

[Ladkin 86] Ladkin, P: *Primitives and Units for Time Specification*, Proc. of 5th AAAI, 1986, S. 354-359.

[Lemke 91] Lemke, Oliver: Quantitatives zeitliches Schließen, Projektarbeit, Uni Kaiserslautern, 1991.

[McDermott 82] McDermott, Drew: *A Temporal Logic for Reasoning about Processes and Plans*, Cognitive Science, 6, 1982, S. 101-155.

[Rit 86] Rit, Jean-Francois: *Propagating Temporal Constraints for Scheduling*, Proc. of 5th AAAI, 1986, S. 383-388.

[Shoham 89] Shoham, Yoav: *Time for Action*, Proc. of 4th IJCAI, Sept. 1989, S. 954-959.

[van Beek 90] van Beek, Peter: *Reasoning about Qualitative Temporal Information*, Proc. of 8th AAAI, 1990, S. 728-734.

[Vere 83] Vere, Steven A.: *Planning in Time: Windows and Durations for Activities and Goals*, IEEE PAMI, Vol. 5, Nr. 3, 1983, S. 246-267.

Temporal Reasoning with Generalized Relations

Gerd Kortüm

IBM Germany, Scientific Center
Institute for Knowledge Based Systems
P.O. Box 80 08 80
7000 Stuttgart 80

Abstract

James Allen formulated an interval-based calculus for maintaining temporal knowledge which is widely applied to temporal reasoning in AI-systems. In this paper we present an extension of existing interval based representations of time which is motivated by requirements stemming from the natural language text understanding project LILOG. For covering temporal quantificational phenomena we introduce the notion of plural intervals, i.e. *sets of intervals*. The main novelty is the definition of *generalized relations* as primitives for describing relationships between sets of intervals. Generalized relations are derived from standard interval relations by implicit "generalized" quantification. Furthermore, we specify inference rules which allow for temporal reasoning with generalized relations. We demonstrate how they can be reduced to Allens's transitivity rules for interval relations.

1 Introduction

In the LILOG project of IBM Germany methods for machine understanding of german natural language texts are being developed. For the purpose of text understanding the necessity of the representation and processing of adequate semantic background knowledge is widely accepted. In the LILOG project the background knowledge is modelled in the logic based representation language L_{LILOG} (see [Pletat and von Luck 90]). The background knowledge consists of general world knowledge, especially knowledge about time and space. Temporal knowledge is used for the reconstruction of the temporal structure of texts and for answering questions concerning temporal phenomena.

For representing temporal knowledge intervals are held to serve as adequate representational primitives. They are considered as projections of situations and events onto time. James Allen [Allen 83] developed a calculus for maintaining knowledge about intervals. For describing the temporal ordering of intervals, he employed 13 basic relations like *meets*, *overlaps* or *equals*. This calculus was given a logical axiomatization in [Allen and Hayes 87] which serves as the basis for the representation of temporal knowledge in LILOG. According to the interval based approach the temporal structure of a text consists of partially ordered intervals each corresponding to an event or state introduced by the text.

Simple intervals, however, are not sufficient to represent temporal knowledge, in general. The following is an example concerning temporal quantification: *The museum is closed on every monday.* In general, quantifiers serve to introduce sets of objects into the discourse domain. We interpret the example as stating a relationship between two sets of intervals. The first consisting of all intervals on which the museum is open, and the second being the set of all mondays. We propose *sets of intervals* as adequate representational primitives for the representation of temporal quantification. In this paper we will concentrate on the development of a formal framework for representing and processing temporal knowledge which is based on such sets of intervals.

The outline of this paper is as follows:
In the next section, we start with a formal definition of 'sets of intervals'.
In section 3, we introduce the notion of *generalized relations* as primitives for describing relationships between sets of intervals. These relations are derived from standard interval relations by implicit "generalized" quantification.
In section 4, the problem of inferencing with generalized relations is investigated. In Allen's interval calculus, inferencing is based exclusively on a set of transitivity rules summarized in his transitivity table. We identify corresponding inference rules for generalized relations and show how these rules can be reduced to the

transitivity rules for intervals. We also investigate conditions for deciding whether knowledge about sets of intervals is inconsistent or not.

2   Sets of Intervals

For constructing temporal set objects we use a lattice theoretic approach (see [Eberle 90]). In the following, we will call the resulting temporal set objects *set-intervals*. We introduce a join operator on set-intervals with the following properties[1]:

- Commutativity: $\forall A, B : A \sqcup B = B \sqcup A$
- Associativity: $\forall A, B, C : A \sqcup (B \sqcup C) = (A \sqcup B) \sqcup C$
- Idempotence: $\forall A : A \sqcup A = A$
- Completeness: $\forall A, B \exists C : A \sqcup B = C$

Additionally, we require the lattice to observe strict complementarity. The lattice operation $\sqcup$ induces a partial ordering on set-intervals which can be interpreted as the part-of relation:

- Part-of-relation: $\forall A, B : A \sqsubseteq B \Longleftrightarrow A \sqcup B = B$

We consider the lattice as atomic and identify intervals with the atomic elements:

- $\forall A : interval(A) \Longleftrightarrow \forall B : (B \sqsubseteq A \Longrightarrow B = A)$

We can now define the element relation to be the restriction of the part-of relation on intervals:

- Element-relation: $\forall A, B : A \in B \Longleftrightarrow interval(A) \wedge A \sqsubseteq B$

In the following, we call intervals for which the element-relation holds *element-intervals* of the corresponding set-interval. As a result of the lattice approach we get the effect that there is no notational difference between true intervals und set-intervals. Thus, each interval is at the same time a set-interval.

3   Generalized Relations

After having introduced and formally defined set-intervals as our representational primitives, we can now state the definition of corresponding temporal relations. We define a class of relations that can hold between set-intervals, and show their utility by giving natural language examples. The relations, which we call *generalized relations*, are derived from standard interval relations by implicit "generalized" quantification. By making implicit the quantification over set-intervals we yield an effectively propositional logic, thus avoiding explicit handling of quantifiers.

Generalized relations are binary relations on set-intervals, which associate element-intervals of two set-intervals on the basis of interval relations. To begin with, let $\mathcal{REL} = \{R_1, \ldots, R_n\}$ be a unique and complete set of interval relations with the following properties holding for all relations $R_i, R_j \in \mathcal{REL}$ and all intervals a,b[2]:

- Uniqueness: $\forall a, b : aR_i b \wedge aR_j b \Longrightarrow R_i = R_j$
- Completeness: $\forall a, b : aR_1 b \vee \ldots \vee aR_n b$

As the result there is exactly one relation out of $\mathcal{REL}$ holding between two given intervals. The set of Allen's 13 interval relations satisfies this condition.

A generalized relation is defined to be the tupel $G = (Q, R)$ where Q is a quantifier and R is an interval relation from $\mathcal{REL}$. We use the prefix-notation $Q_R AB$ to denote that a generalized relation (Q, R) holds between two set-intervals A, B. By restricting our attention to the quantifiers *All*, *Some*, *Not_All* and *No*, we define four generalized relations as follows:

- $All_R AB \Longleftrightarrow \forall a \in A \exists b \in B : aRb$
- $Some_R AB \Longleftrightarrow \exists a \in A \exists b \in B : aRb$
- $Not\_All_R AB \Longleftrightarrow \exists a \in A \forall b \in B : \neg(aRb)$
- $No_R AB \Longleftrightarrow \forall a \in A \forall b \in B : \neg(aRb)$

For instance, generalized relations can be used to represent the fact that two events *always* occur at the same time (*All*) or that two events *never* occur at the same time (*No*). The cooccurrence of two events can be further specified with respect to an interval relation. For instance, the fact that an event always

---

[1] A different approach was undertaken by Peter Ladkin [Ladkin 86a, Ladkin 86b]. He introduces *non-convex intervals* which can be understood as sequences of intervals.

[2] We use upper case symbols to denote set-intervals and lower case symbols to denote true intervals.

starts/ends at the same time as another event can be represented by the relation All_{starts}/All_{ends}. As a concrete example let us show how generalized relations can be applied to the representation of natural language sentences. Consider the following examples:

(1) *Before giving a talk$_A$, Peter is always nervous$_B$.*
(2) *After giving a talk$_A$, Peter is sometimes nervous$_B$.*
(3) *Before giving a talk$_A$, Peter is not always nervous$_B$.*
(4) *During giving a talk$_A$, Peter is never nervous$_B$.*

As the representation of the temporal structure of these sentences we employ two set-intervals, the first (A) corresponding to Peter's talks, and the second (B) corresponding to his state of being nervous. For representing their relationships as expressed in the sentences we make use of the generalized relations. The temporal frequency adverbs *always, sometimes, not always* and *never* correspond to the quantifier of generalized relations. The temporal ordering expressed by the conjunctions *before, after* and *during* can be represented by the corresponding interval relation. Finally, we achieve the following generalized relations as the temporal representation[3]:

(1) $All_{after}AB$
(2) $Some_{before}AB$
(3) $Not\_All_{after}AB$
(4) $No_{contains}AB$

As demonstrated by these examples, we get a relational representation of temporal quantification.

Generalized relations are considered to be primitives for describing relationships between set-intervals. In contrary to simple interval relations they do not form a unique and complete set of relations: for two given set-intervals, a conjunction of generalized relations is required for a complete characterization of their relationship. This situation is illustrated graphically in the following picture.

$$A \quad \rule{1cm}{0.4pt} \quad \rule{0.8cm}{0.4pt} \quad \rule{1.2cm}{0.4pt}$$

$$B \quad \rule{1cm}{0.4pt} \quad \rule{1.2cm}{0.4pt} \quad \rule{1.5cm}{0.4pt}$$

Among others, the following generalized relations hold between the set-intervals A and B: $Some_{ends}AB$, $Some_{starts}AB$, $No_{equals}AB$, $Not\_All_{starts}AB$. Even an exhaustive enumeration of all the generalized relations that hold between the set-intervals shown in the figure cannot fully describe the illustrated situation. In fact, a complete description is never intended as far as all important aspects are covered.

4 A Calculus for Generalized Relations

To do temporal reasoning with generalized relations we need two prerequisites. Firstly, we have to specify rules of inference to explicate relations which are only given implicitly. In the interval calculus a set of transitivity rules is used for this task. We will show how transitivity rules for generalized relations can be reduced to these rules. Secondly, we have to identify situations containing inconsistent information. In the interval calculus inconsistent situations can be detected very easily by determining whether the set of all possible relations between two intervals is empty. Because generalized relations do not form a complete and unique set of relations checking inconsistencies is not so trivial in this case. However, we are able to specify rules to detect some inconsistencies that might occur in the description of a relationship.

4.1 Inference Rules

A transitivity rule for generalized relations has the following form where Q_1, Q_2, Q_3 each range over the quantifiers *All, Some, Not_All* and *No* and R_1, R_2, R_3 range over interval relations:

$$\frac{Q_{1_{R_1}} AB \qquad Q_{2_{R_2}} BC}{Q_{3_{R_3}} AC}$$

---

[3] In order to capture the correct meaning of the example sentences we have to represent the conjunctions like *before* or *during* directly opposed to the language surface by the interval relations *after* and *contains*.

The question here is which combination of quantifiers Q and interval relations R yields a valid transitivity rule. The following example gives us an intuitive plausible inference:

$$\frac{\begin{array}{c} \textit{Before giving a talk}_A,\ \textit{Peter is always nervous}_B. \\ \textit{When Peter is nervous}_B,\ \textit{he always smokes a cigarette}_C. \end{array}}{\textit{Before giving a talk}_A,\ \textit{Peter always smokes a cigarette}_C.}$$

If we use the relations $All_{after}AB$ and $All_{contains}BC$ for the representing of the temporal structure of the two first sentences, this inference determines the relationship between the set-intervals A and C as $All_{after}AC$. We obtain the following transitivity rule for generalized relations:

$$\frac{\begin{array}{c} All_{after}AB \\ All_{contains}BC \end{array}}{All_{after}AC}.$$

If we systematically apply the definitions of our generalized relations we can reduce the conclusion of the transitivity rules to Allen's transitivity function for intervals. The resulting transitivity rules for generalized relations are summarized in the following figure[4].

$\mathrm{trans}(G_1,G_2)$	$All_{R_2}BC$	$Some_{R_2}BC$
$All_{R_1}AB$	$All_{trans(R_1,R_2)}AC$	no info
$Some_{R_1}AB$	$Some_{trans(R_1,R_2)}AC$	no info
$Not\_All_{R_1}AB$	$Some_{trans(\overline{R_1},R_2)}AC$	$Some_{trans(\overline{R_1},R_2)}AC$
$No_{R_1}AB$	$All_{trans(\overline{R_1},R_2)}AC$	$All_{trans(\overline{R_1},R_2)}AC$

$\mathrm{trans}(G_1,G_2)$	$Not\_All_{R_2}BC$	$No_{R_2}BC$
$All_{R_1}AB$	no info	$No_{trans(R_1,\overline{R_2})}AC$
$Some_{R_1}AB$	no info	$Not\_All_{trans(R_1,\overline{R_2})}AC$
$Not\_All_{R_1}AB$	$Not\_All_{trans(\overline{R_1},\overline{R_2})}AC$	$Not\_All_{trans(\overline{R_1},\overline{R_2})}AC$
$No_{R_1}AB$	$No_{trans(\overline{R_1},\overline{R_2})}AC$	$No_{trans(\overline{R_1},\overline{R_2})}AC$

Figure 1: Transitivity table for generalized relations

As a further example, we can obtain the following valid inference rule from this table where $\overline{after}$ is the disjunction consisting of all other 12 interval relations:

$$\frac{\begin{array}{c} Not\_All_{after}AB \\ Some_{contains}BC \end{array}}{Some_{trans(\overline{after},contains)}AC}$$

4.2 Checking Inconsistencies

In order to successfully employing the inference rules given above, we need to know whether information obtained in the inference process is inconsistent or not. We have to specify conditions that must be satisfied by any description of a relationship between set-intervals. The following are two conditions which can be derived from the properties of the set $\mathcal{REL} = \{R_1,\ldots,R_n\}$:

- For two arbitrary set-intervals, there holds at least one generalized relation involving the $Some$-quantifier: $Some_{R_1}AB \lor Some_{R_2}AB \lor \ldots \lor Some_{R_n}AB$
- It is never the case that all generalized relations involving the No-quantifier hold at the same time: $\neg(No_{R_1}AB \land No_{R_2}AB \land \ldots \land No_{R_n}AB)$

Looking at the two generalized relations All_{after} and No_{after} we recognize another valuable condition: All_{after} and No_{after} can never hold between two set-intervals A and B at the same time. This is due to the contradictory status of these relations: $All_RAB \iff \neg(Not\_All_RAB)$.

---

[4] We use the following notational conventions: $trans(R_1,R_2)$ denotes the transitivity function on interval relations used by Allen. For expressing the negation of interval relations, we use the complement operation $\overline{R}$ on relations: $\neg(aRb) \iff a\overline{R}b$. In both definitions we take for granted that they naturally extend to disjunctions of interval relations.

Entries in the table marked with the label 'no info' indicate the impossibility of inferring any information about the corresponding relation.

By systematically investigating the properties of our generalized relations we are able to detect more conditions which are intuitive plausible:

- $\neg(No_RAB \wedge Some_RAB)$
- $\neg(All_RAB \wedge Not\_All_RAB)$
- $\neg(No_RAB \wedge All_RAB)$
- $No_RAB \vee Some_RAB$
- $All_RAB \vee Not\_All_RAB$

After having developed inference rules and consistency conditions for generalized relations we are able to specify a constraint propagation algorithm that can detect an unsatisfiable set of relations efficiently. We can adopt well-known techniques already used for temporal reasoning (e.g. [Allen 83] and [van Beek 90]). In [Kortüm 91] we show how the inference techniques used for temporal reasoning in the interval calculus are to be modified for reasoning about generalized relations.

5 Summary

Starting with the observation that certain temporal phenomena in natural language concerning quantification are not adequately expressible in terms of simple intervals we have introduced both the notion of set-intervals and of generalized relations. In general, descriptions of relationships between arbitrary set-intervals are conjunctions of several generalized relations which serve as representational primitives. Furthermore, we have transferred the transitivity rules for intervals to corresponding rules for set-intervals. Inference rules for generalized relations have then been augmented by conditions for evaluating inferences.

For the time being, we are only able to give an incomplete set of conditions for consistency checking. As a result, we obtain an incomplete calculus for generalized relations so far. What our approach needs most at this point is more inquiry of its inferential capabilities and computational properties. We suppose that for efficient reasoning with generalized relations it might be necessary to develop approximate algorithms which compute partial solutions (see e.g. [van Beek 89]).

We believe that the most striking advantage of our framework results from the fact that it combines efficient inference techniques with more expressive power than simple interval-based approaches can provide.

References

[Allen 83] James F. Allen: Maintaining Knowledge About Temporal Intervals. *Communications of the ACM*, 26(11) S. 832–843, November 1983.

[Allen and Hayes 87] James F. Allen and Patrick J. Hayes: *Moments and Points in an Interval-Based Temporal Logic*. Technical Report 180, Departments of Computer Science, University of Rochester, Rochester, NY, Dezember 1987.

[Eberle 90] Kurt Eberle: Eventualities in a Natural Language Understanding System. In K.H. Bläsius, U. Hedstück and C.-R. Rollinger (Hrsg.), *Sorts and Types in Artificial Intelligence*, S. 209–239, Springer-Verlag, Berlin, West Germany, 1990.

[Hayes and Allen 87] Patrick J. Hayes and James F. Allen: Short Time Periods. In *Proceedings of the 10th International Joint Conference on Artificial Intelligence*, Milan, Italy, 1987.

[Kamp 79] H. Kamp: Events, Instants and Temporal Reference. In R. Baeuerle, U. Egli and A. von Stechow (Hrsg.), *Semantics from Different Points of View*, S. 376–417, Springer, Berlin, 1979.

[Kortüm 91] Gerd Kortüm: *Temporales Schließen in einem natürlichsprachlichen System*. LILOG-Report 162, IBM Deutschland, Stuttgart, Mai 1991.

[Ladkin 86a] Peter Ladkin: Primitives and Units for Time Specification. In *Proceedings of the 5th National Conference of the American Association for Artificial Intelligence*, S. 354–359, Philadelphia, Pa., 1986.

[Ladkin 86b] Peter Ladkin: Time Representation:A Taxonomy of Interval Relations. In *Proceedings of the 5th National Conference of the American Association for Artificial Intelligence*, S. 360–366, Philadelphia, Pa., 1986.

[Pletat and von Luck 90] Udo Pletat and Kai von Luck: Knowledge Representation in LILOG. In K.H. Bläsius, U. Hedstück and C.-R. Rollinger (Hrsg.), *Sorts and Types in Artificial Intelligence*, S. 140–164, Springer-Verlag, Berlin, West Germany, 1990.

[Schmiedel 88] Albrecht Schmiedel: *Temporal Constraint Networks*. KIT Report 69, Department of Computer Science, Technische Universität Berlin, Berlin, West Germany, November 1988.

[van Beek 89] Peter van Beek: Approximation Algorithms for Temporal Reasoning. In *Proceedings of the 11th International Joint Conference on Artificial Intelligence*, S. 1291–1296, Detroit, Mich., 1989.

[van Beek 90] Peter van Beek: Reasoning about Qualitative Temporal Information. In *Proceedings of the 9th National Conference of the American Association for Artificial Intelligence*, S. 728–734, 1990.

[van Benthem 83] Johan van Benthem: *The Logic of Time*. Reidel, Dordrecht, Holland, 1983.

MODEL REPRESENTATION AND TAXONOMIC REASONING
IN CONFIGURATION PROBLEM SOLVING

by
Rüdiger Klein
Institute of Artificial Intelligence
(IfKI/ZKI)
Kurstraße 33
O–1086 Berlin

Abstract

Object–level knowledge representation in configuration problem solving often needs highly expressive means. Meeting these requirements within formal, logic–based knowledge representation schemes seems to be impossible (due to the encountered complexity). As a way out, some well–defined restriction in knowledge representation expressiveness will be suggested: relational terms are excluded from concept definitions, instead relations will be defined including concept assignments to their arguments as a kind of consistency conditions. In this way, an adequate representation of the well–structured object–level knowledge, which is characteristic of configuration problems, can be achieved, providing a "background theory" for more general knowledge (represented for instance as a set of clauses).

The constructive problem solving (CPS) will be outlined as an abductive approach to configuration problem solving. Taxonomic reasoning, which is an essential part of the overall configuration problem solving, can be formalized within this paradigm.

A small configuration example will be given as an illustration of this knowledge representation and problem solving approach.

I. Introduction

An essential point in configuration problem solving is the high requirements to object–level knowledge representation. Normally an *explicit model* of the objects involved – including their (relevant) attributes, relations between them, various abstractions and constraints – will be needed (fig.1).

A central issue in recent AI research is the developement of formal, well–defined knowledge representation schemes [Levesque 86]. Such a scheme should provide *epistemologically adequate* representational capabilities [Brachman, Schmolze 85], a *declarative* (Tarski–style) semantics, and a set of explicitly specified inference rules, which allow to address soundness, completeness and complexity issues.

In recent years, in order to get a formal, logic–based knowledge representation various approaches have been developed : for instance order–sorted logic [Walther 87; Cohn 87], feature logic [Smolka 88; Schmidt–Schauß, Smolka 88], term–description languages (TDL) in the tradition of KL–ONE [Brachman, Schmolze 85] or approaches integrating various schemes (for instance [Pletat, Luck 89; Ait–Kaci, Podelski 91]).

Recent results of theoretical investigations in these formal knowledge representation schemes revealed a basic conflict between expressiveness and inferential complexity [Nebel 90; Nebel 90a; Hollunder, Nutt 90]. Every scheme providing sufficient expressiveness (for instance in configuration problems) may easily result in intractability (or even undecidability [Schild 88; Patel–Schneider 89]) of the inference operations.

As a consequence, in recent years considerable interest has been grown in *hybrid reasoning* techniques [Baader et al. 90; Frisch, Cohn 91], integrating various knowledge representation and reasoning techniques in a *well–formalized* way.

Two main questions arise with such hybrid schemes:

- Which knowledge may be represented in which way?
- How may the various forms of knowledge interact?

The second question has been addressed in some general theoretical approaches: for instance theory resolution [Stickel 85], the substitutional frame concept [Frisch 89] as a generalization of order–sorted unification [Walther 87, Cohn 87], or constraint resolution [Bürckert 90; Baader et al. 90]. Of course, their *applicability* will be affected by the answer found to the first question.

The goal of this paper is not to formulate a new theoretical approach, but to demonstrate such a hybrid knowledge representation scheme including *taxonomic* and *general* domain knowledge.

In order to retain the formal foundation of knowledge representation and to avoid unnecessary complexity, this hybrid representation will include some *well–defined restrictions* in the representational capabilities and in the inferences [Klein 91]. Configuration problems provide a suitable testbed [Klein 91b] (compared with other fields of application, as for instance natural language understanding, vision, or common sense reasoning) for the investigations of such well–formalized hybrid approaches, because object–level knowledge in configuration problems will mainly be well–structured, exact and (relatively) complete.

The paper is organized as follows: In the next chapter we will discuss some of the knowledge representation aspects in configuration problems. Chapter 3 outlines a formal definition of the syntax and the declarative semantics of our knowledge representation. Chapter 4 contains a description of the taxonomic reasoning needed in configuration problem solving. An example will be introduced in chapter 5 as an illustration of our ideas, followed by a discussion in the final chapter 6.

II. Knowledge Representation Issues in Configuration Problems

In the literature, in various ways the requirements of object–level knowledge representation in configuration problems have been formulated [Cunis et al. 88; Searls, Norton 89; Tank et al. 89; Coyne et al. 90; Klein 90a]. They may be summarized as follows:

- A clear distinction will be needed between a priori *definitional knowledge* describing the domain *in general* (the object classes, their relations and constraints), and *assertional knowledge* characterizing the concrete objects and their relations.
- An epistemologically adequate representation of the definitional (as well as the assertional) knowledge implies the provision of a *rich variety of representational constructs* (see fig. 1).

definitional knowledge	object descriptions
• super classes and inheritance • feature specifications • relation specifications • part_of relations • constraints: logical, algebraic	• class assignments • feature values • relations between objects

Fig.1: Some aspects of object–level knowledge in configuration problems

It seems to be impossible to formalize a knowledge representation scheme, which could include all these requirements (fig.1) in *one uniform way* (for instance in the form of term description languages) . Already the integration of logical expressions (such as clauses on concept expressions [Owsnicki 88; Schild 89] or on role expressions [Quantz 90]) into the concept description capabilities will greatly increase the computational complexity of inference operations. But just this integration of class–related (taxonomic) inferences with general logical operations will be essential for an adequate problem solving in configuration tasks [Klein 90a; Owsnicki 88; Peltason 89;].

Thus the question arises, *whether* a hybrid reasoning system (the theoretically well–founded *integration* of various knowledge representation and reasoning schemes) would be adequate here, and, if there is a positive answer, *how* such a system should be formulated.

In order to get a formal representation of at least *some aspects* of the knowledge, which can be relevant in configuration problems, two points, which characterize this special problem class, will be taken into account:

- In configuration problems, object classes can be defined *per se*, i.e., by their own features (attributes), internal structures etc., but *not* necessarily with respect to other objects (i.e., by relations). In contrast, relations may be characterized by class specifications of their arguments, in order to express a kind of *consistency conditions* (see also the example in chapter 5).

- Due to the synthetic type of configuration problem solving, a major part of the problem solving will be *solution generation*. This includes instantiation of a–priori defined objects, refinement of object descriptions, of relations between them, etc. Thus, the main point will be to keep the generated solution *consistent*. As a result, a *shift of emphasis* may occur from definitional to assertional inferences.

We suggest the following scheme of the definitional knowledge:

- The *object–centered knowledge representation* (concept descriptions) will include Boolean expressions on other concepts, feature terms (selections), and feature (dis–)agreements [Smolka 88; Schmidt–Schauß, Smolka 88]. But in contrast to other term description languages, concept–defining terms will *not* contain *any relational expressions* (like $\exists$rel.c or $\forall$rel.c)[1].

- As part of the *definitional* knowledge, relations will be defined including concept assignments to their arguments (in analogy to order–sorted logic [Walther 87; Cohn 87]). These concept assignments provide *necessary pre–conditions* for objects to be in such a relation to each other.

- Both concept and relational expressions may be included in clauses, expressing general logical constraints.

The overall representation scheme of the definitional knowledge adopted here has been outlined in fig. 2.

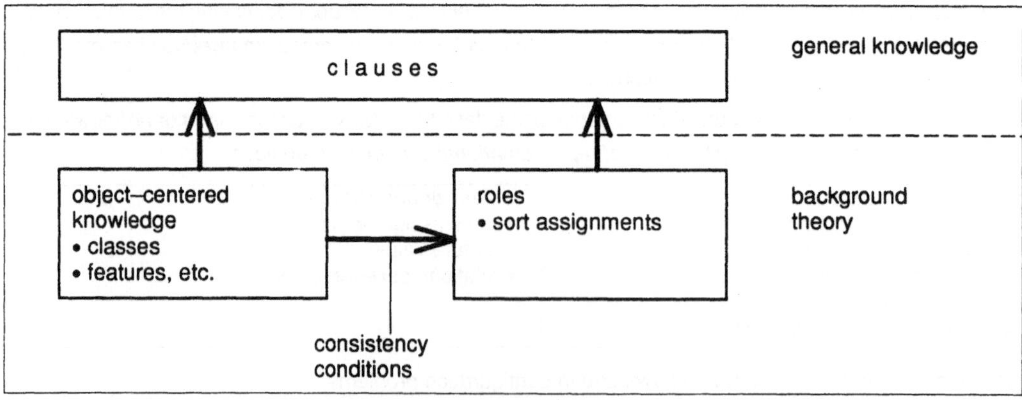

Fig. 2: An outline of the definitional knowledge representation

The restrictions in the concept description capabilities mentioned above (no relational expressions in concept descriptions) will be accompanied with a *restriction of the terminological inferences*: no relational ex-

1. The distinction between *features* and *relations* (roles) as taken here will not be only a formal one (functional versus relational expressions), but basically one reflecting the *different intended meaning*: a feature will uniquely be assigned to one of the objects, whereas a role specifies a relation between various objects (see for instance the example described in chapter 5.).

pressions could be used in subsumption calculations. But this restriction will be compensated by an increased inferential power on the side of logical expressions, which involve concept and role expressions (as a background theory, for instance, to a modified[2] constraint resolution [Bürckert 90; Baader et al. 90]). This will be described in chapter 4.

III. Formal Definition of Object–Level Knowledge Representation

As a subset[3] of the requirements to the object–level knowledge representation (as outlined in fig.1), we define the following representation scheme [Klein 91]:

- The object class descriptions will be represented by a sort[4] hierarchy SH;

- A set REL^{SH} of relations with SH sort assignments to their arguments (representing consistency conditions);

- A set CL+^{SH} and a set CL–^{SH} of of definite and of negative clauses[5], respectively, on sort and relational expressions, representing general logical connections.

Object Class Representations

We start with the specification of the object–class representation in a sort hierarchy SH:

Definition: sort signature

A sort signature Σ is a triple: $\Sigma = <S, \tilde{F}, A>$, with
- S = a set of sort symbols (concepts);
- F = an S–family of sets of feature symbols: $F_{s,s'}$; and
- A = an S–family of sets of atoms (constants): A_s

Out of these primitive building blocks more complex *sort expressions* may be formulated:

Definition: sort expressions

Given a sort signature $\Sigma = <S, F, A>$, a set SE of sort expressions may be defined from this signature as follows:
- every sort symbol is a sort expression: $S \subseteq SE$;
- se $\wedge$ se' will be in SE;
- se $\vee$ se' will be in SE;
- $\neg$se will be in SE;
- $\{a_1, a_2, ... a_n\}$ will be in SE;
- f:se will be in SE; and
- p=q and p≠q will be in SE

with se, se' being sort expressions, f a feature symbol, p and q being feature paths [Smolka 88], and every a_i a constant.

A further increase in expressiveness will be gained by the specification of a set SC of *sort constraints* allowing to relate different sort expressions. Two forms of sort constraints will be provided: *sort definitions* (':=') in analogy to KL–ONE's defined concepts [Brachman, Schmolze 85], and *sort restrictions* (':<'), comparable to *primitive concepts* in KL–ONE.

2. As will be explained in chapter 4, configuration problem solving will be described in terms of abductive reasoning, which implies some modifications of standard resolution and unification [Klein 91a].
3. This scheme can not fulfil all the demands listed in fig.1. For instance part–of relations or algebraic constraints can not be expressed. But the scheme will suffice to demonstrate the *idea* of hybrid representation followed–up here.
4. The notions sort and concept will be used synonymously.
5. The restriction to definite and negative (Horn) clauses will be motivated in the next chapter.

Finally, a *sort hierarchy* can be defined on these representational means as a representation of a taxonomic hierarchy:

Definition: sort hierarchy

A sort hierarchy SH is a pair SH = < Σ, SC>, with

- Σ being a sort signature; and
- SC being a set of sort constraints.

These representational means of object classes are basically a conjunction of feature logic constructs with term description capabilities [Pletat, Luck 89].

Relations

A set REL^{SH} of relations will be specified as part of the *definitional* knowledge. Each relation in REL^{SH} (or for short, SH–relation) will be provided with SH sort assignments of its arguments (in analogy to order–sorted logic [Walther 87]). These assignments will be interpreted as necessary pre–conditions for every object, which can be included in such a relation. Relational expressions (like $\exists$rel.c or $\forall$rel.c) will be excluded from concept definitions.

Definition: relations

Given a sort hierarchy SH, a set REL^{SH} of relations will be defined. Each SH–relation rel in REL^{SH} will be assigned a string s1,s2,..., sn of sort expressions (s1,s2,...,sn$\in$ SE):

$$rel_{s1, s2, \dots, sn}$$

specifying the sort assignments to each of its n arguments.

Semantics

Based on these syntax specifications, a declarative Tarski–style, set–theoretic semantics may be defined as usual. We start with the definition of an *interpretation*:

Definition: interpretation

Given a sort signature $\Sigma = $ <S, F, A>, a sort hierarchy SH , and a set REL^{SH} of SH–relations, an interpretation I is a pair I = <Δ^I, I·>, with Δ^I being a set (the *domain* of the interpretation), and I· being an *interpretation function* having the following properties:

- every sort expression se $\in$ SE will be assigned a subset Δ^I_{se} of the domain Δ^I:

$$I(se) = \Delta^I_{se}, \text{ with } \Delta^I_{se} \subseteq \Delta^I ;$$

- every feature $f_{s,se} \in$ F will be assigned a function $f^I_{s,s'}$, mapping elements of its domain interpretation I(s) to elements of its range interpretation I(s'):

$$I(f_{s,s'}) = f^I_{s,s'} : I(s) \rightarrow I(s');$$

- every attribute $a_s \in A_s$ will be assigned an element of the corresponding sort interpretation I(s):

$$I(a_s) = a^I_s, \text{ with } a^I_s \in I(s); \text{ and}$$

- every relation $r_{s1,s2,...,sn} \in REL^{SH}$ will be assigned a subset of the Cartesian product on the corresponding sort interpretations:

$$I(r_{s1,s2,...,sn}) \subseteq I(S_1) \times I(S_2) \times ... \times I(S_n) .$$

Of course we are normally not interested in *any* interpretation, but in those fulfilling the conditions specified by sort expressions and sort constraints [Nebel 90a; Pletat, Luck 89; Schmidt–Schauß, Smolka 88]. Any such interpretation will be called a *model* of SH.

A sort hierarchy SH will be called *inconsistent* if it contains a sort symbol, which in every model interpretation will be assigned the empty set as only possible interpretation. Inconsistent sort hierarchies will not be considered in the following.

Based on these semantical considerations, the *subsumption* relation between sort expressions can be defined (in the usual TDL manner):

Definition: subsumption

Given a sort hierarchy SH, a sort expression $se \in SE$ will be said to *subsume* (or SH–subsume) another sort expression $se' \in SE$, iff for any interpretation $I = <\Delta^I, I>$ being a model of SH holds:

$$I(se') \subseteq I(se)$$

This subsumption relation between se and se' will be written

$$se' \leq_{SH} se .$$

Though in configuration problems the object–level knowledge normally will be well–structured, which implies that superclass–subclass relations will be known "in advance", it can be useful to have this *semantically defined* notion of superclass–subclass relations.

This notion of subsumption also provides the *semantical foundation* to the consistency conditions of *relational expressions* and *clauses*: having for instance a relation rel *defined* in REL^{SH} with sort assignments s1,s2,...,sn to its n arguments:

$$rel_{s1,s2,...,sn} \in REL^{SH}$$

any relational term rel(o1,o2,..,on) will only be consistent, if each of its arguments o_i (i = 1,...,n) has a sort assignment s_i' (i = 1,...,n) fulfilling the *well–sortedness conditions* [Frisch 89][6]:

$$s_i' \leq_{SH} s_i \quad (\forall i = 1,...,n)$$

Thus the sort hierarchy SH will be used as a *sort theory*, which has to be fulfilled by every semantics. The resulting *hybrid entailment* will be written (as usual) $|=_{SH}$.

IV. The Constructive Problem Solving (CPS) Approach

Configuration problem solving is mainly a *synthetic* process: a solution will be generated, which allows to fulfil the goals formulated as well as some constraints defining consistency.

As a basis of our discussion we'll outline a formal approach to configuration problem solving (introduced in [Klein 90]), called *constructive problem solving* (CPS):

Definition: constructive problem solving

- The *definitional knowledge* characterizing a configuration domain will be represented by a sort hierarchy SH, a set REL^{SH} of relation specifications and sets CL+^{SH} and CL–^{SH} of definite and negative clauses, respectively, on sort and relational expressions.

- A *concrete configuration problem* will be represented by a set GOAL^{SH} of atomic goal expressions (interpreted as conjunction).

- *Solving* a configuration problem formulated in this way means to generate a solution SOL^{SH} being a set of assertions (a database of ground atomic expressions representing objects and relations between them). This set SOL^{SH} has to fulfil the following *formal conditions* in order to be a correct solution:

  - $$SOL^{SH} \cup CL+^{SH} |=_{SH} GOAL^{SH} \qquad ;;; \text{the goal has to be fulfilled}$$
  - $$\forall c \in CL–^{SH}: \qquad SOL^{SH} \cup CL+^{SH} |=_{SH} c \qquad ;;; \text{the constraints must be fulfilled}$$

---

6. This provides a semantical extension of the original, synactically defined well–sortedness of order–sorted logic [Walther 87; Cohn 87].

Up to now there is no comprehensive formalization of this basically *abductive*[7] approach. This is at least in part due to a missing general theory of abduction (on the predicate logic level) [O'Rorke 90+91; Levesque 89; Selman, Levesque 90].Of course, also some meta–criteria should be fulfilled by the abductive reasoning process. The generated solution database SOL^{SH} has to fulfil, for instance, a kind of minimality criterion with respect to the set of objects introduced and to relations specified between them.

The restriction of the clauses to definite and negative ones may significantly reduce complexity (without loosing too much in expressiveness [Kowalski 90]): the negative clauses allow to represent inconsistency explicitly, without affecting the "positive side" of the problem solving[8] (realized by the definite clauses). The set of definite clauses will be treated as a *complete decription* of the positive literals contained [Klein 90; Console et al. 90].

These and other formal issues of the CPS approach will be discussed elsewhere [Klein 91a].

The solution database SOL^{SH} will formally be defined as follows:

Definition: solution SOL^{SH}

Given a sort hierarchy SH and a set REL^{SH} of relation definitions, a solution database SOL^{SH} is a set of assertions (ground atomic expressions):

- object descriptions: $a{:}s$ – with a being an object and s being a sort expression: $s \in SE$; and

- relational expressions : $rel(o_1,...,o_n)$ – with $rel_{s1,...,sn} \in$ REL^{SH} being a relation, and $o_1{:}s_1'... o_n{:}s_n'$ being objects in SOL^{SH} fulfilling the well–sortedness conditions:
  $$\forall i = 1,...,n: s_i' \leq_{SH} s_i$$

The semantics may be extended in the usual way in order to capture the assertional terms, hybrid entailment, etc. [Nebel 90a].

One of the essential points with this kind of constructive problem solving is *database consistency*: having an object description
$$a{:}s_1$$
in the solution database SOL^{SH}, and an assertion
$$r(a,b)$$
with $r_{s,s'} \in$ REL^{SH} being a relation defined as part of the definitional knowledge, the object a has to have a sort assignment $s_1 \wedge s$ in order to have a *consistent* database SOL^{SH}:

$$\{a{:}s_1, r(a,b) ... \} \models a{:} s_1 \wedge s$$

Of course, $s_1 \wedge s$ has to be consistent, too.

Exactly this specification of objects and relations between them will be done by the abductive inferences in the constructive problem solving. This results in a kind of *taxonomic reasoning* by monotonicly restricting the sort expressions of the objects in order to keep the solution database consistent.

Of course, this is only a *very restricted form* of interaction between a background theory of definitional knowledge, and more general logical expressions in configuration problem solving.

---

7. For a discussion of abductive reasoning in configuration problem solving and the relation between deductive and abductive inferences see for instance [Coyne et al. 90; Poole 90; Klein 90] and references cited there.
8. At least as long as the solution generated will be consistent.

V. An Example

The following small example should demonstrate the knowledge representation and problem solving capabilities of the approach defined in the preceding chapters.

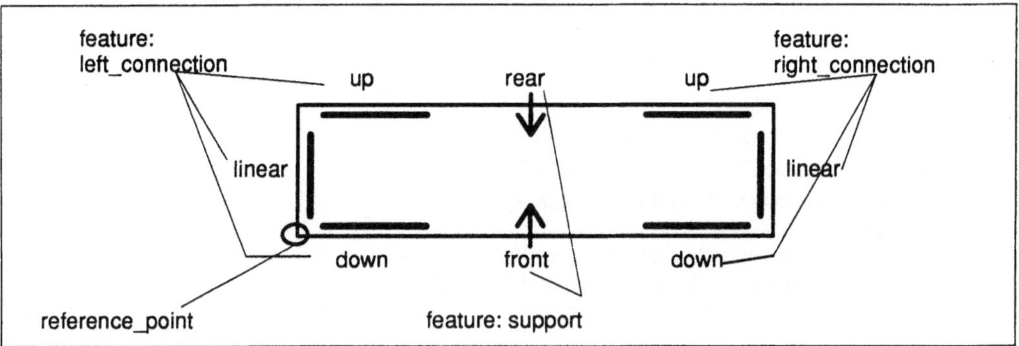

Fig. 3: A sketchy representation of the sort *module* with its three features *left_connection*, *right_connection* and *support*.

```
sort signature  Σ = <S, F, A>, with
              S = {module, connection_mode, support_mode, module_at, module_al,
                    module_m, module_n, module_l, module_k}
              A = {connection_mode = {up, down, linear},
                    support_mode = { front, rear} }

              F = {left_connection(module,connection_mode),
                    right_connection(module,connection_mode),
                    support(module,support_mode)}
```

sort constraints SC:

module_at := right_connection:linear ∧ left_connection:linear ∧ support:front

module_al := right_connection:linear ∧ left_connection:linear ∧ support:rear

module_m := right_connection:up ∧ left_connection:up ∧ support:front

module_n := right_connection:down ∧ left_connection:down ∧ support:rear

module_k := right_connection:linear ∧ left_connection:down ∧ support:rear

module_l := right_connection:down ∧ left_connection:linear ∧ support:rear

relations REL^{SH} = {right_neighbor(module,module),

right_up1(right_connection:linear,right_connection:down),

right_up2(right_connection:linear,left_connection:up),

linear(right_connection:linear,left_connection:linear),

inverse_linear(right_connection:linear,right_connection:linear),

right_down1(right_connection:linear,left_connection:down)

right_down2(right_connection:linear,right_connection:up), ... }

Fig. 4a: Sort signature and sort constraints composing the example sort hierarchy SH_{module}

We assume a configuration problem, in which certain kinds of building blocks (called *modules*) and certain qualitative geometric relations between them are given. The modules will be characterized intensionally (see fig. 3) by a set of features, reflecting their own properties and internal structures (which latter will not be considered here explicitly).

definite clauses:

        right_neighbor(X,Y) :– right_up1(X,Y).
        right_neighbor(X,Y) :– right_up2(X,Y).
        right_neighbor(X,Y) :– linear(X,Y).
        right_neighbor(X,Y) :– inverse_linear(X,Y).
        right_neighbor(X,Y) :– inverse_linear(Y,X).
        right_neighbor(X,Y) :– right_down1(X,Y).
        right_neighbor(X,Y) :– right_down2(X,Y). etc.

negative clauses

        right_neighbor(X,Y), right_neighbor(X,Z), Y≠Z → ⊥.
        right_neighbor(Y,X), right_neighbor(Z,X), Y≠Z → ⊥.

Fig. 4b: Some of the definite and negative clauses of the module example

In fig. 4b some of the clauses characterizing *logical constraints* between relational expressions (see also fig. 6) have been shown.

In fig. 4a we give the formal concept definitions in a sort hierarchy SH_{module} and a set REL^{SH} of defined relations. The two features *left_connection* and *right_connection* have as their range the attribute set *connection_mode* containing the three members *linear, up* and *down*. The feature *support* covers the attribute set *support_mode* with *rear* and *front* as elements. The reference point has been introduced as an additional feature in order to break left–right symmetry, resulting in increased representation demands.

In fig.5 the sort hierarchy is shown, which results from the sort constraints given in fig.4a. The three features *left_connection, right_connection,* and *support* each define (by the feature selections shown) a *complete partition* of the extension of the *module* root concept. The resulting sort lattice provides the formal basis for taxonomic reasoning as an essential part of configuration problem solving. Two sort expressions will be considered *disjoint,* if none of them subsumes the other one and there is no common subsort to them.

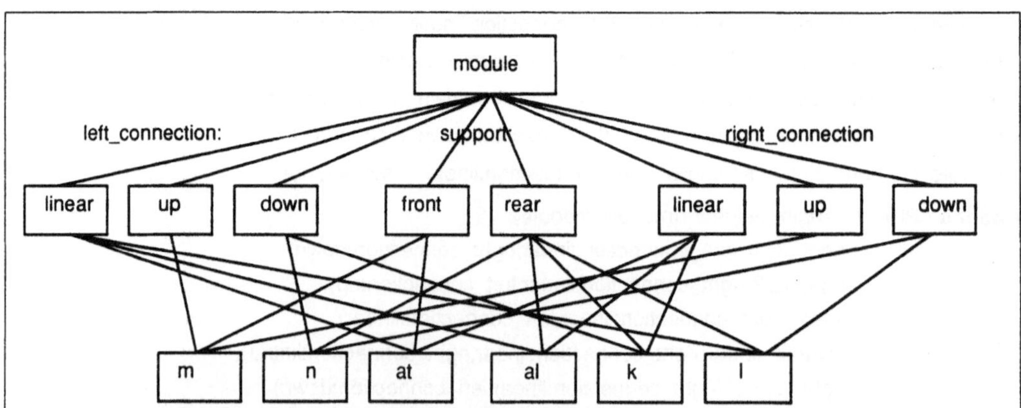

Fig. 5: The sort hierarchy as defined in fig. 3a comprises a lattice

In fig.7 an example problem solving process has been protocolled, demonstrating the role of taxonomic inferences:

- At first, three modules have been specified, together with their sort assignments.

- In the next step, adding a relational assertion causes new constraints on the sort assignments of the objects involved in order to keep the overall solution consistent.

- In the last step, due to the sort assignment of the module m1, the only way to specify the right_neighbor relation is to specify a right_up1 relation[9]. Again, in order to save overall solution consistency, new sort restrictions result from this role specification, causing m3, which initially had been defined as any module, to have a linear right_connection feature.

VI. Discussion

The development of well–formalized hybrid knowledge representation schemes, which allow the integration of different knowledge representation aspects in a well–formalized way, (for instance general and "background" knowledge) is a promising task [Frisch, Cohn 91].

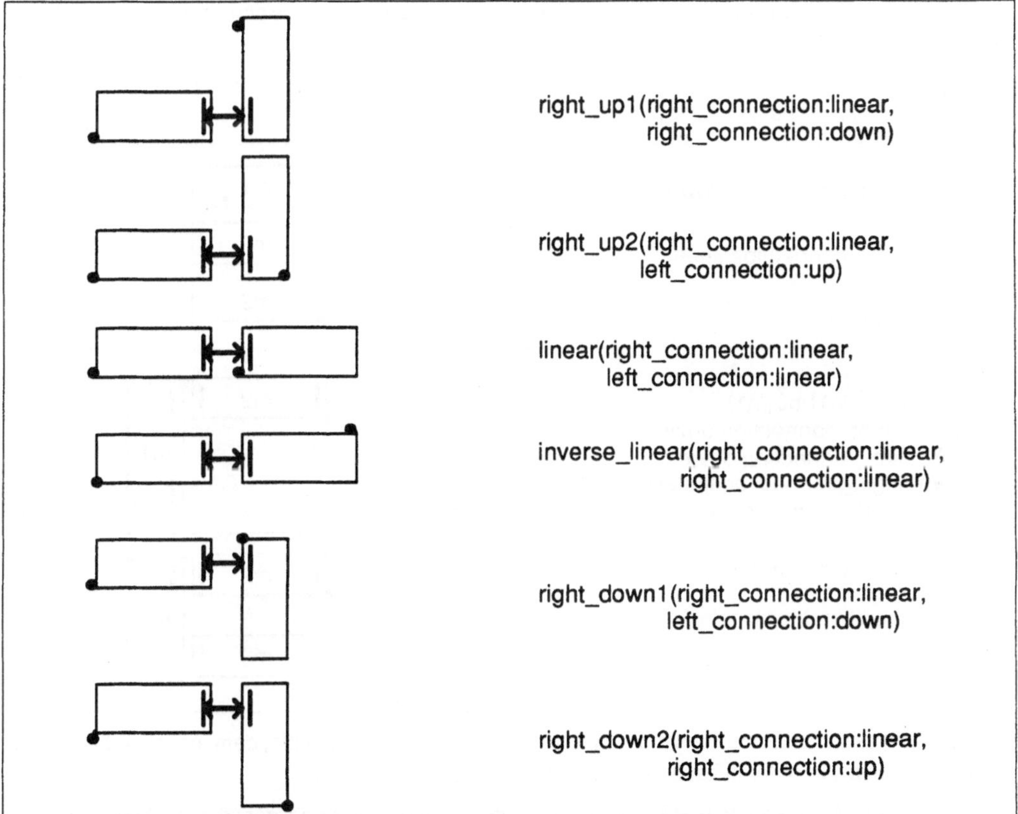

Fig. 6: Some of the qualitative geometric relations in the "module world", including the sort restrictions of their arguments

The approach to formal knowledge representation suggested here has been mainly based on a well–defined restriction in the expressiveness of the definitional knowledge: relations (roles) have been excluded from concept definitions. This seems to be adequate in (many) configuration problems: due to the well–structuredness of the object level knowledge, which allows for object definitions *per se*, without reference to other

9. using the completeness assumption w.r.t. the right_neighbor relation as basis of the abductive inference

objects. This well–structuredness also implies, that it is useful to define relations in conjunction with concept assignments to their arguments (providing a kind of consistency information). This enables the integration of this "background" definitional knowledge into more general logical expressions, (in order to represent the various logical connections and constraints being relevant here).

Of course, the knowledge representation scheme adopted here, can only be a partial one: many aspects of object–level knowledge can not be represented within this scheme. Neither relational expressions (like ∀rel.c or ∃rel.c), which have been excluded with purpose from concept definitions, nor part–of hierarchies, algebraic constraints etc. can be taken into account.

How could we get things as *expressive* as needed (see fig.1), and keep them *theoretically well–defined*? Here, as in many other cases of hybrid inference systems, the main problem seems to be the *control of inferences*: this may keep the *practical* complexity tractable. Take for instance subsumption inferences: knowing a:s, we may answer a question, whether a:s' holds, by searching for a subsumption relation between sorts s and s': s ≤ s'. But answering this question may be done by deducing a:s' directly (only for the special case of object a), too, which could be much less expensive[10]. In our approach, we have generally excluded relational expressions from concept descriptions (without any possibility of control). Having a suitable way to *control* the inference process, this may allow to take relations (roles) into account as concept defining terms in *some special cases*, without increasing complexity *in general*.

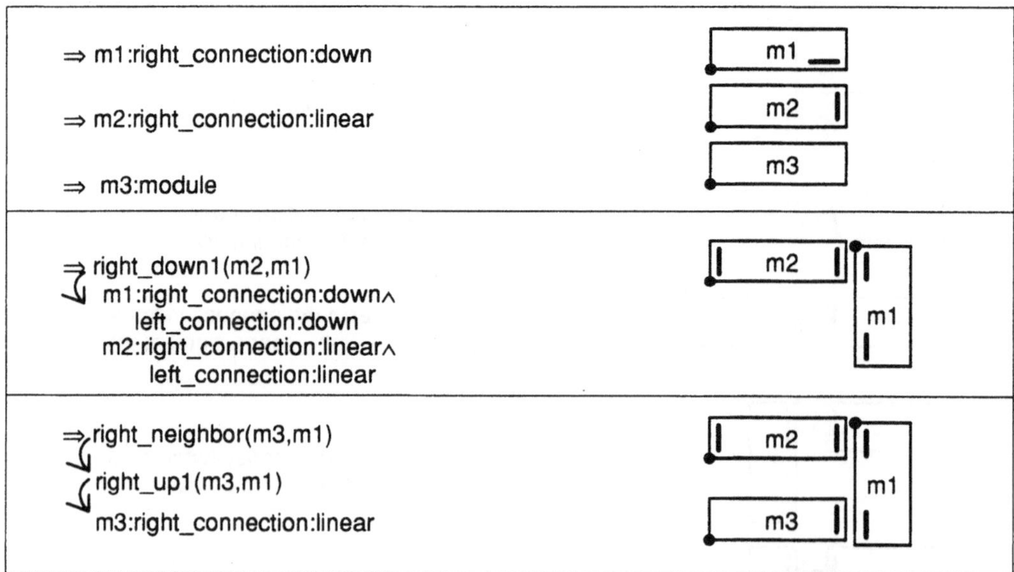

Fig. 7: A sketchy protocoll of the constructive problem solving process example, demonstrating the role of taxonomic inferences in order to keep the overall solution consistent

The constructive problem solving (CPS) approach has been used as a formal description of configuration problems. Due to the lack of a general theory of abduction (at least on the predicate–logic level), only some aspects of this approach could be demonstrated here. Other essential aspects (like variable treatment, minimum model semantics, inference rules) are under way [Klein 91a].

Acknowledgements

Many thanks to the collegues from the ESPRIT project KIT–BACK at TU Berlin, especially Jochen Quantz, for some very helpful discussions.

10. though the opposite case may be true as well

References

[Ait-Kaci, Podelski 91]
Ait-Kaci, H., and Podelski, A.: Is there a Meanng to LIFE?, 2nd International Workshop on Terminological Logic, Schloß Dagstuhl, May 1991, Statements of Interest, IBM Report, IWBS Stuttgart, 1991.

[BACK 87]
Luck, K.v. et al.: "The Anatomy of the BACK System", KIT-Report 41, TU Berlin, 1987

[Baader et al. 90]
Baader, F., Bürckert, H.-J., Hollunder, B., Nutt, W., and Siekmann, J.H.: Concept Logic, in: [Lloyd 90], pp. 177-201.

[Bürckert 90]
Bürckert, H.-J.: A Resolution Principle for Clauses with Constraints, in: M. Stickel (ed.): Proc. 10th Conf. on Autom Deduction, Kaiserslautern, 1990.

[Brachman, Schmolze 85]
R.J. Brachman, J.G. Schmolze: An Overview of the KL-ONE Knowledge Representation System, Cognitive Science 9 (85) 171-216.

[Cohn 87]
A.G. Cohn: "A More Expressive Formulation of Many-Sorted Logic", J. of Autom. Reasoning, 3/2 (87) 113

[Console et al. 90]
Console, L., et al.: A Completion Semantics for Object-Level Abduction, in: [O'Rorke 90], pp. 72-76.

[Coyne et al. 90]
Coyne, R., et al.: Knowledge-Based Design Systems, Addison Wesley, Reading (Mass.), 1990._

[Cunis et al. 88]
Cunis, R., et al.: PLAKON - Modellierung von technischen Domänen mit BHIBS, in: M. Hein et al. (eds.): Proc. Third Workshop "Planen und Konfigurieren", GMD-Bericht 388, St. Augustin, May 1988.

[Frisch 89]
Frisch, A.: A General Framework of Sorted Deduction, in: Brachman, R., Levesque, H., and Reiter, R. (eds.): Proc. of the First International Conference on Principles of Knowledge Representation, Toronto, May 1989, pp. 126-136, Morgan Kaufman Publ., 1989.

[Frisch, Cohn 91]
Frisch, A., and Cohn, A.: Thoughts and Afterthoughts on the 1988 Workshop on Hybrid Reasoning, AI Mag. (Special Issue), Jan. 1991, pp.77-87.

[Hollunder, Nutt 90]
Hollunder, B. and Nutt, W.: Subsumption Algorithms for Concept Languages, Report 90-04, DFKI.

[Klein 90]
Klein, R. : Problem solving as database construction, Proc. 4. Workshop "Planen und Konfigurieren", FAW Bericht, Ulm, April 1990.

[Klein 90a]
Klein, R.: Towards an Integration of Knowledge Based Systems with Computer-Aided Design, in: U. Geske, D. Koch (eds.): Contributions to AI, Akademie-Verlag, Berlin, 1990.

[Klein 91]
Klein, R.:An Approach to the Integration of Term Description Languages and Clauses, 2nd Intern. Workshop on Terminological Logics, Schloß Dagstuhl, May 1991, IBM Report, Stuttgart 1991.

[Klein 91a]
Klein, R.: Constructive Problem Solving, subm. to the 8th Deduction Workshop, Berlin, Oct. 1991.

[Klein 91b]
Klein, R.: Towards a Logic-Based Model Representation in Configuration Problems, ÖGAI91 Workshop on Model Based Reasoning, Wien, Sept. 91.

[Kowalski 90]
Kowalski, R.: Problems and Promisses of Computational Logic, in: [Lloyd 90], pp. 1-36

[Levesque 86]
Levesque, H.: Making Believers out of Computers, AI30/1(1986)81-108.

[Levesque 89]
Levesque, H.: A knowledge-level account of abduction, Proc. IJCAI-89, pp.1061-1066, Detroit, 1989

[Lloyd 90]

Lloyd, J.W.: Computational Logic, Proc. of the ESPRIT Basic Reasaerch Activities Symposium, Bruxels, Nov. 1990, Springer, Berlin, 1990.

[Nebel 90]

Nebel, B.: Terminological Reasoning is Inherently Intractable, AI Journal 43/2(1990)235–250.

[Nebel 90a]

Nebel, B.: Reasoning and Revision in Hybrid Representation Systems, Lecture Notes in AI 422, Springer, Berlin, 1990.

[O'Rorke 90]

O'Rorke, P.: Automated Abduction, Working Notes, 1990 AAAI Spring Symposium, Stanford–Univ., TR–90–32

[O'Rorke 91]

O'Rorke, P.: Review of AAAI–90 Spring Symposium on Automated Abduction, SIGART Bulletin 1/3(1991), pp.12–17.

[Owsnicki 88]

Owsnicki–Kleve, B.: Configuration as a consistency–maintenance task, in: W. Hoeppner (Hrsg.): Künstliche Intelligenz, Informatik–Fachberichte 181, Springer, Berlin, 1988.

[Patel–Schneider 89]

Patel–Schneider, P.: Undecidability of Subsumption in NIKL, AI 39(1989)263–272.

[Peltason 89]

Peltason, C.: "Wissensrepräsentation für Entwurfssysteme", Diss. TU Berlin, 1989.

[Pletat, Luck 89]

Pletat, C. und v. Luck, K.: Die Wissensrepresentationssprache SORT–LILOG, IWBS–Report 89, IBM Stuttgart, 1989

[Poole 90]

Poole, D.: Hypo–Deductive Reasoning for Abduction, Default Reasoning and Design, in: [O'Rorke 90], pp. 106–110.

[Quantz 90]

Quantz, J.: Modeling and Reasoning with Defined Roles in BACK, KIT–BACK Report 84, TU Berlin, 1990.

[Schild 88]

Schild, K.: Undecidability of Subsumption in U, KIT–Report 67, TU Berlin, Oct. 88

[Schild 89]

Schild, K.: Towards a Theory of Frames and Rules, KIT–Report 76, TU Berlin, Dec. 89

[Schmidt–Schauss, Smolka 88]

Schmidt–Schauss, M. and Smolka, G.: Attributive Concept Description with Unions and Complements,SEKI Report 88–21, Universitaet Kaiserslautern, Dec. 88

[Searls, Norton 90]

Searls, D.B. and Norton, L.M.: Logic–Based Configuration with a Semantic Network, Journal of Logic Progr. 8(1990)53–73.

[Selman, Levesque 90]

Selman, B., and Levesque, H.: Abductive and Default Reasoning: A Computational Core, Proc. AAAI–90 , pp.343–348.

[Smolka 88]

Smolka, G.: A Feature Logic with Subsorts, IBM Report 33, IWBS Stuttgart, May 1988.

[Stickel 85]

Stickel, M.: Automated Deduction by Theory Resolution, J. Autom. Reas, 1(85) 333

[Tank et al. 90]

Tank, W., et al.: AMOR – eine Wissensrepräsentationssprache für die technische Klärung von Aufträgen, in: H. Krallmann (Hrsg.): Innovative Anwendungen, Oldenburg–Verlag, München, 1990.

[Walther 87]

Walther, C.: A Many–Sorted Calculus with Resolution and Paramodulation, Morgan–Kaufman Publ., 1987.

6. EXPERTENSYSTEME

Improving Case Based Classification with Expert Knowledge

Frank Puppe, Klaus Goos
Karlsruhe University
Institute for Logic, Complexity and Deduction
P.O. Box 6980, W-7500 Karlsruhe, Germany

Abstract: While pure case based classification systems can take little advantage of heuristic expert knowledge, heuristic classification systems have much difficulty to adapt themselves with case knowledge. There are three integration strategies: Combine two independent problem solvers, learn rules from cases, or incorporate heuristic knowledge into the case based approach. Pursuing the last alternative, we present a case comparison language (CCL) designed for incremental refinement with knowledge from domain experts. Nevertheless CCL needs considerably less knowledge than is usually necessary for probabilistic rules in heuristic classification. The key features of CCL are combining static and dynamic weighting of symptoms, providing several schemes for computation of partial similarities between symptoms, and a categorical rule language with abstraction layers for inferring the domain terminology from the raw symptoms. Its simplicity, adaptability, and explainability, its strong dependence on domain terminology, its high potential for parallelism, and its incremental approach to knowledge acquisition seem to make it a candidate for a model of human classification problem solving in experience-rich domains. CCL is implemented as a component named CCC+ of the diagnostic expert system shell D3.

1. Introduction

Case based reasoning for knowledge based systems has received much attention during the last few years. The idea is to overcome the knowledge acquisition bottleneck by reasoning directly on known cases without attempting to abstract generic knowledge like correlations or rules from them.

While pure case based classification systems like those using the nearest neighbour method [Stanfill 86] can take little advantage of expert knowledge, pure heuristic [Clancey 85] or causal classification systems have much difficulty to adapt themselves, if case knowledge becomes available. There are three integration strategies: (1) Combine two independent problem solvers, (2) learn abstractions from cases or (3) incorporate expert knowledge in the case based approach. The first approach of combining two different problem solvers has been pursued by e.g. [Rissland 89] and [Koton 88]. In [Rissland 89], a rule based and a case based approach are used to find out discrepancies between them (e.g. a rule which did not fire, but whose conclusion has been stated in a very similar case or vice versa) yielding a focus on further reasoning. In [Koton 88], a case based approach is used for generating hypotheses which are then tested by a causal problem solver. The main effects of combination approaches are to enhance efficiency by exploiting the different compromises between accuracy and efficiency of the original problem solvers and/or the potential to choose the better solution from several high quality offers. However since the different kinds of knowledge cannot cross-fertilize (or disturb) each other the combination approaches yield a rather small profit at low risks.

The second integration strategy of abstracting knowledge from cases is currently the dominant approach. Comparisons of the different techniques (Bayesian approaches, neural nets, inductive learning algorithms like ID3) are given in e.g. [Mooney 89, Weiss 89]. It is also possible, to abstract knowledge from cases for generating a similarity measure [Althoff 90]. While this approach is promising in domains where formalized expert knowledge does not exist or is very difficult to get, it stands in competition rather than cooperation with available heuristic expert knowledge. In subsymbolic approaches, heuristic knowledge cannot be integrated into a trained neural net. In Bayesian or inductive approaches there is no straightforward way to combine generated rules or decision trees with those formalized by experts, because it is not easy to detect the better ones. Therefore this abstraction strategy also fails to cross-fertilize the two different knowledge sources.

The third integration strategy avoids abstracting knowledge from cases, but allows experts to incorporate their knowledge in the similarity measure for comparing cases. Since the cases and the expert knowledge are preserved in their original, rather different form, there is not a competitive but rather a symbiotic relation between them, since they depend on each other. In particular, new cases or additional similarity knowledge can be added without regard to the respective other part. The prerequisite is, that the weights of symptoms are not statically given, but dynamically inferred depending on the context and the expert knowledge. Dynamic computation of the similarity measure has been done e.g. in HYPO [Ashley 88]. However, the context dependence in HYPO results primarily from different viewpoints lying outside the cases to be compared. In case-based classification, the context consists only of the features of the two cases to be compared and the solution of the known case.

The incorporation of expert knowledge in a similarity measure requires that the similarity measure is both expressive and easy to understand for experts. For illustration of the discussion in the rest of this paper, Fig. 1 shows the basic situation in case-based classification.

	new-case	old-case-1	old-case-2	old-case-3
type of car	type A	type B	type A	type C
km driven	100 000	110 000	95 000	105 000
gas consumption l/100km	7	8	8	13
engine rotates uneven	yes	yes	no	yes
car does not start	usually	sometimes	always	usually
noises	pinking	pinking + slight detonations	nothing	unknown
solution	?	spark-plug defect	battery empty	C-Turbo defect

Fig. 1. Basic situation in case-based classification.

A new case is a vector of symptoms (type of car, km driven, etc.) with values (type A, 100 000, etc.) without a solution. An old case is a vector together with a solution. In case based classification, a solution to a new case is found simply by taking over the solution of a known case, if the similarity between both cases is great enough. Therefore it is much simpler than cased-based construction, where the solution must be modified (as e.g. in [Kolodner 87, Hammond 89]).

In a very simple world, where all symptoms are equally important and have just the boolean values "True" and "False", it would be sufficient for computing the similarity between two cases to divide the number of alike values of corresponding symptoms through the number of all symptoms. If symptoms are not of equal importance, it is necessary to introduce a weight. If this weight is not a constant but depends on the actual value of the symptom or on the diagnosis of the known case, it must be computed dynamically. If symptoms have more values than just True and False, it is necessary to compute a partial similarity (i.e. a number between 0 and 1) between them, which might also depend on the diagnosis of the known case. The total similarity between two cases is now computed by weighting partial similarities between corresponding symptoms.

The knowledge for the assignment of the weights and the computation of partial similarities should come from experts, since it is very sensible knowledge and experts usually can tell easily, whether differences between cases are important or not. Although this introduces a new knowledge acquisition problem, it has become much smaller compared to a rule based approach. With n diagnoses and m symptoms, each having on the average k different relevant values, and even without combinations of symptoms in a rule, $n * m * k$ symptom-value-to-diagnosis rules have to be taken into account. This is much more than the m symptom declarations (together with some modification depending on diagnoses) which would be necessary in the case based approach.

The bridge between heuristic and case-based knowledge are the diagnosis specific modifications of the weights in the case-based approach. If a specific weight of every symptom value for every diagnosis is required, the amount of heuristic knowledge would be equivalent in both approaches. While this requirement is necessary e.g. in PROTOS [Porter 90], which tries to automatically generate these weights, our approach emphasizes the symptom specific knowledge (static weight, dynamic weight depending on the actual symptom value, partial similarity) thus reducing the need for diagnostic modifications. However, they remain necessary for exclusion conditions such as, e.g., *if* "C-Turbo defect" *then* the "type of the car" must be "C".

As a general rule in expert systems, experts must be allowed to use their domain terminology, since it contains valuable knowledge. Therefore some inference facilities for deriving symptom-abstractions from the raw data together with a mechanism for managing different abstraction layers are necessary. As Clancey [85] pointed out, this "data abstraction" is much simpler than the "heuristic match" between symptom values and diagnoses. The relevant knowledge is readily available from the experts and also in the literature causing little knowledge acquisition problem.

We have designed a case comparison language (CCL) for describing this knowledge and implemented a case comparing component (CCC+, the successor of CCC [Hestermann 90]) integrated in the expert system shell D3 [Bamberger 91], the successor of MED2 [Puppe 87, 91] for heuristic classification. In chapter 2, we describe the underlying assumptions and the knowledge representation. The reasoning mechanism is given in chapter 3. Chapter 4 shows an example and a discussion follows in chapter 5. More details of the knowledge representation and the reasoning strategy are given in [Puppe 90, Chapter 12].

2. Knowledge Representation

The goal for our case comparing component is to find the most similar case to a new case from a database of old cases and to return its solution, if the similarity exceeds both a certain absolute and relative threshold. To avoid linguistic problems, the cases in the data base should be described in the same terminology as the new case. Therefore the terminology must be defined first, and the case descriptions are entered afterwards by a comfortable dialogue interface generated automatically from the terminology. Changes in the terminology require an adaptation of the case descriptions in the data base. The maintenance is supported by a renaming facility, by setting new terms to "unknown", and by removing obsolete terms in the data base. Despite these maintenance aids, large changes in the terminology may seriously affect the usefulness of a data base, so that domains with an unstable terminology are rather ill-suited for the approach.

In the following description of the knowledge representation, we focus on the three requirements for an expressive similarity measure identified in chapter 1:
(1)   computing partial similarities between symptom´s values,
(2)   dynamic weighting, and
(3)   dealing with symptom-abstractions.

ad 1: In some classification systems only boolean symptoms are allowed, such as in e.g. INTERNIST [Miller 82] (an example for a boolean symptom is "engine rotates uneven" in Fig. 1). This restriction excludes the local computation of partial similarities between symptom values like "car does not start = sometimes" and "car does not start = usually", since they would be syntactically represented as two different symptoms. Therefore more complex ranges[1] of symptoms than "True" and "False" should be allowed. This would also help in structuring the knowledge base and increasing its expressive power. More complex ranges include scalar types where the range is ordered along a kind of numerical dimension, and checklist types where the range consists of a list of items without internal structure. Scalar types may have a *numerical* range where the value is a number (see "km driven" and "gas consumption (quantitative)" in Fig. 1) or an ordinal *one-choice* range where the value is one item of an ordered list of items (see "car does not start" in Fig. 1, with the range of "never, sometimes, usually, always"). Checklist types may have an arbitrary *one-choice* range, where the value must be exactly one item of a list (see "type of car" in Fig. 1 with the range "type A, type B, type C") or a *multiple-choice* range, where the value may be none, one or several items of a list (see "noises" in Fig. 1 with the range "pinking, slight detonations, ..."). For computing partial similarities between two values A and B of a symptom, CCL provides three basic schemes:

---

[1]   In the following discussion of ranges, the value "unknown" is implicitly included as an additional alternative.

- **individual** (for all types): if $A = B$ then *1* else *0*.
- **functional** (for scalar types only): $f(A)/f(B)$ or $1 - |f(A) - f(B)| / K$, where the function f and the constant K are given in the *similarity specification* (see below) by an expert[2]. In the simplest case for a numerical range, f is the identity function. If a constant is used and the formula would produce a negative result, it is set to 0. In a frequent special case, f is a stepwise linear function defined by a list of points and K is the distance between the lowest and the highest y-coordinate of the points. A slightly modified version of this is used for ordinal one-choice ranges, where a number (corresponding to an y-coordinate) is assigned to each item of the range.
- **grouped** (for checklist types only): if $A = B$ then *1*, else if *A and B belong to the same group*, then *x* else *0*. The groups and their similarities x are given in the *similarity specification* by an expert. If the range is multiple-choice and A and B denote several items, each item resp. item group is treated separately and the singular results are averaged to one number.

The type "grouped" allows expressing a restricted logical "or". It simplifies the treatment of different terms for similar observations in the predefined domain terminology. In Fig. 1 the two values "pinking" and "slight detonations" for the symptom "noises" in the old-case-1 mean similar things and should therefore be grouped resulting in a high similarity compared to the value "pinking" in the new-case.

CCL provides two properties for each symptom expressing the knowledge about partial similarities: a *similarity type* (individual, functional or grouped with some specializations) and a *similarity specification*. While the similarity type determines the formula to be used for computing the partial similarity, the *similarity specification* provides concrete values to the parameters and functions used in the formula. For ease of knowledge editing, default values are predefined where possible. Examples appear in Chap. 4. The exact definitions are given in [Puppe 90, Chap. 12].

ad 2: Other properties allow the assignment of weights to symptoms and the dynamic modification of the weights. Each symptom is given a property *static weight* describing its relative importance. While for some symptoms like the "km driven" in Fig. 1 a static weight might be sufficient, other symptoms like "engine rotates uneven" should be treated differently: If two cases are similar with respect to the fact that their engines rotate normally (i.e. "engine rotates uneven = no"), this is of far less significance than in the abnormal case (i.e. "engine rotate uneven = yes"). The reason is that, especially in troubleshooting but also in other classification domains, most measurements are "normal" and only the few abnormalities are important for classification. Therefore CCL provides a property *abnormality* assessing the relative normality or abnormality of the possible values for a symptom. It requires that the range be partitioned. The abnormality assigns each partition a number, where 1 denotes the most abnormal partition(s) and the smallest number denotes the normal partition(s). These numbers are used to modify the *static weight* depending on the actual value of the symptom by multiplication, thus lowering the weight more or less drastically if the value lies in the normal partition. If there were no dynamic weighting to emphasize the abnormal values, the similarities between two arbitrary cases would directly increase with the number of measurements taken, since most possible measurements usually yield normal values, and thus the selectivity of the similarity measure would decrease.

The other dynamic modification of the weight is motivated by peculiarities of the solution. Consider the situation, that a particular diagnosis (e.g. "C-turbo defect") occurs only in cars of type C. While in general, the symptom "type of car" is unimportant and should have a low weight, if the diagnosis "C-turbo defect" is taken into account, the correct value of "type of car" is a necessary precondition for inferring the solution. However, such necessary preconditions cannot be represented in a pure case-based approach. There are two principal remedies: either representing the needed knowledge as solution-dependent modifications of the weights or representing it separately (e.g. as rules) for ruling out candidate solutions. In CCL both methods or combinations of them are allowed. Using solution-dependent weights has the advantage that CCL can represent not only exclusion conditions but also less drastic modifications of the weights, if for a particular solution some symptoms are relatively more or less important than usual. Using rules has the ad-

---

2   For scalar types $f(A)$ is assumed to be smaller than $f(B)$.

vantage of a more explicit representation. They are interpreted as dominating the comparison results, i.e. they may exclude solutions and the corresponding cases. The disadvantage is that only categorical rules may be used, since probabilistic rules cannot easily be integrated in the case comparison approach. Therefore the "less drastic solution-dependent modifications" can not be expressed by separate rules.

CCL allows one to associate with each diagnosis a *similarity modification* consisting of a list of symptoms with modifications of the *static weight* and/or of the *similarity specification*. If a new case is compared with an old case, the first thing to be checked is whether the solution of the old-case has a *similarity modification*. If true, the *static weight* and *similarity specification* of those symptoms given in the *similarity modification* are replaced by the solution specific knowledge. If the purpose of the modification is the exclusion of improper cases, negative weights must be allowed. They are interpreted in a slightly different way than usual: if the two values of corresponding symptoms have no similarity (i.e. 0), the negative solution specific weight is used; if they have complete similarity (i.e. 1), the original positive *static weight* is used; and if they have a partial similarity, an interpolation between both extremes is used (see Fig. 6). In addition, CCL allows one to specify categorical rules for excluding or establishing solutions directly from the symptom values (similar rules are also used for dealing with symptom-abstractions; see ad 3).

ad 3: Finally, CCL must provide mechanisms for inferring symptom-abstractions from the raw data for establishing the domain terminology. Otherwise, it can happen that superficially similar values of corresponding symptoms mean different things and vice versa. A typical example is the "gas consumption (quantitative)" from Fig. 1. Since many types of cars have a different normal gas consumption, the values from different types are incompatible and have to be normalized. The normalization is a simple arithmetic operation, yet in standard case-based-reasoning, there are no mechanisms for this. Therefore, CCL provides a simple rule language for deriving such abstractions including arithmetic operations. The CCL rule language differs from the rule language in heuristic classification, in that it allows only categorical reasoning (i.e. no probabilities).

However, the existence of symptom-abstractions (like "gas consumption (qualitative)"; see Fig. 2) introduces the problem, that one measurement might be counted more than once: as raw data and as part of various symptom-abstractions. Therefore, CCL allows the expert to fill out for each symptom and symptom-abstraction a property named *abstraction layer*. At the beginning of a case comparison, one particular *abstraction layer* must be chosen and all symptoms and symptom-abstractions not belonging to this abstraction layer will be ignored. By choosing different abstraction layers for the same case comparison, the actual benefits of inferring the domain terminology can be easily tested. The *abstraction layer* may also be used for defining different views of the cases, e.g. focusing on electrical symptoms and disregarding all other symptoms.

3. Reasoning Strategy

We assume for the following description of the reasoning strategy, that the symptoms with values, the symptom-abstractions and the solution of the known cases are stored in a conventional data base. The basic algorithm consists of the following steps:

Input: Symptoms and values of a new case and an *abstraction layer*.
Output: Solution of a "sufficient" similar known case (see step 6) or "unknown".

1. Derive the symptom-abstractions in the new case.
2. Ignore all symptoms and symptom-abstractions not having the given *abstraction layer*.
3. Preselect candidate cases from the database of known cases in three steps. First, determine the key symptoms in the new case having the highest weights. Second, compute intervals from the values of the key symptoms based on a look ahead of the resulting partial similarities. Third, choose the best n known cases with the most symptom values inside those intervals, where n can be adapted to various compromises between accuracy and efficiency and load them from the database into main-memory. With parallel hardware, the necessity of making compromises could be minimized (see Chap. 5).

4. Check the rules for excluding solutions and eliminate the candidate cases with excluded solutions.

5. For all remaining candidate cases do:

5.1 Change temporarily the *static weights* and the *similarity specifications* of all symptoms having a *solution modification* from the solution of the current candidate case.

5.2 Compute the actual weights (maximal possible points) of all symptoms by taking into account the *abnormality*. Depending on the more abnormal value from the new case and the current candidate case, the *solution modified static weight* from step 5.1 is adapted by multiplication with the relevant factor from the *abnormality*.

5.3 Compute the partial similarities between all pairs of corresponding symptom values. Depending on the *similarity type* and the *similarity specification*, the appropriate formula is used to compute a number between 0 and 1.

5.4 Multiply for all corresponding symptoms the actual weight with the partial similarity to compute their actual points.

5.5 Compute the global similarity between the two cases by dividing the sum of all actual points by the sum of all maximal possible points.

6. Rank the candidate cases according to their global similarities. If both the absolute similarity and the difference between the best candidate case and its strongest competitor having a different solution is high enough, report the solution of the best candidate case as solution to the new case. Otherwise report "unknown" and give the user the list of competitors for his or her own interpretation.

It is also possible to assess a degree of confidence for the whole procedure. If at the end, two cases are both absolutely and relatively very similar, but the similarity is based on only a few or rather unimportant symptoms in common, while other symptoms have been incomparable because their values were unknown in one of the cases, this can be detected by the absolute value of the sum of actual weights (computed in step 5.5). The higher this value both in absolute terms and in relation to the sum of the weights of all unknown symptoms in both cases, the more reliable is the result.

4. Example

To illustrate the knowledge representation and reasoning strategy, we give an example relevant for comparing the cases in Fig.1. The complete knowledge base necessary for the example is shown in Fig. 2a and 2b.

The example is implemented in our shell CCC+. Another test knowledge base exists for the domain of finding similar workpieces from a data base for a new workpiece to be produced [Hestermann 90]. While these small knowledge bases show promising results, we currently lack a large scale application.

<table>
<tr><td>

Additional Knowledge is necessary for deriving the symptom-abstraction "gas consumption (qualitative)" from the "gas consumption (quantitative)" and the "type of car" being specified with a hidden symptom-abstraction "normal gas consumption (quantitative)", 4 rules, and an interval scheme:

If type of car = A, <u>then</u> normal gas consumption (quantitative) <u>is</u> 6.

If type of car = B, <u>then</u> normal gas consumption (quantitative) <u>is</u> 7.

If type of car = C, <u>then</u> normal gas consumption (quantitative) <u>is</u> 12.

If gas consumption (quantitative) = known and normal gas consumption (quantitative) = known,

<u>then</u> gas consumption (qualitative) points <u>is</u> gas consumption (quantitative) - normal gas consumption (quantitative).

The gas consumption (qualitative) points are transformed by an interval scheme (0 1 3) in one of the four categories "normal" (points < 0), "slightly too high" ($0 \leq$ points < 1), "too high" ($1 \leq$ points < 3) and "much too high" (points ≥ 3).

</td></tr>
<tr><td>

Additional Knowledge is necessary to adjust the static weight of the type of car, if the diagnosis C-Turbo defect is taken into account. Since other types than C must be excluded, the static weight is given a negative value:

C-Turbo defect.solution modifications (Type of car :*static weight* -100).

</td></tr>
</table>

Fig. 2b.[3] Knowledge base for similarity measure for cases in Fig. 1. (part 2).

---

3 For layout reasons, Fig 2b is shown before Fig. 2a, but should be read in the reverse order.

Symptoms and Values / Properties	Range Type	Similarity Type	Static Weight	Abnorm-ality	Similarity Specification	Abstract. Layer
Type of Car	one-choice	individual	1			
= Type A						
= Type B						
= Type C						
Gas Consumption (quantitative)	numerical	functional	2			1
Gas Consumption (qualitative)	one-choice	functional	5			2
= Normal				0.2	0	
= Slightly too high				0.4	2	
= Too high					8	
= Much too high					10	
Km driven	numerical	functional	1		(K = 100000)	
Engine rotates uneven	yes/no	individual	5			
= Yes						
= No				0.2		
Car does not start	one-choice	functional	10			
= Never				0.1	0	
= Sometimes				0.4	4	
= Usually				0.6	8	
= Always					20	
Noises	multiple-choice	grouped	5		(((1 2) 0.95))	
= Pinking						
= Slight detonations						
= Hammering						
= None				0.1		

(Window title: Properties for Case-Comparison)

Fig. 2a. Knowledge base for similarity measure for cases in Fig. 1. (part 1). Each symptom must have a range type, a similarity type and a static weight. The other properties are optional. The default for abnormalities is 1. The abnormality values will be multiplied with the static weight. The kind of similarity specification depends on the type properties. For the one-choice symptoms, the symptom values are mapped onto the specified numbers. For the numerical functional symptoms, the function f is the identity function by default. For the multiple-choice grouped symptoms, the values are mapped onto groups: in this example the first and the second value are grouped with a similarity of 0.95 (95%). For individual symptoms, no similarity specification is allowed. The default abstraction layer is "all", being equivalent in this example to the abstraction layer (1 2).

The final results of the comparison of the new case with the three old cases from Fig. 1 is given in Fig. 3. The abstraction layer is set to "2". The detailed comparison results of each compared case are shown in Fig. 4, 5 and 6.

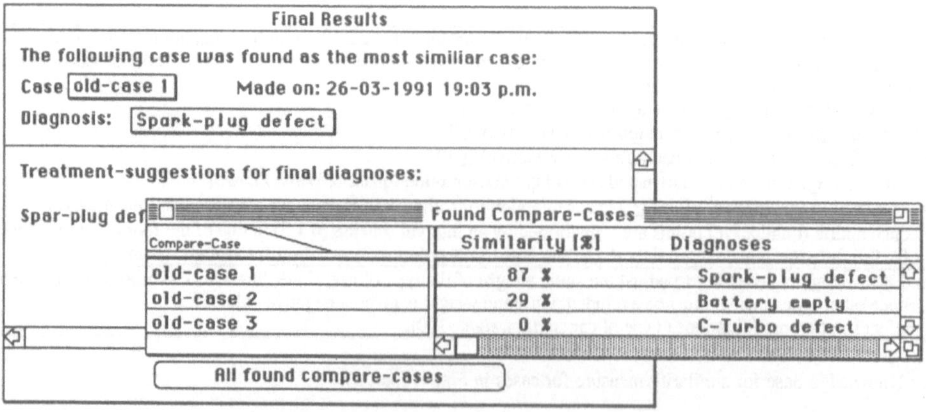

Final Results

The following case was found as the most similiar case:

Case [old-case 1]   Made on: 26-03-1991 19:03 p.m.

Diagnosis: [Spark-plug defect]

Treatment-suggestions for final diagnoses:

Spar-plug def

Found Compare-Cases

Compare-Case	Similarity [%]	Diagnoses
old-case 1	87 %	Spark-plug defect
old-case 2	29 %	Battery empty
old-case 3	0 %	C-Turbo defect

All found compare-cases

Fig. 3. Results found from CCC+ when comparing the new case with the three old cases from Fig.1. Explanations of the computed similarities are shown in Fig. 4, 5 and 6.

Results of the comparison between "new-case" and "old-case 1"	Actual-value	Compare-value	Max points	Similarity [%]	Actual points
Case	new-case	old-case 1	20.00	87 %	17.45
General			20.00	87 %	17.45
Type of Car	Type A	Type B	1.00	0 %	0.00
Km driven	100000.0	110000.0	1.00	90 %	0.90
Gas Consumption (quantitative)	7.0	8.0	–	–	–
Engine rotates uneven	Yes	Yes	5.00	100 %	5.00
Car does not start	Usually	Sometimes	6.00	80 %	4.80
Noises	Pinking	Pinking	5.00	95 %	4.75
		Slight detonations			
Gas Consumption (qualitative)	Slightly too high	Slightly too high	2.00	100 %	2.00

The overall similarity between both cases is 87 %.

The diagnosis of the compare-case is: Spark-plug defect

Fig. 4. Case comparison between the new-case and the old-case-1 resulting in an overall similarity of 87 %.

Results of the comparison between "new-case" and "old-case 2"	Actual-value	Compare-value	Max points	Similarity [%]	Actual points
Case	new-case	old-case 2	27.00	29 %	7.95
General			27.00	29 %	7.95
Type of Car	Type A	Type A	1.00	100 %	1.00
Km driven	100000.0	95000.0	1.00	95 %	0.95
Gas Consumption (quantitative)	7.0	8.0	–	–	–
Engine rotates uneven	Yes	No	5.00	0 %	0.00
Car does not start	Usually	Always	10.00	40 %	4.00
Noises	Pinking	None	5.00	0 %	0.00
Gas Consumption (qualitative)	Slightly too high	Too high	5.00	40 %	2.00

The overall similarity between both cases is 29 %.

The diagnosis of the compare-case is: Battery empty

Fig. 5. Case comparison between the new-case and the old-case-2 resulting in an overall similarity of 29 %.

Results of the comparison between "new-case" and "old-case 3"	Actual-value	Compare-value	Max points	Similarity [%]	Actual points
Case	new-case	old-case 3	15.00	0 %	-86.05
General			-86.00	0 %	-86.05
Type of Car	Type A	Type C	(1 -100)	0 %	-100.00
Km driven	100000.0	105000.0	1.00	95 %	0.95
Gas Consumption (quantitative)	7.0	13.0	–	–	–
Engine rotates uneven	Yes	Yes	5.00	100 %	5.00
Car does not start	Usually	Usually	6.00	100 %	6.00
Noises	Pinking	Unknown	–	–	–
Gas Consumption (qualitative)	Slightly too high	Slightly too high	2.00	100 %	2.00

The overall similarity between both cases is 0 %.

The diagnosis of the compare-case is: C-Turbo defect

Fig. 6. Case comparison between the new-case and the old-case-3 resulting in an overall similarity of 0 %. Old-case-3 has the solution "C-Turbo defect" modifying the weight of "type of car" to -100 in the case of no similarity. If there would be 100% similarity, the old static weight of 1 would be used as max points. The purpose of using a negative weight is to express an exclusion condition not interfering with the normal computation of similarities. If the sum of the actual points is less than 0, then the result is set to 0 %.

The result is, that the new case is both absolutely and relatively very similar to the old-case-1, so that its solution "spark-plug defect" is inferred.

5. Discussion

Building a case based classification system with CCL, experts can contribute their knowledge in several ways without impairing the automatic knowledge acquisition inherent in case-based-reasoning: they can define their domain specific terminology, provide a basic similarity measure, enter text book cases, increase the selectivity of the similarity measure depending on diagnoses, and add categorical rules representing well defined knowledge about diagnoses. These mechanisms allow one to express much knowledge represented by the probabilistic rules in heuristic classification systems in a rather natural manner.

Usually, the relation between a symptom value and a diagnosis is expressed by two rules: 1) Evoking strength: *If* <symptom value> *then* <diagnosis> *with evidence* <x>. 2) Frequency: *If* <diagnosis> *then* <symptom value> *with degree* <y > (see INTERNIST [Miller 82]). The frequency is approximated in heuristic classification by a doubly negated rule: *if not* <symptom value> *then not* <diagnosis> *with evidence* <y'>. The two degrees x and y (resp. y') are independent; for example, there may be symptom values which occur in many diagnoses thus having a low evoking strength but are mandatory for a particular diagnosis thus having a high frequency (a concrete example from the medical domain is the relation between high fever and measles). While the knowledge about the evoking strength is captured in the cases of case based classification, high frequencies are often understated, if the concerned symptom values are not unusual thus having a low weight. CCL allows compensating such understatements by solution-dependent modifications of the symptom´s weights.

For expressing the knowledge about combinations of symptoms in rules, CCL provides two mechanisms: 1) grouping of symptom values to express a restricted logical "or" and 2) defining new terms called symptom-abstractions with categorical rules. The latter is rather common in experience-rich domains such as medicine, where important combinations of symptoms are often given a name of their own.

In summary, CCL has a number of attractive features:

- *Inherent parallelism*: The efficiency of case based classification can be drastically increased by parallel hardware, since both the comparison of the new case to the known cases from the data base and the comparison of corresponding symptoms inside a pair of cases can be executed concurrently. The resulting efficiency gain would diminish the problem of preselection (step 3 in the algorithm in chapter 3) to a large extent.

- *Hypothesis for human learning*: Case based classification may be a good model for some aspects of human learning: Both start with a basic domain terminology, a simple similarity measure and text book cases. Refinement takes place in all three levels: The initial domain terminology becomes enriched by more and more symptom-abstractions and their definitions. The integrity is maintained simply by adapting the abstraction layers. The initial simple similarity measure is complemented by adding categorical rules and improved by adapting the static weights and introducing dynamic weighting with abnormalities and peculiarities from solutions. It should be noted, that the need to deal with arithmetic functions for computing partial similarities can be avoided by qualitative abstractions of numerical values (e.g. a numerical value for "gas consumption (quantitative)" can be abstracted to a symptom-abstraction with the values "normal", "slightly too high", "too high", "much too high"). The initially learned text book cases which provide a starting point for case-based classification are incrementally enlarged by more and more cases representing the actual variations of diagnoses.

- *Feasible and incremental knowledge acquisition*: The definition of the domain terminology is necessary in any classification problem solving method and seems to be no problem for experts. The definition of the knowledge for the similarity measure is still difficult, but much simpler than stating rule probabilities, since the number of heuristic assessments is proportional only to the number of symptoms and not to the number of symptom-diagnosis-rules. In addition, the problem solving capacity improves automatically with every new case, if the correct solution to the case is known. An incremental quality improvement is also possible by enriching the similarity measure in a controlled manner: the knowledge added for dynamic weighting and dynamic computation of partial similarities with solution modifications as well as for inferring new symptom-abstractions has rather local effects (as opposed to e.g. changing the static weights).

- *Explanation facility*: Case-based classification can justify the overall similarity of two cases by tracing it back to similarities of individual symptoms and their relative importance. It also has similar exploratory power to rule-based classification, since "pseudo-rules" can easily be inferred from a selected similar case; i.e. just look at the symptom values contributing most to the overall similarity and state them as rules. In our example from Fig. 1 - 6, the justification for the solution "spark plug defect" could be stated as because 1) "engine rotates uneven = yes", 2) "Noises = pinking" and to a lesser degree 3) "Car does not start = usually". Similar, the justification of not choosing the solution "C-Turbo defect" can be stated simply by "The type of car is not C!", relying strongly on the additional expert knowledge. If several similar old cases to a new case with the same solutions were found, the rules could be stated with a higher confidence. There is an interesting coincidence, that precise rule probabilities cannot be deduced in this way and experts usually refuse to give them even if they are urged in rule based approaches (however the expert system could easily compute the exact statistical correlation based on its data base if requested).

Planned future work includes (1) examining methods to automatically infer the knowledge for dynamic weighting from statistical, heuristic or causal knowledge, (2) selecting or abstracting model cases to reduce the total number of cases to be searched in the database, (3) fully integrating the case based with the other well studied problem solving methods for classification on all levels, and most importantly (4) testing the method with large knowledge bases in the laboratory and in routine use. It should be noted, that the conceptual limits of heuristic classification extend to those of our case-based classification approach. In particular the problem of multiple interacting diagnoses [Patil 87] cannot be resolved in general without a causal model of the domain, since too many combinations are possible and thus probably adequate comparison cases to a new case will be missing.

6. References

Althoff, K.-D., de la Ossa, A., Maurer, F., Stadler, M. and Weß, S.: *Case based Reasoning for Real World Applications*, Internal Report, Kaiserslautern University, 1990.

Ashley, K. and Rissland, E.: *Waiting on Weighting: A Symbolic Least Commitment Approach*, AAAI-88, 239-244, 1988.

Bamberger, S., Gappa, U., Goos, K., Meinl, A., Poeck, K. and Puppe, F.: *The Diagnostic Expert System Shell D3* (in German), Handbook, Version 1.0, Karlsruhe University, 1991.

Clancey, W.: *Heuristic Classification*, AI-Journal 27, 289-350, 1985.

Hammond, K.: *Case-Based-Planning: Viewing Planning as a Memory Task*, Academic Press, 1989.

Hestermann, C.: *CCC: Design and Implementation of an Expert System Component for Case Comparison and its Use for Similarity Searching of Prismatic Workpieces* (in German), Diploma Thesis, Karlsruhe University, 1990.

Kolodner, J.: *Capitalizing on Failure through Case-Based-Inference*, in: Proc. of the Conference on the Cognitive Science Society, 1987.

Koton, P.: *Using Experience in Learning and Problem Solving*, PhD-Thesis, Department of Electrical Engineering and Computer Science, MIT, 1988.

Mooney, R., Shavlik, J., Towell, G., and Gove, A.: *An Experimental Comparison of Symbolic and Connectionist Learning Algorithms*, ICJAI-89, 775-780, 1989.

Miller, R., Pople, H., and Myers, J.: *INTERNIST1, an Experimental Computer-Based Diagnostic Consultant for General Internal Medicine*, New England Journal of Medicine 307, 468-476, 1982.

Patil, R.: *A Case Study on Evolution of System Building Expertise: Medical Diagnosis*, in Grimson, E. and Patil, R. (eds.): AI in the 1980s and Beyond, MIT Press, 75-108, 1987.

Porter, B., Bareiss, R., and Holte, R.: *Concept Learning and Heuristic Classification in Weak-Theory Domains*, AI-Journal 45, 229-263, 1990.

Puppe, F.: *Requirements of a Classification Shell and Their Realization in MED2*, Applied Artificial Intelligence 1, 163-171, 1987.

Puppe, F.: *Problem Solving Methods in Expert Systems* (in German, translation to English in preparation), Springer, 1990.

Puppe, F., Legleitner, T., and Huber, K.: *DAX / MED2 - A Diagnostic Expert System for Quality Assurance of an Automatic Transmission Control Unit*, to appear in Zarri, G. (ed.): Operational Expert Systems in Europe, Pergamon Press, 1991.

Rissland, E. and Skalak, D.: *Combining Case-Based and Rule-Based Reasoning: A Heuristic Approach*, IJCAI-89, 524-530, 1989.

Stanfill, G. and Waltz, D.: *Toward Memory-Based Reasoning*, CACM 29, 1213-1228, 1986.

Weiss, S. and Kapoulas, I.: *An Empirical Comparison of Pattern Recognition, Neural Nets and Machine Learning Classification Methods*, IJCAI-89, 781-787, 1989.

Reflection and competent problem solving

Angi Voß$^\diamond$, Werner Karbach$^\diamond$, Uwe Drouven$^\diamond$
Brigitte Bartsch-Spoerl†, Bert Bredeweg‡
$^\diamond$German National Research Center for Computer Science (GMD)
P.O. Box 1240, D-5205 Sankt Augustin
†BSR Consulting
Wirtstrasse 38, D-8000 Muenchen 90
‡University of Amsterdam
Roeterstraat 15, NL-1018 WB Amsterdam

e-mail: avoss@gmdzi.gmd.de; karbach@gmdzi.gmd.de

Abstract

Most of today's knowledge based systems are far from being competent. They do not
degrade gracefully, they provide no basis for adequate explanations, tutoring or really cooperative problem solving. We present an approach that aims at improving the competence of
given problem solvers. For that purpose, we view competence assessment and improvement as
a reflective activity which is essentially situated at the knowledge level. Our approach suggests
a terminology and basic inference steps to describe competence assessment and improvement.[1]

1 The pieces of the mosaic

Competent problem solvers need not be perfect. They need not know every detail about their
domain and they may even expose certain weaknesses [Voß, Karbach, Drouven, Lorek 90]. But
a competent system knows whether it understands a problem at all and solves it as well and
as cheaply as possible. Being aware of insufficiencies like missing, incomplete, or contradictory
knowledge, it degrades gracefully.

A generic approach Most of today's expert systems do not behave very competently. So, to
improve the competence of a given, arbitrarily (in)competent system, to be called the object system,
a generic and conservative approach is needed. The gradual enhancement of competence should
leave the system as intact as possible, so as to minimize re-programming and re-testing. Thus, we
aim at a clear separation between the object system and the competence improving add-ons. In
other terms, we want to achieve competent behaviour by adding competence improving behaviour.

A reflective approach Competence improvement requires stepping back and viewing the object
system from the outside in order to detect its defects. Hence, assessment is a prerequisite activity.
Both, competence assessment and improvement may be regarded as reflective behaviours, the
inspection and modification of the object system by itself.

---

[1]The research reported here was carried out in the course of the REFLECT project. This project is partially
funded by the Esprit Basic Research Programme of the Commission of the European Communities as project number
3178. The partners in this project are the University of Amsterdam (NL), the German National Research Institute
for Computer-Science GMD (D), the Netherlands Energy Research Foundation ECN (NL), and BSR Consulting(D).

We are elaborating this view in the ESPRIT basic research action REFLECT [Bartsch-Spoerl, Reinders 90]. Our central idea is to place the add-ons into a separate metasystem, or more precisely, into a reflective component. This is a metasystem that does not directly operate on the object system, but on a model thereof, constituting the self-representation of the system [Maes 88]. Model and object system must be causally connected so that modifications in one of them are reflected in the other. Via the model, the reflective component may have an abstract view on the object system, focusing on important aspects and leaving out the irrelevant ones. Reflective component, object system, self-representation, and the causal connections together constitute a reflective system.

To reply to a recurring question – of course we could directly build the competence improvement into the object system, by the way getting rid of the self-representation and the causal connections. But this would work only for a particular object system, while we aim at a generic and modular approach that can easily be applied or adapted to other systems.

The model of the object system should at least distinguish the input or problem statement, the working memory and the output, answer or solution. In addition, there is the program which in turn can be differentiated into code and interpreter. In [Bartsch-Spoerl, Reinders 90] we have used this scheme to classify different kinds of reflective behaviours.

Classifying competence improvement as reflective behaviours In our classification, we distinguish reflective behaviours by the components being accessed, and by the type and time of access. Competence improvement falls into several categories, all of which require write access to the object system: The competence of a problem solver may be improved statically, i.e. independently of a particular problem, which is a kind of transformation task. Dynamic competence improvement modifies the object system so as to cope with a particular input problem. Here we can further distinguish a configuration task which is performed prior to starting the object system, from a repair task which happens during the object system's execution, and even from post mortem optimization. Competence assessment, in contrast, is a purely diagnostic task which requires no write access to the object system. Like improvement, assessment may be (in)dependent (on) of a particular problem, and it may take place before, during, or after the execution of the object system.

A knowledge level approach Competence improvement may be concerned with conceptual aspects of the system as well as with implementational ones (where the latter already touch the boundary to optimizations). From work in automatic theorem proving it is well known that the crucial ideas of a program often cannot be recovered from the code, which gave rise to the verify-while-develop paradigm in software engineering [Beierle, Olthoff, Voß 86]. This is why, in the RE-FLECT project, we concentrate on conceptual aspects rather than on implementational ones. To speak with Newell, we study competence improvement at the knowledge level, not at the symbol level [Newell 82].

Applications Our work in REFLECT is guided by three very different object systems, a qualitative reasoner GARP [Bredeweg, Reinders, Wielinga 90], a cover-and-differentiate diagnosis system [Karssen 90] and an assignment system that deals with a special type of synthesis problems [Voß et al. 90]). For each of these systems we have started to develop reflective modules to cope with special types of incompetence. Towards the end of the project, they will be joined into integrated demonstrator systems that cover a large spectrum of (in)competence in a hopefully generic way.

Contents In this paper, we will present our approach to dynamically improve the competence of the assignment application in the REFLECT project. We develop a conceptual description of a reflective system whose metacomponent assesses the competence of the object problem solver on the knowledge level and tries to improve it dynamically. In the final section we will discuss the generality of our approach and address the questions we are currently tackling.

2 The assignment application

The synthetic application in REFLECT is called OFFICE-PLAN [Karbach, Linster, Voß 89] [Voß et al. 90]. Given a description of employees and rooms, and a set of requirements, the system generates a constraint network with employees as variables and rooms as values, which it then tries to satisfy by constraint propagation. OFFICE-PLAN is divided into an application-specific part and into a generic one. The latter represents a shell for arbitrary assignment problems and we currently apply it to school time table construction.
OFFICE-PLAN does not behave very competently. It takes too much time to solve complex problems and it finds no solution for overspecified ones. In case of missing knowledge, it always assumes the best case, and it does not detect inconsistent nor redundant requirements. Thus, we will try to detect, analyze and cope with overcomplex and overspecified problems, with missing knowledge, and with inconsistent and redundant requirements.

3 A knowledge level framework for reflection

The KADS framework To describe problem solvers at the knowledge level, we use the four layer scheme for conceptual models proposed by the KADS knowledge acquisition methodology [Wielinga, Breuker 86] [Breuker, Wielinga 89]. The bottom layer contains all domain-specific information in terms of concepts and relations, the inference layer describes the basic inference steps in terms of knowledge sources that operate on so-called metaclasses. The latter describe the roles domain concepts may play during the problem solving process, e.g. observations, causes or hypotheses. The flow of control between knowledge sources is described on the task layer in terms of tasks and goals. On the highest layer, strategies may be formulated to adjust the flow of control dynamically. This layer is often obsolete. We will use the term "control layer" to denote any of the upper two layers.

The self-representation The KADS four layer scheme provides an appropriate level of abstraction to model the object system in the reflective component. However, by addressing only static aspects, the original scheme covers only the program component. In addition we classify both the metaclasses and the domain layer into input, output and working memory. To describe the state of control, we introduce an agenda of pending tasks on the task layer as part of the working memory. Although we recommend the object system to be modeled in KADS, its implementation may deviate, if only the causal connections can be established. Thus the intermediate model acts as an interface between object system and reflective component.

The competence component The competence component may be viewed as a problem solver of its own whose domain is (a model of) another object system. To describe it at the knowledge level, we can again use the KADS four layer scheme [2]. As shown in figure 1, we thus obtain a KADS scheme for the reflective component with another KADS scheme on its domain layer that is causally connected to the object system. Additionally, the reflective domain layer may contain

---

[2]More precisely, we only use the three lower layers, since all strategic reasoning shall be carried out by the reflective component.

knowledge that is not explicitly contained in the object system such as "integrity constraints" as known from databases.

The reflective inference, task and strategy layers are to a large extent independent of the particular object system model at the domain layer. We might exchange it for a model of another object system as long as it can be connected to the inference layer of the reflective component. Hence, due to the KADS separation of problem-specific and application-specific knowledge, our approach is per se generic and applicable to a broader range of object systems – at least at the knowledge level.

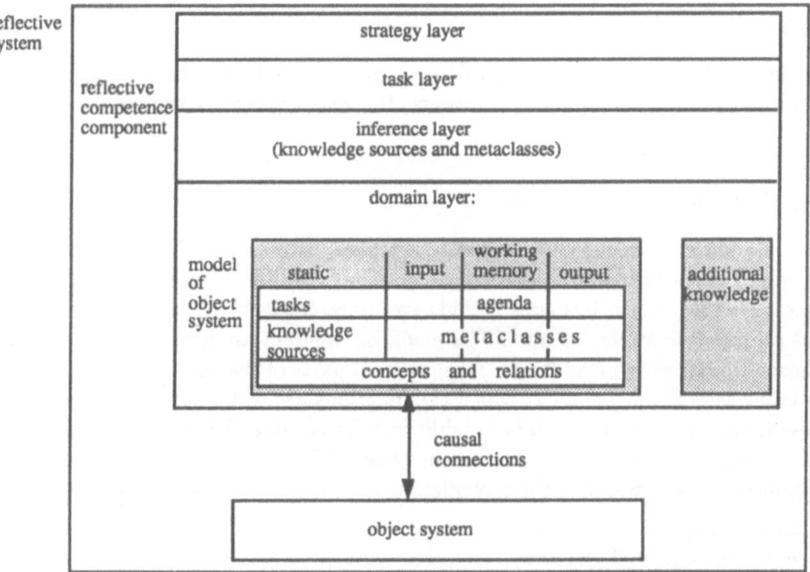

Figure 1: A knowledge level view of reflective systems

In the following sections we will present a conceptual description of a reflective component that assesses and improves the competence of our assignment problem solver when confronted with a particular problem. We will indicate which parts of the description are specific to our type of problem solver (written **sans serif**), which parts are general and which have been implemented so far.

4 A reflective competence component

4.1 The control layers

Dynamic competence assessment and improvement means inspecting and analyzing an object system that is confronted with a particular problem and to modify it so as to better cope with that problem. This can be done either before, during, or after execution of the object system leading to the following control sequence:

1. Read the input problem of the object system.

2. Analyze it and interpret the findings so as to assess the capabilities of the object system to solve that problem. If the result is unsatisfactory, refuse the problem, relax it, or adapt the object system itself.

3. If the problem has not been refused, start the object problem solver.

4. Monitor its execution.

5. If the object system runs into impasses like deadends or loops, analyze its working memory, interpret the findings, and either stop the system or modify its working memory and reset it suitably.

6. When the object system has terminated, analyze the solutions, interpret the findings, and output the solutions if they are ok, otherwise modify them or even modify the working memory and reset the object system.

How to detect the events where the reflective component has to become active, and how to organize the distributed flow of control between the two systems is the subject of our ongoing tasks.

4.2 The inference structure

In any case, the basic reactions to all events are alike: analyze the object system, interpret the findings, arrive at an assessment, propose repair measures and select one of them. They constitute the inference structure shown in figure 2. This structure can be further refined, in particular the analyze and propose knowledge sources. There will be different analyze and propose functions for the different malfunctions to be addressed, the different parts of the object system to be considered, and the different assessment points at which the functions are to be activated from the task layer. Each of these functions may need access to additional knowledge like the afore-mentioned integrity constraints, or potential problem relaxations or reasonable default assumptions. In the following we will explain in more detail first the metaclasses and then the knowledge sources.

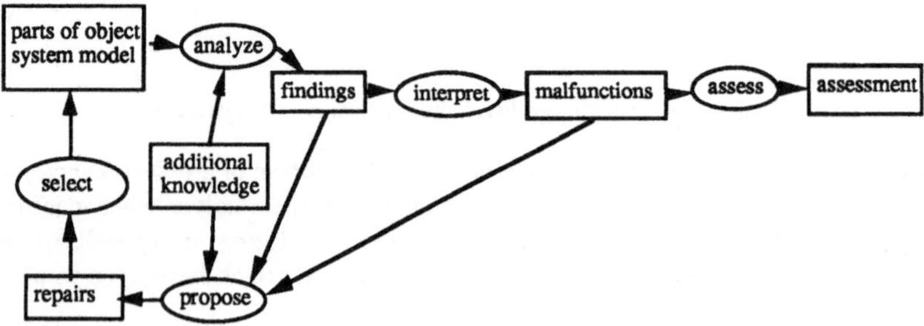

Figure 2: An inference structure for competence assessment and improvement in the reflective component

4.2.1 Metaclasses

Assessment Dynamic competence assessment means judging the potential ability of a problem solver to solve a particular problem or class of problems. These judgements answer four types of questions: Does the object system understand the problem statement? Can it solve the problem? Will the quality of its solutions be acceptable? Will the amount of computing resources needed be acceptable?

Problem understanding: In order to handle a given input problem, the system must be able to parse (syntactical understanding) and to interpret (semantical understanding) it. It should know whether the interpretation is unambiguous and complete, and how reliable it is.

Solvability of the problem: Next, a meaningful problem may be unsolvable, in principle or in practice. Overspecified or inconsistent problems, like the map colouring problem, are unsolvable in principle, i.e. independent of a particular problem solver.

On the other hand, a particular problem solver may fail to solve a principally solvable problem in practice, because the quality of the solutions or of the solution process is insufficient.

If the problem solver can solve a problem, it is important to know how many solutions it will produce, whether it will find all solutions, or the best ones, or whether the solutions may be approximative or uncertain.

The problem solving process: There may be different ways (strategies or heuristics) to solve a principally and practically solvable problem. The alternatives may differ wrt. time, space, number of interactions or whatever resources are scarce.

Malfunction categories   Our work in REFLECT [Bartsch-Spoerl, Reinders 90] suggests that, on the knowledge level, there are essentially six categories of malfunctions that may be responsible for a system's incompetence wrt. a given problem: incompleteness, uncertainty, inconsistency, overcomplexity, irrelevancy and redundancy. – Further categories like sufficiency of computing resources or parsability are already situated at the implementation level. – The six categories can apply to all components of the object system model: input, working memory, output and static parts. We will use the term "knowledge" to refer to any of them.

Knowledge is incomplete if it lacks some information the problem solver needs to solve the problem. On the domain layer and in the input, incompleteness may mean missing concepts and relations, concepts with missing attributes or relations with missing tuples. A special case of incomplete input are underspecified problems which contain too little information to reasonably restrict the number of solutions.

Uncertain knowledge is unreliable and not always safe to use. Often, uncertainties are expressed by associating certainty factors to the knowledge. Uncertain knowledge usually leads to unreliable solutions.

Knowledge is inconsistent if it contains contradictions. Integrity constraints, as known from databases, allow to formulate necessary conditions for consistency. A particularly interesting case of inconsistent input are overspecified problems which contain contradictory information so that no solution can be derived.

Knowledge is overcomplex for the system if it cannot come up with a solution in reasonable time. In synthesis applications, problems are often overcomplex because the artefact to be constructed is too big or too complicated.

Knowledge is irrelevant if it is not needed for solving the particular problem.

Knowledge is redundant if it can be derived from other information.

As mentioned before, OFFICE-PLAN does not find any solutions in the presence of inconsistent requirements and when confronted with overspecified problems. It will slow down when tackling overcomplex problems and it will make opportunistic assumptions for missing knowledge that may lead to unacceptable results. Since OFFICE-PLAN provides no means to express uncertainties, we will not deal with this type of malfunction. Neither will we deal with irrelevant knowledge, since it does no harm to the system.

Parts of the object system model   As shown in figure 1 we distinguish input, working memory, output, and static parts. The KADS scheme provides an orthogonal classification into domain, inference, and task layers. Wrt. OFFICE-PLAN, we will inspect the problem statement in the input metaclasses, the solutions in the output metaclasses, and the static descriptions on the domain layer. We will inspect and modify the transformation of the input into a constraint problem contained in the working memory metaclasses.

Findings   Wrt. OFFICE-PLAN, we compare available and needed resources like square meters of space or computing equipment. We determine the complexity of the constraint problem derived from the input and observe the number of solutions being produced. We determine missing domain knowledge, in particular incomplete descriptions of the employees. We further identify redundant or inconsistent requirements or constraints, e.g. two employees may have to share a room because they work in the same project, and they may have to be in different rooms because one is a smoker and the other is not.

Additional knowledge   Additional knowledge strongly depends on the analyze or propose functions being employed. Wrt. OFFICE-PLAN we use knowledge about mutual exclusion and containment of relations, integrity constraints, priorities of requirements and employees, relaxations of requirements and constraints, abstractions of problems and evaluation criteria for comparing solutions [Voß, Karbach, Drouven, Lorek 90].

4.2.2   Knowledge Sources

analyze is decomposed into eight functions, each producing a special sort of finding as indicated in figure 3.

interpret concludes from these findings the malfunction categories shown in figure 4.

assess concludes from certain malfunctions to categories of (in)competence as shown in figure 5.

propose The judgements produced by assess are intended to be communicated to the human user. If any incompetence has been detected, repair measures should be proposed. For that purpose, the results of assess are on too high a level of abstraction, so that we better rely on the more detailed findings analyzed and the malfunctions recognized. For OFFICE-PLAN, we split the propose knowledge source into six functions, one for each malfunction category. Figure 6 gives a survey.

select There are cases where we may have to deal with mulpiple faults. Then it is likely that several repair measurements will be proposed. We will prefer the more reliable ones, i.e. we prefer REMOVE-RED to DECO and ASSUME or REMOVE-CONTRA to RELAX.

4.3   The domain layer

The domain layer has to supply the knowledge about OFFICE-PLAN that goes into the metaclasses "parts of object system model" and "additional knowledge". For the knowledge sources we have already indicated which parts they have to access and what type of knowledge they need. Here are some concrete examples from OFFICE-PLAN.

priorities between requirements It is more important to place the secretary next to the head of group than the heads of projects near to the head of group; or separating smokers is more important than joining project members.

abstractions We may readily abstract from our students, but not from the head of group.

relaxations If there are not enough rooms, first reduce the size claimed by the employees, then allow more employees to share a room, and in the worst case, leave some employees out of consideration. If there is not enough computing equipment, let some machines be shared by several employees, then assume new machines to be acquired.

model parts to be accessed	analyze function	imple-mented	findings	additional knowledge
input problem, domain-layer	FEASI	+	available vs needed resources	necessary conditions for solvability
input problem, domain-layer	MISS	+	missing attributes and relations (tuples)	---
input problem, domain-layer	RED-R		implications between requirements	subsumption between relations
transformed problem, domain layer	RED-C	+	implications between constraints	subsumption between relations
input problem, domain-layer	CONTRA-R		inconsistencies between requirements	exclusion between relations
transformed problem, domain layer	CONTRA-C	+	inconsistencies between constraints	exclusion between relations
transformed problem	QUANTO		#constraints: #variables:#values	----
output	SOL?		#solutions	---

Figure 3: Analysis functions with input and output and the additional domain knowledge

findings of	malfunction category
FEASI , QUANTO, SOL?	overcomplex input, underspecified input, overspecified input
MISS	incomplete knowledge
CONTRA -R, CONTRA-C	inconsistent knowledge
RED-R, RED-C	redundant knowledge

Figure 4: How findings are interpreted in terms of malfunction categories

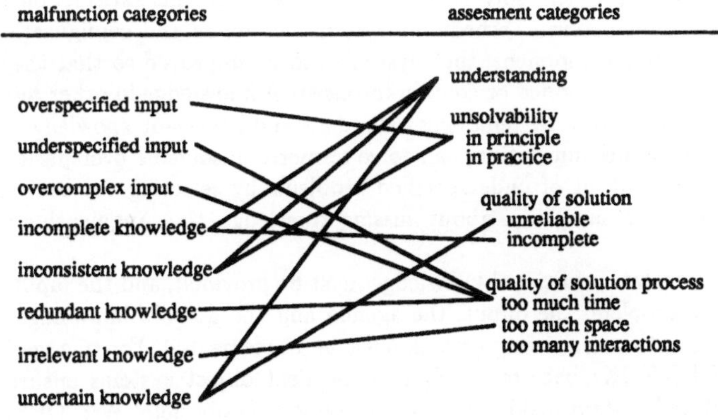

Figure 5: Malfunctions and their consequences in terms of assessment categories

malfunction category	findings of	model parts to be modified	propose functions	additional knowledge
overcomplex input	FEASI, SOL?	transformed problem	DECOmpose	abstractions, priorities
underspecified input	FEASI , SOL?	transformed problem, output	RESTRICT	priorities, preference criteria
overspecified input	FEASI	transformed problem	RELAX	relaxations
incomplete input	MISS, SOL?	transformed problem	ASSUME	defaults, statistical averages
inconsistent input	CONTRA-C CONTRA -R	transformed problem input problem	REMOVE-CONTRAdictions	
redundant input	RED-C RED-R	transformed problem input problem	REMOVE-REDundancies	

Figure 6: Propose repair knowledge sources for OFFICE-PLAN with input, output and additional knowledge

preference criteria Prefer solutions with a minimal number of moves.

defaults In the default case, assume that an employee is an ordinary researcher rather than a student or secretary, that (s)he does not smoke, and that (s)he will need a Macintosh. About his/her project or hobbies no reasonable assumptions can be made.

Concerning the model of the object problem solver, we are still discussing whether to include the full conceptual description (as given in [Voß et al. 90]), or whether the model should be minimal. In the latter case, it just has to contain the input problem, the transformed problem, the ouput, the agenda, and the domain layer knowledge, as can be inferred from the description of the knowledge sources.

5   Outlook

We presented a conceptual description of a reflective component to assess and improve the competence of an object system when confronted with a particular problem. As currently elaborated, our approach is applicable to problem solvers implementing a constraint satisfaction method. These can be assignment problem solvers, scheduling systems, planners and configuration systems. By the addition of a reflective component, such systems can be improved so that they do not try to solve problems that are overspecified or contain inconsistent knowledge in other respects, speed up their problem solving procedure by removing redundant and irrelevant knowledge, solve overcomplex problems quicker by decomposition, can solve formerly unsolvable overspecified problems by relaxation, improve the output of underspecified problems by selecting the best solutions, make reasonable and conscious assumptions about missing knowledge, thus augmenting the reliablity of their solutions.

To be applicable, certain additional knowledge must be provided, and the input problem statement, the constraint problem, the ouput, the agenda and the domain knowledge of the systems must be accessible, i.e. the causal connections must be implemented. For this we have developed the language MODEL-K [Karbach et al. 90] to implement object systems ensuring the isomorphy between model and system making the causal connection obsolete. Wrt. OFFICE-PLAN, we already have implemented versions of FEASI, RED-R, RED-C, CONTRA-R, CONTRA-C and QUANTO [Karbach, Hofbauer 90]. Reflective modules for tackling more types of redundancies, for decomposing overcomplex problems and for time management of problem solving steps are to be finished soon.

Acknowledgements   We would like to thank Joachim Hertzberg for providing helpful comments on earlier drafts of this paper.

References

[Bartsch-Spoerl, Reinders 90] Bartsch-Spoerl, B.; Reinders, M. (eds.): *A Tentative Framework for Knowledge-level Reflection.* REFLECT Project Document RFL/BSR-ECN/I.3/1, Deliverable IR.2, 1990.

[Beierle, Olthoff, Voß 86] Beierle, C.; Olthoff, W.; Voß, A.: *Towards a formalization of the software development process.* In: Software Engineering 86, IEEE Computing Series 6, London: Peter Peregrinus Ltd, 1986.

[Bredeweg, Reinders, Wielinga 90] Bredeweg, B.; Reinders, M.; Wielinga, B.: *GARP: A Unifying Approach to Qualitative Reasoning.* Technical Report, Amsterdam: University of Amsterdam, 1990.

[Breuker, Wielinga 89] Breuker, J.; Wielinga, B.: *Models of Expertise in Knowledge Acquisition.* In: Guida, G., Tasso, C. (eds.): Topics in Expert System Design, Amsterdam: North-Holland, 1989, 265–295.

[Karbach, Linster, Voß 89] Karbach, W.; Linster, M.; Voß, A.: *OFFICE-Plan: Tackling the Synthesis Frontier.* In: Proceedings of GWAI-89, Berin: Springer Verlag, 1989, 379–387.

[Karbach, Hofbauer 90] Karbach, W.; Hofbauer, Th.: *Reflective Modules tackling inconsistent, redundant and missing knowledge in OFFICE-PLAN.* REFLECT Project Report RFL/GMD/II.1/2, Sankt Augustin, 1990.

[Karbach et al. 90] Karbach, W.; Voß, A.; Drouven, U.; Schuckey, R.: *MODEL-K: Prototyping at the Knowledge Level.* Proceedings of the 11th International Workshop Expert Systems & Their Applications, Avignon 91.

[Karssen 90] Karssen, Z.: *Cover-and-Differentiate and AHEAD.* REFLECT Project Report RFL/UvA/I.2/2b, Amsterdam, 1990.

[Maes 88] Maes, P.: *Issues in Computational Reflection.* In: P. Maes, D. Nardi (eds.): Meta-Level Architectures and Reflection, Amsterdam: Elsevier, 1988, 21 – 36.

[Newell 82] Newell, A.: *The Knowledge Level.* Artificial Intelligence 18(1982), 82–127.

[Voß, Karbach, Drouven, Lorek 90] Voß, A., Karbach, W.; Drouven, U.; Lorek, D.: *Competence Assessment in Configuration Tasks.* Proceedings of the 9th European Conference on Artificial Intelligence, London: Pitman, 1990, 676 – 681.

[Voß et al. 90] Voß, A.; Karbach, W.; Drouven, U.; Lorek, D.; Schuckey, R.: *Task I.2.1 Report: Operationalization of a synthetic problem.* REFLECT Project Report RFL/GMD/I.2/5, Sankt Augustin, 1990.

[Wielinga, Breuker 86] Wielinga, B.; Breuker, J.: *Models of expertise.* Proceedings of ECAI-86, Brighton, 1986.

FRESCO: EINE BANKENAPPLIKATION ALS TESTBED FÜR DIE FÖDERATIVE KOOPERATION VON EXPERTENSYSTEMEN

Stefan Kirn, Gunther Schlageter
FernUniversität Hagen, Praktische Informatik I, Postfach 940, 5800 Hagen 1
kirn@fuhasch.fernuni-hagen.de

Föderative Ansätze bieten Möglichkeiten, heute verfügbare Konzepte der Kooperation intelligenter Agenten wesentlich zu flexibilisieren. Ziel ist es, Kooperationsverhalten von Agenten an wechselnde Anforderungen von Aufträgen anzupassen. Der Aufsatz beschreibt das Konzept föderativer Kooperation und stellt das Testbed FRESCO vor. Es folgt eine Diskussion der Eigenschaften, die ein XPS besitzen muß, um bedarfsabhängig kooperieren zu können sowie eine detaillierte Erläuterung lokalen Kooperationsmanagements.

1. EINLEITUNG

Aktuell in der DAI diskutierte Kooperationskonzepte gehen im allgemeinen davon aus, daß die gewünschte Form der Zusammenarbeit durch den Programmierer weitgehend "fest verdrahtet" wird. Flexible Kooperationskonzepte sollte es jedoch ermöglichen, daß intelligente Systeme ihren Kooperationsbedarf selbst erkennen, nach Art und Umfang spezifizieren und artikulieren können, um dann zu versuchen, ihn im Verein mit anderen Expertensystemen des Verbundes zu befriedigen. Mit anderen Worten: *Intelligente Agenten sollten in die Lage versetzt werden, intelligent zu kooperieren.* Hier setzt das Konzept der föderativen Kooperation an. Agenten eines föderativen Systems ermitteln ihren Kooperationsbedarf nach Art und Umfang selbständig. Sie entscheiden selbst, bei welchen Auftragsgranulaten und mit welchen bzw. wie vielen Partnern eine Zusammenarbeit erfolgen soll. Sie wählen die für ein Problem nach ihrer Meinung geeignetste Form der Kooperation aus. Damit wird der Lösungsweg durch die Suche nach "günstigen" Auftragszerlegungen, Entscheidungen über "geeignete" Kooperationsverfahren und die Auswahl von Kooperationspartnern determiniert. Dabei sind jedoch folgende Aspekte zu berücksichtigen:

* im allgemeinen besitzt kein Agent eine generelle Kompetenz für die Bearbeitungsplanung über mehrere dezentralisierte Bearbeitungsschritte hinweg,
* Kooperationsformen müssen ggfs. dynamisch gewechselt werden,
* Auftragszuordnungen basieren auf einem Vergleich abstrakter Beschreibungen von Aufträgen und XPS; daraus entsteht ein Fehlerrisiko, das zu verbundweitem Backtracking führen kann,
* eine explizite globale Koordination der Auftragsbearbeitung über mehrere Bearbeitungsschritte ist normalerweise ebenfalls nicht möglich und
* im allgemeinen besitzt kein Agent a priori vollständiges Wissen über die im Verbund vorhandenen Fähigkeiten und deren Verteilung auf die Agenten.

Deshalb gibt es in der Regel keine verbundweit gültigen Lösungspläne, die die gesamte Auftragsbearbeitung vorab beschreiben. Stattdessen wird die Bearbeitungssteuerung dezentralisiert und lokal durch die jeweiligen Agenten durchgeführt. Das setzt voraus, daß diese dezidiertes Wissen über Art, Umfang und Ablauf von Kooperationsprozessen besitzen, um ihr Kooperationsverhalten dynamisch an die Belange der Auftragsbearbeitung anzupassen. Das ist jedoch nur möglich, wenn sie kooperationsfähig sind, d.h., wenn es ihnen möglich ist, auf Basis eigener Entscheidungen in Kooperationsprozesse einzugreifen, um diese konstruktiv (im Sinne eigener und auf Verbundebene definierter) Ziele voranzubringen.

Um die aus diesem Ansatz resultierenden Fragen auch auf einer technischen Ebene untersuchen zu können, wurde die Bankenapplikation FRESCO entworfen. FRESCO besteht derzeit aus sechs Expertensystemen und einem als Kontraktnetz realisierten Nachrichtentransportsystem. Jeder Agent verfügt über umfangreiches Domänenwissen. Die den Systemen zugewiesenen Aufgabenbereiche überlappen sich zum Teil wechselseitig. So verfügen z.B. sowohl das Anlageberatungs- als auch das Konjunkturprognosesystem über Wissen zu grundsätzlichen Zusammenhängen zwischen gesamtwirtschaftlichem Wachstum und Kapitalmarktrenditen. FRESCO wird auf SUN´s unter Verwendung von Prolog, Oracle und C implementiert.

2. DYNAMISCHE BEARBEITUNGSPLANUNG

Die *Dynamische Bearbeitungsplanung* faßt alle Aktivitäten zusammen, die der Steuerung der verbundweiten Auftragsbearbeitung dienen. Aufträge werden an beliebigen Knoten des Verbundes definiert. Das angesprochene System überprüft den neuen Auftrag durch eine Auftragsanalyse auf gegebene Bearbeitungsalternativen. Kann der Auftrag lokal nicht bearbeitet werden, dann wird versucht, diesen an einen anderen Agenten des Verbundes abzugeben.Soll er zwar lokal bearbeitet werden, ist es jedoch nicht möglich oder nicht zweckmäßig, ihn direkt an eine Inferenz zu übergeben, dann wird er in Teilaufträge zerlegt. Hier kommt es darauf an, eine für die weitere Bearbeitung möglichst günstige Auftragszerlegung zu finden. Da die Agenten das dazu erforderliche Wissen über Existenz, Verfügbarkeit und Verteilung der im Verbund vorhandenen Kompetenzen nicht a priori besitzen, muß dieses dynamisch ermitteln werden. Deshalb erarbeitet die Zerlegungsplanung lediglich einen Zerlegungsvorschlag, der vor der weiteren Bearbeitung mit der Auftragsanalyse und der Zuordnungsplanung abgestimmt werden muß. Danach kann die geplante Verteilung der erzeugten Teilaufträge verbindlich gemacht werden. Generell gilt: Entscheidungen können sich später als zweckmäßig oder unzweckmäßig erweisen. Letzteres muß durch Ergebniskontrollen möglichst früh erkannt werden. Falls ungeeignete Entscheidungen getroffen wurden, müssen diese rückgängig gemacht werden können. Das kann zu Backtracking-Prozessen im verbundglobalen Lösungsraum führen. Die *Dynamische Bearbeitungsplanung* stellt folgende Funktionalitäten bereit:

* **Datenimport/-export:** Kooperation bedingt erhebliche Kommunikation innerhalb der *Dynamischen Bearbeitungsplanung* sowie zwischen dieser und dem Anwender, mit anderen Agenten des Verbundes und dem lokalen *Kern-XPS*. Da Agenten über unterschiedliche lokale Auftragsbeschreibungsprachen verfügen, sind Übersetzungen und eine Verwaltung der gesamten Kommunikation erforderlich.
* **Kooperationsmanagement:** Ein *Kooperationsmanager* koordiniert alle zur lokalen und globalen Steuerung der Auftragsbearbeitung erforderlichen Bearbeitungsschritte im Hinblick auf die globale Kohärenz der Auftragsbearbeitung (Details vgl. Kapitel 3).
* **Zugriffskontrolle:** Zugriffe auf lokales Wissen können direkt oder über einen Kooperationspartner erfolgen. Das macht Zugriffskontrollen erforderlich. Diese können derzeit lediglich auf Ebene von Wissensbasen, nicht jedoch auf Prädikaten und Fakten realisiert werden.
* **Auftragsanalyse:** Die *Auftragsanalyse* stellt Einschätzungen der (Un-) Lösbarkeit und Zerlegbarkeit eines Auftrags sowie der Möglichkeiten, diesen ggfs. an einen anderen Agenten des Verbundes zu übergeben, zur Verfügung und bereitet so die weitere Bearbeitung vor.
* **Zerlegungsplanung:** Aufträge werden unter Verwendung syntaxgesteuerter Definitionen [AhoS 88] formuliert. Diese erlauben (über Semantikregeln) eine weitgehend freie Definition von Beziehungen

zwischen verschiedenen Auftragsteilen. Gleichzeitig steht so eine formale Sprache zur Verfügung, auf deren Grundlage Aufträge syntaxbasiert zerlegt werden können.

- **Zuordnungsplanung:** Die *Zuordnungsplanung* übernimmt eine Menge von Aufträgen und versucht, diese geeigneten Agenten so zuzuordnen, daß jeder Auftrag erfolgreich bearbeitet werden kann. Sie basiert, dem Kontraktnetzansatz entsprechend, auf dem Vergleich abstrakter Beschreibungen von Aufträgen und XPS-Kompetenzen. Aus Platzgründen muß hier darauf verzichtet werden, auf die Form dieser Beschreibungen näher einzugehen; eine ausführliche Darstellung des Ansatzes ist jedoch enthalten in [KiSc 91]. Das Ergebnis der Zuordnungsplanung wird dem *KM* als Vorschlag zurückgegeben.
- **Ergebniskontrolle:** Dient der Auswertung von Statusmeldungen und der Überprüfung, inwieweit vorgegebene Anforderungen an ein Ergebnis erreicht wurden. Resultate der Ergebniskontrolle werden als Statusinformationen in der Bearbeitungszustandstabelle abgelegt.

3. KOOPERATIONSMANAGER (KM)

Der *KM* koordiniert alle Maßnahmen, die für die abschließende Bearbeitung von Nachrichten erforderlich sind. Er wird aktiviert, wenn eine neue Nachricht in die Importtabelle eingetragen wurde.Dazu müssen während der Auftragsbearbeitung alle relevanten Informationen zwischengespeichert werden (Bearbeitungszustandstabelle) und den für ihre Auswertung bzw. Weiterverarbeitung zuständigen Komponenten des Agenten zur Verfügung stehen. Der *KM* terminiert, wenn alle aus der Nachricht resultierenden Arbeiten abgeschlossen sind. Das ist dann der Fall, wenn diese aus der Bearbeitungszustandstabelle ausgetragen wurde. Bearbeitungszustände werden beschrieben durch:

- <KONTRAKT_ID>: Schlüssel für Eintrag in die Importtabelle ("<...>": Term des Kontraktprotokolls)
- Variablenliste: Enthält die einer <NACHRICHT> zugehörigen Variablen und deren Belegung,
- *time out*-Vorgaben und (noch unbearbeitete) Statusmeldungen,
- aktuelle Bearbeitungsstation: lokales *Kern-Expertensystem*, Submodule der *Dynamischen Bearbeitungsplanung* oder Kontraktor,
- Informationen zur lokalen / globalen Lösbarkeit, Zerlegbarkeit, Delegierbarkeit des Auftrags,
- Verweise auf die aus dem Auftrag erzeugten Subaufträge sowie den übergeordneten Auftrag.

Im einzelnen übernimmt der *Kooperationsmanager* folgende Aufgaben:

- Übernahme der jeweils neu in der Importtabelle abgelegten <NACHRICHT>.
- Auswertung der durch die *Auftragsanalyse, Zerlegungsplanung, Zuordnungsplanung, Ergebniskontrolle* und *Kompetenzeinschätzung* erzielten Bearbeitungsresultate.
- Festlegung des nächsten Bearbeitungsschrittes in Abhängigkeit vom Typ und dem aktuellen Bearbeitungszustand einer <NACHRICHT>, den Rückmeldungen / Ergebnissen der Submodule der *Bearbeitungsplanung* sowie seiner eigenen, lokalen Kooperationsintelligenz.
- Auslösen des nächsten lokalen Arbeitsschritts (oder Datenübergabe an den *Import-/Export-Managers*).
- Führen der Bearbeitungszustandstabelle.
- Koordinierung aller zur Abarbeitung einer <NACHRICHT> erforderlichen Arbeitsschritte.
- Veranlassen des Zurücksetzens einer Auftragszerlegung dann, wenn diese zu keinem Ergebnis geführt hat und der Anwender Zerlegungsbacktracking grundsätzlich zugelassen hat.

Um diese Aufgaben erfüllen zu können, benötigt der *Kooperationsmanger*

- Wissen über das I/O-Verhalten aller Komponenten der Dynamischen Bearbeitungsplanung sowie der Kompetenzabschätzung,
- Wissen über das lokale Zielsystem des Agenten,
- Wissen über Kooperationsverhalten und Kooperationsstrategien sowie
- Kontrollwissen zur Koordination der für die Auftragsbearbeitung erforderlichen Tätigkeiten.

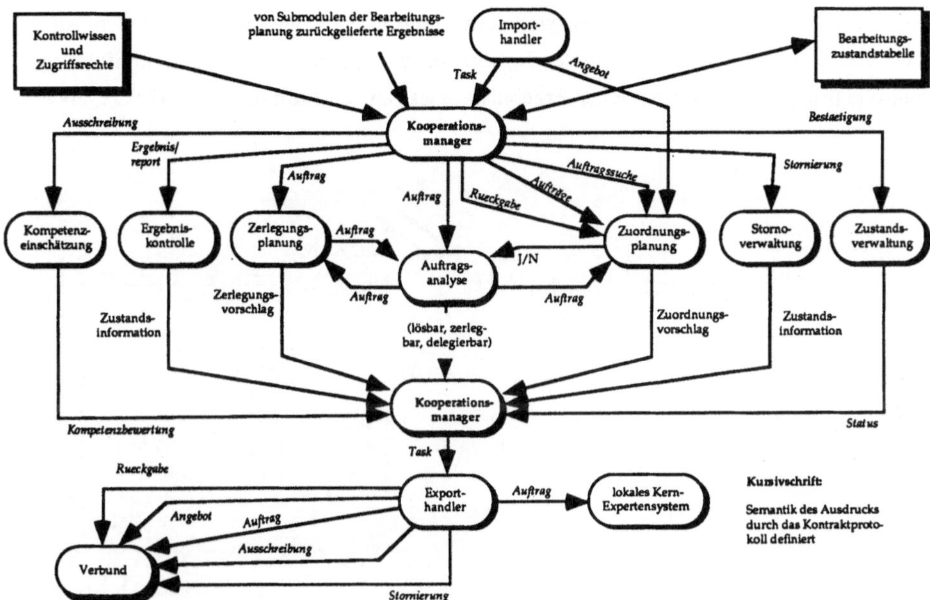

Dieses Wissen definiert die Kooperationsintelligenz eines Agenten und steht dem *KM* in einer Wissensbasis zur Verfügung. Damit kann Kooperationswissen dynamisch evaluiert werden.Agenten können nun durch Modifikation dieses Wissens ihr Kooperationsverhalten ändern, d.h. (unter Beachtung ihrer Ziele) an wechselnde Erfodernisse der Auftragsbearbeitung anpassen können. In FRESCO eröffnet das Möglichkeiten, durch Veränderungen von Kooperationswissen Kooperationsverhalten von Agenten zu beeinflussen und so den Zusammenhang zwischen Kooperationswissen, lokalem Kooperationsverhalten und globalem Kooperationsverlauf zu untersuchen. Die zu koordinierenden Vorgänge zeigt das obige Bild.

4. DAS FRESCO-AGENTENMODELL

Eines der Ziele von FRESCO bestand darin, die Agenten so aufzubauen, daß bereits bestehende XPS durch einen wenigstens teilweise automatisch ablaufenden Konfigurationsvorgang kooperationsfähig gemacht werden können. Das hat zu dem in nachfolgendem Bild dargestellten modularen Aufbau geführt. Das Kern-Expertensystem wird durch ein herkömmliches (*stand alone-*) XPS definiert, das in eine Schale eingebettet wird, die alle für die Kooperationsfähigkeit wesentlichen Funktionalitäten enthält. Verschiedene XPS eines Verbundes unterscheiden sich damit lediglich in ihren *Kern-Expertensystemen* sowie dem Inhalt ihrer *Meta-Wissensbasen* voneinander.

Der Anwender kommuniziert mit dem Gesamtsystem via lokaler oder universeller Dialogschnittstelle. Während erstere beim Entwurf des *Kern-Expertensystems* aufgebaut wird, bietet die *universelle Dialog-schnittstelle* Möglichkeiten, weitgehend frei formulierbare Anfragen an den Verbund zu richten. Diese werden mit Hilfe des globalen data dictionary einer Kontrolle unterzogen, um eindeutig außerhalb der Leistungsfähigkeit des Verbundes liegenden Anfragen bereits bei der Eingabe zurückweisen zu können.Über die universelle Dialogschnittstelle eingegangene oder nach positiver Kompetenzabschätzung von anderen Agenten übernommene Aufträge werden der Dynamischen Bearbeitungsplanung übergeben. Diese entscheidet über die weitere Bearbeitung einer Anfrage und vergibt den Auftrag (bzw. die erzeugten Teilaufträge) entweder an das *lokale Kern-Expertensystem* oder, falls das nicht möglich ist, an andere Agenten des Verbundes. Von dort kommen die abgeleiteten Ergebnisse zurück und werden nach Durchführung der Ergebniskontrolle und der ggfs. erforderlichen Ergebnissynthese an den Auftraggeber zurückgegeben.

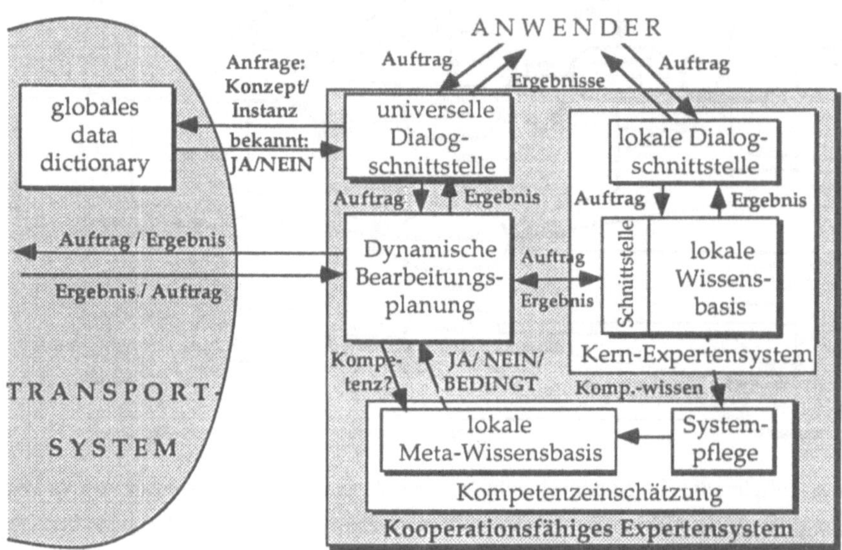

LITERATUR

[AhoS 88] Aho, V.A.; Sethi, R.; Ullman, J.: Compilerbau, Band I, II, Addison-Wesley, Bonn, Reading /Mass. et. al., 1988.

[Durf 87] Durfee, E.H.; Lesser, V.L.; Corkill, D.: Coherent Cooperation Among Communicating Problem Solvers, IEEE Trans. on Computers, C-36, 1987, pp. 1275

[Find 87] Findler, N.V.; Gao, J.: Dynamic Hierarchical Control for Distributed Problem Solving, Data & Knowledge Engineering 2(1987) pp. 285-301.

[Gass 88] Gasser, L.: Distribution and Coordination of Tasks among Intelligent Agents, Proc. 1st Scandinavian Conf. on AI, 1988, pp. 177.

[Kirn 90] Kirn, St. et.al.: Expertensysteme beim Einsatz in Föderativen Umgebungen: Ein Problemaufriß, FernUniv. Hagen, Informatikbericht Nr.90, 2/1990.

[KiSc 90] Kirn, St.; Schlageter, G.: Federated Expert Systems: Concepts and Implementation, 1st CKBS, Keele, Great Britain, Oct. 3-5, 1990.

[KiSc 91] Kirn, St.; Schlageter, G.: Competence Evaluation in Federative Problem Solving - How to Make Expert Systems Cooperative, 11th conference on 2nd generation expert systems, Avignon, France, May 28-31, 1991.

[Klet 89] Klett, G.: Kooperierende Expertensysteme mit Kontraktnetzarchitektur und ihr Einsatz in technischen Anwendungen, Dissertation, Hagen 1989.

Graphische Wissensrepräsentationen

Ute Gappa
Universität Karlsruhe, Institut für Logik, Komplexität und Deduktionssysteme
Postfach 6980, D-7500 Karlsruhe
e-mail: gappa@ira.uka.de

– Kurzfassung –

Graphische Wissensrepräsentationen haben das Potential, Experten das selbständige Programmieren von Expertensystemen in ihrem Anwendungsbereich zu ermöglichen, wenn sie gleichzeitig hinreichend auf den Bereich oder die Problemlösungsmethode zugeschnittene Wissensmodelle beinhalten. In dem Beitrag zeigen wir, daß sich der überwiegende Teil der in Wissensakquisitionssystemen benutzten graphischen Wissensrepräsentationen auf die vier Grundtypen *Hierarchie*, *Graph*, *Formular* und *Tabelle* zurückführen läßt. Daher lohnt es sich, diese Grundtypen als generische Graphikprimitive durch Spezifikation ihrer Parameter zu formalisieren. Auf der Basis dieser graphischen Wissensrepräsentationsprimitive läßt sich ein allgemeines Muster für den graphischen Wissenserwerb ableiten, das darin besteht, zunächst die Terminologie und Taxonomie des Anwendungsbereichs in Hierarchien und Graphen einzugeben, lokale Informationen und Eigenschaften zu den Begriffen durch Ausfüllen objektspezifischer Formulare hinzuzufügen und drittens die Relationen und Inferenzen, die nicht durch die Taxonomie abgegolten sind, überwiegend durch Tabellen und Graphen zu repräsentieren. Diese Methodik haben wir in verschiedenen Wissensakquisitionssystemen realisiert, u.a. in CLASSIKA für die Klassifikation, an welchem wir die Mächtigkeit und Effektivität graphischer Wissensrepräsentationen verdeutlichen.

1 Einleitung

Das derzeitige Spektrum von Wissensakquisitionsmethoden reicht von indirekten Methoden über Wissensingenieure, direkten Methoden, bei denen Experten ihr Wissen selbst aufbereiten und eingeben bis zu den induktiven Verfahren des Maschinellen Lernens. Wissensakquisitionssysteme, die sich direkt an den Experten wenden, verwenden entweder graphische Wissensrepräsentationen, in denen Experten ihr Wissen graphisch repräsentieren, und/oder Fragestrategien, die neu Wissenseinträge aktiv erfragen. Die Vorteile, wenn Experten ihre Expertensysteme selbst entwickeln können, sind naheliegend: Aufwand und Kosten der Erstellung von Expertensystemen sind geringer, da der Wissensingenieur nicht oder nur gelegentlich, z.B. zu Beginn bei der Wissensanalyse und Auswahl eines geeigneten Shells, zu Rate gezogen werden muß, die Fehleranfälligkeit ist geringer, und nicht zuletzt entwickeln die Experten ein größeres Verantwortungsbewußtsein für die von ihnen selbst erstellten Expertensysteme.

Die wichtigste Voraussetzung für Wissensakquisitionssysteme für Experten ist, daß das zugrundegelegte Wissensmodell hinreichend gut auf den Anwendungsbereich und/oder dessen Problemlösungsverfahren ausgelegt ist, so daß es für den Experten leicht nachvollziehbar ist. Dabei können gut gewählte graphische Wissensrepräsentationen die Verständlichkeit des Wissensmodells und damit die Modellbildung des Experten entscheidend unterstützen. Der notwendige Zuschnitt eines Wissensmodells läßt sich nicht nur an der graphischen Wissenserwerbsoberfläche, sondern auch an der Formalisierung des Wissensmodells, also an der internen Wissensrepräsentation, ablesen. Denn je weitgehender die verwendeten Objekttypen, Attribute von Objekten, Regeltypen, Prädikate zur Auswertung der Objektattribute etc. fest eingebaut sind, desto besser kann ein voll-graphisches Wissensakquisitionssystem zu dem Wissensmodell bzw. zu der Wissensrepräsentation erstellt werden, in dem lediglich die Terminologie und optionale Erklärungen als freier Text eingetippt werden brauchen und alles weitere vollständig durch Menüauswahl mit Öffnen und Ausfüllen vorgegebener Fenster eingegeben werden kann.

Ein Beispiel für ein ausgefeiltes graphisches Wissensakquisitionssystem ist OPAL [Musen et al. 87, Musen 89b], das die Behandlungsrichtlinien („Protokolle") direkt nachahmt, die Ärzte zur Therapie von Krebspatienten benutzen. OPAL nutzt eine graphische Flußdiagrammsprache zur Beschreibung der zeitlichen Abfolge von Chemotherapien, Radiotherapien und Untersuchungen. Die Chemotherapien werden anhand von Formularen präzisiert, in denen die beteiligten Medikamente durch Menüauswahl eingetragen und deren Dosis und Verabreichungsform angegeben wird. Auch Regeln werden über Formulare eingegeben, wobei zur Auswertung von Labordaten und Patientensymptomen teilweise Tabellen benutzt werden, in die die Regelaktionen wiederum durch Menüauswahl eingetragen werden. Diese hochstrukturierte Wissenseingabe in OPAL ist nur möglich, weil mit der Erstellung der graphischen Wissensrepräsentationen und Eingabeformen ein Wissensmodell geschaffen wurde, das starke Annahmen über den Anwendungsbereich ausnutzt.

Wenn auch die Vorteile graphischer Wissensrepräsentationen auf der Hand liegen, ist ihre Realisierung mit enormem Zeitaufwand verbunden. Der Aufwand lohnt sich in der Regel nur dann, wenn ein Großteil der implementierten Graphikfunktionalität wiederverwendet werden kann. Mit genau diesem Ziel der Wiederverwendbarkeit haben wir vier Grundtypen graphischer Eingabeformen identifiziert. In Kapitel 2 geben wir eine Kurzanalyse der in Wissensakquisitionssystemen benutzten Graphikformen und führen den Großteil auf die identifizierten Grundtypen zurück. Ihre Struktur beschreiben wir detaillierter in Kapitel 3. Wir geben eine Theorie ihrer Anwendbarkeit und leiten aus ihnen ein allgemeines Muster für den graphischen Wissenserwerb ab. Ein auf der Basis der Graphikprimitive entstandenes Wissensakquisitionssystem wird mit CLASSIKA in Kapitel 4 illustriert. Der Beitrag schließt mit einer Diskussion in Kapitel 5.

2 Rückführung graphischer Wissensrepräsentationen auf Graphik–primitive

Ziel dieses Kapitels ist es, eine Kurzanalyse über die wichtigsten *graphischen Wissensrepräsentationen* zu geben, die in verschiedenen *graphischen Wissensakquisitionssystemen* eingesetzt werden (siehe Tabelle in Abb. 1). Obwohl der Hauptzweck der graphischen Repräsentationen die Verkörperung der Semantik des Wissensmodells ist, wollen wir uns mehr auf die syntaktische Struktur und Manipulationsformen der graphischen Repräsentationen konzentrieren, um sie auf grundlegende Graphikprimitive, wie *Graph* bzw. *Hierarchie*, *Formular* und *Tabelle* zurückzuführen. Dabei reicht uns zunächst ein intuitives Verständnis dieser Begriffe aus.

Die wichtigsten graphikorientierten Wissensakquisitionssysteme, die ihr Wissen interaktiv direkt vom Experten akquirieren, sind das eingangs erwähnte OPAL, mit PROTÉGÉ [Musen 89a] erstellte Wissensakquisitionssysteme im Bereich der Planbeschreibung, die auf dem Konstruktgitterverfahren basierenden Systeme AQUINAS [Boose et Bradshaw 87] und KSS0 [Shaw et Gaines 87], sowie TDE/TEST [Kahn et al. 87, ESS 88] für die Klassifikation mit erweiterten Entscheidungsbäumen und CLASSIKA [Gappa 89, D3 91] für die heuristische und fallvergleichende Klassifikation. Dem System PROTÉGÉ kommt eine Sonderstellung zu, da es sich erst in der zweiten Wissensakquisitionsphase direkt an einen Bereichsexperten richtet und die erste Phase von einem Wissensingenieur in Zusammenarbeit mit dem Experten geleistet wird.

Die auf dem Konstruktgitterverfahren basierenden Systeme wurden nur bedingt in die Tabelle (Abb. 1) aufgenommen, da sie den Experten nicht direkt mit der Semantik des Wissensmodells zur Problemlösung konfrontieren und insofern ein implizites Wissensmodell benutzen [Musen 89b]. Dahinter steckt die Grundannahme, daß Experten ihr Wissen nicht direkt ausdrücken können, sondern in geeigneter Form danach gefragt werden müssen. So dienen die in den Systemen benutzten Konstruktgitter, Klassifikationshierarchien und Herleitungsgraphen nur der Visualisierung vom System hergeleiteter Zusammenhänge, können aber häufig nicht durch den Benutzer modifiziert werden.

Wissensakquisitionssystem	Graphische Wissensrepräsentationen	Semantik der graphischen Repräsentation	"Grundtyp" der graph. Rep.
OPAL	Graphische Flußdiagrammsprache mit Kontrollelementen wie Verzweigung, Iteration, Parallelausführung und Abbruchbedingung.	Zeitliche Abfolge von Therapieformen (Chemo-, Radiotherapien und Untersuchungen), u.a. abhängig davon, wie stark der Patient auf die Behandlung anspricht.	Graph
	Formulare für Chemotherapien und Medikamente	Dauer einer Chemotherapie, beteiligte Medikamente, deren Dosis und Verabreichungsform	Formular
	Regelformular mit Menüauswahl für die Aktion der Regel. Mehrere Bedingungen und zugehörige Aktionen werden mehrspaltig eingegeben. Für spezielle Konditionskonstellationen wird eine Tabelle benutzt, in die die zugehörige Aktion in Abhängigkeit zweier Parameter eingetragen wird.	Modifikation der Behandlungsprotokolle und Therapieformen in Abhängigkeit des klinischen Zustandes des Patienten, u.a. Labordaten. Mögliche Aktionen sind z.B. das Abbrechen oder Aussetzen einer Chemotherapie, Ersetzen eines Medikamentes, Ändern der üblichen Dosis etc.	Formular und Tabelle
PROTÉGÉ	2-stufiges Wissensakquisitionssystem: 1) Formularbasierte Sprache zur Anpassung an das Bereichsmodell	Definition der Planeinheiten und Beziehungen, die einen Plan ausmachen, Attribute der Planeinheiten, Aktionen, die einen Plan modifizieren können und Eingabedaten, auf die sich die Aktionen gründen	im wesentlichen Formular
	2) Graphische Flußdiagrammsprache, Formulare für Objekte und Regeln teilweise mehrspaltig oder tabellenartig (analog zu OPAL)	Abfolge von Planeinheiten, Definition der Attribute der Planeinheiten und Regeln, die den Plan modifizieren (analog zu OPAL)	Graph, Formular, teilweise mehrspaltig oder tabellenartig
ETS/ AQUINAS	Konstruktgitter (nicht manipulierbar)	Charakterisierung von Objekten durch die Ausprägung ihrer Merkmals	Tabelle
	Implikationsgraph, Merkmals- und Klassifikationshierarchien (jeweils nicht manipulierbar)	vom System hergeleitete Implikationen und Ähnlichkeiten zwischen den Merkmalen	Hierarchie / Graph
KSSO	zusätzlich zu AQUINAS: Verschiedene graphisch manipulierbare Balkenrepräsentationen zur Eingabe des Konstruktgitters	Balkenrepräsentationen zur Einordnung der Klassifikationsobjekte, direkter Vergleich zweier Merkmale, zweier Klassifikationsobjekte etc.	keine Entsprechung
TDE/TEST	Graphisch manipulierbare Fehlerhierarchie	Fehlerzustände mit Angabe der möglichen Ursachen für einen Fehlerzustand in einer Hierarchie	Hierarchie / Graph
	Attributgraph	Graphische Visualisierung einiger Attribute eines Fehlerzustandes wie Tests und Reparaturanweisungen	Hierarchie / Graph
	Formularartiges Textfenster für Fehlerzustände	Alle Attribute eines Fehlerzustandes (u.a. die aus der Fehlerhierarchie und dem Attributgraphen)	Formular
CLASSIKA	Symptom- und Diagnoschierarchie	Taxonomie des Anwendungsbereichs, u.a. Strukturierung der Symptome in Fragebögen, Fragen, Folgefragen und Symptomabstraktionen	Hierarchie
	Formulare mit fest vorgegebenen Attributen für jeden Objekt- und Regeltyp, die außer bei freien Texten über Mausklicks angegeben werden	• lokale Objekteigenschaften, wie z.B. Fragetext, Antworttyp, Wertebereich bzw. Antwortalternativen von Symptomen; • Regeltypen zur Herleitung von Symptomabstraktionen, Diagnosen, Vorschlägen, zur Dialogsteuerung, Plausibilitätskontrolle etc.	Formular
	Regeltabellen mit unterschiedlichem Abstraktions/Detaillierungsgrad, die über Menüauswahl ausgefüllt werden	Kompaktere und übersichtlichere Eingabe des mit obigen Regeltypen repräsentierten heuristischen Diagnosewissens	Tabelle
	Zeilenweise Eingabe der Zusatzattribute in einer Tabelle	Ähnlichkeitsmaß von Symptomen, relative Wichtigkeit, Abstraktionsebene etc., die eine fallvergleichende Problemlösung unterstützen	Tabelle

Abb. 1 Graphische Wissensrepräsentationen in graphischen Wissensakquisitionssystemen

MORE [Kahn 88, Marcus 88], MOLE [Eshelman 88, Marcus 88] und ASK [Gruber 89] sind ebenfalls Beispiele für Wissensakquisitionssysteme, die eine systemgesteuerte Wissenserfragung präferieren und sogar auf graphische Wissensrepräsentationen vollständig verzichten. MORE benutzt acht verschiedene sog. Fragestrategien aufgrund statischer Analysen der Wissensbasis, die jedoch häufig zu irrelevanten Fragen führen, so daß nur eine der Fragestrategien in das Nachfolgesystem MOLE übernommen wurde. In einer anderen Weiterentwicklung von MORE ist man dazu übergegangen, verstärkt dem Benutzer die Initiative beim Wissensbasisaufbau einzuräumen und hat dafür graphisch manipulierbare Wissensrepräsentationen bereitgestellt. TDE/TEST läßt eine wechselnde Initiative vom Benutzer und System beim Wissensbasisaufbau zu, in dem Anfänger überwiegend die aktiven Fragestrategien benutzen, während Fortgeschrittene die direkte Manipulation der Fehlerzustandshierarchien und Objektattribute vorziehen.

MOLE und ASK haben sich verstärkt dynamischen Analysen der Wissensbasis zugewendet. Sie nutzen für die systemgestützte Wissensbefragung den Kontext der vom Expertensystem nicht-korrekt gelösten Aufgaben aus, um dem Experten bezüglich der Fehlersuche und Korrektur der Wissensbasis zu assistieren. Teilweise benutzen sie induktive Verfahren zur Anpassung der Wissensbasis. Die analoge Prozedur bei passiven Wissensakquisitionssystemen wie TDE und CLASSIKA ist, daß Experten sich die Begründung für die Lösungen bzw. nicht herausgefundene Lösungen oder Zwischenschritte des Systems anzeigen lassen, die Wissensbasis graphisch korrigieren und den gleichen Fall unter der geänderten Wissensbasis vom Problemlöser wiederholen lassen.

In dem Zusammenhang graphischer Wissenseditoren ist wichtig festzuhalten, daß aktive Wissenserwerbssysteme nicht notwendigerweise den gleichen Anspruch an graphische Wissensrepräsentationen und deren Modifikationsmöglichkeiten stellen wie interaktiv-passive Systeme, da sie einen bestimmten Wissenseintrag erfragen und die Antwort auch direkt auf die interne Repräsentation abbilden können.

In der obigen Tabelle (Abb. 1) ist die Rückführung der jeweils wichtigsten in Akquisitionssystemen benutzten graphischen Wissenseditorfenster auf graphische Grundrepräsentationen dargestellt. Dabei ist die Zuordnung der graphischen Wissensrepräsentationen zu diesen Typkategorien nicht immer eindeutig, da der Übergang von Formular und Tabelle beispielsweise durch mehrspaltig angeordnete Formulare, wie sie z.B. in PROTÉGÉ und OPAL teilweise verwendet werden, durchaus fließend ist. Zusammenfassend läßt sich sagen, daß die in den verschiedenen Systemen verwendeten graphischen Wissensrepräsentationen, die ja jeweils eine spezielle Semantik in ihrem Wissensmodell repräsentieren, zwar unterschiedliche graphische Ausprägungen und Anordnungen haben, aber doch auf die gleichen Grundtypen rückführbar sind.

Auch wenn nicht alle Wissensakquisitionssysteme, die die Voraussetzungen für graphische Wissensakquisition, nämlich eine starkes Modell der Problemlösung [Puppe 90] mitbringen, graphische Wissensrepräsentationen verwenden, wäre es trotzdem für sie von Vorteil. Zum Beispiel wäre es eine deutliche Verbesserung für SALT [Marcus 88], dem als Wissensmodell die Vorschlagen-und-Verbessern-Strategie für Konfigurierung zugrundeliegt, wenn das Abhängigkeitsnetz von Parametern, Constraints und Korrekturen, das in Veröffentlichungen graphisch dargestellt ist, durch einen Graphen visualisiert und editierbar gemacht würde.

3 Generische graphische Repräsentationen und deren Nutzung für den Wissenserwerb

In diesem Kapitel werden die bisher „intuitiv" eingeführten Begriffe Graph, Hierarchie, Formular und Tabelle durch Spezifikation entsprechender *generischer graphischer Grundprimitive* präzisiert. Der Zweck der Graphikprimitive ist nicht nur die Visualisierung und Inspektion der Wissensbasis, sondern auch die Definition und direkte Manipulation des darin repräsentierten Wissens.

Hierarchie und *Graph*:

Hierarchie und Graph repräsentieren Knoten bzw. Objekte und deren Abhängigkeiten durch Linien oder Pfeile (vgl. 1. Teil der Abb. 2). Der Hauptunterschied zwischen einer graphischen Hierarchie und einem Graphen besteht unserer Terminologie zufolge darin, daß die Knoten in einem Graphen vom Benutzer positioniert werden, während die Knotenanordnung in Hierarchien automatisch vom System erfolgt. Für den interaktiven Aufbau der Graphikformen hat das u.a. zur Folge, daß bei der Hierarchie nur angegeben werden muß, hinter welches/welche Objekte ein oder mehrere neue Objekte angehängt werden, während bei der Konstruktion eines Graphen ein neues Objekt zuerst plaziert und dann erst durch Einzeichnen von Linien mit anderen Objekten in Beziehung gesetzt wird. Außer solchen Unterschieden, die direkt oder indirekt aus der unterschiedlichen Handhabung der Plazierung resultieren, werden Hierarchie und Graph durch identische Parameter charakterisiert, wie • Nachfolgerfunktion, • Typisierung von Knoten und Linien mit Assoziieren eines bestimmten graphischen Layouts, • zusätzliche Markierungsarten für Objekte, • Selektionstyp, ob Objekte und/oder Linien anklickbar sind und wenn, ob mehrere auf einmal, • Funktionen, die bei Einfach- oder Doppelklick auf Knoten aufgerufen werden, • Kontrolle der Benutzermodifikationen, • assoziierte Funktionen, die die Modifikationen der graphischen Repräsentation auf der internen Wissensrepräsentation (Wissensbasis) durchführen, u.v.m.

Formular:

Formulare sind das graphische Äquivalent zu Objekt-Attribut-Repräsentationen („filler-and-slot"). Ein generisches Formular ist wie folgt aufgebaut (vgl. 2. Teil der Abb. 2):
• statische Namen der Attribute, • evtl. aus mehreren Graphikelementen zusammengesetzte Graphikformen zur Eingabe von Attributwerten. Benutzbare Graphikelemente sind Editierfelder für freie Texte oder Zahlenangaben, statische Texte, Pop-up-Menüs, Auswahlpunkte („radio-buttons") und Objektfelder zum Eintragen von Objekten der Wissensbasis durch Auswählen aus anderen Fenstern, beispielsweise einer graphischen Hierarchie, • optionale Tastenzeile für zusätzliche Attribute, deren Integration in das Hauptformular nicht sinnvoll ist. Ein Beispiel ist ein Dialogfenster zum Einzeichnen sensitiver Felder auf Bildern sowie • Standard-Tastenfelder für „OK", d.h. Übernehmen der Einträge in die Wissensbasis, „Abbrechen" und wahlweise für „Löschen" und „Kopieren" des Objektes.
Außer diesen Angaben zum „statischen Aufbau" des Formulars und allgemeinen Layout-Spezifikationen werden in dem Formular auch die Abhängigkeiten zwischen Attributwerten berücksichtigt. Z. B. ist der Wertebereich einer Frage vom Antworttyp abhängig; ist dieser „one-choice" oder „multiple-choice", wird der Wertebereich als Aufzählung der einzelnen Antwortalternativen eingegeben, ist der Antworttyp „numerisch", ist der Wertebereich beispielsweise ein Intervall etc.

Tabelle:

Die generische Tabelle (vgl. 3. Teil der Abb. 2) besteht aus • der Beschriftung für die Zeilen und Spalten und deren Überschriften, • der eigentlichen Tabelle und • einer optionalen Tastenzeile am unteren Rand des Tabellenfensters. Zur weiteren Einteilung der Tabelle können die Spalten in Unterspalten unterteilt und die Zeilen in einer Hierarchie angeordnet werden. Die Tabelle benutzt ein internes „Feld", auf der sich alle für ein Tabellenfeld relevanten Informationen speichern lassen. Zur Darstellung des internen Feldwertes kann man eine Darstellungsfunktion angeben.
Die Tabelle kann entweder durch Ankreuzen, Texteingabe oder Menüauswahl ausgefüllt werden. Wenn der Benutzer einen Tabelleneintrag ändert, wird eine benutzerdefinierte „Updatefunktion" aufgerufen, die die Änderung auf der Wissensbasis durchführt. Möglichkeiten der Zeilen- und Spaltenindexierung sind die Position, die Beschriftung oder ein mit einer Beschriftung assoziierter interner Wert. Die Tabelle ist entweder als Graphikelement verfügbar, das in ein anderes Fenster gesetzt werden kann, oder als eigenständiges Fenster, bei dem sich die Tabelle automatisch an die Fenstergröße anpaßt.

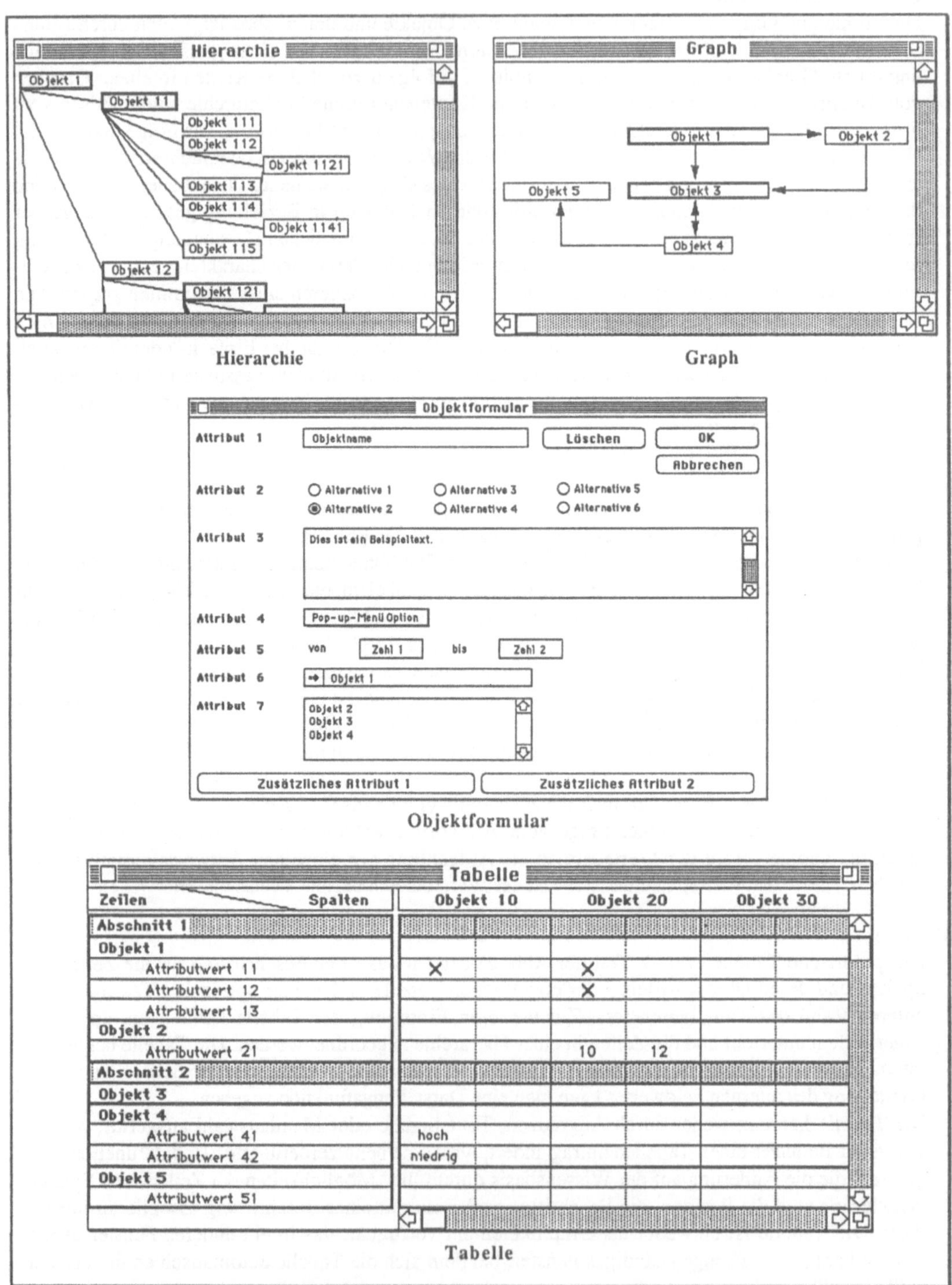

Hierarchie

Graph

Objektformular

Tabelle

Abb. 2   Generische graphische Grundprimitive

Die hier skizzierten generischen Graphik-Grundtypen sind unter Allegro Common Lisp auf dem Macintosh implementiert und voll darin eingebettet. Insbesondere werden das Objektsystem und die von der Programmiersprache angebotenen Graphikprimitive verwendet. Eine ausführlichere Beschreibung der hier entwickelten generischen Graphikprimitive bis auf die Parameterebene findet sich in [Gappa 91], das auch die Integration verschiedener etwas weniger mächtiger Graphikwerkzeuge in einer Graphik-bibliothek für Wissenseditoren beinhaltet.

Die generischen graphischen Primitive machen noch keinerlei Annahmen über die Semantik des Wissensmodells, das mit ihnen repräsentiert wird, sondern beschreiben nur deren graphische Syntax. Zu der Anwendbarkeit der graphischen Wissensrepräsentationen kann man Kriterien angeben, wann welche am besten geeignet ist und ein Muster für die Vorgehensweise beim graphischen Wissenserwerb ableiten.

Sowohl die Hierarchie als auch der Graph eignen sich für die Visualisierung von Objektabhängig-keiten, wenn ein Objekt überwiegend von einem oder wenigen anderen Objekten abhängt und nicht allzu-viele zirkuläre Beziehungen bestehen. Beide sollten möglichst wenig querverlaufende Linien aufweisen, wobei Ausnahmen tolerierbar sind. Während mit einer Hierarchie am besten 1:n-Relationen zwischen einem Objekt und seinen Nachfolgern dargestellt werden können, erlaubt ein Graph eher die Repräsentation von n:m-Beziehungen, wenn n und m klein sind und nur lokale Cluster vorhanden sind.

Die Tabelle ist die geeignete Darstellungsform von n:m-Beziehungen, bei denen viele Elemente der einen Menge mit denen der anderen Menge in Verbindung stehen. Eine typische Situation dafür ist beispielsweise, wenn viele Regeln sich auf gleiche Objekte beziehen. Eine Tabelle kann sowohl für einen Vergleich von Objekten (Spalten) durch ihre Merkmale (Zeilen) benutzt werden als auch zur Definition von Kondition-Aktion-Relationen, die auf die gleichen Objekte referieren, wie beispielsweise in Ent-scheidungstabellen. Im Vergleich zu Hierarchien und Graphen sind in Tabellen Abhängigkeiten über mehrere Stufen nur unübersichtlich darstellbar.

Formulare bieten sich an zur Charakterisierung eines Objektes durch seine Attribute. Je mehr die Wissensrepräsentation typisiert ist, desto leichter läßt sich ein Formular entwerfen, das bis auf Texte rein durch Auswählen mit der Maus ausgefüllt werden kann. Wenn die Attributwerte keine lokalen Objekt-eigenschaften, sondern andere Objekte beinhalten, d.h. Beziehungen darstellen, sind andere graphische Notationen, wie Hierarchien, Graphen und Tabellen in der Regel besser geeignet. Da Formulare immer nur die Sicht auf ein singuläres Objekt erlauben, sollten sie nur zur Angabe objektlokaler Informationen eingesetzt werden.

Setzt man die graphischen Repräsentationen zusammen mit ihren Manipulationsmöglichkeiten in der skizzierten Art voraus, ergibt sich folgendes Muster für den graphischen Wissenserwerb:
❶ Eingabe und Strukturierung der Terminologie des Anwendungsbereichs in Hierarchien oder Graphen, ❷ Hinzufügen lokaler Informationen und Eigenschaften zu den Begriffen in objektspezifi-schen Formularen, ❸ Angabe der Relationen und Inferenzen, die nicht durch die Taxonomie abgedeckt sind, in Tabellen und Graphen.

Das impliziert nicht, daß man zuerst alle Begriffe eingegeben haben *muß*, bevor man Beziehungs-wissen eingeben kann, da die Wissensbasis jederzeit inkrementell erweitert werden kann. Hierarchien und Graphen eignen sich am besten zur Eingabe der Begriffe, da neue Begriffe im Kontext der bestehen-den gesehen werden, aber gleichzeitig nicht zu viele zusätzliche Angaben verlangt sind, wie bei Formu-laren oder Tabellen. Vor Eingabe des Beziehungswissens sind die Objekte bekannt und brauchen nur durch Auswählen in den graphischen Hierarchien oder Graphen in die Zeilen- und Spaltenbeschriftungen von Tabellen eingesetzt und deren Beziehungen durch Ausfüllen der Tabellenfelder etabliert werden.

4 Beispiel eines graphischen Wissensakquisitionssystems auf der Basis der generischen Graphikrepräsentationen

CLASSIKA [D3 91] und COKE [Poeck 91] sind Beispiele von Wissensakquisitionssystemen, die auf der Basis der vorgestellten generischen Graphikprimitive entwickelt wurden. Da diese nicht für Wissens-akquisitionssysteme spezifisch sind, konnten wir sie auch in anderen Benutzeroberflächen einsetzen,

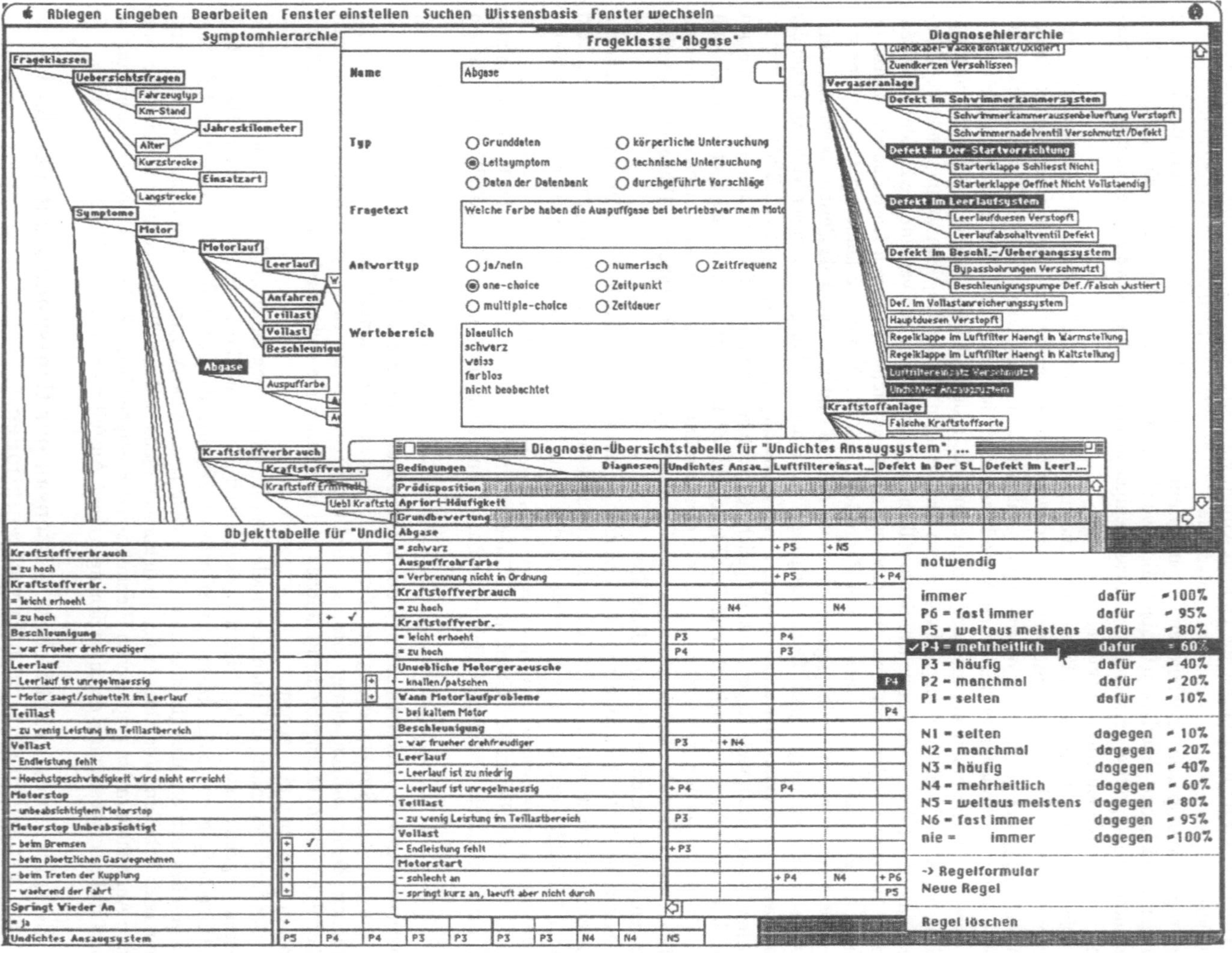

Objekttabelle für "Undic									
Kraftstoffverbrauch									
= zu hoch									
Kraftstoffverbr.									
= leicht erhoeht									
= zu hoch	+	√							
Beschleunigung									
- war frueher drehfreudiger									
Leerlauf									
- Leerlauf ist unregelmaessig	+								
- Motor saegt/schuettelt im Leerlauf	+								
Teillast									
- zu wenig Leistung im Teillastbereich									
Vollast									
- Endleistung fehlt									
- Hoechstgeschwindigkeit wird nicht erreicht									
Motorstop									
- unbeabsichtigtem Motorstop									
Motorstop Unbeabsichtigt									
- beim Bremsen	+	√							
- beim ploetzlichen Gaswegnehmen	+								
- beim Treten der Kupplung	+								
- waehrend der Fahrt	+								
Springt Wieder An									
= ja	+								
Undichtes Ansaugsystem	P5	P4	P4	P3	P3	P3	P3	N4	N4	NS

Abb. 3 Graphische Wissensrepräsentationen in CLASSIKA

z.B. für ein Tutorsystem, das die Problemlösungsfähigkeit mit CLASSIKA erstellter Expertensysteme ausnutzt.

Der Einsatzbereich von CLASSIKA ist die heuristische und seit neuestem auch fallvergleichende Diagnostik (Klassifikation), bei der die Diagnosen (Lösungen) aufgrund von Symptomen (Merkmalen) ausgewählt werden. Der Aufbau der Wissensbasis folgt dem oben dargestellten Vorgehensmuster für den graphischen Wissenserwerb.

Die wichtigsten dabei verwendeten graphischen Wissensrepräsentationen (vgl. Abb. 3) stehen für folgendes Wissensmodell (Semantik). Die in der Diagnosehierarchie im oberen rechten Fenster angegebenen Diagnosen sind die möglichen Lösungen des Expertensystems. Demgegenüber werden die Eingabedaten für das Expertensystem in Fragebögen zusammengefaßt und in der Symptomhierarchie repräsentiert. Fragebögen, wie z.B. "Übersichtsfragen" sind aus Standardfragen und eventuell Folgefragen und hergeleiteten Symptomabstraktionen, wie im Beispiel "Jahreskilometer" aufgebaut, deren Vorbedingung bzw. Art der Herleitung durch Doppelklick auf die Hierarchielinie präzisiert werden kann. Zu allen Objekten kann man ein Objektformular öffnen, um die objektlokalen Informationen, wie Fragetext, Antworttyp und Wertebereich anzugeben. Der Bildschirmauszug zeigt das Objektformular zum Fragebogen "Abgase". Das eigentliche heuristische Beziehungswissen zwischen Symptomen und Diagnosen wird in Regeltabellen angegeben, wobei entweder eine Übersichtstabelle zum direkten Vergleich mehrerer Objekte benutzt werden kann oder eine Objekttabelle, die sich auf Herleitung nur eines einzigen Objektes konzentriert, dafür aber eine detailliertere Darstellung komplexerer Regelbedingungen zuläßt. Außer den Tabellen zur Herleitung von Diagnosen sind analoge Tabellen zur Herleitung von Symptomabstraktionen, von Vorschlägen, zur Plausibilitätskontrolle sowie zur Dialogsteuerung verfügbar. Letztere ist aus verschiedenen Tabellenabschnitten zusammengesetzt und erlaubt die Spezifikation einer Kosten/Nutzen-Analyse zur Auswahl der optimalen nächsten Frageklasse.

Neben der allgemeinen Wiederverwendbarkeit besteht der Vorteil der Graphikbibliothek für CLASSIKA vor allem in einer aufgrund der Modularisierung besseren Wartbarkeit sowie in einer größeren Einheitlichkeit für den Endbenutzer, da alle Tabellen, Hierarchien, Formulare etc. gleichartig aufgebaut sind. Diese Aspekte sind bei großen Programmen – CLASSIKA besteht derzeit aus ca. 1,5 MB kompiliertem LISP-Code – mit verteilter Programmierung von nicht zu unterschätzendem Nutzen.

5 Diskussion

Das Erstellen leistungsfähiger graphischer Wissensakquisitionssysteme ist mit enormem Zeitaufwand verbunden, obwohl die auf den verschiedenen Plattformen verfügbaren Werkzeuge zur Erstellung graphischer Benutzeroberflächen, wie z.B. Macintosh User-Interface, OSF-MOTIF auf Unix, Presentation Manager auf IBM OS/2, Microsoft Windows auf IBM-AT und CLIM in letzter Zeit erheblich mächtiger geworden sind. Um den Zeitaufwand für graphische Wissensakquisitionssysteme zu reduzieren, haben wir verschiedene graphische Grundtypen identifiziert und als wiederverwendbare generische Graphikprimitive implementiert. Da sie nicht auf die Anwendung in Wissensakquisitionssystemen beschränkt sind, sind sie mit den oben genannten allgemeinen Graphikwerkzeugen vergleichbar, haben jedoch eine höhere Abstraktionsebene.

Der Vorteil für die Realisierung graphischer Wissensakquisitionssysteme besteht darin, daß die Hauptfenster zur Wissenseingabe und -manipulation vorgegeben sind und nur noch durch Instantiierung der Parameter auf das jeweilige Wissensmodell ausgelegt werden brauchen. Dadurch kann der Implementierungsaufwand für graphische Wissenserwerbsoberflächen auf die wirklichen Applikationsspezifika reduziert werden. Es gibt jedoch immer auch sinnvolle spezielle Graphikrepräsentationen, wie z.B. die graphische Flußdiagrammsprache in OPAL, die mit ihrer Umrandungsmöglichkeit zur Zusammenfassung mehrerer Knoten des Graphen zur Repräsentation von Iterationen und Parallelausführungen und deren Beschriftung über die derzeitige Parameterspezifikation der von uns spezifizierten generischen Graphikprimitive hinausgehen.

Die Voraussetzung für graphische Wissensakquisitionssysteme ist die Verwendung einer auf die Anwendungsaufgabe zugeschnittenen Problemlösungsmethode, um durch geeignete graphische Wissensrepräsentationen eine modellbasierte Wissensakquisition unterstützen zu können. Graphische Wissensakquisitionssysteme erfordern eine zu den graphischen Wissensrepräsentationen zugehörige interne Wissensrepräsentation, aus der sie wiederum die Graphik aufbauen können. Einige Systeme wie beispielsweise OPAL, AQUINAS, KSSO mußten dafür eine eigene Zwischenrepräsentation einführen, die in eine andere Wissensrepräsentation „herunterkompiliert" werden muß, um sie durch den Problemlöser interpretieren zu lassen. Dies ist dann problematisch, wenn die Problemlösung nicht mehr mit den gleichen Begriffen und auf der gleichen Ebene wie das für die Wissensakquisition benutzte Wissensmodell Erklärungen liefern kann, wie das z.B. in den Systemen AQUINAS und KSSO passiert. Demgegenüber verwenden TDE/TEST und CLASSIKA nur eine einzige interne Wissensrepräsentation, die direkt vom Problemlöser interpretiert wird. Es findet keine Übersetzung in ein anderes Wissensmodell statt und das eingegebene Wissen kann sofort getestet, geändert und wieder getestet werden.

Eine der Perspektiven, die wir mit der Verfügbarkeit solcher generischen Graphikrepräsentationen sehen, ist, daß die Zeit eines Zyklus vom Vorschlagen eines Wissensmodelles für ein Expertensystem zu dessen Evaluierung sich entscheidend verkürzt, da graphische Wissensrepräsentationen viel schneller erzeugt und das Wissensmodell sodann durch die Bereichsexperten selbst evaluiert werden kann.

Danksagung

Ich bedanke mich bei Frank Puppe, Klaus Goos und insbesondere Karsten Poeck für die hilfreichen Kommentare zu einer vorherigen Version des Papiers. Mein Dank gilt auch allen Studenten, in erster Linie Andrea Bernhard, Wolfgang Eger, Matthias Nolle, Frank Rieg und Karin Zipf, die an der Implementierung der Graphikwerkzeuge und ihrer Anwendungen mitgewirkt haben.

Literatur

[Boose et Bradshaw 87] J. H. Boose, J. M. Bradshaw: *Expertise transfer and complex domains: using AQUINAS as a knowledge acquisition workbench for knowledge-based systems*; International Journal of Man-Machine Studies, Vol. 26, 1987

[D3 91] S. Bamberger, U. Gappa, K. Goos, A. Meinl, K. Poeck, F. Puppe: *Die Diagnostik-Expertensystem-Shell D3*; Handbuch, Version 1.0, Universität Karlsruhe, 1991

[Eshelman 88] L. Eshelman: *MOLE: A knowledge acquisition tool for cover-and-differentiate systems*; in: S. Marcus (ed.): Automating Knowledge Acquisition for Expert Systems, pp. 37-80, Kluwer Academic Publishers, 1988

[ESS 88] *Two problem-specific tools for diagnosis*, Expert System Strategies 4, No. 12, 7-12, 1988

[Gappa 89] U. Gappa: *CLASSIKA: A knowledge acquisition tool for use by experts*; Proceedings of the AAAI-Workshop on Knowledge Acquisition, Banff, Kanada, 1989

[Gappa 91] U. Gappa: *A toolbox for generating graphical knowledge acquisition environments*, zur Veröffentlichung eingereicht.

[Gruber 89] T. Gruber: *The Acquisition of Strategic Knowledge*, Academic Press, 1989.

[Kahn et al. 87] G. Kahn, E. Breaux, P. DeKlerk, R. Joseph: *A mixed-initiative workbench for knowledge aquisition*; International Journal of Man-Machine Studies, Vol 27, 1987

[Kahn 88] G. Kahn: *MORE: From observing knowledge engineers to automating knowledge acquisition*, in: S. Marcus (ed.): Automating Knowledge Acquisition for Expert Systems, pp. 7-35, Kluwer Academic Publishers, 1988

[Marcus 88] S. Marcus (ed.): Automating Knowledge Acquisition for Expert Systems, Kluwer Academic Publishers, 1988. S. Marcus: *SALT: A knowledge acquisition tool for propose-and-revise systems*, pp. 81-123

[Musen et al. 87] M. Musen, L. Fagan, D. Combs, E. Shortliffe: *Use of a domain model to drive an interactive knowledge-editing tool*; International Journal of Man-Machine Studies, Vol. 26, 1987

[Musen 89a] M. Musen: *An editor for the conceptual models of interactive knowledge-acquisition tools*, International Journal of Man-Machine Studies, Vol. 31, 673-698, 1989

[Musen 89b] M. Musen: *Automated Generation of Model-Based Knowledge Acquisition Tools*, Morgan Kaufmann Publishers, Pitman, London, 1989

[Poeck 91] K. Poeck: *COKE: An expert system shell for assignment problems*; Beiträge zum 5. Workshop "Planen und Konfigurieren", LKI-M-1/91, Universität Hamburg, 1991

[Puppe 87] F. Puppe: *Diagnostisches Problemlösen mit Expertensystemen*, Springer, 1990

[Puppe 90] F. Puppe: *Problemlösungsmethoden in Expertensystemen*, Springer, 1990

[Shaw et Gaines 87] M. L. G. Shaw, B. R. Gaines: *KITTEN: Knowledge initiation and transfer tools for experts and novices*; International Journal of Man-Machine Studies, Vol. 27, 1987

B. Petkoff, D. Kraus
Research Group Expert Systems, CT Biomed,
Center for Technology Transfer Biomedicine
Brahmsstr. 2, D-4970 Bad Oeynhausen

Abstract

The problematic aspects of knowledge acquisition, representation and maintenance, the development of modular, extendable, flexible, reflective and explainable systems can only be addressed with reasonable hope of success if an appropriate conceptual structure of the system has been attained. The ACCORD-methodology provides an interpretation framework for the mapping of domain facts - constituting the world model of the expert - onto conceptual models which can be expressed in formal representations. The MACCORD framework allows a stepwise and inarbitrary reconstruction of the problem solving competence of medical experts as a prerequisite for an appropriate architecture of both medical knowledge bases and the "reasoning device". ACCORD thus shows a way to bridge the large conceptual gap between the mental models of human experts and formal representations in programming languages or shell systems.

1. The need for a methodology of problem solving

Over the past fifteen years a great deal of research has been directed towards the development of knowledge based systems (*expert systems* resp. *xps*) for problem solving in complex domains. Several research groups have tried to formulate practical advice in "standard" textbooks and/or more advanced conceptualisations: generic task concept [Chandrasekaran 83], KADS methodology [Breuker 87] etc., but there is still no means for bridging the large conceptual gap between domain concepts and representational formalisms, which renders knowledge engineering an art rather than a science.

There are many reasons for the knowledge acquisition bottleneck:

(1) **interpretation problem** - knowledge engineers are unable to understand the world model of the experts;

(2) **representation problem** - experts are unable to understand the representation language of the knowledge engineers;

(3) **conceptualisation problem** - experts and knowledge engineers have different approaches to problem solving;

We claim that the *ACCORD (Acquisition Cooperative Cognitive Organized Reasoning Device) conceptual models* offer a methodological framework for interpreting unstructured data allowing the choice of appropriate formal representation by reconstructing the expert´s knowledge [Petkoff 83-88]:

• as a prescriptive tool it emphasizes the dynamic properties of the knowledge acquisition process, governed by the logic and methods within certain medical domains, and offers epistemologically motivated structuring and processing principles.

• as a descriptive tool it allows the meaningful reconstruction and correlation of different medical domains or different medical tasks like diagnosis & therapy in *expert systems* - and is a basis for the development of comprehensive classification schemes.

In the case of a medical domain this modelling requires an in depth epistemological analysis of the medical reasoning process which is not supported by any common approach. This analysis has to include the identification, formalization and represention of the relevant concepts, notions and phenomena of the domain and their interrelations. These models of expertise have to comprise knowledge of various categories and at different levels of abstraction, according to the cognitively and epistemologically different problem solving activities, in order to enable effective communication between medical experts and knowledge engineers during the knowledge acquisition process.

2. Theoretical foundations of ACCORD

The ACCORD-metamodel has two major sources: the Experiential Learning Modell (ELM) - developed by Lewin, Lippitt and White (1939), elaborated by Kolb and Fry [Kolb et al, 75] and the epistemological studies of the structuralist philosophers [Sneed 71] and [Balzer et al, 87]. Through the integration of both views a conceptual framework is yielded which allows a dynamic description of individual or collective learning & problem solving processes. Under the assumption that what a human problem solver is doing when confronted with a problematic situation can be interpreted as *learning*, this framework can be used as an epistemological structure for knowledge based systems.

2.1 Experiential Learning Model (fig. 1)

The basic idea of the ELM is fairly self evident, namely that learning and problem solving, i.e. the accumulation and modification of knowledge, is best facilitated by a process consisting of four phases:
(1) here-and-now experience
(2) the collection of data and observations about that experience
(3) the analysis and formations of abstract concepts, with the conclusions of this analysis
(4) used for modification of behavior and choice of new experiences
Learning and problem solving is basically a cyclic process ridden with tension and conflict.

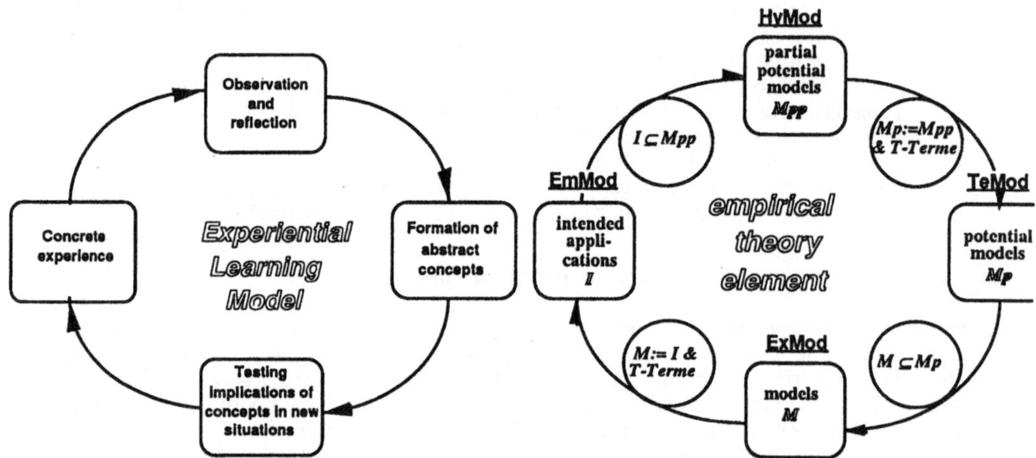

fig. 1: the four phases of the experiential learning model   fig. 2: the four items of an empirical theory

2.2 Structuralist approach to empirical theories (fig. 2)

The structuralists, especially Sneed, Balzer, Moulines and Stegmüller, have developed a form for describing empirical theories, which can be modified and simplified in order to be made applicable to "medical" theories [Balzer et al, 87]. According to the structuralist point of view, one can attempt to answer the question "what is an empirical theory?" by reconstructing the way in which theories are actually established. Roughly speaking, this is done using a framework analogous to that of the ELM.

• Some concrete phenomena I - *intended applications* (CE: concrete experience in ELM) - become of vital interest to scientists, i.e. experts. The latter want to 'explain' or 'understand' these phenomena. First they try to discover some features common to all *intended applications* in order to have a general frame excluding other phenomena they are not interested in .

• These common features describe a class of phenomena called M_{pp}- *partial potential models* (RO: reflective observation in ELM). In order to explore the field of *partial potential models* they try to find similarities and dissimilarities between them. On the one hand they try to classify the *partial potential models* according to some standards of similarity. This procedure amounts to establishing several similarity classes.

• On the other hand they try to find structures 'intrinsic' to the *partial potential models*. The second procedure amounts to finding 'theoretical' terms, which when added to the *partial potential models* yield new structures for which laws or axioms can be formulated. *Partial potential models* supplemented by theoretical terms are called M_p- *potential models* (AC: Abstract Conceptualisation in ELM).

• Potential models which also satisfy the special axioms peculiar to the class of phenomena considered are called M- *models* (AE: Active Experimentation in ELM).

According to Sneed, the main use of an established empirical theory (from which other applications may be derived) is to formulate an empirical claim. This is a sentence which is claimed to be true and which expresses what the empirical theory says about its range of intended applications. Empirical theories in this sense are formal representations of intellectual structures, i.e. expert knowledge.

Theory elements are the intellectual focus of the social activity of expert problem solving. Expert communities may be organized around theory elements and/or collections of closely linked, "neighbouring" theory elements - "empirical theories" in the larger sense of the word.

3. Maccord: methodology for medical knowledge based systems

The ELM and the results of the structuralists make similar propositions about the nature of learning and problem solving. An essential common ground of these approaches is the circular nature of the problem solving process which is illustrated by the hypothetico-deductive cycle (fig 3)

ACCORD now tries to integrate both approaches into what can be called a "methodology of knowledge based systems" [Petkoff 83-88]. Developing a medical knowledge based system using the ACCORD-model means: reconstructing the problem solving behavior of the medical expert in terms of empirical, hypothetical, theoretical or experimental models at various levels of abstraction, and the transitions between these.

The very nature of medicine makes it extremely hard merely to *represent* the knowledge categories of medical reasoning appropriately. Consider for example the following (partial) transcript of a cardiological consultation:

the patient suffers from chest pain - being asked, she gives more detailed information concerning location, quality and duration of the pain - in the current context (sex, age, high-risk factors) degenerative heart diseases are the most frequent cause of such pains - the hypothesis "degenerative coronary disease" induces asking about the trigger of the pain - the (unexpected) answer that the pain occurs at rest causes a change of hypothesis: an oesophageal disease (sliding hernia) becomes probable - again this hypothesis is rejected because the pain occurs in sitting position (which is very untypical), and the previous hypothesis ("degenerative coronary disease") is reactivated - this disease leads to a low supply of oxygen to the heart muscle - this can be proved by several techniques - one of these, a special form of ECG, is performed since it is the least uncomfortable and relatively specific-...

Several areas of medical knowledge are touched upon here: clinical knowledge, nosology, epidemiology, etiology; pathophysiology, anatomy and knowledge about testing procedures (specifity and sensitivity, invasiveness, etc.).

As one tries to apply the evolving concepts to a domain as complex as medicine one inevitably becomes confronted with the notion of conceptual levels. One reason for these is often "meta"-considerations or "meta"-decisions are often involved. For instance, compared to the decision in favour of a certain form of therapy, the decision to treat the patient at all is a metadecision. Another argument for conceptual levels is the idea that when reasoning reaches an impassè this has to be resolved at a somewhat "higher" level.

Furthermore, problem solving activities under different circumstances (scarce resources, time constraints, limited availability of data) tend to utilize knowledge located on levels that vary according to categories such as "heuristic vs. deterministic", "causal vs. associative" or "shallow vs. deep models".

All levels (strategic, tactical, operative) have the form of hypothetico-deductive cycles, extended by backward leading transitions and are linked via (empirical, hypothetical, theoretical, experimental) columns (fig 4).

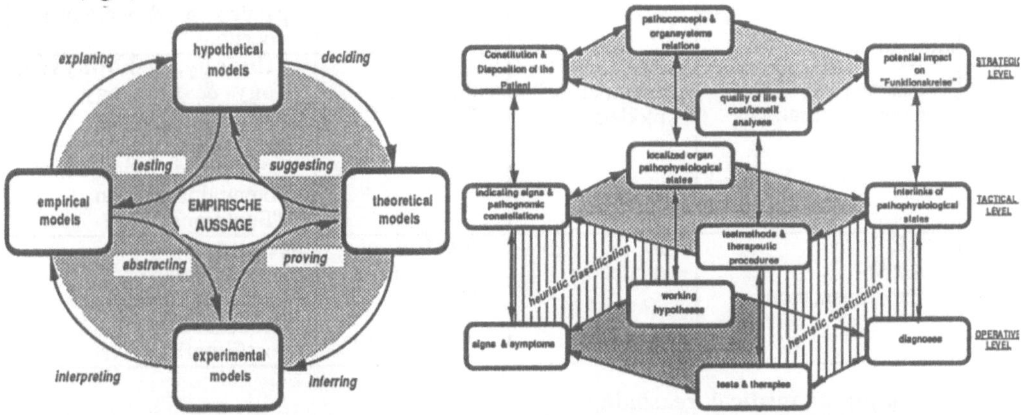

<table>
<tr><td>fig. 3: the hypothetico-deductive cycle
in the 2-D ACCORD model</td><td>fig. 4 : the structure of diagnostic-therapeutical
reasoning in the 3-D ACCORD model</td></tr>
</table>

The highest **strategical level** deals with knowledge of the environment in which problem solving takes place. With regard to medicine this may be the constitutional or situative factors of the patient (expositions, psychic and social situation), seasonal or epidemiological circumstances and the like, moreover the "never changing" anatomical and etiological categories, but also the ("meta-") criteria for the evaluation of procedural methods (specifity, sensitivity, invasiveness, risk...) and the patient´s health status (comfort, abilities, development potential).

The knowledge provided by medical *specialties* is mainly found at the **tactical level**: pathognomonic constellations of findings and principal signs, specific knowledge concerning the etiological nature of disorders at various anatomical sites, detailed pathophysiological knowledge (...).

Knowledge organized at the lowest, the **operative level** is most concrete: the raw, uninterpreted observations, specific hypotheses as well as diagnoses or particular tests and therapies are found at the operative level.

Similar to the intuitive notion of **levels** /consisting of frames and rule-sets/, one may circumscribe the meaning of the **columns** that develop from the "poles" of the circle by juxtaposing several levels:

The **empirical column** simply contains /as classes and objects/ everything that is observable: concrete signs and symptoms as well as abstract historical facts or epidemiological constellations.

The **hypothetical column** is the location of structures /as classes and objects/ which can be *assumed* on the basis of observations. Such assumptions may concern anatomical localizations of varying precision (such as *hepatobiliary system* and *ductus choledochus*) or etiological classes (such as *infectious disease* and *inborn metabolic disturbance*).

Theoretical concepts can be found /in the net of interlinked classes and objects/ in the **theoretical column**. In clinical medicine, what we mean by theoretical concepts are mainly physiological or pathophysiological notions describing functional properties of the human body.

The **experimental column** contains the elements /objects and methods/ which render medicine as an actional science oriented towards influencing the signs & symptoms of the patient. These are tests & therapies, procedural classes (such as *substitution, provocation, determination*) that are subject to "meta"-criteria such as *sensitivity, specifity, invasiveness* and the like.

It should be clear that *heuristic classification* and *heuristic construction* [Boose H.89] can be localized as vertical planes in the Maccord framework .The concepts of ELM, the structuralists´view (STR), ACCORD and its interpretation within medicine Maccord can also easily be compared:

ELM	STR	ACCORD	Maccord
CE Concrete Experience	**I** intended applications	**EmMod** empirical O-/T-/S- models	**observable data & facts** • signs & symptoms • syndromes • situative context

RO
Reflective
Observation
	$\mathbf{M_{pp}}$
	partial
	potential
	models
		HyMod
		hypothetical
		O-/T-/S-
		models
			etiology & anatomy
			• working hypotheses
			• localized pathological
			  states
			• pathic states & anatomical
			  locations

AC
Abstract
Conceptualisation
	$\mathbf{M_p}$
	potential
	models
		TeMod
		theoretical
		O-/T-/S-
		models
			pathology,pathophysio-
			logy & nosology
			• tentative diagnoses
			• interinks of
			  pathophysiological states
			• potential impact on
			  "Funktionskreise"

AE Active Experimentation	**M** models	**ExMod** experimental O-/T-/S- models	**actions** • tests & therapies • testing & therapeutic procedures • cost/benefit analyses

4. Example of medical reasoning

These concepts are easier to comprehend when applied to the field of medicine, i.e what can be considered as medical theory and how medical theories are applied in order to make diagnoses.The above example of a cardiological consultation can be described in full detail using the terminology of this methodological structure (note that medical concepts appear <u>underlined</u>, instances of these in *italics* and the transitions in **bold** face):

The patient exhibits the <u>signs</u> of *pain* in the *chest region,* which can be subsumed under the <u>principal sign</u> *thoracodynia*. For a <u>sign</u> to be *thoracodynia* it has to have a specific location, quality and duration. The _principal sign_ at hand has to be evaluated in the individual (_sex, age, exposition, risk factors_) and situative (_seasonal, epidemiological_) context. One has to adopt for the time being an hypothesis about what may have caused the pain. This may be selected from the following classes: _cardial, oesophageal, vertebragene, pleural_ (...) causes. This selection can only be made with consideration to various pathogenetic modes (e.g. _degenerative, inflammatory, neoplastic_ ...), from which, in turn, one has to be provisionally adopted with respect to the context (as, for example, infants are unlikely to suffer from degenerative diseases). In the current case of a, say, 55 year old woman, who smokes heavily, the pathoconcept _degenerative_ is chosen, which induces the location _cardial site_ to be the suspected "locus morborum" (since the most frequent degenerative diseases which cause thoracal pain are cardial); the most probable instance under these circumstances is _degenerative coronary disease_, which is now established as a working hypothesis. This working hypothesis can be validated or disproved by employing the knowledge of the obligatory and facultative signs it produces; it is in this case (amongst other things) likely that the _pains are triggered by stress_. The unexpected answer that the _pain occurs at rest_ gives rise to the new principal sign _thoracal rest pain_. The previous assumption about the localisation is discarded and replaced by "_oesophageal_"; the new working hypothesis is "_sliding hernia_". Disproving this by the observation that the _pain occurs in sitting position_ leads to the reactivation of the old hypothesis _degenerative coronary disease_. This disease leads to a low supply of oxygen to the heart muscle, causing the pathophysiological state "_cardial hypoxia_". There are several testing procedures for _cardial hypoxia_ including _provocative tests_ and _image producing procedures_. In order to decide which procedure to apply in the given situation one has to engage medical test theory (_sensitivity, specifity_ of tests) and other test attributes such as _risk, invasiveness, side effects_. In the example the _exercise electrocardiogram_ is performed, since it is able to combine well high specifity of the result and low discomfort for the patient...

It should then be possible to say that **Maccord** _shows a way to the rational and comprehensible restructuring of medical knowledge_, i.e. **domain knowledge** (concepts and relations of the universe of discourse) and the **problem solving knowledge** (acting in specific situations of interest), than _the entire diversity of medical reasoning can be described adequately in a formal terminology_ derived from epistemology and cognitive science regardless of the medical application..

5. Conclusion

To summarize, the ACCORD-methodology stands as an interpretation framework for the mapping of domain struktures onto conceptual models which can be expressed in formal representations, and which are thus a step nearer to implementational constructs.

The use of rigorous mathematical and logical methods in this framework can produce important theoretical and practical results. This is because the distributed knowledge base of ACCORD takes into consideration the complex character of the cognition process as a multi-level phenomenon and tries to satisfy the requirements of the formal reconstruction of intelligent behavior with an arhitecture facilitating Computer Supported Cooperative Work. The structure for knowledge bases provided by the general ACCORD - framework may play a very important heuristic role for the Hypermedia Human Computer Interaction by the knowledge acquisition, storage and utilization process. Moreover existing programming tools such as KEE, KAPPA, BABYLON, etc. support efficiently the ACCORD paradigm for problem solving and can be adopted in order to build "second generation" expert systems.

References:

Balzer W., Moulines C.U. Sneed J.D. (1987) An Architectonic for Science - The Structuralist Program, D.Reidel Publishing Company
Boose H.,(1989) A Survey of Knowledge Acqusition Techniques and Tools, Knowledge Acqusition Vol 1, Nr. 1 , Academic Press
Breuker J. et al (1987) Model-Driven Knowledge Acquisition: Interpretation Models Esprit Project 1098, Memo 87, University of Amsterdam, The Netherlands
Bylander, T.; Chandrasekaran, B.(1987): Generic Tasks for Knowledge-Based Reasoning: The "Right" Level of Abstraction for Knowledge Acquisition., Int. Journal of Man-Machine Studies 26
Kolb D. A., Fry R.(1975): Towards an Applied Theory of Experiential Learning, in: Cooper C. (ed): Theories of group processes, New York
Petkoff B. (1983) Kybernetisches Modell der wissenschaftlichen Forschung. 7th Int. Cong. "Logic, Methodology and Philosophy of Science", Salzburg.
Petkoff B. (1985) Artificial Intelligence and Computer Simulation of Scientific Discovery. Artificial Intelligence - Methodology, Systems, Applications, Proc. AIMSA 84 , North-Holland, Amsterdam.
Petkoff B. (1988) ACCORD - a metamodel for II. generation expert systems Artificial Intelligence - Methodology, Systems, Applications, Proc. AIMSA 88, North-Holland, Amsterdam
Sneed, D.(1971) The Logical Structure of Mathematical Physics

7. AUTOMATISCHES PROGRAMMIEREN

Constructing Programs From Input-Output Pairs[*]

Kurt Ammon[†]
Universität Hamburg
Windmühlenweg 27
D-2000 Hamburg 52

Abstract

This paper introduces a learning procedure which constructs programs from input-output pairs. The programs are represented in a declarative language including universal propositions and set constructors. The input of the procedure contains simple axioms giving the domains and ranges of elementary functions and predicates which form the building blocks of the programs in its output. The application of the axioms yields compositions of the elementary functions and predicates. Special operators use these compositions to form universal propositions, set constructors, and programs. The procedure is controlled by syntactic and semantic constraints for the propositions, set constructors, and programs, by data such as the input-output pairs, and by partial programs previously produced.

1 Introduction

An approach to automatic programming is the construction of programs from input-output pairs. Examples of input-output pairs for a program producing the maximum of a finite set of natural numbers are $(\{1,2\},2)$ and $(\{2,3\},3)$. They say that the maximum of the set $\{1,2\}$ is 2 and the maximum of $\{2,3\}$ is 3. Section 3 describes a learning procedure that constructs programs from input-output pairs. These programs are represented in a declarative language which is introduced in Section 2. The procedure is illustrated by a detailed description of the construction of a maximum program from the input-output pairs given above.

2 Language

Programs are represented in the functional language CL. They contain universal propositions and set constructors whose variables refer to finite sets.

Let S be a finite set and P be a computable predicate defined on S. A universal proposition $\forall x(x \in S \rightarrow P(x))$, which says that $P(x)$ holds for all $x \in S$, is evaluated by successively substituting each element of S for the variable x in $P(x)$ and evaluating the resulting propositions. If all propositions yield true, the universal proposition is true. Otherwise, it is false. A set constructor $\{x : x \in S \wedge P(x)\}$ is also evaluated by successively substituting each element of S for the variable x in $P(x)$ and evaluating the resulting propositions. The set of elements $x \in S$ for which $P(x)$ holds is the set represented by the set constructor.

[*] This work, in whole or in part, describes components of machines or processes protected by one or more patents or patent applications in Europe, the United States of America, or elsewhere. Further information is available from the author.

[†] This work was supported in part by the German Science Foundation (DFG).

A program can be regarded as a binary relation $R(x,y)$ that uniquely determines an output y for every input x, i.e., for every x, there is a unique y such that $R(x,y)$ holds. Such relations can be used to represent programs of the form

$$f : x \mapsto y \tag{1}$$
$$y \in S \wedge R(x,y), \tag{2}$$

where f is the name of the program and S is the set of output data. The left side of the barred arrow in (1) gives the variable x denoting an input of the program and its right side the variable y denoting an output. The variables x and y occur free in the proposition $y \in S \wedge R(x,y)$ in (2). The output $y \in S$ of an input x is computed by evaluating $R(x,y)$ for x and each $y \in S$. The first $y \in S$ that yields true is the output of the input x. An example of a such program in CL is the program

$$maximum : S \mapsto m$$
$$m \in S \wedge \forall n(n \in S \rightarrow n \leq m), \tag{3}$$

which computes the maximum of a finite set S of natural numbers. According to the procedure for evaluating universal propositions, the universal proposition $\forall n(n \in S \rightarrow n \leq m)$ in (3) is evaluated for each element $m \in S$. The first $m \in S$ for which this universal proposition yields true is the maximum of the set S. For example, the application of the *maximum* program to the set $\{1,2\}$ yields 2. Another example of a program in CL is the finding program

$$find : (i, S) \mapsto m$$
$$m \in S \wedge |\{n : n \in S \wedge n \leq m\}| = i, \tag{4}$$

where S is a finite set of natural numbers, i is a number that is less than or equal to the number of elements of S, and $|\{n : ...\}|$ is the number of elements of the set $\{n : ...\}$. This program finds the ith smallest element of S. For example, the value of $find(2, \{1,3,4\})$ is 3.

3 Learning Procedure

The learning procedure constructs programs in the language CL from input-output pairs and axioms giving the domain and ranges of elementary functions and predicates. The programs in its output are composed of the elementary functions and predicates. This section describes a simple specific embodiment of the procedure. The next section discusses its general mode of operation.

Let $E = \{(x_1, y_1), (x_2, y_2), ..., (x_n, y_n)\}$, where n is a natural number, be a set of input-output pairs. A relation $R(x,y)$ is called *consistent* with E if $R(x_i, y_i)$ holds for all $i \in \{1, 2, ..., n\}$. The learning procedure produces a relation $R(x,y)$ which is consistent with a set E of input-output pairs and which uniquely determines an output y for every input x, i.e., for every input x, there is a unique y such that $R(x,y)$ holds. According to Section 2, such a relation $R(x,y)$ represents a program (1) and (2). Because $R(x,y)$ is consistent with E, this program produces the output y_i from every input x_i for all input-output pairs $(x_i, y_i) \in E$. The learning procedure constructs the relation $R(x,y)$ in four stages. The *first* stage *initializes* a proof by introducing variables. The *second* stage applies axioms giving the domains of predicates to the proof which yields *propositions* and tests whether the propositions only containing variables for inputs and outputs are consistent with the input-output pairs. The *third* stage generates *universal propositions* that are consistent with the input-output pairs from the propositions in the proof. The *fourth* stage constructs a relation representing a *program* from the propositions produced by the second and the third stage. The construction of the propositions and programs is controlled by the input-output pairs and syntactic and semantic constraints. The procedure is illustrated by a detailed description of the construction of a maximum program from the input-output pairs $E = \{(\{1,2\}, 2), (\{2,3\}, 3)\}$.

1.	$S \in power\text{-}set(N)$	variable S for an input
2.	$m \in N$	variable m for an output
3.	$n \in N$	additional variable n
4.	$is\text{-}a\text{-}proposition(m \in S)$	because of steps 1 and 2 and axiom (6)
5.	$is\text{-}a\text{-}proposition(n \in S)$	because of steps 1 and 3 and axiom (6)
6.	$is\text{-}a\text{-}proposition(m \leq n)$	because of steps 2 and 3 and axiom (7)
7.	$is\text{-}a\text{-}proposition(n \leq m)$	because of steps 3 and 2 and axiom (7)

Table 1: Proof for constructing propositions

The arguments of the learning procedure give a name for the program to be constructed and denotations for the set of its inputs and outputs. An example: Let N be the set $\{1, 2, 3\}$. The arguments

$$maximum : power\text{-}set(N) \rightarrow N \tag{5}$$

of the learning procedure say that it should construct a program whose name is *maximum*, whose input is an element of the power set of N, i.e., a subset of N, and whose output is an element of N. The procedure initializes a proof by introducing variables for an element of the set of inputs and an element of the set of outputs which yields the first two proof steps in Table 1. Furthermore, additional variables are introduced for an element of each set in the arguments of the procedure that is not denoted by a compound term. These variables are bound by quantifiers in the third stage of the procedure. Because N is a set in (5) that is not denoted by a compound term, a variable is introduced for an element of the set N which yields the third proof step in Table 1.

The second stage of the learning procedure applies axioms giving the domains of predicates to the proof which yields propositions. An example of an axiom is

$$\forall A, B, x \, (A \in power\text{-}set(B) \wedge x \in B \rightarrow is\text{-}a\text{-}proposition(x \in A)), \tag{6}$$

which says that if A is a subset of B and x is an element of B, the expression "$x \in A$" is a proposition. It introduces the element relation "$\in$". Another example of an axiom with regard to the set $N = \{1, 2, 3\}$ is

$$\forall x, y \, (x \in N \wedge y \in N \rightarrow is\text{-}a\text{-}proposition(x \leq y)), \tag{7}$$

which says that if x and y are elements of N, the expression "$x \leq y$" is a proposition. It introduces the inequality relation "$\leq$". The application of these axioms to the initial proof in Table 1 yields the fourth, fifth, sixth, and seventh proof step in Table 1. A semantic constraint is that propositions that only contain variables for inputs or outputs are not added to the proof because such propositions cannot be used to represent a program. For example, the application of axiom (7) to the second proof step yields the proposition "$m \leq m$" which is not added to the proof because it only contains the variable m for an output. If a proposition that only contains variables for inputs and outputs is added to the proof, the learning procedure tests whether such a proposition is consistent with the input-output pairs. In our example, the proposition "$m \in S$" in the fourth proof step in Table 1 only contains the variables S and m for an input and output. It is consistent with the input-output pairs E because $m \in S$ for $S = \{1, 2\}$ and $m = 2$ and for $S = \{2, 3\}$ and $m = 3$. Such consistent propositions are processed by the fourth stage of the learning procedure which produces programs.

Some of the propositions in the proof contain an additional variable, i.e., a variable which does not denote an input or an output. If such a proposition is added to the proof, a *universal operator* uses it to construct universal propositions that are consistent with the input-output pairs. It forms an implication whose consequent is such a proposition and whose antecedent is a proposition in a preceding proof step which also contains this additional variable. A syntactic constraint is that the two propositions together must contain variables for inputs and outputs. The universal operator binds the additional variable by a universal quantifier and tests whether the resulting proposition is consistent with the input-output pairs. If it is not consistent, another proposition from the proof is added to the antecedent of its implication and the test is repeated. If it is consistent with the input-output pairs, it is processed by the fourth stage of the learning procedure which produces programs. In our example, the proposition $"n \leq m"$ in the seventh proof step in Table 1 contains the additional variable n. Thus, it is used as a consequent. The propositions $"n \in S"$ and $"m \leq n"$ in the fifth and the sixth proof step also contain the additional variable n. Because the proposition $"m \leq n"$ and the consequent $"n \leq m"$ do not contain a variable for an input, $"m \leq n"$ is abandoned. The proposition $"n \in S"$ and the consequent $"n \leq m"$, which contain the variables S and m for an input and an output, are used to form the universal proposition $\forall n(n \in S \rightarrow n \leq m)$ which is consistent with the input-output pairs E.

The fourth stage of the learning procedure tests whether the propositions $R(x, y)$ from the second and the third stage, which are consistent with the input-output pairs, uniquely determine an output y for every input x, i.e., it tests whether for every input x, there is a unique output y such that $R(x, y)$ holds for all consistent propositions $R(x, y)$. If this is true, these consistent propositions represent a program which computes the output from the input of each input-output pair. Otherwise, the second and the third stage of the procedure produce further consistent propositions $R(x, y)$. In our example, the second and the third stage of the learning procedure produce the consistent propositions $m \in S$ and $\forall n(n \in S \rightarrow n \leq m)$. Therefore, the procedure tests whether for all inputs $S \in \textit{power-set}(N)$, there is a unique output $m \in N$ such that these two propositions hold. Because this is true, the procedure constructs the maximum program (3) which is represented by the conjunction of these two propositions. In a computer experiment, its construction from the set E of input-output pairs took some thirty seconds.

In another experiment, the learning procedure constructed an infimum program. Its input contained one axiom saying that $"xy \in I"$ is a proposition for all $x \in S$ and $y \in S$, where $S = \{a, b, c, d, e\}$ and $I = \{aa, ae, ba, bb, be, ca, cc, ce, da, db, dc, dd, de, ee\}$ is a binary relation on S.[1] The relation I defines a partial ordering of S (see Birkhoff and MacLane, 1953). For example, the elements of S may be interpreted as sets and the notation $"ae"$ in I may be read $"a$ includes $e"$. The input-output pairs were the set

$$E \;=\; \{(aa, a), (ab, a), (ac, a), (ad, a), (ae, a), (bb, b), (bc, a), (bd, b),$$
$$(be, e), (cc, c), (cd, c), (ce, e), (dd, d), (de, e), (ee, e)\}. \tag{8}$$

Thus, the task of the learning procedure was to develop a program that computed the right side z of any pair $(xy, z) \in E$ from its left side xy. It took some three minutes to construct the program

$$\textit{infimum} : xy \mapsto z$$
$$z \in S \wedge xz \in I \wedge yz \in I \wedge$$
$$\forall z'(z' \in S \wedge xz' \in I \wedge yz' \in I \rightarrow zz' \in I). \tag{9}$$

It says that the *infimum* of two elements $x \in S$ and $y \in S$ is an element $z \in S$ such that x and y include z and z inludes any z' that is included by x and y.

4 Discussion

Between 1962 and 1986, Amarel (1986) developed various approaches to the automatic construction of programs from input-output pairs. An automatic synthesis of an infimum program is out of reach because there are difficult open problems such as the "model-finding problem" (see Amarel, 1986,

---

[1]The inclusion relation I and the input-output pairs E in (8) were taken in part from Amarel (1986, p. 504).

pp. 503, 537, and 566–567). To my knowledge, this paper describes the first automatic synthesis of an infimum program from input-output pairs.

The axioms in Section 3, which are used to produce propositions, give the domains of predicates. The learning procedure also processes axioms giving the domains and ranges of functions. Thus, its second stage produces propositions that are composed of functions and predicates. Besides the universal operator in Section 3, it contains further operators such as a set operator which produces set constructors. The construction of the maximum program (3) and the infimum program (9) are simple applications of the learning procedure. In a more complex experiment, its application to a proof of the simple theorem that $(x^{-1})^{-1} = x$ holds for all elements of a group produced a theorem-proving program which was represented by two set constructors.[2] The automatic development of the program took some three hours. In an experiment, it generated proofs of nine further theorems in group theory such as $x^2 = 1$ implies group commutativity and a proof of SAM's Lemma without any human intervention. The theorem that $x^2 = 1$ implies group commutativity, is "the limit of the capability" of the heuristic theorem prover ADEPT developed at MIT in the mid-sixties (Loveland, 1984, p. 13). The Markgraf Karl Refutation Procedure is one of the largest software projects in the history of automatic theorem proving. After fifteen years of development, Ohlbach and Siekmann (1989, p. 58) give SAM's Lemma as the only "more difficult" theorem that their theorem prover has proved. ADEPT and the Markgraf Karl Refutation Procedure were developed manually. In contrast, the learning procedure automatically developed the "ideas" for the theorem prover on the basis of elementary knowledge, implemented them in a program in the language CL, and applied the resulting theorem prover to the new theorems without any human intervention.

5 Conclusion

We have described a learning procedure which constructs programs in the language CL from input-output pairs. Its input contains simple axioms giving the domains and ranges of elementary functions and predicates. The application of these axioms yields compositions of the functions and predicates. Special operators use these compositions to form universal propositions and set constructors which are composed of the elementary functions and predicates in the input. The programs in the output are represented by these propositions and set constructors. The generality and the power of the procedure were illustrated by experiments such as the construction of an infimum program and a powerful automatic theorem-proving program. These achievements are significantly beyond the capabilities of conventional systems for automatic programming.

References

Amarel, S. 1986. Program synthesis as a theory formation task: Problem representations and solution methods. In R. S. Michalski, J. G. Carbonell, and T. M. Mitchell (Eds.) *Machine Learning: An Artificial Intelligence Approach*, Vol. II, Morgan Kaufmann, Los Altos, California.

Ammon, K. 1988. The automatic acquisition of proof methods. *Proceedings of the Seventh National Conference on Artificial Intelligence*, August 21–26, St. Paul, Minnesota, pp. 558–563.

Birkhoff, G., and MacLane, S. 1953. *A Survey of Modern Algebra*. New York: Macmillan.

Loveland, D. W. 1984. Automated theorem proving: a quarter century review. In W. W. Bledsoe and D. W. Loveland, *Automated Theorem Proving: After 25 Years*. Providence, R.I.: American Mathematical Society.

Ohlbach, H. J., and Siekmann, J. 1989. The Markgraf Karl Refutation Procedure. University of Kaiserslautern, Department of Computer Science, SEKI Report SR-89-19.

---

[2] Ammon (1988) describes an earlier comparable experiment which also produced a theorem-proving program from a simple proof in group theory.

8. KONNEKTIONISMUS

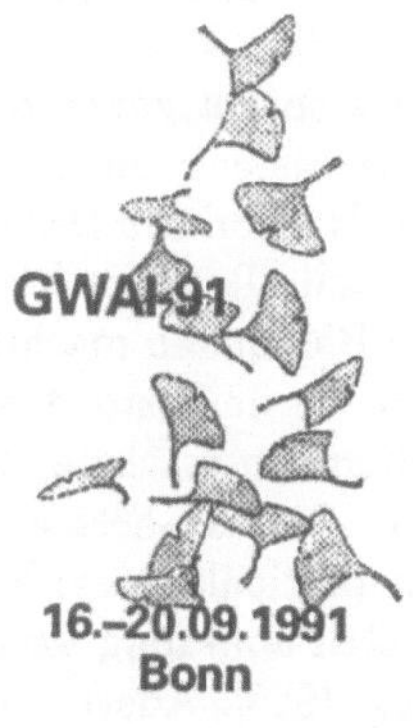

Transforming Constraint Relaxation Networks into Boltzmann Machines*

Joachim Hertzberg   *Hans Werner Guesgen*

German National Research Center for Computer Science (GMD)
Schloß Birlinghoven, D-5205 Sankt Augustin 1, F.R.G.

Abstract

We describe how to transform constraint networks—which may involve a particular form of constraint relaxation—into corresponding Boltzmann machines, thereby viewing constraint satisfaction as a problem of combinatorial optimization. We discuss feasibility and order preservingness of the consensus function used and give a necessary and sufficient condition for a locally optimal configuration to correspond to a solution of the constraint network.

1   Motivation

Solving constraint satisfaction problems (CSPs) has been approached from various directions. A straightforward technique is backtracking which tries to instantiate the variables of a given problem successively until a solution is found. In general, this is a desperate approach. So other techniques have been developed among which is Waltz filtering that not only improves backtracking significantly but also allows implementing constraint satisfaction techniques on parallel hardware easily. Kasif [1989], Rosenfeld [1975], and Samal & Henderson [1987] have introduced such parallel versions of filtering. Moreover, there are also massively parallel algorithms: AC Chip which can be implemented directly in VLSI and computes arc-consistent solutions to CSPs almost instantaneously, and ACP which has been designed for SIMD computers like the Connection Machine (see [Cooper and Swain, 1988] as reference for both algorithms). They are closely related to Mohr and Henderson's AC-4 algorithm [Mohr and Henderson, 1986], which is optimal for computing 2-consistency on single-processor machines.

However, filtering algorithms in general do not guarantee a solution of the CSP but result in some level of local consistency such as 2-consistency in the case of Mackworth's AC-x algorithms [1977] or 3-consistency in the case of Allen's algorithm [Allen, 1983]. An aim here is to present an approach that both actually solves CSPs and allows for being implemented on massively parallel hardware. The basis for this approach are Boltzmann machines.

Moreover, as Boltzmann machines can be understood as a technique for combinatorial optimization, transforming a CSP into a Boltzmann machine also shows an elegant way for handling constraint relaxation where one issue is to find the best among possibly many solutions. We are not aware of other work having gone this particular way; however, the work of Boltz and Wittur [1990] has influenced us. They use simulated annealing for solving CSPs, which is closely related to Boltzmann machines [Aarts and Korst, 1989]. Adorf and Johnston [1989; 1990] use a similar formulation of CSPs as Hopfield networks of which Boltzmann machines are an extension; their work does not, however, deal with relaxation.

---

*This work is partially funded by the German Federal Ministry for Research and Technology (BMFT) in the joint project TASSO under grant ITW8900A7. TASSO is also part of the GMD *Leitvorhaben* Assisting Computer (AC). Thanks to our colleagues Christoph Lischka and Gerd Paaß for comments on a draft of this paper.

In the following, we first sketch the technical background of this work: constraints and Boltzmann machines; then we present an example of how to transform a constraint network into a Boltzmann machine; after that, we introduce a special form of relaxation into constraint networks; subsequently, we formally define the transformation of constraint networks including relaxation into corresponding Boltzmann machines and state necessary and sufficient conditions for locally optimal configurations of the machines to correspond to solutions of the CSP; and finally, we summarize our findings.

2 Background: Constraints and Boltzmann Machines

In this section, we give a very brief introduction to the relevant notions from the areas of constraint satisfaction and Boltzmann machines. We refer to [Guesgen, 1989; Aarts and Korst, 1989] for more details. The reader who is fit in these areas may safely skip the respective subsections.

2.1 Constraints

A k-ary *constraint* C is a decidable relation over a domain $D_1 \times \cdots \times D_k$, where the places of the relation are represented by variables $V_1, \ldots, V_k$ with values from the domains $D_1, \ldots, D_k$, respectively. A member of the constraint relation is called a *relation element*. Different constraints are tied to *constraint networks* by sharing variables: A constraint network on variables $V_1, \ldots, V_m$ consists of constraints $C_1, \ldots, C_n$, the variables of each C_i being a subset of $V_1, \ldots, V_m$.

A *solution* of a constraint network consists of an assignment of single values—taken from their domains—to all variables of the network such that all constraints are satisfied; more exactly: A tuple $(d_1, \ldots, d_m)$ satisfies a constraint C_i if the subsequence of $(d_1, \ldots, d_m)$ that corresponds to the variables of C_i is a relation element of C_i. A solution of a constraint network that is given by constraints $C_1, \ldots, C_n$ on variables $V_1, \ldots, V_m$ over domains $D_1, \ldots, D_m$ is a tuple $(d_1, \ldots, d_m) \in D_1 \times \cdots \times D_m$ that satisfies the constraints.

The task of finding one, some, or every solution(s) of a constraint network is called *constraint satisfaction problem* (CSP); we sometimes use the terms constraint network and CSP interchangebly if this causes no confusion.

2.2 Boltzmann Machines

A Boltzmann machine[1] is a graph $B = (U, K)$, where U is the finite set of *units* and K is a set of unordered pairs of elements of U, the *connections*, each connection written as $\{u, v\}$, for $u, v \in U$. K includes all *bias connections*, i.e., connections connecting a unit with itself. In short: $\{\{u, u\} \mid u \in U\} \subset K$. The units are binary, i.e., they are either *on* or *off*, which is represented as 1 and 0, respectively. A *configuration* of a Boltzmann machine is a 0-1-vector of length $|U|$ describing the state of each unit. If k is a configuration, $k(u)$ denotes the state of u in k.

Connections are either active or passive. A connection between u und v is *active* in a configuration k if both connected units are on, i.e., if $k(u) \cdot k(v) = 1$; else it is *passive*. Every connection $\{u, v\}$ has an associated *connection strength* $s_{\{u,v\}} \in \mathbb{R}$, to be interpreted as the desirability that $\{u, v\}$ is active. The strength of a bias connection $\{u, u\}$ is called the *bias* of u.

The desirability of a whole configuration k, expressed in terms of a *consensus function* is the sum of the strengths of all active connections; hence the consensus function $\kappa(k)$ looks as follows:

$$\kappa(k) = \sum_{\{u,v\} \in K} s_{\{u,v\}} \cdot k(u) \cdot k(v).$$

The objective of a Boltzmann machine is to find a global maximum of the consensus function. In general, a Boltzmann machine can be run sequentially, where units are allowed to change their

---

[1]This description is an excerpt from [Aarts and Korst, 1989]

states only one at a time, and in parallel. For simplicity, we will here use the sequential mode of operation. As before, we refer to [Aarts and Korst, 1989] for further information.

The idea how to arrive at a global maximum is: take an arbitrary configuration as the recent one; generate a neighboring one (by changing the state of one unit); accept it as the recent configuration with some probability depending on the difference of consensus compared to the recent configuration and on run time of the procedure; continue.

To sketch this briefly, given a configuration k, we define a *neighboring configuration k_u* as the one obtained from k by changing the state of the unit u. The *difference in consensus* between k and k_u, is defined as

$$\Delta\kappa_k(u) := \kappa(k_u) - \kappa(k)$$

A configuration k is locally maximal if $\Delta\kappa_k(u) \leq 0$ for all units u, i.e., if its consensus is not increased by a *single* state change. Given a configuration k, assume that neighboring configurations k_u are generated with equal probabilities for all u. The *acceptance criterion* to accept k_u as the recent configuration is

$$\frac{1}{1 + \exp\frac{-\Delta\kappa_k(u)}{c_t}} > random[0, 1),$$

where $c_t > 0$, converging to 0 for increasing t.

3 Transforming Constraint Networks: An Example

We will now show in a simple example the general idea of how to transform a constraint network into a Boltzmann machine. The transformation procedure we use here is similar to the one in [Johnston and Adorf, 1989]; it will be generalized to include relaxation in section 5.

Suppose we have a part of an office involving the six areas $a, \ldots, f$ to be furnished with a desk and a bookcase, where each of these objects must be placed into exactly one of the six areas. There are the constraints that objects must not occlude the door, the bookcase must not occlude the window, and that these two must be placed in different areas. The problem and the constraint network are shown and explained in figure 1.

The idea of the transformation is to have one unit per relation element of every constraint and one unit per domain element of every variable. (This is often called the unit/value principle [Feldman and Ballard, 1982].) To transform the network in figure 1, for instance, we get the units $d\text{-}place = a, \ldots, d\text{-}place = f$ as a transformation of the variable $d\text{-}place$ and three units $bookcase = (b), \ldots, bookcase = (e)$ as the transformation of the $bookcase$ constraint.

Concerning the connections, there are, firstly, the bias connections connecting each unit with itself. Secondly, there must be a link between two units u, v if u represents a relation element of the constraint C and v represents a value of a variable of C; there are connections corresponding to fitting pairs of relation element and one argument (like the connection between the units corresponding to $desk = (a)$ and $d\text{-}place = a$), and there are connections corresponding to non-fitting such pairs (like $desk = (a)$ and $d\text{-}place = b$). We will call these connections *positive* and *negative* connections, respectively. And thirdly, there is a connection between every pair of units representing different elements of the same relation or values of the same variable—like $desk = (a)$ and $desk = (b)$; these are called *intra-relation* connections. The Boltzmann machine contains only the positive, negative, intra-relation, and bias connections. The machine corresponding to the example then looks as shown in figure 2. The connections are associated with the following strengths: positive connections have strength 1, negative and intra-relation ones -1, and bias connections 0. Let k_0 be the following configuration

$$k_0(u) = \begin{cases} 1 & \text{if } u \in \{desk = (a),\, desk = (b),\, d\text{-}place = a,\, neq = (a, c),\, b\text{-}place = c,\, bookcase = (c)\} \\ 0 & \text{else} \end{cases}$$

then the consensus $\kappa(k_0) = 2$. k_0 is not locally maximal; the configuration k_1 we arrive at by deactivating $desk = (b)$ in k_0 has a consensus value of 4. k_1 *is* locally and even globally maximal.

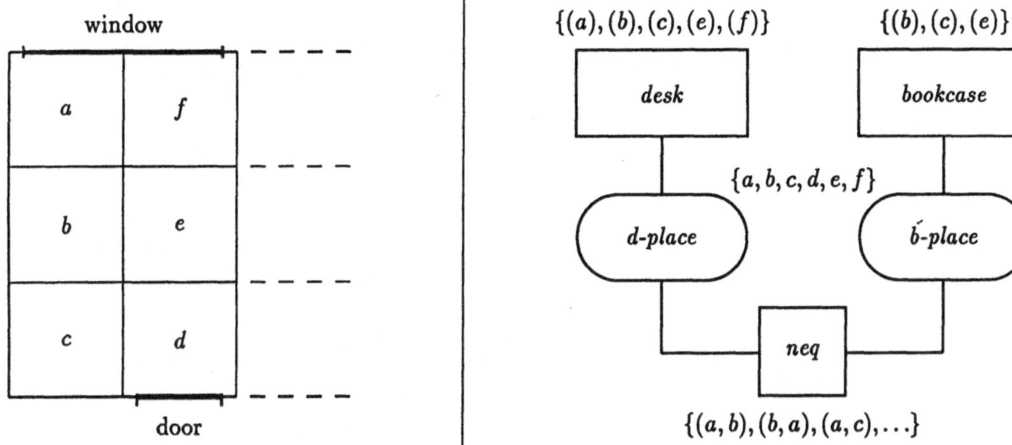

Figure 1: The example problem and its constraint network. Boxes represent constraints, ovals represent variables. The variables *d-place* and *b-place* range over the possible positions for the desk and the bookcase, resp.; the relation elements of the constraints *desk* and *bookcase* enumerate the allowed positions; and the constraint *neq* enumerates all different positions of desk and bookcase.

From the facts that k_1 is globally optimal for the Boltzmann machine in figure 2 *and* that it corresponds to a solution of the corresponding constraint network in figure 1, you might induce that global maxima of Boltzmann machines constructed in analogy to constraint networks in the way described correspond to solutions of the constraint networks. This is nearly right, as will be explained below. Unfortunately, there are *local* maxima of such Boltzmann machines that do *not* correspond to solutions of the constraint network. As an example take the configuration

$$k_2(u) = \begin{cases} 1 & \text{if } u \in \{desk = (b), d\text{-}place = b, b\text{-}place = b, bookcase = (b)\} \\ 0 & \text{else} \end{cases}$$

k_2 is locally maximal; there is no neighboring configuration with a positive consensus difference. On the other hand, k_2 does not correspond to a solution of the associated constraint network.

4   Constraint Relaxation

Before generalizing the transformation of constraint networks into Boltzmann machines, let us first generalize constraint networks to include relaxation[2]. The idea of constraint relaxation is to allow for more and less "hard" constraints in a constraint network. The purpose of constraint relaxation is to make constraints more expressive. In practical problems, a set of constraints is often inconsistent when all constraints are taken literally. However, sometimes you don't want to express more than a preference by a constraint, which should but need not be fulfilled by a solution of the problem so that constraint networks that are inconsistent when taken literally are not when respecting different

---

[2]Note that the term relaxation is overloaded in the relevant literature. We adopt the notion *constraint relaxation* from [Dechter and Pearl, 1987] in the sense explained below. Montanari and Rossi [1991], e.g., use it in the different sense of constraint network preprocessing, which is comparable to the usual sense of *relaxation* in the context of Boltzmann machines.

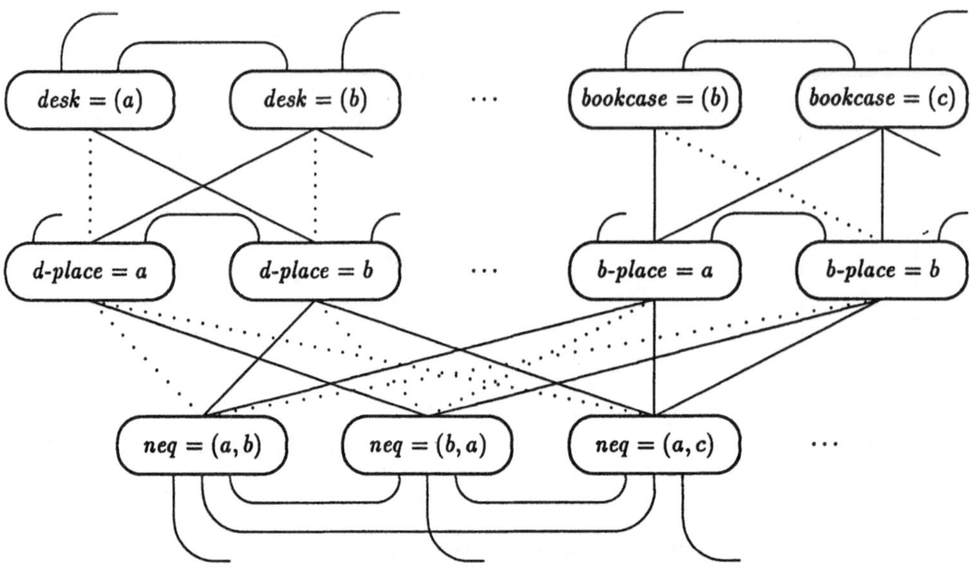

Figure 2: Part of the Boltzmann machine corresponding to the constraint network in figure 1. Positive connections are depicted as dotted lines, negative connections as solid lines, intra-relation connections as round corner lines, and bias connections are omitted for clearness.

---

weights of constraints. But note that dealing with inconsistency is not the only purpose of constraint relaxation: you may want to express that different solutions to the problem are of different quality.

There are a few theoretical formulations of constraint relaxation, e.g., [Hertzberg *et al.*, 1988] or [Freuder, 1989] (who terms it *partial constraint satisfaction*), all of which extend CSPs by—in Freuder's terms—a *problem space* and a *metric,* in one way or another:

- The problem space *PS* includes the original problem; it consists of a set of constraint satisfaction problems over constraint networks with an identical structure plus a partial ordering $\leq$ on them, where for two problems $P, Q \in PS$, $P \leq Q$ is to be interpreted as: P is *weaker* than Q, i.e., every solution of Q is also a solution of P.

- The metric on the problems in *PS* is used to determine a numerical value for the distance between the original problem and a relaxed one.

The idea of a problem space is consistent with the definition of a relaxed constraint in [Dechter and Pearl, 1987]: a constraint is called relaxed if its relation is a superset of the original relation.

Solving a CSP now means to find a solution of a relaxed problem in the problem space that is both minimally different, respecting the metric, and only tolerably different from the original problem (where you have to specify what is tolerable, e.g., in terms of a maximum of the metric).

As an example, let us introduce relaxation into the problem presented in section 3. Given an n-ary relation $R(x_1, \ldots, x_n)$, we generate its relaxed $(n+1)$-ary version $R'(relax, x_1, \ldots, x_n)$, where $relax \geq 0$ is a real variable denoting a *penalty* given for accepting the "proper" argument $(x_1, \ldots, x_n)$ in a solution (the higher $relax$ the less desirable the argument tuple; for easy calculating, we use integer penalties). Constraint networks containing $relax$ constraints will be called relaxation constraint networks or *relaxation networks* for short. Obviously, constraint networks are a special case of relaxation networks. To extend our example, let us introduce variables *relax-desk* and *relax-bookcase* with domains $\{0, \ldots, 3\}$ into the constraint network and define the new versions of the *desk* and *bookcase* relations as

$$desk' = \{(0,a),(2,b),(3,c),(3,e),(1,f)\}, bookcase' = \{(2,b),(0,c),(3,e)\}$$

with the rationale that desks should be close to windows, bookcases should stand in corners and all furniture should be placed along walls. We do not sketch the new constraint network and the corresponding Boltzmann machine for lack of space; they are constructed in the obvious way.

Note that finding a solution to a CSP can now be seen as a problem of combinatorial optimization. It is well known [Aarts and Korst, 1989] that Boltzmann machines can be used as tools to solve such problems, and we will now see how this works, starting with some general remarks about what to expect from such a tool.

5 Transforming Relaxation Constraint Networks

When using Boltzmann machines for solving combinatorial optimization problems, it is usually required that the consensus function be *feasible*, i.e., that all local maxima of the Boltzmann machine correspond to solutions of the problem. As we have seen in configuration k_2, κ is not feasible. This might cause a problem when using a Boltzmann machine as a realization of a constraint network because one is only guaranteed to find a *locally* optimal solution in finite time, and if this does not correspond to finding a solution to the original problem, namely, the CSP, we might ask of what value the transformation of CSPs to Boltzmann machines actually is.

What ways out of this do we have? Either we could try to find another transformation and a feasible consensus function. Or we could look for an appropriate interpretation of local maxima of Boltzmann machines; and this is what we are going to do because we like the relatively close correspondence between constraint networks and Boltzmann machines constructed as described.

To start with, let us define a corresponding Boltzmann machine for a relaxation network. The way to generate it is similar to the procedure used to transform the network in figure 1 into the Boltzmann machine in figure 2; the difference is that we now want to be able to handle *relax* constraints in the network properly. We assume that all *relax* constraints involve a finite number of penalties. Moreover, we assume that all arguments of relations in the networks to follow must correspond to different variables, i.e., for every constraint over variables $V_1, \ldots, V_n$, we require $V_i \neq V_j$ for $i \neq j$. This assumption is in fact not restrictive as every network violating it can be transformed into a fitting different one by renaming the appropriate variables and formulating the respective equality constraints.

Definition 1 (Corresponding Boltzmann machine)
Let N be a relaxation network. If N contains relax variables $V_1, \ldots, V_r$ over domains $D_1, \ldots, D_r$, let p_{max} be the maximum of the penalties occuring in them, let $\overline{p}$ be an upper bound to p_{max}, i.e., $p_{max} < \overline{p}$, and let s be an upper bound for the sum of all penalties of all relax variables. (We will use $s = p_{max} \cdot \sum_{i=1}^{r} |D_i|$ in the following.)
The corresponding Boltzmann machine $B_N = (U_N, K_N)$ is constructed in the following way:

1. *The set U_N of units includes one unit per relation element and one unit per variable domain element of N, and it includes no other units.*

2. *Let C be a constraint in N, V its ith variable, let $(d_1, \ldots, d_m), (e_1, \ldots, e_m)$ be relation elements of C, and let d be a member of the domain of V. The set K_N of connections includes the following and no other connections:*

   - *Bias Connections.*
   - *Positive Connections. These are the connections between all pairs $\{u, v\}$ of units corresponding to fitting pairs of relation elements and arguments, i.e.,*

     $$u \text{ corresponds to } (d_1, \ldots, d_m), v \text{ corresponds to } d \text{ and } d = d_i$$

- Negative Connections. *Connections between all pairs $\{u,v\}$ of units corresponding to non-fitting pairs of relation elements and arguments, i.e.,*

$$u \text{ corresponds to } (d_1,\ldots,d_m), v \text{ corresponds to } d \text{ and } d \neq d_i$$

- Intra-relation Connections. *Connections between all pairs $\{u,v\}$ of units corresponding to different elements of the same relation, i.e.,*

$$u \text{ corresponds to } (d_1,\ldots,d_m), v \text{ corresponds to } (e_1,\ldots,e_m),$$
$$\text{and } (d_1,\ldots,d_m) \neq (e_1,\ldots,e_m)$$

and analogously for the variables.

3. *The connection strengths are set as follows:*

- *The positive connections have strength $\overline{p}$.*

- *The negative connections have strength $-\overline{p}$.*

- *The intra-relation connections have strength $-(c-1)\cdot\overline{p}$, where $c \geq 1$ is the maximal number of positive connections a unit of the Boltzmann machine B_N is involved in.*

- *A bias connection that corresponds to other than* relax *constraints has strength 0.*

- *The bias connections corresponding to a* relax *constraint with a penalty p has strength $\frac{\overline{p}-p-\varepsilon}{s}$ for some real ε such that $\overline{p} - p_{max} > \varepsilon > 0$.*

Let us briefly look at the relaxation example presented in section 4, thinking about the parameters. First, the maximum of positive connections a unit is involved in is 2, corresponding to the fact that we maximally have 2-ary constraints and variables have maximally 2 constraints operating on them. The cardinality of the *relax* variables is 4. We then get the following parameter values:

$$
\begin{array}{rcll}
c & = & 2 & \text{(the maximum of a unit's positive connections)} \\
p_{max} & = & 3 & \text{(the maximum of penalties)} \\
\overline{p} & = & 4 & \text{(an upper bound to } p_{max}) \\
s & = & 24 & \text{(an upper bound for the penalty sum)} \\
\varepsilon & = & \tfrac{1}{2} & \text{(arbitrary)}
\end{array}
$$

Given these values, the biases for the four units representing the *relax-desk* and *relax-bookcase* constraints, respectively, are $\frac{3.5}{24},\ldots,\frac{0.5}{24}$, respectively. The strenghts for positive, negative, and intra-relation connections are $4, -4, -4$, respectively.

Every configuration of the corresponding Boltzmann machine that corresponds to a solution involves 6 active positive connections and no active negative and no active intra-relation connections, corresponding to the links in the original constraint network in figure 1 plus the links to the *relax* variables. In the solution corresponding to the relaxation version of the configuration k_1 described earlier, the contribution of the biases of units corresponding to the *relax* variables to the consensus function is $\frac{3.5+3.5}{24}$, and it is $\frac{0.5+3.5}{24}$ in the solution corresponding to shifting the desk to b. This yields consensus values of $24\frac{7}{24}$ and $24\frac{4}{24}$, respectively, of the configurations corresponding to the two solutions.

Note that the example transformation we used to get the Boltzmann machine in figure 2 is a special case of the one now defined. Consequently, the consensus function is still not feasible under the transformation just described. However, by the very construction of B_N, we can tell whether a given local maximum of the Boltzmann machine corresponds to a solution of N. This is elaborated on in the following two propositions whose proofs, which are given in the appendix, should clarify why the connection strengths in definition 1 are set the way they are.

Proposition 1 (Necessary condition for solution)
Let N be a constraint network, l the sum of arities of all constraints in N, B_N the corresponding Boltzmann machine, k a configuration of B_N, and $\overline{p}$ an upper bound of the penalties of all relax variables in N as defined in definition 1.

If k corresponds to a solution of N, then for the value $\kappa(k)$ of the consensus function

$$\kappa(k) \geq \overline{p} \cdot l \tag{1}$$

The converse of proposition 1 is also true: every configuration k of B_N for which the inequality (1) holds is a solution of N. And, more important, every such k is locally maximal:

Proposition 2 (Sufficient condition for solution)
Let $N, B_N, l, k, \overline{p}$ be defined as in proposition 1. If $\kappa(k) \geq \overline{p} \cdot l$, then k corresponds to a solution of the constraint network N, and k is locally optimal in B_N

The converse of the local optimality part of proposition 2 is wrong; see, e.g., the configuration k_2. This means that there may be local optima k where $\kappa(k) < l \cdot \overline{p}$.

There is another property which one would like a consensus function κ to have: given two solutions S, S' of N with the corresponding configurations k, k' in B_N; if $m(S) < m(S')$ for a given metric m, then one would expect $\kappa(k) < \kappa(k')$. A consensus function for which this property holds is called *order preserving* [Aarts and Korst, 1989], and it holds for κ in the office corner furnishing example using the sum of all values of all *relax* constraints as the metric.

However, order preservingness does not only depend on the consensus function in the Boltzmann machine in question but also on the metric in the problem space, and different metrics may be useful in different spaces. For instance, there is another metric resulting in that relaxing any number of constraints with penalty $p-1$ is preferred to relaxing one constraint with penalty p; this is effectively the metric used in [Hertzberg *et al.*, 1988]. κ from definition 1 is obviously *not* order preserving for this metric. So, if there isn't *the* natural metric on the solution space of your original problem, you cannot expect that one single consensus function mirrors any of them in the corresponding Boltzmann machine.

Finally, let us come back to the problem that κ is not feasible. We have argued above that this may be impractical as we cannot guarantee a Boltzmann machine to deliver a global optimum, and if not every local optimum corresponds to a solution to the original CSP, we cannot be sure about what we have gained by a transformation of a CSP into a Boltzmann machine. However, matters look more friendly now. Propositions 1 and 2 state necessary and sufficient conditions for a configuration to correspond to a solution of the CSP: it must be a local optimum satisfying inequality (1).

If this should not suffice as a criterion for all practical purposes, then there is an alternative. Using the idea of constraint relaxation and some new value $?$ to be added to all domains, you could define for a given network N a "closure" constraint network N', in which every partial solution, i.e., a tuple consisting of locally compatible values where missing values are filled up with $?$s, is a solution which gets a penalty corresponding to the number of involved $?$s. It is easily verified—but we will not do so here—that every local optimum of B_N, i.e., the Boltzmann machine corresponding to the original constraint problem, corresponds to a solution of N', where missing values are filled up with $?$s. We have in fact seen an example for that: the configuration k_2 corresponds to the solution $desk = (b), d\text{-}place = b, b\text{-}place = b, bookcase = b, neq = ?$ in the hypothetical "closure" constraint network of the one in figure 1.

6 Conclusion

To sum up, we have

- generalized the standard notation of constraint networks to relaxation networks which are able to include penalties for relation elements;

- defined corresponding Boltzmann machines for relaxation networks;

- stated necessary and sufficient conditions for a locally optimal configuration of a Boltzmann machine to correspond to a solution of the relaxation network.

By the virtue of a Boltzmann machine to allow for a massively parallel implementation, the definition of corresponding Boltzmann machines as presented yields a framework for such an implementation of constraint satisfaction including relaxation; by its virtue of being an approach to combinatorial optimization, it guarantees for finding optimal or—given finite time—good solutions, if any.

Much work remains to be done. Practically, we have not yet experimented with an implementation of the concept presented here. For this purpose, a translator of relaxation networks (for example in a relaxation version of CONSAT [Guesgen, 1989] syntax) into corresponding Boltzmann machines seems a necessary tool. There could be a problem in principle that the biases of the *relax* variables contribute only very little to the consensus values so that solutions of different qualities differ only very little in their consensus values.

Beyond that, we have not exploited the theory of Boltzmann machines by far. For example, one could consider to use learning mechanisms to adjust the biases of the *relax* variables properly. Moreover, one could think of different correspondence mappings of relaxation networks to Boltzmann machines that are in fact feasible; alternatively, one could examine using subclasses of relaxation networks for which the transformation described in fact results in a feasible consensus function.

A   Appendix: Proofs to the Propositions

Proof of proposition 1. As we assumed that all arguments of relations in N correspond to different variables, l positive connections, each of strength $\bar{p}$, are active in k. By construction of B_N, no negative and no intra-relation connections are active in k; moreover, the bias connections are nonnegative, so that (1) follows.

Proof of proposition 2. Note that the sum of all bias connection strengths in B_N is less than $\bar{p}$. So, by definition of the connection strengths, k must involve activating at least l different positive connections, where a solution of N corresponds to activating *exactly* l of these, by construction of B_N.

Assume that m, where $m > l$, positive connections are active in k. By construction of B_N, this involves activating more than $m - l$ negative and intra-relation connections, yielding a consensus value less than $\bar{p} \cdot l$, because the sum of biases is less than $\bar{p}$, contradicting the assumption in the proposition.

Now assume that k corresponds to a solution of N, i.e., involves activating l positive connections. Assume further that $\kappa(k_u) > \kappa(k)$ by a state change of u. As k corresponds to a solution of N, deactivating an active unit decreases the consensus. So, there must be $v \neq u$ such that $k(v) = k_u(v) = 1$, and v, u correspond to different relation elements of $C \in N$, such that all positive and no negative connections of v are active. As $u \neq v$, u deactivates at least one positive connection and activates at least one negative connection by construction of B_N; moreover, it activates the intra-relation connection to v. That means that k is locally maximal, because if c_u is the number of positive connections u is involved in,

$$\Delta\kappa_k(u) \leq (c_u - c - 1) \cdot \bar{p} + s_{\{u,u\}} < 0.$$

References

[Aarts and Korst, 1989] E. Aarts and J. Korst. *Simulated Annealing and Boltzmann Machines.* John Wiley & Sons, Cichester, England, 1989.

[Adorf and Johnston, 1990] H.M. Adorf and M.D. Johnston. A discrete stochastic neural network algorithm for constraint satisfaction problems. In *Proc. IJCNN-90*, San Diego, California, 1990.

[Allen, 1983] J.F. Allen. Maintaining knowledge about temporal intervals. *Communications of the ACM*, 26:832–843, 1983.

[Bolz and Wittur, 1990] D. Bolz and K. Wittur. Die Umsetzung deklarativer Beschreibungen von Graphiken durch Simulated Annealing. In P. Wißkirchen K. Kansy, editor, *Proc. GI-Fachgespräch Graphik und KI*, pages 68–77, Berlin, Germany, 1990. Springer.

[Cooper and Swain, 1988] P.R. Cooper and M.J. Swain. Parallelism and domain dependence in constraint satisfaction. Technical Report 255, University of Rochester, Computer Science Department, Rochester, New York, 1988.

[Dechter and Pearl, 1987] R. Dechter and J. Pearl. Network-based heuristics for constraint-satisfaction problems. *Artificial Intelligence*, 34:1–38, 1987.

[Feldman and Ballard, 1982] J.A. Feldman and D.H. Ballard. Connectionist models and their properties. *Cognitive Science*, 6:201–254, 1982.

[Freuder, 1989] E.C. Freuder. Partial constraint satisfaction. In *Proc. IJCAI-89*, pages 278–283, Detroit, Michigan, 1989.

[Guesgen, 1989] H.W. Guesgen. *CONSAT: A System for Constraint Satisfaction*. Research Notes in Artificial Intelligence. Morgan Kaufmann; Pitman, San Mateo, California; London, England, 1989.

[Hertzberg et al., 1988] J. Hertzberg, H.W. Guesgen, and H. Voss A. Voss, M. Fidelak. Relaxing constraint networks to resolve inconsistencies. In W. Hoeppner, editor, *Künstliche Intelligenz, GWAI-88*, pages 61–65, Berlin, Germany, 1988. Springer.

[Johnston and Adorf, 1989] M.D. Johnston and H.-M. Adorf. Learning in stochastic neural networks for constraint satisfaction problems. In G. Rodriguez and H. Seraij, editors, *Proc. NASA Conf. on Space Telerobotics*, pages 367–376. JPL Publ., 1989.

[Kasif, 1989] S. Kasif. Parallel solutions to constraint satisfaction problems. In *Proc. KR-89*, pages 180–188, Toronto, Ontario, 1989.

[Mackworth, 1977] A.K. Mackworth. Consistency in networks of relations. *Artificial Intelligence*, 8:99–118, 1977.

[Mohr and Henderson, 1986] R. Mohr and T.C. Henderson. Arc and path consistency revisited. *Artificial Intelligence*, 28:225–233, 1986.

[Montanari and Rossi, 1991] U. Montanari and F. Rossi. Constraint relaxation may be perfect. *Artificial Intelligence*, 48:143–170, 1991.

[Rosenfeld, 1975] A. Rosenfeld. Networks of automata: Some applications. *IEEE Transactions on Systems, Man, and Cybernetics*, 5:380–383, 1975.

[Samal and Henderson, 1987] A. Samal and T.C. Henderson. Parallel consistent labeling algorithms. *International Journal of Parallel Programming*, 16:341–364, 1987.

The SNNS Neural Network Simulator

Andreas Zell, Niels Mache, Tilman Sommer, Thomas Korb
Universität Stuttgart,
Institut für Parallele und Verteilte Höchstleistungsrechner (IPVR),
Breitwiesenstr. 20-22, D-7000 Stuttgart 80,
E-mail: zell@informatik.uni-stuttgart.de

ABSTRACT

SNNS is a neural network simulator for Unix workstations developed at the Universität Stuttgart. It is a tool to generate, train, test and visualize artificial neural networks. The simulator consists of a simulator kernel, a graphical user interface based on X-Windows to interactively construct and visualize neural networks, and a compiler to generate large neural networks from a high level network description language. Applications of SNNS currently include printed character recognition, handwritten character recognition, recognition of machine parts, stock prize prediction, noise reduction in a telecom environment and texture analysis, among others. We also give preliminary design decisions for a planned parallel version of SNNS on a massively parallel SIMD-computer with more than 16,000 processors (MasPar MP-1216) which has been installed at our research institute recently.

Keywords: connectionism, neural networks, network simulators, network description language

1. THE SNNS NEURAL NETWORK SIMULATOR

SNNS (Stuttgart Neural Network Simulator) is an efficient and portable neural network simulation environment for Unix workstations. It is a software tool to generate, train, test and visualize artificial neural networks. The simulator consists of three major components: a simulator kernel that operates on the internal representation of the neural networks, a graphical user interface to interactively construct and change small neural nets, and a compiler to generate the internal representation of large neural networks from a high level network description language. The whole network simulator has been developed in C on various Unix workstations. The graphical user interface was implemented under X-Windows X11 Release 4.0 with the MIT Athena widget set, for maximal portability.

As was already mentioned, our simulator consists of 3 components: simulator kernel, graphical user interface and network compiler. The simulator kernel operates on the internal representation of the neural networks and performs all operations of the learning and recall phase. It is loosely coupled with the network compiler by a network description file containing an intermediate form of the network and more closely with the graphical user interface via an interface of function calls. The definition of learning and propagation rules is part of the network definition program, learning can be supervised or not. The simulator kernel is written in C for efficiency and portability and has already been ported to a number of architectures (Sun 3 and Sun 4 under SunOS 4.0, DECStation 2100 / 3100 under Ultrix-32, HP 9000/345 under Unix Sys V.3 and BSD 4.3, IBM PC 386 under AT&T Unix Sys. V and SCO Xenix V, IBM RISCSystem/6000 under AIX). With more than 1,100,000 CPS (connections per second) on a DECStation 3100 and more than 2,200,000 CPS on an IBM R/6000 Model 520 it is a rather fast general purpose workstation simulator.

The graphical user interface, based on X-Windows, is a tool to construct the topology and visualize and modify small to medium sized nets interactively with an integrated graphical editor. It can also be used to generate and save test patterns for small networks. To economize on screen space the display elements are kept in separate windows and thus can be arbitrarily arranged or hidden if desired. There are various ways to display or modify nodes and links or selected sets of them. An integrated help facility aids the novice with the interface. Networks can be modified through the user interface during simulation. Units can be introduced, removed, or have their activation values changed, connections among the units can be inserted, deleted, redirected, or have their strengths modified. In contrast to most other simulators the modifications can be done in a simple manner directly in the visual representation of the network topology.

Our network description language Nessus is a high level procedural language. Its main task is to describe the topology of the network being simulated. We are able to specify parameters like network topology, activation functions and graphical display information of regular topologies, in a convenient way. However, the ASCII network description file can also be generated by any other program which can generate an file in the intermediate form.

The compiler can generate the internal representation of large neural networks from a high level procedural language with elements of Pascal, C and Modula2. The Nessus compiler was implemented in C with the aids of lex and yacc and can generate large networks very rapidly. In fact, most of the time of generating large networks with this compiler is attributable to writing the often several megabytes of the network description file for large networks. We have successfully generated networks with more than 10.000 nodes and more than one million weights with the compiler but have not attempted to train these networks.

The structure of the whole SNNS simulator can be visualized as in figure 1.

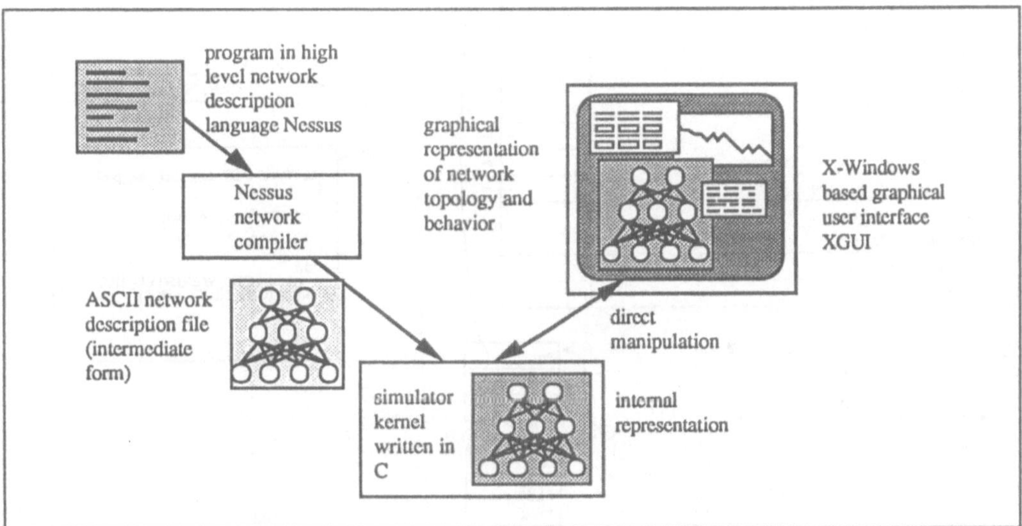

Fig. 1: Structure of the SNNS network simulator consisting of 3 parts: simulator kernel, graphical user interface and network compiler

2. SIMULATOR KERNEL

The kernel performs activation propagation and learning. Learning can be supervised or not. Networks can be modified through the user interface during simulation. Units may be introduced, removed, or have their activation values changed. Connections among the units may be inserted, deleted, redirected, or have their strengths modified, if needed.

2.1. Simulator kernel layers

The simulator kernel is structured into four layers of increasing abstraction. The innermost layer are the memory management functions. They provide functions for the allocation and disallocation of data structures in large blocks of contiguous memory, thus enhancing the standard Unix memory management. The next layer comprises all functions that modify the network, including propagation and learning functions. The next layer consists of the functions that the kernel provides as interface between itself and the X graphical user interface. The fourth layer consists of the file I/O interface to the network compiler.

2.2. Internal data structures

A dynamic unit array was chosen for efficiency reasons to hold the contents of the units. If more units are requested than are available in the unit array, the SNNS memory management demands a new larger array from the operating system and efficiently copies all data and pointers to substructures to the new array, disallocating the old unit array. The main internal data structures are represented graphically in fig. 2.

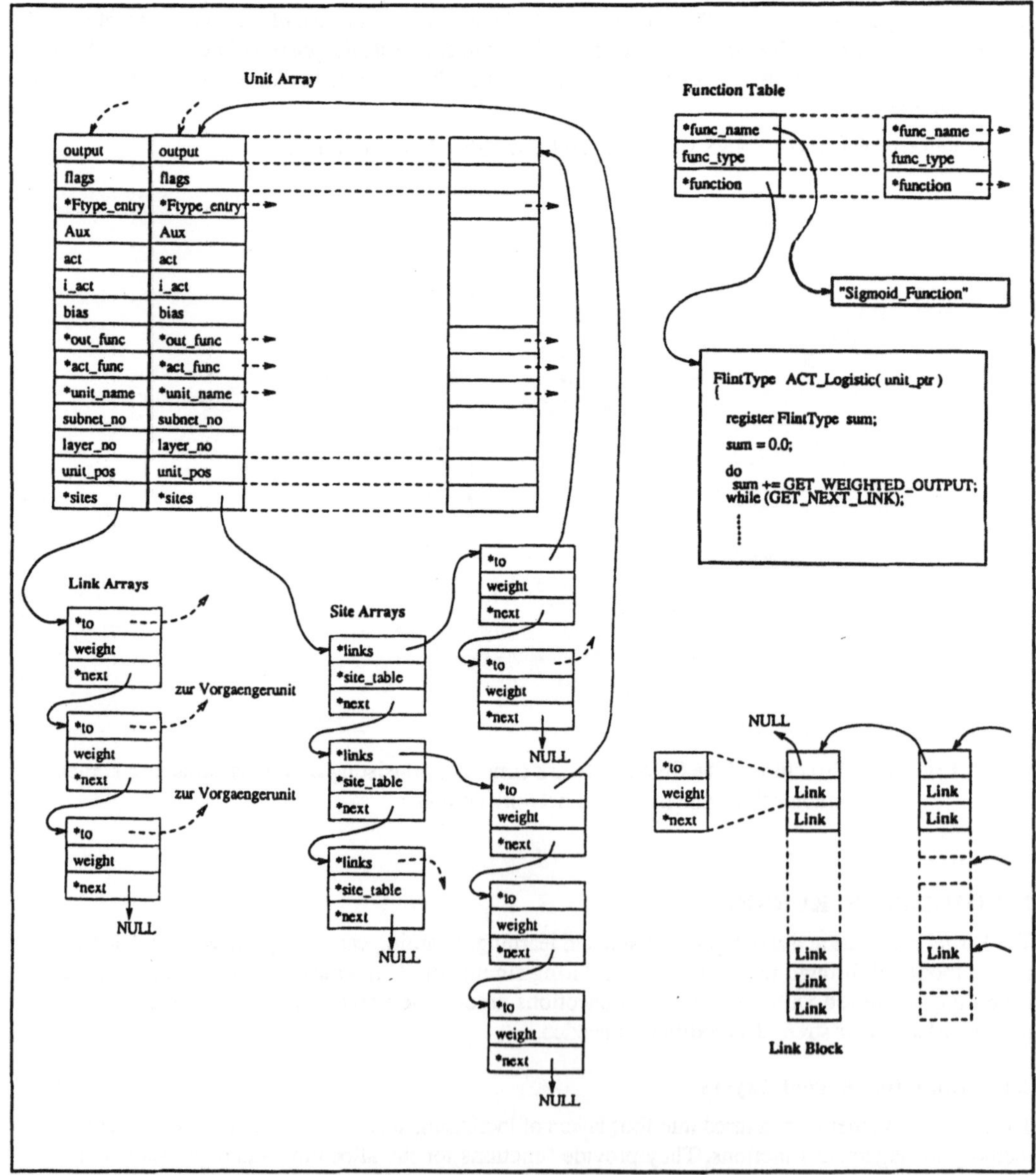

Fig. 2:   SNNS simulator kernel internal data structures (simplified)

Currently about a dozen activation and output functions are already supplied with the simulator, but it is very easy to write other transfer functions in C, then compile and link them to the simulator kernel. They then show up in the user interface and can be chosen from a menu.

Five different modes of forward dynamic activation spreading can be selected: synchronous firing, random order, random permutation, topologic order, and fixed order. In synchronous mode, all cells (quasi) simultaneously compute their new activation, then they all change their output. In random order one cell is chosen at random, its new activation and output values are computed and propagated before any other cell is updated. In random permutation a permutation of the cell numbers guarantees that every cell is updated after one full sweep through the network). In fixed order, the cells are updated according to their internal cell number, while topologic order first performs a topologic sort of the network (provided it is acyclic). This guarantees that a change of activation in the input layer is reflected all way up to the output layer in one sweep through the network.

The simulator allows the generation of new links or units at run time. For testing purposes any property of a cell or connection may be inspected or changed between cycles at run time.

The kernel does not differentiate between feedforward and feedback networks since we wanted to allow experimentation with feedback networks as well. It is the task of the user to guarantee the feedforward property if he wants to work with learning rules like standard back-propagation. Also, the simulator kernel does not possess a layer concept, but regards the network as flat. This concept is imprinted on the network either by the user or by the network compiler.

3. SNNS GRAPHICAL USER INTERFACE

Even for small neural networks a text-based or a numerical representation of the network and its activities is usually inadequate. A graphical representation of the network is necessary to display the dynamics of the simulation. But for larger networks with many units and connections even a graphical display can be rather confusing. Therefore, a graphical user interface must contain appropriate tools to efficiently constrain the number of objects and the amount of information displayed.

3.1. Network visualization

The graphical user interface consists of the following windows which can be positioned and controlled independently:

- a *manager panel* with info panel (above), below the menu button GUI, with which other windows may be opened, a message line and a status information line
- several *graphical displays* of the network
- a *remote panel* to control the activity of the simulator (like with a TV remote control)
- a *control panel* which is used to control learning and to test the network
- several *help windows* for context sensitive help

A number of popup windows (transient shells) are only visible on request and block all other windows of SNNS. These are

- a *file panel* to load and store networks and patterns
- a *setup panel* to control the graphical appearance of the networks
- a *confirmer* to demand user confirmations and to display important messages
- a *list panel* to choose several alternatives from a list
- a *layer panel* to individually select the layer of units (note our layers are unlike the usual hierarchical layers of neural networks: they have nothing to do with network topology but only with the visual display. They are similar to overhead transparencies such that units may belong to several layers. One or many layers of units may be displayed in a window.

Figure 3 shows a version of the current graphical user interface. Not visible here are a help panel with context sensitive help, a text panel to record a session with the simulator which can be loaded and replayed and a setup panel to control the display of units and links.

Units are usually displayed as growing boxes or growing bars in a raster of positions. The user can control the raster size of the graphic window, the visual representation of units (activation values, output values, number, name) and the display of links (directed, undirected, weight). Connections and units can be displayed selectively, i.e. the user may choose to display only those units whose activations or outputs exceed a given display threshold or only those links whose weights are in a certain range. This allows watching the growth of units and the establishing or deterioration of strong links during learning.

Until recently our simulator was limited to a black and white display since nearly all workstations in our department were B/W. With the proliferation of color workstations our simulator now can utilize color displays. It then gives a color coded display of the units activations or outputs and uses color to indicate weight sign and strength. This is not only an improvement of looks but can convey more information in the same area.

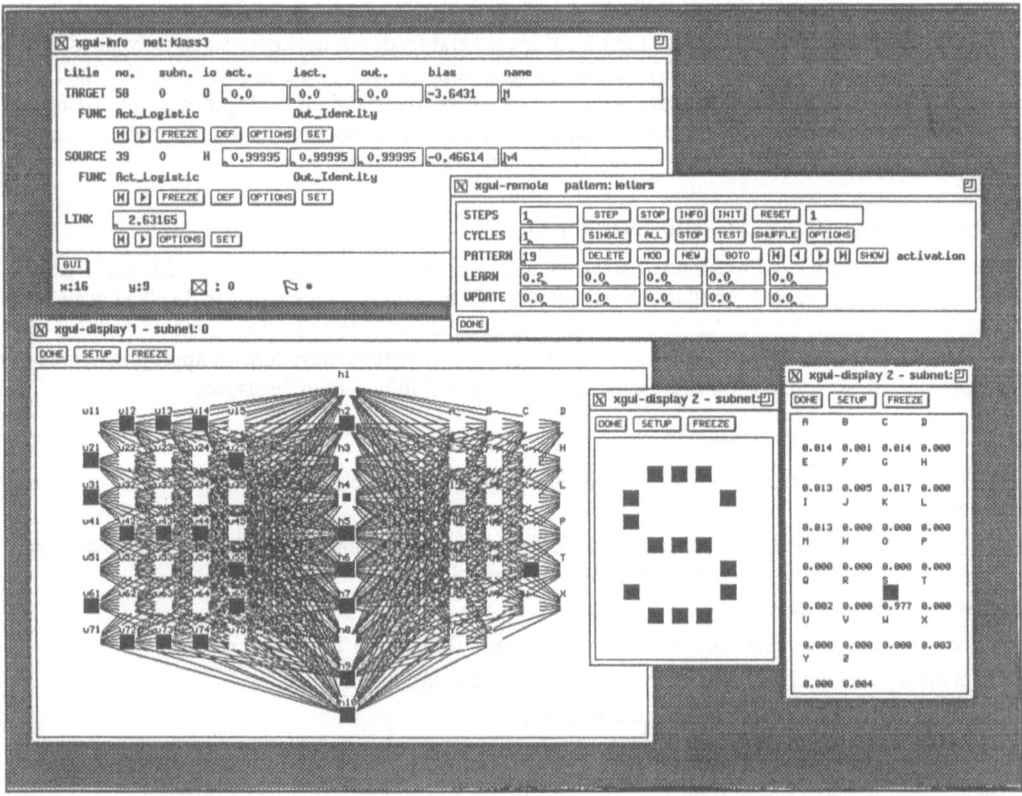

Fig. 3: Graphical user interface: manager panel, remote panel and three graphical network displays

3.2. Network editing

The graphical interface is not only used to display a neural network but to generate and manipulate it as well. Therefore, the user has a powerful set of operations (insertion, deletion, copying, moving) at his use. These operations may be applied to individual units or to selections of units and may affect links as well, like 'copy all selected units with their input links' or 'delete all links into the selected units'. These operations allow a quick and convenient generation of networks. For networks which fit on a display screen and have a regular topology it is is usually more convenient to use the graphical interface of the simulator to generate the networks than to use the network compiler The powerful network editing facilities are especially useful for networks with simple or repetitive but not completely regular topology.

4. NEURAL NETWORK DESCRIPTION LANGUAGE NESSUS

4.1. The Nessus Language

Nessus is a procedural language especially suited to describe the topology of neural networks. It was developed after experiences we gained with the implementation of a declarative language, Nesila. This earlier language had some nice features like topology descriptions in a set theoretic notation with so called *where clauses* specifying arbitrary and even nested conditions for groups of nodes to be connected. It also eliminated the necessity to declare variables before their use and even allowed the use of variables before their declaration. This was made possible by the single assignment rule of the language and a two phase compiler. However, this language was hard to implement and took too long to generate large networks, for which it was originally designed. Therefore we fell back to a standard procedural language which is now implemented very efficiently.

A Nessus program is divided into the following parts: program header, constant definition part, type definition part, structure definition part, variable declaration part and topology modification part. The interesting and unusual parts are the structure definition part and the topology modification part. The idea here is to define regular topologic structures in the structure definition part which can be later combined, extended and modified in various ways in the topology modification part.

The program in fig. 4 describes the simple letter recognition network displayed in fig. 3.

```
network recogLetter();       {network recognizes a capital letter displayed by a 5*7 input matrix}
const  Letters = ["A".."Z"];  {output units are named "A", "B", .. "Z"}
typedef                      {unit type without sites - same for all units}
     unit with actfunct Act_Logistic, outfunc OutThreshold05, act random: stdUnit;
structure
     cluster[35] of stdUnit with iotype input matrix (5,7) at (2,7): inLayer;
                             {5x7 matrix to display letters}
     cluster[10] of stdUnit plane | at (8,7): hidLayer;
                             {hidden layer, ten units, vertically displayed, center (8,7), default type}
     clique[26] of stdUnit with  iotype output  get name from Letters
                             matrix (4,7) at (13,7) by -1.0: outLayer
                             {output layer: 26 char units in a wta-network, 4x7 matrix, center (13,7)}
var      unit: x, y;
begin                        {define connectins between layers}
     foreach x in inLayer do
         foreach y in hidLayer do
             x-> y : 1.0      {fully connect input to hidden layer}
         end
     end;
     foreach x in hidLayer do
         foreach y in outLayer do
             x-> y : 1.0      {fully connect hidden to output layer}
         end
     end
end.
```

Fig. 4: Nessus program to generate simple letter recognition network

4.2. The Network Compiler

Our compiler performs the following tasks:

- translation of a network definition into an input file for the simulator kernel
- combining of source files and intermediate representation files to networks, and
- computing the layout of the generated networks for the graphical interface.

We used Lex and Yacc to construct the scanner and the LALR-parser, mainly because the language was undergoing several changes during implementation. The programmer can define output and activation functions or learning rules as C functions which are included in a library. These functions are linked to the simulator kernel by the compiler.

The compiler supports debugging of Nessus programs indicating the positions of detected errors in the source file. The format of error messages is compatible with the EMACS editor, thus providing a comfortable programming environment. If compilation is initiated from within EMACS, the editor automatically positions on the line in which the first error occurred, even for files that are linked in.

5. RECENT MODIFICATIONS TO SNNS

Since the simulator kernel and graphical user interface are now efficient enough in our view, the inclusion of other popular network paradigms other than the numerous variations of back propagation is given priority now. We already have implemented Hopfield networks, ART 1 [Carpenter, Grossberg 88], Quickprop and Counterpropagation [Hecht-Nielsen 88]. We continue to implement further network paradigms.

At the same time we are trying to facilitate installation and porting SNNS to other Unix workstation platforms that we can access in our department and that support X11R4. We are considering a port to OSF/Motif.

It is planned to distribute SNNS via anonymous ftp free of charge under a GNU-style copyright and license agreement, including source code. We only need to charge a nominal fee for the printed user manuals and postage. Currently all written documentation is in German, but we hope to have an English version of the documentation by the time this article appears.

6. APPLICATIONS OF SNNS

SNNS is used by a number of co-workers and students in our department as well as some cooperating research institutions. Some applications so far include

- *printed character recognition*: the goal is here to recognize printed individual characters of a variety of fonts in different sizes scanned by an OCR scanner. The characters are already segmented and are rotated only slightly. The neural net models examined here are various variants of backpropagation, counterpropagation and quickprop.
- *handwritten character recognition*: scale and position invariant recognition of single handwritten characters. The same models are examined plus more specialized models like the neocognitron.
- *recognition of machine parts*: two dimensional binary and gray scale images of relatively flat machine parts are to be recognized with a neural net classifier system. The machine parts may be rotated to any degree. Part of the image preprocessing will be done with conventional technology.
- *stock prize prediction*: based on the previous time behaviour of selected stock and economic indices, a short term prediction of selected stock values and direction of movement is being investigated. Here, the adaline, madaline and backpropagation models will be compared for this task.
- *recognition and classification of exogenic and endogenic components of event correlated brain potentials*: this research is done in collaboration with a medical psychology research group in Tübingen who is in charge of the experimental setup and the choice of network model.

- *noise reduction in natural language communication in a telecom environment*: together with an industry partner specializing in telefone and mobile phone equipment, the application of neural networks for noise reduction and later on for recognition of a limited subset of spoken language in a noisy telecom environment is being investigated.
- *texture and object recognition.* This larger joint project with another federal research institution and an industry partner will use SNNS for research on texture and object recognition for real world vision problems, like materials inspection and image segmentation of objects differentiated by textures. Here SNNS will be used to evaluate various neural network models which will later be trained on a massively parallel neural network simulation system on a SIMD computer (see below).

The first of these applications are performed as student projects, the last three are cooperation projects. It is expected that the range of applications of SNNS will further increase considerably.

7. A PARALLEL NEURAL NETWORK SIMULATION ENVIRONMENT

In a successor project a massively parallel simulation system for neural networks on a SIMD-computer with more than 16.000 processors (MasPar MP-1216) is being developed. The goal is to enable the simulation of large neural networks for the tasks of image processing, feature extraction and pattern and object recognition.

The MasPar MP-1216 delivers a peak performance of 30,000 MIPS (32 bit addition) and 1,500 resp. 600 MFLOPS (32 bit resp. 64 bit). Communication bandwidth is up to 1500 MB/s peak global router and up to 24 GB/s peak X-net communication. It can be programmed with parallel versions of C (MPL) and Fortran. MPPE (MasPar parallel programming environment), an integrated graphical tool set based on X-Windows, facilitates program development and debugging. An overview of the MasPar MP-1216 architecture is given in fig. 5.

The sequential neural network simulator SNNS will be the starting point for the parallel simulator to be implemented. The parallel simulator will consist of a massively parallel simulator kernel running on the MasPar, an X-Windows based graphical user interface to visualize the networks on graphic workstations, and a modified description language. Tools for the analysis of network performance, for measurements of learning behaviour and for tests about scalability of the models will be developed and integrated into the system.

We are currently investigating the benefits of different approaches to parallelization of the kernel, as given in [Singer 90], [Grajski et al. 90], [Chinn et al. 90] and [Zhang et al. 89]. The studies of [Grajski et al. 90] showed that 9.8 M CUPS (connection updates per second) for learning and 18.4 M CUPS during recall can be obtained with "vanilla" backpropagation benchmarks on a 16K PE MasPar MP-1. These studies suggest that for networks with regular topology, between a tenfold and a hundredfold increase in performance of a massively parallel SIMD system against a workstation simulator can be obtained.

The implementation of the parallel simulator will be done in MPL, a parallel extension of C.

8. ACKNOWLEDGEMENTS

Some ideas in the simulator were inspired by the Rochester Connectionist Simulator RCS, [Goddard et al. 89], some also by the Esprit II Research Project 2059 Pygmalion Neurocomputing Simulator [Pygmalion 90 a-c]. Other popular simulators, like P3 [Zipser, Rabin 86], the PDP-Simulators [McClelland 86] and NeuralWorks Professional II [NeuralWare 90] and the Axon language [Hecht-Nielsen 88] were analyzed but did not have a great impact on our own system.

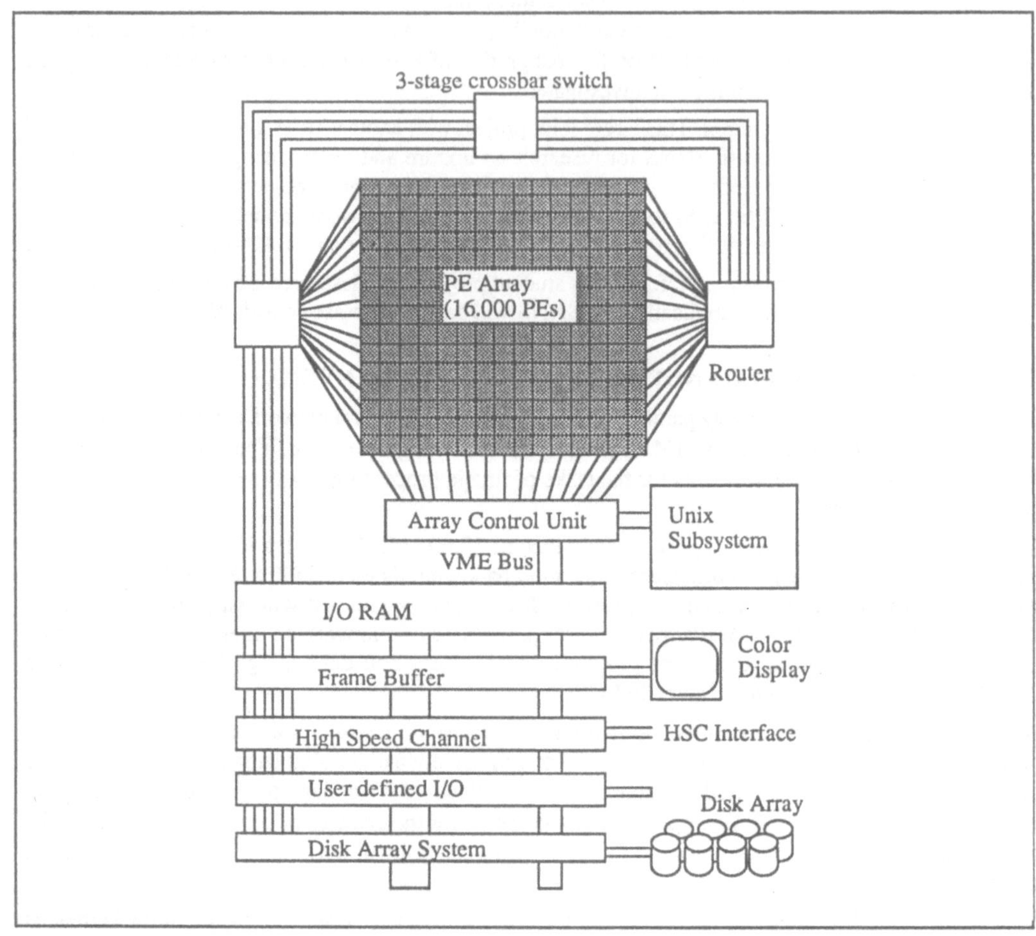

Fig. 5: MasPar MP-1 architecture

REFERENCES

[Carpenter, Grossberg 88] Carpenter, G.A., Grossberg, S.: The ART of Adaptive Pattern Recognition by a Self Organizing Neural Network, IEEE Computer, March 1988, pp. 77-88

[Chinn et al. 90] G. Chinn, K.A. Grajski, C. Chen, C. Kuszmaul, S. Tomboulian: Systolic Array Implementations o Neural Nets on the MasPar MP-1 Massively Parallel Processor, MasPar Corp. Int. Report

[Eckmiller 90] R. Eckmiller (Ed.): Advanced Neural Computers, North Holland, 1990

[Eckmiller et al. 90] R. Eckmiller, G. Hartmann, G. Hauske (Ed.): Parallel Processing in Neural Systems an Computers, North Holland, 1990

[Goddard et al. 89] Goddard, N.H., Lynne, K.J., Mintz, T., Bukys, L.: The Rochester Connectionist Simulator: Use Manual, Tech Report 233 (revised), Univ. of Rochester, NY, 1989

[Grajski et al. 90] K.A. Grajski, G. Chinn, C. Chen, C. Kuszmaul, S. Tomboulian: Neural Network Simulation on th MasPar MP-1 Massively Parallel Processor, Internat. Neural Network Conference, Paris, France, 1990

[Hecht-Nielsen 88] Hecht-Nielsen, R.: Neurocomputing, Addison-Wesley, 1990

[Hinton 89] Hinton, G.E.: Connectionist Learning Proceedures, Artificial Intelligence 40 (1989), p. 185-234

[NeuralWorks 90a, b, c] NeuralWorks Professional II: Neural Computing, Users Guide, Reference Guide, NeuralWa Inc., 1990

[McClelland, Rumelhart 87] McClelland, J.A., Rumelhart, D.E., the PDP Research Group: Explorations in Parall Distributed Processing, MIT Press, Cambridge MA, 1987

[Pygmalion 90a] M. Hewetson: Pygmalion Neurocomputing, Graphic Monitor Tutorial v 1.1 & Graphic Monitor Manual, Dept. Comp. Science, University College, London

[Pygmalion 90b] J. Taylor: Pygmalion Neurocomputing, Algorithm Library v 1.0, ditto

[Pygmalion 90c] M. B. R. Vellasco: Pygmalion Neurocomputing, nC Tutorial & nC Manual v 1.02, ditto

[Recce, Treleaven 89] Recce, M., Treleaven, P.C.: Parallel Architectures for Neural Computers, Neural Computers, Springer, 1989, pp. 487-495

[Rumelhart, McClelland 86] Rumelhart, D.E., McClelland, J.A., the PDP Research Group: Parallel Distributed Processing, Vol. 1, 2, MIT Press, Cambridge MA, 1986

[Singer 90] A. Singer: Implementations of Artificial Neural Networks on the Connection Machine, Thinking Machines Corp. Tech. Rep. RL 90-2, Jan. 1990 (also to appear in Parallel Computing, summer 1990)

[SNNS 91a] A. Zell, Th. Korb, N. Mache, T. Sommer: SNNS, Stuttgarter Neuronale Netze Simulator, Benutzerhandbuch, Universität Stuttgart, Fakultät Informatik, Bericht Nr. 1/91, (in German)

[SNNS 91b] A. Zell, Th. Korb, N. Mache, T. Sommer: SNNS, Stuttgarter Neuronale Netze Simulator, Nessus-Handbuch, Universität Stuttgart, Fakultät Informatik, Bericht Nr. 3/91, (in German)

[Touretzky 89] Touretzky, D.: Advances in Neural Information Processing Systems 1, Morgan Kaufmann, 1989

[Touretzky et al. 88] Touretzky, D., Hinton, G., Sejnowski, T.: Proc. of the 1988 Connectonist Models Summer School, June 17-26, Carnegie Mellon University, Morgan Kaufmann, 1988

[Zhang et al. 89] X. Zhang, M. Mckenna, J.P. Mesirov, D. L. Waltz: An efficient implementation of the Back-propagation algorithm on the Connection Machine CM-2, Thinking Machines Corp. TR

[Zell et al. 89] A. Zell, Th. Korb, T. Sommer, R. Bayer: NetSim, ein Simulator für Neuronale Netze, Informatik Fachberichte 216, D. Metzing (Hrsgb.) GWAI-89, 13th German Workshop on Artificial Intelligence, Eringerfeld, Sept. 89, Springer, pp. 134-143 (in German)

[Zell et al. 90] A. Zell, Th. Korb, T. Sommer, R. Bayer: A Neural Network Simulation Environment, Proc. Applications of Neural Networks Conf., SPIE Vol. 1294, pp. 535-544

[Zell et al. 91] A. Zell, Th. Korb, N. Mache, T. Sommer: Recent Developments of the SNNS Neural Network Simulator, Proc. Applications of Neural Networks Conf., SPIE Vol. 1294, 1991

[Zipser, Rabin 86] D. Zipser, D.E. Rabin: P3: A Parallel Network Simulation System, in [Rumelhart, McClelland 86]

„wahrscheinlich sind meine Beispiele soo sprunghaft
und und und eh ehm zu zu telegraph" –
Konnektionistische Modellierung von „covert repairs"[*]

Ulrich Schade

Hans-Jürgen Eikmeyer

Fakultät für Linguistik und Literaturwissenschaft

Universität Bielefeld

Universitätsstraße 25

D-4800 Bielefeld 1

Zusammenfassung

In diesem Beitrag wird eine spezielle Klasse von Phänomenen gesprochener Sprache, die sogenannten „covert repairs", mit ihren Relationen zum kognitiven Prozeß der Planung und Produktion von Äußerungen und zum interaktiven Prozeß der Verteilung des Rederechts („turn taking") diskutiert. Ausgehend von diesen Bezugspunkten werden Regeln für die Produktion von „covert repairs" formuliert, in die Diskursbedingungen eingehen. Die Regeln werden in einem konnektionistischen Produktionsmodell integriert, das zuvor eingeführt wird. Die Integration liefert ein einfaches Modell auch für Sequenzen von „covert repairs", das die empirischen Daten adäquat beschreibt und erklärt.

1. „Covert repairs" und kognitive Modellierung

Wiederholungen, Hesitationen („eh(m)") und Pausen („..") sind charakteristische Eigenschaften gesprochener Sprache, die nur scheinbar irregulär sind. In diesem Beitrag wird versucht, einfache Bedingungen für ihre Produktion anzugeben. In Anlehnung an die Klassifikation von Levelt (1983) werden alle drei vorstehend genannten Typen von Phänomenen gemeinsam als „covert repairs" bezeichnet. Der folgende Ausschnitt aus einem Transkript zeigt mehrere von ihnen *in situ* und macht insbesondere deutlich, daß „covert repairs" auch in Sequenzen auftreten:

[*] Die Arbeiten zu diesem Beitrag wurden von der DFG im Rahmen der DFG-Forschergruppe „Kohärenz" an der Universität Bielefeld gefördert.

(1)   ich weiß- ich weiß- ich weiß- ich weiß- ich weiß- ich weiß jetzt wir habn- ich eh
      habe Sie zu schnell unterbrochen & s war meine Schuld & aber ich weiß jetzt was
      ich Sie (k) wo eh in welchem Sinn welchem Sinn nach ich Sie unterbrechen wollte,
      Sie haben gesagt, eh wie man auch immer .. wie man auch immer darauf reagiert hat,
      <u>wer</u>, das ist nämlich die Stichfrage, <u>wer</u>?

Seit Anfang der fünfziger Jahre wird — insbesondere in den Arbeiten von Goldman-Eisler (eine Zusammenfassung findet sich in Goldman-Eisler 1967) — ein Zusammenhang zwischen „covert repairs" und dem Prozeß der Planung von Äußerungen gesehen. In diesen ersten Arbeiten wurden jedoch zu starke Annahmen über diesen Zusammenhang gemacht. So ist etwa die These, Pausen seien notwendig für die Planung, und Sprechen ohne Pause sei gar nicht möglich, viel zu stark (vgl. Brotherton 1979). Diese These ist von der Vorstellung einer seriellen Organisation des Sprachproduktionsprozesses geprägt, die heute als obsolet zu gelten hat (vgl. Bock 1982).

Ein Zusammenhang zwischen Planungsprozessen und „covert repairs" wird natürlich nicht bezweifelt, die — im Vergleich zur Vergangenheit weit vorsichtigere — aktuelle Formulierung besagt jedoch in etwa, daß „covert repairs" *Planungsprobleme* signalisieren. Daneben haben sie in dialogischen Situationen die Funktion, dem Sprecher das Festhalten am Rederecht zu ermöglichen, obwohl er Planungsprobleme hat (vgl. Siegman 1979). „Covert repairs" sind also in der Lage Situationen zu verhindern, die in dem Transkript (1) von einem der Beteiligten angesprochen werden, daß nämlich einer den anderen unterbrechen kann, wenn dieser in seiner Rede nicht flüssig fortfährt. Alle drei Typen von „covert repairs" erlauben das Festhalten am Rederecht, auch Pausen. Dies erscheint zwar auf den ersten Blick paradox, aber nicht jede Pause führt eben zu einem Verlust des Rederechtes wie auch an obigem Transkript zu sehen ist. Von graduellen Unterschieden in der Effizienz der drei Typen von „covert repairs" ist allerdings auszugehen; diese Unterschiede wurden auch experimentell nachgewiesen (vgl. Beattie 1979).

Bei der Behandlung von „covert repairs" kann man sich nicht auf die Betrachtung des Produzenten beschränken; die Diskurssituation und das „turn taking"-System, d.h. die Regularien für die Verteilung des Rederechts, müssen ebenfalls berücksichtigt werden (vgl. Sacks, Schegloff & Jefferson 1974). Damit schließt man an bereits gut etablierte Bereiche der KI an, die sich mit der Diskurssituation, Partnermodellierung u.ä. auseinandersetzen. Aus der Sicht der kognitiven Modellierung besteht ein besonderes Interesse an Phänomenen wie „covert repairs", da sie zum einen erlauben, aus der Betrachtung eines gestörten Systems auf seine Funktion im Normalfall zurückzuschließen, und zum anderen einen Mechanismus zur Prävention von Störungen darstellen.

2. Eine Modellvorstellung für die Produktion von „covert repairs"

Für die Produktion von „covert repairs" muß es nach dem bereits gesagten einen *Anlaß* geben. Dieser Anlaß wird hier identifiziert mit einem Planungsproblem, d.h. dem Sprecher ist es nicht gelungen, seine folgende Äußerung soweit zu planen, daß er bereits etwas äußern könnte. Um dennoch am Rederecht festzuhalten, produziert er ein „covert repair". Unter den drei möglichen *Realisationsformen* (Pausen, Hesitationen und Wiederholungen) wird eine aufgrund der geltenden *Diskursbedingungen* gewählt. Die erste dabei zu berücksichtigende Regeln ist die

(2) *Siegman-Beattie-Regel*
In bezug auf das Festhalten am Rederecht sind Wiederholungen effektiver als Hesitationen, letztere sind ihrerseits effektiver als Pausen.

Für die Beschreibung von Sequenzen von „covert repairs" kommt eine zweite Regel hinzu, die einen Kumulierungseffekt postuliert:

(3) *Sequenz-Regel*
Wenn das letzt Produktionsresultat bereits ein „covert repair" war und das Planungsproblem fortbesteht, so darf das aktuell zu produzierende „covert repair" nicht efektiver sein als das vorherige. Vielmehr kann das aktuell zu produzierende „covert repair" isoliert betrachtet an Effektivität abnehmen. In Verbindung mit dem zuletzt produzierten wird dessen Effektivität trotzdem fortgeschrieben.

Mit Hilfe der letzten Regel ist das Beispiel aus dem Titel beschreibbar, in dem auf zwei Wiederholungen von „und" zwei Hesitationen folgen („eh ehm"). Sie beschreibt auch Fälle wie (4), in denen auf eine Hesitation („äh") eine Pause folgt:

(4) `ja ich habe auch irgendwie gleichzeitig .. das Gefühl daß es äh .. jetzt ja daß es`
     `aber allen schwer fällt`

Zu den Diskursbedingungen für die Produktion von „covert repairs" gehören zwei triviale Bedingungen: (i) der Sprecher hat das Rederecht und (ii) er intendiert, am Rederecht festzuhalten. Bemerkt der Sprecher dann, daß er (iii) ein Planungsproblem hat, wird er nach den beiden vorstehenden Regeln eine Realisationsform wählen. Die Wahl hängt nach der hier vertretenen Modellvorstellung von der

Einschätzung des Sprechers ab, wie groß die Gefahr ist, das Rederecht zu verlieren. Bei Einbeziehung der Regel (2) allein wird er bei großer Gefahr eine Wiederholung produzieren, bei mittelgroßer Gefahr eine Hesitation und bei geringer Gefahr eine Pause. Durch die Regel (3) ist es aber auch möglich, bei mehreren Planungsproblemen in Folge in der Hierarchie ‚Wiederholung > Hesitation > Pause‘ zu niedrigeren Realisationsformen zu greifen.

Die Realisationsform eines zu produzierenden „covert repair" — Wiederholung, Hesitation oder Pause — wird bestimmt durch die Relation eines Parameters p_i zu zwei Schwellwerten t_1 und t_2 ($0 \leq t_1 < t_2 \leq 1$). Wenn zum Zeitpunkt i gilt, daß $0 < p_i \leq t_1$ ist, wird eine *Pause* produziert. Wenn $t_1 < p_i \leq t_2$ gilt, entsteht eine *Hesitation* und bei $t_2 < p_i \leq 1$ eine *Wiederholung*.

Der Parameter p_i ist eine Funktion von der Einschätzung des Sprechers über die Gefahr, das Rederecht zu verlieren und der Anzahl der bisher produzierten „covert repairs". Die Einschätzung der Gefahr, das Rederecht zu verlieren hat eine langsame Dynamik, d.h. sie ändert sich nach Brotherton (1979) nur im Bereich mehrerer Minuten. Es wird daher angenommen, daß diese Einschätzung für die Dauer einer Äußerung konstant ist.

Die vorstehend skizzierte Modellvorstellung ist noch unabhängig von einer konkreten Realisierung durch ein Modell einer bestimmten Klasse (symbolverarbeitend vs. konnektionistisch) zu sehen. Eine Realisierung im symbolverarbeitenden Paradigma liegt mit Eikmeyer (1987, 1989) vor. Im folgenden wird eine Realisierung diskutiert, die in ein konnektionistisches Sprachproduktionsmodell integriert ist.

3. Ein konnektionistisches Sprachproduktionsmodell

Für die kognitive Fähigkeit der Sprachproduktion existieren in der Literatur konnektionistische Modelle in der Tradition von Gary Dell (Dell & Reich 1980; Dell 1985, 1986, 1988; Stemberger 1985a, 1985b, 1990; Berg 1986, 1988; MacKay 1987; Schade 1988, 1990). Die verschiedenen Modelle unterscheiden sich in der Repräsentation syntaktischer Regeln und der damit verbundenen Realisation der Sequentialisierung linguistischer Einheiten wie Wörter, Silben und Phoneme während des Produktionsprozesses. Alle diese Modelle sind lokale konnektionistische Modelle (nach der Terminologie von Rumelhart und McClelland 1986), da sie jede der genannten linguistischen Einheiten, also jedes Wort, jede Silbe, jedes Phonem aber auch jedes phonologische Merkmal, durch einen Knoten eines konnektionistischen Netzwerks repräsentieren.

Grundsätzlich bestehen konnektionistische Modelle aus einem Netzwerk miteinander verbundener Knoten, die über einen Aktivierungswert verfügen. Übersteigt der Aktivierungwert eines Knotens seinen Schwellwert, so kann der Knoten an seine Nachbarn Aktivierung weiterleiten. Die Menge der Aktivierung, die ein Knoten weiterleitet, hängt dabei von zweierlei Faktoren ab: Sie ist zum einen proportional zu der Aktivierung des sendenden Knotens, und sie ist zum anderen proportional zu der Stärke der Verbindung zwischen dem sendenden Knoten und dem Empfänger. Aufgrund der eingehenden Aktivierung verändern sich die Aktivierungswerte der Knoten.

Die Knoten der konnektionistischen Modelle für die Sprachproduktion sind in Ebenen angeordnet. Es gibt beispielsweise eine Ebene mit Wortknoten, eine Ebene mit Silbenknoten, eine Ebene mit Phonemknoten und mehrere Ebenen mit Knoten für phonologische Merkmale. In dem hier zugrunde gelegten Modell sind alle Knoten einer Ebene paarweise durch inhibitorische Leitungen verbunden. Inhibitorische Leitungen sind Verbindungen zwischen Knoten, die zu einer Verkleinerung des Aktivierungswertes beim empfangenden Knoten führen, ihn also hemmen. Inhibitorische Verbindungen ergeben sich aus linguistisch paradigmatischen Relationen und beschreiben Wahlmöglichkeiten für bestimmte strukturelle Positionen: Zu einer bestimmten Zeit kann immer nur ein Wort, nur eine Silbe und nur ein Phonem geäußert werden.

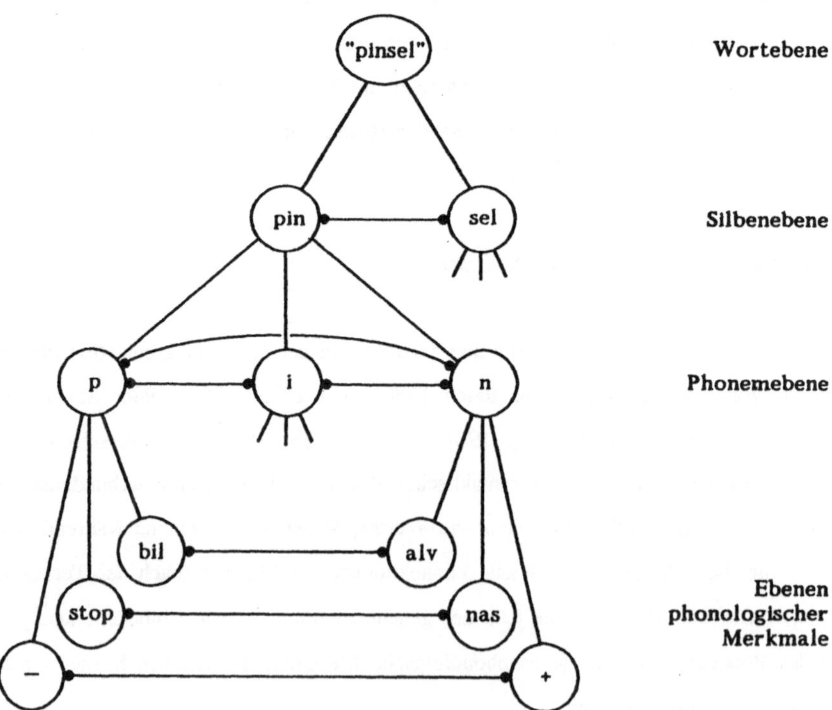

Abbildung 1: Ausschnitt aus einem konnektionistischen Netzwerk zur Sprachproduktion

Anders als bei den inhibitorischen Leitungen, die von Dell und MacKay nicht vorgesehen sind, stimmen die Modelle bezüglich der exzitatorischen Leitungen (Verbindungen, über die Aktivierung weitergeben wird, die zur Vergrößerung des Aktivierungswertes des empfangenden Knotens führt) überein. Exzitatorische Leitungen ergeben sich aus syntagmatischen Relationen zwischen den linguistischen Einheiten und verbinden stets Knoten benachbarter Ebenen: beispielsweise ist ein Silbenknoten mit denjenigen Knoten der Phonemebene verbunden, die die Phoneme der entsprechenden Silbe repräsentieren (vgl. Abbildung 1). Alle exzitatorischen und inhibitorischen Verbindungen sind symmetrisch, so daß bei einer Produktion Feedbackeffekte auftreten (vgl. Dell 1985).

Wird mit der Hilfe eines konnektionistischen Netzwerkes der beschriebenen Art Sprachproduktion modelliert, so wird derjenige Knoten auf einen hohen Aktivierungswert gesetzt, der die zu äußernde linguistische Einheit repräsentiert; dies kann beispielsweise ein Knoten auf einer der semantischen Ebenen sein, wenn der entsprechende semantische Gehalt in einer Äußerung wiederzugeben ist. Nach dieser „Initialisierung" des Netzwerkes breitet sich im Netz Aktivierung aus. Aufgrund der daraus entstehenden Aktivierungsverteilung erfolgen dann — in bestimmten Zeitabständen — Selektionen von Wörtern bzw. deren Teilen. Bei der Produktion eines (nächsten) Wortes muß beispielsweise zunächst das Wort selbst durch die Selektion ausgewählt werden, später dann eine seiner Silben bzw. deren Phoneme. Selektion auf der Wortebene bedeutet beispielsweise die Versorgung eines Teilnetzes mit Aktivierung, das letztlich die Realisierung der Phonemkette des entsprechenden Wortes steuert. Ebenso wie für die Weitergabe von Aktivierung muß der Aktivierungswert eines Knotens einen Schwellwert überschreiten, bevor eine Selektion dieses Knotens bzw. der durch den Knoten repräsentierten linguistischen Einheit erfolgen kann.

4. Eine konnektionistische Modellierung der Produktion von „covert repairs"

In einem konnektionistischen Produktionsmodell ergibt sich der Anlaß zur Produktion eines „covert repairs" dadurch, daß eine Selektion stattfinden sollte, ohne daß ein Knoten der betrachteten linguistischen Ebene seine Selektionsschwelle überschritten hat. In einem solchen Fall hat der Planungsprozeß, der durch die zuvor erfolgte Aktivierungsausbreitung modelliert wird, noch nicht zu einem selegierbaren Resultat geführt. Im Beispiel aus dem Titel dieses Beitrags etwa liegt nach der Produktion der Konjunktion „und" kein weiteres Wort vor, das produziert werden könnte.

Das Fehlschlagen einer Selektion bewirkt in dem der Sequentialisierung dienenden syntaktischen Teilnetz des Produktionsmodells (vgl. Schade 1990), daß erneut eine Selektion von der Art vorbereitet wird wie die zuletzt fehlgeschlagene. Des weiteren wird dem Knoten D erlaubt seine Aktivierung in das Teilnetz einzuspeisen, das die Produktion steuert. Der Knoten D repräsentiert die für unsere Fragestellung zentrale Diskursbedingung, nämlich die Einschätzung der Gefahr, daß das Rederecht für das Produktionssystem verloren geht. Je höher die Aktivierung dieses Knotens ist, desto höher wird diese Gefahr eingeschätzt. Entsprechend der in Abschnitt 2 dargelegten Überlegungen ist die Aktivierung von D für die Simulation einer Äußerung konstant.

Der Knoten D aktiviert bei einem vorliegenden Planungsproblem den Knoten CR (vgl. Abbildung 2), der die Realisierung eines „covert repair" steuert. Bleibt dessen Aktivierungswert unterhalb seiner Aktivationsschwelle, so kann CR selbst keine Aktivierung weitergeben, und eine Produktion unterbleibt. Der Fluß der Gesamtproduktion wird also in diesem Fall durch eine Pause unterbrochen. Die Aktivationsschwelle von CR entspricht damit dem in Abschnitt 2 postulierten Schwellwert t_1.

Liegt die Aktivierung von CR über der Aktivierungsschwelle t_1, so werden die Knoten H und W von CR aktiviert. Die Aktivationsschwelle des Knotens W ist identisch mit dem in Abschnitt 2 postulierten Schwellwert t_2. Liegt die von CR an W abgegebene Aktivierung unterhalb dieser Schwelle, so kann W keine Aktivierung weiterleiten. Da der Knoten H ebenso wie CR die Aktivierungsschwelle t_1 besitzt, kann er in diesem Fall die Produktion einer Hesitation initiieren. Liegt dagegen die Aktivierung von W über der Schwelle t_2, so kann W die Produktion einer Wiederholung einleiten. Da in diesem Fall W gleichzeitig H hemmt, ist gesichert, daß die Produktion einer Hestitation unterbleibt (vgl. Abbildung 2).

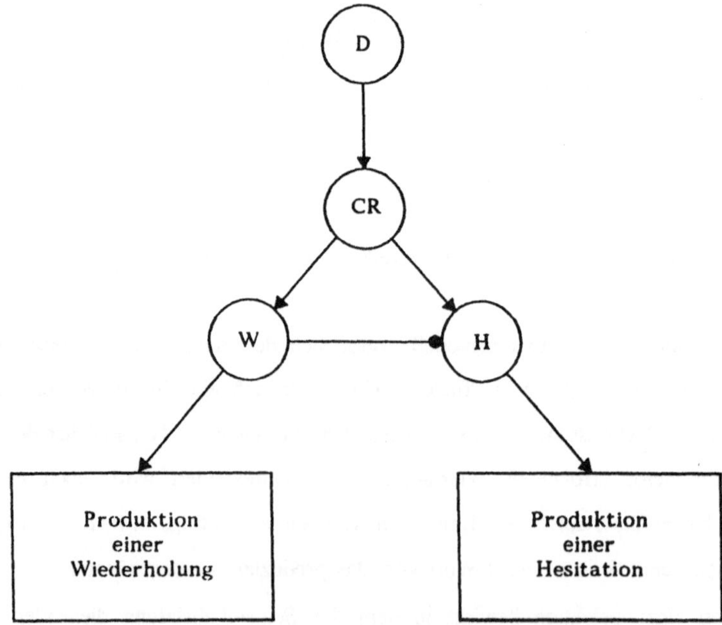

Abbildung 2: Teilnetz für die Realisierung von „covert repairs"

Der Aktivierungsverlauf des Knotens CR ist so gewählt, daß solange „covert repairs" zu Selektionszeitpunkten erzeugt werden, bis auf der betrachteten linguistischen Ebene der Aktivierungswert eines Knotens seinen Selektionsschwellwert überschritten hat und die linguistische Einheit, die dieser Knoten repräsentiert, realisiert wird. Im Beispiel aus dem Titel beendet die Produktion von „zu" die Sequenz der „covert repairs". Abbildung 3 zeigt den entsprechenden Aktivierungsverlauf. Da während der Zeit, in der die „covert repairs" produziert werden, der Aktivierungswert von CR dem normalen (langsamen) Zerfallsprozeß unterworfen ist, der auf die Aktivierungswerte aller Knoten wirkt, ergibt sich die in Abschnitt 2 diskutierte Folge von „covert repairs" abfallender Mächtigkeit: Der Abfall der Aktivierung unter den Wert t_2 bewirkt die Produktion von Hesitationen statt Wiederholungen, und der Abfall der Aktivierung unter den Wert t_1 bewirkt die Produktion von Pausen.

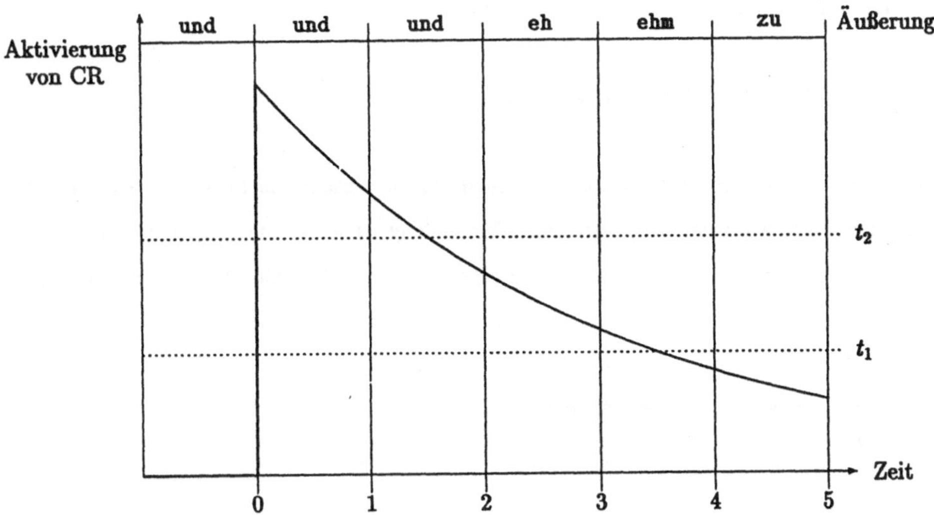

Abbildung 3: Aktivierungsverlauf von CR während einer Beispielsequenz

5. Abschließende Bemerkungen

Das im vorangehenden Abschnitt diskutierte Modell für die Produktion von „covert repairs" läßt sich in ähnlicher Form auch symbolverarbeitend realisieren (vgl. Eikmeyer 1987, 1989). Für eine konnektionistische Realisierung sprechen jedoch zwei Gründe: Zum einen läßt sich die konnektionistische Lösung leicht in bekannte konnektionistische Produktionsmodelle (vgl. Abschnitt 3) integrieren, zumal diese bereits über das Konzept der Produktionsschwelle zur Modellierung von Planungsproblemen verfügen, daß den Anlaß für die Produktion von „covert repairs" darstellt. Zum anderen läßt sich aus der konnektionistischen Modellierung eine interessante Vorhersage über den Zusammenhang von Sprechgeschwindigkeit und Sequenzen von „covert repairs" ableiten. Da die Zerfallsrate, die den Zerfall der Aktivierung des Knotens CR — wie auch aller anderer Knoten — bestimmt, eine konstante Größe ist, ergibt sich aus dem vorgestellten Modell die Vorhersage, daß eine Vergrößerung der Sprechgeschwindigkeit die Länge von Sequenzen von „covert repairs" vergrößert. Anhand dieser Vorhersage kann das Modell, das die empirisch abgeleitete Sequenz-Regel (vgl. Abschnitt 2) adäquat abbildet, empirisch getestet werden.

Sowohl das vorgestellte konnektionistische Modell als auch das o.a. symbolverarbeitende Modell beschreiben nicht alle Vorkommen von „covert repairs". Ausgenommen sind zum einen „covert repairs" als Bestandteile von größeren Strukturen wie etwa „error repairs" (vgl. Levelt 1983), da sie in solchen Fällen (vgl. (5)) eine reparatureinleitende Funktion haben.

(5)   wir kommen jetzt zum Anfang ähh zum Ende

Zum anderen sind Fälle wie (6) problematisch, da in ihnen die absteigende Folge der Realisationsformen unterbrochen wird. Nach der hier vertretenen Vorstellung ist jedoch das zweite Vorkommen von „das war" in (6) keine Wiederholung des ersten Vorkommens, sondern ein „fresh start" (vgl. Levelt 1989, S. 490ff.).

(6)   das war eh eh das war ein Selbstgespräch

Anmerkung

Wir danken Klaus Kinski für die Produktion des Beispiels im Titel sowie von (1) und (6) im Verlauf einer denkwürdigen Talkshow. Beispiel (4) ist einem Therapiegespräch entnommen; Beispiel (5) wurde nach der Realität konstruiert.

Literatur

Beattie, G. (1979). The Modifiability of the Temporal Structure of Spontaneous Speech. In: Siegman & Feldstein (1979), 115–148.

Berg, T. (1986). The Problems of Language Control: Editing, Monitoring, and Feedback. *Psychological Research*, 48, 133–144.

Berg, T. (1988). *Die Abbildung des Sprachproduktionsprozesses in einem Aktivierungsflußmodell*. Tübingen: Niemeyer.

Bock, J.K. (1982). Towards a Cognitive Psychology of Syntax: Information Processing Contributions to Sentence Formulation. *Psychological Review*, 89, 1–47.

Brotherton, P. (1979). Speaking and Not Speaking: Processes for Translating Ideas into Speech. In: Siegman & Feldstein (1979), 179–209.

Dell, G.S. (1985). Positive Feedback in Hierarchical Connectionist Models: Applications to Language Production. *Cognitive Science*, 9, 3–23.

Dell, G.S. (1986). A Spreading-Activation Theory of Retrieval in Sentence Production. *Psychological Review*, 93, 283–321.

Dell, G.S. (1988). The Retrieval of Phonological Forms in Production: Tests of Prediction from a Connectionist Model. *Journal of Memory and Language*, 27, 124–142.

Dell, G.S. & Reich, P.A. (1980). Toward a Unified Model of Slips of the Tongue. In: V.A. Fromkin (Hrsg.), *Errors in Linguistic Performance*, 273–286. New York, NY: Academic Press.

Eikmeyer, H.-J. (1987). Die Simulation der Produktion von „covert repairs". Ms., Universität Bielefeld.

Eikmeyer, H.-J. (1989). Ein Prozeßmodell für die Produktion von „covert repairs". Ms., Universität Bielefeld.

Goldman-Eisler, F. (1967). Sequential Temporal Patterns and Cognitive Processes in Speech. *Language and Speech*, 10, 122–132.

Levelt, W.J.M. (1983). Monitoring and Self-Repair in Speech. *Cognition*, 14, 41–104.

Levelt, W.J.M. (1989). *Speaking: From Intention to Articulation*. Cambridge, MA; London: MIT-Press.

MacKay, D.G. (1987). *The Organisation of Perception and Action*. New York, NY: Springer.

Rumelhart, D.E. & McClelland, J.L. (1986). *Parallel Distributed Processing: Explorations in the Microstructure of Cognition, Vol. 1: Foundations*. Cambridge, MA: MIT-Press.

Sacks, H., Schegloff, E. & G. Jefferson (1974). A Simplest Systematics for the Organization of Turn-taking for Conversation. *Language*, 50, 696–735.

Schade, U. (1988). Ein konnektionistisches Modell für die Satzproduktion. In: J. Kindermann & C. Lischka (Hrsg.), *Workshop Konnektionismus*, Arbeitspapiere der GMD, 329, 207–220. St. Augustin.

Schade, U. (1990). Konnektionistische Modellierung der Sprachproduktion. Dissertation, Universität Bielefeld.

Siegman, A. (1979). Cognition and Hesitation in Speech. In: Siegman & Feldstein (1979), 151–178.

Siegman, A. & S. Feldstein (Eds.) (1979), *Of Speech and Time. Temporal Speech Patterns in Interpersonal Contexts*. Hillsdale, NJ: Erlbaum.

Stemberger, J.P. (1985a). An Interactive Activation Model of Language Production. In: A.W. Ellis (Hrsg.), *Progress in the Psychology of Language*, Vol. 1, 143–186. London: Erlbaum.

Stemberger, J.P. (1985b). *The Lexicon in a Model of Language Production*. New York, NY: Garland Publishing.

Stemberger, J.P. (1990). Wordshape Errors in Language Production. *Cognition*, 35, 123–157.

Band 240: D. Tavangarian, Flagorientierte Assoziativspeicher und -prozessoren. XII. 193 Seiten. 1990.

Band 241: A. Schill, Migrationssteuerung und Konfigurationsverwaltung für verteilte objektorientierte Anwendungen. IX, 174 Seiten. 1990.

Band 242: D. Wybranietz, Multicast-Kommunikation in verteilten Systemen. VIII, 191 Seiten. 1990.

Band 243: U. Hahn, Lexikalisch verteiltes Text-Parsing. X, 263 Seiten. 1990.

Band 244: B. R. Kämmerer, Sprecherunabhängigkeit und Sprecheradaption. VIII, 110 Seiten. 1990.

Band 245: C. Freksa, C. Habel (Hrsg.), Repräsentation und Verarbeitung räumlichen Wissens. VIII, 353 Seiten. 1990.

Band 246: Th. Bräunl, Massiv parallele Programmierung mit dem Parallaxis–Modell. XII, 168 Seiten. 1990

Band 247: H. Krumm, Funktionelle Analyse von Kommunikationsprotokollen. IX, 122 Seiten. 1990.

Band 248: G. Moerkotte, Inkonsistenzen in deduktiven Datenbanken. VIII, 141 Seiten. 1990.

Band 249: P. A. Gloor, N. A. Streitz (Hrsg.), Hypertext und Hypermedia. IX, 302 Seiten. 1990.

Band 250: H. W. Meuer (Hrsg.), SUPERCOMPUTER '90. Mannheim, Juni 1990. Proceedings. VIII, 209 Seiten. 1990.

Band 251: H. Marburger (Hrsg.), GWAI-90. 14th German Workshop on Artificial Intelligence. Eringerfeld, September 1990. Proceedings. X, 333 Seiten. 1990.

Band 252: G. Dorffner (Hrsg.), Konnektionismus in Artificial Intelligence und Kognitionsforschung. 6. Österreichische Artificial-Intelligence-Tagung (KONNAI), Salzburg, September 1990. Proceedings. VIII, 246 Seiten. 1990.

Band 253: W. Ameling (Hrsg.), ASST'90. 7. Aachener Symposium für Signaltheorie. Aachen, September 1990. Proceedings. XI, 332 Seiten. 1990.

Band 254: R. E. Großkopf (Hrsg.), Mustererkennung 1990. 12. DAGM-Symposium, Oberkochen-Aalen, September 1990. Proceedings. XXI, 686 Seiten. 1990.

Band 255: B. Reusch, (Hrsg.), Rechnergestützter Entwurf und Architektur mikroelektronischer Systeme. GME/GI/ITG-Fachtagung, Dortmund, Oktober 1990. Proceedings. X, 298 Seiten. 1990.

Band 256: W. Pillmann, A. Jaeschke (Hrsg.), Informatik für den Umweltschutz. 5. Symposium, Wien, September 1990. Proceedings. XV, 864 Seiten. 1990.

Band 257: A. Reuter (Hrsg.), GI–20. Jahrestagung I. Stuttgart, Oktober 1990. Proceedings. XVIII, 602 Seiten. 1990.

Band 258: A. Reuter (Hrsg.), GI–20. Jahrestagung II. Stuttgart, Oktober 1990. Proceedings. XVIII, 602 Seiten. 1990.

Band 259: H.-J. Friemel, G. Müller-Schönberger, A. Schütt (Hrsg.), Forum '90 Wissenschaft und Technik. Trier, Oktober 1990. Proceedings. XI, 532 Seiten. 1990.

Band 260: B. J. Frommherz, Ein Roboteraktionsplanungssystem. XI, 134 Seiten. 1990.

Band 261: W. Zimmermann, Automatische Komplexitätsanalyse funktionaler Programme. VII, 194 Seiten. 1990.

Band 262: W. Gerth, P. Baacke (Hrsg.), PEARL 90 - Workshop über Realzeitsysteme. 11. Fachtagung, Boppard, November 1990. Proceedings. X, 187 Seiten. 1990.

Band 263: H. Eckhardt, Entwurfstransaktionen für modulare Objektsysteme. VIII, 144 Seiten. 1990.

Band 264: T. Härder, H. Wedekind, G. Zimmermann (Hrsg.), Entwurf und Betrieb verteilter Systeme. Fachtagung, Dagstuhl, September 1990. Proceedings. XII, 283 Seiten. 1990.

Band 265: U. Herrmann, Mehrbenutzerkontrolle in Nicht-Standard-Datenbanksystemen. VIII, 183 Seiten. 1991.

Band 266: R. Cunis, A. Günter, H. Strecker (Hrsg.), Das PLAKON-Buch. VIII, 279 Seiten. 1991

Band 267: W. Effelsberg, H. W. Meuer, G. Müller (Hrsg.), Kommunikation in verteilten Systemen. GI/ITG-Fachtagung, Mannheim, Februar 1991. Proceedings. X, 589 Seiten. 1991.

Band 268: J. Raczkowsky, Multisensordatenverarbeitung in der Robotik. X, 168 Seiten. 1991.

Band 269: G. Hommel (Hrsg.), Prozeßrechensysteme '91. Berlin, Februar 1991. Proceedings. XIV, 449 Seiten. 1991.

Band 270: H.-J. Appelrath (Hrsg.), Datenbanksysteme in Büro, Technik und Wissenschaft. GI-Fachtagung, Kaiserslautern, März 1991. Proceedings. XIII, 507 Seiten. 1991.

Band 271: A. Pfitzmann, E. Raubold (Hrsg.), VIS '91, Verläßliche Informationssysteme. GI-Fachtagung, Darmstadt, März 1991. Proceedings. VIII, 355 Seiten. 1991.

Band 272: R. Grebe, C. Ziemann, Parallele Datenverarbeitung mit dem Transputer. Aachen, September 1990. Proceedings. X, 300 Seiten 1991.

Band 273: M. Timm (Hrsg.), Requirements Engineering '91. VIII, 208 Seiten. 1991.

Band 274: R. Denzer, H. Hagen, K.-H. Kutschke (Hrsg.), Visualisierung von Umweltdaten. Workshop, Rostock, November 1990. Proceedings. VII, 97 Seiten. 1991.

Band 276: H. Maurer (Hrsg.), Hypertext / Hypermedia '91. Tagung der GI, SI und OCG, Graz, Mai 1991. Proceedings. VIII, 299 Seiten. 1991.

Band 277: U. Borgolte, Flexible, realzeitfähige Kollisionsvermeidung in Mehrroboter-Systemen. XIII, 105 Seiten. 1991.

Band 278: H. W. Meuer (Hrsg.), SUPERCOMPUTER '91. Proceedings. VIII, 266 Seiten. 1991.

Band 279: G. Schwichtenberg (Hrsg.), Organisation und Betrieb von Informationssystemen. 9. GI — Fachgespräch über Rechenzentren, Dortmund, März 1991. Proceedings. IX, 337 Seiten. 1991.

Band 280: B. Westfechtel, Revisions- und Konsistenzkontrolle in einer integrierten Softwareentwicklungsumgebung. X, 321 Seiten. 1991.

Band 281: W. Emde, Modellbildung, Wissensrevision und Wissensrepräsentation im Maschinellen Lernen. XI, 204 Seiten. 1991.

Band 282: P. Buchholz, Die strukturierte Analyse Markovscher Modelle. VII, 192 Seiten 1991.

Band 283: M. Dal Cin, W. Hohl (Hrsg.), Fault-Tolerant Computing Systems. 5th International GI/ITG/GMA Conference, Nürnberg, September 1991. Proceedings. XII, 425 Seiten. 1991.

Band 284: R. Stadler, Ausführbare Spezifikation von Directory-Systemen in einer logischen Sprache. X, 142 Seiten. 1991.

Band 285: T. Christaller (Hrsg.), GWAI-91. 15. Fachtagung für Künstliche Intelligenz, Bonn, September 1991. IX, 273 Seiten. 1991.

Band 286: A. Lehmann, F. Lehmann (Hrsg.), Messung, Modellierung und Bewertung von Rechensystemen. 6. GI/ITG-Fachtagung, Neubiberg, September 1991. Proceedings. VIII, 338 Seiten. 1991.

Band 287: H. Kaindl (Hrsg.), 7. Österreichische Artificial-Intelligence-Tagung, Wien, September 1991. Proceedings. VIII, 180 Seiten. 1991.